Managing a Microsoft® Windows NT® Network

Microsoft Press

PUBLISHED BY
Microsoft Press
A Division of Microsoft Corporation
One Microsoft Way
Redmond, Washington 98052-6399

Library of Congress Cataloging-in-Publication Data
Microsoft Corporation.
    Managing a Microsoft Windows NT Network / Microsoft Corporation.
       p. cm.
    Includes bibliographical references (p.   )
    ISBN 0-7356-0647-1
    1. Microsoft Windows NT. 2. Operating systems. I. Title.
  QA76.76.O63M486   1999
  005.4'469--dc21   98-52142
                                        CIP

Printed and bound in the United States of America.

  2 3 4 5 6 7 8 9   QMQM   4 3 2 1 0 9

Distributed in Canada by Penguin Books Canada Limited.

A CIP catalogue record for this book is available from the British Library.

Microsoft Press books are available through booksellers and distributors worldwide. For further information about international editions, contact your local Microsoft Corporation office or contact Microsoft Press International directly at fax (425) 936-7329. Visit our Web site at mspress.microsoft.com.

Acquisitions Editor: Anne Hamilton
Project Editor: Thom Votteler

Contributors

We dedicate this volume to the authors, contributors, and reviewers who generously gave their time, experience, and vast knowledge to make this title a reality.

Program Manager

Michael Ohata

Senior Technical Editor

Bob Haynie

Contributors

Anthony Baron, Miles Burkart, Nigel Cain, Tom Dodds, Tom Fuchs, Jeff Hamer, Brian Karasawa, Andreea Leonard, Michael Lyons, David Millett, Gary Milne, Eric Miyadi, David Skinner, Matthew D. Storer, Rick Varvel, and Alan von Weltin

Additional Contributors & Technical Review

Michael Andrade, Jason Bakke, David Bright, Adam Gordon, Loren Kaneshige, Bruce Jones, Mark Lawrence, Bryan Miller, Bruce MacNaughton, Laura Payne, and Gavin Schiff

Technical Writer

Kelly Chalfant

Technical Editor & Production Specialist

Heidi Wrightsman

Indexer

Richard S. Shrout

Project Editor

Thom Votteler

Welcome

In this day of rapidly evolving technology and growing complexity in network computing, Information Technology professionals can find it tough to keep up with daily troubleshooting, long-range planning, and frequent systems integration projects—let alone ride the leading edge of the technological wave. At Microsoft, we know about your problems: every day, Microsoft Consulting Services works in the field with IT professionals like you to build network infrastructure so your organization can keep up *and* stay ahead. The *Notes from the Field* series captures this experience, tried-and-tested best practices, and wealth of knowledge.

There is no shortage of references and resources for the IT pro, and for that we can all be thankful. Our copies of the compendiums and encyclopedias are usually well-thumbed, because we often need to find accurate information quickly. But we also need help when it comes to *doing* things, and this is information of a different kind.

The *Notes from the Field* series offers practical information derived from real-world experience—and you know there is no substitute for experience—all of which has been worked out and tested in the field. The complexity of network management arises from the interconnectedness of planning, testing, management, and troubleshooting—all those currents that keep you in constant motion. This series provides you with a tactical tool to sort through the issues and keep moving ahead.

Managing a Microsoft Windows NT Network starts with the basics (a simple management process) and works through topics ranging from security to automated installation and software distribution. It provides methods, safeguards, and examples that help you accomplish the routine tasks and objectives of managing a system effectively and efficiently. With Windows 2000 on the horizon, the solidification of infrastructure and the extension of your Windows NT 4.0 network are *strategic* goals in preparing your platform for the next enterprise solution.

Sincerely,

Frank Artale
General Manager,
Windows NT Server and Enterprise

Contents

Part 2   Desktop Lockdown, Security, and Failover Scenarios

Chapter 4   Locking Down the Desktop at Microsoft's Professional Developer Conference   163

Part 3   Deploying Windows NT—Automated Installation

Part 4   Just a Little More Before You Head out the Door

Introduction

Welcome to *Managing a Microsoft Windows NT Network,* fourth in the *Notes from the Field* series, featuring best practices from Microsoft Consulting Services. Designed for information technology (IT) and information systems (IS) professionals, this book condenses and organizes the broad expertise of field consultants and support engineers, and offers you the benefit of their real-world experiences. Most of the chapters use specific fictitious companies to provide a single frame of reference for understanding the discussion, but all of the material in this book derives from actual customer scenarios or an amalgamation of several technical implementations during which consultants tested and proved their approaches and techniques.

You should use this book as a supplement to the Microsoft Windows NT Server and Workstation 4.0 product documentation and the *Microsoft Windows NT Server 4.0 Resource Kit.* The resource kit contains a collection of tools essential to optimizing and managing Windows NT networks, and a wealth of information, ranging from high level (Windows NT architecture) to fine detail (installing, configuring, and using point-to-point tunneling protocol—PPTP). The book you are reading now often refers you to it for general and background information.

No single book can cover every necessary management topic for a product as complex as Windows NT Server, and this book doesn't try to. Instead, it focuses tightly on administering and supporting a network. It deals with Microsoft Systems Management Server (SMS) from several points of view, beginning with the basic (how to use SMS to improve the quality of management while cutting its cost) to the complex (how to use SMS to configure remote control settings). It discusses backup and failover strategies and methods, looks at security inside and outside of the firewall, explains how to lock down environments, and shows how to deal with software distribution within them once they are locked down. It addresses the considerable challenge of automating software distribution in networks of ever-increasing size and organizational complexity. In sum, it assumes that you are already responsible for a large network, then proceeds to examine management areas that you may not have yet explored or mastered.

The third *Notes from the Field* volume, *Optimizing Network Traffic*, explains how to build the framework for analyzing, optimizing, and troubleshooting Windows NT-based traffic.

What's in This Book

Part 1: Managing Your Network Infrastructure

More specifically: how to deal with mounting infrastructure complexity by using Microsoft Systems Management Server (SMS) as your *management system.* Chapter 1 reviews operational roles and procedures, then recommends daily, weekly, and monthly tasks. Chapter 2 looks at an SMS deployment using site hierarchy to manage future growth and minimize network bandwidth utilization. Chapter 3 drills down into planning and executing the backup and recovery of your SMS data, so that you have a contingency plan in the event of an outage.

Part 2: Desktop Lockdown, Security, and Failover Scenarios

Chapter 4 looks at some concepts you can use to create a desktop environment that is adaptable to the needs of many users, but resists hacking and inappropriate modification. Chapters 5 and 6 discuss, respectively, securing internal and external networks—the segments inside or outside the firewall. Returning to more general management tasks, Chapter 7 describes three ways to use SMS Installer to simplify software distribution in secure environments. Chapter 8 troubleshoots a potential issue with user authentication in distributed environments. Chapter 9 explains how you can use Microsoft Cluster Server to boost system availability and reliability.

Part 3: Deploying Windows NT—Automated Installation

This section details two of the best methods. Chapter 10 walks you through the Microsoft Automated Installation Framework (MSIF)—a collection of components developed by MCS to make PC installation and configuration automatic and dynamic. Chapter 11 provides a template for an unattended modular build of Windows NT, service packs, and application software. These chapters provide enough details, tips, and code samples to make mastering these tools easy.

Part 4: Just a Little More Before You Head out the Door

This last section returns to SMS, explaining how to use it even more effectively. Chapter 12 describes two simple issues and provides tools for configuring remote control settings and getting the right information to help desk staff. Chapter 13 looks at the workaround procedure for configuring a Novell 4.1x server to function as an SMS logon and distribution server.

Additional Information

Appendix A lists references and resources, including support offerings, Web sites, white papers, and Microsoft Technical Support Knowledge Base articles on Windows NT Server, including a complete list of the fixes in Service Pack 4 (SP4). Appendix B explains how to configure the Server Proxy Feature for Exchange Server 4.0 - 5.5.

The last thing in the book may be the first thing you'll want to take advantage of: a Microsoft TechNet sample CD that includes a representative selection of one issue's contents *and* the sample code files and tools mentioned in Chapters 4, 7, 10, 12, and 13. For a book such as this one, drawn from first-hand accounts and experience, TechNet is the obvious companion piece: it is *the* support resource for professionals in the trenches. Each month, it provides subscribing IT professionals with in-depth information on evaluating, deploying, managing, and supporting Microsoft products and technologies.

Conventions Used

Convention	Description
ALL CAPITALS	Acronyms, filenames, and names of commands.
bold	Menus and menu commands, command buttons, property page and dialog box titles and options, command-line commands, options, and portions of syntax that must be typed exactly as shown. First occurrences of special terms, and book titles.
Initial Capitals	Names of applications, programs, servers, windows, directories, and paths.
Italic	Information you have to enter. Used also for emphasis as dictated by context.
`monospace type`	Sample command lines, program code, and program output.
Q123456, Title: How to Use SMS to Manage a Windows NT Network	Knowledge Base article titles. Search for them on Microsoft TechNet or at http://support.microsoft.com/support/a.asp?M=F using the "Q" number (no spaces).

Icons That Highlight Text

These sidebar icons provide you with simple signposts:

Icon	Description
	Caution or **Warning**. Advises you to take or avoid specific action to avoid potential damage.
	Note. Emphasizes, supplements, or qualifies points in the text.
	Best Practices or **Guidelines**. Highlights proven practices, techniques, or procedures from MCS real-world experiences.
	Tools. Indicates sample code, Windows NT utilities, or tools provided on the companion CD.

Some Important Business

The example companies, organizations, products, people and events depicted in this book are fictitious. No association with any real company, organization, product, person or event is intended or should be inferred.

Warning Throughout this book you'll find recommendations for optimizing or tuning the Windows NT registry using the Registry Editor. Using the Registry Editor incorrectly can cause serious, system-wide problems that require you to reinstall Windows NT. Microsoft cannot guarantee that any problems resulting from the use of Registry Editor can be solved. Use this tool at your own risk.

And one more thing...

Note Microsoft does not guarantee the performance of *Windows NT Resource Kit* utilities, performance rates, or bugfixes to tools, although it does offer customer assistance on the utilities though Knowledge Base articles and other Microsoft Technical Support options. For a listing of support phone numbers, please refer to *Your Guide to Service and Support*, included with Windows NT. You can also send comments to the RKINPUT@MICROSOFT.COM alias, which is monitored by Microsoft Press.

Managing Your Network Infrastructure

You can't even remember it happening, but it did. Your organization's network has grown so quickly in size and complexity that your title of Management Information Systems Administrator—which in the beginning seemed almost honorary—now hangs over your head like the sword of Damocles. And it stays there, somehow, no matter how much you run: troubleshooting daily service disruptions, dashing off to a planning meeting, even holing up in your office to check on the latest upgrade distribution. Is it just a matter of time before that sword drops? What will snap the hair that holds it? Some unforeseen catastrophe? Or merely the increasing weight of compounding system complexity?

Catastrophes can be guarded against, even if the unforeseen is, all too often, unforeseeable. This book details a number of safeguards you can put in place to protect against random occurrences. Complexity, however, is ironically simpler to deal with. This section helps you understand how. It looks at managing your enterprise network infrastructure, using Microsoft Systems Management Server as your *management system*. Chapter 1 reviews common operational roles and procedures, then recommends daily, weekly, and monthly operational tasks. Chapter 2 looks at an SMS deployment using site hierarchy to manage future growth and minimize network bandwidth utilization. And Chapter 3 drills down into planning and executing the backup and recovery of your SMS data, providing you with a contingency plan during an outage.

C H A P T E R   1

Working Practices—Using SMS at The Frugal Company

By Anthony Baron, MCS— United Kingdom

Microsoft Systems Management Server (SMS) is a useful system management tool, and its value can increase as systems become more complex and the need for careful control increases. But tools alone aren't enough: effective system management also requires a solid foundation. This chapter looks at some basic safeguards, practices, and processes that can help you use SMS to lower costs, to improve service, and to protect your system's stability, availability, and reliability.

In Focus

Enterprise

The Frugal Company is a temporary employment agency specializing in matching young inexperienced workers to short-term contracts that provide them with the chance to begin developing workplace skills.

Network

Windows NT 4.0 Server and Workstation, Windows 95, Office 97. Each of five regional offices has a server and about 30 workstations.

Challenge

Update workstation software (Office 97) with Service Release 2 (SR2) for Y2K compliance.

Solution

The problem provided a good opportunity to work through the MCS process for managing changes using Microsoft Systems Management Server. The Frugal Company used this process to design, test, and implement the upgrade.

What You'll Find In This Chapter

- How to use SMS effectively to support and control changes to the IT infrastructure.

- How to separate tasks (such as software distribution) into definable and manageable phases for SMS.

- How to document the process thoroughly for process and quality control.

- How to organize and complete testing before, during, and after deployment.

Support Model

How you design your Systems Management Server (SMS) system depends on how you want to handle administration, security, and control. You have to distribute tasks in some way, and the SMS hierarchy will necessarily reflect distribution of control to separate business areas, administrator groups, or locations. Once you decide to implement SMS, you have to consider working practices and processes if you want to use it effectively to lower costs and improve service.

Distribute Responsibilities

The IT group needs clearly defined lines of responsibility and accountability for SMS. An established and effective practice is to create two roles for the information technology (IT) group: an *operational support* team responsible for maintaining the current environment and a *development* team responsible for improvement and change.

The operational support team plans and tests changes before they are implemented in the production environment. Their mandate is to ensure operational stability.

The development team identifies and evaluates *necessary* changes. This is challenging enough under normal circumstances; it is especially so when business pressures demand rapid implementation, putting the development team on the spot. The team needs a clear set of best practices and guidelines to maintain quality under real-world constraints. The Microsoft Solutions Framework (MSF) is a good place to look for ideas and methods.

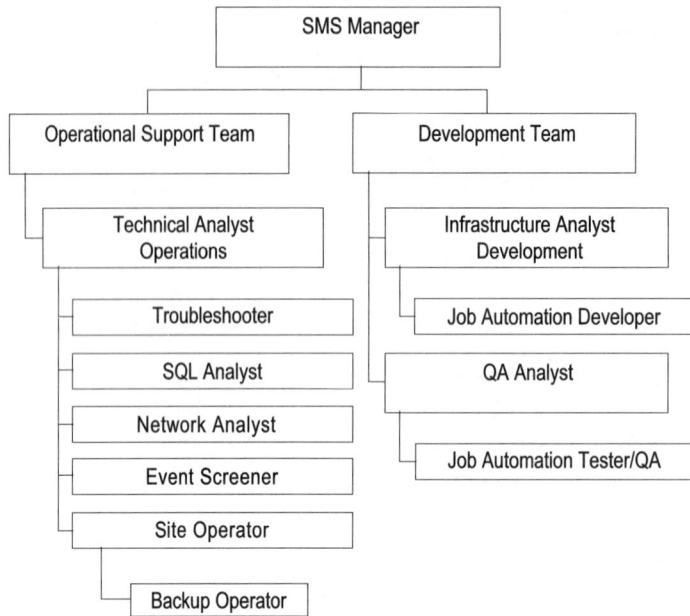

Figure 1.1 Functional hierarchy for systems management and operations.

Effective SMS implementation and ongoing support require a correctly planned operational process that addresses your organization's characteristics, meets your business's requirements, and provides accountability and change control. This is another reason to separate responsibilities for ongoing environment management from those of development and quality assurance.

Key Tasks

Most organizations implement SMS to:

- Reduce the total cost of ownership
- Improve system availability
- Allow the organization to be more responsive to change
- Provide tools to the organization to manage and control its systems investment

To help you accomplish these goals, you need to use SMS to support:

Inventory. Providing comprehensive details of deployed hardware and software—the IT group needs current and accurate information to make sound technical decisions.

Software distribution. Controlling software changes and additions to your IT infrastructure to minimize confusion and manual intervention for normal and rapid rollouts.

Helpdesk. Providing tools that IT support staff can use to monitor, control, and troubleshoot the above tasks as well as daily operation.

Key Phases within a Task

You need to break down and structure tasks to ensure delegation and accountability. Separate initial effort (designing, building, and testing) from final effort (deployment) for each task you want to accomplish. Before making any significant change, you should define your requirements, then design and complete acceptance testing. The goal is to apply only necessary changes of acceptable quality.

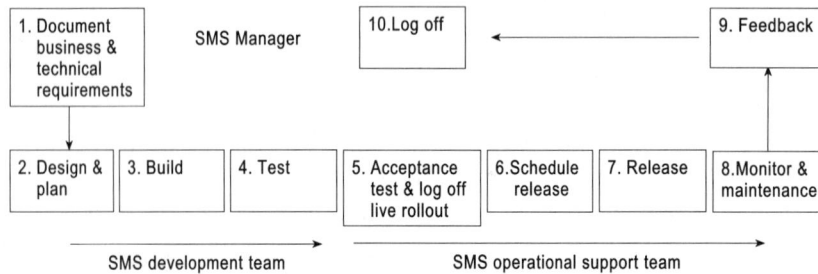

Figure 1.2 Task deployment process.

Requirements Phase (1)

First, ask why a task is necessary. If it is, then determine its business or technical requirements. Documenting these and agreeing on them up front helps the development team create a clear understanding with users.

A requirements document is essential. An example is provided below to give you some ideas of what to document and how. Documents vary in detail depending on the type of job, but any good one describes what needs to be done, why it needs to be done, and the possible effects of *not* doing it. In its simplest form, it details a change request.

At the Frugal Company, the Director of Finance decided, after reading up on the Year 2000 problem, that Office 97 workstations needed to be upgraded to Y2K compliance by applying Service Release 2 (SR2). That request was submitted and the IT group began the change process.

Requirements document example.

SMS requirement	Explanation
Requirement	Update Microsoft Office 97 workstation software for Year 2000 by applying Service Release 2 (SR2)
Requested By	Director of Finance
Required Date	Before 20th May 1999
Users Affected	All users across enterprise
Implication of Failure	All systems will fail to perform correctly from Jan 1st 2000 and some may experience problems earlier
Responsibility for Completion	SMS Manager

When it is completed, the requirements document is signed off by the SMS Manager and passed to the development team.

Development Phases (2,3,4)

This phase comprises three sets of tasks: designing, building, and testing. In the first, the development team works out what they need to do to meet the requirements, and identifies the technical characteristics of a successful implementation (so it can be tested for on completion). Example: testing the version of an executable after a software distribution. The design also needs to account for a failed distribution by identifying a rollback procedure to restore the environment to its previous state. The table below shows how this phase incorporates and augments the requirements defined above.

Design document example.

SMS design factor	Explanation
Does the design meet the requirements?	Update Microsoft Office 97 workstation software for Year 2000 by applying SR2.
Timeframe for updating	Task needs to complete between Jan 1st 1999 and before 20th May 1999.
Users affected	All users across enterprise these include all 200 company locations and all 12,000 PC's running *Windows NT* 4 and Windows 98.
Constraints	No more than 10 users/day/ location should be updated.
	No updates should be performed between April 5th 1998 and April 25th due to end of tax year.
	Some users do not log onto network.
	Some locations have only 64-K lines.
Design imperatives	Correct versions of updated executables are released to different OS.
	Job checks for critical success and does a rollback on failure, also reports this to operations.
	Software should be successfully delivered to local site servers at least 14 days before applying patches.
	The correct country/language version of a software package should be delivered to a PC.
	The job should be designed so that it does not exceed the maximum network bandwidth available for SMS.

Design document example.   *(continued)*

SMS design factor	Explanation
Design considerations	Is compression needed or is software already compressed?
	Should fan-out be used? That is: send the job to top level primaries first, and to the child primary sites from there.
Implication of failure	All systems will fail to perform correctly from Jan 1st 2000 and some may experience problems earlier.
Description of design	This task will result in a number of SMS software packages being prepared containing the correct country/language and OS version of the Y2K patch for Office 97 (SR2). Each package will also contain the logic for the distribution of software, special instructions for deployment, tests against critical successes, and a procedure for ensuring that each workstation can roll back to a stable condition.
Responsibility for Completion of design	Infrastructure Development Analyst
Responsibility for sign off of design	SMS Manager

The next development task is to build the job. In this, the outputs from the design and planning task are used to build the task so that it meets the design requirements and fully addresses all constraints and imperatives. For software distributions, this task includes the packaging of the software, the automated script to apply the package, the rollback script to undo the applied change should a failure occur, and any special testing and deployment instructions.

The third development task is to test the change. Testing should try to mirror the way the change will be deployed in the live environment. For this, the team must use a standard testing rig that reflects the live environment as far as possible and includes, at the very least, server and workstation configurations identical to the live environment. A test lab can be costly, but it can pay for itself in the effort and expense it saves. (Configured test hardware is also a handy source of emergency replacements for production machines.)

The testing requirements section below details how to construct an ideal testing infrastructure. Initial testing is the responsibility of the Job Automation Tester/QA; it should document disk space requirements and how much network traffic the job will place on the infrastructure. When this testing is complete, the task is handed off to the Technical Operations Analyst for acceptance testing.

Acceptance Testing (5)

In this phase, the work done by the development team is reviewed, then tested against the requirements to confirm its acceptability for release to the live environment. The team in this phase acts as a gatekeeper—it can accept jobs that meet requirements and reject jobs that don't. The Technical Operations Analyst is ultimately accountable for the task working or failing, so this phase must ascertain the job's acceptability completely and accurately. The Analyst must be prepared to push back on the design team if tests indicate that the job will not work. The need for thoroughness makes a checklist essential.

Checklist example.

SMS acceptance testing factor	Explanation
Does the design meet the requirements?	How has this been proven?
Is the documentation set complete?	Requirements?
	Design/Planning?
	Testing?
Are the effects of the live infrastructure understood and documented?	How has this been done?
Does the job have a disaster recovery (rollback) procedure?	Documented?
	Rollback script?
	Test procedure?
What will the effect be on helpdesk?	Are they aware of this job?
	Do they have the staff and skills to support it?
Has each responsible party signed off?	User?
	SMS Manager?
	Development Analyst?
	QA Analyst?
	Helpdesk Manager?
Responsibility for Acceptance Testing	Technical Analyst Operations

Schedule (6)

Once the Operations Team accepts the task, it needs to be scheduled for release into the live environment. Coordination is essential and this usually requires negotiation with the user community and helpdesk. Normally rollouts are staggered so that at first only a few workstations receive the change. This is done to ensure that the job is stable before distributing it to large numbers of systems. Each successive deployment stage can increase the number of target workstations, but the number should never be increased to the point where problems can become paralyzing or tracking too complex. An unattended modular rollout is a possibility (see Chapter 11).

Document the finalized roll out schedule and distribute it to users. Explain any effects they may experience: new dialog boxes appearing, slower system speeds for a few minutes each morning, etc. The schedule should also include review points so that any issues that come to light during the rollout can be fed back to the development team for correction.

Split the schedule into two stages: delivery of source software to distribution servers, followed a few days later by delivery of the release trigger. This method helps ensure that the job has successfully arrived at all locations, even those with low bandwidth or far down in a large SMS hierarchy.

The schedule should pick one of each type of user (ideally a friendly one) for initial deployment. When this has been successfully completed, scale the deployment gradually up to larger numbers.

An example rollout schedule:

Week 1 – day 1 => Distribute job to all servers

Week 2 – day 1 => Distribute job trigger for 5 named users

Week 2 – day 4 => Distribute job trigger for 15 more named users

Week 3 – day 1 => Distribute job trigger for whole of IT department

Weed 3 – day 2 => Distribute job trigger for HR and Accounts

Week 3 – day 3 => Distribute job trigger for Sales, Transport, Research

Week 3 – day 4 => Distribute job trigger for remaining departments

When scheduling rollout to remote locations without local IT support, start with the nearest site. You may have to send someone over quickly if a problem develops.

Remember to keep the helpdesk involved from the beginning. They may have to staff up, and they may also require training to prepare for a major software release.

Release (7)

This phase should follow the two-stage scheduling process. Don't release any software until all previous phases are successfully completed.

Monitor (8)

When release is successfully completed, you can boost your chances of success by performing live monitoring. Key areas to monitor:

- SMS senders—Are they functioning correctly?
- Distribution points—Has the job arrived?
- Client—Has the job arrived? Been installed successfully?
- Network bandwidth—Are traffic levels acceptable?
- Site server and responsiveness—Has the job seriously affected server performance and network performance?
- Scheduler—Did the job run on time? Are the outbox rules functioning correctly?
- Helpdesk—Are call levels acceptable? Manageable? Are repeat problems being reported?
- Rollbacks—Did any occur? Why?

Feedback (9)

Once the task has been completed, perform a review so that you can learn from any issues that came up during the life cycle of the task. No sense solving the same problems again next time.

Sign Off (10)

One more phase: determine if the requirements defined at the beginning of the process were met. If the job was successful, understand why; if not, understand why. System changes and software distributions are recurrent—use each task as a learning experience to perfect your technique.

Task signoff form example.

SMS task sign off factor	Explanation
Original Requirement	Update Microsoft Office 97 workstation software for Year 2000 by applying SR2
Requested by	Director of Finance
Required date	Before 20th May 1999
Users affected	All users across enterprise
Implication of failure	All systems will fail to perform correctly from Jan 1st 2000 and some may experience problems earlier
Responsibility for Completion.	SMS Manager

Task signoff form example.   *(continued)*

SMS task sign off factor	Explanation
Was the task successfully & requirements delivered	User
	Development Analyst
	QA Analyst
	Helpdesk Manager
	Technical Analyst Operations
If not, what areas caused problems?	The job failed to install on one type of PC
What lessons can be learned?	Improve future testing against this configuration
Follow up actions	QA Analyst to update test lab to include this configuration and test.
	SMS Manager to review this test at next month's meeting.

You have to learn from mistakes if you want to use SMS to deliver a more reliable environment.

Requirement for Testing

Pre-deployment testing is critical when integrating changes in the enterprise environment—essential when integrating complex products. You need to understand the environment's operating characteristics fully if you are going to manage the process of introducing changes in it. The software industry tests products thoroughly before release, but you still need to test if any of these conditions obtain:

- Use of a complex set of tools.
- Implementation across distributed locations including limited WAN links.
- Integration with third-party products.
- Significant amounts of tailored code.
- Need for a high level of reliability and availability.

Inadequate testing can affect reliability, availability, productivity, and cost.

Testing Skills

The test team leader must understand the test process, the enterprise infrastructure, and software development. Development skills are important because test teams often must write automated tests. Test plans and procedures for client-server systems can be complex; they must take into account network issues, connectivity issues, and the user-configurable nature of the desktop. They can become even more complex with event-driven programming, multiple network transports, target servers, mainframe or back room system interoperability issues, and data and database administration issues. The testing team must understand the intricate interaction between application configurations.

High Level Approach

To implement changes in any complex client-server environment you should carefully plan regression testing that allows for:

- Creation of a **test lab** that resembles (*exactly*, if possible) the live environment. The degree of resemblance of course depends on the complexity of that environment, but it also depends on how much time and money you can commit to the effort. Regardless of degree, the lab should make it possible to complete end-to-end testing, even if it is simulating just one user in one site attaching to a server in a remote location and traversing routers and WAN links.

- Designing and building a **test script** that tests critical functionality and can run automatically and repeatedly, ensuring that the tailored environment can perform its tasks reliably over extended periods. These tests should be constructed from numerous simple but functional tests such as creating a document, entering large amounts of text, reformatting, repaginating, and saving. You should be able to rerun this test indefinitely, as you change configurable environmental options such as network load, server load, and concurrency. The more you test, the more reliable your results.

- Archiving all test results as resources for diagnosing problems in a live environment.

Suggested Network Topology

The maximum test configuration is a complete second environment for testing—which of course you cannot create if your system is of any size. What is the minimum? The network topology below provides the minimum hardware necessary to test a desktop and server environment using Microsoft Office and BackOffice in a distributed head office and branch environment.

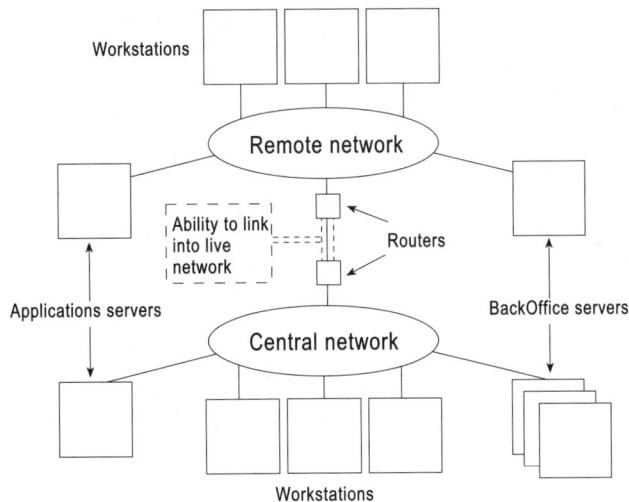

Figure 1.3 Minimum test hardware for desktop and server environment.

Hardware

Minimum hardware for comprehensive pre-deployment testing.

Hardware	Quantity
Workstations	6
Servers	6—the types are listed below:
	2 applications servers
	1 central Exchange server
	1 central domain controller, Windows Internet Naming Service (WINS), Dynamic Host Configuration Protocol (DHCP)
	1 central backup domain controller and file server
	1 remote backup domain controller and general BackOffice server
Network Hubs	2
WAN Routers	2

Memory, CPUs, and other characteristics should match the hardware in the live environment.

Regression Testing

Below are the basic roles and responsibilities of a well-thought-out test group. As part of your testing arsenal, don't overlook the many third-party regression testing tools.

Roles and responsibilities.

Role	Responsibilities	Training and knowledge needs	Workload variables
SMS Manager *Owns the service level agreement.*	Manages other SMS staff. Works with upper management on SMS strategy, and on implementing other management information service (MIS) strategies using SMS.	Requires an operational understanding of SMS, but this is primarily a non-technical role. Ideally an SMS Microsoft Certified Professional (MCP).	Number of staff to manage. Degree of control over staff who want to use the SMS Administrator utility. Responsiveness of remote site administrators. Other departments' willingness to use SMS
Technical Analyst *Owns technical design and management of platform.*	Sets up accounts. Designs hierarchy, defines groups, queries, alerts, packages, jobs. Designs package and application inventory. Designs database views. Acts as gatekeeper between development and rollout into live environment.	Requires high level of technical skill with SMS. Must see the "big picture" from a technical perspective. Needs Microsoft Certified Systems Engineer (MCSE).	Growth rate of SMS hierarchy. Frequency of network and domain reorganizations.

Roles and responsibilities.   *(continued)*

Role	Responsibilities	Training and knowledge needs	Workload variables
Troubleshooter *Can also be included in role of technical analyst.*	Installs sites. Tracks error events. Troubleshoots job failures reported by site.	Highly skilled with SMS. Comprehensive knowledge of client platforms, such as Windows NT, Windows 95, etc. General troubleshooting skills. Needs SMS, Windows NT/W95 MCP training.	Size and growth rate of SMS hierarchy. Frequency of problem reports. Responsiveness of remote operators.
SQL Analyst *Can also be included in role of technical analyst.*	Installs and maintains SQL Server.	Skilled and experienced with SQL Server. Needs SQL, Windows NT MCP training.	Size and growth rate of SMS hierarchy. Frequency of account changes.

Roles and responsibilities.   *(continued)*

Role	Responsibilities	Training and knowledge needs	Workload variables
Network Analyst *Can also be included in role of technical analyst.*	Installs senders and related hardware. Uses Network Monitor and other tools to monitor and troubleshoot network and communication links.	General SMS knowledge with focus on senders. Detailed knowledge of network and communications hardware, and Windows NT. Needs Windows NT and SMS MCP training.	Number and type of senders in use Stability of network and communications hardware.
Event Screener *Can also be included in role of technical analyst.*	Reads, responds to, and deletes SMS events.	Strong SMS skills: understands how SMS works "under the hood." Good troubleshooting skills. Needs SMS and Windows NT MCP training.	Number of events, which depends on network stability, client stability, and how well SMS sites are maintained. SMS Administrator utility response time, which depends on number of events, speed of administrative machine and SQL Server machine, and load on those machines.

Roles and responsibilities.   *(continued)*

Role	Responsibilities	Training and knowledge needs	Workload variables
Site Operator *Can also be included in role of technical analyst.*	Adds and removes group members. Sends packages and jobs. Sets up views. Runs reports and queries. Reports problems to site installer/troubleshooter	Knowledge of SMS Administrator utility. Knowledge of Windows NT. Can recognize and report problems. Needs SMS and Windows NT MCP training.	Number of job, package, site, group, and client changes per month. Additional customization required. Response time of the SMS Administrator utility.
Backup Operator *Can also be included in role of technical analyst or site operator*	Backs up data. Troubleshoots hardware problems. Restores data after crashes.	General support skills for SMS and Windows NT. Ideally SMS and Windows NT MCP training.	Size and growth rate of SMS hierarchy. Reliability of hardware. Frequency of backups. Frequency of restores.

Roles and responsibilities.   *(continued)*

Role	Responsibilities	Training and knowledge needs	Workload variables
Job Automation Developer This development role should NOT be included in the role of technical operator or site operator.	Prototypes packages and jobs using the standard PC configuration, and delivers working models to site operators.	Highly skilled with SMS, with particular focus on package and job creation. Comprehensive knowledge of client and server platforms, such as Windows NT, Windows 95, etc. Ideally MCSE.	Volume of new packages and jobs. Frequency and complexity of job and package customization.
Job Automation Tester/QA	Test packages and jobs to ensure that solution meets specifications and requiremenst for job.	Highly skilled with SMS, with particular focus on package and job creation. Comprehensive knowledge of client and server platforms, such as Windows NT, Windows 95, etc. Ideally MCSE.	Volume of new packages and jobs. Frequency and complexity of job and package customization.

Operational Tasks: Administrator Checklist

Finally, to keep SMS running smoothly, you need to make sure that certain tasks are completed regularly.

Daily Tasks

- Check the SMS Event log. Look for errors that have not recovered. Find and fix any recurring problems. If possible, fix conditions generating warnings. Delete unneeded old events.

  Responsibility: Event Screener

- Check the SMS Jobs window for jobs that have not completed as expected. Determine cause and fix problems.

  Responsibility: Site Operator

- Back up the SMS and Master databases. Verify that the backup occurred.

  Responsibility: Backup Operator

- Check the messages in the SQL Server Messages window in SMS Administrator. Many of these messages are not logged—they appear only if the window is open, so keep it open. (From the **File** menu select **Open**, then **SQL Server Messages**.) You can use the **Customize Toolbar** option to add this icon to the toolbar.

  Responsibility: Event Screener

- Run Performance Monitor to check the status of critical components on the site servers and the SQL Server. See the volume called "Optimizing Windows NT" in the *Microsoft Window NT 3.5 Resource Kit* for information on performance monitoring.

  Responsibility: Site Operator

- Run Network Monitor to check the available bandwidth and error rates on the networks used by the SMS hierarchy.

  Responsibility: Network Analyst

Weekly Tasks

- Check the SMS database to be sure that the devices and logs are not full.

  Responsibility: SQL Analyst

- Check the drive space on the SMS site servers and the SQL Server to make sure SMS has ample free disk space. If any directories are filling up, determine why and fix the problem if possible.

  Responsibility: Site Operator

- Use DBCLEAN to check for duplicate machines in the SMS database. Delete older duplicates, and fix any problems that may be causing duplicate machines to appear.

  Responsibility: Site Operator

Monthly Tasks

- Use DBCLEAN to check for and delete Unused Records and Abandoned Collected Files.

  Responsibility: Site Operator

- Restore a backup to verify that the daily backups are working.

  Responsibility: Backup Operator

- Use the SQL Server DBCC utility to verify SMS database consistency (as needed).

  Responsibility: SQL Analyst

CHAPTER 2

SMS Infrastructure and Deployment Strategy at Pretty Good Health Care Centers

By Jeff Hamer, MCS— MidAmerica

Microsoft Systems Management Server (SMS) allows you to organize your existing network structure into logical groupings called sites, by managing hardware and software inventory, and software updates and distribution. Typically, you can group computers located in a single geographical area as a single site. Network administrators at Pretty Good Health Care Centers (PGHCC) headquartered in Chicago, designed multiple sites using a site hierarchy based on organizational and management needs. This distributed administration duties between sites, reduced network traffic between geographical areas, and provided maximum scalability for future growth. This chapter takes a high-level look at the design and deployment of an SMS version 1.2 infrastructure.

In Focus

Enterprise
Pretty Good Health Care Centers, with headquarters office in Chicago, and branch offices in Alabama, Missouri, and Indiana.

Network
12,000 PCs spread across 13 geographic locations, with the largest concentration of workstations (about 5,000) residing in the central metro site.

Challenge
Deploying a management infrastructure that can help inventory hardware and software, and distribute software, including updates. Designing an infrastructure that will be minimally affected by future growth.

Solution
Implement SMS 1.2 using site hierarchy over a phased deployment.

What You'll Find In This Chapter

- Overview of SMS site hierarchy and site server roles.

- Ideas for an infrastructure deployment strategy.

- Description of the phased deployment and recommendations.

- Best practices for setting up software distribution and SMS maintenance.

- Sample scripts and files.

Warning This chapter makes recommendations for tuning the Windows NT registry using the Registry Editor. Using the Registry Editor incorrectly can cause serious, system-wide problems that require you to reinstall Windows NT. Microsoft cannot guarantee that any problems resulting from the use of Registry Editor can be solved. Use this tool at your own risk.

Infrastructure Design Overview

The PGHCC SMS site hierarchy defines geographical areas based on specific site roles: *primary, central,* or *secondary* (see Figure 2.1, page 34). A **primary** site has its own Microsoft SQL Server (which stores SMS information for the workstations in that site and for workstations in the sites beneath it in the hierarchy) and SMS administrative tools that allow direct management of the primary site and those beneath it: SMS Administrator, Network Monitor, Database Manager, Security Manager, Sender Manager, and Service Manager. Of these, Network Monitor is a valuable tool for detecting and troubleshooting problems on local area networks (LANs) and wide area networks (WANs) that use Microsoft Remote Access Service (RAS) to connect to LANs.

The primary site at the top of the site hierarchy acts as the **central** site. At PGHCC, the central site server is named PGH-SMS-001. It is in the PGHCC domain, located in the PGHCC Metro data center. Network administrators designed the server to support 5000 SMS-enabled workstations in the central site, with 250 KB of inventory data for each workstation reporting weekly. This minimum requirements configuration requires:

- Pentium, Alpha, or MIPS CPU
- Windows NT Server 4.0 SP3, configured as a domain controller
- Access to a CD-ROM drive
- 4-GB system partition, hardware RAID 1
- 4-GB transaction partition, hardware RAID 1
- NTFS volume with 1 GB of free disk space, configured as multiple drives or drive array for faster disk input/output
- 128 MB RAM with SQL Server on the same computer
- Microsoft SQL Server 6.5 SP4

An SMS **secondary** site does not have its own SQL Server—it forwards inventory and status information to its primary site for processing and storage. Secondary sites do not have administrative tools for direct site management. Administrators connect to and administer a secondary site through its primary site, including the central site.

For more information on site hierarchy, refer to "Chapter 3—Understanding Sites" in the *Microsoft Systems Management Server Planning Guide,* and "Chapter 3—Installing and Upgrading Sites, Servers, and Clients" in the *Microsoft Systems Management Server 1.2 Resource Guide* of the *BackOffice Resource Kit, Second Edition.*

SMS Site Hierarchy Strategy

PGHCC network administrators deployed SMS throughout the network, arranging the site hierarchy geographically, following the configuration of the PGHCC Windows NT Domain whenever possible. The current domain structure consists of approximately 12,000 PCs spread across 13 geographic locations, with the largest concentration of PCs (about 5,000) residing in the central Metro site. All networked PCs in the enterprise are managed by an SMS site based on their physical location. PGHCC can group and manage distributed hardware and software assets according to location or specific business unit requirements.

The central site server and central SMS database reside on a dedicated machine in the PGHCC Metro data center. From this point they can be used to support physical security, monitoring, and scheduled backup cycles. Because you can install SMS administrator tools on any Windows NT-based PC with network access, you centralize or distribute SMS administration. If for some reason you do not want to administer SMS from a central site, you can manage the SMS site hierarchy from a Windows NT Workstation in a remote site.

Second-level primary site servers exist in branch offices named after their geographic area—Missouri, Indiana, and Alabama—for easier management. In the PGHCC implementation, administrators assigned unique SMS site codes (capitalized 3-letter strings) for each branch office (labeled BRN), as shown below.

SMS site codes and server names.

Geographic location	SMS site code	Server name
PGHCC Metro Data Center	PGH	PGH-SMS-001
Missouri BRN	MOB	BRN-MO
Indiana BRN	INB	BRN-IN
Alabama BRN	ALB	BRN-AL
Crimson Tide	CTB	BRN-CT

Figure 2.1 shows the basic PGHCC site hierarchy. Crimson Tide is the only field location specified as a secondary site server because it contains so many client workstations.

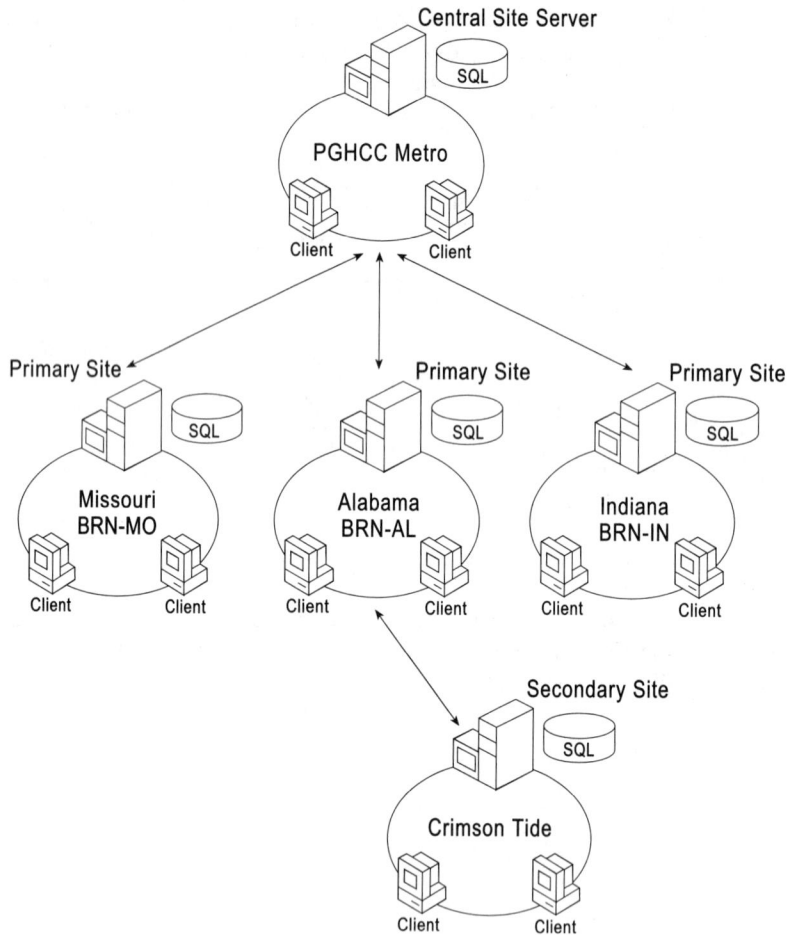

Figure 2.1 PGHCC site hierarchy with primary sites based on geographic areas.

Scalable Administration

You can manage inventory reporting and software distribution based on a computer's association with its Windows NT domain. At PGHCC, all servers and workstations reside in the master domain called PGHCC. The domain controller in each BRN location is configured as an SMS primary site server, reporting to its central site server parent site. All site locations report to and can be managed from their nearest BRN location.

A PGHCC Metro-based administrator handles all SMS site administration centrally. As the organization grows, network designs change, or administrators are added at field locations, the PGHCC can decentralize administration without changing the SMS infrastructure. For example, an administrator in the Missouri BRN location could be given permissions to manage only the client systems in the Burnstead, Ocean City, and Bloomington locations (see Figure 2.3, page 41). And of course the Metro-based administrator can always manage all sites.

Scaling the Infrastructure

PGHCC's site hierarchy allows for maximum scalability for future growth or changes in network design. As field locations grow, you can add secondary site servers to handle the additional load. As the number of users in a location increases, distribution servers can be added on existing server hardware to accommodate software update and distribution requirements.

As shown in Figure 2.1, PGHCC administrators planned the Crimson Tide location as a secondary site server. This was done to reduce the amount of network bandwidth required to collect inventory, distribute software, install SMS client software, and remotely control systems.

Distribution servers (designated at the building level) do not require dedicated SMS servers because SMS can use existing resource servers already configured for local print and file services. PGHCC provided dedicated SMS computers at primary and secondary-level sites, including the central site and database computers.

Bandwidth Efficiency

Designing the SMS hierarchy with primary site servers at each of the four major BRN locations minimized network traffic across WAN links, keeping most SMS activities within a site's routed subnets, and minimizing costs by using existing resource servers.

Within each primary site, inventory data collected from client PCs is stored in the local primary site server database. Each night when network utilization is at a minimum, inventory data is transferred over the WAN to the central site server.

Administrators can also create software distribution packages at the central site and send them to the four remote primary site locations during times of low network utilization. Once distributed throughout the SMS site hierarchy, packages can be quickly and efficiently installed on client PCs over the LAN.

SMS Client and Server Network Configuration

While the PGHCC Windows NT account domain manages user accounts, client computers belong to (and can be managed by) SMS sites, in this case based on geographic locations. Account domain controllers automatically detect new networked client computers upon successful authentication of each user, through the logon script.

PGHCC network administrators used the user logon process to balance SMS load activities across servers, greatly reducing single points of failure. They controlled the SMS rollout process, by "turning on" SMS for new client machines only through the logon and authentication of new Windows NT users, rolling out SMS, new desktops, and by extension *the network,* simultaneously.

The first time users turn on new workstations and log on to the Windows NT network, SMS is loaded and their inventory is reported. As PGHCC expands, more desktops come online, and the SMS system grows, SMS functions as a real-time management mechanism for the new environment.

SMS was activated on workstations by executing SMSLS.BAT from a logon server. Clients executed SMSLS.BAT automatically from a site server upon being validated by the preconfigured account domain controllers. SMSLS.BAT determines if SMS client code is already resident on the client machine, and if so, moves on to the inventory collection phase. If SMS is not resident on the machine, SMSLS.BAT initiates the client installation process and collects initial inventory. Refer to the "Sample Files Used in the PGHCC Implementation" to see the file used during the PGHCC pilot.

To ensure that each client machine runs SMSLS.BAT, a standard network logon script named LOGON.BAT connects clients to SMS servers and executes the SMSLS.BAT file during every user's network logon. Local sites can implement their own logon scripts by creating a LOCAL.BAT file, which is called by the standard network logon script after SMSLS.BAT.

The master LOGON.BAT file resides on (and is managed from) \\PGH-PDC. PGHCC administrators configured the Windows NT Replicator Service on this computer to distribute (or export) this standard logon script to all account domain controllers.

When any domain controller performs logon authentication for any client in the enterprise, it always calls LOGON.BAT—an approach that assures that new machines are discovered by the SMS system (as they are added), are mapped to the appropriate site servers, and are never inadvertently excluded from the inventory process.

SMSLS.BAT executes setup routines to install client components and report inventory. One of these routines, SETLS.EXE, checks the configuration file (SMSLS.INI) for any custom SMS settings. This text file maps each computer's inventory to the *resource* domain it belongs to, rather than to the *account* domain where the user logged on (which is the SMS default) because many users are authenticated across the WAN.

The master SMSLS.INI file resides on (and is managed from) \\PGH-PDC. Administrators also configured Windows NT Replicator Service on this server to distribute (or export) this file to all account domain controllers.

Deployment Strategy

General Recommendations and Best Practices

Some recommended steps for ensuring that the deployment succeeds:

- Thoroughly test before deploying new software or using new features.
- Properly train and prepare support and administrative teams for the deployment.
- Inform users about your deployment plans and be sure that they understand the product (to the degree appropriate for your organization).
- Phase your deployment efforts, proceeding slowly and cautiously at each step. Create backup plans to recover from problems.
- Schedule major SMS activities for off-hours.
- Do not enable SMS features unless they are required.

Some things to consider as you try to minimize the impact of your deployment on users:

- PGHCC had not uses Windows NT logon scripts before, so they introduced a very simple, user-friendly logon script well before they enabled SMS in the logon script. This gave users time to adjust to scripts, and provided time to resolve any issues introduced by the scripts themselves.
- When you enable SMS in logon scripts, customize them so users know what is happening. For instance, you can add a support contact and phone number for problems, the last revision reason and date, a short description of the SMS features you are providing, and so on.

PGHCC added this functionality to their logon scripts during the SMS pilot phase using the KiXTart scripting utility (KIX32.EXE—found in the *Microsoft Windows NT 4.0 Resource Kit, Supplement 3*) to enhance functionality.

Note See the "Sample Files Used in the PGHCC Implementation" section (page 49) for script details and descriptions.

- Consider customizing scripts for different users, using environment variables or file existence checks to trigger particular actions. For instance, you can have a script run in a verbose mode for less experienced users, and provide a script for seasoned users that runs with little or no feedback.

- Give users time to accept SMS. Do not schedule major work using SMS right away. Try not to schedule intrusive or time-consuming jobs unless you are sure that your users need the functionality provided by the job.

- Inform and educate your users about SMS before you deploy it to their computers. SMS includes a sample file (CLIENT.WRI) that you can customize and distribute to users, describing what SMS is, why a company might want to use it, and how it affects clients.

Phased Deployment Plan

You can control risk by implementing the SMS site infrastructure using a phased approach. The PGHCC network design inherently provided well-defined areas in which a phased deployment took place. For example, network administrators configured a single BRN and verified client data collection before moving to the next BRN.

A phased deployment also allows you to test the hierarchy before adding clients, or moving on to additional site locations, or implementing more complicated SMS functionality. You can even disable all of the client software when you add your clients, which causes SMS to install the client portions but run only hardware inventory. You can enable SMS client software as you need it, again, phasing in new functionality and thereby reducing risk.

Here's PGHCC's four-phase model to build the SMS site infrastructure:

Deployment Phase I: PGHCC Metro Data Center

The PGHCC deployment team planned an SMS pilot project to set up the central site server and SQL Server database configurations to handle all client data collection for the Metro area (Chicago). In addition, they configured all Windows NT domain controllers as logon servers to handle all possible user authentication and SMS client installation scenarios across WAN links.

```
     Central Site Server
        Site Code: PGH
   SMS Domain: PGHCC
```

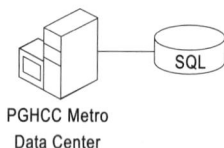

PGHCC Metro
Data Center

Figure 2.2 Deployment Phase I established the central site SMS server.

Deployment Phase II: Missouri BRN

Phase II established the branch office in Missouri, following these steps:

1. Procure and install a dedicated SMS server for the Missouri BRN location.
2. Install and configure SQL Server.
3. Install and configure SMS as a primary site, reporting to the central site server (\\PGH-SMS-001).
4. Configure additional senders and addresses.
5. Configure existing backup domain controllers (BDCs) in Burnstead, Ocean City, and Bloomington as distribution servers.
6. Verify the integrity of the site infrastructure.
7. Add Burnstead clients.
8. Verify client data collection.
9. Add Ocean City clients.
10. Verify client data collection.
11. Add Bloomington clients.
12. Verify client data collection.

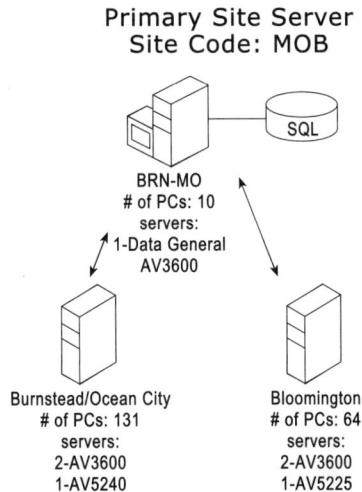

Primary Site Server
Site Code: MOB

SQL

BRN-MO
# of PCs: 10
servers:
1-Data General
AV3600

Burnstead/Ocean City
# of PCs: 131
servers:
2-AV3600
1-AV5240

Bloomington
# of PCs: 64
servers:
2-AV3600
1-AV5225

Figure 2.3 Schematic of the Missouri site, established in Phase II.

Deployment Phase III: Indiana BRN

Phase III established the branch office in Indiana:

1. Procure and install a dedicated SMS server for the Indiana BRN site.
2. Install and configure SQL Server.
3. Install and configure SMS as a primary site, reporting to the central site server (\\PGH-SMS-001)
4. Configure additional senders and addresses.
5. Configure existing BDCs in Carver, Columbus, and Bedford/New Amsterdam as distribution servers.
6. Verify the integrity of the site infrastructure.
7. Add Carver clients.
8. Verify client data collection.
9. Add Columbus clients.
10. Verify client data collection.
11. Add Bedford clients.
12. Verify client data collection.
13. Add New Amsterdam clients.
14. Verify client data collection.

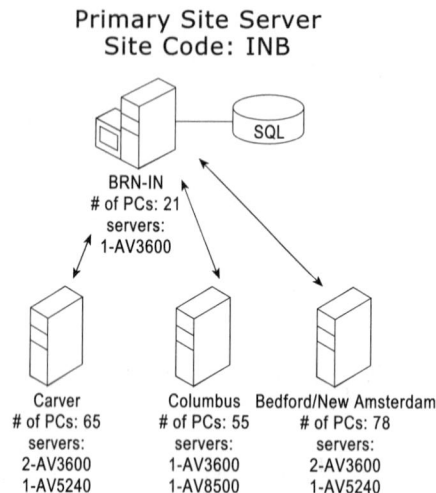

Figure 2.4 Adding the Indiana primary site.

Deployment Phase IV: Alabama BRN

Phase IV established the branch office in Alabama:

1. Procure and install a dedicated SMS server for the Alabama BRN location.
2. Install and configure SQL Server.
3. Install and configure SMS as a primary site, reporting to the central site server (\\PGH-SMS-001)
4. Configure additional senders and addresses.
5. Configure existing BDCs in Fayetteville, Bloomington, and Gardner as distribution servers.
6. Verify the integrity of the site infrastructure.
7. Add Fayetteville clients.
8. Verify client data collection.
9. Add Bloomington clients.
10. Verify client data collection.
11. Add Gardner clients.
12. Verify client data collection.
13. Install and configure *secondary SMS site* at Crimson Tide.
14. Configure senders and addresses.
15. Verify site communication to BRN-AL.
16. Add Crimson Tide clients.
17. Verify client data collection.

Primary Site Server
Site Code: ALB

BRN-AL
# of PCs: 15
servers:
1-AV3600

Secondary Site Server
Site Code: CTB

Fayetteville
# of PCs: 64
servers:
2-AV3600
1-AV5240

Gardner
# of PCs: 78
servers:
2-AV3600
1-AV9500

Crimson Tide
# of PCs: 218
servers:
1-AV3600
2-AV3650r
1-AV8500

Bloomington
# of PCs: 52
servers:
1-AV3600

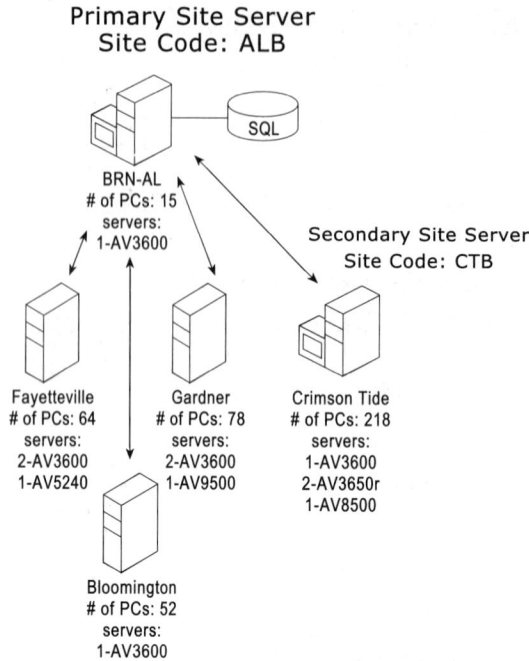

Figure 2.5 Establishing the Alabama and Crimson Tide sites during Phase IV.

SMS Administration

A well-designed infrastructure goes a long way toward successful use of SMS in the daily administration of your enterprise. Ongoing maintenance of the SMS database is an important part of maintaining it as a finely tuned and efficient management tool.

Software Distribution Best Practices

Standardizing software across any enterprise is crucial to software distribution. Keep in mind that SMS provides only the *distribution mechanism* for software packages: it does not eliminate the need for thorough application compatibility testing, package creation and deployment testing, and certification.

For SMS design purposes, you can categorize client software as standard or non-standard. **Standard** software is company or business unit-wide software (Windows 9*x*, Windows NT, and Microsoft Office, including other vendor-provided applications) installed from the loadset with some variations to accommodate departmental or business unit needs. **Non-standard** software is used by few, or is not supported by the enterprise.

You can use SMS to distribute standard enterprise software when:

- The manufacturer upgrades the standard software.
- A computer has a technical problem that requires software re-installation.
- A new computer is set up without the standard loadset.

Although your enterprise might distribute standard software infrequently, you should still copy distribution packages *to each SMS site server.* Having multiple servers provides backup for application installations is particularly useful in disaster recovery should a site server or client PCs need to be rebuilt without access to a local SMS distribution server. Whenever a user requests a standard software load, you can schedule an immediate SMS job to run the installation from the user's local SMS site server, which already has the standard software in uncompressed form. If the user's site server is down, you can redirect the installation to run from the nearest working site server.

This approach uses more disk space on site-level servers, but can save bandwidth by not transmitting standard software across the WAN to satisfy user requests. It also circumvents the delay (several hours) from the time you create a new SMS package to the time it arrives and is decompressed on the distribution server. This way, users can install standard software within 15 minutes of requesting it. You can stage non-standard software on distribution servers if the number of users justifies the increased disk usage.

Here are some recommendations and best practices for staging standard software or distributing a new version to many users:

- Distribute the SMS package to site servers in phases to minimize (or at least stagger) network bandwidth utilization across the WAN.

- Schedule the distribution of these packages for weekend nights to avoid interfering with normal workday network traffic and weekday evening backup and maintenance routines.

- When scheduling installation for large numbers of users, schedule the client job distribution to run the standard software installation in staggered phases. For example, once the new standard software exists on each site server, schedule client installation for some users in each branch office area each day, minimizing use of network bandwidth and site server CPU time during work hours.

By default, SMS distribution jobs target computers, or groups of computers for distribution and installation of software. Groups can be created easily by querying the SMS database. For example, query on the machines running Word 6.0, and then target that group for Word 97 installation.

Here's a list of software distribution practices that PGHCC implemented, and their benefits:

- Install the initial standard loadset prior to delivery of a new PC.

  Benefit: Network bandwidth use is reduced.

- Make all standard software available through the SMS site hierarchy infrastructure.

  Benefit: Existing workstations have access.

- Stage all standard software on all SMS site servers.

  Benefit: Network bandwidth use and distribution delays are minimized.

- Provide SMS site servers with adequate disk resources to house staged standard software.

  Benefit: Significant savings by not requiring more dedicated SMS servers (despite any additional cost for disk space *on resource servers* depending on size of standard software packages).

- Manage non-standard software installations on a case-by-case basis.

  Benefit: The business justification must consider the cost of your SMS administrators creating and managing non-standard software distribution.

- Schedule software distribution across the WAN during off-peak hours.

  Benefit: This significantly reduces network bandwidth use, but does not accommodate *immediate, real-time* distribution. Devise a contingency plan for emergency distribution of non-standard or new standard software.

SMS Maintenance Recommendations

The central SQL database server requires regular backup, but since it resides in the central data center you can easily add this job to a network administrator's regular duties. Perform a full backup each week and incremental backups throughout the week.

The SMS system itself requires minimal maintenance, providing operational stability. If any portion of the system other than the central database goes down, you'll lose minimal functionality.

- If a site server goes down and the central database stays up, most management functions are not interrupted. You can run the SMS Administrator utility from any Windows NT workstation or server.

- Although SMS collects inventory data at every user logon, inventory reporting to the central site typically takes place only once a day. Changes in inventory are infrequent, and it isn't critical to maintain up-to-the-minute inventory data. The SMS administrator can configure the frequency in which inventory data is relayed up to the central site server.

- When a downed site server comes back online, it automatically begins collecting inventory again, and synchronizes with the central database during the next scheduled synchronization. In this respect SMS is a "self correcting" management system.

- As long as the central database is running, helpdesk staff can still remotely control users—even users in a site with a downed server.

- Package distribution is load-balanced across many distribution servers, so users in a site with a downed server can still execute any jobs that have already been sent. They experience an interruption in current jobs only if the downed server is *the only* distribution server targeted for that package. Otherwise, other distribution servers are used until the downed server is restored. New distribution jobs must wait for the site server to come back online.

- Program groups controlled by SMS continue to work if a site server is down, but distribution of new program groups must wait for the site server to come back online.

Use Windows NT Performance Monitor regularly to assess performance of various system components for retuning as needed, including processor utilization percentages, memory utilization, and physical disk access. Of course, a well-managed Windows NT network should include backup and recovery plans for all major systems. Chapter 3 discusses how to back up and recover your SMS infrastructure.

Sample Files Used in the PGHCC Implementation

To enhance logon script functionality, PGHCC used KiXTart scripting language to expose system variables and settings not available through traditional batch file programming. Here are some commented examples of the scripts and files used in the PGHCC SMS pilot deployment.

ISLOGON.BAT

```
@ECHO OFF
CLS
ECHO.
ECHO One moment while your login script runs ...

REM  Check what OS the user is running.
if "%OS%" == "Windows_NT" SET XCOPYDIR=%windir%\system32
if "%OS%" == "" SET XCOPYDIR=%windir%\command
if "%OS%" == "" %0\..\WINSET XCOPYDIR=%windir%\command
if "%XCOPYDIR%" == "" SET XCOPYDIR=%windir%\command

REM  Copy CHECKRAS,KIX32 & KIX DLLs to user's local temp drive
REM  and subdirectory for much faster execution, especially
REM  in remote access scenarios

%XCOPYDIR%\xcopy %0\..\CHECKRAS.EXE %TEMP%\CHECKRAS.exe /C /Q   /D
/I<%0\..\f.txt >NUL

%XCOPYDIR%\xcopy %0\..\KIX32.EXE %TEMP%\KIX32.exe /C /Q /D
/I<%0\..\f.txt >NUL

%XCOPYDIR%\xcopy %0\..\KX16.DLL %TEMP%\KX16.DLL /C /Q /D
/I<%0\..\f.txt >NUL
```

```
%XCOPYDIR%\xcopy %0\..\KX32.DLL %TEMP%\KX32.DLL /C /Q /D
/I<%0\..\f.txt >NUL

%XCOPYDIR%\xcopy %0\..\CHOICE.EXE %TEMP%\CHOICE.EXE /C /Q /D
/I<%0\..\f.txt >NUL

REM  Map drive L: for LaserArc users.

call %0\..\LARC

REM  Install SMS Client.

call %0\..\SMSLS2

REM  Synchronize time with domain controller.

net time \\PGH-PDC /SET /YES

************* End of ISLOGON.BAT Listing **************
```

SMSLS2.BAT

```
@echo OFF
cls

REM  Check for a Dial-Up Networking/RAS Connection
REM  (NOT A BRIDGE/RTR)

SET RASAPI=0


IF EXIST %windir%\system\rasapi32.dll SET RASAPI=1
```

This code is spaced so that it is easier to read. Lines are broken for layout only: entries should be on a single line. If you want to skip this section, go to page 64.

SMSLS2.BAT   *(continued)*

```
IF EXIST %windir%\system32\rasapi32.dll SET RASAPI=1

IF "%RASAPI%" == "0" goto NODUN

%TEMP%\checkras>nul

if errorlevel 1 goto RAS

goto NODUN

:RAS

echo.

echo Remote access detected ... SMS client will not run !

pause

goto END

:NODUN

REM  Launch the KixScript to check for SMS Pilot Participation.

dir>%TEMP%\NOTINSMS.TMP

%TEMP%\kix32.exe %0\..\kixdosms.scr

REM  Since environment variables don't work right, temp files
REM  are deleted by KS when user is in SMS PILOT group.
```

This code is spaced so that it is easier to read. Lines are broken for layout only: entries should be on a single line. If you want to skip this section, go to page 64.

```
IF EXIST %TEMP%\NOTINSMS.TMP SET NOTINSMS=1

IF NOT EXIST %TEMP%\NOTINSMS.TMP SET NOTINSMS=0

if "%NOTINSMS%" == "1" goto END

REM Copy the most recent SMSWIN.INI for DMI/TopTools.

%XCOPYDIR%\xcopy %0\..\smswin.ini C:\DMI\Win32\Bin\SMSWIN.INI /C /Q
/D /I<%0\..\f.txt >NUL

REM  Create TEMP files on user's local drive to denote
REM  OPTIONAL/MANDATORY and REMOTE/LOCAL BRIDGE/RTR access
REM  for KixScript.

dir>%TEMP%\SMSTEMP.DIR

dir>%TEMP%\HSACCESS.DIR

REM  Check for variable on user's system for SMS to NEVER
REM  execute. USE THIS SPARINGLY.

if "%SMSNEVER%" == "1" goto END

REM  Launch the KixScript (kixscript.scr) to check for
REM  remote access and optional execution of SMS.

%TEMP%\kix32.exe %0\..\kixscr~1.scr


REM  Since environment variables don't work right, KS deletes
REM  temp files when OPTIONAL and REMOTE ACCESS is found.

IF EXIST %TEMP%\SMSTEMP.DIR SET SMSMAND=1
```

> This code is spaced so that it is easier to read. Lines are broken for layout only: entries should be on a single line. If you want to skip this section, go to page 64.

SMSLS2.BAT   *(continued)*

```
IF NOT EXIST %TEMP%\SMSTEMP.DIR SET SMSMAND=0

IF EXIST %TEMP%\HSACCESS.DIR SET HSACCESS=1

IF NOT EXIST %TEMP%\HSACCESS.DIR SET HSACCESS=0

REM  Check the EV set directly above by the presence or
REM  absence of temp files for HIGH SPEED or REMOTE.

echo.

if "%HSACCESS%" == "0" goto END

REM  Check the EV set directly above by the presence or absence
REM  of temp files for MANDATORY or OPTIONAL.


echo.

if "%SMSMAND%" == "0" goto MAYBE

if "%SMSMAND%" == "1" goto YES

if "%SMSMAND%" == "" goto YES

goto YES

REM  Optional execution.

echo.
```

This code is spaced so that it is easier to read. Lines are broken for layout only: entries should be on a single line. If you want to skip this section, go to page 64.

SMSLS2.BAT *(continued)*

```
:MAYBE

%TEMP%\CHOICE Run SMS? /T:Y,15

if errorlevel 2 goto END

REM  Mandatory execution.


:YES

REM  Copyright (C) 1994-1995 Microsoft Corporation.

REM

REM  This batch file is the Systems Management Server (SMS)
REM  logon script for workstations logging in to a Windows NT
REM  or LAN Manager server. It installs the SMS client components
REM  and collects hardware and software inventory data.

echo.

echo Microsoft Systems Management Server (SMS)

echo.


REM Checking for HP TopTools SMS Client ...
```

This code is spaced so that it is easier to read. Lines are broken for layout only: entries should be on a single line. If you want to skip this section, go to page 64.

SMSLS2.BAT   *(continued)*

```
if "%OS%" == "Windows_NT" goto SKIPSMSWIN

echo Checking for HP TopTools SMS Client ...

IF NOT EXIST C:\SMS.INI goto :skipsmswin

IF NOT EXIST C:\DMI\Win32\Bin\SMSWIN.EXE goto :skipsmswin

START /W c:\dmi\win32\bin\SMSWIN.EXE

ECHO HP TopTools SMS Client found and executed.

echo.

goto next

:skipsmswin

ECHO HP TopTools and/or SMS Client not present and/or configured.

echo.

:next

REM  If the SMSLS environment variable is set on the workstation
REM  (for example, set SMSLS=1), verbose output is enabled
REM  for SETLS16, CLI_DOS, and INVDOS or SETLS32, CLI_NT and
REM  INVWIN32.
```

This code is spaced so that it is easier to read. Lines are broken for layout only: entries should be on a single line. If you want to skip this section, go to page 64.

```
if "%SMSLS%" == "" goto START

set SMS_VERBOSE=/v

echo Executing SMS logon script.

goto START

REM  Determine the binary files directory on the SMS logon server
REM  by checking environment variables for operating system and
REM  processor architecture. Set environment variables for this
REM  directory and for the OS type. The directory this file
REM  exists in and the platform-specific directory beneath it
REM  are added to the path so that the proper version of SETLS
REM  and NLSMSG can be called.

:START

REM  Check to see if we can save path and reserve the necessary
REM  environment space before continuing.
```

This code is spaced so that it is easier to read. Lines are broken for layout only: entries should be on a single line. If you want to skip this section, go to page 64.

SMSLS2.BAT   *(continued)*

```
set SMS_P=%PATH%

set SMS_TEMP=123456789012345678901234567890123456789012345

if "%SMS_TEMP%"=="123456789012345678901234567890123456789012345"
goto FIND_OS

goto LOW_ENV

:FIND_OS

set SMS_TEMP=

if "%OS%" == "Windows_NT" goto NT_BIN

REM  Determine the MS-DOS version and exit if OS/2 1.3 or
REM  greater.

%0\..\dosver

if errorlevel 13 goto OS2


:DOS_BIN

set SMS_OS=16

set SMS_BIN=x86.bin

goto RUN_FROM

:NT_BIN
```

> This code is spaced so that it is easier to read. Lines are broken for layout only: entries should be on a single line. If you want to skip this section, go to page 64.

SMSLS2.BAT   *(continued)*

```
if "%PROCESSOR_ARCHITECTURE%" == "ALPHA" goto NT_ALPHA

if "%PROCESSOR_ARCHITECTURE%" == "MIPS"  goto NT_MIPS

if "%PROCESSOR_ARCHITECTURE%" == "x86"   goto NT_X86

if "%PROCESSOR_ARCHITECTURE%" == "PPC"   goto NT_PPC

echo.

echo Unable to determine operating system or processor architecture.

echo.

echo Consult your network administrator.

echo.

Pause

goto END

:NT_ALPHA

set SMS_BIN=alpha.bin

set SMS_OS=32

goto RUN_FROM


:NT_MIPS
```

This code is spaced so that it is easier to read. Lines are broken for layout only: entries should be on a single line. If you want to skip this section, go to page 64.

SMSLS2.BAT   *(continued)*

```
set SMS_BIN=mips.bin

set SMS_OS=32

goto RUN_FROM

:NT_X86

set SMS_BIN=x86.bin

set SMS_OS=32

goto RUN_FROM

:NT_PPC

REM  The PowerPC is not supported in this release.


goto END

:RUN_FROM

if "%OS%" == "Windows_NT"    set PATH=%PATH%;%0\..\%SMS_BIN%

if not "%OS%" == "Windows_NT" set

PATH=%0\..;%0\..\%SMS_BIN%;"%PATH%"

REM  Check for a slow network connection to the NETLOGON share
```

This code is spaced so that it is easier to read. Lines are broken for layout only: entries should be on a single line. If you want to skip this section, go to page 64.

SMSLS2.BAT *(continued)*

```
REM  and possibly exit. If not, the SETLS program is run during
REM  NETLOGON to a Windows NT or LAN Manager server and is used
REM  to find the correct SMS logon server and spawn the
REM  executable files for CLI_DOS and INVDOS or CLI_NT and
REM  INVWIN32 located on this server.

Netspeed

if not errorlevel 1 goto RUN_SETLS

if not errorlevel 2 goto RESTORE

if errorlevel 2 NLSMSG%SMS_OS% 6 /C YN,101 /# 1,30 /M "Slow network
detected. Continue"

if not errorlevel 2 goto RUN_SETLS

goto RESTORE

:RUN_SETLS

if "%OS%" == "Windows_NT" goto RUN_NT

:RUN_DOS

setls%SMS_OS% -m:E -i -p:%SMS_BIN%\CLI_DOS.EXE pa:/p:%%SMS_UNC%%\ -
pa:%SMS_VERBOSE% %SMS_VERBOSE%
```

This code is spaced so that it is easier to read. Lines are broken for layout only: entries should be on a single line. If you want to skip this section, go to page 64.

```
setls%SMS_OS% -m:E -i -p:%SMS_BIN%\INVDOS.EXE -pa:/l:%%SMS_UNC%%\ -
pa:/i -pa:%SMS_VERBOSE% %SMS_VERBOSE%

goto RESTORE

:RUN_NT

setls%SMS_OS% -m:E -i -p:%SMS_BIN%\CLI_NT.EXE -pa:/p:%%SMS_UNC%%\ -
pa:%SMS_VERBOSE% %SMS_VERBOSE%

setls%SMS_OS% -m:E -i -p:%SMS_BIN%\INVWIN32.EXE -pa:/l:%%SMS_UNC%%\
-pa:/e -pa:/t0 -pa:/i -pa:%SMS_VERBOSE% %SMS_VERBOSE%

goto RESTORE

:OS2

echo.

%0\..\x86.bin\NLSMSGo2 5 /M "Please run SMSLS.CMD from an OS/2
window"

echo.

Pause

goto END

REM  SMSLS was unable to reserve the necessary amount of
REM  environment space and was unable to complete successfully.
```

This code is spaced so that it is easier to read. Lines are broken for layout only: entries should be on a single line. If you want to skip this section, go to page 64.

```
REM Increase available environment space and repeat logon.

:LOW_ENV

set SMS_TEMP=

REM  Try to start a new command shell to procure more environment
REM  space, but only once to avoid extra recursion.

if "%1" == "" goto newshell

echo.

%0\..\x86.bin\NLSMSG16 7 /M "Not enough environment space"

%0\..\x86.bin\NLSMSG16 8 /M "Use the /E parameter on the shell=
command in config.sys"

%0\..\x86.bin\NLSMSG16 9 /M "to increase the amount of environment
space available."

Pause

goto END

:newshell
```

This code is spaced so that it is easier to read. Lines are broken for layout only: entries should be on a single line. If you want to skip this section, go to page 64.

SMSLS2.BAT   *(continued)*

```
command /e:2048 /c %0 retry

goto END

:RESTORE

REM  Restore the previous path setting.

PATH=%SMS_P%

goto END

REM  Clean up the environment variables and reset the errorlevel.

:END

set SMS_P=

set SMS_BIN=

set SMS_VERBOSE=

set NOTINSMS=

set SMSMAND=

set HSACCESS=

set RASAPI=

if exist %TEMP%\SMSTEMP.DIR del %TEMP%\SMSTEMP.DIR
```

This code is spaced so that it is easier to read. Lines are broken for layout only: entries should be on a single line. If you want to skip this section, go to page 64.

```
if exist %TEMP%\HSACCESS.DIR del %TEMP%\HSACCESS.DIR

if exist %TEMP%\NOTINSMS.TMP del %TEMP%\NOTINSMS.TMP

if exist %TEMP%\XCOPY.EXE del %TEMP%\XCOPY.EXE

if exist %TEMP%\XCOPY32.EXE del %TEMP%\XCOPY32.EXE

if errorlevel 1 %0\..\clrlevel

************ End of SMSLS2.BAT Listing ***************
```

KIXSCRIPT.SCR

```
CLS

COLOR y+/n

? "You were authenticated by the ("+@LSERVER+") NT server ..."

IF INGROUP("User Debug")=1

COLOR w+/n

?

? "You are in DEBUG MODE ..."

?
```

This code is spaced so that it is easier to read. Lines are broken for layout only: entries should be on a single line. If you want to skip this section, go to page 70.

KIXSCRIPT.SCR   *(continued)*

```
? "Logged-in User Full Name : @FULLNAME"

? "Logged-in User UserID    : @USERID"

? "Logged-in User Comment   : @COMMENT"

? "Logged-in User O/S        : @INWIN (1=NT,2=95)"

? "Computer O/S SubDir      : @LANROOT"

? "Computer NETBIOS Name    : @WKSTA"

? "Network Card MAC Address : @ADDRESS"

? "Current NT Domain        : @DOMAIN"

? "Logon Domain             : @LDOMAIN"

? "Logon Server             : @LSERVER"

? "Current Logon Server Ver : @DOS"

? "NETLOGON Drive           : @LDRIVE"

? "KiXtart Version          : @KIX"

?

at (23,26) "<any key to continue>"
```

This code is spaced so that it is easier to read. Lines are broken for layout only: entries should be on a single line. If you want to skip this section, go to page 70.

```
get $x

?

?

ENDIF

COLOR r+/n

?"Greetings, @FULLNAME, today is @DAY, day @MDAYNO of @MONTH @YEAR
..."

?

SLEEP 1

COLOR w/n

$IPA0=ReadValue("HKEY_LOCAL_MACHINE\System\CurrentControlSet\Service
s\Class\NetTrans\0000","IPAddress")

$IPA1=ReadValue("HKEY_LOCAL_MACHINE\System\CurrentControlSet\Service
s\Class\NetTrans\0001","IPAddress")

$IPA2=ReadValue("HKEY_LOCAL_MACHINE\System\CurrentControlSet\Service
s\Class\NetTrans\0002","IPAddress")

$IPA3=ReadValue("HKEY_LOCAL_MACHINE\System\CurrentControlSet\Service
s\Class\NetTrans\0003","IPAddress")
```

This code is spaced so that it is easier to read. Lines are broken for layout only: entries should be on a single line. If you want to skip this section, go to page 70.

KIXSCRIPT.SCR   *(continued)*

```
$IPA4=ReadValue("HKEY_LOCAL_MACHINE\System\CurrentControlSet\Service
s\Class\NetTrans\0004","IPAddress")

$IPRA0 = INSTR($IPA0,"123.456.789")

$IPRA1 = INSTR($IPA1,"123.456.789")

$IPRA2 = INSTR($IPA2,"123.456.789")

$IPRA3 = INSTR($IPA3,"123.456.789")

$IPRA4 = INSTR($IPA4,"123.456.789")

$IPRA5 = INSTR($IPA0,"0.0.0.0")

$IPRA6 = INSTR($IPA1,"0.0.0.0")

$IPRA7 = INSTR($IPA2,"0.0.0.0")

$IPRA8 = INSTR($IPA3,"0.0.0.0")

$IPRA9 = INSTR($IPA4,"0.0.0.0")

IF $IPRA0 = 1

 $Selection=MessageBox("Remote access detected -- SMS will not run
!","Alert!",0)

 DEL "%TEMP%\HSACCESS.DIR"

ENDIF
```

This code is spaced so that it is easier to read. Lines are broken for layout only: entries should be on a single line. If you want to skip this section, go to page 70.

```
IF $IPRA1 = 1


  $Selection=MessageBox("Remote access detected -- SMS will not run
!","Alert!",0)

  DEL "%TEMP%\HSACCESS.DIR"

ENDIF

IF $IPRA2 = 1

  $Selection=MessageBox("Remote access detected -- SMS will not run
!","Alert!",0)

  DEL "%TEMP%\HSACCESS.DIR"

ENDIF

IF $IPRA3 = 1

  $Selection=MessageBox("Remote access detected -- SMS will not run
!","Alert!",0)

DEL "%TEMP%\HSACCESS.DIR"

ENDIF

IF $IPRA4 = 1

  $Selection=MessageBox("Remote access detected -- SMS will not run
!","Alert!",0)
```

This code is spaced so that it is easier to read. Lines are broken for layout only: entries should be on a single line. If you want to skip this section, go to page 70.

```
    DEL "%TEMP%\HSACCESS.DIR"

ENDIF

IF INGROUP("SMS Optional")=1

? "SMS-O"

DEL "%TEMP%\SMSTEMP.DIR"

ENDIF

IF INGROUP("SMS Mandatory")=1

? "SMS-M"

ENDIF

EXIT

***************** End of KIXSCRIPT.SCR Listing *******************
```

This code is spaced so that it is easier to read. Lines are broken for layout only: entries should be on a single line. If you want to skip this section, go to page 70.

KIXDOSMS.SCR

The KIXDOSMS.SCR is called from the :NODUN section of the SMSLS2.BAT file. It was implemented for the SMS pilot only. This script tests for inclusion in the Window NT group "SMS Pilot" and if not present will not install the SMS client software.

```
*************** Start KIXDOSMS.SCR listing *****************

IF INGROUP("SMS Pilot")=1

 DEL "%TEMP%\NOTINSMS.TMP"

ENDIF

EXIT

**************** End KIXDOSMS.SCR listing ******************
```

CHAPTER 3

Backup and Recovery of an SMS Infrastructure at River City Power

By Nigel Cain, MCS—United Kingdom, and David Millett, MCS—Northern California

The information (inventory, software packages, and job status) contained in a successful Microsoft Systems Management Server (SMS) implementation is a significant investment—in money *and* the time and effort required to collect it. To protect this resource against loss, you need to perform regular maintenance checks and implement a disaster recovery policy. This chapter explains how to create a policy, describes a number of troubleshooting steps, and discusses the consequences of restoring from backup media. It also details how to make a secure backup in a real-world situation using an automated process that regularly backs up all relevant SMS data.

In Focus

Enterprise

River City Power provides power to three states. Its headquarters is in Portland, Oregon.

Network

Three SMS sites: a central and primary site located on the same LAN, another primary site connected via a WAN link.

Challenge

The IT group wants to avoid the expense and management problems associated with having a tape backup unit for each SMS site server.

Solution

As detailed in the second half of this chapter, the IT group created an automated process to back up all site information on a single server, and build a stable image for use during recovery.

What You'll Find In This Chapter

- An explanation of backup processes and strategies for Systems Management Server.

- How to create a reliable backup image.

- Troubleshooting steps for backup and restore operations.

- An explanation of the consequences of restoring from backup media.

- How to make a secure backup in a real-world situation using an automated process that regularly backs up all relevant SMS data on SMS site and logon servers.

Warning This chapter makes recommendations for tuning the Windows NT registry using the Registry Editor. Using the Registry Editor incorrectly can cause serious, system-wide problems that require you to reinstall Windows NT. Microsoft cannot guarantee that any problems resulting from the use of Registry Editor can be solved. Use this tool at your own risk.

In general, Systems Management Server (SMS) requires little maintenance: with regular checks on the log files, Windows NT events and the SQL database, you can avoid most common problems. Even if serious problems occur, SMS may still continue to function. If a site server fails but the SMS database is still available, management functions may continue uninterrupted, and administrators or helpdesk technicians can run the SMS Administrator program from any Windows NT computer.

Inventory reporting, collected locally at each logon, is transferred to a primary site server only once a day. Amendments to machine inventory are infrequent and it is not critical to keep this information up-to-date. Once a site server is back online, it begins recapturing any inventory changes. And package distribution can be load balanced across a number of servers, so that applications and jobs can be accessed even if one of the servers fails.

Although it may be possible for SMS to recover from many of these situations, there may be circumstances where you have no other option than to restore from backup media. In these cases, a dependable system backup, comprehensive documentation, and an awareness of the recovery process may mean the difference between a live operational system and re-installing SMS.

Documenting the Site

In many organizations, SMS has been implemented with little or no supporting documentation. Little information is recorded on site settings and configuration changes are made without reference to site server loading or the potential impact on network bandwidth. But lack of adequate documentation can make it more difficult to manage even a simple SMS hierarchy, and recovering from a failure, even if regular backups are taken, may force you to restore more than should be necessary.

As a minimum, you should create and maintain documents that detail the SMS design, the physical implementation of the design within the organization (deployment document), and each site server's configuration. Configuration settings should be subject to some form of change control to ensure that the site can be recovered in the event of a systems failure.

Making a Manual Backup

Making an SMS backup is not simple, although the process is relatively straightforward. A typical implementation includes at least one primary site server, several secondary site servers, and a number of logon and distribution servers. The backup procedure for each of these server "types" is discussed in turn below.

Primary Site Server

A primary site has its own SQL Server database to store the system, package, inventory, and status information for the primary site and the sites beneath it in the hierarchy. It also has administrative tools to directly manage all sites in the site hierarchy.

Making a clean backup of an SMS primary site server is a crucial task, which must be performed in two phases: the first is concerned with the SMS database, and the second with the Windows NT file system and registry. The nature of the backup process and the amount of data being written to backup media may keep the primary site server offline for two or more hours. You can speed this up by installing backup devices into each primary site server.

The steps below outline the backup process, the Windows NT services that need to be shut down for the duration of the backup task, and the order in which you should carry this out.

1. Stop all SMS services by creating a batch file containing the following commands or by issuing them directly from the Windows NT command line.

   ```
   NET STOP SMS_CLIENT_CONFIG_MANAGER

   NET STOP SMS_EXECUTIVE

   NET STOP SMS_HIERARCHY_MANAGER

   NET STOP SMS_INVENTORY_AGENT_NT

   NET STOP SMS_PACKAGE_COMMAND_MANAGER_NT

   NET STOP SMS_SITE_CONFIG_MANAGER
   ```

2. After all SMS services have been successfully shut down, back up the SQL databases. Note that along with the SMS database, you should also back up the master, model, and MSDB databases to tape.

3. Stop all SQL Server services to allow the file system backup to take place.

   ```
   NET STOP MSSQLSERVER

   NET STOP SQLEXECUTIVE
   ```

4. Create a copy of the SMS site server's registry keys using Registry Editor (included with Windows NT). If you use REGBACK to copy registry keys then you'll have to delete any old Windows NT Server registry backup files in the Windows NT Server registry backup directory, because the REGBACK utility cannot overwrite old backup files (see page 99).

   ```
   IF EXIST C:\WINNT\SMS.REG DEL C:\WINNT\SMS.REG

   REGEDIT /E C:\WINNT\SMS.REG HKEY_LOCAL_MACHINE\SOFTWARE\Microsoft\SMS
   ```

5. Back up the complete file system to tape, including the database device (.DAT) files and the SMS configuration file, SMS.INI.

6. Restart SQL Server.

```
NET START MSSQLSERVER
NET START SQLEXECUTIVE
```

7. Restart all SMS services.

```
NET START SMS_CLIENT_CONFIG_MANAGER
NET START SMS_EXECUTIVE
NET START SMS_HIERACHY_MANAGER
NET START SMS_INVENTORY_AGENT_NT
NET START SMS_PACKAGE_COMMAND_MANAGER_NT
NET START SMS_SITE_CONFIG_MANAGER
```

Once the backup has completed, check the Windows NT event logs to ensure that all SMS and SQL Server services started successfully and that the site is operational. Make a test restore at frequent intervals to ensure that data was actually written to the storage media.

Along with the backup tape, you should also maintain an **isql** script that will re-create the structure of a restored SMS database. Make sure this script is updated whenever the size or structure of the SMS database is changed, because restoration is impossible without it. A sample database creation script is shown below.

Check for available device numbers by running **sp_helpdevice** and noting the ones used by any existing device files. User files must be assigned a unique number between 0 and 255.

Create the SMS database devices.

```
DISK INIT
    NAME = 'SMSDBData'
    PHYSNAME = 'D:\MSSQL\DATA\SMSDBData.DAT'
    VDEVNO = Obtain next unique number from sp_helpdevice
    SIZE = 102400 (200 Mb)

DISK INIT
    NAME = 'SMSDBLog'
    PHYSNAME = 'D:\MSSQL\DATA\SMSDBLog.DAT'
    VDEVNO = Obtain next unique number from sp_helpdevice
    SIZE = 20480 (40 Mb)
```

Create the SMS database and extend the size (if required).

```
CREATE DATABASE SMS
    ON SMSDBData = 100
    LOG ON SMSDBLog = 20
ALTER DATABASE SMS
    ON SMSDBData = 200
ALTER DATABASE SMS
    ON SMSDBLog = 40
```

You should also make a point of running the **sp_helpdevice** and **sp_helpdb** stored procedures on the SMS database and database devices whenever changes are made to the database. Record the results in an SMS change log, because this information will greatly aid recovery.

```
SP_HELPDEVICE SMSDBData

SP_HELPDEVICE SMSDBLog

SP_HELPDB SMS
```

The primary site server should be backed up each day; more frequently when changes are made to the site configuration. Besides making physical backups, make sure that all changes to the site are managed and documented to ensure that a successful recovery is possible.

Secondary Site Server

A secondary site forwards its system, package, inventory, and status information to its primary site for processing and storage in the SQL Server database. It does not store this information locally. Nor does it have administrative tools, since it must be administered through one of its parent sites.

In most cases, secondary site servers are not dedicated to SMS. Typically, they provide file and print services to a local user community and may even be used to run business-critical applications. You can use the steps below to back up a secondary site server regardless of whether it is dedicated to SMS:

1. Stop all SMS services by creating a batch file containing the following commands or by issuing them directly from the command line.

```
NET STOP SMS_CLIENT_CONFIG_MANAGER

NET STOP SMS_EXECUTIVE

NET STOP SMS_HIERACHY_MANAGER

NET STOP SMS_INVENTORY_AGENT_NT

NET STOP SMS_PACKAGE_COMMAND_MANAGER_NT

NET STOP SMS_SITE_CONFIG_MANAGER
```

2. Create a copy of the SMS site server's registry keys using Registry Editor (included with Windows NT).

```
IF EXIST C:\WINNT\SMS.REG DEL C:\WINNT\SMS.REG

REGEDIT /E C:\WINNT\SMS.REG_HKEY_LOCAL_MACHINE\SOFTWARE\Microsoft\SMS
```

3. Back up the SMS directory on the server. Also back up the SMS.INI file in the root directory. If the secondary site server is also acting as a distribution point, you have to back up the SMS_PKGx directory. Later, take a file system backup that excludes these directories. This approach significantly reduces the amount of time the secondary site server will be offline and provides a greater time window for software distribution.

4. Restart all SMS services.

```
NET START SMS_CLIENT_CONFIG_MANAGER

NET START SMS_EXECUTIVE

NET START SMS_HIERACHY_MANAGER

NET START SMS_INVENTORY_AGENT_NT

NET START SMS_PACKAGE_COMMAND_MANAGER_NT

NET START SMS_SITE_CONFIG_MANAGER
```

Logon (Instruction) Server

For SMS purposes, a logon server is not necessarily the same as a domain controller, although it typically is. (The exception to this would be a Novell logon server. See Chapter 13 for a discussion of configuring Novell servers to function as SMS logon servers.) A logon server holds a copy of the client support files and information necessary for the client to obtain package instructions. It also provides a location for the client to deposit inventory information.

It is assumed that the SMS components will be backed up during a full system backup. Primary and secondary site servers that have been configured as logon servers (the default) should be backed up as described above. You don't have to back up the logon server components separately.

The only steps required over and above a standard backup operation are listed below:

1. Stop all SMS services by creating a batch file containing the following commands or by issuing them directly from the command line.

```
NET STOP SMS_CLIENT_CONFIG_MANAGER

NET STOP SMS_EXECUTIVE

NET STOP SMS_INVENTORY_AGENT_NT

NET STOP SMS_PACKAGE_COMMAND_MANAGER_NT
```

2. Create a copy of the SMS site server's registry keys using Registry Editor (included with Windows NT).

```
IF EXIST C:\WINNT\SMS.REG DEL C:\WINNT\SMS.REG

REGEDIT /E C:\WINNT\SMS.REG_HKEY_LOCAL_MACHINE\SOFTWARE\Microsoft\SMS
```

3. Back up the complete file system including the SMS configuration file, SMS.INI.

4. Restart all SMS services.

```
NET START SMS_CLIENT_CONFIG_MANAGER

NET START SMS_EXECUTIVE

NET START SMS_INVENTORY_AGENT_NT

NET START SMS_PACKAGE_COMMAND_MANAGER_NT
```

Distribution Server

A distribution server is a computer on which the source files of an SMS package are stored and made available to the target clients. An SMS client connects to one of these servers whenever the user wants to run a network-served application.

It is assumed that you will back up the software applications distributed to the server by SMS during a full system backup. Primary and secondary site servers that have been configured as logon servers (the default) should be backed up as described above. You don't have to back up the distribution server components separately.

If the server is running SMS components (indicated by the presence of SMS_EXECUTIVE in the active services list) you have to stop those components as well as other services that are running before backing up the distribution directory (SMS_PKG*x*). Restart the services after the backup has completed.

Is Recovery Really Necessary?

Recovering SMS from backup media should be considered only in a worst-case scenario. In many cases, you can restore SMS to full functionality without resorting to backup tapes or the installation media. What might appear to be a catastrophic system failure may have been caused by incorrect settings in SQL Server or in the SMS Administrator UI. It may even have been caused by problems elsewhere in the network.

The initial point of reference should be the Windows NT event logs and, if available, the SQL event window in SMS. The SMSTRACE utility, included on the SMS CD, is also useful. With these tools you should be able to find the probable cause of the error.

If access to the SMS database is slow or denied, it could be due to reasons not requiring a restore. Check the SQL event logs for warnings about the number of locks, open objects, physical memory allocation, or full transaction logs. You can correct the majority of these conditions with SQL Enterprise Manager. The procedure for clearing a full transaction log is documented in the Knowledge Base article Q125487, Title: SMS Administrator Unable To Retrieve Machine List.

As an initial guideline, Microsoft recommends that you set the number of open objects to 5,000 and user connections to a minimum of 50. For more information, see Knowledge Base article Q110352, Title: Optimizing Microsoft SQL Server Performance.

The amount of memory allocated to SQL Server depends on the physical memory installed and whether the server is also running SMS. You should certainly increase it from its default value of 8,192 (2-KB) pages: the SMS Administrator program can fail if insufficient resources are allocated to SQL Server. Typical results include missing machine information or the user interface hanging during information retrieval.

Recovery from Backup Media

If SMS cannot be recovered and you have to restore some, or all, of the server components from backup media, how much data you must recover depends on the type and nature of the error.

Primary Site Server

Two circumstances can require recovery: the file system and registry keys have been corrupted or the SMS database has failed. Database errors necessitate recovering either the database device (.DAT) files, or the database and tables. System component failure requires recovering the Windows NT registry, the file system, and the SMS database.

SMS Database Recovery

Prior to recovering the database, you have to shut down all SMS site services either through the SMS Service Manager or by issuing a NET STOP command for each service in turn (as noted in the backup procedure above).

Database Device Files

The fastest way to restore the database is to recover the database device (.DAT) files from the backup tape. To achieve this, stop the MSSQLServer service either from the command line or by using the SQL Server Service Manager. Then recover the SMS database and log files from the backup device. The database device files are typically called SMSDBDATA.DAT and SMSDBDATA.LOG. If the database spans more than one device file, restore these database device files at the same time.

After the file restore has been completed, restart SQL Server and check the SQL Server error log and Windows NT event logs to determine whether the database was successfully recovered. If there are no errors in the event log, check the database structure by issuing a DBCC CHECKDB statement to ensure data integrity. If the database has been restored successfully, restart SMS and check the Windows NT event logs again.

This approach will succeed only if there have been no changes to the structure and size of the database since the backup was made. The master database records the database size, the extents, and the number and type of devices on which the SMS database is located. If the information in the master database does not match the physical structure of the SMS database, recovery fails.

Device or File System Error

You can recover the database records directly, if you don't want to use the .DAT device file (recommended method). To do this, you need to delete the database and database device file from within SQL Enterprise Manager.

Then re-create the database, transaction logs, and device file(s) either through SQL Enterprise Manager or through the **isql** scripts maintained during the lifetime of the system.

You must re-create and size the database and transaction logs to match the original versions. This is best accomplished by using the **isql** scripts maintained during the lifetime of the SMS database. After you have re-created the database structure, restore the records using the information on the backup media.

After the database restore has completed, check the SQL Server error log to determine whether the database was successfully recovered. If there are no errors in the event log, check the database structure by issuing a DBCC CHECKDB statement to ensure data integrity.

Full SQL Server Recovery

If the master database does not accurately reflect the structure of the SMS database, the previous recovery methods will fail and you will have to rebuild and recover the entire SQL Server, including the master, MSDB, and model databases, along with the SMS database.

The process for recovering an entire SQL Server is documented in the *Microsoft SQL Server Administrator's Guide*.

File System Recovery

In the worst case, the site server itself fails and you have no choice but to recover SMS from backup storage. Although you may be able to recover just the system files and registry entries from the backup tape, leaving the SMS database intact, this approach is not recommended.

To recover the server, build a base image of Windows NT Server and install the backup software. Then perform a full system recovery, to include all system and data files, together with the databases necessary to bring SQL Server and the SMS database back on line. After the system has been recovered, check the event logs for error messages relating to SQL Server or SMS. Resolve these errors before putting the server back into the production environment.

Secondary Site Server

To recover the server, build a base image of Windows NT Server and install the backup software. Then perform a full system recovery, including all system and data files. After the system has been recovered, check the event logs for error messages and resolve these errors before putting the server back into the production environment.

This full recovery process is fine only if you can completely reinstall the target server. In most cases, however, you can't use this approach because user data and other systems have been placed on the server's hard disk. In this case, you have to restore the SMS files and registry keys.

Stop all SMS services and recover the SMS directory from the backup media. You may also have to restore the configuration file, SMS.INI, to the system root directory. When you have done this, reapply the registry keys saved in the SMS.REG file. Finally, restart the SITE_CONFIGURATION_MANAGER service to bring the server back online. You may have to start the other SMS services manually. You *cannot* perform a site reset on a secondary site server.

Check the event logs carefully for warning messages and information about inactive SMS components. If the SMS directory and registry settings exist but the service components are missing, manually add the SITE_CONFIGURATION_MANAGER service into Service Control Manager— it automatically installs all other SMS services. This site resetting procedure is fully documented in Knowledge Base article Q138347, Title: SMS: Procedure for Backing up and Restoring a Secondary site.

Logon Server

You can recover a logon server by performing a site reset at the SMS parent site, which forces SMS to check each logon server and redistribute client support files and Windows NT services as necessary. Performing a site reset temporarily takes the site off line and may also create wide area network (WAN) or local area network (LAN) traffic.

You can also recover the server from backup tape to preserve client inventory files or package and job status information. If you do this, you should restore the server in its entirety, including the SMS.INI file, rather than recovering just the SMS components.

Whenever you restore an SMS logon server from backup tape, you should prevent SMS Maintenance Manager from detecting it until the registry, file system, and site services have been restored. If Maintenance Manager detects the server before the restore is complete it automatically allocates a new SMSID range to the server.

When you recover from a backup tape, duplicate SMSIDs may be issued, especially if a number of new computers were added to the inventory list since the backup was taken. The only way to monitor this and determine whether a problem exists is to run the DBCLEAN.EXE utility on a regular basis. Delete the SMS.INI file on the duplicate computers so that SMS can allocate a new (and unique) number.

To assure that no duplicate SMSIDs are allocated while reinstalling the site you can check the registry, note the last allocated ID range, then place a sufficiently high value in the registry to ensure that duplicate SMSIDs are not issued. The registry entry is stored as a REG_SZ type in the following key:

```
HKEY_LOCAL_MACHINE\SOFTWARE\Microsoft\Systems Management
Server\Components\SMS_MAINTENANCE_MANAGER\Next Systems Management
Server Unique ID
```

Distribution Server

If the server is running SMS services, you have to stop them before restoring the package files and restart them once recovery is complete. You have to put the package files and directories on the same logical drive letter they were backed up from. You may also have to recover the SMS.INI file to the root of the system drive.

It should also be possible to recover files on the package server by creating a separate **Distribute only** job to redistribute each package to it. If you have to create packages on a number of failed servers, create a machine group.

Potential Recovery Issues

Although recovery from tape seems relatively simple, a number of problems may become apparent when the server is brought back into the SMS hierarchy. These problems will be more obvious if new domains or logon servers were added to the site prior to the server failure and the changes are not reflected in the backup. The sections below discuss some potential issues.

Missing Logon Servers

Logon servers that were added to the site hierarchy prior to the failure will still function correctly. New client computers are issued an SMSID and client software is checked and installed as necessary, but inventory information for clients validated by these servers may not be passed back to the SMS site server responsible for the domain. This is because the SMS Maintenance Manager, which retrieves these files from the Sms_shr\Inventory.box directory, ignores the new servers if they are not configured as one of the available logon servers.

Note This particular scenario does not apply when the **Detect All Available Logon Servers** option has been set for a domain. You should *never* set this option for domains that span more than one SMS site.

Orphaned Secondary Sites

A new secondary site whose primary site server is offline (orphaned secondary site) continues to function normally, but the Site Reporter service will log errors whenever it attempts to communicate with the primary site server until the relationship with the parent site is restored. Any packages and jobs issued to the secondary site prior to the failure are still offered to clients in the normal way.

To recover the secondary site into the SMS hierarchy after the primary server is back online, add the secondary site's address to the site address list on the primary site server and perform a site reset from the Systems SMS Setup program. This should restore the relationship and add the secondary site to the SMS Administrator UI. Stop and restart the SMS_EXECUTIVE service at the secondary site to send a full inventory record back to the primary site. Reporting asset information for all the clients maintained at the secondary site takes some time—it is not instantaneous.

Missing Packages and Jobs

The status of **Package Distribution**, **Run Command On Workstation**, **Share Command On Server**, or **Remove Package From Server** tasks will be difficult to determine. Tasks that were active on other servers within the SMS hierarchy will continue to be processed, and users can still install software applications and run shared applications. But if the primary site server receives a status message for a task of which it has no record it creates an event in the Windows NT event log. If many computers are affected by the task, the number of messages could be substantial. Set the event log **Overwrite Events As Needed** option on the primary site server to prevent the event log from becoming full.

Unfortunately, there is no method to recover from this condition other than to wait for the task to complete. Furthermore, jobs that were active when the server was backed up to tape are re-instantiated during the restore, possibly offering clients a package they have already been offered.

Completing Recovery

You must reapply any amendments that were made to the site configuration after the backup was taken and check the event logs to ensure that the amendments have been successfully made. This brings the discussion back to the importance of adequate documentation: without it you will find this process exceptionally difficult and you may end up reinstalling more than is actually required.

Automated Backup of SMS Site and Logon Servers

Now that the backup and recovery process has been explored in some depth, this section explains how to make a secure backup in a real-world situation using an automated process that regularly backs up all relevant SMS data on SMS site and logon servers.

The Scenario

As a sample scenario, this section takes a look at River City Power's three SMS sites, one of which acts as the central site server. One primary site is located on the same LAN as the central site server, and the other is connected to the central site by a WAN link. All site servers have four SMS logon servers reporting to them. River City Power has a dedicated centralized backup server and wants to take advantage of after-hours network availability to move all backup images to that machine. They also want to have an on-disk image of each server, in addition to the tape backup, to improve recovery speed.

Keep in mind that the approach outlined here assumes there is available network bandwidth to support copying files over the network to a centralized backup server. An alternative to this centralized backup method is a local backup approach, which would require local backup devices installed on each remote machine and local administration staff to manage these backups.

The example case assumes that all SMS site servers are running Windows NT Server 4.0 Service Pack 3, SMS 1.2 Service Pack 2, and SQL Server 6.5 Service Pack 1, and that you have a copy of the *Microsoft Windows NT Server 4.0 Resource Kit.*

The discussion assumes that you have an advanced knowledge of Windows NT Server 4.0, SMS version 1.2, and some understanding of SQL Server 6.5 and Transact-SQL statements.

Although the discussion focuses on a specific case, you can easily adapt the process to suit your own requirements.

The Problem

Overall, River City Power wants to avoid the expense and management problems associated with having a tape backup unit installed on each SMS site server. More specifically, the IT group wants to take advantage of after-hours network availability to create a process that moves each SMS site server's backup information to a dedicated centralized backup server equipped with a backup tape device. This will create two current copies of the backup—one on disk and the other on tape.

This backup procedure offers several advantages:

- Automatic regular backup of all SMS site server file systems, the Windows NT Server registry, and SQL Server and SMS site server databases.
- Centralized backup, which requires one backup server with one backup tape device and less administration staff.
- Redundant backups stored on both disk and tape.
- Backups performed while the SMS system is shut down, which enables known-state backups to be performed.
- Logging of all backup processes.
- Copying of only file deltas across the network, which reduces network load and backup time.

The Steps

Determine the Size of the Backup Server

The first task is to calculate the size of the central backup server.

- Calculate the total of each SMS site server's SMS file system. All SMS file system files have to be copied, not just selected ones, to ensure a synchronized state after restoring a backup. Make sure to estimate and add some space to accommodate growth from SMS package distribution.

- Add the sizes of each SMS and SQL Server database for each SMS site server—the master, msdb, tempdb, and SMS databases—to save the complete state of the systems by backing up all relevant SQL Server databases. Use the maximum size of each SQL Server database device to make sure that enough space will be available on the backup server as the SMS inventory grows.

- Add the total size of the Windows NT Server registry backup files from each SMS site server. The entire registry has to be backed up, not just selected parts.

Because multiple simultaneous network write operations are performed during the backup process, the backup server must be connected to the network by a high speed network adapter card and have sufficient system memory and I/O capacity to perform adequately.

Site Server Backup

Backing up the site servers is a fairly complicated process. Here is an overview of the steps:

1. Schedule a regular backup task to run at 12:00 A.M. each morning. On primary site servers, you can do this with the SQL Server Scheduler.

2. Stop all SMS services before starting the backup to ensure that the state of the SMS site server is static before the backup is started.

3. Dump the master, msdb, tempdb, and SMS databases into one SQL Server backup device file, using Microsoft SQL Server Transact-SQL statements.

4. Dump the Windows NT Server registry by using the REGBACK tool from the Windows NT Server 4.0 Resource Kit.

5. Copy the complete SMS file system, the SQL Server backup device file, and the Windows NT Server registry files from the site server to the backup server, by using the ROBOCOPY tool from the Windows NT Server 4.0 Resource Kit.

6. Restart all SMS services.

Create Backup Directories

Create two directories on each site server to store the SQL Server dump device and the Windows NT Server registry backups. For convenience, place these directories in the site server's SMS root directory. For example, you can use the following commands at a command prompt to create directories to store the SQL Server dump device and the Windows NT Server registry backup:

```
md d:\sms\sql
md d:\sms\reg
```

Distribute the ROBOCOPY and REGBACK Utilities

The simplest way to distribute these utilities is to use the Windows NT Directory Replication system, which must be established to distribute the SMS logon scripts. Placing these two utilities into the Winnt\System32\Repl\Import\Scripts directory on the Windows NT Server master Directory Replication server causes them to be replicated to all Windows NT Server Directory Replication partners. The assumption here is that all SMS site servers are configured as Windows NT Server Directory Replication partners.

Create an SQL Server Backup Dump Device

To do this:

1. Create a subdirectory under the main SMS directory to store the SQL Server backup dump device. This makes sure that all files to be backed up are located in one directory structure. For example, use this command at a command prompt to create a directory:

   ```
   md d:\sms\sql
   ```

2. On the SQL Enterprise Manager application **Tools** menu, click **Database Backup/Restore** and create a backup device located in the directory you just created. For example, create a backup device called "SMSP," which creates a file named SMSP.DAT in the Sms\Sql directory.

Create and Test SQL Server Stored Procedures

The next step is to create on each primary site server four SQL Server stored procedures containing instructions to dump the SQL Server master, msdb, and tempdb databases, and the SMS database. On the SQL Enterprise Manager application **Tools** menu, click **SQL Query Tool**. From this window, test the Transact-SQL statements you plan to use to dump the four databases before creating the SQL Server stored procedures. For example, use the following command, where SMSP is the name of the SQL Server dump device:

```
DUMP DATABASE master TO SMSP VOLUME = 'SS0011' WITH NOUNLOAD, STATS =
10, INIT, NOSKIP
```

Note that the first DUMP command initializes the dump device. This clears old backups before starting the new dumps. This Transact-SQL statement must always be executed before the other statements.

```
DUMP DATABASE msdb    TO SMSP VOLUME = 'SS0011' WITH NOUNLOAD, STATS =
10, NOINIT, NOSKIP

DUMP DATABASE SMS     TO SMSP VOLUME = 'SS0011' WITH NOUNLOAD, STATS =
10, NOINIT, NOSKIP

DUMP DATABASE tempdb TO SMSP VOLUME = 'SS0011' WITH NOUNLOAD, STATS =
10, NOINIT, NOSKIP
```

Note that the other three dump commands do not initialize the dump device.

After you have tested your Transact-SQL statements, you can create the SQL Server stored procedures to be used by the automated backup process. For example, use the following commands:

```
create proc Backup_tempdb

as

DUMP DATABASE tempdb TO SMSP VOLUME = 'SS0011' WITH NOUNLOAD, STATS =
10, NOINIT, NOSKIP
```

The label **Backup_tempdb** is the name of the SQL Server stored procedure you created. Create stored procedures for each dump command for each database on each site server. After you have created all the SQL Server stored procedures, you can check them for correctness by executing these Transact-SQL statements:

```
sp_help


exec Backup_master

exec Backup_msdb

exec Backup_SMS

exec Backup_tempdb
```

The **sp_help** command displays your SQL Server stored procedures. The **exec** command runs them.

Create Windows NT Server Command Procedures

You must create two Windows NT Server command procedures that will be executed by each site server. The first stops SMS services on the site server, the second:

1. Deletes old Windows NT Server registry backup files from the Windows NT Server registry backup directory. This must be done because the REGBACK utility cannot overwrite existing backup files.
2. Backs up the Windows NT Server registry to the backup directory.
3. Copies the entire SMS directory file structure to the backup server.
4. Restarts all stopped SMS services on the site server.

Both of these procedures are called from the SQL Server Scheduler and run in the context of the SQL Server Windows NT Server service account.

Store both procedures on each site server in a well-known directory, for example in the Windows NT Server directory replication system. For example name them SMSP1.CMD and SMSP2.CMD, and store them in the Windows NT Server Directory Replication system in the Winnt\System32\Repl\Import\Scripts directory. They will then be replicated to each site server:

First Windows NT Server Command Procedure

This command procedure stops all SMS services running on the site server. Here is an example:

```
REM  ------------------------------------------------------------
REM SMS site server backup script section one.
REM The site backup is done by the SQL Server Scheduler.
REM See the SQL Server on each site server.
```

```
REM -----------------------------------------------------------
REM Stop all Systems Management Server site server services.
REM -----------------------------------------------------------
NET STOP   SMS_CLIENT_CONFIG_MANAGER
NET STOP   SMS_EXECUTIVE
NET STOP   SMS_HIERARCHY_MANAGER
NET STOP   SMS_INVENTORY_AGENT_NT
NET STOP   SMS_PACKAGE_COMMAND_MANAGER_NT
NET STOP   SMS_SITE_CONFIG_MANAGER
```

Second Windows NT Server Command Procedure

This command procedure is called after the SQL Server databases have been dumped. It is more complicated than the first, and is explained in more detail below.

The first command deletes any old Windows NT Server registry backup files in the Windows NT Server registry backup directory, because the REGBACK utility cannot overwrite old backup files. Note that the Windows NT Server command procedure variable **computername** is used so that this command procedure can be generic. Furthermore, the **/q** option is used with the Windows NT Server **delete** command to make it run in quiet mode.

```
REM -----------------------------------------------------------
REM Systems Management Server site server backup script.
REM This is run after the SQL Server has dumped the databases.
REM -----------------------------------------------------------
REM Delete old backed up registry files and back up current.
REM -----------------------------------------------------------
del     \\%computername%\sms_shrd\reg /q
```

The next command procedure performs a fresh Windows NT Server registry backup to the Windows NT Server registry backup directory. Note that it uses the SMS share rather than a hard coded physical name, because this name may differ on different servers.

```
%windir%\system32\repl\import\scripts\regback
\\%computername%\sms_shrd\reg
```

The next command performs a ROBOCOPY backup from the site server to the backup server. After the initial backup is made, subsequent backups will copy only deltas (files that have changed) to the centralized backup on the backup server. This reduces the amount of time required for a regular backup, and greatly reduces network traffic. These ROBOCOPY switches are needed:

- The **/e** option copies all subdirectories, including empty ones.
- The **/purge** option deletes destination files and directories that no longer exist at the source.
- The **/r:10** and **/w:10** options make sure the copy times out if something goes wrong.

The command procedure variable **computername** is used to ensure that each backup from each site server is placed in a unique directory on the backup server.

```
REM -----------------------------------------------------------
REM Copy all Systems Management Server files to the backup
REM server SMSTEST.
REM -----------------------------------------------------------
%windir%\system32\repl\import\scripts\robocopy
\\%computername%\sms_shrd \\smstest\smsdumps\%computername% /e /purge
/r:10 /w:10
```

The next set of commands restarts all of the stopped SMS services on the site server.

```
REM -----------------------------------------------------------
REM Start all Systems Management Server site server services
REM -----------------------------------------------------------
NET START SMS_CLIENT_CONFIG_MANAGER
NET START SMS_EXECUTIVE
NET START SMS_HIERARCHY_MANAGER
NET START SMS_INVENTORY_AGENT_NT
NET START SMS_PACKAGE_COMMAND_MANAGER_NT
NET START SMS_SITE_CONFIG_MANAGER
```

Schedule a Regular Backup

Because the SQL Server Scheduler is going to be used to perform the backup on each site server, you must ensure that both the SQL Executive and MSSQLServer services are started using a valid Windows NT Server domain service account. Ensure that this service account is a member of the Windows NT Server Domain Admins global group. This is required because the SQL Server Scheduler must copy files from the site server to the backup server. By default, these two SQL Server services are started using the local Windows NT Server system account, and this account does not have access rights to the backup server. Make these changes using the Services Control Panel.

On the SQL Enterprise Manager application **Tools** menu, click **Task Scheduling** to open the Task Scheduling window and establish the required schedule.

After you have established the task schedule, return to the New Task window and ensure that the **Type** is set to **TSQL**. In the **Command** box, type your automated backup commands.

Note that the Transact-SQL statement **xp_cmdshell** is used. This stored procedure allows Windows NT Server commands to be called from within the Transact-SQL job. Also notice that the first Windows NT Server command procedure is executed and the output from the procedure is placed in a log file located in the root directory of the system drive. This facilitates troubleshooting and creates a record of each backup run.

```
exec xp_cmdshell "c:\winnt\system32\repl\import\scripts\smsp1.cmd >
c:\smsp1.log"
```

The next set of Transact-SQL statements executes the stored procedures you created earlier to dump the SQL Server databases.

```
exec Backup_master

exec Backup_msdb

exec Backup_SMS

exec Backup_tempdb
```

The second Windows NT Server command procedure is now run, and the output from the procedure is placed in a log file located in the root directory of the system drive. This once again facilitates troubleshooting and creates a record of each backup run.

```
exec xp_cmdshell "c:\winnt\system32\repl\import\scripts\smsp2.cmd >
c:\smsp2.log"
```

Summary of the Site Server Backup Process

Here is a flow chart of the major steps performed to back up a site server.

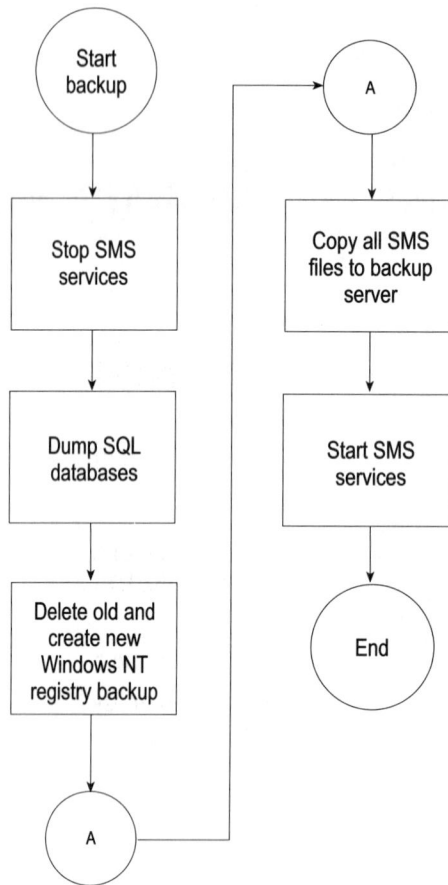

Figure 3.1 Flow chart of site server backup process.

Logon Server Backup—Create Backup Directories

Unlike the procedure for the site server backup, this requires that you create only one directory, the Windows NT Server registry backup directory, on each SMS logon server. For convenience, create this directory under the site server's SMS main directory. For example, you can use the following command to create a directory to store the Windows NT Server registry backup:

```
md d:\sms\reg
```

Distribute the ROBOCOPY and REGBACK Utilities

Distribute these utilities as outlined in the same section in the first half of this chapter: "Distribute the ROBOCOPY and REGBACK Utilities."

Create a Windows NT Server Command Procedure

You must create one command procedure that will be executed by each logon server. This Windows NT Server command procedure will:

1. Stop all SMS services on the logon server.
2. Delete old Windows NT Server registry backup files from the Windows NT Server registry backup directory, because the REGBACK utility cannot overwrite existing backup files.
3. Back up the Windows NT Server registry to the backup directory.
4. Copy the entire SMS directory file structure to the backup server.
5. Restart all of the stopped SMS services on the logon server.

This command procedure will be run by the Windows NT Server Schedule service, and will run in the context of the Windows NT Server Schedule service. You must therefore ensure that the Schedule service is started on each logon server and that it uses a service account that is a member of the Windows NT Server Domain Admins global group.

Store the Windows NT Server command procedure on each logon server in a well-known directory. For example, you can place it in the Windows NT Server Directory Replication system. In this example, the procedure is named SMSL.CMD and stored in the Winnt\System32\Repl\Import\Scripts directory of the Directory Replication system. It is replicated to each logon server:

The Logon Server Windows NT Server Command Procedure

The first function of this Windows NT Server command procedure is to stop all SMS services running on the logon server. Here is an example:

```
REM ------------------------------------------------------------
REM Systems Management Server logon server backup script
REM ------------------------------------------------------------
REM Stop all Systems Management Server logon server services.
REM ------------------------------------------------------------
NET STOP   SMS_CLIENT_CONFIG_MANAGER
NET STOP   SMS_INVENTORY_AGENT_NT
NET STOP   SMS_PACKAGE_COMMAND_MANAGER_NT
```

The next command deletes any old Windows NT Server registry backup files in the Windows NT Server registry backup directory, because the REGBACK utility cannot overwrite old backup files. Note that the Windows NT Server command procedure variable **computername** is used so that the Windows NT Server command procedure can be generic. Furthermore, the **/q** option is used with the Windows NT Server **delete** command to make it run in quiet mode.

```
REM ---------------------------------------------------------
REM Delete old backed up registry files and back up current.
REM ---------------------------------------------------------
del      \\%computername%\sms_shrd\reg /q
```

The next command performs a fresh Windows NT Server registry backup to the Windows NT Server registry backup directory. The SMS share is used rather than a hard-coded physical name because the name may differ on different servers.

```
%windir%\system32\repl\import\scripts\regback
\\%computername%\sms_shrd\reg
```

The next command performs a ROBOCOPY backup from the logon server to the backup server. After the initial backup is made, subsequent backups will copy only deltas (files that have changed) to the backup on the backup server. This reduces the amount of time required for a regular backup, and greatly reduces network traffic. These ROBOCOPY switches are needed:

- The **/e** option copies all subdirectories, including empty ones.
- The **/purge** option deletes destination files and directories that no longer exist at the source.
- The **/r:10** and **/w:10** options make sure the copy times out if something goes wrong.

```
REM -----------------------------------------------------------
REM Copy all Systems Management Server files to the backup
REM server SMSTEST.
REM -----------------------------------------------------------
%windir%\system32\repl\import\scripts\robocopy
\\%computername%\sms_shrd \\smstest\smsdumps\%computername% /e /purge
/r:10 /w:10
```

The next set of commands restarts all of the stopped SMS services on the logon server.

```
REM -----------------------------------------------------------
REM Start all Systems Management Server logon server services
REM -----------------------------------------------------------
NET START SMS_CLIENT_CONFIG_MANAGER
NET START SMS_INVENTORY_AGENT_NT
NET START SMS_PACKAGE_COMMAND_MANAGER_NT
```

Schedule a Regular Backup of a Logon Server

To perform a regular backup on the SMS logon servers, use the Command Scheduler tool from the Windows NT Server 4.0 Resource Kit. It allows you to remotely schedule regular backups on each logon server. Schedule this command on each SMS logon server:

```
c:\winnt\system32\repl\import\scripts\sms1.cmd > c:\sms1>log
```

This runs the backup script and sends the output to a log file in the root directory of the system drive.

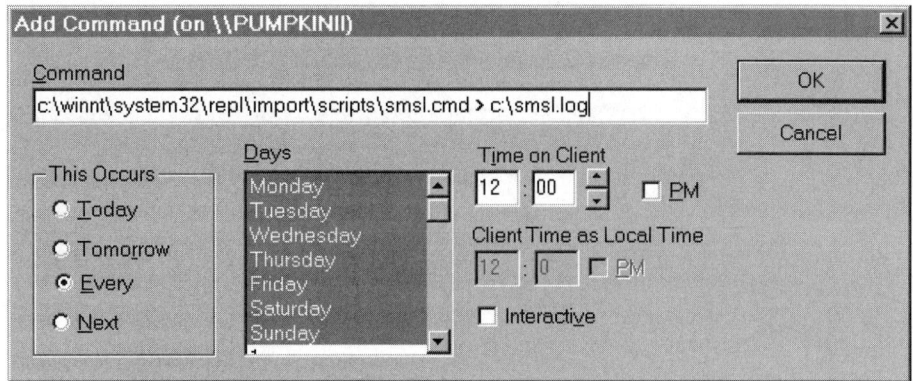

Figure 3.2 AT Command Scheduler for SMS logon servers.

Central Server Backup to Tape

After all SMS site and logon servers have backed up their files to the backup server, you can create an automated process on the backup server that regularly performs a backup of the SMS backup files to a specific tape device. You can do this with the Windows NT Server Backup utility or a third-party tool.

To maintain a complete SMS system backup history on tape, create a regular tape backup performed after all SMS site and logon servers have completed their backups to the backup server.

Reporting and Logging

There are three ways to determine whether a backup has occurred as scheduled. First, look at the log files on each SMS system root directory. Each site server will have two log files, and each logon server will have one. A good way to manage access to all of these log files is to create a folder on your management workstation that contains Windows shortcuts to each of these log files. Examples of these log files are presented below.

Smsp1.log Log File

This log file is generated when the SQL Executive runs the first site server
Windows NT Server command procedure.

```
D:\SMSsoft\SMSBAC~1>REM ---------------------------------------------

D:\SMSsoft\SMSBAC~1>REM SMS Site Server Backup Script section one.

D:\SMSsoft\SMSBAC~1>REM The Site backup is done by the SQL Server
Scheduler

D:\SMSsoft\SMSBAC~1>REM see the SQL Server on each site server

D:\SMSsoft\SMSBAC~1>REM ---------------------------------------------

D:\SMSsoft\SMSBAC~1>REM Stop all Systems Management Server site server
services.

D:\SMSsoft\SMSBAC~1>REM ---------------------------------------------

D:\SMSsoft\SMSBAC~1>NET STOP  SMS_CLIENT_CONFIG_MANAGER

The SMS_CLIENT_CONFIG_MANAGER service was stopped
successfully.D:\SMSsoft\SMSBAC~1>NET STOP  SMS_EXECUTIVE

The SMS_EXECUTIVE service was stopped
successfully.D:\SMSsoft\SMSBAC~1>NET STOP  SMS_HIERARCHY_MANAGER

The SMS_HIERARCHY_MANAGER service was stopped
successfully.D:\SMSsoft\SMSBAC~1>NET STOP  SMS_INVENTORY_AGENT_NT

The SMS_INVENTORY_AGENT_NT service was stopped
successfully.D:\SMSsoft\SMSBAC~1>NET STOP
SMS_PACKAGE_COMMAND_MANAGER_NT

The SMS_PACKAGE_COMMAND_MANAGER_NT service was stopped
successfully.D:\SMSsoft\SMSBAC~1>NET STOP  SMS_SITE_CONFIG_MANAGER

The SMS_SITE_CONFIG_MANAGER service is stopping.
```

This code is spaced so that it is easier to read. Lines are broken for layout only: entries
should be on a single line. If you want to skip this section, go to page 134.

```
The SMS_SITE_CONFIG_MANAGER service was stopped
successfully.D:\SMSsoft\SMSBAC~1>REM -------------------------------
D:\SMSsoft\SMSBAC~1>REM The SQL Server will now dump the SQL databases

D:\SMSsoft\SMSBAC~1>REM --------------------------------------------
```

Smsp2.log Log File

This log file is generated when the SQL Executive runs the second site server
Windows NT Server command procedure.

```
D:\SMSsoft\SMSBAC~1>REM --------------------------------------------------

D:\SMSsoft\SMSBAC~1>REM Systems Management Server site server backup
script.

D:\SMSsoft\SMSBAC~1>REM This is run after the SQL Server has dumped the
databases.

D:\SMSsoft\SMSBAC~1>REM --------------------------------------------

D:\SMSsoft\SMSBAC~1>REM Delete old backed up registry files and back up
current.

D:\SMSsoft\SMSBAC~1>REM --------------------------------------------

D:\SMSsoft\SMSBAC~1>del      \\SMSTEST\sms_shrd\reg /q

D:\SMSsoft\SMSBAC~1>C:\WINNT\system32\repl\import\scripts\regback
\\SMSTEST\sms_shrd\reg

saving SECURITY to \\SMSTEST\sms_shrd\reg\SECURITY

saving SOFTWARE to \\SMSTEST\sms_shrd\reg\software

saving SYSTEM to \\SMSTEST\sms_shrd\reg\system

saving .DEFAULT to \\SMSTEST\sms_shrd\reg\default
```

This code is spaced so that it is easier to read. Lines are broken for layout only: entries
should be on a single line. If you want to skip this section, go to page 134.

```
saving SAM to \\SMSTEST\sms_shrd\reg\SAM

***Hive = \REGISTRY\USER\S-1-5-21-2144011916-71395201-114579206-6019

Stored in file
\Device\Harddisk1\Partition2\WINNT\Profiles\SQLadmin\NTUSER.DAT

Must be backed up manually

regback <filename you choose> users S-1-5-21-2144011916-71395201-
114579206-6019

***Hive = \REGISTRY\USER\S-1-5-21-2144011916-71395201-114579206-1005

Stored in file
\Device\Harddisk1\Partition2\WINNT\Profiles\bblyler.000\NTUSER.DAT

Must be backed up manually

regback <filename you choose> users S-1-5-21-2144011916-71395201-
114579206-1005

***Hive = \REGISTRY\USER\S-1-5-21-1004933954-1864521944-1415713722-1001

Stored in file
\Device\Harddisk1\Partition2\WINNT\Profiles\bblyler\NTUSER.DAT

Must be backed up manually

regback <filename you choose> users S-1-5-21-1004933954-1864521944-
1415713722-1001

D:\SMSsoft\SMSBAC~1>REM -------------------------------------------------

D:\SMSsoft\SMSBAC~1>REM Copy all SMS files to backup server SMSTEST

D:\SMSsoft\SMSBAC~1>REM -------------------------------------------------

D:\SMSsoft\SMSBAC~1>C:\WINNT\system32\repl\import\scripts\robocopy
```

> This code is spaced so that it is easier to read. Lines are broken for layout only: entries should be on a single line. If you want to skip this section, go to page 134.

```
\\SMSTEST\sms_shrd \\smstest\smsdumps\SMSTEST /e

--------------------------------------------------------------------

ROBOCOPY v 1.71  :  Robust File Copy for Windows NT  :  by
kevina@microsoft.com

--------------------------------------------------------------------

Started : Fri May 30 13:29:33 1997

Source : \\SMSTEST\sms_shrd\

    Dest : \\smstest\smsdumps\SMSTEST\

    Files : *.*

  Options : *.* /S /E /R:1000000 /W:30
```

```
                               2   \\SMSTEST\sms_shrd\

        *EXTRA Dir            -1   \\smstest\smsdumps\SMSTEST\sms\

                               0   \\SMSTEST\sms_shrd\helper.srv\

                               3   \\SMSTEST\sms_shrd\helper.srv\X86.BIN\

                               1
\\SMSTEST\sms_shrd\helper.srv\X86.BIN\00000409\

                               1
\\SMSTEST\sms_shrd\helper.srv\X86.BIN\ERRORHIS\

        Newer                      184  SMS_CLIE.HIS  0%  100%

                              20   \\SMSTEST\sms_shrd\logon.srv\
```

> This code is spaced so that it is easier to read. Lines are broken for layout only: entries should be on a single line. If you want to skip this section, go to page 134.

SMSP2.LOG   *(continued)*

```
              Newer                        1429   DOMAIN.INI  0%  100%

                                    0
\\SMSTEST\sms_shrd\logon.srv\appctl.box\

                                    0
\\SMSTEST\sms_shrd\logon.srv\appctl.box\database\

                                    0
\\SMSTEST\sms_shrd\logon.srv\appctl.box\inifiles\

                                    0
\\SMSTEST\sms_shrd\logon.srv\appctl.box\scripts\

                                    0   \\SMSTEST\sms_shrd\logon.srv\ccr.box\

                                    0
\\SMSTEST\sms_shrd\logon.srv\ccr.box\retry\

                                    0
\\SMSTEST\sms_shrd\logon.srv\despoolr.box\

                                    3
\\SMSTEST\sms_shrd\logon.srv\invencfg.box\

                                    4
\\SMSTEST\sms_shrd\logon.srv\inventry.box\

            *EXTRA File              67332   00000000.RAW

                                    0
\\SMSTEST\sms_shrd\logon.srv\isvmif.box\
```

This code is spaced so that it is easier to read. Lines are broken for layout only: entries should be on a single line. If you want to skip this section, go to page 134.

SMSP2.LOG   *(continued)*

```
                                           3   \\SMSTEST\sms_shrd\logon.srv\MAC.BIN\

                                           8
\\SMSTEST\sms_shrd\logon.srv\MAC.BIN\00000409\

                                          32   \\SMSTEST\sms_shrd\logon.srv\mstest\

                                           5
\\SMSTEST\sms_shrd\logon.srv\mstest\ALPHA.BIN\

                                           5
\\SMSTEST\sms_shrd\logon.srv\mstest\MIPS.BIN\

                                           5

\\SMSTEST\sms_shrd\logon.srv\mstest\X86.BIN\

                                           1   \\SMSTEST\sms_shrd\logon.srv\NCDTREE\

                                          31
\\SMSTEST\sms_shrd\logon.srv\pcmins.box\

                                           0
\\SMSTEST\sms_shrd\logon.srv\pcmpkg.src\

                                           1   \\SMSTEST\sms_shrd\logon.srv\SMSID\

                                         118   \\SMSTEST\sms_shrd\logon.srv\X86.BIN\

                                          51
\\SMSTEST\sms_shrd\logon.srv\X86.BIN\00000409\

                                          30   \\SMSTEST\sms_shrd\LOGS\

        Newer                           120455   alerter.log   0%    51%   100%

        Newer                            43907   appman.log    0%   100%
```

This code is spaced so that it is easier to read. Lines are broken for layout only: entries should be on a single line. If you want to skip this section, go to page 134.

SMSP2.LOG   *(continued)*

```
Newer                              48777   clicfg.log  0%  100%

Newer                             120996   datalodr.log  0%   50%  100%

Newer                              93127   despool.log  0%   65%  100%

Newer                              23440   hman.log  0%  100%

Newer                              95211   invagent.log  0%   64%  100%

Newer                              67489   invproc.log  0%   91%  100%

Newer                              66092   lansend.log  0%   92%  100%

Newer                             114923   maintman.log  0%   53%  100%

Newer                             113088   pacman.log  0%   54%  100%

Newer                             107069   sched.log  0%   57%  100%

Newer                             110238   siterept.log  0%   55%  100%

Newer                              16110   smsexec.log  0%  100%

                        0   \\SMSTEST\sms_shrd\NETMON\

                       14   \\SMSTEST\sms_shrd\NETMON\X86\

                        4   \\SMSTEST\sms_shrd\NETMON\X86\CAPTURES\

                       43   \\SMSTEST\sms_shrd\NETMON\X86\PARSERS\

                        0   \\SMSTEST\sms_shrd\PRIMSITE.SRV\

                        2   \\SMSTEST\sms_shrd\PRIMSITE.SRV\AUDIT\

                        1
\\SMSTEST\sms_shrd\PRIMSITE.SRV\AUDIT\PACKAGE\

                        1
```

This code is spaced so that it is easier to read. Lines are broken for layout only: entries should be on a single line. If you want to skip this section, go to page 134.

SMSP2.LOG   *(continued)*

```
\\SMSTEST\sms_shrd\PRIMSITE.SRV\AUDIT\PACKAGE\ALPHA.BIN\

                          1
\\SMSTEST\sms_shrd\PRIMSITE.SRV\AUDIT\PACKAGE\ALPHA.BIN\00000409\

                          1
\\SMSTEST\sms_shrd\PRIMSITE.SRV\AUDIT\PACKAGE\MIPS.BIN\

                          1
\\SMSTEST\sms_shrd\PRIMSITE.SRV\AUDIT\PACKAGE\MIPS.BIN\00000409\

                          2
\\SMSTEST\sms_shrd\PRIMSITE.SRV\AUDIT\PACKAGE\X86.BIN\

                          2
\\SMSTEST\sms_shrd\PRIMSITE.SRV\AUDIT\PACKAGE\X86.BIN\00000409\

                          0
\\SMSTEST\sms_shrd\PRIMSITE.SRV\IMPORT.SRC\

                         150
\\SMSTEST\sms_shrd\PRIMSITE.SRV\IMPORT.SRC\ENU\

                          0
\\SMSTEST\sms_shrd\PRIMSITE.SRV\IMPORT.SRC\ENU\ACS200\

                          5
\\SMSTEST\sms_shrd\PRIMSITE.SRV\IMPORT.SRC\ENU\ACS200\SMSPROXY\

                          3
\\SMSTEST\sms_shrd\PRIMSITE.SRV\IMPORT.SRC\ENU\ACS200\SMSPROXY\MSACCESS\

                          0
\\SMSTEST\sms_shrd\PRIMSITE.SRV\IMPORT.SRC\ENU\ACS200\SMSPROXY\MSAPPS\

                          1
\\SMSTEST\sms_shrd\PRIMSITE.SRV\IMPORT.SRC\ENU\ACS200\SMSPROXY\MSAPPS\
MSGRAPH5\
```

This code is spaced so that it is easier to read. Lines are broken for layout only: entries should be on a single line. If you want to skip this section, go to page 134.

```
                            1
\\SMSTEST\sms_shrd\PRIMSITE.SRV\IMPORT.SRC\ENU\ACS200\SMSPROXY\MSAPPS\
MSINFO\

                            0
\\SMSTEST\sms_shrd\PRIMSITE.SRV\IMPORT.SRC\ENU\EXC50A\

                            5
\\SMSTEST\sms_shrd\PRIMSITE.SRV\IMPORT.SRC\ENU\EXC50A\SMSPROXY\

                            3
\\SMSTEST\sms_shrd\PRIMSITE.SRV\IMPORT.SRC\ENU\EXC50A\SMSPROXY\EXCEL\

                            0
\\SMSTEST\sms_shrd\PRIMSITE.SRV\IMPORT.SRC\ENU\EXC50A\SMSPROXY\MSAPPS\

                            1
\\SMSTEST\sms_shrd\PRIMSITE.SRV\IMPORT.SRC\ENU\EXC50A\SMSPROXY\MSAPPS\
MSINFO\

                            1
\\SMSTEST\sms_shrd\PRIMSITE.SRV\IMPORT.SRC\ENU\EXC50A\SMSPROXY\MSAPPS\
MSQUERY\

                            0
\\SMSTEST\sms_shrd\PRIMSITE.SRV\IMPORT.SRC\ENU\EXC50C\

                            5
\\SMSTEST\sms_shrd\PRIMSITE.SRV\IMPORT.SRC\ENU\EXC50C\SMSPROXY\

                            2
\\SMSTEST\sms_shrd\PRIMSITE.SRV\IMPORT.SRC\ENU\EXC50C\SMSPROXY\EXC50C\

                            0
\\SMSTEST\sms_shrd\PRIMSITE.SRV\IMPORT.SRC\ENU\EXC50C\SMSPROXY\MSAPPS\
```

This code is spaced so that it is easier to read. Lines are broken for layout only: entries should be on a single line. If you want to skip this section, go to page 134.

SMSP2.LOG   *(continued)*

```
                              1
\\SMSTEST\sms_shrd\PRIMSITE.SRV\IMPORT.SRC\ENU\EXC50C\SMSPROXY\MSAPPS\
MSINFO\

                              1
\\SMSTEST\sms_shrd\PRIMSITE.SRV\IMPORT.SRC\ENU\EXC50C\SMSPROXY\MSAPPS\
MSQUERY\

                              0
\\SMSTEST\sms_shrd\PRIMSITE.SRV\IMPORT.SRC\ENU\OFF42A\

                              5
\\SMSTEST\sms_shrd\PRIMSITE.SRV\IMPORT.SRC\ENU\OFF42A\SMSPROXY\

                              0
\\SMSTEST\sms_shrd\PRIMSITE.SRV\IMPORT.SRC\ENU\OFF42A\SMSPROXY\MSAPPS\

                              1
\\SMSTEST\sms_shrd\PRIMSITE.SRV\IMPORT.SRC\ENU\OFF42A\SMSPROXY\MSAPPS\
ARTGALRY\

                              1
\\SMSTEST\sms_shrd\PRIMSITE.SRV\IMPORT.SRC\ENU\OFF42A\SMSPROXY\MSAPPS\
EQUATION\

                              1
\\SMSTEST\sms_shrd\PRIMSITE.SRV\IMPORT.SRC\ENU\OFF42A\SMSPROXY\MSAPPS\
MSGRAPH5\

                              1
\\SMSTEST\sms_shrd\PRIMSITE.SRV\IMPORT.SRC\ENU\OFF42A\SMSPROXY\MSAPPS\
MSINFO\
```

This code is spaced so that it is easier to read. Lines are broken for layout only: entries should be on a single line. If you want to skip this section, go to page 134.

```
                                    1
\\SMSTEST\sms_shrd\PRIMSITE.SRV\IMPORT.SRC\ENU\OFF42A\SMSPROXY\MSAPPS\
MSQUERY\

                                    1
\\SMSTEST\sms_shrd\PRIMSITE.SRV\IMPORT.SRC\ENU\OFF42A\SMSPROXY\MSAPPS\
ORGCHART\

                                    1
\\SMSTEST\sms_shrd\PRIMSITE.SRV\IMPORT.SRC\ENU\OFF42A\SMSPROXY\MSAPPS\
WORDART\

                                    7
\\SMSTEST\sms_shrd\PRIMSITE.SRV\IMPORT.SRC\ENU\OFF42A\SMSPROXY\MSOFFICE\

                                    0
\\SMSTEST\sms_shrd\PRIMSITE.SRV\IMPORT.SRC\ENU\OFF42C\

                                    5
\\SMSTEST\sms_shrd\PRIMSITE.SRV\IMPORT.SRC\ENU\OFF42C\SMSPROXY\

                                    0
\\SMSTEST\sms_shrd\PRIMSITE.SRV\IMPORT.SRC\ENU\OFF42C\SMSPROXY\MSAPPS\

                                    1
\\SMSTEST\sms_shrd\PRIMSITE.SRV\IMPORT.SRC\ENU\OFF42C\SMSPROXY\MSAPPS\
ARTGALRY\

                                    1
\\SMSTEST\sms_shrd\PRIMSITE.SRV\IMPORT.SRC\ENU\OFF42C\SMSPROXY\MSAPPS\
EQUATION\

                                    1
\\SMSTEST\sms_shrd\PRIMSITE.SRV\IMPORT.SRC\ENU\OFF42C\SMSPROXY\MSAPPS\
MSGRAPH5\
```

> This code is spaced so that it is easier to read. Lines are broken for layout only: entries should be on a single line. If you want to skip this section, go to page 134.

```
                         1
\\SMSTEST\sms_shrd\PRIMSITE.SRV\IMPORT.SRC\ENU\OFF42C\SMSPROXY\MSAPPS\
MSINFO\

                         1
\\SMSTEST\sms_shrd\PRIMSITE.SRV\IMPORT.SRC\ENU\OFF42C\SMSPROXY\MSAPPS\
MSQUERY\

                         1
\\SMSTEST\sms_shrd\PRIMSITE.SRV\IMPORT.SRC\ENU\OFF42C\SMSPROXY\MSAPPS\
ORGCHART\

                         1
\\SMSTEST\sms_shrd\PRIMSITE.SRV\IMPORT.SRC\ENU\OFF42C\SMSPROXY\MSAPPS\
WORDART\

                         7
\\SMSTEST\sms_shrd\PRIMSITE.SRV\IMPORT.SRC\ENU\OFF42C\SMSPROXY\OFF42C\

                         0
\\SMSTEST\sms_shrd\PRIMSITE.SRV\IMPORT.SRC\ENU\OFP43_\

                         5
\\SMSTEST\sms_shrd\PRIMSITE.SRV\IMPORT.SRC\ENU\OFP43_\SMSPROXY\

                         0
\\SMSTEST\sms_shrd\PRIMSITE.SRV\IMPORT.SRC\ENU\OFP43_\SMSPROXY\MSAPPS\

                         1
\\SMSTEST\sms_shrd\PRIMSITE.SRV\IMPORT.SRC\ENU\OFP43_\SMSPROXY\MSAPPS\
ARTGALRY\

                         1

\\SMSTEST\sms_shrd\PRIMSITE.SRV\IMPORT.SRC\ENU\OFP43_\SMSPROXY\MSAPPS\
EQUATION\
```

This code is spaced so that it is easier to read. Lines are broken for layout only: entries should be on a single line. If you want to skip this section, go to page 134.

```
                                    1
\\SMSTEST\sms_shrd\PRIMSITE.SRV\IMPORT.SRC\ENU\OFP43_\SMSPROXY\MSAPPS\
MSGRAPH5\

                                    1
\\SMSTEST\sms_shrd\PRIMSITE.SRV\IMPORT.SRC\ENU\OFP43_\SMSPROXY\MSAPPS\
MSINFO\

                                    1
\\SMSTEST\sms_shrd\PRIMSITE.SRV\IMPORT.SRC\ENU\OFP43_\SMSPROXY\MSAPPS\
MSQUERY\

                                    1
\\SMSTEST\sms_shrd\PRIMSITE.SRV\IMPORT.SRC\ENU\OFP43_\SMSPROXY\MSAPPS\
ORGCHART\

                                    1
\\SMSTEST\sms_shrd\PRIMSITE.SRV\IMPORT.SRC\ENU\OFP43_\SMSPROXY\MSAPPS\
WORDART\

                                    8
\\SMSTEST\sms_shrd\PRIMSITE.SRV\IMPORT.SRC\ENU\OFP43_\SMSPROXY\MSOFFPRO\

                                    0
\\SMSTEST\sms_shrd\PRIMSITE.SRV\IMPORT.SRC\ENU\OFP43C\

                                    5
\\SMSTEST\sms_shrd\PRIMSITE.SRV\IMPORT.SRC\ENU\OFP43C\SMSPROXY\

                                    0
\\SMSTEST\sms_shrd\PRIMSITE.SRV\IMPORT.SRC\ENU\OFP43C\SMSPROXY\MSAPPS\

                                    1
\\SMSTEST\sms_shrd\PRIMSITE.SRV\IMPORT.SRC\ENU\OFP43C\SMSPROXY\MSAPPS\
ARTGALRY\
```

> This code is spaced so that it is easier to read. Lines are broken for layout only: entries should be on a single line. If you want to skip this section, go to page 134.

SMSP2.LOG   *(continued)*

```
                                 1
\\SMSTEST\sms_shrd\PRIMSITE.SRV\IMPORT.SRC\ENU\OFP43C\SMSPROXY\MSAPPS\
EQUATION\

                                 1
\\SMSTEST\sms_shrd\PRIMSITE.SRV\IMPORT.SRC\ENU\OFP43C\SMSPROXY\MSAPPS\
MSGRAPH5\

                                 1
\\SMSTEST\sms_shrd\PRIMSITE.SRV\IMPORT.SRC\ENU\OFP43C\SMSPROXY\MSAPPS\
MSINFO\

                                 1
\\SMSTEST\sms_shrd\PRIMSITE.SRV\IMPORT.SRC\ENU\OFP43C\SMSPROXY\MSAPPS\
MSQUERY\

                                 1
\\SMSTEST\sms_shrd\PRIMSITE.SRV\IMPORT.SRC\ENU\OFP43C\SMSPROXY\MSAPPS\
ORGCHART\

                                 1
\\SMSTEST\sms_shrd\PRIMSITE.SRV\IMPORT.SRC\ENU\OFP43C\SMSPROXY\MSAPPS\
WORDART\

                                 8
\\SMSTEST\sms_shrd\PRIMSITE.SRV\IMPORT.SRC\ENU\OFP43C\SMSPROXY\OFP43C\

                                 0
\\SMSTEST\sms_shrd\PRIMSITE.SRV\IMPORT.SRC\ENU\PPT40A\

                                 5
\\SMSTEST\sms_shrd\PRIMSITE.SRV\IMPORT.SRC\ENU\PPT40A\SMSPROXY\

                                 0
\\SMSTEST\sms_shrd\PRIMSITE.SRV\IMPORT.SRC\ENU\PPT40A\SMSPROXY\MSAPPS\
```

This code is spaced so that it is easier to read. Lines are broken for layout only: entries should be on a single line. If you want to skip this section, go to page 134.

```
                                    1
\\SMSTEST\sms_shrd\PRIMSITE.SRV\IMPORT.SRC\ENU\PPT40A\SMSPROXY\MSAPPS\
ARTGALRY\

                                    1
\\SMSTEST\sms_shrd\PRIMSITE.SRV\IMPORT.SRC\ENU\PPT40A\SMSPROXY\MSAPPS\
EQUATION\

                                    1
\\SMSTEST\sms_shrd\PRIMSITE.SRV\IMPORT.SRC\ENU\PPT40A\SMSPROXY\MSAPPS\
MSGRAPH5\

                                    1
\\SMSTEST\sms_shrd\PRIMSITE.SRV\IMPORT.SRC\ENU\PPT40A\SMSPROXY\MSAPPS\
MSINFO\

                                    1
\\SMSTEST\sms_shrd\PRIMSITE.SRV\IMPORT.SRC\ENU\PPT40A\SMSPROXY\MSAPPS\
ORGCHART\

                                    1
\\SMSTEST\sms_shrd\PRIMSITE.SRV\IMPORT.SRC\ENU\PPT40A\SMSPROXY\MSAPPS\
WORDART\

                                    5
\\SMSTEST\sms_shrd\PRIMSITE.SRV\IMPORT.SRC\ENU\PPT40A\SMSPROXY\POWERPNT\

                                    0
\\SMSTEST\sms_shrd\PRIMSITE.SRV\IMPORT.SRC\ENU\PPT40C\

                                    5
\\SMSTEST\sms_shrd\PRIMSITE.SRV\IMPORT.SRC\ENU\PPT40C\SMSPROXY\
```

This code is spaced so that it is easier to read. Lines are broken for layout only: entries should be on a single line. If you want to skip this section, go to page 134.

SMSP2.LOG   *(continued)*

```
                                 0
\\SMSTEST\sms_shrd\PRIMSITE.SRV\IMPORT.SRC\ENU\PPT40C\SMSPROXY\MSAPPS\

                                 1
\\SMSTEST\sms_shrd\PRIMSITE.SRV\IMPORT.SRC\ENU\PPT40C\SMSPROXY\MSAPPS\
ARTGALRY\

                                 1
\\SMSTEST\sms_shrd\PRIMSITE.SRV\IMPORT.SRC\ENU\PPT40C\SMSPROXY\MSAPPS\
EQUATION\

                                 1
\\SMSTEST\sms_shrd\PRIMSITE.SRV\IMPORT.SRC\ENU\PPT40C\SMSPROXY\MSAPPS\
MSGRAPH5\

                                 1
\\SMSTEST\sms_shrd\PRIMSITE.SRV\IMPORT.SRC\ENU\PPT40C\SMSPROXY\MSAPPS\
MSINFO\

                                 1
\\SMSTEST\sms_shrd\PRIMSITE.SRV\IMPORT.SRC\ENU\PPT40C\SMSPROXY\MSAPPS\
ORGCHART\

                                 1
\\SMSTEST\sms_shrd\PRIMSITE.SRV\IMPORT.SRC\ENU\PPT40C\SMSPROXY\MSAPPS\
WORDART\

                                 5
\\SMSTEST\sms_shrd\PRIMSITE.SRV\IMPORT.SRC\ENU\PPT40C\SMSPROXY\PPT40C\

                                 0
\\SMSTEST\sms_shrd\PRIMSITE.SRV\IMPORT.SRC\ENU\PRJ40_\
```

> This code is spaced so that it is easier to read. Lines are broken for layout only: entries should be on a single line. If you want to skip this section, go to page 134.

```
                                  5
\\SMSTEST\sms_shrd\PRIMSITE.SRV\IMPORT.SRC\ENU\PRJ40_\SMSPROXY\

                                  0
\\SMSTEST\sms_shrd\PRIMSITE.SRV\IMPORT.SRC\ENU\PRJ40_\SMSPROXY\MSAPPS\

                                  1
\\SMSTEST\sms_shrd\PRIMSITE.SRV\IMPORT.SRC\ENU\PRJ40_\SMSPROXY\MSAPPS\
MSINFO\

                                  3
\\SMSTEST\sms_shrd\PRIMSITE.SRV\IMPORT.SRC\ENU\PRJ40_\SMSPROXY\WINPROJ\

                                  0
\\SMSTEST\sms_shrd\PRIMSITE.SRV\IMPORT.SRC\ENU\WWD60A\

                                  5
\\SMSTEST\sms_shrd\PRIMSITE.SRV\IMPORT.SRC\ENU\WWD60A\SMSPROXY\

                                  0
\\SMSTEST\sms_shrd\PRIMSITE.SRV\IMPORT.SRC\ENU\WWD60A\SMSPROXY\MSAPPS\

                                  1
\\SMSTEST\sms_shrd\PRIMSITE.SRV\IMPORT.SRC\ENU\WWD60A\SMSPROXY\MSAPPS\
EQUATION\

                                  1
\\SMSTEST\sms_shrd\PRIMSITE.SRV\IMPORT.SRC\ENU\WWD60A\SMSPROXY\MSAPPS\
MSGRAPH\

                                  1
\\SMSTEST\sms_shrd\PRIMSITE.SRV\IMPORT.SRC\ENU\WWD60A\SMSPROXY\MSAPPS\
MSINFO\
```

This code is spaced so that it is easier to read. Lines are broken for layout only: entries should be on a single line. If you want to skip this section, go to page 134.

SMSP2.LOG   *(continued)*

```
                              1
\\SMSTEST\sms_shrd\PRIMSITE.SRV\IMPORT.SRC\ENU\WWD60A\SMSPROXY\MSAPPS\
WORDART\

                              3
\\SMSTEST\sms_shrd\PRIMSITE.SRV\IMPORT.SRC\ENU\WWD60A\SMSPROXY\WINWORD\

                              0
\\SMSTEST\sms_shrd\PRIMSITE.SRV\IMPORT.SRC\ENU\WWD60C\

                              5
\\SMSTEST\sms_shrd\PRIMSITE.SRV\IMPORT.SRC\ENU\WWD60C\SMSPROXY\

                              0
\\SMSTEST\sms_shrd\PRIMSITE.SRV\IMPORT.SRC\ENU\WWD60C\SMSPROXY\MSAPPS\

                              1
\\SMSTEST\sms_shrd\PRIMSITE.SRV\IMPORT.SRC\ENU\WWD60C\SMSPROXY\MSAPPS\
EQUATION\

                              1
\\SMSTEST\sms_shrd\PRIMSITE.SRV\IMPORT.SRC\ENU\WWD60C\SMSPROXY\MSAPPS\
MSGRAPH\

                              1
\\SMSTEST\sms_shrd\PRIMSITE.SRV\IMPORT.SRC\ENU\WWD60C\SMSPROXY\MSAPPS\
MSINFO\

                              1
\\SMSTEST\sms_shrd\PRIMSITE.SRV\IMPORT.SRC\ENU\WWD60C\SMSPROXY\MSAPPS\
WORDART\

                              2
\\SMSTEST\sms_shrd\PRIMSITE.SRV\IMPORT.SRC\ENU\WWD60C\SMSPROXY\WWD60C\
```

This code is spaced so that it is easier to read. Lines are broken for layout only: entries should be on a single line. If you want to skip this section, go to page 134.

SMSP2.LOG *(continued)*

```
                                 0
\\SMSTEST\sms_shrd\PRIMSITE.SRV\RMOTECFG.BOX\

                                 0
\\SMSTEST\sms_shrd\PRIMSITE.SRV\RMOTESRC.BOX\

                                 5   \\SMSTEST\sms_shrd\Reg\

              Newer                    73728   default  0%   83%   100%

              Newer                    36864   SAM   0%   100%

              Newer                    49152   SECURITY   0%   100%

              Newer                  1384448   software  0%    4%    8%
  13%   17%   22%   26%   31%   35%   39%   44%   48%   53%   57%   62%
  66%   71%   75%   79%   84%   88%   93%   97%  100%

              Newer                   995328   system  0%    6%   12%   18%
  24%   30%   37%   43%   49%   55%   61%   67%   74%   80%   86%   92%
  98%  100%

                                 0   \\SMSTEST\sms_shrd\SITE.SRV\

                                 0   \\SMSTEST\sms_shrd\SITE.SRV\appmgr.box\

                                 0
\\SMSTEST\sms_shrd\SITE.SRV\dataload.box\

                                 0
\\SMSTEST\sms_shrd\SITE.SRV\dataload.box\deltamif.col\

          *EXTRA File                66677   00000000.MIF

                               100
\\SMSTEST\sms_shrd\SITE.SRV\dataload.box\deltamif.col\BADMIFS\

                                 0
\\SMSTEST\sms_shrd\SITE.SRV\dataload.box\deltamif.col\process\
```

This code is spaced so that it is easier to read. Lines are broken for layout only: entries should be on a single line. If you want to skip this section, go to page 134.

SMSP2.LOG   *(continued)*

```
                              0
\\SMSTEST\sms_shrd\SITE.SRV\dataload.box\files.col\

                              0
\\SMSTEST\sms_shrd\SITE.SRV\despoolr.box\

                              0
\\SMSTEST\sms_shrd\SITE.SRV\despoolr.box\receive\

                              2
\\SMSTEST\sms_shrd\SITE.SRV\despoolr.box\store\

                              0
\\SMSTEST\sms_shrd\SITE.SRV\inventry.box\

                             58
\\SMSTEST\sms_shrd\SITE.SRV\inventry.box\history\

        Newer                 65193  TL100001.hms  0%  100%

                    0  \\SMSTEST\sms_shrd\SITE.SRV\isvmif.box\

                              3
\\SMSTEST\sms_shrd\SITE.SRV\MAINCFG.BOX\

                              0
\\SMSTEST\sms_shrd\SITE.SRV\MAINCFG.BOX\APPCTL.SRC\

                              0
\\SMSTEST\sms_shrd\SITE.SRV\MAINCFG.BOX\APPCTL.SRC\DATABASE\

                              0
\\SMSTEST\sms_shrd\SITE.SRV\MAINCFG.BOX\APPCTL.SRC\INIFILES\

                              0
\\SMSTEST\sms_shrd\SITE.SRV\MAINCFG.BOX\APPCTL.SRC\SCRIPTS\
```

This code is spaced so that it is easier to read. Lines are broken for layout only: entries should be on a single line. If you want to skip this section, go to page 134.

```
                                17
\\SMSTEST\sms_shrd\SITE.SRV\MAINCFG.BOX\CLIENT.SRC\

                                3
\\SMSTEST\sms_shrd\SITE.SRV\MAINCFG.BOX\CLIENT.SRC\MAC.BIN\

                                8
\\SMSTEST\sms_shrd\SITE.SRV\MAINCFG.BOX\CLIENT.SRC\MAC.BIN\00000409\

                               118
\\SMSTEST\sms_shrd\SITE.SRV\MAINCFG.BOX\CLIENT.SRC\X86.BIN\

                                51
\\SMSTEST\sms_shrd\SITE.SRV\MAINCFG.BOX\CLIENT.SRC\X86.BIN\00000409\

                                0
\\SMSTEST\sms_shrd\SITE.SRV\MAINCFG.BOX\invdom.box\

                                1
\\SMSTEST\sms_shrd\SITE.SRV\MAINCFG.BOX\invdom.box\SMSLAB.000\

                                3
\\SMSTEST\sms_shrd\SITE.SRV\MAINCFG.BOX\invdom.box\SMSLAB.000\
invencfg.box\

                                31
\\SMSTEST\sms_shrd\SITE.SRV\MAINCFG.BOX\MSTEST\

                                5
\\SMSTEST\sms_shrd\SITE.SRV\MAINCFG.BOX\MSTEST\ALPHA.BIN\

                                5
\\SMSTEST\sms_shrd\SITE.SRV\MAINCFG.BOX\MSTEST\MIPS.BIN\

                                5
\\SMSTEST\sms_shrd\SITE.SRV\MAINCFG.BOX\MSTEST\X86.BIN\
```

This code is spaced so that it is easier to read. Lines are broken for layout only: entries should be on a single line. If you want to skip this section, go to page 134.

```
                                0
\\SMSTEST\sms_shrd\SITE.SRV\MAINCFG.BOX\pcmdom.box\

                               31
\\SMSTEST\sms_shrd\SITE.SRV\MAINCFG.BOX\pcmdom.box\SMSLAB.000\

                                1
\\SMSTEST\sms_shrd\SITE.SRV\MAINCFG.BOX\PKGRULE\

                                0
\\SMSTEST\sms_shrd\SITE.SRV\schedule.box\

                                0    \\SMSTEST\sms_shrd\SITE.SRV\sender.box\

                                0
\\SMSTEST\sms_shrd\SITE.SRV\sender.box\requests\

                                2
\\SMSTEST\sms_shrd\SITE.SRV\sender.box\requests\LAN_DEFA.000\

           Newer                         20  00000000.CPB  0%  100%

                                0
\\SMSTEST\sms_shrd\SITE.SRV\sender.box\requests\RAS_ASYN.000\

                                0
\\SMSTEST\sms_shrd\SITE.SRV\sender.box\requests\RAS_ISDN.000\

                                0
\\SMSTEST\sms_shrd\SITE.SRV\sender.box\requests\RAS_X25_.000\

                                0
\\SMSTEST\sms_shrd\SITE.SRV\sender.box\requests\SNA_BATC.000\

                                0
\\SMSTEST\sms_shrd\SITE.SRV\sender.box\requests\SNA_INTE.000\
```

This code is spaced so that it is easier to read. Lines are broken for layout only: entries should be on a single line. If you want to skip this section, go to page 134.

SMSP2.LOG   *(continued)*

```
                                    2
\\SMSTEST\sms_shrd\SITE.SRV\sender.box\tosend\\\SMSTEST\sms_shrd\SITE.SR

                                    1
\\SMSTEST\sms_shrd\SITE.SRV\SITECFG.BOX\

                                    0
\\SMSTEST\sms_shrd\SITE.SRV\siterep.box\

          *EXTRA File                66713   00000000.MIF

          *EXTRA File                95137   00000000.UMF

                               88  \\SMSTEST\sms_shrd\SITE.SRV\X86.BIN\

                                    27
\\SMSTEST\sms_shrd\SITE.SRV\X86.BIN\00000409\

                                    1
\\SMSTEST\sms_shrd\SITE.SRV\X86.BIN\ERRORHIS\

                               1   \\SMSTEST\sms_shrd\Sql\

------------------------------------------------------------------------

              Total    Copied    Skipped  Mismatch    FAILED    Extras

    Dirs :      199        0        199        0         0         1

   Files :     1286       23       1263        0         0         4

   Bytes :   264.9 m    3.5 m    261.4 m        0         0    288.9 k

   Times :   0:14.000  0:03.745                     0:00.000  0:10.255

Ended : Fri May 30 13:29:47 1997

D:\SMSsoft\SMSBAC~1>REM -------------------------------------------------
```

This code is spaced so that it is easier to read. Lines are broken for layout only: entries should be on a single line. If you want to skip this section, go to page 134.

```
D:\SMSsoft\SMSBAC~1>REM Start all SMS Site Server Services

D:\SMSsoft\SMSBAC~1>REM -------------------------------------------------

D:\SMSsoft\SMSBAC~1>NET START SMS_CLIENT_CONFIG_MANAGER

The SMS_CLIENT_CONFIG_MANAGER service is starting.

The SMS_CLIENT_CONFIG_MANAGER service was started successfully.

D:\SMSsoft\SMSBAC~1>NET START SMS_EXECUTIVE

The SMS_EXECUTIVE service is starting.

The SMS_EXECUTIVE service was started successfully.

D:\SMSsoft\SMSBAC~1>NET START SMS_HIERARCHY_MANAGER

The SMS_HIERARCHY_MANAGER service is starting.

The SMS_HIERARCHY_MANAGER service was started successfully.

D:\SMSsoft\SMSBAC~1>NET START SMS_INVENTORY_AGENT_NT

The SMS_INVENTORY_AGENT_NT service is starting.

The SMS_INVENTORY_AGENT_NT service was started successfully.

D:\SMSsoft\SMSBAC~1>NET START SMS_PACKAGE_COMMAND_MANAGER_NT

The SMS_PACKAGE_COMMAND_MANAGER_NT service is starting.

The SMS_PACKAGE_COMMAND_MANAGER_NT service was started successfully.

D:\SMSsoft\SMSBAC~1>NET START SMS_SITE_CONFIG_MANAGER

The SMS_SITE_CONFIG_MANAGER service is starting..

The SMS_SITE_CONFIG_MANAGER service was started successfully.
```

This code is spaced so that it is easier to read. Lines are broken for layout only: entries should be on a single line. If you want to skip this section, go to page 134.

Smsl.log Log File

This log file is generated when the Windows NT Scheduler runs the Windows NT Server command procedure at an SMS logon server.

```
D:\SMSsoft\SMSBAC~1>REM --------------------------------------------


D:\SMSsoft\SMSBAC~1>REM SMS Logon Server Backup Script


D:\SMSsoft\SMSBAC~1>REM --------------------------------------------


D:\SMSsoft\SMSBAC~1>REM Stop all SMS Logon Server Services


D:\SMSsoft\SMSBAC~1>REM --------------------------------------------
```

> This code is spaced so that it is easier to read. Lines are broken for layout only: entries should be on a single line. If you want to skip this section, go to page 159.

SMSL.LOG   *(continued)*

```
D:\SMSsoft\SMSBAC~1>NET STOP  SMS_CLIENT_CONFIG_MANAGER


The SMS_CLIENT_CONFIG_MANAGER service was stopped successfully.


D:\SMSsoft\SMSBAC~1>NET STOP  SMS_INVENTORY_AGENT_NT


The SMS_INVENTORY_AGENT_NT service was stopped successfully.


D:\SMSsoft\SMSBAC~1>NET STOP  SMS_PACKAGE_COMMAND_MANAGER_NT


The SMS_PACKAGE_COMMAND_MANAGER_NT service was stopped successfully.


D:\SMSsoft\SMSBAC~1>REM -----------------------------------------------


D:\SMSsoft\SMSBAC~1>REM Delete old backed up registry files and back up
current


D:\SMSsoft\SMSBAC~1>REM -----------------------------------------------
```

> This code is spaced so that it is easier to read. Lines are broken for layout only: entries should be on a single line. If you want to skip this section, go to page 159.

```
D:\SMSsoft\SMSBAC~1>del        \\SMSTEST\sms_shrd\reg /q


D:\SMSsoft\SMSBAC~1>C:\WINNT\system32\repl\import\scripts\regback
\\SMSTEST\sms_shrd\reg

saving SECURITY to \\SMSTEST\sms_shrd\reg\SECURITY

saving SOFTWARE to \\SMSTEST\sms_shrd\reg\software

saving SYSTEM to \\SMSTEST\sms_shrd\reg\system

saving .DEFAULT to \\SMSTEST\sms_shrd\reg\default

saving SAM to \\SMSTEST\sms_shrd\reg\SAM


***Hive = \REGISTRY\USER\S-1-5-21-2144011916-71395201-114579206-6019

Stored in file
\Device\Harddisk1\Partition2\WINNT\Profiles\SQLadmin\NTUSER.DAT

Must be backed up manually

regback <filename you choose> users S-1-5-21-2144011916-71395201-
114579206-6019




***Hive = \REGISTRY\USER\S-1-5-21-2144011916-71395201-114579206-1005

Stored in file
\Device\Harddisk1\Partition2\WINNT\Profiles\bblyler.000\NTUSER.DAT
```

This code is spaced so that it is easier to read. Lines are broken for layout only: entries should be on a single line. If you want to skip this section, go to page 159.

Must be backed up manually

regback <filename you choose> users S-1-5-21-2144011916-71395201-
114579206-1005

***Hive = \REGISTRY\USER\S-1-5-21-1004933954-1864521944-1415713722-1001

Stored in file
\Device\Harddisk1\Partition2\WINNT\Profiles\bblyler\NTUSER.DAT

Must be backed up manually

regback <filename you choose> users S-1-5-21-1004933954-1864521944-
1415713722-1001

***Hive = \REGISTRY\USER\S-1-5-21-2144011916-71395201-114579206-5584

Stored in file
\Device\Harddisk1\Partition2\WINNT\Profiles\SMSAdmin\NTUSER.DAT

Must be backed up manually

regback <filename you choose> users S-1-5-21-2144011916-71395201-
114579206-5584

This code is spaced so that it is easier to read. Lines are broken for layout only: entries should be on a single line. If you want to skip this section, go to page 159.

SMSL.LOG   *(continued)*

```
D:\SMSsoft\SMSBAC~1>REM --------------------------------------------


D:\SMSsoft\SMSBAC~1>REM Copy all SMS files to backup server SMSTEST


D:\SMSsoft\SMSBAC~1>REM ---------------------------------------------


D:\SMSsoft\SMSBAC~1>C:\WINNT\system32\repl\import\scripts\robocopy
\\SMSTEST\sms_shrd \\smstest\smsdumps\SMSTEST /e



-------------------------------------------------------------------

ROBOCOPY v 1.71  :  Robust File Copy for Windows NT  :  by
kevina@microsoft.com

-------------------------------------------------------------------



   Started : Fri May 30 13:20:37 1997


    Source : \\SMSTEST\sms_shrd\

      Dest : \\smstest\smsdumps\SMSTEST\

     Files : *.*

   Options : *.* /S /E /R:1000000 /W:30
```

This code is spaced so that it is easier to read. Lines are broken for layout only: entries should be on a single line. If you want to skip this section, go to page 159.

```
------------------------------------------------------------

                                 2   \\SMSTEST\sms_shrd\

        *EXTRA Dir              -1   \\smstest\smsdumps\SMSTEST\sms\

                                 0   \\SMSTEST\sms_shrd\helper.srv\

                                 3   \\SMSTEST\sms_shrd\helper.srv\X86.BIN\

                                 1
\\SMSTEST\sms_shrd\helper.srv\X86.BIN\00000409\

                                 1
\\SMSTEST\sms_shrd\helper.srv\X86.BIN\ERRORHIS\

                                20   \\SMSTEST\sms_shrd\logon.srv\

            Newer               1429  DOMAIN.INI  0%  100%

                                 0
\\SMSTEST\sms_shrd\logon.srv\appctl.box\

                                 0
\\SMSTEST\sms_shrd\logon.srv\appctl.box\database\

                                 0
\\SMSTEST\sms_shrd\logon.srv\appctl.box\inifiles\
```

This code is spaced so that it is easier to read. Lines are broken for layout only: entries should be on a single line. If you want to skip this section, go to page 159.

SMSL.LOG   *(continued)*

```
                                     0
\\SMSTEST\sms_shrd\logon.srv\appctl.box\scripts\

                             0   \\SMSTEST\sms_shrd\logon.srv\ccr.box\

                             0
\\SMSTEST\sms_shrd\logon.srv\ccr.box\retry\

                             0
\\SMSTEST\sms_shrd\logon.srv\despoolr.box\

                             3
\\SMSTEST\sms_shrd\logon.srv\invencfg.box\

                             4
\\SMSTEST\sms_shrd\logon.srv\inventry.box\

        *EXTRA File              67332   00000000.RAW

        New File                 64458   00000003.tmp   0%   100%

                             0
\\SMSTEST\sms_shrd\logon.srv\isvmif.box\

                             3   \\SMSTEST\sms_shrd\logon.srv\MAC.BIN\

                             8
\\SMSTEST\sms_shrd\logon.srv\MAC.BIN\00000409\

                            32   \\SMSTEST\sms_shrd\logon.srv\mstest\

                             5
\\SMSTEST\sms_shrd\logon.srv\mstest\ALPHA.BIN\
```

> This code is spaced so that it is easier to read. Lines are broken for layout only: entries should be on a single line. If you want to skip this section, go to page 159.

```
                          5
\\SMSTEST\sms_shrd\logon.srv\mstest\MIPS.BIN\

                          5
\\SMSTEST\sms_shrd\logon.srv\mstest\X86.BIN\

                         1   \\SMSTEST\sms_shrd\logon.srv\NCDTREE\

                         31
\\SMSTEST\sms_shrd\logon.srv\pcmins.box\

                          0
\\SMSTEST\sms_shrd\logon.srv\pcmpkg.src\

                         1   \\SMSTEST\sms_shrd\logon.srv\SMSID\

                       118   \\SMSTEST\sms_shrd\logon.srv\X86.BIN\

                        51
\\SMSTEST\sms_shrd\logon.srv\X86.BIN\00000409\

                        30   \\SMSTEST\sms_shrd\LOGS\

       Newer                 45326   clicfg.log    0%   100%

       Newer                 91249   invagent.log  0%    67%   100%

       Newer                 65624   invproc.log   0%    93%   100%

       Newer                 51836   lansend.log   0%   100%
```

This code is spaced so that it is easier to read. Lines are broken for layout only: entries should be on a single line. If you want to skip this section, go to page 159.

SMSL.LOG   *(continued)*

```
Newer                    60731  maintman.log  0%  100%

Newer                   110623  pacman.log  0%   55% 100%

Newer                   105625  siterept.log  0%   58% 100%

              0  \\SMSTEST\sms_shrd\NETMON\

             14  \\SMSTEST\sms_shrd\NETMON\X86\

              4  \\SMSTEST\sms_shrd\NETMON\X86\CAPTURES\

             43  \\SMSTEST\sms_shrd\NETMON\X86\PARSERS\

              0  \\SMSTEST\sms_shrd\PRIMSITE.SRV\

              2  \\SMSTEST\sms_shrd\PRIMSITE.SRV\AUDIT\

              1
\\SMSTEST\sms_shrd\PRIMSITE.SRV\AUDIT\PACKAGE\

              1
\\SMSTEST\sms_shrd\PRIMSITE.SRV\AUDIT\PACKAGE\ALPHA.BIN\

              1
\\SMSTEST\sms_shrd\PRIMSITE.SRV\AUDIT\PACKAGE\ALPHA.BIN\00000409\

              1
\\SMSTEST\sms_shrd\PRIMSITE.SRV\AUDIT\PACKAGE\MIPS.BIN\

              1
\\SMSTEST\sms_shrd\PRIMSITE.SRV\AUDIT\PACKAGE\MIPS.BIN\00000409\

              2
\\SMSTEST\sms_shrd\PRIMSITE.SRV\AUDIT\PACKAGE\X86.BIN\

              2
\\SMSTEST\sms_shrd\PRIMSITE.SRV\AUDIT\PACKAGE\X86.BIN\00000409\
```

This code is spaced so that it is easier to read. Lines are broken for layout only: entries should be on a single line. If you want to skip this section, go to page 159.

```
                          0
\\SMSTEST\sms_shrd\PRIMSITE.SRV\IMPORT.SRC\

                         150
\\SMSTEST\sms_shrd\PRIMSITE.SRV\IMPORT.SRC\ENU\

                          0
\\SMSTEST\sms_shrd\PRIMSITE.SRV\IMPORT.SRC\ENU\ACS200\

                          5
\\SMSTEST\sms_shrd\PRIMSITE.SRV\IMPORT.SRC\ENU\ACS200\SMSPROXY\

                          3
\\SMSTEST\sms_shrd\PRIMSITE.SRV\IMPORT.SRC\ENU\ACS200\SMSPROXY\MSACCESS\

                          0
\\SMSTEST\sms_shrd\PRIMSITE.SRV\IMPORT.SRC\ENU\ACS200\SMSPROXY\MSAPPS\

                          1
\\SMSTEST\sms_shrd\PRIMSITE.SRV\IMPORT.SRC\ENU\ACS200\SMSPROXY\MSAPPS\
MSGRAPH5\

                          1
\\SMSTEST\sms_shrd\PRIMSITE.SRV\IMPORT.SRC\ENU\ACS200\SMSPROXY\MSAPPS\
MSINFO\

                          0
\\SMSTEST\sms_shrd\PRIMSITE.SRV\IMPORT.SRC\ENU\EXC50A\

                          5
\\SMSTEST\sms_shrd\PRIMSITE.SRV\IMPORT.SRC\ENU\EXC50A\SMSPROXY\

                          3
\\SMSTEST\sms_shrd\PRIMSITE.SRV\IMPORT.SRC\ENU\EXC50A\SMSPROXY\EXCEL\
```

This code is spaced so that it is easier to read. Lines are broken for layout only: entries should be on a single line. If you want to skip this section, go to page 159.

```
                              0
\\SMSTEST\sms_shrd\PRIMSITE.SRV\IMPORT.SRC\ENU\EXC50A\SMSPROXY\MSAPPS\

                              1
\\SMSTEST\sms_shrd\PRIMSITE.SRV\IMPORT.SRC\ENU\EXC50A\SMSPROXY\MSAPPS\
MSINFO\

                              1
\\SMSTEST\sms_shrd\PRIMSITE.SRV\IMPORT.SRC\ENU\EXC50A\SMSPROXY\MSAPPS\
MSQUERY\

                              0
\\SMSTEST\sms_shrd\PRIMSITE.SRV\IMPORT.SRC\ENU\EXC50C\

                              5
\\SMSTEST\sms_shrd\PRIMSITE.SRV\IMPORT.SRC\ENU\EXC50C\SMSPROXY\

                              2
\\SMSTEST\sms_shrd\PRIMSITE.SRV\IMPORT.SRC\ENU\EXC50C\SMSPROXY\EXC50C\

                              0
\\SMSTEST\sms_shrd\PRIMSITE.SRV\IMPORT.SRC\ENU\EXC50C\SMSPROXY\MSAPPS\

                              1
\\SMSTEST\sms_shrd\PRIMSITE.SRV\IMPORT.SRC\ENU\EXC50C\SMSPROXY\MSAPPS\
MSINFO\

                              1
\\SMSTEST\sms_shrd\PRIMSITE.SRV\IMPORT.SRC\ENU\EXC50C\SMSPROXY\MSAPPS\
MSQUERY\

                              0
\\SMSTEST\sms_shrd\PRIMSITE.SRV\IMPORT.SRC\ENU\OFF42A\

                              5
\\SMSTEST\sms_shrd\PRIMSITE.SRV\IMPORT.SRC\ENU\OFF42A\SMSPROXY\
```

This code is spaced so that it is easier to read. Lines are broken for layout only: entries should be on a single line. If you want to skip this section, go to page 159.

```
                              0
\\SMSTEST\sms_shrd\PRIMSITE.SRV\IMPORT.SRC\ENU\OFF42A\SMSPROXY\MSAPPS\

                              1
\\SMSTEST\sms_shrd\PRIMSITE.SRV\IMPORT.SRC\ENU\OFF42A\SMSPROXY\MSAPPS\
ARTGALRY\

                              1
\\SMSTEST\sms_shrd\PRIMSITE.SRV\IMPORT.SRC\ENU\OFF42A\SMSPROXY\MSAPPS\
EQUATION\

                              1
\\SMSTEST\sms_shrd\PRIMSITE.SRV\IMPORT.SRC\ENU\OFF42A\SMSPROXY\MSAPPS\
MSGRAPH5\

                              1
\\SMSTEST\sms_shrd\PRIMSITE.SRV\IMPORT.SRC\ENU\OFF42A\SMSPROXY\MSAPPS\
MSINFO\

                              1
\\SMSTEST\sms_shrd\PRIMSITE.SRV\IMPORT.SRC\ENU\OFF42A\SMSPROXY\MSAPPS\
MSQUERY\

                              1
\\SMSTEST\sms_shrd\PRIMSITE.SRV\IMPORT.SRC\ENU\OFF42A\SMSPROXY\MSAPPS\
ORGCHART\

                              1
\\SMSTEST\sms_shrd\PRIMSITE.SRV\IMPORT.SRC\ENU\OFF42A\SMSPROXY\MSAPPS\
WORDART\
```

This code is spaced so that it is easier to read. Lines are broken for layout only: entries should be on a single line. If you want to skip this section, go to page 159.

```
                              7
\\SMSTEST\sms_shrd\PRIMSITE.SRV\IMPORT.SRC\ENU\OFF42A\SMSPROXY\MSOFFICE\

                              0
\\SMSTEST\sms_shrd\PRIMSITE.SRV\IMPORT.SRC\ENU\OFF42C\

                              5
\\SMSTEST\sms_shrd\PRIMSITE.SRV\IMPORT.SRC\ENU\OFF42C\SMSPROXY\

                              0
\\SMSTEST\sms_shrd\PRIMSITE.SRV\IMPORT.SRC\ENU\OFF42C\SMSPROXY\MSAPPS\

                              1
\\SMSTEST\sms_shrd\PRIMSITE.SRV\IMPORT.SRC\ENU\OFF42C\SMSPROXY\MSAPPS\
ARTGALRY\

                              1
\\SMSTEST\sms_shrd\PRIMSITE.SRV\IMPORT.SRC\ENU\OFF42C\SMSPROXY\MSAPPS\
EQUATION\

                              1
\\SMSTEST\sms_shrd\PRIMSITE.SRV\IMPORT.SRC\ENU\OFF42C\SMSPROXY\MSAPPS\
MSGRAPH5\

                              1
\\SMSTEST\sms_shrd\PRIMSITE.SRV\IMPORT.SRC\ENU\OFF42C\SMSPROXY\MSAPPS\
MSINFO\

                              1
\\SMSTEST\sms_shrd\PRIMSITE.SRV\IMPORT.SRC\ENU\OFF42C\SMSPROXY\MSAPPS\
MSQUERY\

                              1
\\SMSTEST\sms_shrd\PRIMSITE.SRV\IMPORT.SRC\ENU\OFF42C\SMSPROXY\MSAPPS\
ORGCHART\
```

This code is spaced so that it is easier to read. Lines are broken for layout only: entries should be on a single line. If you want to skip this section, go to page 159.

SMSL.LOG   *(continued)*

```
                                   1
\\SMSTEST\sms_shrd\PRIMSITE.SRV\IMPORT.SRC\ENU\OFF42C\SMSPROXY\MSAPPS\
WORDART\

                                   7
\\SMSTEST\sms_shrd\PRIMSITE.SRV\IMPORT.SRC\ENU\OFF42C\SMSPROXY\OFF42C\

                                   0
\\SMSTEST\sms_shrd\PRIMSITE.SRV\IMPORT.SRC\ENU\OFP43_\

                                   5
\\SMSTEST\sms_shrd\PRIMSITE.SRV\IMPORT.SRC\ENU\OFP43_\SMSPROXY\

                                   0
\\SMSTEST\sms_shrd\PRIMSITE.SRV\IMPORT.SRC\ENU\OFP43_\SMSPROXY\MSAPPS\

                                   1
\\SMSTEST\sms_shrd\PRIMSITE.SRV\IMPORT.SRC\ENU\OFP43_\SMSPROXY\MSAPPS\
ARTGALRY\

                                   1
\\SMSTEST\sms_shrd\PRIMSITE.SRV\IMPORT.SRC\ENU\OFP43_\SMSPROXY\MSAPPS\
EQUATION\

                                   1
\\SMSTEST\sms_shrd\PRIMSITE.SRV\IMPORT.SRC\ENU\OFP43_\SMSPROXY\MSAPPS\
MSGRAPH5\

                                   1
\\SMSTEST\sms_shrd\PRIMSITE.SRV\IMPORT.SRC\ENU\OFP43_\SMSPROXY\MSAPPS\
MSINFO\

                                   1
\\SMSTEST\sms_shrd\PRIMSITE.SRV\IMPORT.SRC\ENU\OFP43_\SMSPROXY\MSAPPS\
MSQUERY\
```

This code is spaced so that it is easier to read. Lines are broken for layout only: entries should be on a single line. If you want to skip this section, go to page 159.

1
```
\\SMSTEST\sms_shrd\PRIMSITE.SRV\IMPORT.SRC\ENU\OFP43_\SMSPROXY\MSAPPS\
ORGCHART\
```

1
```
\\SMSTEST\sms_shrd\PRIMSITE.SRV\IMPORT.SRC\ENU\OFP43_\SMSPROXY\MSAPPS\
WORDART\
```

8
```
\\SMSTEST\sms_shrd\PRIMSITE.SRV\IMPORT.SRC\ENU\OFP43_\SMSPROXY\MSOFFPRO\
```

0
```
\\SMSTEST\sms_shrd\PRIMSITE.SRV\IMPORT.SRC\ENU\OFP43C\
```

5
```
\\SMSTEST\sms_shrd\PRIMSITE.SRV\IMPORT.SRC\ENU\OFP43C\SMSPROXY\
```

0
```
\\SMSTEST\sms_shrd\PRIMSITE.SRV\IMPORT.SRC\ENU\OFP43C\SMSPROXY\MSAPPS\
```

1
```
\\SMSTEST\sms_shrd\PRIMSITE.SRV\IMPORT.SRC\ENU\OFP43C\SMSPROXY\MSAPPS\
ARTGALRY\
```

1
```
\\SMSTEST\sms_shrd\PRIMSITE.SRV\IMPORT.SRC\ENU\OFP43C\SMSPROXY\MSAPPS\
EQUATION\
```

1
```
\\SMSTEST\sms_shrd\PRIMSITE.SRV\IMPORT.SRC\ENU\OFP43C\SMSPROXY\MSAPPS\
MSGRAPH5\
```

1
```
\\SMSTEST\sms_shrd\PRIMSITE.SRV\IMPORT.SRC\ENU\OFP43C\SMSPROXY\MSAPPS\
MSINFO\
```

This code is spaced so that it is easier to read. Lines are broken for layout only: entries should be on a single line. If you want to skip this section, go to page 159.

SMSL.LOG   *(continued)*

```
                              1
\\SMSTEST\sms_shrd\PRIMSITE.SRV\IMPORT.SRC\ENU\OFP43C\SMSPROXY\MSAPPS\
MSQUERY\

                              1
\\SMSTEST\sms_shrd\PRIMSITE.SRV\IMPORT.SRC\ENU\OFP43C\SMSPROXY\MSAPPS\
ORGCHART\

                              1
\\SMSTEST\sms_shrd\PRIMSITE.SRV\IMPORT.SRC\ENU\OFP43C\SMSPROXY\MSAPPS\
WORDART\

                              8
\\SMSTEST\sms_shrd\PRIMSITE.SRV\IMPORT.SRC\ENU\OFP43C\SMSPROXY\OFP43C\

                              0
\\SMSTEST\sms_shrd\PRIMSITE.SRV\IMPORT.SRC\ENU\PPT40A\

                              5
\\SMSTEST\sms_shrd\PRIMSITE.SRV\IMPORT.SRC\ENU\PPT40A\SMSPROXY\

                              0
\\SMSTEST\sms_shrd\PRIMSITE.SRV\IMPORT.SRC\ENU\PPT40A\SMSPROXY\MSAPPS\

                              1
\\SMSTEST\sms_shrd\PRIMSITE.SRV\IMPORT.SRC\ENU\PPT40A\SMSPROXY\MSAPPS\
ARTGALRY\

                              1
\\SMSTEST\sms_shrd\PRIMSITE.SRV\IMPORT.SRC\ENU\PPT40A\SMSPROXY\MSAPPS\
EQUATION\

                              1
\\SMSTEST\sms_shrd\PRIMSITE.SRV\IMPORT.SRC\ENU\PPT40A\SMSPROXY\MSAPPS\
MSGRAPH5\
```

This code is spaced so that it is easier to read. Lines are broken for layout only: entries should be on a single line. If you want to skip this section, go to page 159.

SMSL.LOG   *(continued)*

```
                           1
\\SMSTEST\sms_shrd\PRIMSITE.SRV\IMPORT.SRC\ENU\PPT40A\SMSPROXY\MSAPPS\
MSINFO\

                           1
\\SMSTEST\sms_shrd\PRIMSITE.SRV\IMPORT.SRC\ENU\PPT40A\SMSPROXY\MSAPPS\
ORGCHART\

                           1
\\SMSTEST\sms_shrd\PRIMSITE.SRV\IMPORT.SRC\ENU\PPT40A\SMSPROXY\MSAPPS\
WORDART\

                           5
\\SMSTEST\sms_shrd\PRIMSITE.SRV\IMPORT.SRC\ENU\PPT40A\SMSPROXY\POWERPNT\

                           0
\\SMSTEST\sms_shrd\PRIMSITE.SRV\IMPORT.SRC\ENU\PPT40C\

                           5
\\SMSTEST\sms_shrd\PRIMSITE.SRV\IMPORT.SRC\ENU\PPT40C\SMSPROXY\

                           0
\\SMSTEST\sms_shrd\PRIMSITE.SRV\IMPORT.SRC\ENU\PPT40C\SMSPROXY\MSAPPS\

                           1
\\SMSTEST\sms_shrd\PRIMSITE.SRV\IMPORT.SRC\ENU\PPT40C\SMSPROXY\MSAPPS\
ARTGALRY\

                           1
\\SMSTEST\sms_shrd\PRIMSITE.SRV\IMPORT.SRC\ENU\PPT40C\SMSPROXY\MSAPPS\
EQUATION\

                           1
\\SMSTEST\sms_shrd\PRIMSITE.SRV\IMPORT.SRC\ENU\PPT40C\SMSPROXY\MSAPPS\
MSGRAPH5\
```

This code is spaced so that it is easier to read. Lines are broken for layout only: entries should be on a single line. If you want to skip this section, go to page 159.

SMSL.LOG   *(continued)*

```
                            1
\\SMSTEST\sms_shrd\PRIMSITE.SRV\IMPORT.SRC\ENU\PPT40C\SMSPROXY\MSAPPS\
MSINFO\

                            1
\\SMSTEST\sms_shrd\PRIMSITE.SRV\IMPORT.SRC\ENU\PPT40C\SMSPROXY\MSAPPS\
ORGCHART\

                            1
\\SMSTEST\sms_shrd\PRIMSITE.SRV\IMPORT.SRC\ENU\PPT40C\SMSPROXY\MSAPPS\
WORDART\

                            5
\\SMSTEST\sms_shrd\PRIMSITE.SRV\IMPORT.SRC\ENU\PPT40C\SMSPROXY\PPT40C\

                            0
\\SMSTEST\sms_shrd\PRIMSITE.SRV\IMPORT.SRC\ENU\PRJ40_\

                            5
\\SMSTEST\sms_shrd\PRIMSITE.SRV\IMPORT.SRC\ENU\PRJ40_\SMSPROXY\

                            0
\\SMSTEST\sms_shrd\PRIMSITE.SRV\IMPORT.SRC\ENU\PRJ40_\SMSPROXY\MSAPPS\

                            1
\\SMSTEST\sms_shrd\PRIMSITE.SRV\IMPORT.SRC\ENU\PRJ40_\SMSPROXY\MSAPPS\
MSINFO\

                            3
\\SMSTEST\sms_shrd\PRIMSITE.SRV\IMPORT.SRC\ENU\PRJ40_\SMSPROXY\WINPROJ\

                            0
\\SMSTEST\sms_shrd\PRIMSITE.SRV\IMPORT.SRC\ENU\WWD60A\

                            5
\\SMSTEST\sms_shrd\PRIMSITE.SRV\IMPORT.SRC\ENU\WWD60A\SMSPROXY\
```

This code is spaced so that it is easier to read. Lines are broken for layout only: entries should be on a single line. If you want to skip this section, go to page 159.

```
                              0
\\SMSTEST\sms_shrd\PRIMSITE.SRV\IMPORT.SRC\ENU\WWD60A\SMSPROXY\MSAPPS\

                              1
\\SMSTEST\sms_shrd\PRIMSITE.SRV\IMPORT.SRC\ENU\WWD60A\SMSPROXY\MSAPPS\
EQUATION\

                              1
\\SMSTEST\sms_shrd\PRIMSITE.SRV\IMPORT.SRC\ENU\WWD60A\SMSPROXY\MSAPPS\
MSGRAPH\

                              1
\\SMSTEST\sms_shrd\PRIMSITE.SRV\IMPORT.SRC\ENU\WWD60A\SMSPROXY\MSAPPS\
MSINFO\

                              1
\\SMSTEST\sms_shrd\PRIMSITE.SRV\IMPORT.SRC\ENU\WWD60A\SMSPROXY\MSAPPS\
WORDART\

                              3
\\SMSTEST\sms_shrd\PRIMSITE.SRV\IMPORT.SRC\ENU\WWD60A\SMSPROXY\WINWORD\

                              0
\\SMSTEST\sms_shrd\PRIMSITE.SRV\IMPORT.SRC\ENU\WWD60C\

                              5
\\SMSTEST\sms_shrd\PRIMSITE.SRV\IMPORT.SRC\ENU\WWD60C\SMSPROXY\

                              0
\\SMSTEST\sms_shrd\PRIMSITE.SRV\IMPORT.SRC\ENU\WWD60C\SMSPROXY\MSAPPS\

                              1
\\SMSTEST\sms_shrd\PRIMSITE.SRV\IMPORT.SRC\ENU\WWD60C\SMSPROXY\MSAPPS\
EQUATION\
```

This code is spaced so that it is easier to read. Lines are broken for layout only: entries should be on a single line. If you want to skip this section, go to page 159.

SMSL.LOG   *(continued)*

```
                                   1
\\SMSTEST\sms_shrd\PRIMSITE.SRV\IMPORT.SRC\ENU\WWD60C\SMSPROXY\MSAPPS\
MSGRAPH\

                                   1
\\SMSTEST\sms_shrd\PRIMSITE.SRV\IMPORT.SRC\ENU\WWD60C\SMSPROXY\MSAPPS\
MSINFO\

                                   1
\\SMSTEST\sms_shrd\PRIMSITE.SRV\IMPORT.SRC\ENU\WWD60C\SMSPROXY\MSAPPS\
WORDART\

                                   2
\\SMSTEST\sms_shrd\PRIMSITE.SRV\IMPORT.SRC\ENU\WWD60C\SMSPROXY\WWD60C\

                                   0
\\SMSTEST\sms_shrd\PRIMSITE.SRV\RMOTECFG.BOX\

                                   0
\\SMSTEST\sms_shrd\PRIMSITE.SRV\RMOTESRC.BOX\

                          5   \\SMSTEST\sms_shrd\Reg\

             Newer                  73728   default  0%   83%   100%

             Newer                  36864   SAM   0%   100%

             Newer                  49152   SECURITY   0%   100%

             Newer               1384448   software  0%    4%    8%
13%    17%    22%    26%    31%    35%    39%    44%    48%    53%    57%    62%
66%    71%    75%    79%    84%    88%    93%    97%   100%

             Newer                995328   system  0%    6%   12%   18%
24%    30%    37%    43%    49%    55%    61%    67%    74%    80%    86%    92%
98%   100%
```

> This code is spaced so that it is easier to read. Lines are broken for layout only: entries should be on a single line. If you want to skip this section, go to page 159.

```
                                       0   \\SMSTEST\sms_shrd\SITE.SRV\

                                       0   \\SMSTEST\sms_shrd\SITE.SRV\appmgr.box\

                                       0
\\SMSTEST\sms_shrd\SITE.SRV\dataload.box\

                                       0
\\SMSTEST\sms_shrd\SITE.SRV\dataload.box\deltamif.col\

            *EXTRA File                66677  00000000.MIF
                                     100
\\SMSTEST\sms_shrd\SITE.SRV\dataload.box\deltamif.col\BADMIFS\

                                       0
\\SMSTEST\sms_shrd\SITE.SRV\dataload.box\deltamif.col\process\

                                       0
\\SMSTEST\sms_shrd\SITE.SRV\dataload.box\files.col\

                                       0
\\SMSTEST\sms_shrd\SITE.SRV\despoolr.box\

                                       0
\\SMSTEST\sms_shrd\SITE.SRV\despoolr.box\receive\

                                       2
\\SMSTEST\sms_shrd\SITE.SRV\despoolr.box\store\

                                       0
\\SMSTEST\sms_shrd\SITE.SRV\inventry.box\

                                      58
\\SMSTEST\sms_shrd\SITE.SRV\inventry.box\history\

                                       0   \\SMSTEST\sms_shrd\SITE.SRV\isvmif.box\
```

This code is spaced so that it is easier to read. Lines are broken for layout only: entries should be on a single line. If you want to skip this section, go to page 159.

```
                              3
\\SMSTEST\sms_shrd\SITE.SRV\MAINCFG.BOX\

                              0
\\SMSTEST\sms_shrd\SITE.SRV\MAINCFG.BOX\APPCTL.SRC\

                              0
\\SMSTEST\sms_shrd\SITE.SRV\MAINCFG.BOX\APPCTL.SRC\DATABASE\

                              0
\\SMSTEST\sms_shrd\SITE.SRV\MAINCFG.BOX\APPCTL.SRC\INIFILES\

                              0
\\SMSTEST\sms_shrd\SITE.SRV\MAINCFG.BOX\APPCTL.SRC\SCRIPTS\

                             17
\\SMSTEST\sms_shrd\SITE.SRV\MAINCFG.BOX\CLIENT.SRC\

                              3
\\SMSTEST\sms_shrd\SITE.SRV\MAINCFG.BOX\CLIENT.SRC\MAC.BIN\

                              8
\\SMSTEST\sms_shrd\SITE.SRV\MAINCFG.BOX\CLIENT.SRC\MAC.BIN\00000409\

                            118
\\SMSTEST\sms_shrd\SITE.SRV\MAINCFG.BOX\CLIENT.SRC\X86.BIN\

                             51
\\SMSTEST\sms_shrd\SITE.SRV\MAINCFG.BOX\CLIENT.SRC\X86.BIN\00000409\

                              0
\\SMSTEST\sms_shrd\SITE.SRV\MAINCFG.BOX\invdom.box\

                              1
\\SMSTEST\sms_shrd\SITE.SRV\MAINCFG.BOX\invdom.box\SMSLAB.000\
```

This code is spaced so that it is easier to read. Lines are broken for layout only: entries should be on a single line. If you want to skip this section, go to page 159.

```
                              3
\\SMSTEST\sms_shrd\SITE.SRV\MAINCFG.BOX\invdom.box\SMSLAB.000\invencfg.b
ox\

                             31
\\SMSTEST\sms_shrd\SITE.SRV\MAINCFG.BOX\MSTEST\

                              5
\\SMSTEST\sms_shrd\SITE.SRV\MAINCFG.BOX\MSTEST\ALPHA.BIN\

                              5
\\SMSTEST\sms_shrd\SITE.SRV\MAINCFG.BOX\MSTEST\MIPS.BIN\

                              5
\\SMSTEST\sms_shrd\SITE.SRV\MAINCFG.BOX\MSTEST\X86.BIN\

                              0
\\SMSTEST\sms_shrd\SITE.SRV\MAINCFG.BOX\pcmdom.box\

                             31
\\SMSTEST\sms_shrd\SITE.SRV\MAINCFG.BOX\pcmdom.box\SMSLAB.000\

                              1
\\SMSTEST\sms_shrd\SITE.SRV\MAINCFG.BOX\PKGRULE\

                              0
\\SMSTEST\sms_shrd\SITE.SRV\schedule.box\

                              0    \\SMSTEST\sms_shrd\SITE.SRV\sender.box\

                              0
\\SMSTEST\sms_shrd\SITE.SRV\sender.box\requests\

                              2
\\SMSTEST\sms_shrd\SITE.SRV\sender.box\requests\LAN_DEFA.000\
          Newer                         20  00000000.CPB  0%  100%
```

This code is spaced so that it is easier to read. Lines are broken for layout only: entries should be on a single line. If you want to skip this section, go to page 159.

```
                                   0
\\SMSTEST\sms_shrd\SITE.SRV\sender.box\requests\RAS_ASYN.000\

                                   0
\\SMSTEST\sms_shrd\SITE.SRV\sender.box\requests\RAS_ISDN.000\

                                   0
\\SMSTEST\sms_shrd\SITE.SRV\sender.box\requests\RAS_X25_.000\

                                   0
\\SMSTEST\sms_shrd\SITE.SRV\sender.box\requests\SNA_BATC.000\

                                   0
\\SMSTEST\sms_shrd\SITE.SRV\sender.box\requests\SNA_INTE.000\

                                   2
\\SMSTEST\sms_shrd\SITE.SRV\sender.box\tosend\

                                   1
\\SMSTEST\sms_shrd\SITE.SRV\SITECFG.BOX\

                                   2
\\SMSTEST\sms_shrd\SITE.SRV\siterep.box\

                                  88   \\SMSTEST\sms_shrd\SITE.SRV\X86.BIN\

                                  27
\\SMSTEST\sms_shrd\SITE.SRV\X86.BIN\00000409\

                                   1
\\SMSTEST\sms_shrd\SITE.SRV\X86.BIN\ERRORHIS\

                                   1   \\SMSTEST\sms_shrd\Sql\
```

> This code is spaced so that it is easier to read. Lines are broken for layout only: entries should be on a single line. If you want to skip this section, go to page 159.

```
---------------------------------------------------------------

              Total    Copied   Skipped  Mismatch    FAILED    Extras

    Dirs :      199        0       199          0         0         1

   Files :     1288       15      1273          0         0         2

   Bytes :   265.0 m    2.9 m   262.0 m         0         0    130.8 k

   Times :  0:11.937  0:01.872                    0:00.000  0:10.065

   Ended : Fri May 30 13:20:49 1997


D:\SMSsoft\SMSBAC~1>REM --------------------------------------------------

D:\SMSsoft\SMSBAC~1>REM Start all SMS Logon Server Services

D:\SMSsoft\SMSBAC~1>REM --------------------------------------------------

D:\SMSsoft\SMSBAC~1>NET START SMS_CLIENT_CONFIG_MANAGER

The SMS_CLIENT_CONFIG_MANAGER service is starting.

The SMS_CLIENT_CONFIG_MANAGER service was started successfully.

D:\SMSsoft\SMSBAC~1>NET START SMS_INVENTORY_AGENT_NT

The SMS_INVENTORY_AGENT_NT service is starting.

The SMS_INVENTORY_AGENT_NT service was started successfully.

D:\SMSsoft\SMSBAC~1>NET START SMS_PACKAGE_COMMAND_MANAGER_NT

The SMS_PACKAGE_COMMAND_MANAGER_NT service is starting.

The SMS_PACKAGE_COMMAND_MANAGER_NT service was started successfully.
```

> This code is spaced so that it is easier to read. Lines are broken for layout only: entries
> should be on a single line. If you want to skip this section, go to page 159.

Check Schedulers

You can check the SQL Server Scheduler by using the SQL Enterprise Manager application and looking at the Task History window.

You can check the Windows NT Scheduler by using the Command Scheduler utility from the *Windows NT Server 4.0 Resource Kit* and connecting to each SMS logon server.

## PART 2

Desktop Lockdown, Security, and Failover Scenarios

Now that the basics are out of the way, it's time to look at some specifics. Plenty of books bigger than this one deal with desktop lockdown, security, and failover—they are big topics—and you haven't got the time (or maybe even the inclination) to embark on a course of study that makes you an expert in three vast, though related, areas. After all, there is more than enough to do in the course of a day already. Why read book after book looking for useful information? Here's some good news: you don't have to. These books are references, resources. They're handy if you need them.

Even better news is that you don't need to know everything about these topics; you just need some information and ideas on how to get things *done*. It turns out that this can be covered nicely in six chapters. Chapter 4 looks at some concepts that you can use to create a desktop environment that is adaptable to the needs of many users, but resists hacking and inappropriate modification. Chapters 5 and 6 discuss, respectively, securing internal and external networks—the segments inside or outside the firewall. Chapter 7 moves back to the topic of management tasks: it offers three ways to use SMS Installer to simplify software distribution within a secure environment. Chapter 8 is short, but it troubleshoots a potential issue with user authentication in distributed environments. Finally, failover. As is pointed out above, a lot has been written about this. Chapter 9 narrows the focus to explain how you can use Microsoft Cluster Server to boost system availability and reliability. It is only one component of a fault-tolerant system, but it's a useful one.

C H A P T E R   4

Locking Down the Desktop at Microsoft's Professional Developer Conference

By Miles Burkart, Andreea Leonard and Michael Lyons— Lante Corporation

At Microsoft's yearly Professional Developer Conference (PDC) nearly 7,500 application developers and information technology (IT) managers spend a week devoted to technical training. To provide attendees with a useful, compelling, content-rich environment that keeps them in touch with their home offices, Lante Corporation, a Microsoft Certified Solution Provider, implements and supports a PDC Communications Network (ComNet). Composed of 15 servers supporting 260 workstations, ComNet is a temporary network home to thousands of users during the week-long event. This chapter explains how Lante ensures ComNet's security, focussing on how roaming profiles and system policies are used to lock down some settings and to provide the same look and feel to all users.

In Focus

Enterprise

The PDC ComNet, modeling a locked-down network for any organization.

Network

260 workstations and 15 servers, supporting some 7500 roaming users.

Challenge

Providing a content-rich environment with a consistent look and feel in a secure, locked-down environment.

Solution

Implementing a combination of user profiles, systems policies, and NTFS restrictions.

What You'll Find In This Chapter

- **Description of the functional requirements for the ComNet locked-down environment.**

- **An overview of system policies.**

- **How to define user *types* for use in system design.**

- **How to implement roaming user profiles.**

- **Best practices for using the default user profile, and implementing user profiles.**

- **How to lock down the desktop with system policies.**

- **Best practices and considerations for implementing Systems Policies.**

- **How to use NTFS to lock down the desktop.**

- **How to map users to a network printer and automatically point to their mail server.**

Warning This chapter makes recommendations for tuning the Windows NT registry using the Registry Editor. Using the Registry Editor incorrectly can cause serious, system-wide problems that require you to reinstall Windows NT. Microsoft cannot guarantee that any problems resulting from the use of Registry Editor can be solved. Use this tool at your own risk.

The Communications Network

Like any system accessible to the public, ComNet must be secure. It must also flexible enough to allow knowledgeable users to customize workstation configurations to their liking and maintain those settings as they log on to other ComNet PCs. This is the challenging part—securing a personal computer (PC) that has more flexibility than a simple task-oriented workstation. Professional Developer Conference (PDC) attendees typically are "power users," adept at computing and at personalizing workstations. And they use (and thus expect) a variety of software products to access external e-mail accounts: POP3, Telnet, Microsoft Outlook, Outlook Web Access, Hotmail, and so forth. Together, attendees' expertise and requirements create a challenging atmosphere for designers who want to allow users latitude yet enforce system standards and security.

Each application loaded onto the system introduces the possibility of users controlling the local settings, and, as any helpdesk technician can testify, the more control an end user has over a PC's system, the more likely a helpdesk technician will be called on to correct a user-induced system problem. ComNet users want lots of tools, but by providing users with access to only the tools they *need*, ComNet can minimize system errors, reduce support needs, and maximize overall system uptime.

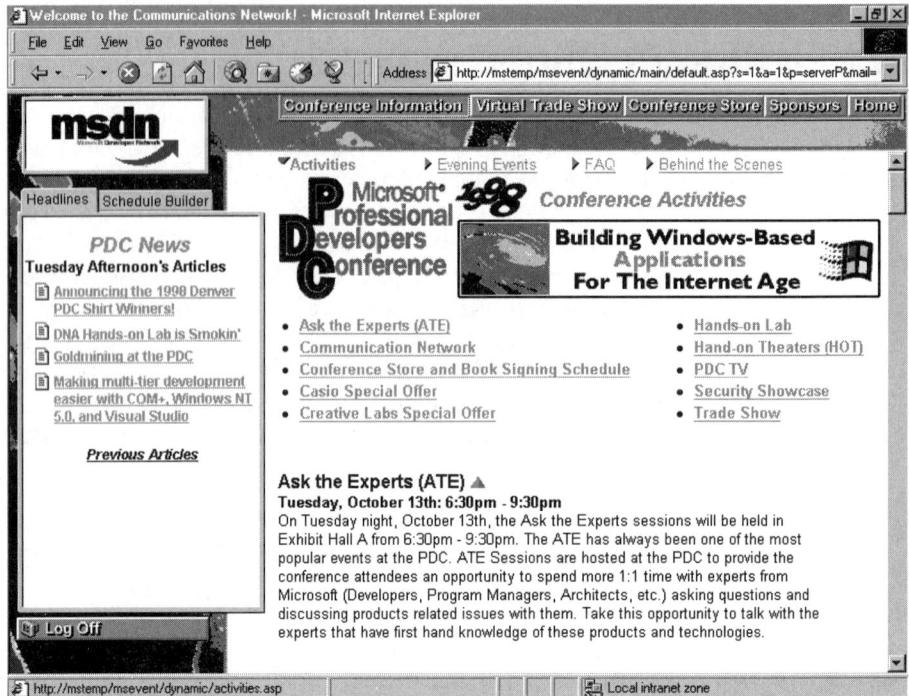

Figure 4.1 Communications Network homepage provides a content-rich environment.

The conference environment also means Lante must take network security very seriously. As with any college or high school network, some users may see ComNet as an opportunity to test the administrator's network security, attempting to bypass it and hack away. Fortunately, most security breaches are limited to events such as attempting to change background display properties, or installing a game software demo. However, a design that misses some of the key policy settings or Windows NT File System (NTFS) permissions can make the system vulnerable to a serious security threat. For this reason Lante hides, locks down, or removes anything that might compromise the security of ComNet desktops.

Network Environment Requirements

Before network administrators can implement profiles, policies, and secure the system, they must define overall levels of security, a standard desktop configuration, and how to set up user accounts. A PDC workstation comprises a standard installation of Windows NT 4, Internet Explorer 4.01 (IE 4.01), and Outlook 98. The network system also provides viewers with Microsoft Word, Microsoft PowerPoint, and Microsoft Excel as well as Telnet, Microsoft Chat, and Outlook Express. Users have access to all applications when they log on with their Windows NT account.

Note The PDC system integrated beta versions of Windows 2000, Internet Explorer 5 (IE 5), and Outlook 2000 in some areas. Except where noted, Lante applied the same strategies and methods to secure the workstations running this software.

The Windows NT accounts on the PDC system have several items associated with them: membership in the PDC domain users group, profile directories to store the user's roaming profile, home directories for miscellaneous documents, and a mailbox on one of the two Microsoft Exchange messaging servers.

Because the PDC workstations are intended to provide only communications and conference information access, they have a limited functionality. Users can see only available applications with shortcuts on the desktop, start menu, and task bar. ComNet administrators removed the shortcuts that gave access to all other system items.

Standard application setup for items such as Outlook often requires user configuration guided by an installation wizard. In a conference (and roaming-user) environment, many users may not know what to enter or may enter incorrect values, so ComNet administrators pre-set these system defaults to provide a pre-configured environment. This saves end users time and frustration. And it saves administrators the chore of correcting user errors.

Providing Default User Profile Functionality

A pre-configured, locked-down environment requires a well-planned default profile for first-time users. Lante accomplishes this by copying a pre-configured user profile with desired settings into the local machine's default user profile or on the nearest domain controller (DC). When a user logs on for the first time, Windows NT detects that they do not yet have a profile and forces the default profile. This provides a consistent interface. As users customize settings then log off, the profile is copied up to their home directory. Saved there for future logons, it follows them from workstation to workstation.

After defining desktop, application, and default user functionality, Lante carefully audited the network design for potential security liabilities, and further locked down the workstations by removing access to the run command, control panel, file system, and registry. Using a combination of system policies, NTFS, and registry settings, the solution provides administers a secure environment with minimal user support. Policies and the registry provide the primary tools for hiding parts of the operating system, and NTFS locks down executables such as CMD.EXE, REGEDIT.EXE, and NET.EXE.

Overview of User Profiles

A profile is the local representation of certain user-related desktop, application, and computer settings on a Windows NT workstation. Profiles offer a wide variety of options for Windows NT administrators who need to customize the look and feel of Windows NT workstations.

The user profile includes a Windows NT registry hive (NTUSER.DAT) and a set of profile directories. The NTUSER.DAT file maps to the HKEY_CURRENT_USER portion of the registry when users log on. The NTUSER.DAT file maintains user environment settings when users log on to workstations, storing settings such as control panel configurations (desktop patterns, mouse preferences, and so on), application-specific configurations, and settings that maintain network connections. The profile directories store shortcut links, desktop icons, startup applications, application data, and so on. Together, these two components record and store all user-configurable settings that can migrate from computer to computer in a Windows NT environment.

A Windows NT environment supports three kinds of user profiles:

- **Local Profile.** Specific to a computer. Users who have a local profile on a particular computer gain access to that profile only when logged on to that computer.

- **Roaming Profile.** Stored on a network share and accessible from any networked computer. Users with roaming profiles can log on to any networked computer where that profile is valid and access the profile.

- **Mandatory Profile.** Pre-configured roaming profile that users cannot change. Network administrators can assign this to one or more users who require a common interface and standard workstation configuration.

For all profile types, a Windows NT workstation stores the user profile locally in the *%systemroot%\profiles\%username%* directory. Windows NT creates the contents of profiles on the local drive or has them copied down from a server location, depending on the profile type associated with user accounts.

Note The %systemroot% environment variable represents the root directory containing Windows NT files on a workstation. The %systemroot%\profiles points to a folder that contains user profiles for each user of the computer. Another environment variable, %username%, represents the user account ID for the current logged-on user.

When a user logs off from a workstation, Windows NT handles different types of profile differently. It automatically copies a roaming profile back up to its share location, ensuring that the user can access the most recent profile from any workstation. It maintains a local profile on the workstation, updating it only when the same user logs back onto the workstation. It does not save any changes that a user makes to a mandatory profile.

The All Users Shared Profile

The All Users profile directory exists on every Windows NT 4.0 workstation and you can configure it specifically for a particular workstation. It contains common groups that apply to all users logging onto the workstation, providing programs and shortcuts available to all users, in addition to the programs and shortcuts that users already have in their own profile. In planning a pre-configured, locked-down workstation, you should specify programs, shortcuts, or file directories that everyone needs, and place them in that workstation's All Users directory.

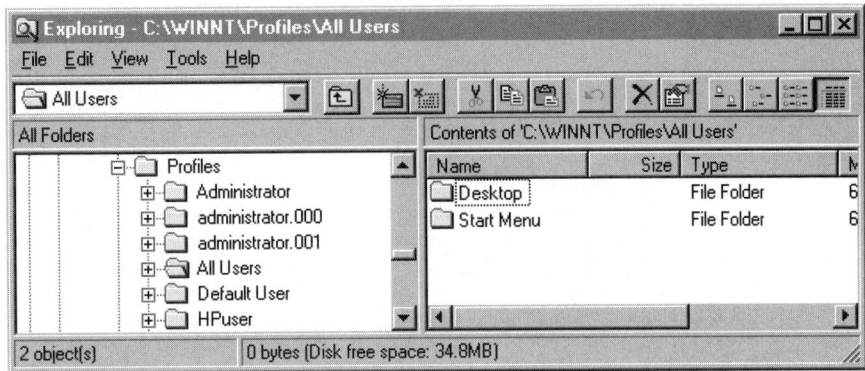

Figure 4.2 All Users profile directory on Windows NT 4.0.

However, if the network requires establishing domain-wide common groups and settings, you can use the System Policy Editor to modify registry entries on remote workstations so that they point to server directories for common items, instead of pointing to the local All Users profile. As environment requirements change, you can remove domain-wide settings, pointing users to local All Users profiles. This entails using the System Policy Editor to change any default directory paths back to their original settings.

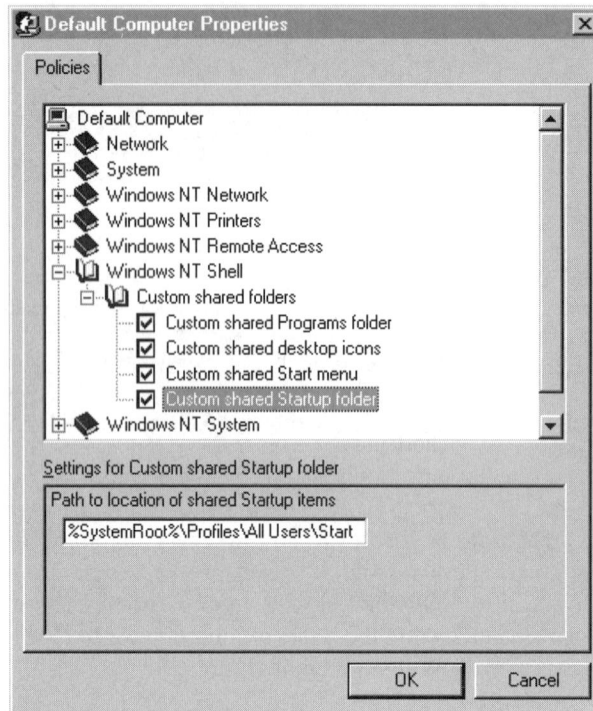

Figure 4.3 Using Systems Policy Editor to modify All Users to point to server directories.

Note You can find a description of user profiles and their contents, and additional details on configuring the all users profile in the "Guide To Windows NT 4.0 Profiles and Policies," available on http://www.microsoft.com/ntserver.

Implementing Roaming Profiles

Adding, deleting, and modifying the contents of Windows NT roaming profiles can confuse some administrators because of how modifications propagate depending on whether a user has logged on. The chart below gives some examples of how roaming profiles work.

How roaming profiles propagate modifications.

Action	Effect on roaming profile directory on server after logoff
Users add or modify a file in the root of %systemroot%\profiles\%username%	The added file is copied to the user's profile directory on the server, and the modified file overwrites the one on the server.
Users remove a file from the root of %systemroot%\profiles\%username%	The file is not deleted from the user's profile directory on the server.
Users add or modify a file or shortcut on their desktop on a workstation	The change propagates to the user's profile directory on the server.
Users remove a file or shortcut from their desktop on a workstation	The change propagates to the user's profile directory on the server.

Note In this table, assume changes to *%systemroot%\profiles\%username%* (the local profile) take place only when a user has logged on. Also assume that the latest cached local user profile exists on the workstation and system policies are not enabled.

Cached copies of user profiles will exist on a workstation for each user that has logged on unless policies are set to delete them. **Cached profiles** are local profiles and they reduce the time it takes Windows NT to log users on and load their profile.

If you modify the contents of a user's network profile directory and a user logs on to a workstation containing the user's latest locally cached profile, the changes will be lost. The last change timestamp on the NTUSER.DAT will be the same for both the network roaming profile and the locally cached profile, in which case the cached profile is used, overwriting the network profile when the user logs off.

If you modify the contents of a user's network profile directory while the user is logged on, the user's locally cached profile will be copied up to the profile directory and overwrite the changes when the user logs off. Make sure that users are not logged on before modifying their network profile directory contents.

You should also realize that workstation software, system policies, and share and profile permissions can also affect roaming profiles. Test their behavior thoroughly before rolling them out in a production environment.

Roaming Profiles in the PDC Communications Network

Because a Windows NT roaming profile environment typically allows only certain settings to follow users as they log on and off computers, you must find a way to permit user-specified custom settings. The PDC ComNet uses a combination of roaming profiles, home directories, policies, and customized local applications to create a consistent look and feel for roaming users while still allowing them to customize some settings.

When a user logs on to a Windows NT Workstation, the system checks to see if the user's account has a profile path declared. If a roaming profile path exists, the system checks that network path for the user's profile, then checks for a locally cached copy. If both the network roaming profile and the locally cached profile exist, the system compares timestamps on the profiles and loads the most current one for the user. If the timestamps are the same, the system loads the locally cached profile.

When only one profile is available, the system uses that one. If both profiles are unavailable (not found), the system builds the user's profile locally using the Default User profile in the workstation's *%systemroot%\profiles\default user* directory. When the user logs off, the locally cached profile is copied up to its server location until requested again.

Note   You can find additional information on how user profiles operate in the "Guide To Windows NT 4.0 Profiles and Policies," available on http://www.microsoft.com/ntserver.

Why Not Mandatory Profiles?

Mandatory profiles can force all users to have the same look and feel across workstations, *but they do not allow users to customize and save settings.* For example, if users need to configure Outlook 98 to have multiple mailbox profiles—one for PDC-specific e-mail and another for their corporate e-mail— mandatory profiles would prevent saving profile changes.

Roaming profiles permit user changes to follow users as they log in to different workstations. For ComNet, Lante's network administrators used roaming profiles, providing a flexible environment that allows some user customization, and system policies to lock down other settings, providing the same look and feel for all users.

Home Directories and Roaming Profiles

The PDC ComNet provides a kiosk environment—260 workstations supporting approximately 7,500 users. In a typical roaming-profile environment, cached copies of user profiles reside on each machine a user has logged on to. Even though the latest version of a user's roaming profile resides on a server, older cached versions of the profile will exist locally on every computer the user has logged on to. User profiles can be several hundred KB, quickly consuming disk space on a workstation shared by many users.

To prevent local-workstation caching, ComNet administrators implemented the *Delete cached copies of roaming profiles* system policy, which causes the system to remove the user's locally cached profile from the Windows NT workstation when the user logs off. Because cached copies of user profiles are automatically deleted from workstations when users log off of ComNet, logging on forces Windows NT to copy the entire contents of the user's network profile to the workstation on every logon.

ComNet administrators also provided users with greater flexibility on the Windows NT network through designated **Home Directories**—directories, accessible to users, containing their files and programs. A home directory can be assigned to a single user or to a group.

Lante developed a custom application called Account Management System (AMS) for creating and updating customized Windows NT user accounts on a large scale. When kiosk users log on, their customized Windows NT account maps the home directory to the workstation, providing users (and any local workstation applications) access to home directory contents. System policies are used to hide viewing and access to both the Network Neighborhood and the local workstation drives on kiosks. The custom PDC Logon Application (also developed by the ComNet team) resides on each workstation, with permission to access setting files from user home directories.

On ComNet, user profile directories exist *within* each user's home directory. For example, for user Bob Kay (alias BobK), the user profile path appears as \\mshome\users\bobkhome\bobk:

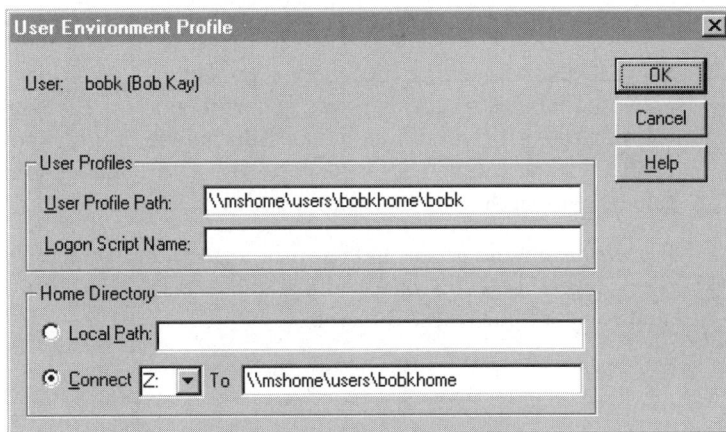

Figure 4.4 Profile path to user's home directory.

ComNet administrators created a network share (\\mshome\users) containing the home directory for *bobk,* labeled *bobkhome*. Within the home directory, they specified the user's profile directory, *bobk*.

Note Make sure to set permissions on the parent directory of the roaming user profiles so that users have at least Add and Read permissions for Windows NT.

ComNet implements a custom .INI file containing a user's home e-mail server name, that lives in each user's home directory. When users log on, the PDC Logon Application reads the mail server name from the .INI file and automatically configures a MAPI profile. This allows ComNet administrators to "load balance" Exchange servers on ComNet. It also ensures that users have the proper mail configuration no matter where they log on, even if they manually changed personal mail settings during a previous ComNet session.

You can also add setting files to the Application Data folder within a user's network roaming profile directory so that it copies to the workstation *%systemroot%\profiles\%username%* during logon. This provides custom applications or scripts with local access to setting files in user Application Data folders, without having to access the files over the network.

If users have write access to their profile and home directories (in order to save files), several potential bandwidth and disk space issues can arise, depending on how you configure these directories.

If the home directory resides within a user's network profile directory and files are placed in the user home directory, they become part of that user's roaming profile. The files are transferred across the network when the user logs on and off workstations. If the home directory and user profile directory point to the same path for a user account, all files placed in the home directory may disappear when a user logs out. Both of these scenarios can cause slow network logon times because of the potential for large files moving across the network. You should place user profile directories inside of home directories when a home directory is needed for each user.

Windows 2000 allows you to set disk quotas on directory sizes, and policies allow you to limit user profile sizes. These features give you more power to regulate the amount of disk space and network bandwidth taken up by roaming users much more effectively.

Summary of Benefits

Roaming profiles in the PDC ComNet provide:

- **Consistent workstation look-and-feel.** Users can log on to any ComNet kiosk and get the same functionality, the same desktop, and the same startup menu items. And they don't have to worry about previous users re-configuring kiosk workstations.

- **Personalized settings that follow users from kiosk to kiosk.** Users don't have to re-configure settings every time they log on. If a user personalizes e-mail settings by adding servers or visits Web sites that generate cookies, these settings and files are stored in their roaming profile.

- **Centralized administration of user profiles.** Network administrators can simply delete a user profile from a central network location if for any reason it becomes corrupt. The Windows NT kiosk creates fresh profiles the next time the user logs on to ComNet.

Default User Profile Implementation

Administrators need to understand how to implement a well-designed default user profile because it provides the template for the creation of new *user profiles*. The default user profile builds the initial profile for new network and workstation users.

There are two basic implementations of a default user profile: **workstation default user** and **network default user**. A workstation default user profile exists on every Windows NT workstation in the *%systemroot%\profiles\default user* directory. The Windows NT setup program automatically builds this profile during installation. You can create a network default user profile by placing a profile in the NetLogon share *(%systemroot%\system32\repl\import\scripts)* of each domain controller on a network. The folder must be named *Default User* in order to be downloaded from the server.

When new users log on to a Windows NT workstation and do not have either a local or server-based profile, Windows NT first looks for a network default user profile to use in the validating domain controller's NetLogon directory. If one exists, it becomes the template for the user logging on. If one is not found, the workstation default user profile becomes the template for creating the user's profile.

ComNet administrators customized workstation default user profiles to ensure correct initial configuration of all user profiles (see "Customizing a Default User Profile" below). Of the nearly 7,500 conference attendees potentially logging on to over 260 kiosks, most represent first-time ComNet users. Workstation default user profiles save a large amount of network bandwidth and speed up the logon process for new users because all profile creation is done locally.

Removing Potential Difficulty

You can trace *network* default user profile issues to a central location (a domain controller) very easily. Tracing issues with *workstation* default user profiles can be more difficult. If you configure a workstation default user profile incorrectly for users with roaming profiles, then every first-time user logging on has this *mis*-configuration. The problem becomes difficult to track down when users move from workstation to workstation.

ComNet administrators removed the potential for bad profiles in two ways. First, they used an imaging process to "clone" every workstation so each had the same software and settings (configuration). Second, the PDC Logon Application can copy, move, and delete files on a kiosk as a user logs on. If administrators needed to replace the workstation default user profile on every kiosk, they could put the latest copy onto a network share and the new profile would be updated automatically. This allows ComNet administrators to focus on roaming profile issues on a user-by-user basis.

Customizing a Default User Profile

ComNet administrators customized the workstation default user profile to provide users with specific desktop settings and shortcuts that appear whenever they log on. Most of the workstation default user profile configuration was done manually by logging onto the domain using a template user. ComNet administrators created a domain user called "001" that had no roaming profile. To do this, they:

1. Logged on as 001 and received the workstation default user profile (because it was a first-time logon).

2. Manually added and deleted shortcut items and changed the desktop until the desktop environment met user requirements.

3. Logged off 001, logged back on as *Administrator*, and manually deleted the contents of *%systemroot%\profiles\default user*.

4. Copied the entire contents of the 001 user profile (*%systemroot\profiles\001*) to the default user profile directory, replacing the workstation default user profile with the updated version on the workstation.

5. Logged off the *Administrator* account, and created several fresh domain user accounts, testing the new default user profile on the workstation to make sure it had been configured correctly.

Other Approaches

The approach used on ComNet works well for managing the creation of workstation default user profiles but there are other Windows NT tools available that can simplify profile management. See the "Guide to Windows NT 4.0 Profiles and Policies" available on http://www.microsoft.com/ntserver for more information.

You can change settings in a user's NTUSER.DAT portion of the profile by using REGEDT32.EXE to load the file into the HKEY_USERS hive in the registry. Once the .DAT file is loaded, you can edit the portions of HKEY_USERS that represent the .DAT file. Finally, unload the hive from the registry and save changes to the NTUSER.DAT file. This method works well for making updates to workstation or network default user profiles as well as for regular users. Remember that you must make changes to a user profile only when the user is not logged on.

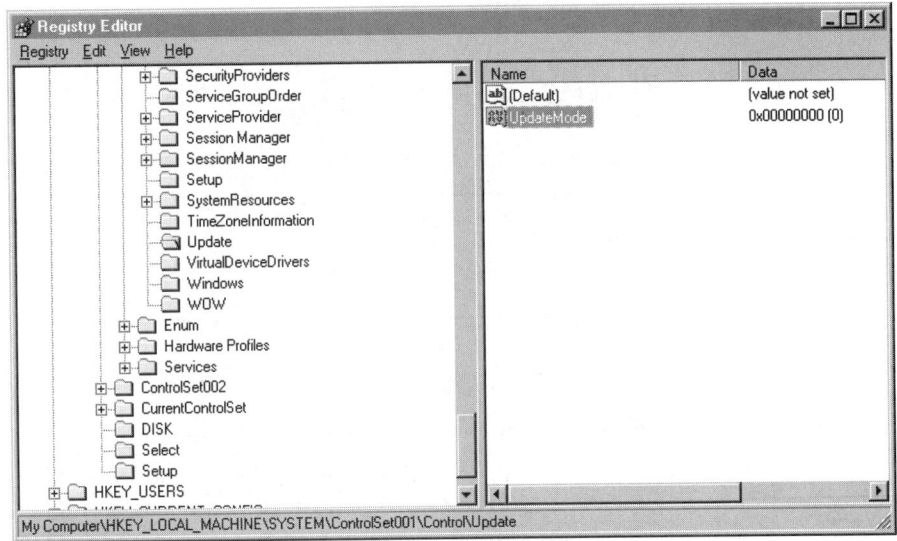

Figure 4.5 Using REGEDT32.EXE to modify default user profile.

The Control Panel System Properties in Windows NT 4.0 also provides a tool to manage user profiles. The *User Profiles* tab allows you to view user profiles that reside on a particular computer, and to delete them, copy them, or modify the profile type.

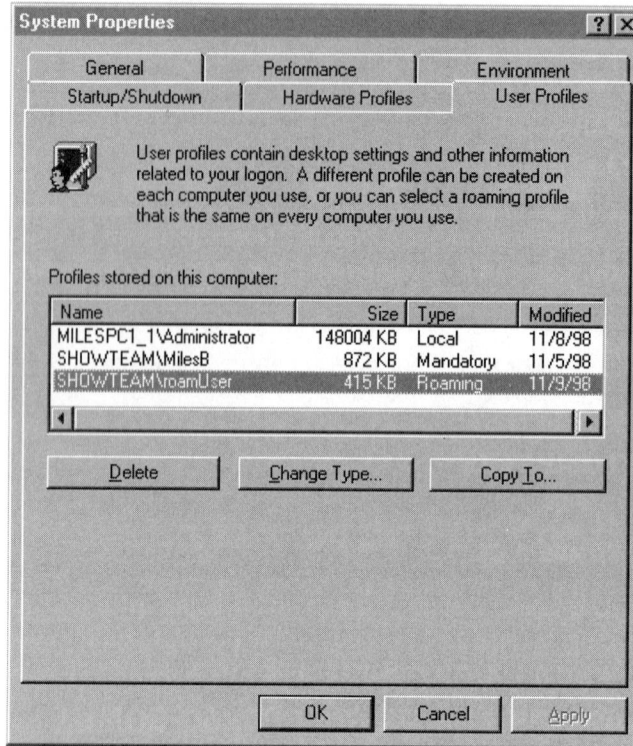

Figure 4.6 Using System Properties (in Control Panel) to manage user profiles.

Issues in User Profile Creation on the PDC ComNet

When implementing any of the options in the System Policy Editor (including clearing every check box), the behavior of profiles in relation to the directory structure changes slightly, causing a user's folders to operate in an unexpected manner.

For example, when users download files to their desktop, they may expect to save to the profile directory's desktop folder on the local computer (%systemroot%\profiles\%username%\desktop). Because ComNet uses roaming profiles, the file should copy up to the server profile directory when users log out. However, because Lante used System Policy Editor to lock down desktops, files that get saved to the desktop actually get saved to a common desktop folder on the local machine (%systemroot%\desktop). This allows any user logging on to the machine to see and access the downloaded applications of another user.

To avoid letting the desktop of each workstation get cluttered with files, ComNet administrators used NTFS file security to restrict the rights to Read Only, which prevents saving files to the desktop. Instead, the administrators can provide users with a shortcut to their home directory on the desktop and from this location they can save downloaded programs and other files.

This approach saves network bandwidth and time during the logon because the profiles do not roam with large files that belong in the home directory. (Refer to the "Home Directories and Roaming Profiles" section above.) This also allows administrators to keep the desktop in a perpetually "clean" state, ensuring the consistency of each user's experience.

How Changing Software Changes Profiles

Changes to software force administrators to discover where new entries are stored in the registry that affects the user. This is important to know so that any logon applications or scripts can modify and configure settings appropriately for each user. Typically, even though application versions change, their corresponding registry keys or sections generally change very little. This makes administering profiles and policies a much easier task as software becomes obsolete and is upgraded or replaced.

Windows 2000 and User Profiles

Windows 2000 profiles function in the same manner as Windows NT 4.0 profiles: desktop shortcuts save to the *%systemroot%\profiles\all users\desktop* subdirectory, and start menu programs save to the *%systemroot%\profiles\default user\start menu\programs* subdirectory.

Although users have a true roaming profile, saving on bandwidth or disk space are not issues because the Windows 2000 Group Policy Editor allows you to restrict the size of user profiles, and specify what profile directories can roam with them. In Windows NT 4.0 you can customize the programs folders for the system by using the System Policy Editor; in Windows 2000 you can do it by using the Group Policy Editor.

User Profiles Implementation Considerations

Slow Network Connections

Windows NT has automatic methods to deal with slow network speeds. When it detects a slow network connection, it prompts users with the option of either downloading the existing profile, or using locally cached information, which can significantly decrease the time it takes to logon.

You can adjust the time setting that Windows NT requires to determine a slow network speed by using the System Policy Editor to edit the *Slow network connection timeout* setting. (See Figure 4.14 on page 197.)

Permissions on User Profiles

When troubleshooting or preparing to roll out user profiles, pay attention to permissions on the Windows NT File System (NTFS) and share levels. Mandatory profiles require that the user account have at least Read permissions on the network share where the user's user profile is stored. Roaming profiles require that the user have Change permissions (or better) because the client needs to write the changes back to the central profile on the shared network drive during logoff.

If roaming profiles are stored on an NTFS partition, you can remove the Delete permission from the default Change permissions at the NTFS level.

The parent directory containing roaming user profiles needs at least Add and Read permissions for Windows NT to read profiles correctly. Using only Add permissions causes a Windows NT profile check to fail because it looks for the path first and this requires Read rights.

You must also set permissions on client computers where users log on. Errors can occur if Windows NT is installed in an NTFS partition on the client computer and the user does not have at least default permissions. (See the *Windows NT Server Concepts and Planning Guide*.) For example, incorrect permissions on the system directory root create this message: "Can't access this folder—the path is too long." A blank desktop is displayed and the user must log off.

If permissions are set incorrectly in the *%systemroot%*, *%systemroot%\System*, *%systemroot%\System32*, or *%systemroot%\System32\Config* directories, the following message appears: "Unable to log you on because your profile could not be loaded."

System Policies

A **system policy** represents a set of registry settings that define computer resources available to one or more users. Policies specify the various parts of the desktop environment that administrators need to control, such as Control Panel options, network settings, and so forth. To implement system policies for computers, all users, specific users, or user groups, use the System Policy Editor program (POLEDIT.EXE), a graphical tool provided with Windows NT Server 4.0.

You can create a file that contains registry settings that write to the user or local computer portion of the registry database. This file saves as NTCONFIG.POL in the NetLogon share of all of the domain controllers in the domain, and comprises two template (.ADM) files for Windows NT: COMMON.ADM and WINNT.ADM. You can customize .ADM files to place restrictions on applications developed in-house, and there are template files available for Microsoft products such as Outlook and Word.

User-specific profile settings for users who log on to a given workstation or server, write to the registry subkey under HKEY_CURRENT_USER. Computer-specific settings write to the subkey under HKEY_LOCAL_MACHINE.

When you apply a system policy, the file overwrites existing registry settings, implementing restrictions on the client computer and end user. With a properly implemented policy, regardless of where a user logs on, you can customize a user's environment to business and network specifications, in spite of the user's preference. For example, if one user saves a background as wallpaper, the policy settings for a background that you specify are applied when the next user logs onto the machine. The settings available in the system policy can cover a variety of options to manage the environment.

Implementing Policies on the ComNet

Policies allow ComNet administrators to shut out any external system options that can compromise network security, thereby increasing system uptime, and reducing administrative burden.

Locking down the workstation provides a higher level of security for the local computer, discouraging any efforts to render a machine or a group of machines inoperable. Occasionally, curious users feel the need to experiment or to test theories on system flaws that they would consider too risky on their own PCs ("What will happen if I try to delete the *system32* directory?"). With hundreds of computers available, ComNet looks like the perfect hands-on lab.

Policies provide additional security for network servers and any computers on the network not managed by the ComNet team. An attack on a server could potentially cripple the system. Policies prevent the users browsing through the Network Neighborhood. If users can't see servers, they are less likely to stumble across an open share. ComNet administrators also set up share protection using NTFS, but hiding the Network Neighborhood prevents a great deal of unwanted exploration. Additionally, at the PDC, ComNet administrators often find that some users connect their own laptop to the network, with fully shared hard drives and folders. Network policies provide these naïve users with the only protection they have from being at the mercy of everyone on the system.

Locking Down a Desktop with Policies

The application shown in the following figures is the System Policy Editor (POLEDIT), one of the Administrative Tools (Common) found on any standard installation of Windows NT server. To implement a new policy select **New** from the **File** menu. You are presented with two icons: **Default Computer** and **Default User**. To set system policies for all users, double-click the Default User icon to display the **Default User Properties** dialog box. This lists all the system policies you can set for the user. To set system policies for all client computers, double-click Default Computer to display the **Default Computer Properties** dialog box, then go through and check off the policies you want. When you're finished, save the settings (as a .POL file) to the appropriate network share (most likely the NetLogon share of the domain controllers). Save the file as NTCONFIG.POL to apply the policies to Windows NT workstations.

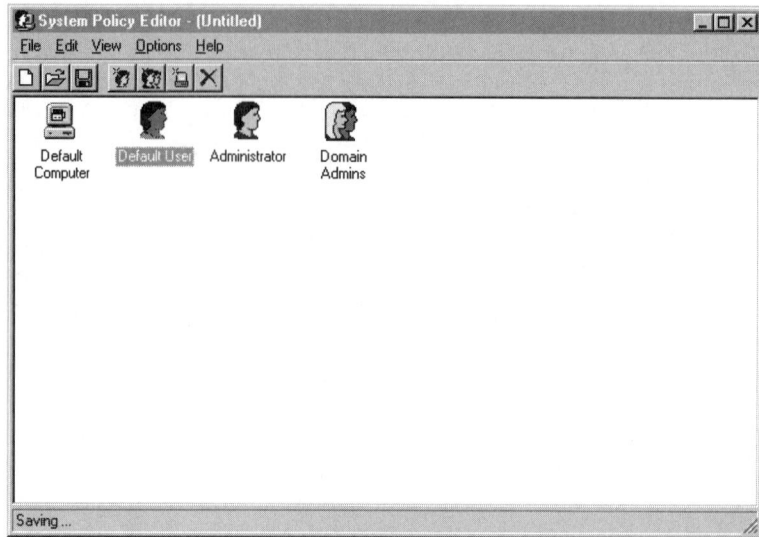

Figure 4.7 System Policy Editor window.

To add policies for a specific group or user, click on **Add User** or **Add Group** option in the **Edit** menu. In the dialog, type in the name of the user or group. A new icon will be created for that group.

When applying policies, if the check box is:

- **Checked** it is implemented.
- **Cleared** it is not implemented.
- **Grayed out** the setting is ignored and unchanged from the first time the user logged on.

Setting User Policies

Here are some ComNet user policies:

- **Control Panel.** Restrict or deny access to the display settings. Some settings available in the User Policy Editor get very specific. This allows administrators to limit which tabs are available to the user in the display dialog.

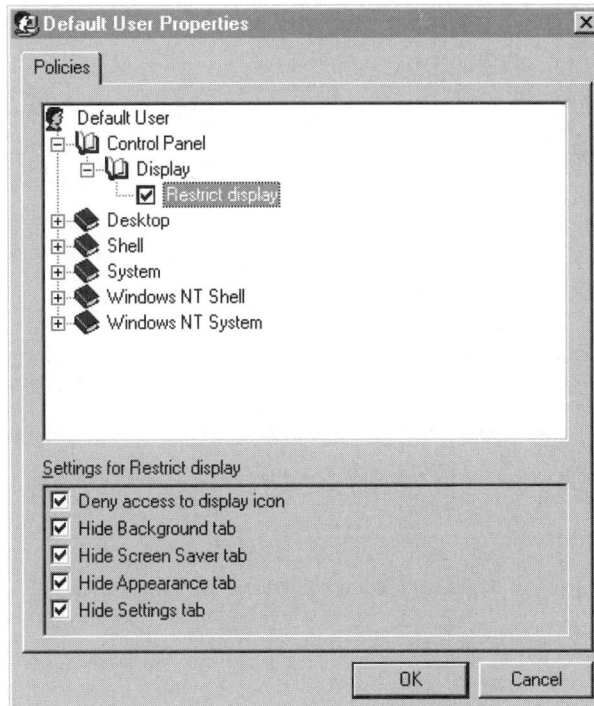

Figure 4.8 Restricting display settings access through Policy Editor.

- **Desktop.** Enforce standard wallpaper and color schemes on the desktop. This policy prevents the user from customizing the workstation's background in any way. It allows administrators to specify a file as the user's default background.

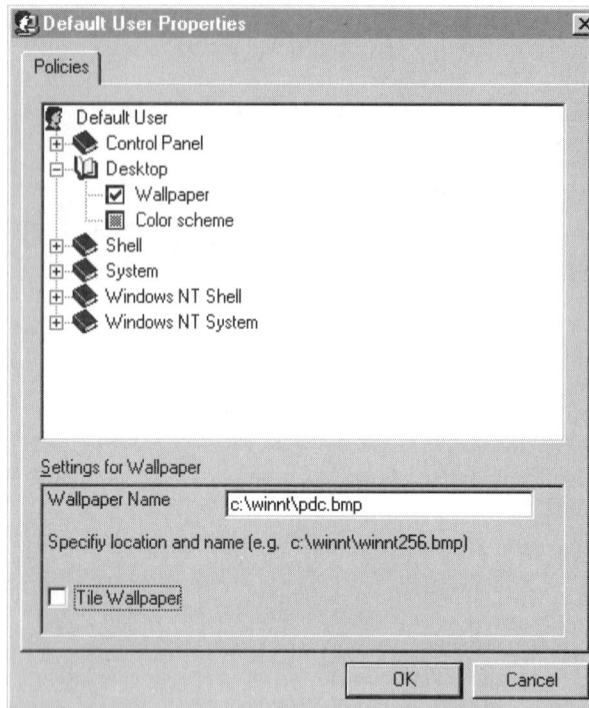

Figure 4.9 Enforcing a standard wallpaper.

Note You can also use NTFS permissions to prevent users from customizing the wallpaper .BMP file.

- **System.** Disable the Windows NT Registry Editor (REGEDT32.EXE). Prevents users from manually editing any of the registry files. Administrators can also provide a list of available Windows-based applications. Any application not on the list is unavailable to users.

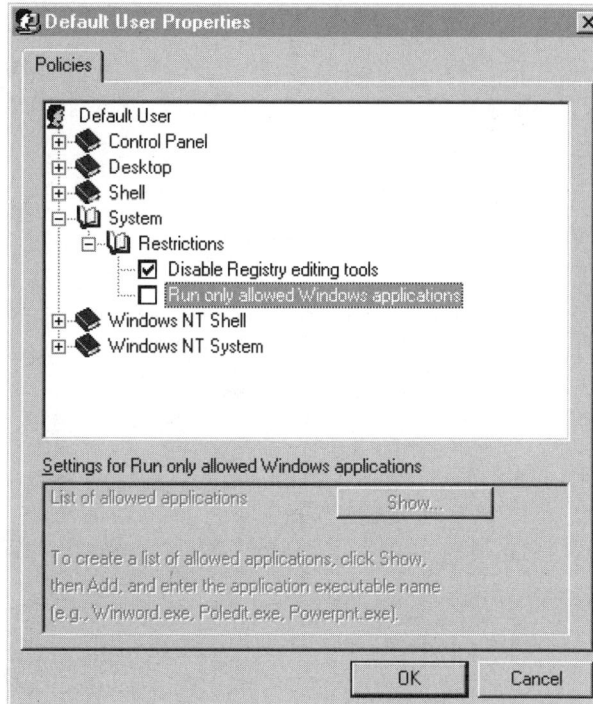

Figure 4.10 Preventing users from modifying registry files.

- **Shell.** The Shell and Windows NT Shell contain a list of very useful restrictions you can impose to prevent users from accessing system functions. You can also use this area of the Policy Editor to modify the Windows NT Shell, creating a custom user interface instead of EXPLORER.EXE.

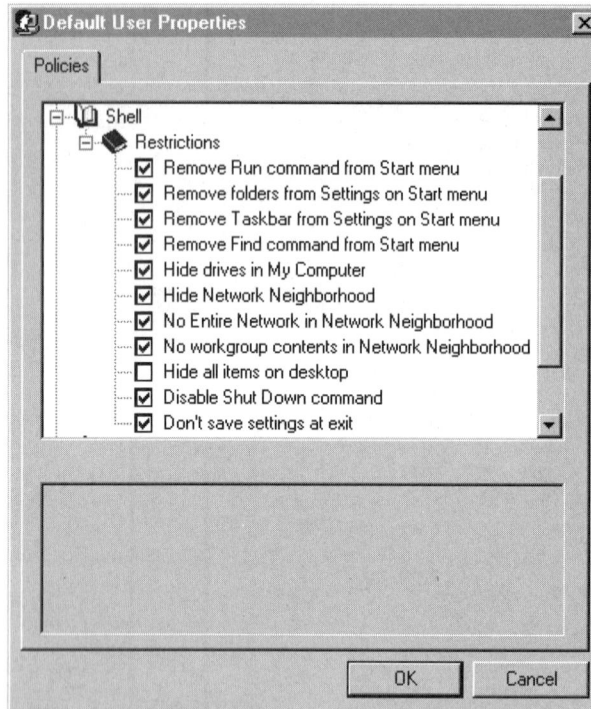

Figure 4.11 Customizing the user interface by modifying the Windows NT Shell.

Setting Computer Policies

Administrators wanting a locked-down environment should establish a default computer system policy that complements the user policy. If the policies conflict, *the user policy overrides computer policy.* Computer settings in system polices prevent users from modifying the system configuration settings for the operating system, ensuring that the operating system starts in a predictable way.

Some featured systems policies for ComNet computers are:

- **Network.** Entering a path to a different policy file enables manual update of the policy file from a location other than the domain controller's NetLogon share. This provides load balancing and prevents bottlenecks on large networks when many users try to access the same policy file. Administrators can configure the network to display an error message when a policy cannot be applied.

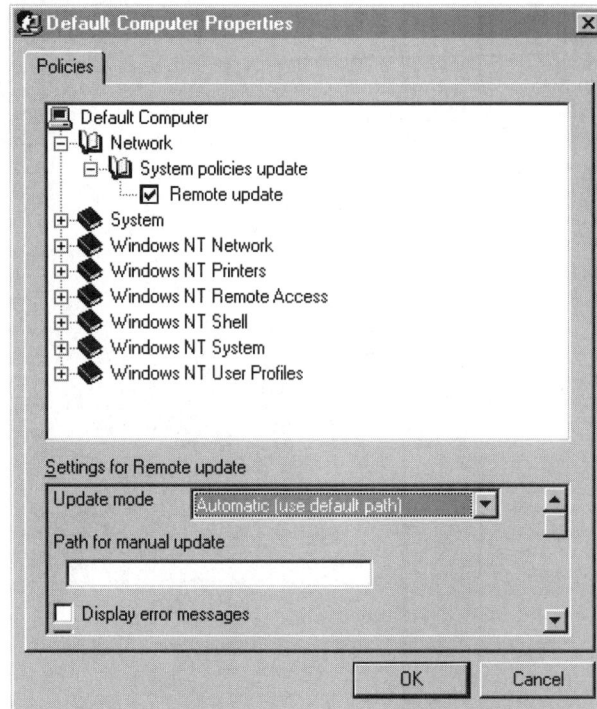

Figure 4.12 Enabling manual update of policy files.

- **Windows NT System.** Not displaying the user name of the last logged on user is very helpful in a busy, roaming-user environment. It also helps protect the accounts of users that don't password-protect their account. Disabling shutdown prevents users from shutting down a workstation out of habit.

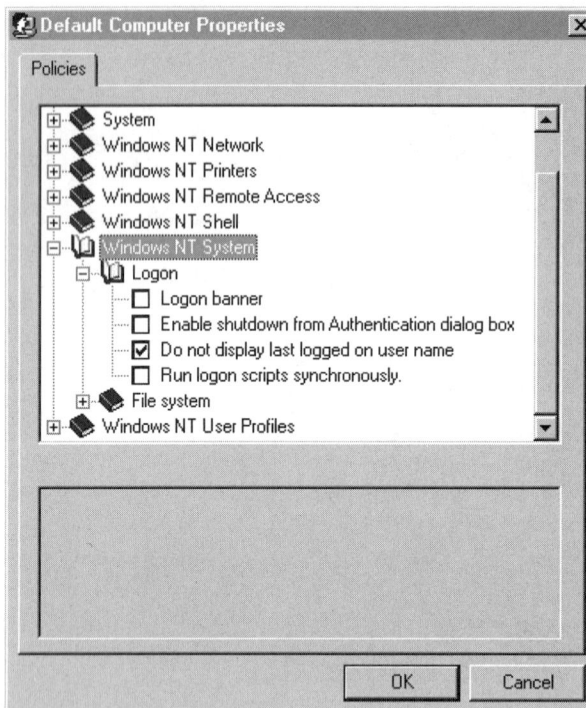

Figure 4.13 Blocking last logged on user display.

- **Windows NT User Profiles.** You can use policies to modify several profile settings. You can adjust the amount of time before the user receives a slow-network-connection dialog, and delete cached copies of the roaming profile to guarantee that users download their latest version every time they log on.

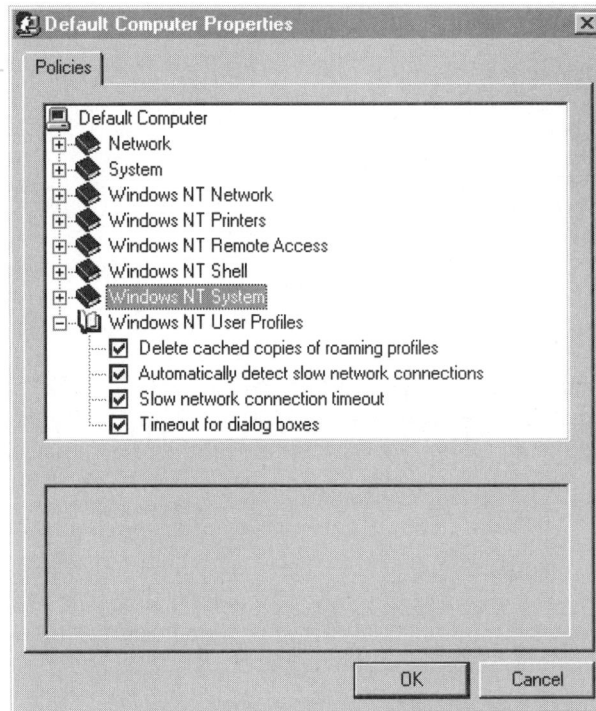

Figure 4.14 Modifying profiles to account for slow network connections.

Customizing Application Settings

Sometimes you need to configure an application that does not provide its own policy template, or that provides a template without the setting needed. In this case, you must either modify an existing template or create one, which requires knowledge of the application and how the application uses the registry to store configuration data.

WINDIFF, found in the *Microsoft Windows NT Server Resource Kit version 4.0,* can compare exported registry files for differences. This still entails a bit of guesswork because it requires identifying the correct registry key where the change takes place.

To create a customized application template:

1. Open the application.
2. Run REGEDIT and export the registry hive.
3. Make the change in the application.
4. Close the application. This is usually when an application saves information to the registry.
5. Export the registry hive again.
6. Run WINDIFF, comparing the two files.

You might have to repeat this process depending on how many options are configured in the registry key. For example, if one registry setting records the display of all toolbars and stores this information in a hexadecimal format, then test a few configurations to understand which values represent various toolbar configurations.

Customizing a template helps define a specific set of registry settings in system policies, including settings not definable by default through System Policy Editor. For example, you might need system policy settings for corporate-specific applications, such as an in-house database or a custom front-end application. After a template has been customized, you can load the template and use it to set values in the registry.

To use a template other than the default template:

1. In **System Policy Editor**, close all policy files.
2. From the **Options** menu, click on **Policy Template**.
3. In the **Policy Template Options** dialog box, click **Add**.
4. In the **Open Template File** dialog box, specify the name of the .ADM file to use a template to begin setting policies. Click **Open**.

To create customized templates that can be read by System Policy Editor, use a text editor such as WordPad to write and edit an .ADM file.

System Policy Implementation Considerations

One limitation of system policies is that they cannot disable the execution of MS-DOS and MS-DOS-based programs such as CMD.EXE, NET.EXE, or CACLS.EXE. Nor do they restrict running REGEDIT.EXE. ComNet administrators used NTFS restrictions on particular system files to restrict access. With FAT-partitioned systems, they remove the files entirely. This process is discussed in more detail in the "NTFS versus FAT" section below.

By default, System Policy Editor includes the policy for Default Users and Default Computers (see Figure 4.7, page 190). These policies apply to all users and all computers in the domain unless specified otherwise. To avoid having these policies lock down the administrators, create policy files to protect the *Administrator* and *Domain Admin* groups. This way, Default User and Default Computer lock-down policies do not apply when administrators log on to a computer.

There are two ways to prevent servers in the domain from being affected by Default Computer policies:

- Create policy files for each server in the domain and disable all of the settings
- Set up the server to ignore any further registry changes by policies

To do the latter:

1. Run REGEDIT.EXE.

2. Navigate to the **HKEY_LOCAL_MACHINE\System\CurrentControlSet001\Control\ Update** subkey.

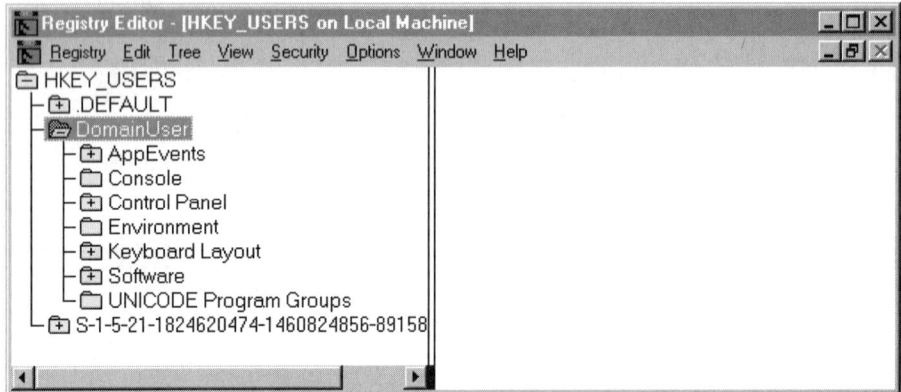

Figure 4.15 Blocking default computer polices from affecting servers.

3. In the right-hand window, double click on **Update Mode**.

4. Change the value to **0**.

5. Close REGEDIT.EXE.

In effect, this registry value prevents any further form of policies from affecting the local machine. *You must complete this change before you turn policies on.*

System Polices and Windows 2000

Currently, Windows NT 4.0 policies also apply to any Windows 2000 workstation in the domain. You can also use the Windows 2000 Group Policy Editor (GPE) to apply policies. GPE policies, however, apply only to Windows 2000 workstations. If the environment includes both operating systems, you still have to use Policy Editor to lock down the Windows NT 4.0 workstations, and copy the NTCONFIG.POL file to the NetLogon share of all of the domain controllers.

GPE policies provide more functionality than those for Windows NT 4.0. In fact, Windows NT 4.0 restrictions represent only a subset of those supported by Windows 2000. With the Windows 2000 Beta 2 release, apply Windows NT 4.0 policies first, then GPE policies. *After Beta 2 the order will be reversed.* You can disable the use of Policy Editor altogether for Windows 2000 workstations (using GPE). In order for GPE to be effective, workstations must be registered with a Windows 2000 server running the Domain Name Server (DNS) service.

Locking Down Desktops Beyond Policies

NTFS versus FAT

There are two ways to lock down a desktop beyond system policies:

- For NTFS partitioned systems: restrict access to selected files using NTFS
- For FAT partitioned systems: totally remove selected files from the workstation

Though both methods are effective, NTFS restrictions provide the additional flexibility of ensuring that the common desktop does not become cluttered with downloaded programs and or any other files.

To set NTFS permissions on a file:

1. In EXPLORER.EXE, right mouse click on the file you want to restrict.
2. Click on **Properties**.
3. Click on the **Security** tab.

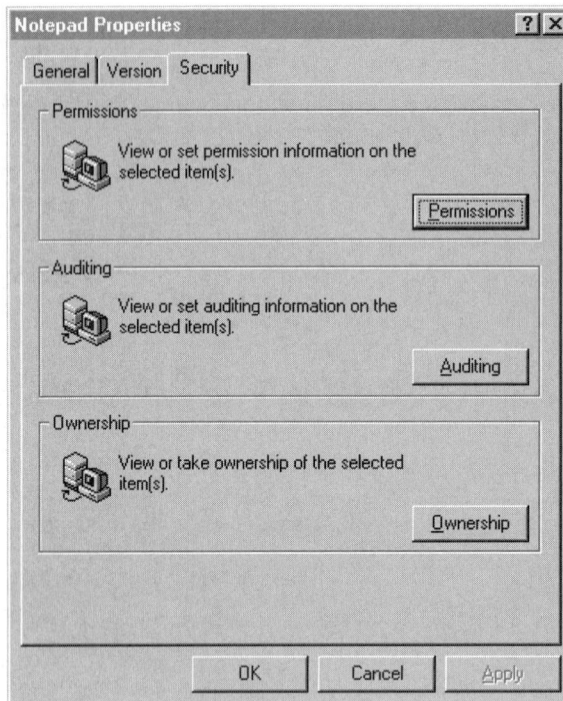

Figure 4.16 Using NTFS to restrict file access.

4. Click on the **Permissions** button.

5. Remove the **Everyone** global group.

6. Add the **Domain Admin** group, and give the group full control rights.

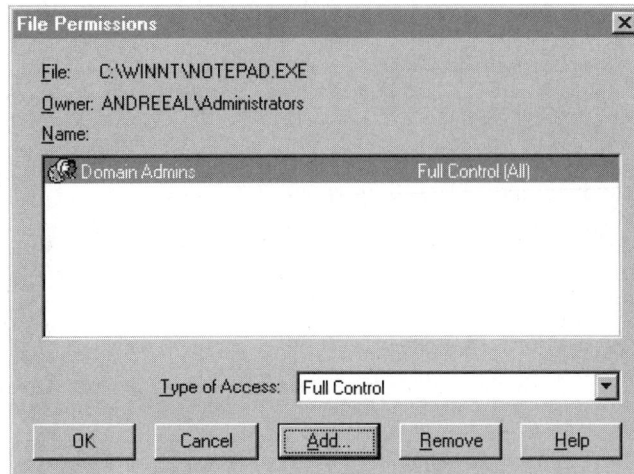

Figure 4.17 Adding the Domain Admin group.

7. Select **OK**.

8. Close the **Properties** page.

PDC attendees often download programs or save files onto their desktop. Instead of the applications roaming with the user profiles, they are placed on the desktop of the local machine and therefore can be seen and accessed by anyone who logs onto that machine. To keep the desktop "clean" ComNet administrators enforce Read-only NTFS permissions on the desktop for the Domain Users group.

To set NTFS on the hidden desktop folder:

1. Double-click on **My Computer**.
2. From the **File** menu, click on **View**, then **Folder Options**.
3. Check the option to "**Show All Files**."
4. Right-mouse-click on *%systemroot%*\desktop.
5. Click on **Properties**.
6. Click on the **Security** tab.
7. Click on the **Permissions** button.
8. Remove the **Everyone** global group.
9. Add the **Domain Admin** group and give the group *Full Control* rights.
10. Add the **Domain Users** group and give the group *Read (RX)* rights.
11. Select **OK**.
12. Close the **Properties** page.

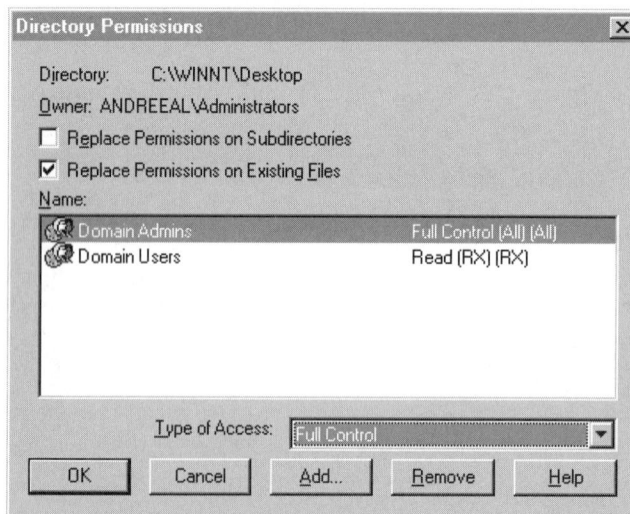

Figure 4.18 Using NTFS to restrict access to the common desktop.

Which System Files Can be Safely Locked-down?

Below is a list of applications that may open the system to security breaches. Use NTFS file permissions to restrict users from these applications. If you have a FAT-partitioned system, you can simply delete them from the PC.

In *%systemroot%*:

- _default
- REGEDIT.EXE
- NOTEPAD.EXE

In *%systemroot%*\system32\:

Caution Removing or restricting CMD.EXE and COMMAND.EXE can prevent some applications and logon scripts from executing.

- ATTRIB.EXE
- CACLS.EXE
- REGEDT32.EXE
- CMD.EXE
- REGEDIT.EXE
- MUSRMGR.EXE
- COMMAND.EXE
- WINFILE.EXE
- EDLIN.EXE

- PROGMAN.EXE
- FORMAT.EXE
- XCOPY.EXE
- EVENTVWR.EXE
- NET.EXE
- FTP.EXE

Scripts and Custom Executables

Some of the settings for applications fall between the cracks of what Windows NT allows you to configure automatically for users. Depending on the level of pre-configuration that you want to provide for the user, you'll eventually run into a setting that can't be set in the default profile or through system policies. For these settings you need to run logon script files or custom executables.

Logon scripts can be a very powerful tool in the network environment. They automatically run during the logon process and can help set up the working environment for the user by copying files, creating connections, and launching applications.

Many of today's corporate networks use the scripts because they're easy to create, edit, and administer. Also, they can be assigned to single users or groups by entering the script name in the user manager for domains. The scripts are placed in the domain controller's NetLogon share (*%systemroot%\system32\rep\import\scripts*) and can be set up to replicate across all domain controllers for ease of administration.

One difficulty with ComNet is that the administrators must prevent users from accessing the command line and this prevents users from running a script file. Therefore, a custom executable was created (The PDC Logon Application) that provides the same functionality as a script file (and more), and still maintains a high level of security. Below are the steps that the PDC Logon Application runs through to configure workstations:

1. Determine the current user alias and machine name.

2. Perform any file manipulations: copy, move, delete

3. Set up applications as necessary: IE—custom registry settings; Outlook—mail profile

4. Set up printer based on machine name.

5. Open Internet Explorer for the user.

Most of these tasks can be coded fairly simply into a VB application, although editing the registry through code requires some knowledge of how to make system API calls.

The PDC Logon Application has two very useful features: automatic creation of a default printer connection for a user, and automatic configuration of the user's e-mail. Both are very handy customizations to ComNet's network environment. They can greatly improve the user's experience when logging on to an unfamiliar network.

Adding a Default Printer Connection for the User

Automatically attaching a network printer to each machine is required for two reasons. The first is that it guarantees that the user uses the right printer. In a large network with hundreds of workstations and dozens of printers, you need to ensure each user gets connected to a nearby printer. If users log on somewhere on row 3 of the network, they most likely will want use a printer in that row. However, in a roaming profile environment, they may have printer 15 (or any other printer they've already used) set up as their default. This can be very frustrating for users if it goes unnoticed.

The second reason is that it relieves users of any administrative work on the system, which, in turn, saves trouble for administrators. By automatically setting up the desired printer for the user, administrators can lock users out of the Control Panel and printer settings.

Automatically setting up machine-based printers in a roaming profile environment is slightly more complicated than it sounds. Windows NT 4.0 has no built-in means to do this effectively. Since the user profile is where the printer information is stored, you need a way to change the default printer based on which machine the user has logged onto. ComNet designers did this with a small Microsoft Visual Basic application.

Note Windows 2000 incorporates a new feature in policies that allows domain administrators to map default printers to groups of workstations or "organizational units."

The application runs each time a user logs onto the machine. (You can find this sample application, including the Microsoft Visual Basic project to create it on the companion CD under the \SetPrinter directory.) The application first finds out the local computer name (such as Workstation3A), then uses the computer (machine) name to figure out which printer should be associated with it (through a strict naming convention or a simple lookup table).

It then uses this information to make a connection using the AddPrinterConnection API. After that is completed the application must modify the HKEY_CURRENT_USER portion of the registry to set that printer connection as the default. The code sample below shows how to create a connection to a printer and edit the appropriate registry key for a Windows NT 4.0 workstation. It was written in Visual Basic 6.0.

```
'********************************************************

Declare Function AddPrinterConnection Lib "winspool.drv" Alias
"AddPrinterConnectionA" _

(ByVal pName As String) As Long


Declare Function RegOpenKeyEx Lib "advapi32.dll" Alias "RegOpenKeyExA" _

(ByVal hKey As Long, ByVal lpSubKey As String, ByVal ulOptions As Long,
ByVal samDesired As Long, phkResult As Long) As Long
```

```
Declare Function RegSetValueEx Lib "advapi32.dll" Alias "RegSetValueExA"
(ByVal hKey As Long, ByVal _ lpValueName As String, ByVal Reserved As
Long, ByVal dwType As Long, lpData As Any, ByVal cbData As Long) As Long

REM  Note that if you declare the lpData parameter as String, you must
REM  pass it By Value.


Declare Function RegCloseKey Lib "advapi32.dll" (ByVal hKey As Long) As
Long

'********************************************************


Function SetDefaultConnection(lsPrinterName As String)

REM  The code below is for an NT4 workstation.


REM  Use the API to connect the printer to this PC by network name.
REM  For example: \\PrintServer\Printer1

    Dim lbSuccess As Boolean

    lbSuccess = AddPrinterConnection(lsPrinterName)


    If Not lbSuccess Then

        MsgBox ("The printer " & lsPrinterName & " was not found.")

        Exit Function
```

```
    End If



REM  Now you need to edit the registry and make the connection
REM  that was just created the default connection for this user.
REM  Note: You'll want to add error handlers for your own code.

    Dim llOpenRegistryHandle As Long

    Dim lsStringValue As String


    Call RegOpenKeyEx(HKEY_CURRENT_USER, "Software\Microsoft\Windows
NT\CurrentVersion\Windows", _

0, 6, llOpenRegistryHandle)

    lsStringValue = Trim$(lsPrinterName) & ",winspool,Ne00:"

REM  This string value may change for your printer.
REM  You can find the proper value at:

REM  HKEY_CURRENT_USER\Software\Microsoft\Windows
REM  NT\CurrentVersion\Devices


    Call RegSetValueEx(llOpenRegistryHandle, "Device", 0, 1, ByVal
lsStringValue, Len(lsStringValue))


    Call RegCloseKey(llOpenRegistryHandle)
    MsgBox "done!"


End Function

'*********************************************************
```

Configuring User's Mail Profile

Automatically configuring the user's e-mail profile is one of the best ways to ensure that the user has a trouble-free experience. In an environment such as the PDC, you simply cannot educate so many new users on how to set up e-mail profiles properly. The many Macintosh, UNIX, and OS/2 users coming in to use ComNet can't be expected to know how to point their Outlook client at the appropriate Exchange server. The setup wizard can be very complicated and confusing for a first-time user. Options such as connection type and offline storage can greatly affect how the user's e-mail is stored and sent. To avoid this confusion, a way was devised to avoid setup wizards and present users with their inbox, ready to go, as soon as they fire up Outlook.

The first need is to create the user's mail profile—the series of settings in the current user's registry that **MAPI** uses to connect the mail client with the server. (MAPI is a standard set of messaging APIs that are used by the client application, the messaging subsystem and the Information Service.) This profile can be created programmatically by making calls to the MAPI common architecture. This would prove to be a fairly complex program. Fortunately, though, Microsoft has provided a utility that can create the profile for you.

The NEWPROF.EXE and PROFGEN.EXE, found in the *Microsoft Office 97 Resource Kit,* can be used in conjunction to automatically create a new default profile each time a user logs in. NEWPROF is the application that does most of the work. It accesses an information file (OUTLOOK.PRF—found with NEWPROF.EXE) to make the desired registry changes. All that was needed was to set up the .PRF file so that it points users to their mailbox on ComNet's Microsoft Exchange Server. The default .PRF file was edited this way:

```
;***********************************************************

; Section 2 - Services in profile.

[Service List]

Service1=Microsoft Outlook Client

;Service2=Personal Folders              ➡ Comment out this line

;Service3=Outlook Address Book

;Service4=Internet E-Mail



;Commented out to assist those who wish to use the Exchange server as a
default profile

Service2=Microsoft Exchange Server     ➡ Uncomment this line



[Service2]

ConversionProhibited=TRUE

HomeServer=ExchangeSRV1                 ➡ Further down in the file,
                                          define our mail server

MailboxName=bobk                        ➡ and the user's mailbox name
```

Note Only the Microsoft Outlook Client and Microsoft Exchange Server are listed in the Service List. You need to comment out personal folders as a service by placing a semi-colon before that line. You also need to specify the user's Exchange server and mailbox name in the Service2 section.

The following command line options are very helpful when running and testing NEWPROF:

NEWPROF [-P <Path to .PRF file>] [-S] [-X] [-Z]

Where:

-P <Path to .PRF file> is the .PRF file with the complete path.

-S causes the NEWPROF.EXE to program to bring up a window, allows the user to choose a .PRF file, and displays status and error messages in this window.

-X causes NEWPROF.EXE to start execution automatically when the -S option is used, without waiting for a .PRF file to be selected. This option requires the -P option or that the DEFAULT.PRF file be present in the Windows directory.

-Z causes NEWPROF.EXE to display MAPI error codes in case any errors are encountered. This option requires the -S option. NEWPROF.EXE does not generate any log files.

The sample code on page 213 creates a default profile that connects the user to the mailbox **bobk** on the Exchange server **ExchangeSRV1**. After this code has been run, Outlook should open directly to that mailbox.

This allows two choices: create a .PRF file for every user in the network and have NEWPROF run against that file as a user logs on, or create a template .PRF file and insert the user's information during the logon. The latter option is exactly what PROFGEN is for.

PROFGEN can modify the OUTLOOK.PRF file before it gets used by NEWPROF. PROFGEN replaces the existing mailbox name in the .PRF file with the logon name of the current Windows NT user. This is exactly what is needed, since the ComNet system is set up so that the Windows NT account name is the same as the user's mailbox name (Windows NT logonName = mailboxName).

The mailserver name does not need to be edited on a user-level basis. Even if there are multiple Exchange servers on the network with mailboxes split between them, just one of them can be used as the mail server in the .PRF file. This is because NEWPROF uses the server name as a point of contact to the Global Address List, then uses the information found for the user in the GAL to create the profile. Therefore, if the user's mailbox is on ExchangeSRV2 but the .PRF file has ExchangeSRV1 listed, the profile still is set up correctly.

More Information

Headquartered in Chicago, Lante Corporation also has offices in New York, San Francisco, and Seattle, and can be reached at http://www.lante.com.

CHAPTER 5

Designing and Planning Internal Security at Big Kahuna Burger

By Brian Karasawa, Tom Fuchs, Eric Miyadi, MCS— Southern California

In today's distributed, client-server environment, corporate data is stored on server platforms, where it is expected to be at once available *and* secure. The degree to which these mutually antagonistic goals are achieved is often a measure of the success and viability of your business. Security must be a serious component of any design discussion, a need that this chapter addresses by outlining the tasks required to create a security policy that maximizes the reliability, availability, and supportability of all systems and data on an internal network—that portion of the Windows NT network within the firewall.

In Focus

Enterprise

Big Kahuna Burger (Slogan: *My, that is a tasty burger*) is a fast food franchise organization with outlets throughout the United States and Canada. The headquarters site is in Los Angeles, CA.

Network

Windows NT 4.0 operating system. Workstations running Windows NT, and Windows 95. Microsoft Exchange, Outlook 98, and Internet Explorer 4.

Challenge

Assess security requirements in order to secure an internal Windows NT network.

Solution

A root certificate server with individual certificate servers in each site. The root certificate was created at the corporate headquarters in Los Angeles, and a subordinate was also created for use with Exchange. Canadian sites coming online must install the certificate authority server at the site and create trust between the root and the new subordinate.

What You'll Find In This Chapter

- Levels of security available in Windows NT.

- How to secure the domain, the registry, RAS, and e-mail.

- Available security auditing tools.

- Explanation of encryption and signing methods.

- HW/SW requirements for a suggested Exchange security configuration.

- Issues in establishing certificate authority.

- A complete checklist of Windows NT security options, with syntax, default values, and recommendations.

Warning This chapter makes recommendations for tuning the Windows NT registry using the Registry Editor. Using the Registry Editor incorrectly can cause serious, system-wide problems that require you to reinstall Windows NT. Microsoft cannot guarantee that any problems resulting from the use of Registry Editor can be solved. Use this tool at your own risk.

Securing the internal network begins with choosing an appropriate level of security for the Windows NT domain. This decision makes it possible to evaluate security needs for specific system areas so that you can evaluate the options available for protecting them.

Securing the Windows NT Domain

Windows NT allows you to establish security ranging from none (not recommended) to C2 level security required by many government agencies.

How much is enough? This is not easy to determine. If security is too lax, the problems are obvious. But there can be problems when security is too tight, too, although they sometimes are as simple as users trying to circumvent safeguards just to get work done. For example, if password policy requires complex and hard to remember passwords, some users will write them down, increasing the chance that they will be misappropriated. If file restriction is extremely tight, users blocked from files they want to use may prevail on their colleagues to "lend" their passwords. These seemingly minor breaches can sometimes create major problems. There has to be a workable and tolerable level of security.

First you must accurately assess your needs. When you have identified them, you can choose and implement security elements. You have to educate users in why security is important and what they have to do to maintain it. Finally, you should monitor the system and make adjustments as needed.

C2-Level Security

C2-level security enforces some practical requirements:

- **Discretionary access control.** The owner of a resource (such as a file) must be able to control access to it.

- **Object reuse.** The operating system must protect data stored in memory for one process so that it is not randomly reused by other processes. For example, Windows NT Server protects memory so that its contents cannot be read after it is freed by a process.

In addition, when a file is deleted, users must not be able to access its data even when its disk space is allocated by another file. This protection must also extend to the disk, monitor, keyboard, mouse, and any other devices.

- **Identification and authentication.** All users must uniquely identify themselves. Windows NT Server requires each user to type in a unique logon name and password before gaining entry to the system. The system uses this identification to track users' activities.

- **Auditing.** System administrators must be able to audit security-related events and the actions of individual users. Access to this audit data must be limited to authorized administrators.

If you decide to set up a C2-certifiable system, review the "Microsoft Report on C2 Evaluation of Windows NT" (at http://www.microsoft.com/security). It contains a frequently updated list of hardware configurations on which Windows NT has been evaluated. It also specifies the features implemented for C2 evaluation (basically the high-level security recommendations) so that you can duplicate them.

Survey the security features described in this document, in the Windows NT documentation, and in the *Windows NT Resource Kit*, and choose the setup that fits your combination of resources, personnel, workflow, and perceived risks. Appendix D, "Security In a Software Development Environment," in the Version 3.51 Update to the *Windows NT Resource Kit*, is useful if you use custom or in-house software. It also provides information on managing and interpreting the security log, and technical details on special-case auditing (for example, auditing base objects).

Once you decide on the features you want to implement, you can use the C2Config application (C2CONFIG.EXE, in the *Windows NT Resource Kit*) to choose from the settings used in evaluating Windows NT for C2 security.

Protecting the Registry

If you want to create a high-security installation, you should consider setting protections on certain registry keys.

There are default protections on the various registry components that provide standard level security. You can tighten security by assigning access rights to specific registry keys, but this requires caution because user programs often need access to certain keys. For more information, see Chapter 11, "Registry Editor and Registry Administration," in the *Windows NT 3.5 Resource Guide*. A common approach is to change the protections on the keys below so that the group *Everyone* is allowed only *QueryValue*, *Enumerate Subkeys*, *Notify*, and *Read Control* accesses.

In the HKEY_LOCAL_MACHINE on Local Machine dialog:

- \Software\Microsoft\RPC (and its subkeys)
- \Software\Microsoft\Windows NT\CurrentVersion
- And under the \Software\Microsoft\Windows NT\CurrentVersion\ subtree:
  - AeDebug
  - Compatibility
  - Drivers
  - Embedding
  - Fonts
  - FontSubstitutes
  - GRE_Initialize
  - MCI
  - MCI Extensions
  - Port (and all subkeys)
  - Profile List
  - WOW (and all subkeys)
- Windows3.1MigrationStatus (and all subkeys)
- In the HKEY_CLASSES_ROOT on Local Machine dialog:
  - \HKEY_CLASSES_ROOT (and all subkeys)

Setting Security Policies

User Profiles

As part of the internal security design, you have to decide how much control to exert over the user desktops. Once you decide on a level, an efficient way to exert this control is by implementing user profiles, which contain user-specific information such as settings and configuration specifics. Each user profile is created from system policies (described below, these define which settings are configurable and which are not) and from settings the end user configures.

There are three types of user profiles:

- **Roaming** profiles allow user settings to "follow" users to any workstation they log on to. Usually these settings are stored on the server.

- **Local** profiles are copies stored on a particular workstation. These settings do not follow the user.

- **Mandatory** profiles, usually stored on the server, allow an administrator to prevent changes to the user settings. Any changes that *are* made (many are prevented by system policies) are lost the next time the user logs off and logs on.

For more information on user profiles, see the Microsoft Windows NT White Paper "Guide to Microsoft Windows NT 4.0 Profiles and Policies," on (http://microsoft.com/ntserver/management) and the *Microsoft Windows NT Server Concepts and Planning Guide*.

To use or not to use? Consider how much control you want over the desktop. If for some users and applications it makes sense to control tightly what is on the desktop, consult the *Microsoft Zero Administration Kit* for tips on how to configure the desktops in a locked-down environment. This level of control is often not necessary, in which case you may want to allow users to configure the settings on their own workstations and to control machine-specific settings. In this case, system policies are a more effective tool than user profiles.

Consider also the line speed of the network client-server link. If you store profile information on a server, a lot of information is downloaded each time each user logs on. This is not efficient unless there is a high-speed client-server link.

Finally, consider the workstation configuration process. For instance, you can use Internet Explorer version 4.*x* to represent the desktop as a Web page. This allows you a lot more control over desktop settings, but requires different configuration procedures than standard Windows NT Workstation or Windows 95 desktop. For more information consult the Internet Explorer Administration Kit Web site, at http://ieak.microsoft.com.

System Policies

System policies are sets of registry settings that define the computer resources available to an individual or a group of users. You can use them in conjunction with or independently of user profiles. To decide which tool to use, consider the scale of the changes you want to implement: system policies work better than individual user settings when configuring a computer, and in fact can override user profiles. And you can implement policies for specific users, groups, computers, or for all users, exerting wide but precise control over the environment.

Consider also what system features you want to control. System policies have some limitations related to logon scripts, NTFS for control of access to individual files, and application-specific issues. For more information and some examples, see Chapter 4, "Locking Down the Desktop at Microsoft's Professional Developer Conference."

In a Windows NT environment, workstations by default look to the server for the System Policy file (NTCONFIG.POL). If a user logs on to a machine in a resource domain, the search for the file is redirected to the validating controller in the account domain.

Mixed environments (those that include Windows NT and Windows 95) present a slight difficulty in that Windows 95 workstations by default always look only to the primary domain controller (PDC) for their policy file: this can be a problem in a networked environment. However, you can update the policy so that after initial logon the workstation looks to the logon server instead. For more information, see Knowledge Base article Q150687, Title: Group Policies Not Applied On Windows NT Domain. Mixed environments also require you to create each workstation's policy file on a machine configured with the corresponding operating system. Again, for more information, consult the Microsoft Windows NT White Paper "Guide to Microsoft Windows NT 4.0 Profiles and Policies" on (http://microsoft.com/ntserver/management), and the *Windows NT Server Concepts and Planning Guide*.

Audit Tools (Microsoft and Third-Party)

In order to monitor the security of Windows NT servers, IT staff should test and qualify a set of tools that can provide feedback on the effectiveness of your corporate Windows NT Server security measures. Some tools:

Microsoft NT Service Pack 4 (SP4)

- **Security Configuration Manager (SCM)** allows administrators to define and apply security configurations for Windows NT Server and Workstation installations. You can also use it to inspect installed systems to locate any degradation in system security.

- **NTLMv2 Security** (in SP4) is an enhancement to NTLM security protocols that significantly improves the NTLM authentication and session security mechanisms.

- **Secure Channel Enhancements** (in SP4) is an enhancement to the secure channel protocols used by member workstations and servers to communicate with their domain controllers, and by domain controllers to communicate with other domain controllers. The enhancements allow you to encrypt these communications and check their integrity.

- **Event Log Security Privilege** (in SP4) is a fix for the Event Log service that requires that the Security privilege be enabled in order to view and manage the security event log. This change requires that administrators be granted the privilege to manage the security log—they cannot manage the log simply because they are members of the Administrators group.

- **SomarSoft**. This contains:

  - **DumpAcl**, a Windows NT program to dump the permissions (ACLs) for the file system, registry, shares, and printers in a concise, readable listbox format, so that "holes" in system security are readily apparent.

  - **DumpEvt**, a Windows NT program to dump the Event Log, in a format suitable for importing into a database. This is a good tool for building an Event Log management system for long-term tracking of security violations, etc. A DLL version allows you to read the formatted event log from Visual Basic, which is useful for tasks such as writing a real-time event monitoring utility.

  - **DumpReg**, a Windows NT and Windows 95 program to dump the registry, making it easy to find keys and values matching a string. You can sort Windows NT by reverse order of last modified time, making it easy to see changes made by recently installed software.

  - **RegEdit.DLL**, which is callable by 32-bit Visual Basic (VB), can be used to view and modify the user registry profile. For example, you can create a 10-line VBA for Excel program that changes the mail server path in the registry profiles of all users at once. This is a useful tool if you can program in VB.

- **ISS** (Internet Security System). This contains:

  - **Internet Scanner**, for quickly finding and fixing security holes with an automated, comprehensive network security vulnerability analysis. It scans and detects vulnerabilities, prioritizes security risks and generates a wide range of meaningful reports ranging from executive-level trend analyses to detailed step-by-step instructions for eliminating security risks.

  - **System Scanner**, a host-based security assessment system that helps manage security risks by thoroughly analyzing internal security weaknesses, comparing your stated security policy with the actual configuration of the host computer. It identifies potential security risks such as missing security patches, dictionary-crackable passwords, inappropriate user privileges, incorrect file system access rights, insecure service configurations, and suspicious activity that might indicate an intrusion.

  - **RealSecure**, an automated, real-time intrusion detection and response system for computer networks. It provides around-the-clock network surveillance and enables you to automatically intercept and respond to security breaches and internal network abuse before systems are compromised. RealSecure unobtrusively monitors network traffic and automatically detects and responds to suspicious activity, providing maximum levels of security across the enterprise.

  - **Kane Security Analyst**, which thoroughly assess the overall security status of a Windows NT network and issues security reports on six areas: password strength, access control, user account restrictions, system monitoring, data integrity, and data confidentiality.

    Based on the expertise of security specialists, KSA streamlines the analysis process, using an embedded expert knowledge base to analyze and assess:

Password vulnerability	User and group permissions across domains
C2 security	Password strength
Trust relationships	Event logs
Scripted passwords	Non-secure partitions
Audit policy compliance	UPS status
Excessive rights	Security report cards
Registry security settings	Guest ID configuration
Logon violations	Windows NT services
Domain security	Domains that can't be administered
Security logs	Down-level authentication

- **BindView** (NOSAdmin for Windows NT) provides hundreds of pieces of information about a Windows NT enterprise. Use it to query your environment for information about users, groups, machines, domains, services, sessions, shares, device drivers, security events, system events, application events, files and directories.

- **DirectManage Suite.** This contains:

  - **DirectAdmin**, a drag-and-drop product that lets you manage all elements of Windows NT networks including delegation, reporting and scripting. It has an interactive Explorer-like interface. Use it to browse and edit the properties of multiple network objects: groups, users, domains, computers, file directories and registries. The result is flexibility in managing distributed resources.

- **DirectScript**, an ADSI-compliant scripting product that lets you create your own tools to reduce labor-intensive administration tasks. It consists of a collection of COM (Component Object Model) objects compatible with Windows NT 2000's Active Directory. These components are used to manage and secure objects such as domains, groups, computers, users, registries, and printers on a network of computers running Windows NT 3.51, 4.0, or 5.0. Because DirectScript is based on COM objects, it can easily be used from common languages such as Visual Basic (VBA and VBS), JavaScript, and Active Server Pages.

Remote Access Security

Microsoft's Remote Access Service (RAS) provides security at the operating system, file system, and network layers, as well as data encryption and event auditing. With its own features and some inherited from Windows NT, RAS allows you to secure every stage of the process—user authentication, data transmission, resource access, logoff, and auditing.

Windows NT Security

Windows NT, the host for RAS, is a secure operating environment. With it you can use software to lock down any Windows NT Server-based computer, provided it is secured physically, so that access to the system requires a password and leaves an audit trail.

Under the single-network-logon model, authenticated users carry access credentials, which the system checks whenever a user attempts to gain access to a resource anywhere on the network. Domains can be configured with trust relationships, allowing users with an account on one server in one domain to access resources in other domains after entering a password once, for initial logon. This model extends to RAS users: RAS access is granted from the pool of all Windows NT user accounts. You can grant dial-in rights to a single user, group of users, or all users. When users use their domain logon to connect via RAS and are authenticated by RAS, they can access resources throughout the domain and in any trusted domains.

Authentication Protocols

RAS uses the Challenge Handshake Authentication Protocol (CHAP) to negotiate the most secure form of encrypted authentication supported by both server and client—a challenge-response mechanism with one-way encryption on the response. CHAP allows the RAS server to negotiate encryption mechanisms downward from most- to least-secure, and protects passwords transmitted in the process.

Of the several types of encryption algorithms supported by CHAP, RAS uses DES (when client and server both use RAS) and RSA Security Inc.'s MD5. DES (Data Encryption Standard) is the U.S. government standard, designed to protect against password discovery and playback. Windows NT 3.51, Windows for Workgroups, and Windows 95 always negotiate DES-encrypted authentication when they communicate.

Security levels and RAS encryption protocols.

Level of security	Type of encryption	RAS encryption protocol
High	One-way	CHAP, MD5
Medium	Two-way	SPAP
Low	Clear-text	PAP

When connecting to other vendors' remote access servers, the RAS *client* can negotiate MD5, an encryption scheme used by various PPP vendors for encrypted authentication. RAS *server* does not support MD5.

When connecting to third-party remote access servers or client software, RAS can negotiate Shiva Password Authentication Protocol (SPAP, a two-way, reversible, encryption) or clear-text authentication if the third party product does not support encrypted authentication. Windows NT Workstation 3.51 uses SPAP when connecting to a Shiva LAN Rover, as do Shiva clients connecting to a Windows NT Server 3.51. SPAP is more secure than clear text, but less secure than CHAP.

PAP uses clear-text passwords and is the least sophisticated authentication protocol. It is typically negotiated if the remote workstation and server cannot negotiate a more secure form of validation. RAS server provides an option that allows administrators to prevent clear-text passwords from being negotiated.

If you are using Windows NT Server RAS server and a Windows NT 4.0 Workstation or Windows 95 client, you will normally use CHAP encryption using the DES algorithm. The only time you would use one of the other protocols is when you use a third-party client or server for authentication or encryption.

Third-party Security Hosts

RAS allows you to enhance security by placing third-party security hosts between remote users and the RAS Server. These require users to present a hardware key of some sort before gaining access to the RAS Server. RAS's open architecture allows you to choose from a variety of third-party security hosts.

Call-back, another RAS security enhancement, enables administrators to require remote users to dial from a specific predetermined location (such as their home telephone number) or to have the system call a user back from any location, in order to use low-cost communications lines. With secured call-back, the user initiates a call and connects with the RAS Server, which then drops the connection and calls back a moment later to the pre-assigned call-back number. This generally thwarts most impersonators.

Network Access Restrictions

The system administrator controls remote access to the network under RAS. In addition to the tools provided with Windows NT Server (authentication, trusted domains, event auditing, C2 security design, etc.), the RAS Admin tool allows you to grant or revoke remote access privileges user by user. Even though RAS runs on a Windows NT Server-based computer, each user must be authorized to enter the network via RAS. This process provides a convenient means for setting call-back restrictions.

Microsoft's RAS provides administrators with a switch that allows access to be granted to all resources that the RAS host computer can see, or just resources local to the computer. This closely controls what information is available to remote users, and limits access even to users who manage to breach security and get in.

Data Encryption

If high security is required, the RAS server allows administrators to force encrypted communications so that all users connecting to that server automatically encrypt all data sent.

E-mail Security (PGP and Key Distribution)

A good information-management strategy allows users to share information with the right people at the right time. Because some of the information being shared may be sensitive or confidential, the strategy must also include some level of security.

This section introduces some e-mail security concepts, goes into the specifics of a high level design using Microsoft Exchange, and concludes with a detailed discussion of what is required to implement the solution in an enterprise with a headquarters site and branch offices.

Security and Encryption

There are two basic cryptographic methods: encryption and signing. Encryption renders text unreadable until it is decrypted by an authorized recipient. Signing is similar to physically signing a document and initialing each section to show that nothing has changed. Verification involves the equivalent of matching the signature to a "signature on file" card, and proving that no portion of the document has changed. Use of both measures ensures that if someone intercepts a message they cannot view its contents without additional information, nor can they alter the contents of the message and pass it on.

Cryptography Basics

Here is some basic information on cryptographic concepts. Encryption is the process of turning plaintext (readable) information or files into a ciphertext (unreadable) format. There are two methods: One is the "secret key" (or "symmetric") method, which uses one key to encode and decode material. The other is the "public key" (or "asymmetric") method, which uses different, matched keys—one called a public key to encode, one called a private key to decode.

A "hash function" (or a "one-way hash") is a calculation performed on a plaintext message that results in a unique identifier for the text. If any of the information is altered even slightly, it will result in a completely different unique identifier and thus be recognized as invalid. Finally a "certificate" is a wrapper around a key that verifies who the key belongs to, what it can be used for, and who issued it.

Certificate Server

Certificate authority (CA) is handled by servers arranged hierarchically: a **root CA** server validates **subordinate CA** certificate servers, which in turn issue certificates to end-users. This allows for better control, and makes it easier to implement new certificate servers without changing policies on other servers.

You should create a subordinate CA server expressly for Exchange Server support, so that you can implement Exchange-specific policies and create additional "subordinate CA" certificate servers for different applications (Web users, external users, etc.). When you apply the custom policy to the Exchange CA server, however, only Exchange Server can create certificates on it. You cannot use a single certificate server for both Exchange and Web users.

The benefits and challenges (there is only a minor one) of a subordinate CA server are:

Benefits	Potential challenge
More control over the creation of the certificates including limiting the validity period.	Creates an additional server to manage.
Allows flexibility for future implementations of certificate servers.	
If multiple certificate servers are used for Exchange, Internet users have to add only a single root certificate to their client in order to decrypt e-mail.	

Exchange Server Options

Exchange Server depends on certificate server to enable security functions. The CA installation, in turn, depends on each site, and each site's requirements.

You can install the CA server locally at the Exchange site or at a central (headquarters) site. The benefits and drawbacks of these options are explained in detail below. Assess your needs and your network and then choose carefully, because if you switch configurations later you will lose the database that stores backup copies of the keys and will have to issue new keys to end users. Or you can decrypt and then re-encrypt all the messages, but it is time consuming. Pick a design you are ready to stick with.

Headquarters Certificate Server

In this configuration, one server issues certificates for all locations, centralizing control. It minimizes hardware requirements and system changes because it requires installing only one server (although you can install more) at headquarters. You have to add software at each site (at least one server per Exchange site) but the service is very small and should not contribute significantly to system load.

Benefits	Potential challenges
Allows for central control of the security functions.	Requires installation of Key Management Server service on other sites.
Upgrade to Exchange 5.5 NOT required on additional sites.	Requires additional work at headquarters to enable e-mail security for remote users.
Issuing certificates can be done ONLY at headquarters, but can be done for anyone in the organization.	

Local Certificate Server

In this configuration, a certificate server is created at one or more remote offices. This allows for local control over the certificate security, but it requires a significant server software upgrade that can take several hours per server. You can put a CA server at every remote site if you want, and in many cases this is desirable because it allows distributed administration of the advanced security functions. It also allows dial-in sites to manage their security configuration independently, without the delay associated with a centralized configuration.

Benefit	Potential challenge
Allows for local control and administration of the security functions.	Requires upgrade to Exchange Server (upgrade to version 5.5, and addition of Service Pack 1), and installation of Key Management Server, as well as installation of Certificate Server.

International Implications

The level of encryption available to Exchange and Outlook e-mail clients is determined by their software because all encryption and digital signing originate on the client machine. Encryption is limited by current US export laws that restrict international distribution of client software, but the U.S. Commerce Department will often grant permission to distribute "high security" products (allowing 128-bit encryption instead of the easier to decode 40-bit encryption) to international offices of US-based companies.

While setting up the security for Exchange, the client indicates its encryption level and that information is stored in the Exchange directory and as part of the certificate. This allows the same server to be used regardless of the security level of the clients. When sending, the Outlook client software automatically detects the encryption capabilities of the recipient when sending the message, and encrypts the message accordingly.

Requirements

Hardware

- Generally, you will want to run the certificate server on the same machine as Exchange server (since the key generation is usually performed for Exchange). The certificate server will not require much processing power, because it is used only to create the keys and revocation lists (the client workstation performs encryption and verification).

- Since the server contains backup copies of users' keys, you should protect this valuable resource with a reliable storage system, such as a disk array or mirrored disks.

- Memory requirements will be the same as for an Exchange server in the site (assuming you are using the same machine for both certificate server and Exchange Server).

Server Software

- Requires Windows NT 4.0 Option Pack, Windows NT 4.0 SP3, PDC or member server (not a backup domain controller (BDC)), and Internet Explorer 4.01.

Client Software

- Requires Outlook 98 to be able to send e-mail to external users
- Exchange client or Outlook 97 for internal e-mail

Networking

- Network connectivity is required to function with the other Exchange servers in the site.

Certificate Server Naming

- A certificate server should be limited to these characters in its relative distinguished name (RDN):

  a-z A-Z 0-9 {space} ()+-./:=?

How Big Kahuna Burger Implemented Certificate Authority

Big Kahuna Burger decided to implement a root certificate server with individual certificate servers in each site. This allowed a single "root certificate authority" to be created for the entire corporation, yet allowed individual offices to create one certificate authority for Web clients and one for e-mail. From the end user perspective, there was only one root authority to trust, although multiple uses were enabled.

As an additional benefit, by using the root certificate authority to issue a "code signing" certificate, the client can digitally sign executables to be distributed via the Web. Moving forward, the same certificate could be used to sign other items, including custom controls or other custom designed executables.

The root certificate was created at the corporate headquarters in Los Angeles, and a subordinate was also created for use with Exchange. Each international site that comes online has to install the certificate authority server at the site (usually on the Exchange server) and trust has to be created between the root and the new subordinate.

The process of creating the trust is documented in the Exchange Server 5.5 Service Pack 1 documentation, as well as in the white paper "Creating Certificate Hierarchies with MS Certificate Server Version 1.0" (available on TechNet or by download from the Microsoft Software Library as "hier3.exe.")

Issues and Things To Watch Out For

You must apply the hotfix described in the Exchange Server 5.5 Service Pack 1 documentation to fix a couple problems in the format and content of default certificates. (You can find it at: FTP://ftp.microsoft.com/bussys/iis/iis-public/fixes/usa/certserv.) *Apply this immediately after creating the certificate server, before any certificates are issued.*

Although the Microsoft Certificate Server 1.0 documentation states that certificate authority hierarchies are not officially supported, it is possible with the current version to create a two-level hierarchy (support for only a root and one subordinate). These are tested only for two level hierarchies, and because the certificate server will include as part of the certificate only the current server's certificate and the certificate of its immediate parent, a complete chain of certificates cannot be maintained for hierarchies with more than two levels.

Scale can also create certificate server design problems. If you create a certificate server for many users (several hundred thousand to millions) you may run into limitations of the certificate specification itself. One of these is the size of the Certificate Revocation List (certificates that have been revoked by the authority).

Each time a certificate is used, it is checked against the list; if the list becomes large (as it can in a large system) things slow down on the server that generates the list and for clients that have to check through the entire list. Perhaps you remember the early days of credit cards. Each clerk had to check your card number against a large book of revoked card numbers. Slow.

Before implementation you should carefully verify the time settings on the Windows NT Server that is acting as the certificate server. Each client's certificate is created with a validity period that starts when the server generates the certificate. If the time settings are somehow not correct on the server, clients may receive certificates that are not yet valid. Result: confusion.

Security Settings

Big Kahuna Burger checked its way through the Windows NT security settings using this table. You can use it to find a topic (such as Backup Strategy) then check the syntax and the Windows NT default. The Comments column offers explanatory detail.

Windows NT security settings.

Item	Syntax	Windows NT default	Comments
Assigning Machine Names to Workstations	Machine name created during installation	Workstation names can consist of any letter or number. Special characters (underscore, dash, etc.) are available but can cause problems with products such as SQL and UNIX. See documentation for additional details.	If a user has multiple machines, increment the names (JoeB1, JoeB2, etc.) Vary combinations of first and last name letters for uniqueness in large environments, but try to do so according to specific rules.

Windows NT security settings.   *(continued)*

Item	Syntax	Windows NT default	Comments
Creating NT User Account	Administrative Tools User Manager Add New User Type in new user name	None: user account creation is usually defined by the administration group.	Consider following the same naming syntax used for workstation naming.
Full Name and Description Fields	Administrative Tools User Manager Open user account Fill in **Full Name** box Fill in **Description** Box	Blank	
Home Directory	Administrative Tools User Manager Open user account Click **Profile** button Home Directory Local Path Connect Drive to Server	Blank	Limit each user's home directory (10 MB is a common size). Windows NT does not enforce quotas, but there are third-party products that do.
Password Maximum Age	Administrative Tools User Manager Policies Account Policy Maximum Password Age	42 days	

Windows NT security settings.   *(continued)*

Item	Syntax	Windows NT default	Comments
Password Minimum Age	Administrative Tools User Manager Policies Account Policy Minimum Password Age	14 days	This prevents users from changing passwords too often—not a big deal but a practice that increases the chance of lost or forgotten passwords.
Password Minimum Length	Administrative Tools User Manager Policies Account Policy Minimum Password Length	Permit Blank Password	
Password Maximum Length	None	14 characters	Consider setting a limit and enforcing it with a policy.
Password Uniqueness	Administrative Tools User Manager Policies Account Policy Password Uniqueness	Do Not Keep Password History	You can configure this to increase the number of previous passwords that are invalid.

Windows NT security settings.   *(continued)*

Item	Syntax	Windows NT default	Comments
After Hours Disconnect	Option 1: WinExit (in the Windows NT Resource Kit) allows you to create an auto logoff screen saver for Windows NT Server Option 2: User Manager, Account Policy, can be set to disconnect remote users from server when logon hours expire. Define Logon Hours under User Manager, Logon Hours. Option 3: Rather than disconnect users, use a screen saver password for protection.	Don't disconnect	Evaluate assets and infrastructure, then configure to meet an appropriate level of security.
Built-in Accounts: Guest	Administrative Tools User Manager Open Guest Account X Account Disabled	No password, account disabled	Disable and rename Guest; assign password.
Built-in Accounts: Administrator	Administrative Tools User Manager Open Administrator Reset Password Close User dropdown Rename Account	Password depends on installation configuration, account enabled.	Reset Administrator password and store settings in a secure location.

Windows NT security settings.   *(continued)*

Item	Syntax	Windows NT default	Comments
Change Password at Next Logon	Administrative Tools. User Manager Open User Account X User must change password at Next Logon	Selected	
User Cannot Change Password	Administrative Tools User Manager Open User Account X User Cannot Change Password	Not selected (except Guest account)	
Password Never Expires	Administrative Tools User Manager Open User Account X User must change password at Next Logon	Not selected	Good idea: don't select this. The longer passwords stay current, the longer they are subject to discovery and misuse.
Account Disabled	Administrative Tools User Manager Open User Account X Account Disabled	Not selected	You can select this for the Guest Account; and consider it case-by-case for others. It is good practice to require all users to be authenticated (using their logon accounts) to gain access to a server's resources.

Windows NT security settings. *(continued)*

Item	Syntax	Windows NT default	Comments
Backup Strategy	Windows NT Server has a built-in backup utility. Administrative Tools Backup Configure Backup Options	Use internal backup	Create a strategy based on your network infrastructure, your assets, work schedule, etc. Store backup tapes in a secure location—offsite if that is feasible.
Disable Run on File Menu	User Profile Editor Define **Permitted to Use** profile X Disable run on File Menu	Not selected	Select this if you want to limit user access to software.
Disable Saved Settings Menu Item and Never Save Settings	User Profile Editor Define **Permitted to Use** profile X Disable saved settings menu item and never save settings	Not selected	Users and administrators can customize workstation and server desktops to meet their needs.
Show Common Program Groups	User Profile Editor Define **Permitted to Use** profile X Show Common Program Groups	Selected	This displays common program groups to all administrators.

Windows NT security settings.   *(continued)*

Item	Syntax	Windows NT default	Comments
Logon Scripts	Created as batch files, defined: Administrative Tools User Manager Open User Account Logon Script Name	No default script	Windows 95 and NT allow auto connection to drives for remote users; you may want to limit the use of logon scripts to home directories, printers, and e-mail databases.
Groups: Local	Windows NT Server has a series of default Local and Global Groups found in: Administrative Tools User Manager Groups	NT has the following built-in groups: *Local:* Account Operators: Default is **No Members** Administrators: Members = **Administrator** Backup Operators: **No Members** Guests: Members = **Domain Guests** Print Operators: **No Members** Replicator: **No Members** Server Operators: **No Members** Users: Members = **Domain Users** *Global:* Domain Admins: **Administrator** Domain Guests: **Guest** Domain Users: **All Domain Users**	Some possibilities: Assign administrators to the Global Admins group Add the Global Admins group to the Local Administrator's group Add Users to security groups based on required privileges Server Operators = All Server Administrators Print Operators = All Print Queue. Managers Backup Operators = Users who need rights to backup and restore files Add users to internal Local groups based on project requirements, and grant groups access to the appropriate shares. Standard naming of these groups can consist of: Application Name; Project Name; Department Name.

Windows NT security settings.   *(continued)*

Item	Syntax	Windows NT default	Comments
Groups: Global	Found in User Manager Console and identified by Users with Globe Icon.	Global Domain Admins: **Administrator** Domain Guests: **Guest** Domain Users: **All Domain Users**	Consider assigning users to Global groups and adding these groups to the proper Local groups to create the proper access. Local Groups contain: Local Users and Global Groups. Global Groups contain users and other Global Groups (refer to the *Windows NT Server Administrative Guide* for details).
File/Directory Permissions	Procedure to create: File Manager Highlight directory to apply permissions Locate **Permissions** key on Toolbar Define required file or directory permissions	Full control	Use NTFS: it is the only file system on Windows NT with complete security enabled.
Directories	Procedure to create: File Manager Highlight Directory to apply permissions Locate **Permissions** key on Toolbar Define required file or directory permissions	Full control	Use NTFS: it is the only file system on Windows NT with complete security enabled.

Windows NT security settings.   *(continued)*

Item	Syntax	Windows NT default	Comments
Shared Files/Directories Across the Network	Procedure to share directories: File Manager Highlight directory to share Locate **Sharing** icon on toolbar (open hand holding a folder) Identify share name and permissions	User shares are created by administrators	Use a standard sharing scheme for each new server. Typical shares on each server can include: Public Users Apps Home
Printers	Created by installing proper drivers on Windows NT Server. Procedure: Open Main Open Print Manager Click Printer dropdown Connect or Create a Printer X Share Printer on the Network Define share name and location	Not shared; can be created only by Administrator.	Share printers and define a security scheme based on the information that will be printed, its level of confidentiality, and the physical security surrounding the printer.
File Structures: FAT	Created during installation	No default file structure	Use NTFS. Use FAT only when necessary for special cases/needs. Syntax to convert FAT to NTFS: Convert {Drive} /FS:NTFS

Windows NT security settings.   *(continued)*

Item	Syntax	Windows NT default	Comments
Replication	Open Administrative Tools Open Server Manager Open Server to configure replication Click **Replication** button Define Server as an Export and/or Import Server. Click OK The Replication Service should now start properly. Refer to *Windows NT Server Admin Guide* for complete details.	Not enabled	Enable where appropriate (for use with logon scripts, etc.). Logon scripting is required when SMS is implemented.
Legal Notice	Use C2 tool in Windows NT 3.51 Resource Kit to enable. Procedure: Install 3.51 resource kit Open C2 Configuration Manager Open Display Logon Message Deselect **Do not Display Logon Message** Add caption and message text	Not enabled	Enable with appropriate message, to protect the system from tampering or malicious activities.

Windows NT security settings.   *(continued)*

Item	Syntax	Windows NT default	Comments
Audit Policy	Use both File Manager and User Manager to audit appropriate events. Syntax:	Not enabled	Consider checking for security violations by auditing for logon failures. Review the logs during normal maintenance.
	Open User Manager		
	Open Policies dropdown		
	Open Audit		
	Define appropriate events		
	For File Manager:		
	Open File Manager		
	Highlight file(s) or directory to audit		
	Open Security dropdown		
	Open Auditing		
	Define appropriate events and directories to audit		
File and Directory Auditing	Open File Manager	Not enabled	Enable where appropriate. Example: audit read and write failures and successes to confidential files.
	Highlight file(s) or directory to audit		
	Open Security dropdown		
	Open Auditing		
	Define appropriate events and directories to audit		

Windows NT security settings.   *(continued)*

Item	Syntax	Windows NT default	Comments
Printers	Use Print Manager to enable auditing as needed. Syntax: Open Main Open Print Manager Highlight Printer Open Security dropdown Open Auditing Define proper audit activities (take ownership, delete, full control etc.)	Not enabled	Auditing of printers may make sense in sensitive areas or to track the use of expensive devices.
Remote Access Server			RAS strategy can include: Controlling RAS access Incorporating both the TCP/IP and IPX protocols Defining connection types (28.8 Kbs, ISDN etc.) Defining user access and security Assigning RAS permissions to users

Windows NT security settings. *(continued)*

Item	Syntax	Windows NT default	Comments
Sizing Security Logs	Open Administrative Tools Open Event Viewer Open Log dropdown Open Log Settings Fill in Overwrite Events	Enabled, don't overwrite events as needed.	Implement procedures to make sure logs are checked before being overwritten. Set initial log size to 4096.
Network Alerts	Generic alerts are sent to computer names. Syntax: Administrative Tools Open Server Manager Open server to configure (find in list and double-click) Click on **Alerts** button Add computer names to send alerts to.	Not enabled	Consider enabling this to send generic alerts to all administrators. The messenger service must be running on Windows 95 and NT machines before they can receive alerts.

Windows NT security settings.   *(continued)*

Item	Syntax	Windows NT default	Comments
Log on Locally (Log on from the Systems Keyboard)	Advanced Policy syntax: Open Administrative Tools Open User Manager Open Policies dropdown Open User Rights X **Show Advanced Rights** Open Right dropdown (click Down arrow on end) Highlight **Logon Locally** Add or remove rights to users and groups	Default: Administrators, Backup Operators, Everyone, Guests, Power Users, and Users	Restrict logon access to Server Console to groups with need to do so, such as Administrators, Backup Operators, Server Operators, etc.

Windows NT security settings.   *(continued)*

Item	Syntax	Windows NT default	Comments
Shut Down the System	Advanced Policy syntax: Open Administrative Tools Open User Manager Open Policies dropdown Open User Rights X **Show Advanced Rights** Open Right dropdown (click Down arrow on end) Highlight **Shut Down the System** Add or remove rights to users and groups	Rights given to Administrators, Backup Operators, Account Operators, Print Operators, Server Operators	Restrict system shutdown capability to groups with need to do so, such as Administrators, Backup Operators, Server Operators, etc.

Windows NT security settings.   *(continued)*

Item	Syntax	Windows NT default	Comments
Access this Computer from the Network (Allows a User to Connect over a Network to the Computer)	Advanced Policy syntax: Open Administrative Tools Open User Manager Open Policies dropdown Open User Rights **X Show Advanced Rights** Open Right dropdown (Click Down arrow on end) Highlight **Access This Computer from the Network** Add or remove rights to users and groups	Initially assigned to Administrators and Everyone	This option allows them to *connect only*. Grant additional share and file rights to enhance, limit, or deny a user's access request.
Back Up Files and Directories	Advanced Policy syntax: Open Administrative Tools Open User Manager Open Policies dropdown Open User Rights **X Show Advanced Rights** Open Right dropdown (click Down arrow on end) Highlight **Backup Files and Directories** Add or remove rights to users and groups	Assigned to Administrators, Backup Operators and Server Operators	

Windows NT security settings.   *(continued)*

Item	Syntax	Windows NT default	Comments
Change the System Time	Advanced Policy syntax: Open Administrative Tools Open User Manager Open Policies dropdown Open User Rights **X Show Advanced Rights** Open Right dropdown (click Down arrow on end) Highlight **Change the System Time** Add or remove rights to users and groups	Administrators and Server Operators	Consider creating a time server with which all servers and workstations can sync their time. See the *Windows NT 3.51 Resource Kit.*
Create a PageFile	Advanced Policy syntax: Open Administrative Tools Open User Manager Open Policies dropdown Open User Rights **X Show Advanced Rights** Open Right dropdown (click Down arrow on end) Highlight **Create a Pagefile** Add or remove rights to users and groups	Assigned to Administrators	

Windows NT security settings.   *(continued)*

Item	Syntax	Windows NT default	Comments
Force a Shutdown from a Remote Machine	Advanced Policy syntax: Open Administrative Tools Open User Manager Open Policies dropdown Open User Rights X Show Advanced Rights Open Right dropdown (click Down arrow on end) Highlight **Force a Shutdown from a Remote Machine** Add or remove rights to users and groups	Assigned to Administrators and Server Operators	Required for remote server reboots. Server and Database Admin staffs require this right.
Increase Scheduling Priority (Boost Execution Priority of a Process)	Advanced Policy syntax: Open Administrative Tools Open User Manager Open Policies dropdown Open User Rights X **Show Advanced Rights** Open Right dropdown (click Down arrow on end) Highlight **Increase Scheduling Priority** Add or remove rights to users and groups	Assigned to Administrators	

Windows NT security settings.   *(continued)*

Item	Syntax	Windows NT default	Comments
Load and Unload Device Drivers	Advanced Policy syntax: Open Administrative Tools Open User Manager Open Policies dropdown Open User Rights X **Show Advanced Rights** Open Right dropdown (click Down arrow on end) Highlight **Load and Unload Device Drivers** Add or remove rights to users and groups	Assigned to Administrators	
Manage Auditing and Security Logs	Advanced Policy syntax: Open Administrative Tools Open User Manager Open Policies dropdown Open User Rights X **Show Advanced Rights** Open Right dropdown (click Down arrow on end) Highlight **Manage Auditing and Security Logs** Add or remove rights to users and groups	Assigned to Administrators	As the network grows, you may want to create other groups (such as Audit Admin) to sub-divide administrative tasks.

Windows NT security settings.   *(continued)*

Item	Syntax	Windows NT default	Comments
Modify Firmware Environment Values	Advanced Policy syntax: Open Administrative Tools Open User Manager Open Policies dropdown Open User Rights X **Show Advanced Rights** Open Right dropdown (click Down arrow on end) Highlight **Modify Firmware Environment Values** Add or remove rights to users and groups	Assigned to Administrators	

Windows NT security settings.   *(continued)*

Item	Syntax	Windows NT default	Comments
Restore Files and Directories	Advanced Policy syntax: Open Administrative Tools Open User Manager Open Policies dropdown Open User Rights X **Show Advanced Rights** Open Right dropdown (click Down arrow on end) Highlight **Restore Files and Directories** Add or remove rights to users and groups	Assigned to Administrators, Backup Operators, and Server Operators	
Take Ownership of Files or Other Objects (Files, Directories, Printers and Other Objects on the System)	Advanced Policy syntax: Open Administrative Tools Open User Manager Open Policies dropdown Open User Rights X **Show Advanced Rights** Open Right dropdown (click Down arrow on end) Highlight **Take Ownership of Files or Other Objects** Add or remove rights to users and groups	Assigned to Administrators	Only Administrators should be able to take ownership of a user's files.

Windows NT security settings.   *(continued)*

Item	Syntax	Windows NT default	Comments
Virus Protection		None	Develop a plan for virus protection and then select an appropriate product.
Ability to Submit Jobs to the AT Scheduling Command	Defined in the registry: HKEY_LOCAL_MACHINE \CurrentControlSet\Control \Lsa Name: Submit Control Add right	Initially assigned to Administrators only	Server Operators can be given this right by adding an entry into the registry. (Outlined in the *Windows NT 3.51 Resource Kit* addendum)
Don't Allow Windows NT to Display the Username of the Last Person to Logon.	Open Resource Kit Open C2 Security Config Open **Last Username** display X **Hide the Last Username to Log On**	Not enabled	Although this may seem to be a security hole, it's easier for users if all they have to type in during logon is their passwords.

Windows NT security settings.   *(continued)*

Item	Syntax	Windows NT default	Comments
Allow Boot from Floppy and Secure Floppy Drive during Operating Hours	1) Enabled in BIOS ROMs of server hardware. Refer to server hardware configuration 2) Use FLOPLOCK.EXE from *Windows NT Resource Kit* to restrict access to administrators. Follow the procedure to configure the floplock service.	Not enabled	If you do not lock server floppy drives, then the screen saver, NCC security, and admin passwords should protect against intrusion.
Announce Presence		Default is for both workstations and servers to announce their presence to their local browse master for peer-to-peer and server-based networking.	
Limit the Duration of Passwords Granted to Third Parties or Consultants with an Expiration Flag.	Set in the Admin tools. Syntax: Open Administrative Tools Open User Manager Create or open account Click **Account** button Set **Account Expires** to 90 days from creation date	Not enabled	Prevents inadvertent persistence of permissions.

Windows NT security settings.   *(continued)*

Item	Syntax	Windows NT default	Comments
Print Out All Security Equivalences for Each User or Group (User, Group and Access Rights)	1) Perms: Used to display a user's permissions (utility in resource kit) 2) Net User: used to display a list of all users. Use with Perms to get a listing of permissions by user.	Not enabled	
All Severs Require an Emergency Repair Diskette	Create an emergency repair diskette during installation and establish a procedure to keep this disk current. Syntax: Administrative Tools Disk Administrator Partition dropdown Configuration **Save to Floppy Disk**	At installation time each server should by default create an emergency repair diskette.	Institute administrative procedures to make sure emergency repair disks are created and kept current.
Server Recovery of Deleted Files	Not Supported, C2 violation	Not Supported	The ability to recover deleted files is considered a breach under C2 security

Windows NT security settings.   *(continued)*

Item	Syntax	Windows NT default	Comments
Automatic Screen Saver Logoff of Windows NT Servers	WinExit, included in the *Windows NT Resource Kit*, allows you to create an auto ogoff screen saver for Windows NT Server	Not enabled	
Automatic creation of hidden shares for each server volume (c$ for croot, d$ for droot etc.)	Created by default. Syntax to check all server shares: Open Administrative Tools Open Server Manager Click **Shares** button Hidden Shares are identified by c$, d$ etc.	Enabled. Administrators have access to these shares.	Control these shares so that only administrators have access rights.
Default System File and Directory permissions c:\NTDetect	Use File Manager to set file permissions. Syntax: Open Main Open File Manager Point to the proper drive by selecting it on the toolbar Highlight the file to check or set permissions on. Click on the key on the toolbar or open the Security dropdown and highlight **Permissions** Set the proper permissions	Default: Everyone: Full control Attributes: Read Only, System	

Windows NT security settings.   *(continued)*

Item	Syntax	Windows NT default	Comments
Default System File and Directory Permissions c:\NTLDR	Use File Manager to set file permissions. Syntax: Open Main Open File Manager Point to the proper drive by selecting it on the toolbar Highlight the file to check or set permissions on Click on the key on the toolbar or open the Security dropdown and highlight **Permissions** Set the proper permissions	Default: Everyone: Full control Attributes: Read Only, System	
Default System File and Directory permissions c:\Boot.ini	Use File Manager to set file permissions. Syntax: Open Main Open File Manager Point to the proper drive by selecting it on the toolbar Highlight the file to check or set permissions on Click on the key on the toolbar or open the Security dropdown and highlight **Permissions** Set the proper permissions	Default: Everyone: Full control Attributes: Read Only, System	

Windows NT security settings. *(continued)*

Item	Syntax	Windows NT default	Comments
Default System File and Directory Permissions c:\autoexec.bat	Use File Manager to set file permissions. Syntax: Open Main Open File Manager Point to the proper drive by selecting it on the toolbar Highlight the file to check or set permissions on Click on the key on the toolbar or open the Security dropdown and highlight **Permissions** Set the proper permissions	Default: Everyone: Full control Attributes: None	
Default System File and Directory Permissions c:\config.sys	Use File Manager to set file permissions. Syntax: Open Main Open File Manager Point to the proper drive by selecting it on the toolbar Highlight the file to check or set permissions on Click on the key on the toolbar or open the Security dropdown and highlight **Permissions** Set the proper permissions	Default: Everyone: Full control Attributes: None	

Windows NT security settings.   *(continued)*

Item	Syntax	Windows NT default	Comments
Protecting the Registry Access to Regedt32	Use File Manager to set file permissions. Syntax: Open Main Open File Manager Point to the proper drive by selecting it on the toolbar Highlight the REGEDT32.EXE file located in the c:\winnt35\system32 directory Click on the key on the toolbar or open the Security dropdown and highlight permissions Set the proper permissions	Default: Everyone	Registry changes can severely affect the system. Restrict registry access rights to Administrators.
Protecting the Registry HkeyLocalMachine	Open Program Manager Open File dropdown Open Run Type **regedt32** in list Open HKEY_LOCAL_MACHINE Highlight Top Folder HKEY_LOCAL_MACHINE Open Security dropdown Open Permissions	Default: Administrators: Full control System: Full control Everyone: Read	Registry changes can severely affect the system. Restrict registry access rights to Administrators.

Windows NT security settings.   *(continued)*

Item	Syntax	Windows NT default	Comments
Protecting the Registry HKEY_LOCAL_MACHINE \Clone	Open Program Manager Open File dropdown Open Run Type **regedt32** in list Open HKEY_LOCAL_MACHINE Highlight Top Folder HKEY_LOCAL_MACHINE Open Clone folder Open Security dropdown Open Permissions	Default: Administrators: Full control System: Full control Everyone: Read	Registry changes can severely affect the system. Restrict registry access rights to Administrators.
Protecting the Registry HKEY_LOCAL_MACHINE \Hardware	Open Program Manager Open File dropdown Open Run Type **regedt32** in list Open HKEY_LOCAL_MACHINE Highlight Top Folder HKEY_LOCAL_MACHINE Open Hardware folder Open Security dropdown Open Permissions	Default: Administrators: Full control System: Full control Everyone: Read	Registry changes can severely affect the system. Restrict registry access rights to Administrators.

Windows NT security settings.   *(continued)*

Item	Syntax	Windows NT default	Comments
Protecting the Registry HKEY_LOCAL_MACHINE \SAM	Open Program Manager Open File dropdown Open Run Type **regedt32** in list Open HKEY_LOCAL_MACHINE Highlight top folder HKEY_LOCAL_MACHINE Open SAM Folder Open Security dropdown Open Permissions	Default: Administrators: Full control System: Full control Everyone: Read	Registry changes can severely affect the system. Restrict registry access rights to Administrators.
Protecting the Registry HKEY_LOCAL_MACHINE \SAM\SAM	Open Program Manager Open File dropdown Open Run Type **regedt32** in list Open HKEY_LOCAL_MACHINE Highlight top folder HKEY_LOCAL_MACHINE Open SAM\SAM folder Open Security dropdown Open Permissions	Default: Administrators: Special access (Write DAC, Read) System: Full control	Registry changes can severely affect the system. Restrict registry access rights to Administrators.

Windows NT security settings.   *(continued)*

Item	Syntax	Windows NT default	Comments
Protecting the Registry HKEY_LOCAL_MACHINE \Security	Open Program Manager Open File dropdown Open Run Type **regedt32** in list Open HKEY_LOCAL_MACHINE Highlight top folder HKEY_LOCAL_MACHINE Highlight Security folder Open Security dropdown Open Permissions	Default: Administrators: Special Access (Write DAC, Read) System: Full control	Registry changes can severely affect the system. Restrict registry access rights to Administrators.
Protecting the Registry HKEY_LOCAL_MACHINE \Software	Open Program Manager Open File dropdown Open Run Type **regedt32** in list Open HKEY_LOCAL_MACHINE Highlight top folder HKEY_LOCAL_MACHINE Open Software folder Open Security dropdown Open Permissions	Default: Administrators: Full control System: Full control Everyone: Read	Registry changes can severely affect the system. Restrict registry access rights to Administrators.

Windows NT security settings.   *(continued)*

Item	Syntax	Windows NT default	Comments
Protecting the Registry HKEY_LOCAL_MACHINE \System	Open Program Manager Open File dropdown Open Run Type **regedt32** in list Open HKEY_LOCAL_MACHINE Highlight top folder HKEY_LOCAL_MACHINE Open System folder Open Security dropdown Open Permissions	Default: Administrators: Full control System: Full control Everyone: Read	Registry changes can severely affect the system. Restrict registry access rights to Administrators.
Protecting the Registry HKEY_CURRENT_USER	Open Program Manager Open File dropdown Open Run Type **regedt32** in list Open HKEY_CURRENT_USER Highlight top folder HKEY_CURRENT_USER Open Security dropdown Open Permissions	Default (All Keys) Administrator: Full control Administrators: Full control System: Full control	Registry changes can severely affect the system. Restrict registry access rights to Administrators.

Windows NT security settings.   *(continued)*

Item	Syntax	Windows NT default	Comments
Protecting the Registry HKEY_CLASSES_ROOT	Open Program Manager Open File dropdown Open Run Type **regedt32** in list Open HKEY_CLASSES_ROOT Highlight top folder HKEY_CLASSES_ROOT Open Security dropdown Open Permissions	Default: Administrators: Full control System: Full control Everyone: Special access (Query and Set Value, Create Keys, Enumerate Subkeys, Notify, Delete, and Read control) Creator Owner: Full control	Registry changes can severely affect the system. Restrict registry access rights to Administrators.
Protecting the Registry HKEY_USERS	Open Program Manager Open File dropdown Open Run Type **regedt32** in list Open HKEY_USERS Highlight top folder HKEY_USERS Open Security dropdown Open Permissions	Default: Administrators: Full control System: Full control Everyone: Read	Registry changes can severely affect the system. Restrict registry access rights to Administrators.

Windows NT security settings.   *(continued)*

Item	Syntax	Windows NT default	Comments
Protecting the Registry HKEY_USERS /(Security Identifier (SID #))	Open Program Manager Open File dropdown Open Run Type **regedt32** in list Open HKEY_USERS Highlight top folder HKEY_USERS Open SID # Subkey Open Security dropdown Open Permissions	Default (All Keys) Administrator: Full control Administrators: Full control System: Full control	Registry changes can severely affect the system. Restrict registry access rights to Administrators.
Protecting the Registry Auditing	Open Program Manager Open File dropdown Open Run Type **regedt32** in list Open Hive or Subkey to Audit Open Security dropdown Open Auditing Set Proper events to audit	Default: Not enabled	Enable registry auditing in special cases, such as when you suspect there has been a break-in.

Windows NT security settings.   *(continued)*

Item	Syntax	Windows NT default	Comments
Default System File and Directory Permissions \Winnt35	Use File Manager to set directory permissions. Syntax: Open Main Open File Manager Point to the proper drive by selecting it on the toolbar Highlight the directory to check or set permissions on. Click on the key on the toolbar or open the Security dropdown and highlight **Permissions** Set the proper permissions	Default: Everyone: Full control	Common settings: Administrators: Full control Creator owner: Full control Everyone: Read System: Full control
Default System File and Directory Permissions \Winnt35\ System	Use File Manager to set directory permissions. Syntax: Open Main Open File Manager Point to the proper drive by selecting it on the toolbar Highlight the directory to check or set permissions on Click on the key on the toolbar or open the Security dropdown and highlight **Permissions** Set the proper permissions	Default: Everyone: Full control	Common settings: Administrators: Full control Creator owner: Full control Everyone: Read System: Full control

Windows NT security settings.   *(continued)*

Item	Syntax	Windows NT default	Comments
Default System File and Directory permissions \Winnt35 System32	Use File Manager to set directory permissions. Syntax: Open Main Open File Manager Point to the proper drive by selecting it on the toolbar Highlight the directory to check or set permissions on Click on the key on the toolbar or open the Security dropdown and highlight **Permissions** Set the proper permissions	Default: Everyone: Full control	Common settings: Administrators: Full control Creator owner: Full control Everyone: Read System: Full control
Default System File and Directory Permissions \Winnt35\ System32\ Config	Use File Manager to set directory permissions. Syntax: Open Main Open File Manager Point to the proper drive by selecting it on the toolbar Highlight the directory to check or set permissions on Click on the key on the toolbar or open the Security dropdown and highlight **Permissions** Set the proper permissions	Default: Everyone: Full control	Common settings: Administrators: Full control Creator owner: Full control Everyone: List System: Full control

Windows NT security settings.   *(continued)*

Item	Syntax	Windows NT default	Comments
Default System File and Directory permissions \Winnt35\ System32\ Drivers	Use File Manager to set directory permissions. Syntax: Open Main Open File Manager Point to the proper drive by selecting it on the toolbar Highlight the directory to check or set permissions on Click on the key on the toolbar or open the Security dropdown and highlight **Permissions** Set the proper permissions	Default: Everyone: Full control	Common settings: Administrators: Full control Creator owner: Full control Everyone: Read System: Full control
Default System File and Directory Permissions \Winnt35\ System32\ Spool	Use File Manager to set directory permissions. Syntax: Open Main Open File Manager Point to the proper drive by selecting it on the toolbar Highlight the directory to check or set permissions on Click on the key on the toolbar or open the Security dropdown and highlight **Permissions** Set the proper permissions	Default: Everyone: Full control	Common settings: Administrators: Full control Creator owner: Full control Everyone: Read Server Operators: Change System: Full control

Windows NT security settings.   *(continued)*

Item	Syntax	Windows NT default	Comments
Default System File and Directory Permissions \Winnt35\ repair	Use File Manager to set directory permissions. Syntax: Open Main Open File Manager Point to the proper drive by selecting it on the toolbar Highlight the directory to check or set permissions on Click on the key on the toolbar or open the Security dropdown and highlight **Permissions** Set the proper permissions	Default: Everyone: Full control	Common settings: Administrators: Full control

More Information

- Q150687, Title: Group Policies Not Applied On Windows NT Domain.
- White paper: "Guide to Microsoft Windows NT 4.0 Profiles and Policies"
- White paper: "Creating Certificate Hierarchies with MS Certificate Server Version 1.0" by Rick Johnson, Program Manager, Windows NT Distributed Systems
- *Windows NT Server Concepts and Planning Guide.*
- Appendix D, "Security In a Software Development Environment," in the Version 3.51 Update to the *Microsoft Windows NT Resource Kit Version 3.5 Update*
- *Windows NT 3.5 Resource Guide*

C H A P T E R   6

Designing and Planning External Security at Bob's Bank

By Tom Dodds, Eric Miyadi, and Tom Fuchs, MCS—Southern California

Security must be a serious component of any design discussion, a need that this chapter addresses by outlining the tasks required to create a security policy that ensures the reliability, availability, and supportability of all systems and data on a Windows NT external network—the part of the network that is unsecured or exposed to the Internet. It is a big topic because developing security is a big job. Like all big jobs, it begins with a single task: creating a general security policy document for the outside network.

In Focus

Enterprise
Bob's Bank is a large financial organization with branch offices throughout the United States.

Network
Windows NT 4.0 operating system. Workstations running Windows NT, Window 95, and Window 98, Microsoft Internet Information Server (IIS), and FrontPage.

Challenge
Plan and configure a large Windows NT network accessible by business partners over Web servers. Provide the needed accessibility while also providing adequate safeguards for network and resource protection.

Solution
Settings (in the registry and elsewhere) adapted the Windows NT servers, IIS, the Windows NT Service Pack 3 hotfixes, and the FrontPage extensions to provide the required protection. These and other modifications are described.

What You'll Find In This Chapter

- The importance of a general security policy and how to create one.

- A discussion of the external network's various facets.

- How to audit the system to ensure that it has not been compromised.

- Detailed description of registry settings and other modifications that can be used to tune access to and security for the external network.

- Examples of configuration options.

Warning This chapter makes recommendations for tuning the Windows NT registry using the Registry Editor. Using the Registry Editor incorrectly can cause serious, system-wide problems that require you to reinstall Windows NT. Microsoft cannot guarantee that any problems resulting from the use of Registry Editor can be solved. Use this tool at your own risk.

Corporate Security Position

Maintaining a secure site is crucial. You must put the proper security policies, procedures, and technologies in place to protect your organization from inadvertent or intentional damage or loss of data.

Perhaps your enterprise is not attractive to hackers and other intruders and thus does not require much in the way of security. This may or may not be true: a recent survey of over 560 companies by the Computer Security Institute (CSI) and the FBI International Computer Crime Squad in San Francisco showed that 75% of the respondents reported financial losses due to security breaches ranging from financial fraud, theft of proprietary information, and sabotage on the high end to computer viruses and laptop theft on the low end. Total estimated losses: $100,119,555. The probability of mischief is high enough that no one can afford to feel immune.

What are you Trying to Secure?

First, you need to know what you are trying to protect. For example, a firewall consists of a number of components and systems between two networks and it is generally implemented to limit access to information from users inside and outside the enterprise. Fair enough, but before this means anything practical to your planners, you need to define *information*. Which information should be limited to internal users? Is there information outside your organization that shouldn't be accessed by users inside? Is there information that is used by one group but not required by others? Should all information be limited based on need to know? You have to define security policies for your enterprise. Only then can you develop the proper testing and auditing facilities that can keep your network secure.

What Level?

The two extremes of enterprise security:

- **Information that is not allowed should not be accessed.** This leaves it to the Information Technology (IT) group to determine who gets to access what information. This is a restrictive arrangement, but a controllable one—so "tight" that it usually discovers security holes or issues with products that require additional effort.

- **Information that is not disallowed can be accessed.** This leaves users primarily responsible for what information they access or are allowed to access. Users prefer this arrangement, but it can be troublesome from a security standpoint—it makes it almost impossible to control data security.

In reality, your company will probably have to adopt a security policy that straddles these extremes—a policy that controls yet promotes data access so that users can get to the information they need.

Assigning permissions is not as simple as it should be. You need a thorough understanding of how your company operates (how it really operates, not just how it is supposed to operate) before you can decide which group or individual needs access to which data. This is complicated when the corporate net is connected to the Internet: should everyone have Internet access, or should it be restricted to those who need the Internet to perform their jobs? Notice that this effort does not actually restrict access: it is simply trying to find out in what ways access should be restricted. Establishing permissions is another task entirely.

Internet-based services such as e-mail bring security risks (for one thing, they facilitate the misuse of information from inside and outside your company) along with inherit design weaknesses if you do not plan and implement them correctly.

Creating a Security Policy

In today's distributed, client-server environment, corporate data is stored on server platforms, where it is expected to be at once available *and* secure. The degree to which these mutually antagonistic goals are achieved is often a measure of the success and viability of your enterprise. This section outlines a general security policy that applies to access, management, and hosting within the network environment. A policy has to address areas of security such as:

- Physical and location security
- Creating a security policy document
- Reacting to a security exposure

The security policy includes guidelines and standards that try to eliminate the common kinds of attacks that threaten most companies. The emphasis is on *try*. The policy attempts to derive and define a workable solution that provides an acceptable level of security. A thorough policy specifies:

- What is acceptable Web conduct and what isn't
- Who has access to the site and who authorizes the access
- Who is responsible for security upgrades, backups, and maintenance
- What kinds of material is allowed on Web server pages
- What needs to be protected on the site and from whom
- How software and pages are tested and evaluated before being installed in production

- How complaints and requests about the server and page content will be handled
- How security incidents will be responded to
- Who is authorized to speak for the organization to members of the press, law enforcement, and other entities in the event of questions or an incident
- Who is contacted in case of an emergency

Physical Security

Physical security means the steps taken to protect the actual machines used to store and process sensitive and/or valuable data. Protecting against accidental or deliberate access (including changes to the way the computer is set up) should not prevent users from doing their work nor should it erect unrealistic or inconvenient barriers to user resources.

Standard Security

For standard security, the computer system must be protected, as any valuable equipment would be. Generally, this involves housing the computer in a building that is locked and out-of-bounds to unauthorized users.

Backups

Regular backups protect data from all sorts of hazards: hardware failures, honest mistakes, viruses, and malicious mischief. The Windows NT Backup utility is described in Chapter 6, "Backing Up and Restoring Network Files" in *Microsoft Windows NT Server Concepts and Planning*. There are also third-party backup solutions.

Because files must be *read* to be backed up, and *written* to be restored, backup privileges should be limited to administrators and backup operators—people who can be trusted with read and write access to all files.

Auditing

Often you don't know about a breach of security until you find it, usually by auditing the network. Effective auditing can also uncover actions that pose a security risk and identify the user accounts from which the actions were taken. Establishing an audit policy requires that you balance the auditing cost (in disk space and CPU cycles) against its advantages. System setup and capacity may dictate how many functions you can audit realistically. At the very least you should audit failed log on attempts, attempts to access sensitive data, and changes to security settings.

High-Level Security

Depending on the level of security required, you can implement additional security measures to create a high-security environment. First you need to identify which computers, if any, contain sensitive data at high risk for theft or intentional violation and disruption. Security for these machines, or their subnet, can be augmented with more stringent security features than those used for the rest of network. You can begin by examining the network's physical links.

Network Level Security

When you put a computer on a network, you add an access route to the computer that should be secured against some level of intrusion—from casual to intentional. User validation and protections on files and other objects are sufficient for standard-level security, but high-level security demands that you secure the physical network.

The main risk is unauthorized network taps. If your network is set up completely within a secure building (a rarity) the risk of unauthorized taps is minimized or eliminated. If the network is not completely within direct physical control, you have to decide on a level of realistic protection and institute it, beginning with physical security. If, for instance, cabling passes through unsecured areas, consider using optical fiber links rather than twisted pair—it is much harder to tap a fiber and siphon off data.

A second, and more common, risk these days is Internet access. The security issue here cuts both ways because this sort of connection provides access *to* and *from* the Internet community. In essence, this means that just about everyone in the world with access to a computer has a shot at your system. To get in, however, they have to come through the outside network, and a later section in this chapter explains how to secure this network and lock down its configuration.

Controlling Access

No computer is ever completely secure if people other than the authorized user can sit down and tinker with it. If you cannot physically secure a computer, try to:

- Disable the floppy-based boot if the computer hardware provides the option. If the computer doesn't require a floppy disk drive, remove it.
- Lock the CPU case with a key that is stored away from the computer.
- Use the Windows NT file system (NTFS) on the entire hard disk.
- Remove the network card if the computer does not need network access.

If possible or practical, keep unauthorized users away from computer power and reset switches. The most secure computers (other than those in locked and guarded rooms) give users access to only the keyboard, monitor, mouse, and printer. You can lock up the CPU and removable media drives and allow only authorized personnel to have access to them.

By default, Windows NT allows any program to access files on floppy disks and CDs. A highly secure, multi-user environment allows only the person interactively logged on to access those devices, so interactive users can write sensitive information to these drives confident that no other user or program can see or modify it.

This mode allocates system floppy disks or CDs to a user as part of the interactive log-on process, then frees them automatically for general use or reallocation when that user logs off. Make it a standard practice to remove sensitive data from the floppy or CD-ROM drives before logging off.

Server Types

Here are some examples of real world solutions implemented by Microsoft Consulting Services:

- Centralized, corporate server farm (most complex)
- Centralized departmental server
- Small office server (least complex)

Physical security requirements differ for each case. The centralized, corporate server farm needs the highest level of security because it handles large amounts of strategic business data. If intruders were to destroy, alter, copy, or kidnap this data, the business would suffer financially and probably be subjected to legal action by its clients and investors. In sum, this network requires very high security. All systems need some kind of security, but most do not need this much.

The discussion begins with the most complex environment and then works back to the simpler ones.

Centralized, Corporate Server Farm

Once upon a time, all processing occurred on a central processor configured with "dumb" remote terminals. This seems primitive by current standards but it certainly was easy to secure. Now, distributed computing environments require security from the end-user desktop, through the departmental server, to the central servers.

Recently, network designers have begun consolidating departmental servers that previously were scattered around the enterprise. Consolidation allows designers to use common hardware platforms, combine workloads, and tighten security for servers and data. The growing demand for high performance, data-rich corporate Web sites has also fuelled the need for Web server farms that connect to the Internet. In addition to the standard security precautions required for Internet connectivity, these systems also need to be centralized and physically secured.

In one case handled by MCS, the location for the Web server farm started out as the telephone patch bay. This tiny room was renamed the "server room," but a new name was not enough to provide the expandability, proper security or ventilation required over time by a Webfarm. The company ended up relocating the farm to an appropriate environment—a costly correction. If you are going to create a "server" room, evaluate your plan by the suggestions and criteria below. Some seem to be general, not security, concerns, but all of them affect the security of the proposed site:

- Build or renovate the room to house the current equipment and provide enough extra space to expand the installation to at least double initial capacity. Make sure it has enough room to maintain, install, relocate, and remove equipment easily.

- Locate the room in the center of the building, or at least in a location that does not use an exterior wall.

- Locate the room in the basement or on one of the upper floors of the building, but not in places that inhibit delivery and removal of equipment.

- Locate the room close to the building cabling ducts that will carry the networking cables to other parts of the building. Ensure that this core "backbone" facility is also secured and that all access points are monitored by the security control room.

- Provide a large enough room to allow the air-conditioning plant to operate effectively.

- Provide a professional air-conditioning system, capable of maintaining a temperature of between 18 and 20 degrees Celsius and sized to cope with a fully loaded room.

- Provide a false floor to accommodate the cabling for the systems and deep enough to allow easy access and reconfiguration.

- Provide solid walls all around. If there is a false ceiling, then extend the walls above the false ceiling to prevent entry from above.

- Provide a secure, fireproof doorway, wide enough to allow easy delivery and removal of the largest piece of equipment.

- Install a sophisticated alarm system with sensors on all doors and at all access points including the ceiling and the false floor. Include smoke detectors and water detectors as well as movement sensors.

- Plan for a nearby security monitoring room. This room needs to be staffed 24x7 and must monitor all access points and all environmental checkpoints relating to the system.

- Employ a professionally trained and experienced security officer and team. If you use a third-party company to handle security, ensure that its personnel pass through the security clearance checks and that they also sign non-disclosure agreements (NDAs).

- Limit access to the computer room to people who *require* access, then run security checks on them—in-house staff as well as support and maintenance staff—and have them sign NDAs.

- Install an access control system that monitors and logs all access to the computer room. Establish a manual backup system to ensure that access is controlled and monitored during periods when the access system is bypassed for maintenance, machine installation, etc.

- Establish a system that records all details relating to the regular removal and delivery of backup media and equipment.

- Ensure that any communication cabling that exits the computer room is secure. If cabling needs to pass through an unsecured area, use fiber optic cable if possible.

- Install an emergency power supply. This may range from a simple uninterruptible power supply (UPS) unit to a full electrical generator. Ensure that this power system is also installed in a secure, controlled environment that is monitored by the security control room.

- If the air conditioning system requires water, provide two independent water connections.

- Ensure that the air conditioning cooling towers are secured and monitored by the security control room.

- Provide a fire-proof safe to store on-site backup media and other essential documentation and equipment. This can be a separate fireproof room leading into the computer room via a safe door. Install monitors and fire and water sensors in this room as well.

- If possible, construct a "dark site" similar to the production computer room but located some distance from it. You can use this to house a fully configured backup system, or to install a replacement system in the event of a disaster. An alternative to this is to make use of a third-party DRP service. In either case, provide duplicate communication links to the backup site.

- Implement a regular audit process that tests all monitor points, access points and environmental checkpoints as well as testing the manual procedures.

- Run regular disaster response exercises to test the validity of the backup media and documentation as well as to minimize time-to-restore.

- Implement a fully functional change control system.

Centralized Departmental Servers

Smaller systems are usually developed by smaller companies that cannot afford all of the measures above. Nor do they need all of them. The basic needs are to control and monitor server access, and to provide servers with a dedicated, secure location, air conditioning, and an uninterruptible power supply.

In you use a smaller departmental Web server to provide additional services such as application processing or data storage, you need to take more stringent security measures. These sorts of server rooms can be considered scaled-down versions of the central server farm computer room described above and you should consult the master list for ideas on protecting the environment, screening personnel, and limiting access and vulnerability.

Small Office Servers

Smaller office servers connected to the Internet provide Web services but they also expose the system to security dangers inherent in Web access. These require many of the same security measures as described for the centralized server farm, although size, budget, and need may make a complete security setup an unrealistic goal.

Install these smaller Web servers in a secure, monitored environment similar to that described for the centralized server farm, then scale the overall mechanisms and methods down appropriately. Instead of monitoring the site with a dedicated security team, use an office supervisor, Internet service provider, or power user. Secure all communication links and routes.

Establish procedures to ensure that backup media are stored safely (on- and off-site), that all movement of media and equipment is monitored and recorded, that backup procedures and media are tested regularly, and that a disaster recovery plan is tested and in place. If necessary, hire a local support company or hardware vendor to ensure that replacement equipment is available in the event of a disaster.

Creating a Security Policy Document

Once you understand how to physically secure the system, the next step is to establish standards in a thorough security policy. For one thing, it helps you plan security logically; for another, it helps you track performance and procedures; for a third, you may need to have things in writing if you take legal action against someone who breaks into your system. The sample policy in this section is based on an MCS engagement with a large financial institution, Bob's Bank. The document began with two direct statements:

1. Access to external Web services as provided by Bob's Bank and its subsidiaries is for authorized company use only.

2. To provide protection of corporate information as required by the Information Security Policy, appropriate precautions must be taken while engaging in any activity on external Web services (including the Internet) to ensure that corporate information is protected from unauthorized access, modification, destruction, or disclosure.

Server Security

The next section detailed the physical access and data backup procedures for their demilitarized zone (DMZ)—the server location designed to provide the best security. Their plan stated that:

No internal Bob's Bank corporate network can be connected to the external DMZ network without firewall protection. Complete firewall architecture is in place to protect the corporate network from the Internet and no internal network is allowed to circumvent this security by directly attaching or multi-homing a server in the DMZ. In particular:

- Any device placed in the Web DMZ (server, router, sniffer, printer, etc.) that is accessible by non-Bob's Bank personnel must be approved by the Security team before it is placed on the network.

- All DMZ servers must be kept in a secured locked location.

- The floppy drives of all DMZ servers must be disabled, and, if possible, removed.

- Server backups and emergency repair disks must be kept in a secure location away from the server.

- No one who is not an employee of Bob's Bank can be given direct access to the DMZ from an internal or external location without authorization from the Security team. All such access must take place through the firewall unless explicitly approved by Security team management.

Classes of Information Allowed on External Web Services

The document next focused on handling information and connections in the DMZ. In particular, the account required:

- **Confidential information.** Only information classified as Public can be posted on the Web server—no confidential or personal information.

- **Restrictions on posting or downloading copyrighted materials.** All users must comply with copyright and software licensing agreements. It is explicitly against the Corporate Information Security Policy to violate such agreements. Uploading or downloading copyright protected material is expressly prohibited. Displaying or posting copyrighted material on any extranet or Internet server is expressly prohibited.

- **Virus precautions.** All information downloaded from external Web services or posted to the Web server must be immediately scanned for viruses using the approved virus-scanning software. A procedure must be put into place on all Web servers to keep virus definition files current. No e-mail message can be passed from any Web server until it has gone through the virus checking procedure. Any e-mail found to contain a virus will be removed from the system.

- **Terminating External Session not Actively in Use.** Sessions not actively in use must be disconnected. A procedure to time-out all idle connections will be put into place. All Windows *9x* and Windows NT users must use a screen saver password and set the default activation to five minutes. Windows NT Workstation users must use the operating system's ability to lock the workstation when not in use. For sensitive systems other security measures will be put into place to protect the data. Some of the physical security measures will include:

- Installing protective covers and case locks on systems
- Using boot passwords and other built-in desktop security features
- Disabling and/or removing floppy drives
- Setting the CMOS to boot only from the local hard drive
- Using Smartcards and Smartcard readers on high-security machines

Password Management

By setting strict controls for password creation and management, the security policy document eliminates ambiguity, imposes standards, and educates users on the value of proper procedures. It also defines password requirements and procedures. Here are some password policy statements taken from the policy document discussed above:

Users must maintain the confidentiality of user accounts and passwords. Users must not use the same passwords for accessing external (Web) and internal (corporate) systems because user accounts and passwords are transmitted over external services, such as the Internet, in clear text and easily intercepted. Strong passwords are required on the external DMZ. For more information see Knowledge Base article Q161990, Title: How to Enable Strong Password Functionality in Windows NT.

Some guidelines for password use:

- Passwords must have at least seven characters and must contain at least one capital letter and one number.
- All passwords used by the built-in Windows NT accounts must be changed to conform to the password standard.
- All accounts must have passwords. Blank passwords are not permitted.
- Passwords must not be shared. Users should change passwords immediately if they are learned by anyone else.
- Passwords must be changed every thirty days. A history of the last six passwords is kept to force users to cycle no less than seven.
- Password must never be written down or sent in e-mail.

Unacceptable Usage

Users have to know what they can and cannot do. A security policy should describe unacceptable activities and inform users that their activities will be monitored and that violations of policy may have repercussions. The Bob's Bank policy characterized as unethical and unacceptable any activity which purposely:

- Seeks to use Web services for private or personal business.
- Seeks to gain unauthorized access to any resources within or outside of Bob's Bank.
- Disrupts the intended use of Bob's Bank and/or the Web service.
- Wastes resources (work time, line capacity, computer time) through such actions.
- Destroys the integrity of or misuses any information assets.
- Compromises the privacy of any other user or department.
- Damages the system.
- Compromises corporate proprietary material.
- Places material on any DMZ platform that is considered inappropriate, offensive, or disrespectful to others.

The policy also states: Bob's Bank reserves the right to monitor any and/or all external Web service related activity. Any users found in violation of this policy are subject to denial of access, and action that may culminate in termination of employment and/or criminal prosecution.

Reacting to a Security Exposure

No matter how tight the security is on an external DMZ there is still a risk of exposure from an external or internal source. Should a violation of security policy occur, you need a plan that will help you react to it. From the Bob's Bank policy:

Any suspicious activity or suspected security compromises to the Web must be reported to the Information Security Department. The security team will take appropriate action to determine the severity of the attack.

In particular, Security will work to completely understand the seriousness of the attack and take the following actions:

- Verify the integrity of the system or systems and take appropriate action
- Shut down all compromised areas to curtail exposure
- Determine the type of attack and its origin
- Take appropriate action to restore systems to normal operation
- Complete necessary steps to eradicate the security hole on all servers to eliminate recurrences
- Categorize the type of attack and if necessary take action against the perpetrator(s) (including legal action)
- If the attack is serious enough, assign a company spokesperson to contact the media to avoid damaging publicity

The actions taken by the security team will depend on the seriousness of the attack and depending on whether it is initiated by an "insider" or an "outsider." For insider violations the security team will take these actions:

- For minor offenses, issue a verbal warning.
- Warn in writing and/or reassign or demote employees who repeatedly violate the security policy.
- Terminate or take legal action against employees who repeatedly violate security or who commit a serious offense (see Unacceptable Usage section above).

For outsider attacks (for example, arising from Internet-based entities or applications) the Internet security team will:

- Find out the identity of the offending application or individual.
- Outline an action plan depending on the severity of the attack. If the attack warrants legal action, provide proper evidence handling.
- Implement and follow change control and testing procedures to plug any security breach.
- Conduct a post-mortem study of the attack. This will help the team improve the security policy, fully document how the incursion occurred, create detailed audit trails in the event of an attack, and finalize any required fixes to the DMZ.

Security Resources

Now that the security team has an internal security policy to enforce, the next challenge is staying current on all the latest security issues. This section outlines a variety of sources that can help with this task.

Microsoft Sources

Microsoft's internal Web site dedicated to the latest security information and issues: http://www.microsoft.com/Security/default.asp

Other Sources

Security Incident Response Teams

- Computer Incident Advisory Capability (CIAC)—http://www.ciac.org/
- Computer Emergency Response Team (CERT) Coordination Center—http://www.cert.org/
- Australian Computer Emergency Response Team (AUSCERT)—http://www.auscert.org.au/
- NASA Automated Systems Incident Response Capability (NASIRC)—http://www-nasirc.nasa.gov/nasa/index.html
- Computer Operations, Audit, and Security Technology (COAST)—http://www.cs.purdue.edu/coast/coast.html

- Computer Security Technology Center (CSTC)—
  http://ciac.llnl.gov/cstc/CSTCHome.html
- Federal Computer Incident Response Capability (FedCIRC)—
  http://www.fedcirc.gov/

Government Security Evaluation Sites

- National Computer Security Center Home Page—http://www.radium.ncsc.mil/
- Cryptographic Standards Validation Program at NIST—
  http://csrc.nist.gov/cryptval/

Standards Organizations

- World-wide Web Consortium (W3C)—http://www.w3.org/
- Internet Engineering Task Force (IETF)—http://www.ietf.org/
- ECMA—http://www.ecma.ch/
- Internet Society—http://info.isoc.org/

Security Organizations

- International Computer Security Association—http://www.ncsa.com/
- Applied Computer Security Associates—http://www.acsac.org/acsa.html
- Association for Computing Machinery Special Interest Group on Security,
  Audit and Control—http://www.acm.org/sigsac/
- Network Security International Association—http://www.netsec-intl.com/
- International Association for Cryptologic Research—
  http://www.swcp.com/~iacr/
- International Information Systems Security Certification Consortium—
  http://www.isc2.org/

Security Standards and Protocols

- IETF Requests for Comment—http://www.rfc-editor.org/

- Secure Electronic Transactions (SET)—http://www.setco.org/
- Kerberos Authentication Protocol—http://web.mit.edu/kerberos/www

Newsgroups

- alt.Security.*—Many different security related newsgroups can be found here
- Alt.2600—An area of newsgroups frequented by the hacker community
- Microsoft.public.windowsnt.*—Newsgroups on Windows NT that often contain security topics
- Comp.security.*—A set of newsgroups relating to security topics
- Microsoft.Public.Proxy—A discussion of issues relating to Microsoft Proxy Server

Other Security-related Web Sites

- htttp://www.ntsecurity.net
- htttp://www.ntbugtraq.com
- htttp://www.gocsi.com/
- htttp://www.icsa.net/
- http://www.somarsoft.com
- http://www.rsa.com/
- http://www.telstra.com.au/pub/docs/security/

Mailing Lists

- NT Security Digest—A monthly synopsis (distributed via e-mail) of the recent security developments and discoveries. To subscribe—
  http://www.ntsecurity.com

- NTBugTraq—A technically focused mailing list dedicated to Windows NT Security issues. To subscribe—htttp://www.ntbugtraq.com/
- Cert Advisory List—A mailing list dedicated to announcing new security issues on all platforms. To subscribe, send e-mail to certadvisory-request@cer.org

Securing the External DMZ—Firewall and Router Security

Connecting servers to the Internet is the prime interest of many networking configurations, and this trend no doubt will continue until virtually every network is in some way connected. For all that this increases communications and opens a world of resources to every desktop, it also creates serious security concerns. And these are well justified given the nature of the Internet today. The days of academic fellowship that shaped the Internet in the early years are long gone, replaced by a competitive environment in which companies showcase themselves and their products to the rest of the world, and hordes of otherwise innocuous people prowl the lines rattling doorknobs in search of an unlocked portal. Companies have reason to worry about their exposure to intrusion, and that reason intensifies each time a break-in is reported—which happens with depressing frequency.

This is the networked world we live in. In response to these challenges, organizations across the Web work tirelessly on security research, design, and enhancement. The good news is this allows companies to learn about issues and provide fixes quickly. The bad news is that this imposes significant demands on security personnel in particular and company resources in general.

You need to provide as much security as is practical and possible "up front," and this section discusses how to secure your DMZ—the area in which your servers are typically placed to provide the best security. As system administrator you are responsible for creating and maintaining this secure environment.

First Step: Some Examples

At the very least, a DMZ requires a router. A more sophisticated design would include two routers and a firewall. How complex your configuration needs to be depends on factors such as:

- How much security you need
- What sort of connectivity your system maintains to other networks (internal—corporate network; external—Internet)
- How many servers you need to protect

The two diagrams below show DMZ configurations common in corporate environments today. Both provide excellent protection for the internal network. Figure 6.1 shows a simpler configuration; the configuration in Figure 6.2 protects the DMZ servers with the same security features used to protect the internal network, controlling DMZ access from the trusted and untrusted sides of the firewall. It is more complex but more secure.

Typical DMZ configurations are shown below:

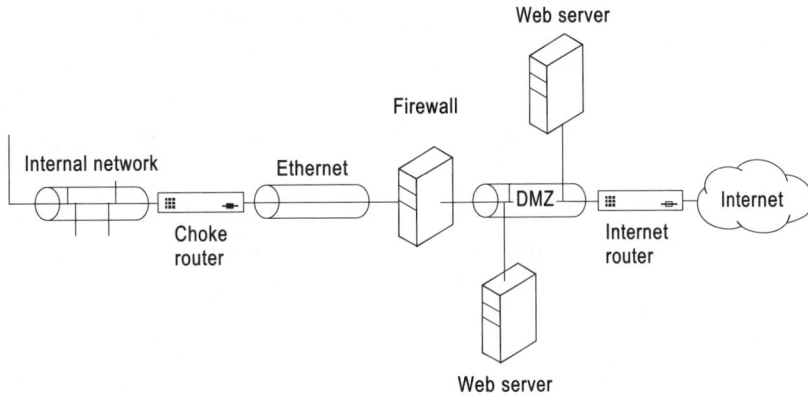

Figure 6.1 Simple DMZ configuration.

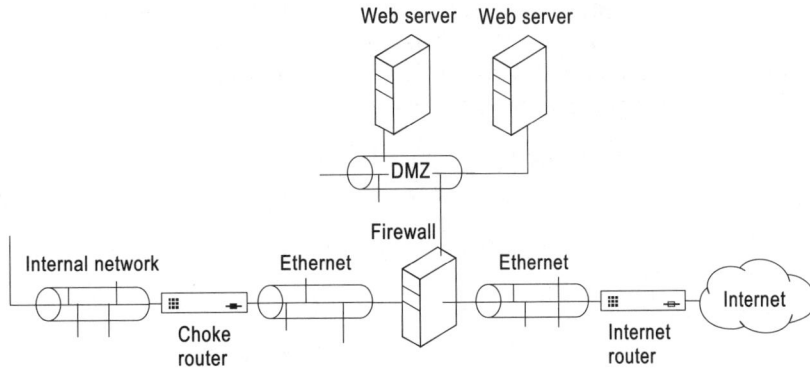

Figure 6.2 DMZ configuration controlling DMZ access from the trusted and untrusted sides of the firewall.

After DMZ topology, the most important step in securing the environment is controlling its traffic. You need to determine who is allowed to connect and who is not, and then enforce those rules, usually with routers and firewalls.

Routers can provide packet filtering, which controls traffic flow between two nodes, but this tends to decrease router performance so you have to be careful not to overuse it. Check your router utilization before and after.

Firewalls protect internal resources from external access. They are more "intelligent" than routers: they can provide packet filtering and stateful inspection (decision-making algorithms that control traffic flow), so they can be used to create and enforce security policies, and to restrict inbound/outbound traffic based on variables such as:

- Protocol ID
- Destination/source port
- Destination/source IP address

The protocol ID is typically Transmission Control Protocol (TCP) or User Datagram Protocol (UDP), although other protocols (GRE, for instance) are sometimes required. The firewall assigns each protocol a series of ports, usually on the basis of a service or task. UDP and TCP are assigned what are called "well known ports." A short list (a subset) of well-known ports starts on the next page. For a full list, see The *Windows NT 4.0 Workstation Resource Kit* ("Port Assignment for Registered Ports"). You can find this on TechNet.

The destination port typically is determined by the type of service that the client is seeking and thus can be discerned before the connection is made. For example, the Post Office Protocol Version 3 (POP3) is defined as port number 110, so clients seeking to retrieve e-mail from the mail server should connect to port 110.

The source port is typically randomly selected from the pool of unassigned ports and typically will be greater than 1024 (as this is presumed to be the last defined port).

The source and destination IP addresses are self-explanatory. If the client has an IP address assigned by Dynamic Host Control Protocol (DHCP) it is impossible to define a filter that would permit this client to connect to an inside resource because you can't always be sure what the client's "true" address is. A solution to this problem would be to create a filter based on a series of pooled addresses or subnets.

Short list of well-known ports.

Port number	Process name	Description
1	TCPMUX	TCP Port Service Multiplexer
5	RJE	Remote Job Entry
20	FTP-DATA	File Transfer Protocol—Data
21	FTP	File Transfer Protocol—Control
23	TELNET	Telnet
25	SMTP	Simple Mail Transfer Protocol
42	NAMESERV	Host Name Server
49	LOGON	Logon Host Protocol
53	DOMAIN	Domain Name System

Short list of well-known ports.   *(continued)*

Port number	Process name	Description
69	TFTP	Trivial File Transfer Protocol
70	GOPHER	Gopher
80	HTTP	HTTP
103	X400	X.400
110	POP3	Post Office Protocol version 3
137	NETBIOS-NS	NetBIOS Name Service
139	NETBIOS-DG	NetBIOS Datagram Service
150	NETBIOS-SS	NetBIOS Session Service
156	SQLSRV	SQL Server
179	BGP	Border Gateway Protocol

Configuring Firewall Security

Typically, you would assume that no traffic needs to cross the firewall. This is the most secure configuration. From there, you proceed to evaluate user needs, which typically will have well defined parameters:

- Destination ports
- Source and destination IP addresses
- Protocol ID

Based on these requirements, you can decide to allow specified kinds of traffic to enter from outside. For example, an e-mail administrator asks that remote users be able upload their e-mail while away from the office. If you decide to allow this traffic, you know that it will have these properties:

- Mail server IP address (fixed)
- Client IP address (variable)
- Port 25 (SMTP) on the mail server (fixed)
- Client source port (variable)

To allow remote users access, you would have to allow all external clients to hit port 25 of the internal mail server. This is referred to as punching holes in the firewall. The more you punch, the more difficult it is to keep your system secure.

Additional Firewall Features

Firewalls can implement more sophisticated services than packet filtering:

- Application proxy
- Circuit-level proxy
- Stateful inspection (intelligent decision-making algorithms that control traffic flow)

The major difference between packet filtering and proxy services (application and circuit-layer) is that the proxy does not let traffic through. Instead, the firewall establishes two connections:

- An internal client (inside of a firewall)
- An external resource (outside of a firewall)

These connections allow the client and server to communicate, but not directly—
the proxy is in the middle. This minimizes security exposure but increased
overhead on the proxy can reduce performance. The good news is that given the
relatively slow nature of the Internet links (T1 compared to 10-MB Ethernet) the
performance reduction is negligible.

There are two common types of proxy services: application and circuit-layer.
Typical firewall software provides both to some degree. Application proxy
services are provided only for certain types of applications because the firewall
has to be designed to accommodate specific protocols such as HTTP or POP3. For
example, when a browser client makes a page request to the proxy server, the
server examines the request and proxies it to the destination server. Circuit-layer
proxy is a "generic application proxy." In this case, the firewall does not need to
handle a protocol for the client-server exchange: it simply takes a request for a
connection from a given port and proxies it to the external server.

Firewalls also provide stateful inspection. This is an umbrella term for intelligent
decision-making algorithms that control traffic flow. The algorithms collect
pertinent information about the connection state from all of the relevant layers of
the stack (current and previous) and assess it to decide whether to permit a packet
to pass. Stateful algorithms can be very sophisticated and they can provide a very
high level of security. The cost for this service is reduced performance.

Packet filtering, proxy services, and stateful inspection require that you
understand DMZ traffic so that you can assess user needs accurately and derive a
sensible security policy that in turn dictates the DMZ configuration.

Other Proxy Security Features

Most proxy servers offer services beyond the standard functionality discussed above. MS Proxy, provides three such features.

Reverse proxy enables proxy server to provide secure access to an internal Web server (not exposing it to the outside) by redirecting external HTTP (application proxy) requests to a single designated machine. This is not suitable for multi-server Web hosting (reverse hosting, described next, takes care of this) but it can be quite valuable when working with a single site.

Reverse hosting allows proxy server to redirect HTTP (application proxy) requests to multiple internal Web servers. Access to multiple servers can be provided as subwebs of one large aggregate Web site or as multiple independent Web servers. More flexible than reverse proxy but equally secure, this method enables you to abstract the physical architecture of your Web sites by mapping multiple servers to a single logical one. Both options benefit from MS Proxy Server's caching functionality.

Server proxy provides the same functionality as reverse proxy and reverse hosting, but unlike these features it works with protocols other than HTTP to provide secure access from the Internet to internal resources such as internal mail or SQL server. To an outside user, the proxy server appears to *be* the mail or SQL server. Basically, server proxy responds to external requests on behalf of the internal servers, which simply have to run the proxy client that redirects the listen directive on a given port to a proxy server. The security benefit is obvious: placing servers behind a proxy prevents direct tampering from the outside and fools would-be attackers into thinking that the proxy server is the box containing the information they want.

Reverse proxy can be very useful. For instance, suppose you need to allow a Web server to query an internal database. There are several ways to do this. You can replicate the database to the outside, if it is not too large, but this puts the contents' integrity at risk. It may make more sense to move the Web and database servers behind the firewall and use reverse proxy or reverse hosting to get at the site. This option is very secure, although the overhead of running multiple Web servers behind the proxy may tax the proxy's ability to service Web requests from internal clients.

A third alternative is better yet: place the Web server in the DMZ and use the server proxy functionality to query the database. This option, shown below in Figure 6.3, provides good security and performance.

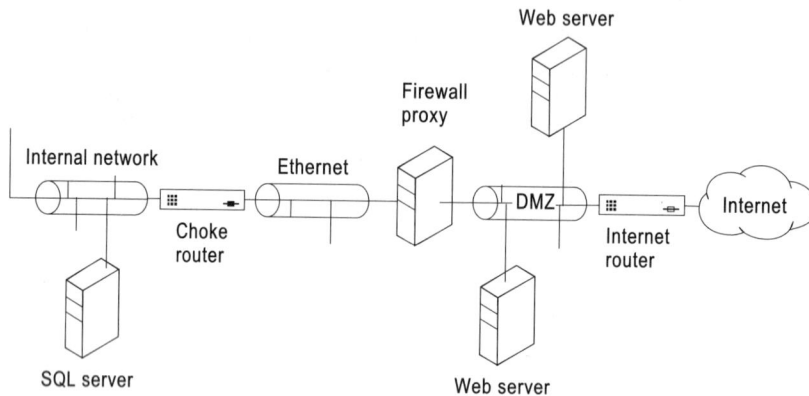

Figure 6.3 Web server in the DMZ; server proxy queries the database.

Before you select any of these options you should analyze your requirements so that you can balance *necessary* security against performance/usability.

Virtual Private Networks and Secure Remote Access

Now that the DMZ is in place, another option corporations are considering is using this outside network to provide secure tunneled access into the corporate network. This solution eliminates the high costs associated with creating and maintaining a private remote access network. Microsoft Consulting Services has been engaged by many accounts to design a solution based on the Point-to-Point Tunneling Protocol (PPTP).

PPTP and the Point-to-Point Protocol (PPP) are supported by the Windows NT 4.0 and Office 2000 Remote Access Service/dial-up networking clients and by Windows 9x dial-up networking (built into Windows 98; Windows 95 requires an upgrade). PPTP uses the Internet as an infrastructure to connect clients or remote networks to a main corporate network. With Remote Access Service (RAS), users have direct dial-up, circuit-based access to a corporate network. With PPTP connection, users first establish direct dial-up, circuit-based connection to an Internet Service Provider (ISP) then use an encrypted "tunnel" over the Internet that connects to a corporate PPTP server. Figure 6.4 shows a PPTP RAS connection:

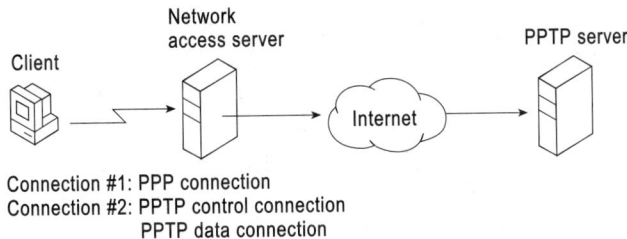

Connection #1: PPP connection
Connection #2: PPTP control connection
PPTP data connection

Figure 6.4 PPTP architecture.

Advantages of PPTP

- Eliminates long distance telephone costs associated with the use of 1-800 or local corporate RAS numbers. The user can dial a local number to access the Internet instead.

- Reduces RAS infrastructure costs such as modem and Integrated Services Digital Network (ISDN) adapter pools. Instead, the ISP handles all modem and ISDN upgrades while the corporation maintains a connection to the Internet to handle PPTP traffic.

- Gives users access to the same applications that they would use over a direct-dial RAS connection.

- Is supported under both Windows NT 4.0 and Windows 9x.

PPTP and Firewalls

PPTP provides secure access to remote private networks by allowing the remote network to authenticate the user as if the user had dialed into a RAS server, and by using the compression and encryption capabilities of the underlying PPP protocol.

There are two approaches to using firewall techniques for protecting a PPTP server and the private network to which it is providing secure internet access: place the PPTP server on the Internet with a firewall behind it to protect the served network, or place a firewall server on the Internet, with the PPTP server between the firewall and the private network.

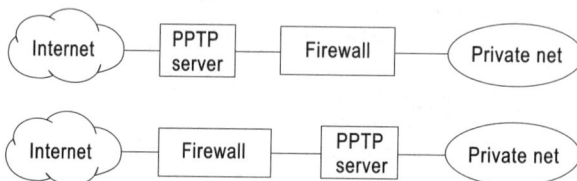

Figure 6.5 PPTP Server location options.

In the first case, the administrator enables PPTP filtering on the PPTP server so that the server receives only PPTP packets. Then, additional filtering in the firewall behind the tunnel server can be applied to admit packets based on source and destination addresses or other criteria.

In the second case, the firewall must be enabled to recognize and pass PPTP packets to and from the PPTP server in addition to any other filter criteria.

The first approach is better because it screens all but PPTP packets from the tunnel server, then submits the data carried in the tunnel to additional filtering after decryption and decompression. The second approach can raise a security issue because the firewall filters cannot look inside the PPTP packet.

Firewall Requirements

PPTP sends data using IP GRE packets (IP protocol 47) and controls the tunnel using a TCP connection to port 1723. To filter PPTP packets through a firewall, you must make these changes:

1. Configure the firewall to allow traffic on IP protocol 47. This enables PPTP GRE packets, which carry the data flow. The data within the GRE frame can be encrypted and/or compressed if the client and server are so configured.

2. Configure the firewall to allow traffic sent to or from TCP port 1723. This is the PPTP control channel for configuring and managing the tunnel between the client and the tunnel server. The packet filter should include the address of the tunnel server. That is, out-bound traffic with port 1723 as the source port or the destination port should be allowed only *from* the tunnel server, and in-bound traffic with port 1723 as the source port or the destination port should be allowed only *to* the tunnel server. This is not necessary, but it enhances firewall security.

Security and Data Encryption

PPTP uses the RAS "shared-secret" encryption process, so called because both ends of the connection share the encryption key. PPTP uses the PPP encryption and PPP compression schemes. The PPP uses Compression Control Protocol (CCP) to negotiate encryption.

The PPTP client provides its user name and password to the PPTP server. A session key is derived (using the RSA RC4 standard) from the hashed password stored on both client and server, then is used to encrypt all data that is passed over the Internet. The remote connection is kept private and secure.

Also, the data in PPP packets is encrypted then encapsulated into a larger IP datagram for routing over the Internet to the PPTP server. If an Internet hacker intercepts an IP datagram, all that is discernible is an indecipherable collection of media headers, IP headers, and the PPP packet containing a block of encrypted data.

Encryption

Communication across the Internet requires both encapsulation and data stream encryption to be viable. PPTP provides multi-protocol encapsulation, or "tunneling" services, allowing IP, Internetwork Packet Exchange (IPX), and NBF packets to be used across the Internet. Microsoft's Point-to-Point Encryption (MPPE, 40- and 128-bit) provides confidentiality for transmitted data.

Microsoft clients and servers can use MPPC (Microsoft Point-to-Point Compression) and/or MPPE (Microsoft Point to Point Encryption) during the CCP negotiation process. When encryption is requested, 40- or 128-bit session key encryption is negotiated.

The user name and password of the PPTP client are available to the PPTP server and supplied by the PPTP client. An encryption key is derived from the hashed password stored on both the client and server. The RSA RC4 standard is used to create this 40-bit (128-bit) session key based on the client password. This key is used to encrypt all data that is passed over the Internet, keeping the remote connection private and secure. A new key is generated after every 256 packets.

Note   Users in the United States and Canada can obtain a 128-bit session key through a cryptography pack for use inside the U.S. The 128-bit key is derived from both the hashed password and the unique MSCHAP challenge. The U.S. Commerce Department will often grant permission to distribute "high security" products (allowing 128-bit encryption) to international offices of U.S.-based companies.

Data in PPP packets is protected as described above. Internet Protocol Security (IPSEC, currently under development), provides encryption, authentication, integrity check and replay protection for IP packets. IPSEC primarily provides network layer security for IP, not tunneling functionality per se, so while it is viable for server-server tunneling (such as between routers) it does not yet provide all the functionality required in client-server tunneling (see the table below).

As a result, IPSEC largely complements, but does not overlap, the functionality provided by PPTP and L2TP. This makes it attractive to combine the flexibility of Layer 2 VPN protocols (PPTP/L2TP) with the security provided by IPSEC. Microsoft will support such a "merged VPN" platform (PPTP or L2TP running over IPSEC) in Windows 2000.

In order to protect existing customer investments, Windows RAS and routing-based VPN solutions provide a smooth migration path from an existing PPTP infrastructure to a platform based on L2TP, IPSEC, and EAP. Windows 2000 will support client/server PPTP and L2TP based VPNs running over IPSEC, as well as server-server tunnels based on PPTP, L2TP, and IPSEC.

Security features.

Features	PPTP	L2TP	IPSEC
Authenticated Tunnels		X	
Compression	X (MPPC)	X (MPPC)	
Token/Smart Card	X (EAP)	X (EAP)	X
Address Assignment	X	X	
Multi-protocol	X	X	
Encryption	X (MPPE)	X (MPPE)	X

Securing a Windows NT Internet Information Server

Securing the Web servers is always a major concern. This section provides guidelines for creating a hacker-resistant Windows NT Web server environment. It documents the process MCS used to secure IIS for Bob's Bank. The following is the set of steps and the template used to document each Internet server's configuration.

Server Hardware Platform

Bob's Bank Web server hardware platform.

System	Compaq Proliant 3000R
Processor	Dual 300-MHz Pentium Pro
Memory	256 MB RAM
	512 K L2 Cache (std.)
Disk Subsystem	3 9-GB Drives in RAID-5 Array
	SMART-2SL Array Controller
	Optional: 4th 9-GB Drive as hot spare
Network	Netelligent 10/100 Controller (on-board)
	Netelligent 10/100 Controller (add-in PCI card)

Disk Subsystem

The disk subsystem was configured for hardware-level RAID and configured the three 9-GB disk drives as a single RAID-5 disk set.

Disk Controller Cache

Battery backup was enabled for the disk controller's cache. Controller caching was set to 75% read and 25% write-back.

Netelligent Network Interface Card

10/100-autodetect was enabled for the NIC.

Use a chart like this to document firmware configuration.

Component	Rev. level

Apply SoftPaq updates as needed to obtain the minimum acceptable revision levels for firmware.

Windows NT Server

These Windows NT features and components were deployed. The table lists sources for the files. MCS installed all major components in the order they are listed.

Windows NT features and components and their source.

Feature/component	Rev. level
Windows NT Server 4.0	Compaq SmartStart CD
Core OS	
Compaq Proliant Multiprocessor HAL	
Compaq SmartArray Driver	
Compaq Network Driver	
Transmission Control Protocol/Internet Protocol (TCP/IP)	
IIS 4.0	
Windows NT Server 4.0 Service Pack 3 or 4 (When it is an approved standard)	Compaq SmartStart CD

Windows NT features and components and their source.   *(continued)*

Feature/component	Rev. level
Internet Explorer 4.01	Required by Option Pack (IIS 4.0)
Standard Installation	
No Active Desktop	
Windows NT 4.0 Option Pack	Windows NT 4.0 Option Pack CD
FrontPage 98 extensions	
Internet Information Server	
Internet Service Manager	
WWW Server	
Data Access Components 1.5	
Data Sources (Jet and Access, SQL Server)	
Index Server	
System Files	
Language Support	
Catalog Directory: D:\Inetpub	
Microsoft Management Console	
Windows NT Option Pack Common Files	

Windows NT features and components and their source.   *(continued)*

Feature/component	Rev. level
Transaction Server	
MTS Core Components	
Install to C:\Program Files\Mts	
Use Local Administration account	
Windows Scripting Host	
Windows NT Hotfixes	Obtain from ftp://ftp.microsoft.com
Compaq SSD Driver Updates	Obtain from http://www.compaq.com

Windows NT SP3 Hotfixes

Until SP4 is an approved standard, Bob's Bank is applying the appropriate SP3 hotfixes to the Web server. Many hotfixes address security and denial-of-service issues. Install the following list of hotfixes to the Web server (note: these hotfixes are included with SP4).

Apply the post SP3 hotfixes in this order (see note on page 320):

Fix folder	Executable date	KB article(s)
Asp-fix	05/28/97 12:00AM	Q165335
Dns-fix	06/09/97 12:00AM	Q142047, Q154984, Q154985, Q167629, Q169461
Iis-fix	06/20/97 12:00AM	Q143484
Lsa-fix	06/25/97 12:00AM	Q154087

Apply the post SP3 hotfixes in this order (see note on page 320):   *(continued)*

Fix folder	Executable date	KB article(s)
Lm-fix	07/11/97 12:00AM	Q147706
Zip-fix	07/14/97 12:00AM	Q154094
Getadmin-fix	07/15/97 12:00AM	Q146965, Q168748, Q170510
Winsupd-fix	08/07/97 12:00AM	Q155701
Ndis-fix	08/08/97 12:00AM	Q156655
Scsi-fix	09/05/97 12:00AM	Q171295
2gcrash	11/01/97 12:00AM	Q173277
Simptcp-fix	11/01/97 12:00AM	Q154460
Ide-fix	11/18/97 12:00AM	Q153296
Wan-fix	11/20/97 12:00AM	Q163251
Roll-up	11/24/97 12:00AM	Q147222
Joystick-fix	12/11/97 12:00AM	Q177668
SAG-fix	12/11/97 12:00AM	Q177471
Pent-fix	12/11/97 12:00AM	Q163852
Iis4-fix	12/12/97 12:00AM	Q169274
Teardrop2-fi	x01/09/98 08:23PM	Q179129
Tapi21-fix	01/12/98 06:29PM	Q179187
Pcm-fix	02/11/98 05:10PM	Q180532
Srv-fix	02/12/98 06:24PM	Q180963
ASPDataFix	07/07/98 08:00PM	Q188806

Note Install the hotfixes in ascending order of the date/time stamps of the self-installing executables. Track all the latest security patches at www.microsoft.com/security.

Windows NT SP4

Installing and testing all these post SP3 hotfixes is costly and time consuming. The better approach is to install Windows NT Service Pack 4, which contains all the SP3 fixes plus the latest year 2000 updates and support for the Euro currency. SP4 is the best solution from a security perspective. For a complete list of the SP4 fixes, see the release notes or Appendix A. Some of the important ones are:

- All public fixes created to resolve customer issues since Windows NT 4.0 released (including the list documented above for SP3).

- All previous service pack updates (SP1, SP2, and SP3). SPs are cumulative and contain all previous service packs and hotfixes.

- The new system key for strong encryption. This tool allows you to configure the Windows NT Accounts Database to enable additional encryption, further protecting the database. Once enabled, this encryption cannot be disabled. For more details see Knowledge Base article Q143475, Title: Windows NT System Key Permits Strong Encryption of the SAM.

- A new utility, SETPRFDC.EXE, and new functionality added to NETLOGON, allow for directing the SC_client to a preferred DC for the secure channel. SETPRFDC.EXE is a command-line utility that can be run in batch or with the AT scheduler in the format: SETPRFDC <TrustedDomain> <ListOfDcsInTrustedDomain> (DC1, DC2, etc.) You do not need to restart your computer when you use SETPRFDC. For more information see Knowledge Base article Q167029, Title: Resource and Master Domain DCs Do Not Load Balance Validation.

- New performance and security updates to PPTP that greatly increase data transfer speeds when run on the PPTP client and server system. A new version of MSCHAP (MSCHAP V2) has been implemented for VPN connections. For more information, see Knowledge Base article Q189595, Title: PPTP Performance & Security Upgrade for WinNT 4.0 Release Notes.

- A bug fix in the Event Log service that requires the SE_SECURITY_NAME privilege, also known as the Security privilege, to be enabled in order to view and manage the security event log. By default, Windows NT grants the privilege to Administrators and local System. However, the privilege must also be enabled in the program accessing the security event log in order to take effect. Prior to this change, members of the Administrators group and services running as local System could open the security log for read or change access without enabling the Security privilege. For more information, see Knowledge Base article Q188855, Title: Security Privilege Must Be Enabled to View Security Event Log.

- Enhancements for the year 2000, including:

  - The User Manager and User Manager for Domains recognize the year 2000 as a leap year.

  - The date/time control panel applet can update the system clock.

  - Find Files supports only numeric character recognition in the decades field.

  - Word document properties recognize both 1900 and 2000 as valid centuries and support years of four digits.

  - The DHCP administrator program supports the years between 2000-2009 with a minimum of two digits.

- The Security Configuration Editor (SCE), which is an integrated security system administrators can use to define and apply security configurations for Windows NT Workstation and Windows NT Server installations. SCE also helps you inspect installed systems to locate any degradation in security. For additional information, see the README file in the MSSCE folder.

System Requirements for SP4

- Service Pack releases are cumulative: SP4 contains all previous Service Pack fixes and any new fixes created after Service Pack 3.

- Windows NT Workstation 4.0, Windows NT Server 4.0 or Windows NT server 4.0 Enterprise Edition.

Note Before you install SP4, read the release notes: they contain vital information as well as installation instructions.

To download SP4 go to: http://www.microsoft.com/ntserver

The security officer should make sure that all the servers in the outside network are up to date, with all the latest security patches. SP4 makes this task much simpler by allowing the administrator to install all post-SP3 hotfixes using a single upgrade. Once testing is completed, SP4 will be a must for MCS client security. Also, the security officer should continue to monitor security standards organizations and related newsgroups, Web sites, mailing lists etc., for alerts, developments, and patches that occur after SP4.

NT System Directory Structure

Bob's Bank installed Windows NT Server to C:\MSWNT, not the default
directory, to provide a layer of security against Trojan horse attacks that assume
the default C:\WINNT directory.

System Settings

System Control Panel settings decided on by Bob's Bank security team.

Properties	Setting
Application performance	Maximum boost
Virtual memory	Single pagefile of 128M on C:
Environment	Accept defaults
System startup	Windows NT Server Version 4.0 (default)
Show list for	3 seconds
System recovery settings	
Write an event to the system log	Enabled
Send an administrative alert	Enabled
Write debugging information to	Enabled; %SystemRoot%\MEMORY.DMP
Overwrite	Enabled
Automatically reboot	Enabled

Directory and File Permissions

Directory permissions applied to the Windows NT directory (C:\MSWNT).

Directory	Permissions
C:\MSWNT And all subdirectories	Administrators: Full control CREATOR OWNER: Full control Everyone: Read Server Operators: Read SYSTEM: Full control

Permissions applied to subdirectories.

Directory	Permissions
C:\MSWNT\REPAIR	Administrators: Full control
C:\MSWNT\SYSTEM32\CONFIG	Administrators: Full control CREATOR OWNER: Full control Everyone: List Server Operators: List SYSTEM: Full control

Permissions applied to subdirectories.   *(continued)*

Directory	Permissions
C:\MSWNT\SYSTEM32\SPOOL	Administrators: Full control
	CREATOR OWNER: Full control
	Everyone: Read
	Server Operators: Change
	SYSTEM: Full control
C:\MSWNT\Cookies	Administrators: Full control
C:\MSWNT\Downloaded Program Files	Not shared
C:\MSWNT\History	Everyone: Special (based on requirements)
C:\MSWNT\Subscriptions	Not shared
C:\MSWNT\Temporary Internet Files	Server Operators: Change
	Administrators: Full control
C:\MSWNT\WEB	SYSTEM: Full control
	Administrators: Full control

Directory and file permissions set in the root-level directory of the boot partition (C:).

Directory	Permissions
\BOOT.INI	Administrators: Full control
	System: Full control
\NTDETECT.COM	SYSTEM: Full control
\NTLDR	
\AUTOEXEC.BAT	Administrators: Full control
\CONFIG.SYS	Everyone: Read
	Administrators: Full control
	SYSTEM: Full control
\TEMP directory	Administrators: Full control
	CREATOR OWNER: Full control
	Everyone: Special (based on requirements)
	Server Operators: Change
	SYSTEM: Full control

Network Configuration

Bob's Bank used the charts below to document each server's network level configuration. The example below outlines the configuration for all of the production Web servers.

Identification chart for production Web servers.

Computer name	XXXXXX
Domain	XXXXXX
Role in domain	XXXXXX

Identification chart for network services.

Service	Properties	Setting
Computer Browser	Other Domains for Browser Service	None (default)
NetBIOS Configuration	LAN adapter (LANA) numbers	Accept defaults as configured by binding analysis
RPC Configuration	Name Service Provider	Windows NT Locator (default)
	Network Address	None (default)
	Security Service Provider	Windows NT Security Service (default)
Server	Optimization	Maximize Throughput for Applications (default)
	LAN-Man 2.x Browser Announcements	Disable (default)
Workstation	No configurable properties	

Also, you should disable commands such as: Finger, Netstat, systat, echo, FTP, Telnet, and the Berkeley "r" commands (rlogin, rsh, rdist, etc.) by either removing them or placing them in a secured directory other than under %SYSTEMROOT%.

Network Protocols and Adapters

Configure TCP/IP only.

The *public* adapter is publicly registered with the Internet Domain Name System (DNS). Web clients on the Internet connect to the Web server on this adapter. Bob's Bank documents the network configuration using this template:

Public adapter configuration.

Properties	Setting
IP Address(es) and masks	x.x.x.x mask: y.y.y.y
Gateways	
Enable PPTP Filtering	Disabled (default)
Enable Security	Enabled
TCP Ports	Permit only: 80, 443
UDP Ports	Permit only: None
IP Protocols	Permit only: TCP, ICMP (based on requirements)
Host Name (Internet)	
Domain (Internet)	
DNS Servers (in searched order)	
Domain Suffix Search Order	Accept defaults
Primary WINS Server	None
Secondary WINS Server	None
Enable IP Forwarding	No

Network Bindings

Bindings determine what network services are available on the network adapter(s). Correctly configuring the bindings is essential to securing the Web server.

Bindings configured in the network control panel.

Adapter	Enabled/disabled
Public	Enabled
TCP/IP Protocol	Enabled
WINS Client (NetBIOS over TCP/IP)	Disabled
NetBIOS Interface	Disabled
Server	Disabled
Workstation	Disabled

Router and Port Changes

Safeguards to consider, based on those instituted by Bob's Bank:

- Filter out ports 137 (nbname), 138 (nbdatagram), 139 (nbsession) on the outside router, to prevent a hacker from port-scanning the Internet router to validate the existence of a Microsoft Network.

- Block all non-essential TCP/IP ports.

- Set up proper packet filters on the routers to prevent security exposures. This requires detailed planning and an intimate knowledge of TCP and UDP port utilization.

- Disable IP forwarding on all Web servers *especially* if there are any multi-homed servers. Multi-homed servers (two network cards, one connected to the internal network and one connected to the external network) are considered a security risk and, as such, require special handling.

Services

Do not allow a secured Windows NT server running IIS to be used to run any other services, it makes the server more vulnerable. Shut down any nonessential services.

Server configuration for Bob's Bank.

Service	Description	Startup
Alerter	Send alert messages, such as *disk full*, to administrators. Depends upon the Messenger service.	Disabled
ClipBook Server	Used for DDE	Disabled
Computer Browser	Used to list Windows Networking computers on the network	Disabled
Content Index	Index Server	Automatic
DHCP Client		Disabled
Directory Replicator	Used to replicate directories with other domain controllers	Disabled
EventLog	Event Log Service	Automatic
FTP Publishing Service		Disabled
IIS Admin Service	Web-based Administration	Automatic
License Logging Service		Automatic
Messenger	Used to send network messages to Windows Network machines and users	Disabled
MSDTC	Microsoft Distributed Transaction Coordinator	Automatic
Network DDE		Disabled
Network DDE DSDM		Disabled
NT LM Security Provider		Automatic

Server configuration for Bob's Bank.   *(continued)*

Service	Description	Startup
Plug and Play		Automatic
Protected Storage	Used by IIS and IE	Automatic
RPC Locator		Automatic
RPC Service		Automatic
Server		Automatic
Site Server Auth. Service		Automatic
Site Server Content Deployment		Automatic
Site Server LDAP Service		Automatic
Site Server List Builder Service		Automatic
Site Server Message Builder Service		Automatic
Spooler		Automatic
Task Scheduler		Automatic
TCP/IP NetBIOS Helper		Disabled
Telephony Service		Manual
UPS		Manual
Workstation		Automatic
WWW Publishing Service		Automatic

User and Group Accounts

It is important to maintain and track all server accounts if you want to maintain a secure environment.

Bob's Bank's current list of accounts and groups.

Account	Purpose	Notes
XXXXX (Administrator)	Account for System Administration	This is the Administrator account created during NT Setup. Rename this account to XXXXX
Guest	Guest access	Disable this account.
IUSR_XXXXX	IIS Anonymous Access	
IAPP_XXXX	IIS Web Application Manager Account	
LDAP_ANONYMOUS	Anonymous account for MP LDAP Server	Used with Membership Server

Local Groups.

Group	Description	Members
Account Operators	Members can administer domain user and group accounts	Administrators
Administrators	Members can fully administer domain controllers	Administrators
Backup Operators	Members can bypass file security to backup files	None

Local Groups.   *(continued)*

Group	Description	Members
GRPAUOMicrosoft	Group for AUO Accounts	None
Guests	Users granted guest access to the computer/domain	Domain Guests
Print Operators	Members can administer domain printers	None
Replicator	Supports file replication in a domain	None
Server Operators	Members can administer the domain servers	None
Users	Ordinary users	Domain Users

Global Groups.

Group	Description	Members
Domain Admins	Designated Administrators of the Domain	Administrators
Domain Guests	All domain guests	Guest
Domain Users	All domain users	All users except Guest

Windows NT User Rights

The default column includes user rights assigned when Windows NT Server, Service Pack 3, and the Windows NT Option Pack are installed.

Bob's Bank's user rights with changes noted.

User right	Default	Changes
Log on locally	Account Operators	Administrators
	Administrators	Backup Operators
	Backup Operators	Server Operators
	Server Operators	IIS Accounts attempting to connect to the Web server
	Print Operators	
Shut down the system	Account Operators	Administrators
	Administrators	
	Backup Operators	
	Server Operators	
	Print Operators	
Access this computer from the network	Administrators	Administrators
		IIS accounts attempting to connect to the Web Server
	Everyone	Backup Operators
		Server Operators
Act as part of the operating system	(None)	

Bob's Bank's user rights with changes noted.   *(continued)*

User right	Default	Changes
Add workstations to the domain	(None)	
Back up files and directories	Administrators	
	Backup Operators	
	Server Operators	
Bypass traverse checking	Everyone	
Change the system time	Administrators	
	Server Operators	
Create a pagefile	Administrators	
Create a token object	(None)	
Create permanent shared objects	(None)	
Debug programs	Administrators	
Force shutdown from a remote system	Administrators	
	Server Operators	
Generate security audits	(None)	
Increase quotas	Administrators	
Increase scheduling priority	Administrators	
Load and unload device drivers	Administrators	

Bob's Bank's user rights with changes noted.   *(continued)*

User right	Default	Changes
Lock pages in memory	(None)	
Log on as a batch job	(None)	
Log on as a service	(None)	
Manage auditing and security log	Administrators	
Modify firmware environment variables	Administrators	
Profile single process	Administrators	
Profile system performance	Administrators	
Replace a process-level token	(None)	
Restore files and directories	Administrators	
	Server Operators	
	Backup Operators	
Take ownership of files or other objects	Administrators	

Passwords

Bob's Bank implemented the Windows NT SP3 password filter to force the use of strong passwords. To turn on high security for all passwords, follow this procedure on all secure domain servers:

1. Install Windows NT 4.0 SP3.

2. Copy PASSFILT.DLL to the %SYSTEMROOT%\SYSTEM32 folder.

3. Use Registry Editor (REGEDT32.EXE) to add the value **Notification Packages** under HKEY_LOCAL_MACHINE\SYSTEM\CurrentControlSet\Control\Lsa, of type REG_MULTI_SZ, under the LSA key. If this key already exists, go to Step 4.

4. Double-click the **Notification Packages** key and, if the value FPNWCLNT is already present, add PASSFILT under it.

5. Click **OK** and then exit Registry Editor.

Shut down and restart the computer running Windows NT Server. For more information see Knowledge Base article Q161990, Title: How to Enable Strong Password Functionality in Windows NT.

Registry Key Changes and Additions

Secure Event Log Viewing

Bob's Bank restricted the Guest account and null logons from accessing the event logs.

Changes to the default registry configuration to restrict Guest account.

Hive	HKEY_LOCAL_MACHINE
Key	\System\CurrentControlSet\Services\EventLog\Application
Value Name	RestrictGuestAccess
Type	REG_DWORD
Value	1

Hive	HKEY_LOCAL_MACHINE
Key	\System\CurrentControlSet\Services\EventLog\Security
Value Name	RestrictGuestAccess
Type	REG_DWORD
Value	1

Hive	HKEY_LOCAL_MACHINE
Key	\System\CurrentControlSet\Services\EventLog\System
Value Name	RestrictGuestAccess
Type	REG_DWORD
Value	1

Require SMB Message Signing

Message signing is an SP3 feature that prevents "man-in-the-middle" attacks using LAN Manager protocols. Even though the security team disabled LAN Manager on the external adapter, the Bob's Bank security team requested message signing for additional layer of security.

Message signing registry settings.

Hive	HKEY_LOCAL_MACHINE
Key	\System\CurrentControlSet\Services\LanManServer\Parameters
Value Name	RequireSecuritySignature
Type	REG_DWORD
Value	1

Hive	HKEY_LOCAL_MACHINE
Key	\System\CurrentControlSet\Services\LanManServers\Paremeters
Value Name	EnableSecuritySignature
Type	REG_DWORD
Value	1

Note You must also apply these settings (along with Service Pack 3) to any other Windows NT Servers or Workstations with which the Web server communicates using SMB (LAN Manager upper-level protocols).

Hide the Previous Logon Name in Winlogon

The configuration at Bob's bank hides the previously used logon from the Logon screen to prevent a hacker from discovering a valid user name.

Hide previous logon name registry setting.

Hive	HKEY_LOCAL_MACHINE
Key	\Software\Microsoft\WindowsNT\CurrentVersion\Winlogon
Value Name	DontDisplayLastUserName
Type	REG_SZ
Value	1

Add a Banner to NT Logon Process

For legal purposes, the Bob's Bank server logon process carries a banner notifying users that the server is a corporate resource, that the network is for authorized use only, and that all activities may be monitored.

Logon banner registry setting.

Hive	HKEY_LOCAL_MACHINE
Key	\Software\Microsoft\WindowsNT\CurrentVersion\Winlogon
Value Name	LegalNoticeText
Text	Sample: All users must be authorized to access Web systems. All activities are monitored.

Auditing

Audit Policy

To maintain a secure environment you must continually monitor systems. Using the Windows NT User Manager, Bob's Bank configured auditing to track the following events:

Auditing settings.

Event	Success	Failure
Logon and Logoff	X	X
File and Object Access		X
Use of User Rights		
User and Group Management	X	X
Security Policy Changes	X	X
Restart, Shutdown, and System	X	X
Process Tracking		

Event Logs

Even though overwriting security events is not recommended, Bob's Bank chose to do so and used these settings for all Windows NT Event Logs (Application, Security and System):

Event log settings.

Max. Log Size	4,096 K
Event Log Wrapping	Overwrite events older than 7 days

Configuring Internet Information Server

Secure Sockets Layer Support

Secure Sockets Layer (SSL) provides an encrypted communications channel for user authentication between the Web server and Web clients. To enable SSL Version 3.0, Bob's Bank requested and installed an X.509 public-key Server ID certificate, available from any Certificate Authority.

For their Web server, they obtained a Global ServerID certificate from Verisign. The Global Server ID supports 128-bit encryption for clients both within and outside the United States and Canada, although you should carefully research export requirements for other countries. The Global Server ID requires an annual renewal. Using Key Manager, they created a new key for the WWW Service.

Bob's Bank template for documenting the key request process.

Request File

Key Name

Password

Bit Length

Organization Name

Organizational Unit   Company Organization or Division

Common Name

Country

State/Province

City/Locality

Your Name

E-mail Address

Phone Number

Configuring Webs in Internet Information Server

IIS creates a default Web site at install time. Bob's Bank retained this Web site for system management purposes.

They created separate Web sites and locations for each site located on the box.

Template for documenting Web sites.

Description	Home
Select IP Address	IP address of external LAN adapter
TCP Port	80
SSL TCP Port	443
Home Directory	D:\Web\wwwroot\Home
Allow Anonymous Access	No
Home Directory Permissions	
Read	Yes
Script	Yes
Execute	No
Write	No
Directory Browsing	No

Overall Web site properties.

Description	Company Internet
IP Address	IP address of external LAN adapter
TCP Port	80
SSL TCP Port	443
Connections	Unlimited
Connection Timeout	900 seconds
Enable Logging	Yes
Active Log Format	W3C Extended Log File Format

Operator Properties.

Operators	Administrators
	SiteServer Administrators

Performance properties.

Estimated Hits per Day	Fewer than 100,000
Bandwidth Throttling	Disabled
Maximum Network Use	N/A
HTTP Keep-Alives	Enabled

Home directory properties.

Content Source	Local Directory
Local Path	D:\Web\WWWroot\Home
Access Permissions	Read Only
Content Control	Log Access Only
Application Settings	
Name	Default Application
Isolated Process	No
Permissions	Execute (including script)

Documents properties.

Enable Default Document	Yes
Default Document List	Default.asp
	Default.htm
Enable Document Footer	No

Directory security properties.

Anonymous Access and Authorization Control	Yes (for unsecured pages)
Secure Communications	Yes
Require Secure Channel	No (this may change)
	Note: Select SSL on a per page basis
Client Cert. Authentication	Do not accept (may be introduced later)
IP Address & DNS Restrictions	None

HTTP headers properties.

Enable Content Expiration	No
Custom HTTP Headers	None
Content Rating	Default
MIME Map	Default

FrontPage Server Extensions

FrontPage is a design tool for Web developers. It also provides a set of extensions that facilitate some of its functionality by installing binaries directly onto the Web server. This allows FrontPage to automatically maintain Web site integrity (prevent broken links) and to add functionality by providing the Web page designer with some runtime controls: Web-bots and Web themes. It also allows users to designate permission for the "FrontPage" Web site: administrator, author, or browser.

These rights are enforced according to permissions granted to the DLLs that perform the functions. They are available locally and remotely (over the Internet). If not set up properly or monitored they can be used to compromise the security of your Web site.

Because of continual problems with administrators not resetting these rights properly, Bob's Bank chose to remove these extensions from the server. The staging servers still use FrontPage extensions but none of the DMZ servers have them installed. To accomplish this they made certain that none of the FrontPage directories are posted to the final production Web site. They removed all directories that FrontPage might have installed, including:

- _vti_bin
- _vti_bin_vti_aut
- _vti_bin_vti_adm
- _vti_pvt
- _vti_cnf
- _vti_txt
- _vti_log (this one will be present only in the root Web server directory)

FrontPage also uses a FRONTPG.INI file to locate any components that might have been installed. It is located in the %SYSTEMROOT% directory.

Tasks for Security Officer

Configuring proper security on an IIS is only one of the major tasks required to create a secure Web presence. Bob's Bank felt that it was equally important that a security officer be appointed to monitor, update, and improve the DMZ, and to maintain the integrity of the security model. Some of the tasks they assigned to this person included:

- Help create the security model and enforce its standards and guidelines.
- Identify and monitor suspicious activity, internal threats, password and account violations, suspicious e-mail activity, access to sensitive information, and security incursions.
- Outline the procedure, protocol, and activities required when responding to a security threat.
- Implement and track Web activities using tools such as packet sniffers, system logs, audit logs, Network Monitor, and Performance Monitor alerts.
- Maintain self-assessment tools that look at the server security and probe for potential weaknesses. Some example tools are: ISS Secure Scanner, Kane's Security Analyst and Security Monitor, BindView, NOSAdmin for NT, and the standard TCP/IP Tools (finger, whois, ping, etc). These tools are described in detail in Chapter 5.
- Discover and respond to new types of security exposures.
- Fully understand the incident reporting process and the use of Incident reporting tools (Internal Process Definition and Computer Emergency Response Team advisories).
- Review news groups, monitor mailing lists, and attend security conferences.
- Monitor Web sites such as WWW.NTSecurity.Com, WWW.NTBugtraq.Com, and WWW.Microsoft.Com/Secuirty for the latest alerts and issues.
- Create the backup and disaster recovery plan for the DMZ.
- Manage secure content updating from the development and staging Web servers to production.
- Approve all CGI scripts that are required by a development team before they are placed on the DMZ Web server (a separate testing model will be created for CGI scripts to address concerns about CGI and security implications).

- Track all servers in the DMZ to make sure they have the latest virus software. Scan all files and put a procedure in place to keep virus definitions up to date.

- Continually monitor all DMZ servers to make sure that the security model is always current and fully intact.

Third-party Audits

After they completed and put their security model in place, Bob's Bank considered having a third party attempt to uncover overlooked issues or security risks. Companies of this type (you can find them on the Internet):

- Scan remotely to try to uncover any security vulnerabilities and look for any of the common hacker signatures in the Web DMZ.

- Supply detailed audits of possible weaknesses in the DMZ security structure.

- Attempt penetration testing by running hacker-like attacks against the DMZ.

- Consult on the design of the DMZ infrastructure and the creation of the security model.

- Analyze firewall security by using various infiltration techniques.

- Evaluate the problem escalation process, backup, and disaster recovery techniques.

There are many risks involved with hosting data on the Web, and they can generate problems despite the best efforts of security teams to protect that data. Third-party evaluation can help assure its integrity, confidentiality, and safety.

Testing and Evaluating the Current Security Level

Security Evaluation Tools

Once you establish a secure DMZ, you have to understand how to monitor and manage changes to the security model to ensure its soundness. Failure to authorize or track changes can result in debilitating security issues. In one case, a developer turned on default author rights for FrontPage extensions, creating a security hole that would have allowed a hacker to overwrite the Web site. (If you can believe this, a hacker identified the hole and reported it, rather than committing any mischief. This company dodged a large-caliber bullet.) And you have to remember that inadvertent damage to information resources (a directory unintentionally destroyed) is just as troublesome and expensive as a commando-style attack. You need to protect your infrastructure and resources against *all* kinds of damage.

Some type of change management is an absolute necessity. The Microsoft Solutions Framework (MSF) formalizes the change management process used at Microsoft. (See www.microsoft.com/solutionsframework for more detail.) Control is the issue: you can create a Web site that allows people to submit change requests for authorization. When permission is given, an engineering change notice is generated and the security document updated. This sort of change management can help you sleep much better.

With change management fully in place, the administrator still needs some tools for ongoing DMZ monitoring. Windows NT Server comes with some utilities useful in this effort:

- **User Manager.** To create a security policy, manage advanced rights and user accounts.
- **Network Monitor.** To capture and diagnose traffic at a protocol level.

- **Server Manager.** To track connections, shares, and server status.
- **Event Viewer.** To study system, security, and application-level events.
- **Performance Monitor.** To track thousands of system and performance level counters to generate alerts, look for errors or issues, and track system capacity. (The *Windows NT 4.0 Resource Kit* has complete details on ways to use PerfMon.)

These tools are helpful but you also need tools that more directly monitor security effectiveness. Third-party tools available for this purpose are described in Chapter 5.

Managing Web Server Changes

This section builds on the previous one by outlining a series of possible solutions to handle archiving and retrieval of changes that occur when new Web sites and applications are installed on Web servers.

The discussions below deal with porting registry information from system to system. This can be successful only when two systems contain identical (or close to identical) hardware; otherwise it is unsupported. Research this carefully before trying it.

Option 1—Standard Windows NT Backup and Tools

This is the low-end solution. It addresses system change issues by physically logging the information being modified, using standard tools such as Rdisk and Regback, and storing the information manually and remotely for recovery after catastrophic failure.

Many third party backup solutions (Cheyenne, Computer Associates, Veritas) include the capability to back up and restore a complete Windows NT system (image backup, registry and file backups etc.). If your security policy calls for on-demand recovery, this option will not meet your needs. Backup solutions can provide an alternative if over-the-network solutions fail, so you might want to consider testing them as you work through security options. The entire registry and file backup process is easy to automate.

Option 2—Windows Scripting Host

The Windows NT Option Pack comes with the Windows Scripting Host (WSH). This is a classical scripting engine that enables JSCRIPT or VBSRIPT to manipulate the IIS admin objects. If the provisioning process is scripted, the information can be entered using an "answer file," that can be processed by a script designed to modify administration objects. You can use these files as a method of collecting change information that can then be automatically moved to a remote server and used remotely to rebuild a down server during the recovery process.

A known limitation of WSH is that it currently can administer IIS only. This will be overcome in Windows 2000, which exposes the administration of all operating system facets through the scripting functionality. In Windows NT 4, however, WSH cannot capture Windows NT configuration information, so you must incorporate other methods with it to create a complete recovery process. Tools available for this are described below.

In addition to the server backups you should also back up the registry, which contains crucial configuration information. Windows NT's RDISK.EXE backs up the registry and creates a floppy disk that setup can use to recover the server after a crash or registry corruption. If all program files are also restored, the server should be fully recovered.

Windows NT system configuration requires administrators to restore the registry specific to a machine, *not the registry of a similar machine*. Even machines that seem to have the same configuration can have subtle hardware differences (BIOS levels, ROM settings etc.) and problems can occur if the wrong registry is restored. Your security team should put in place a procedure to track registry backups box by box.

You have to run RDisk from the console of the system being backed-up. This can be a problem, in which case you can use ERDisk (http://www.aelita.com) to run RDisk over the wire.

When the crashed system and the recovery system run on identical or very similar hardware, you can recover the system remotely by using ERDisk to restore the entire registry or specific portions of it. After the changes are applied to the live box, you can boot it remotely.

You can make configuration changes to accommodate inter-system hardware variance.

A third tool is IntraSoft's KeyVision (http://www.keyvision.com).

KeyVision features.

Feature	Benefit
Centralized Registry Information	Concurrent access to registry settings for all machines and users across the Web Servers
Auditing and Rollbacks of Registry Changes	Thorough histories of registry changes and chronological backtracking speeds diagnosis and recovery of registry issues, so you can get a Web server back online faster.

KeyVision features.   *(continued)*

Feature	Benefit
User-Definable Rules and Notification	Administrators can define specific alert-generating registry events, so corrective action can be taken to prevent potential problems.
Simultaneous Real-time Registry Modifications	Multiple registry changes can be applied simultaneously to multiple systems using KeyVision registry keysets.
Multi-level Windows NT Security Access	Using the Windows NT security structure, Web administrators can be granted three levels of access to registry information: Administrator, Operator, and Read-only User access.

Monitoring Network Health

Along with monitoring configuration changes, you should also monitor issues that affect the system's running state so that administrators can be alerted in the case of a failure.

Option 1—Use the Built-in Performance Monitor and Event Log

Windows NT has some built-in tools to monitor system failures. You can set up the event log and Performance Monitor to alert administrators of critical system resource failure, including system, security, and application events. Windows NT also supports Simple Network Management Protocol (SNMP) and can be integrated with an existing SNMP network management solution.

Option 2—Third-Party Solutions

You can use a third-party solution such as WebWatcher from Avesta Technologies to monitor system health. It monitors Web servers and other network devices, automatically detecting the applications running on Web and FTP servers and testing them in real-time. Administrators can use it to search for any TCP-supported server type. In addition to watching the Web, this tool also watches routers and gateways, and has support for SNMP agents. When a device fails to respond, WebWatcher notifies the appropriate people by e-mail.

Other tools include WebSniffer from Network Associates, which includes agents that gather network protocol and server statistics, a repository that acts as the central database, and software that monitors communications between the Web Server and its users to identify performance problems and provide early warning of slowdowns.

It is important to test these solutions in a lab before choosing one.

The operations described in this section are intrusive and you must thoroughly understand and test them before you use them in your production environment.

Validation Options

When designing security for the DMZ you should also consider user and file level security. The next section outlines three ways that MCS client accounts have built their security to provide secure access to their users:

- Basic security and Secure Sockets Layer (SSL)
- Windows NT challenge-response
- A Lightweight Directory Access Protocol (LDAP)-based directory architecture

Using Basic Security and SSL

Basic authentication uses the local account database to validate remote users, but it does not encrypt this information and the user account and password are passed over the Internet in clear text. The SSL encryption scheme can be used to overcome this shortcoming.

SSL reduces the risk associated with doing business on the Web. It prevents network eavesdropping and sniffer-based attacks. It secures the logon sequence and data, and verifies data integrity. It provides the following benefits:

- The authentication process identifies and directs data to the proper server.
- The encryption and transfer mechanisms ensure that the data is routed properly.
- The process of reading the data at the server verifies that the information has not been tampered with.

In addition, SSL allows administrators to decide if a client-side certificate is required to access a particular virtual server or folder. In this case the server would request an X.509 certificate back from the client in order to validate the identity. For more information on SSL, connect to the RSA data security Web site at htttp://www.rsa.com.

Here's the user logon sequences (Figure 6.6):

1. User directs Web browser to connect to the Web Server (HTTP, TCP port 80).
2. In response to the client request to access a secure area of the site, the Internet Web server establishes a secure, encrypted connection. Over this connection, the Internet Web server presents an SSL-secured logon Web page. (HTTPS, TCP port 443).

3. User enters ID and password, then submits the information to the Web server. (HTTPS, TCP port 443).

4. Web server (Basic Authentication Service) passes the user ID and a password challenge to the Local Security authority for validation.

5. Local Logon Service queries the local account database for account credentials (access and rights) and returns the data to the Authentication Service.

6. Authentication Service verifies user ID and password. Assuming proper validation, the logon page then redirects the client to the application or set of secure pages and sends that information to the Web client.

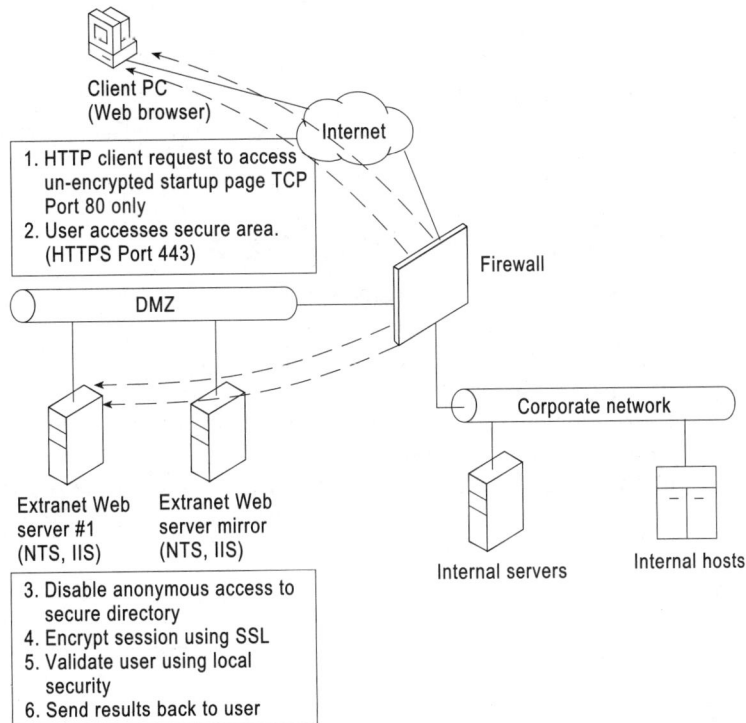

Figure 6.6 Basic security and SSL.

Advantages

- Basic security is supported by most browsers and platforms (Internet Explorer and Netscape in particular).
- It is relatively simple to implement.
- SSL encrypts the password sequence and verifies the accuracy of the data.

Disadvantages

- Accounts must be maintained in the DMZ and on separate servers, obviating a central account database. All accounts are created and administrated server by server.
- Account administrators have to gain direct access to the DMZ to maintain user names, passwords, and security equivalencies.
- Using encryption based on SSL slows performance. Lab testing can verify how much.

Using Windows NT Challenge-Response

Windows NT challenge-response is more secure than the basic authentication method. Challenge-response first attempts to log the user on using the credentials supplied when the user first logged on to the machine. If this fails, the user is prompted with a logon dialog requesting a user name and password, which are then validated against the Windows NT security accounts database. If this succeeds, the user is given an access token that contains all relevant security equivalencies for the domain. Administrators use these security settings to assign proper rights to the Web server's resources.

If both Windows NT challenge-response and basic security are enabled, the Web server uses the highest level of security supported by the Web server: challenge-response if possible, otherwise basic.

Windows NT challenge-response uses a full cryptographic exchange with the user's browser to validate the username and password. The actual password is never transmitted over the Internet, and this protects you against network spies who steal passwords off the wire.

A sample user scenario looks like this (Figure 6.7):

1. User directs Web browser to connect to the Web Server (HTTP, TCP port 80).

2. In response to the client request, the outside Web server establishes a secure, encrypted connection using Windows NT challenge-response.

3. Over this connection, the Web server presents a secured logon Web page and the user enters a user ID and password and submits the information to the Web server.

4. This information is validated against the Windows NT Server Domain Account Database Web Server (Windows NT Logon Service), which passes user ID and a password challenge to the Domain Security authority for validation. This information is not transmitted over the Internet.

5. The Authentication Service verifies the user ID and password. If this succeeds, the Authentication Service constructs a session ID and passes it to the Web client as an access token. The logon page then redirects the client to the application or secure page and sends that information to the Web client.

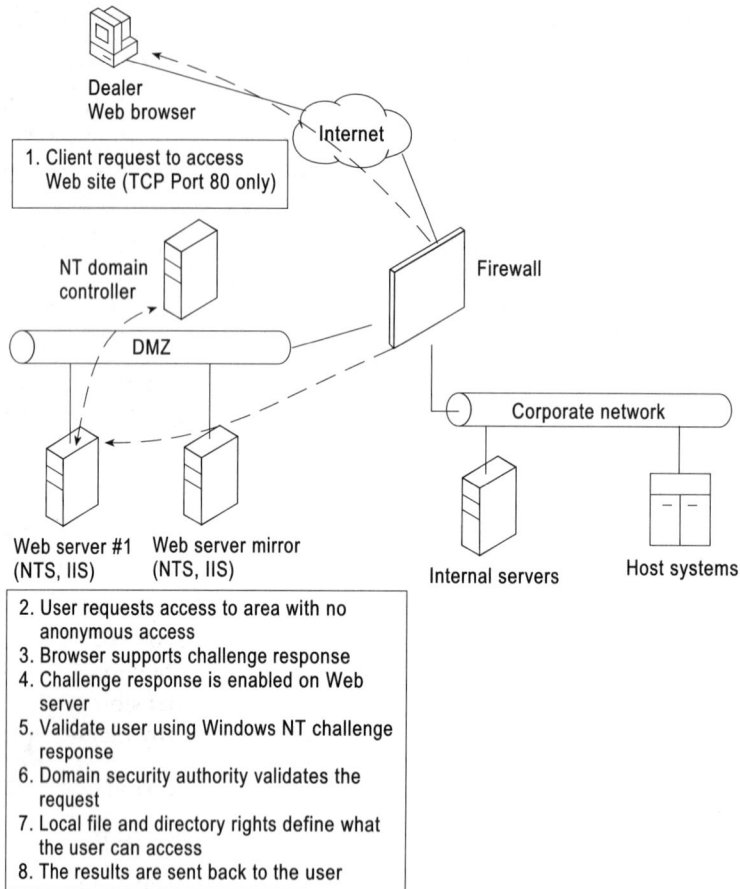

Figure 6.7 Windows NT challenge-response.

Advantages

- Windows NT challenge-response allows you to continue to use standard Windows NT domain architecture.
- Domains allow you to administer all DMZ user accounts centrally and assign rights to servers using this central account database.
- Challenge-response requires no client or browser software changes.

Disadvantages

- Does not support firewalls or proxies.
- Not yet supported by Netscape.
- Does not yet support delegation to secondary servers, so user credentials cannot be passed to another machine. For example, when a request comes in to IIS, the user account credentials cannot be passed to Microsoft SQL Server on a secondary machine.

Using an LDAP Based Directory

The Membership Directory is the Microsoft implementation of a directory service that supports Lightweight Directory Access Protocol (LDAP) which in turn provides the means to communicate with the Membership Directory. With Membership, you can create a centralized, extensible directory structure. It can also allow you to secure the account database by placing it behind the firewall.

With a Membership database, here is a user session sequence (Figure 6.8):

1. User points Web browser to the Web Server (HTTP, TCP port 80).
2. An encrypted connection using SSL is established. The Web server uses it to present a Logon Web page (HTTPS, TCP port 443).

3. User enters ID and password, and they are passed to the Web server (HTTPS, TCP port 443).

4. Extranet Web server (Site Server Authentication Service) passes user ID and a password challenge to the LDAP Service on the Membership and Messaging Server (LDAP, TCP Port 1003).

5. LDAP Service queries the Membership Directory SQL database and returns the data to the Authentication Service on the Web server (ODBC over TCP/IP, TCP port 1344).

6. Authentication Service verifies user ID and password. If they are valid, the Authentication Service constructs a session ID and passes it to the Web client as a cookie with a limited time-to-live (TTL) setting. The logon page then redirects the client to the Web Site or application menu and sends that page to the Web client.

7. Client selects the desired Web-based information, which passes a request for a Web page to the Web server, which passes the front page of the selected Web or application to the client.

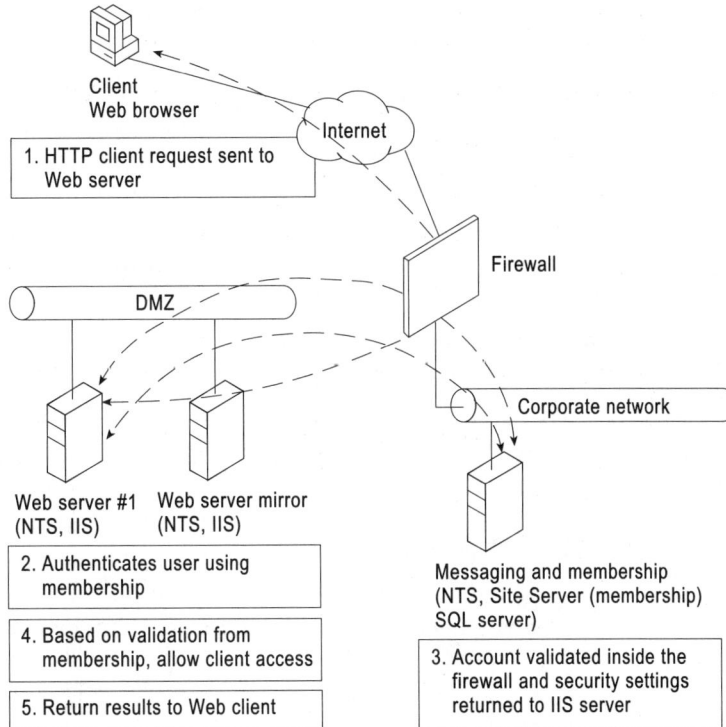

Figure 6.8 Membership database user session sequence.

Advantages

Placing the Membership infrastructure behind the firewall:

- Protects the account database by locating it behind the firewall. You can further enhance security by placing two network cards in the DMZ network—one on the public network and one on a private network. Filters on the firewall would allow traffic from the private network to enter the internal network, and would block all other traffic.

- Makes it possible to scale Membership to thousands of users. This allows you to build expandability into your design.

- Creates a centralized standards-based LDAP directory that can be integrated or migrated to future LDAP infrastructures such as Windows 2000.

- Eliminates the need to punch holes in the firewall because all administration takes place on the corporate network.

Disadvantages

- Requires development skills.

- Creates a separate set of corporate accounts from the existing Windows NT SAM. You would have to understand Membership *and* Windows NT to merge the two databases.

When to Use Each Solution

- Each of these has been implemented in a full production environment. Solutions were chosen based on business and technical requirements.

- A very large company chose to implement basic/SSL to secure its outside presence because:

- They had no control over the type of browser that would connect to the site. The solution had to support Netscape and Internet Explorer, so Windows NT challenge-response could not be used because Netscape does not support it.

- They wanted an off-the-shelf solution that could be implemented quickly with very little development effort. The basic/SSL solution required only that they obtain a key from Verisign and install it in IIS.

- Users connecting to the site must be required to have valid user names and passwords. The configuration used Windows NT Servers (not BDCs or PDCs) for local security and access control lists to manage user accounts and secure area access.

Another MCS client chose to allow business partners to gain access to its infrastructure using Windows NT challenge-response because:

- All accounts needed to be maintained in the central account database. Creating a domain in the DMZ allowed them to do this.

- Site developers could take advantage of additional development features supported by Internet Explorer, including NTLM authentication, enhanced implementation of DHTML, including screen repainting and event bubbling, VB Script, Microsoft Wallet, and some of the personalization settings.

- Administrators could assign security to server data and resources for both internal users and business partners using the DMZ central account database. SQL Server, and Exchange Server could also take advantage of this domain security model.

A large entertainment company used an LDAP-based directory because they:

- Required that the infrastructure support many more accounts than can be currently handled by the Windows NT SAM.
- Required a standard Internet-based security scheme. Using Membership in Microsoft's Site Server product allowed them to build the directory based on the LDAP standard.
- Wanted to centralize all security behind the firewall.

How Some Sample Accounts Use Their DMZ

Companies choose to implement security based on their core business requirements, which means that they choose how they will communicate with business partners by following the requirements outlined in their security policy. This section looks at two rather different examples drawn from MCS cases. In the first, Big Kahuna Burger (a large franchise organization) preferred not to allow business partners direct access to the internal network, opting instead to place content outside the corporate network in the DMZ. In the second, Bob's Bank chose to allow certified business partners to gain direct access to internal servers using the Point-to-Point tunneling protocol. In the third, Pretty Good Health Care Centers, (a mid-size health provider) used server proxy to provide e-mail services over the Internet.

First Example—SSL and Basic Security

As part of their security policy Big Kahuna Burger decided that business partners would not be allowed direct access to the corporate network. All pertinent business partner information would be securely replicated to the DMZ.

Figure 6.9 shows the Big Kahuna Burger security setup: Basic and SSL on all secure sites. Each secure site would register with the InterNIC and obtain a domain name. Each would be assigned a TCP/IP address using the current class C range of addresses obtained from the Internet service provider. Their secure sites would have their domain names and IP addresses housed on a single server in the DMZ.

Using the Key Manager tool, the administrators created a key definition file that was submitted to Verisign. After about two weeks, Verisign returned the key and it was installed onto the server using the same Key Manager tool.

No direct access is allowed from the corporate network to the DMZ. All content is replicated using Site Server's Content Management service. This uses the standard replication model that includes development, staging and production replication servers (Figure 6.9).

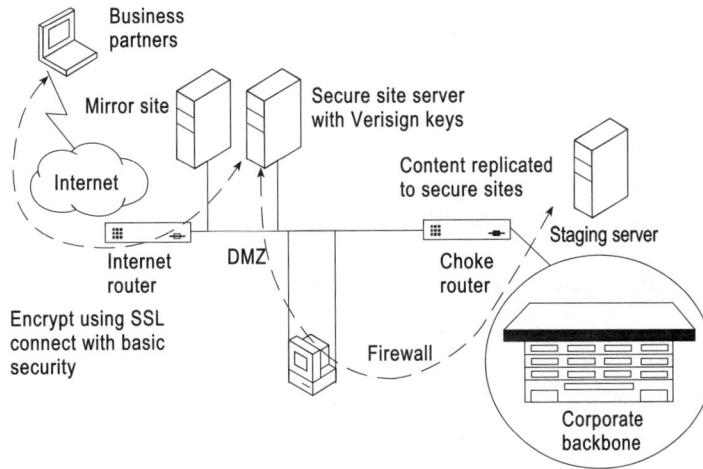

Figure 6.9 Basic and SSL security implementation at Big Kahuna Burger.

Replication Overview

Content Management software transmits content across multiple servers. At Big Kahuna Burger, Content Management sends content to a staging server, where it goes through an approval process, after which changes are replicated to the DMZ on a daily schedule. Big Kahuna Burger's replication architecture is shown below.

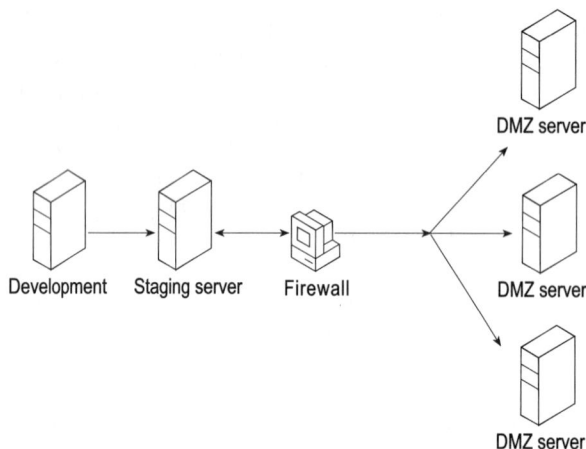

Figure 6.10 Big Kahuna Burger content replication model.

How the Process Works

Content developers replicate updated versions of their content to the staging servers. Content that meets required standards is copied using replication to the proper DMZ server. The firewall makes sure that security is maintained throughout the replication process.

Figure 6.10 shows a firewall that supports a series of internal servers replicating to all required DMZ servers (a many-to-many scenario). In other words, as long as the proper filters are created, any internal server can replicate to any external server. Not all firewalls support this model; research and testing can confirm what methods any individual firewall can support.

Firewalls

Content management can be configured to replicate content through firewalls by allowing outgoing communication over TCP port 507. The source and destination IP addresses will be known in advance as well. The only issue may be that the source TCP port is randomly selected, though most firewalls permit source port numbers over 1024 without restrictions.

Another way to accomplish that is to use the Proxy server. A properly configured client can replicate the content through the proxy server. For complete details see Knowledge Base article Q189746, Title: How to Use Proxy Server with Content Replication System.

Issues

This design worked very well for Big Kahuna Burger, and they are still using it today. There are some issues however:

- Because all accounts are local to the secure server, all administration must take place on that box. And as more business partners require access, account creation and management has become difficult. Big Kahuna Burger has decided to move to an LDAP-based security scheme so they centralize security using the Membership database found in Microsoft Site Server.

- Some content is just too large and cannot be replicated. Big Kahuna Burger plans to address this by using Proxy Server's reverse or server proxy feature to securely present data externally.

- 128-bit SSL cannot be exported outside the United States and Canada and the State Department has not granted Big Kahuna Burger permission to use it on sites requiring international access, so these sites are configured with 40-bit encryption.

The next configuration shows a large financial institution that needed to allow business partners direct access to the corporate infrastructure

Second Example—Using the DMZ with PPTP

Bob's Bank's initial configuration for this new "connected" Internet network used Windows NT 4.0 SP4 as the Server operating system, configured a PPTP VPN Server in the DMZ, and set up a Microsoft 2.0 Proxy Server to protect the internal network. Also, the PPTP Server was configured with two network interface cards to create a multi-homed server architecture (See Figure 6.11).

Using Microsoft 2.0 Proxy Server

To understand the software relationships, think of MS Proxy as a network application while PPTP is a network protocol that requires routing support. Operationally, this means that every packet transmitted to and from the Proxy Server is either sourced or destined with the Proxy Server's IP address. By contrast, PPTP packets use the PPTP server as a router and may have other machines as both the source and destination addresses.

One of the challenges Bob's Bank faced was securely using both the Proxy Server and the PPTP Server. For security reasons, Proxy's user manual recommends turning off IP forwarding for the box on which proxy is installed. This presented a problem, however: PPTP requires IP forwarding because PPTP exposes the local end of the secure, encrypted tunnel as the virtual IP interface. With IP forwarding, Windows NT Server can forward packets correctly from the PPTP tunnel to the internal network. This was solved by installing Service Pack 3 (or higher) on the PPTP Server and enabling PPTP filtering across the Internet interface. PPTP filtering prevents Windows NT Server from accepting non-PPTP packets from the Internet interfaces. The Proxy Server was located internally, in its own network behind the choke router.

DHCP/WINS/DNS Considerations

Another challenge was to define how clients get assigned the proper name server addresses in a PPTP world. Using Figure 6.11 as a reference, you can follow the process:

1. Business partners obtain a PPP connection via RAS to the Internet.

2. Once connected, they launch a Virtual Private Network (VPN) connection that requests an IP address for the PPTP server from the ISP's DNS or that directly connects using the IP address of the outside PPTP server.

3. If multiple PPTP servers exist, the outside DNS completes the look-up and sends the address of one of the PPTP servers back to the RAS client in a round robin fashion.

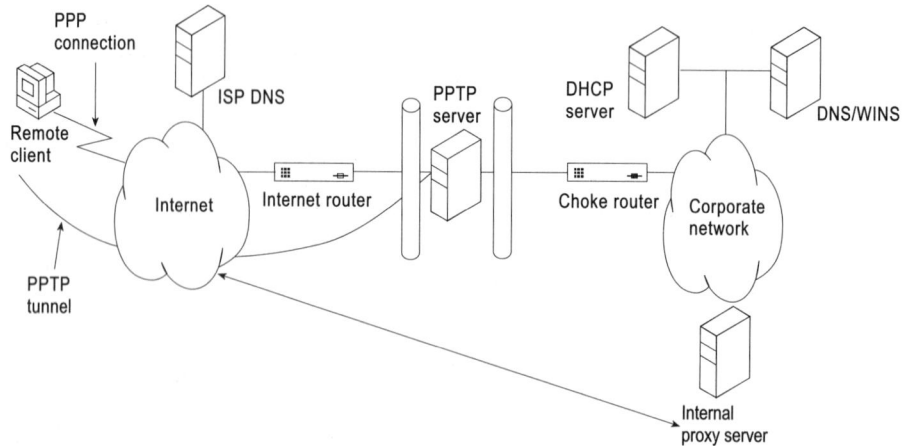

Figure 6.11 PPTP configuration at Bob's Bank.

4. RAS client opens a PPTP tunnel to one of the PPTP servers with its
   Windows NT account information. RAS/PPTP servers provide PPP
   configurations to remote clients using the IPCP protocol. The RAS/PPTP
   server can be configured to acquire IP address from a DHCP server on behalf
   of remote clients, but this is for IP addresses only. Alternatively, the RAS
   server can be configured with a static IP range borrowed from the local subnet.
   In either case, the remote clients will inherit the DNS and WINS configuration
   of the RAS/PPTP server itself. No IP mask or DNS domain name is passed to
   the client for remote connections.

5. If logon is successful, the RAS server passes name resolution information back
   to the client, which becomes a node on the corporate network.

6. At this point the client is an encrypted node on the Bob's Bank corporate network. All transactions take place over the encrypted PPTP tunnel.

7. All access to the Internet is now provided by the internal Proxy Servers and not the ISP. If clients wish to use their ISP's Internet access facilities, they must first drop their VPN connection.

An alternative: A large multi-national client found it necessary to host WINS servers specifically for remote users to prevent them from polluting the internal name space. The WINS servers pull replicas from the enterprise WINS servers, but do not replicate back into the WINS enterprise namespace. This prevents remote users from registering NetBIOS machine names that might conflict with internal naming standards.

Third Example—Using Server Proxy to Provide E-mail

The last example is of an account using server proxy to provide e-mail services over the Internet. The system administrator for Pretty Good Health Care Centers, (a mid-size health provider) placed a Microsoft Exchange Server using the Internet Mail Connector (IMC) on the internal network behind Microsoft Proxy Server. With this configuration, an Exchange Server can provide Internet e-mail service by using the WinSock Proxy client and relying on features of Proxy Server 2.0 for protection. In addition, the Exchange Server computer will not require an additional registered Internet IP address.

The WinSock Proxy Client allows you to bind services or applications to the external network interface of the server computer running Microsoft Proxy Server, which makes them available to hosts on the Internet. The proxy server then listens for connections on their behalf.

For example, if you bind an internal SMTP/POP mail server to the Microsoft Proxy Server, mail clients or SMTP servers on the Internet can contact this mail server by connecting to the Proxy Server's Internet IP address. To remote computers on the Internet, these services appear to be running on the Proxy Server computer.

For information on configuring this option and a full list of well-known ports, see The *Windows NT 4.0 Workstation Resource Kit* ("Port Assignment for Registered Ports"). You can find this on TechNet.

More Information

Here's a list of other Microsoft Knowledge Base articles referenced in the chapter:

- Q143475, Title: Windows NT System Key Permits Strong Encryption of the SAM.
- Q189595, Title: PPTP Performance & Security Upgrade for WinNT 4.0 Release Notes
- Q167029, Title: Resource and Master Domain DCs Do Not Load-Balance Validation
- Q188855, Title: Security Privilege Must Be Enabled to View Security Event Log
- Q161990, Title: How to Enable Strong Password Functionality in Windows NT
- Q189746, Title: How to Use Proxy Server with Content Replication System

C H A P T E R   7

Advanced SMS Installer Software Distribution Techniques at Melis Confectionery Co.

By Gary Milne,
MCS—Minnesota

Microsoft Windows NT Workstation provides security features that allow you to create a controlled environment where users cannot make any significant changes to a workstation, only to their own profile. While this level of control is beneficial, it does pose significant problems when you need to distribute new software, upgrades, and patches that require changes to a workstation's file system, registry, and user profiles. This chapter describes three techniques for using Microsoft Systems Management Server (SMS) Installer to simplify software distribution in a secure environment.

In Focus

Enterprise
Melis Confectionery Co., providing desserts to hotels, restaurants, and grocery stores (such as FoodCo) throughout North America. Its headquarters is in Fargo, North Dakota.

Network
Headquarter offices include four Windows NT Server computers, 5250 clients.

Challenge
Melis Confectionery Co. has a locked-down environment, but it needs to deploy software updates and new applications.

Solution
Working with MCS, IT managers used the SMS Installer, developing three techniques to roll out updates and applications on user workstations.

What You'll Find In This Chapter

- Overview of the concepts and challenges of distribution in locked-down environments.

- How to use the SMS Installer repackaging tool to combine and automate use of Package Command Manager (PCM) and Package Command Manager Service (PCMS).

- Three SMS Installer techniques for distributing applications, updates, and patches in a secure environment.

- Sample code for adding commands to package scripts, with annotations and simple language walkthroughs.

Warning This chapter makes recommendations for tuning the Windows NT registry using the Registry Editor. Using the Registry Editor incorrectly can cause serious, system-wide problems that require you to reinstall Windows NT. Microsoft cannot guarantee that any problems resulting from the use of Registry Editor can be solved. Use this tool at your own risk.

Distributing Software in a Locked-down Environment

For administrators, a major benefit of a locked-down Windows NT environment is centralized control of workstation configurations. Users can control most of the user profile (HKEY_CURRENT_USER) and can customize their desktops (within the restrictions imposed by Windows NT policies), but they cannot make changes to most filesystem areas or to the system registry (HKEY_LOCAL_MACHINE). A major drawback is that because users aren't permitted to change the local machine, they can't install applications. Administrators have to do this.

Systems Management Server (SMS) contains two components for installing workstation software: the Package Command Manager (PCM), which presents users with a list of software available for installation, and the Package Command Manager Service (PCMS, included with SMS 1.2 Service Pack 2), which polls the SMS server for any unattended SMS jobs sent as background, and installs them as required.

PCM allows you to distribute software in a tightly locked-down environment *only* if the package contains changes to the user profile (which is not common). PCMS, on the other hand, implements changes to the file system and the system registry but not to the user profile. This means that you must create two packages for each application installation: one for the user changes and one for the machine.

You can use the SMS Installer repackaging tool to create one package suitable for use with both the PCM and PCMS. It scans a reference machine configuration before and after a new piece of software is installed, determines all changes to files, registry settings, INI files, services, and so forth, then creates a package that can re-create the changes on target client machines that have a common configuration and a valid SMS client license.

The rest of this chapter describes (and provides code samples for) the three techniques developed at Melis Confectionery Co. for distributing and maintaining applications, updates, and patches in a locked-down environment:

- Splitting the package into user and machine components and deploying them separately or together.
- Using scripting to determine which packages have been installed, then installing new ones automatically.
- Creating "Administrative" packages that allow users to perform installations normally requiring hands on work by a workstation administrator.

Technique 1: Split an SMS Installer Package

The technique described in this section requires that workstations already have PCM and PCMS installed.

Applications require numerous system and user registry updates to operate properly. You can use SMS Installer to create a single package with command line options specifying whether to install user and/or machine files and settings.

When it repackages an application, the SMS Installer automatically generates a default script containing all the steps the setup process completes during installation and places it on a reference machine. It can then compile a single executable (for example, MYAPP.EXE) that includes a compressed version of all files and changes to be installed, as well as the installation script. By modifying the script to accept a -M or -U switch in the command line, you can use a single package to install an application instead of creating separate ones for PCM and PCMS.

Sending the PCMS the command MYAPP –M installs all system components. When the SMS status .MIF file indicates installation is complete, you can send the client PCM the command MYAPP -U to modify the user profile and enable the application. Using one script saves time on the packaging process and simplifies script maintenance.

Creating Smart SMS Installer Packages

To use this SMS Installer package technique you must add code to the default installation script. The complete script is displayed at the end of this chapter in the section "SMS Installer Script for Visual Notepad."

Accept Command Line Switches

Add this code to ensure that the package you send to an unattended installation accepts the command line -U and -M switches:

```
REM  Make sure that the command line contains either a
REM  -U or -M option.  Note: This is case sensitive.

If CMDLINE Does Not Contain "-U" then

    If CMDLINE Does Not Contain "-M" then

    Display Message "Invalid Syntax"
```

```
Text: %CMDLINE%  You must provide either a -U,  -M or both to
install the Machine\User components of this package.  Note:  You
must be an administrator to use the -M option.

   End Block

End Block
```

Update the User Profile

Insert this code to have the –U switch run a user profile update. Although this example is for a registry update, you can include entries for associations, shortcuts, or other file system entries.

```
REM  If the command line is a -U then just update the
REM  user's registry.

If CMDLINE Contains "-U" then

   Edit 12 registry keys*

End Block
```

Note* These 12 keys are created when you delete the HKEY_CURRENT_USER entries from the registry information. (See the "Splitting the Registry Information" section below.)

Update the Machine

This code informs the **-M** switch to install the machine portions of an application if the user has administrative privileges; otherwise, the setup exits.

```
REM   If the command line has -M then just update the
REM   machine portions.

If CMDLINE Contains "-M" then

    If System Doesn't Have NT Administrator Rights Abort Installation

    Check Free disk space

    Perform filesystem updates

    Remainder of default generated script here…

    Edit 3 registry keys

    Edit 16 registry keys**

    Self-Register OCXs/DLLs

End Block
```

Note** This includes all of the registry key changes detected by the SMS Installer with the exception of those in the HKEY_CURRENT_USER hive. (See the "Splitting the Registry Information" section below.)

Splitting the Registry Information

Now you have to modify the installation script by splitting the registry information into *user* and *machine* sections. The SMS Installer groups all registry changes and displays them near the bottom of the installation script, when it is viewed in Script Editor mode. To view these changes look for a line that typically reads *Edit XX registry keys*. Double-click this entry to display a list of all hives with modifications.

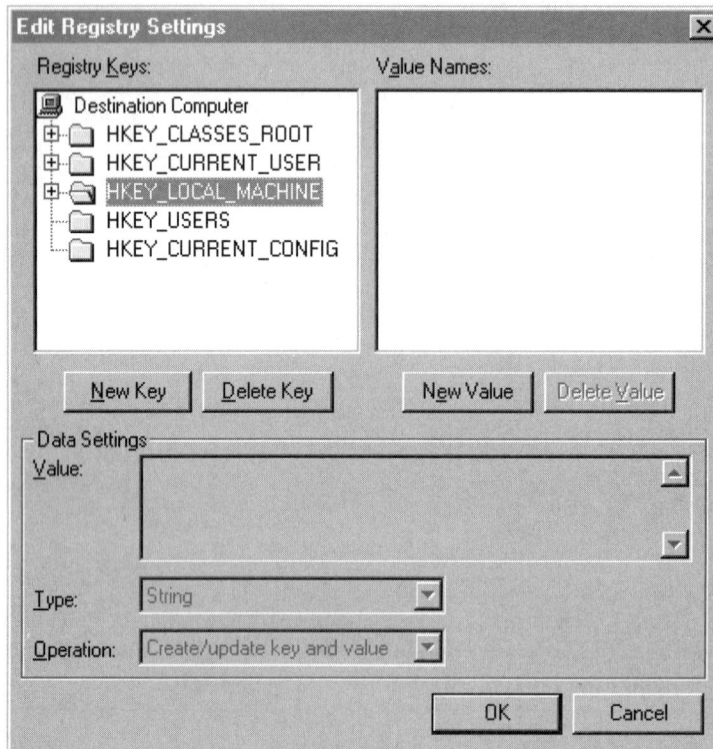

Figure 7.1 Double-click HKEY_LOCAL_MACHINE to display a list of all hives with modifications.

Copy all of the listed registry information using the Edit menu, return to the SMS Installer script, and paste this information in the *user* section. In the *user* section of the Installer script, delete all entries but HKEY_CURRENT_USER; in the *machine* section, delete only HKEY_CURRENT_USER.

You can copy these Visual Notepad sample scripts from the CD included with this book (under the \AdvSMS directory), then cut and paste between two separate instances of the SMS Installer.

- Click to copy the VISNOTE.EXE file. (Rename this file "Visual Notepad.EXE" after copying.)
- Click to copy the VISNOTE.IPF file. (Rename this file "Visual Notepad.IPF" after copying.)
- Click to copy the VISNOTE.WSM file. (Rename this file "Visual Notepad.WSM" after copying.)

After completing these modifications, compile the script into an executable in the normal fashion.

Using the Generated Executable

MYAPP.EXE now accepts the -U and -M command line switches in addition to the standard SMS Installer command line options. If you run MYAPP without a -U or -M switch the application does not install and you receive this dialog box:

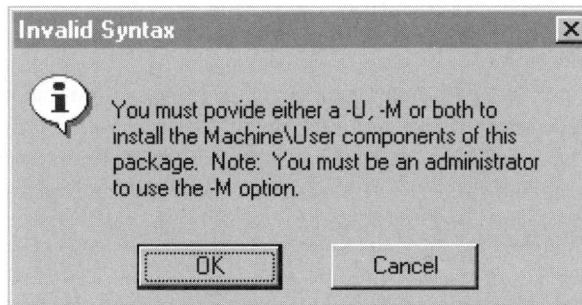

Figure 7.2 Dialog informing you that MYAPP has no -U or -M switches.

The switches provide three options:

- **MYAPP -U** makes changes to the user registry and other entries in the user section of the script, such as user profiles, .INI files, and so forth. These changes are often small and complete very quickly.

- **MYAPP -M** checks whether the user has administrative privileges, and, if so, completes all file system and machine registry changes.

- **MYAPP -U -M** installs both the user and machine package components.

Technique 2: Use Scripting to Launch SMS Installer Scripts

Use this technique to distribute software to clients shared by multiple users.

Because PCMS is on client machines you should be able to distribute the machine portion of an application without any problem. However, if you send an SMS job to the PCM on a client machine, it updates only the profile of the user who executes the job, leaving the machine's other users with an incomplete installation, which can prevent the software from operating.

Building on the previous section, this technique uses scripting to automatically distribute user portions of a package after each user logon installs the machine portion.

Using Version Information

To apply packages automatically when users log on, you need to add software and package version information to the installation script. Add the registry keys and values for the machine and user registry sections of the script (below) after the rest of the registry information. (Select **Edit Registry Key** from the **Script** menu in the SMS Installer script window.)

HKEY_LOCAL_MACHINE\Software\MyCompany\MyAppV1.

Value name	Value	Type	Operation
SoftwareVersion	2.1 (Numeric)	String	Create\Update
PackageVersion	1.0 (Numeric)	String	Create\Update
Installed	Last Installed at %DATETIME%	String	Create\Update

HKEY_CURRENT_USER\Software\MyCompany\MyAppV1.

Value name	Value	Type	Operation
SoftwareVersion	2.1 (Numeric)	String	Create\Update
PackageVersion	1.0 (Numeric)	String	Create\Update
Installed	Last Installed at %DATETIME% by %USERNAME%	String	Create\Update

SoftwareVersion represents the software manufacturer's version number, and PackageVersion indicates a company's internal version of the packaged contents, which can change over time even though the software version may remain the same. Tracking both versions in the user and machine hives allows scripts to identify when the user profile does not match software installed on the machine.

User profiles are updated using a batch, which performs installations and upgrades by querying the user or machine registry to find if a given package is installed. The sample files listed below use KIX32.EXE (a scripting tool from the *Microsoft Windows NT Server 4.0 Resource Kit*). You can also use any scripting tool with registry access, such as Windows Scripting Host with VB Script.

PACKAGE.INI

The PACKAGE.INI file contains version and description information about each package created with the SMS Installer. You can find the PACKAGE.INI file on the CD included with this book in the \AdvSMS directory.

[VISUALNOTEPAD]

SOFTWAREVERSION="1381"

PACKAGEVERSION="2.0"

PACKAGEDESCRIPTION="Microsoft Visual Notepad for NT4 (1381\SP3)"

SOURCE="F:\VISUALNOTEPAD.EXE"

[VISUALCALCULATOR]

SOFTWAREVERSION="1.0"

PACKAGEVERSION="2.0"

PACKAGEDESCRIPTION="Microsoft Calculator for NT4 (1381\SP3)"

SOURCE="F:\VISUALCALCULATOR.EXE"

PACKAGE.SCR

You can find the PACKAGE.SCR file on the CD included with this book under the \AdvSMS directory. This script:

- Reads specific package parameters from the PACKAGE.INI file.
- Queries the USER and MACHINE registry hives, determining whether a package has been installed. The script assumes the last key in the registry path matches the package name. For example, if the package name is MyApp, the registry location is Software\MyCompany\MyApp.
- Identifies which components are outdated and launches the specified SMS Installer package with the appropriate command line switches.
- Provides feedback to the user on updates.

```
; This KIX script checks the HKEY_LOCAL_MACHINE and
; HKEY_CURRENT_USER registries to determine if certain
; SMS Installer packages are installed. If not, they are run
; with the appropriate command line options to update the
; machine, user, or both, depending on the permission of the
; user running the script.

; You must specify a package name on the command line:
; KIX32 PACKAGE.SCR VISUALNOTEPAD

; For a list of valid package names check the PACKAGE.INI



; Color coding standard

; Header / Seperator  m+/n

; Default w+/n (bright white)

; Error messages r+/n (bright red)

; Changes y+/n (bright yellow)

; No Changes g+/n (bright green)
```

This code is spaced so that it is easier to read. Lines are broken for layout only: entries should be on a single line. If you want to skip this section, go to page 392.

PACKAGE.SCR *(continued)*

```
; Configure Constants for your company. This is where package
; version information is stored.

$LMrootkey="HKEY_LOCAL_MACHINE\Software\AcmeCorp"

$CUrootkey="HKEY_CURRENT_USER\Software\AcmeCorp"

Color y+/n

; ***************  Get Package Information  ******************

; Read the package information from the file PACKAGE.INI.

if EXIST(PACKAGE.INI)

        $PackageVersion = ReadProfileString(".\PACKAGE.INI", $PACKAGE,
"PACKAGEVERSION")

        $PackageDescription = ReadProfileString(".\PACKAGE.INI",
$PACKAGE, "PACKAGEDESCRIPTION")

        $SoftwareVersion = ReadProfileString(".\PACKAGE.INI", $PACKAGE,
"SOFTWAREVERSION")

        $Source = ReadProfileString(".\PACKAGE.INI", $PACKAGE, "SOURCE")

else

        Color r/n

        ? "Error: PACKAGE.INI file not found"

        Color w/n

endif

; If we cannot read all of the constants from the file then

; we should not continue.
```

This code is spaced so that it is easier to read. Lines are broken for layout only: entries should be on a single line. If you want to skip this section, go to page 392.

PACKAGE.SCR *(continued)*

```
        If LEN($PackageVersion) >0 AND LEN($PackageDescription) >0 AND
LEN($SoftwareVersion) >0 AND LEN($Source) >0

        color m+/n

        ? "Processing Package: " + $PackageDescription

        color w+/n

else

        color r+/n

        ? "Error reading package information for package:" + $PACKAGE + "
from PACKAGE.INI"

        ? "Package Version: "          $PackageVersion

        ? "Package Description: "      $PackageDescription

        ? "Software Version: "         $SoftwareVersion

        ? "Source: "                   $Source

;       goto end

    Endif

; Read the Install status from the MACHINE and USER registries.

$CUPackageVersion = ReadValue($CUrootkey + "\" + $Package,
"PackageVersion")

$LMPackageVersion = ReadValue($LMrootkey + "\" + $Package,
"PackageVersion")

if $LMPackageVersion = $PackageVersion AND $CUPackageVersion =
$PackageVersion
```

This code is spaced so that it is easier to read. Lines are broken for layout only: entries should be on a single line. If you want to skip this section, go to page 392.

PACKAGE.SCR   *(continued)*

```
; Do Nothing—both HKEY_LOCAL_MACHINE and HKEY_CURRENT_USER
; are up to date.

color g+/n

? "Status: Configuration current for " + $PackageDescription

goto end

endif

if $LMPackageVersion = $PackageVersion and $CUPackageVersion <>
$PackageVersion

        ; HKEY_LOCAL_MACHINE is up to date; run just the user
        ; portion with the -U

        color y+/n

        ? "Status: User installation for " + $PackageDescription

        SHELL $SOURCE + " /S -U "

        goto end

endif

; If we are an Administrator we can use the -M switch if the
; machine is out of date.

If ingroup("Administrators")

        if $LMPackageVersion <> $PackageVersion and $CUPackageVersion <>
$PackageVersion

                ; Both machine and user config are out of date

                color y+/n

                ? "Status: Complete installation for " +
```

This code is spaced so that it is easier to read. Lines are broken for layout only: entries should be on a single line. If you want to skip this section, go to page 392.

PACKAGE.SCR   *(continued)*

```
$PackageDescription

            SHELL $SOURCE + " -M -U"

            goto end

      endif

      if $LMPackageVersion <> $PackageVersion

            ; Only the machine is out of date

            color y+/n

            ? "Status: Machine installation for " +
$PackageDescription

            SHELL $SOURCE + " -M"

            goto end

      endif

endif


; Catch all those that fall through to this point.

? "The Local Machine software is not installed and you are not an
Administrator"

? "The package " + $PackageDescription + "cannot be installed."


:end

? color w/n
```

This code is spaced so that it is easier to read. Lines are broken for layout only: entries should be on a single line. If you want to skip this section, go to page 392.

PACKAGE.BAT

The PACKAGE.BAT file executes the PACKAGE.SCR script for each package listed in the BAT file. You can find the PACKAGE.BAT file on the CD included with this book under the \AdvSMS directory.

```
@ECHO OFF

CLS

KIX32 PACKAGE.SCR $PACKAGE=VISUALNOTEPAD

KIX32 PACKAGE.SCR $PACKAGE=VISUALCALCULATOR
```

Applying the Packages Automatically

Each user logon launches PACKAGE.BAT, which executes the PACKAGE.SCR script for each listed package. The KIX32 script identifies which portions of the package (if any) are already installed and runs MYAPP.EXE with the appropriate command line switches. The table below illustrates this script based on the portions of the package already installed and the user's permissions.

Checking user accounts for installed packages.

Machine portion installed	User portion installed	User has Admin privileges	Action
True	True	Yes	None
True	True	No	None
True	False	Yes	Update user profile with MyApp -U
True	False	No	Update User profile with MyApp -U
False	True	Yes	Update machine with MyApp -M

Checking user accounts for installed packages.   *(continued)*

Machine prtion installed	User portion installed	User has Admin privileges	Action
False	True	No	None (or notify user)
False	False	Yes	Update machine and user with MyApp -M -U
False	False	No	None (or notify user)

Other scenarios to which you can apply this technique:

- Use PCMS to deliver machine portions of software packages and the Windows NT Logon Script to implement user portions. After the machine portion is installed, the user portions install automatically during the next log on.

- Create new workstations using an administrative account to AutoLogon and run the PACKAGE.BAT. This implements all machine portions. When a user logs on and the PACKAGE.BAT runs again, the user's profile is updated.

- Use PCMS to run PACKAGE.BAT on a regular basis. This ensures all machines have updated machine components installed. User logons run PACKAGE.BAT, which updates the user profile after detecting newly installed machine components.

Technique 3: Embed Switch User (SU) in the Installation Script

This technique builds on the previous two, allowing you to create SMS Installer packages for distribution in a locked-down environment that does not use the PCMS. You can use the Switch User utility (SU.EXE) from the *Microsoft Windows NT Server 4.0 Resource Kit—Supplement 2* to switch from a user's account to an administrative one so that you can perform the installation in a secure area of the system.

The packages run MYAPP -U with user permissions and MYAPP -M within the context of a workstation administrative account. This method has two advantages: it allows users without local administrative privileges to initiate complete software installations on a Windows NT Workstation, and it updates the user's profile and the local machine, avoiding the two-stage process outlined in the previous techniques. The steps are listed below.

Installing the SU Service

This technique requires a one-time installation of the SU Service (SUSS.EXE—included in the *Microsoft Windows NT Server 4.0 Resource Kit—Supplement 2*) onto each Windows NT Workstation that receives a package with an embedded SU command. Copy the SUSS.EXE to %SYSTEMROOT%\SYSTEM32 and execute "SUSS –Install". When completed, the SU Service runs using the LocalSystem account. You can perform this installation remotely using the Windows NT Scheduler.

Creating A Domain SU Account

The target client machine uses the domain SU account (named here SUACCT) to perform the machine portion of the installation. Set up this account as a:

- Domain User so that it can read packages from the network.
- Member of a Domain Global Group, which is a member of the Administrators local group on all Windows NT Workstations.

Accounts in the Domain Administrators Global Group meet these criteria by default, but the SU account **must not** be a member of this group—it creates a huge security risk.

Adding Administrative Capability to an SMS Installer Script

The code fragment below shows the main changes made to the SMS Installer script. The REM lines are numbered; the list following the sample explains the changes in each numbered section.

```
REM  1 - This runs the install using SU to elevate the privileges.

If CMDLINE Contains "-SU" then

REM  2 - Install SU executable.

Install File C:\SOURCE\SU.EXE to %TEMP%\SU.EXE

REM  3 - Set up pointers to the network executable.
```

```
Get Environment Variable MYSERVER into Variable
SRCSERVER

Set Variable SRCSHARE to SOURCE

Set Variable SRCEXE to VISUALNOTEPAD.EXE -M

REM  4 - Setup environmental variables required for SU.

Set Variable SETCMD to SET

SU_COMMANDLINE=\\%SRCSERVER%\%SRCSHARE%\%SRCEXE%

Set Variable SETDOM to SET SU_DOMAIN=GARYMIL_PC

Set Variable SETPASS to SET SU_PASSWORD=password

Set Variable SETUSER to SET SU_USERNAME=SUACCT

REM  5 - Place the command line parameters into variables; this
REM      makes them easier to modify.
```

```
Set Variable ARGS to
"%SETUSER%&&%SETPASS%&&%SETDOM%&&%SETCMD%&&START /B
"Installing Application" %TEMP%\SU.EXE -cb -l -e"

REM  6 - Finally, execute the SU command

Execute CMD.EXE /C %ARGS% (Wait)

End Block
```

1. This line adds support for the -SU switch. If you send a package without this switch the remainder of the code is ignored.

2. The SU.EXE copies into the temp directory and expands prior to use. The file can remain on the filesystem permanently or it can be directed to delete itself after use (a security measure).

3. This configuration constructs a path to the network executable allowing users to perform an installation from a nearby server. In this example, %HOMEPATH% (an environmental variable that should already exist) points users back to their home server, but you can also read SMS Server information from the SMS.INI file to produce the same function.

4. SU can receive parameters via the command line or the environment. This section configures the environmental variables with the values required for SU. The "Execute Command" statement cannot be longer than 126 characters. Using variables to contain the arguments gets around this limit and makes it simpler to change the script. (For more information using the SU command line, see the file SU.TXT that accompanies the SU executable in the *Windows NT Server 4.0 Resource Kit.*)

5. This statement links all of the arguments passed to the command shell. Combine multiple commands to CMD with syntax "Command1&&Command2". This populates environmental variables prior to launching SU. Do not use spaces in SET commands: for example,

```
SET VALUE1 =ABC && …
```

results in VALUE1 being equal to "ABC " (with an extra space on the end).

6. This statement executes the whole command string, performing the -M installation.

Running MYAPP with the -SU Switch

In addition to the -U and -M switches, the compiled MYAPP.EXE accepts the -SU switch, which is the equivalent of installing the package with the -M switch when the user has administrative privileges. The -SU option runs the installation twice: once to update user information, and once (using the -M option) to install machine information, which allows all pieces of the SMS Installer package to be installed in the correct user or administrative context. Figure 7.3 displays MYAPP running with various command line switches.

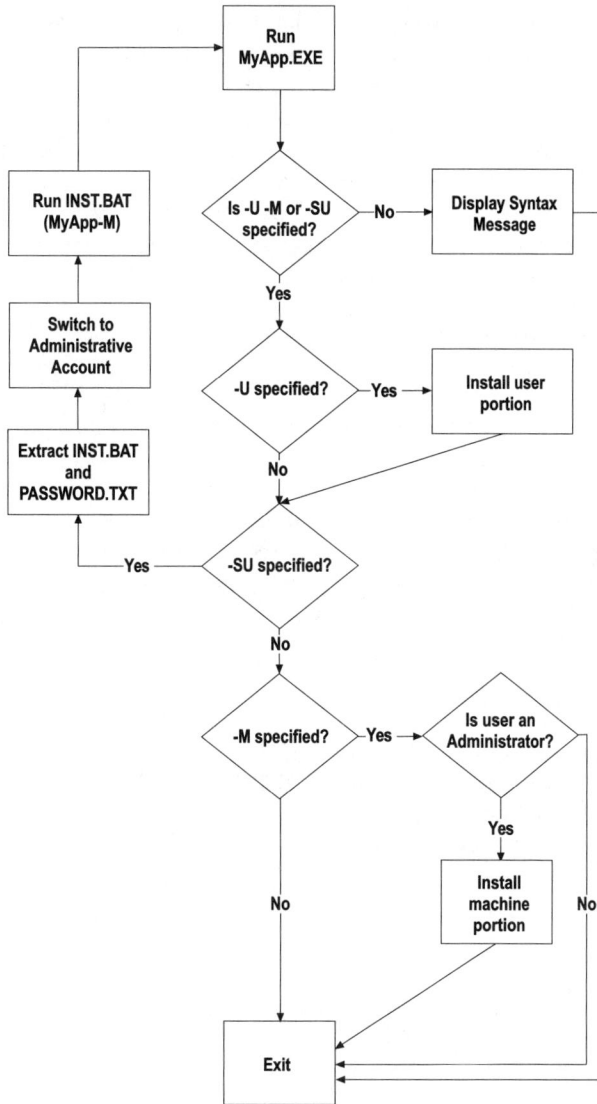

Figure 7.3 MYAPP with various command line switches.

The disadvantage of using this technique is that you must run the package twice for a complete installation, requiring more time and more network bandwidth. You can run the packages in an independent or dependent manner by modifying the "Wait for Program to Exit" parameter for the "Execute" command and the "START" portion of the command line (in the **Execute Program Settings** dialog). Independent execution results in the first instance completing before the second instance begins. Dependent execution reduces time and bandwidth use, but it runs both instances of the package simultaneously and therefore requires more memory on the client computer.

Here are several ways to use this technique:

- Use PCM to deliver the package with -U and -SU switches.
- Deploy a Web page or e-mail to deliver software installations using -U and -SU switches.

Run administrative commands by modifying the value of the CommandLine variable (for example, net config server /srvcomment:"%USERNAME%'s Computer"). This changes the machine description to include the user's logon name, a task that usually requires Power User status on the machine.

Security

The -SU technique represents a compromise between the competing needs of security and software distribution. If simplified distribution is more important to you than absolute security, this is a handy technique. If not, don't use it. It does, however, offer three safeguards:

- The domain SU account (SUACCT) is a domain user and workstation administrator, providing only the domain access required to perform installations.
- The password embedded in the generated SMS Installer package is not in clear-text and cannot be read by people viewing the file contents.
- The password passes to SU through the environment and exists only in client computer memory, not on the disk.

SMS Installer Script for Visual Notepad

Here is an example of the standard code produced by the SMS Installer in plain text. Italicized text indicates additions.

```
Stop writing to installation log

REM  Retreive variables from the environment

Get Environment Variable USERNAME into Variable USERNAME

Get System Information into DATETIME

REM  Make sure that the command line contains either a -U or
REM  a -M option.  Note: This is case sensitive.
```

This code is spaced so that it is easier to read. Lines are broken for layout only: entries should be on a single line. If you want to skip this section, go to page 413.

SMS Installer Script   *(continued)*

```
If CMDLINE Does Not Contain "-SU" then

  If CMDLINE Does Not Contain "-U" then

    If CMDLINE Does Not Contain "-M" then

      Display Message "Invalid Syntax"

      Text: %CMDLINE%  You must povide either a -U or a -M or
both to install the Machine and User

      components of this package.  Note:  You must be an
administrator to use the -M option.

    End Block

  End Block

End Block

Check If Directory not writable %SYS% Start Block

  Set Variable SYS to %WIN%

End Block
```

This code is spaced so that it is easier to read. Lines are broken for layout only: entries should be on a single line. If you want to skip this section, go to page 413.

```
Set Variable APPTITLE to Visual Notepad

Set Variable GROUP to Visual Notepad

Set Variable DISABLED to !

Set Variable MAINDIR to

REM  The SMS Installer sets this value by default.

If System Has Windows 95 Shell Interface Start Block

   Get Registry Key SOFTWARE\Microsoft\Windows\CurrentVersion place
in Variable COMMON

   Get Registry Key SOFTWARE\Microsoft\Windows\CurrentVersion place
in Variable PROGRAM_FILES

   Set Variable MAINDIR to C:\%MAINDIR%

   Set Variable EXPLORER to 1

Else

   Set Variable MAINDIR to C:\%MAINDIR%

End Block

Set Variable BACKUP to %MAINDIR%\BACKUP

Set Variable DOBACKUP to B
```

This code is spaced so that it is easier to read. Lines are broken for layout only: entries should be on a single line. If you want to skip this section, go to page 413.

SMS Installer Script   *(continued)*

```
Set Variable COMPONENTS to

Set Variable BRANDING to 0

If BRANDING Equals "1" then

    Read INI Value from %INST%\CUSTDATA.INI into Variable NAME

    Read INI Value from %INST%\CUSTDATA.INI into Variable COMPANY

    If NAME Equals "" then

        Set Variable DOBRAND to 1

    End Block

End Block

Wizard Block

    If DISPLAY Equals "Select Destination Directory" then

        Set Variable BACKUP to %MAINDIR%\BACKUP

    End Block
```

This code is spaced so that it is easier to read. Lines are broken for layout only: entries should be on a single line. If you want to skip this section, go to page 413.

```
End Block

If DOBACKUP Equals "A" then

    Set Variable BACKUPDIR to %BACKUP%

End Block

If BRANDING Equals "1" then

    If DOBRAND Equals "1" then

        Edit INI File %INST%\CUSTDATA.INI

        [Registration]  NAME=%NAME%  COMPANY=%COMPANY%

    End Block

End Block

Continue/Start writing to installation log

Set Variable COMMON to %COMMON%

Set Variable MAINDIR to %MAINDIR%
```

This code is spaced so that it is easier to read. Lines are broken for layout only: entries should be on a single line. If you want to skip this section, go to page 413.

SMS Installer Script   *(continued)*

```
If System Has Windows 95 Shell Interface Start Block

    Get Registry Key
Software\Microsoft\Windows\CurrentVersion\Explorer\Shell Folders
place in Variable STARTUP

    Get Registry Key
Software\Microsoft\Windows\CurrentVersion\Explorer\Shell Folders
place in Variable DESKTOP

    Get Registry Key
Software\Microsoft\Windows\CurrentVersion\Explorer\Shell Folders
place in Variable STARTMENU

    Get Registry Key
Software\Microsoft\Windows\CurrentVersion\Explorer\Shell Folders
place in Variable GROUPDIR

    Get Registry Key
Software\Microsoft\Windows\CurrentVersion\Explorer\Shell Folders
place in Variable CSTARTUP

    Get Registry Key
Software\Microsoft\Windows\CurrentVersion\Explorer\Shell Folders
place in Variable CDESKTOP

    Get Registry Key
Software\Microsoft\Windows\CurrentVersion\Explorer\Shell Folders
place in Variable CSTARTMENU

    Get Registry Key
Software\Microsoft\Windows\CurrentVersion\Explorer\Shell Folders
place in Variable CGROUPDIR
```

This code is spaced so that it is easier to read. Lines are broken for layout only: entries should be on a single line. If you want to skip this section, go to page 413.

SMS Installer Script   *(continued)*

```
    Set Variable CGROUP_SAVE to %GROUP%

    Set Variable GROUP to %GROUPDIR%\%GROUP%

End Block

REM  If the command line is a -U, just update the user's registry.

If CMDLINE Contains "-U" then

    Edit 12 registry keys

    Edit 3 registry keys
REM  These three are manually added to the package when it is
REM  created; you can query these keys to determine the
REM  installation status of a given piece of software. This is
REM  what we are doing in the PACKAGE.SCR script.

End Block

REM  This section runs the install using SU to elevate
REM  the privileges.

If CMDLINE Contains "-SU" then

REM  Install SU executable.

Install File C:\SOURCE\SU.EXE to %TEMP%\SU.EXE

REM  Set up pointers to the network executable.
```

This code is spaced so that it is easier to read. Lines are broken for layout only: entries should be on a single line. If you want to skip this section, go to page 413.

```
REM  Set up the variables for pointing to the UNC.

Get Environment Variable MYSERVER into Variable SRCSERVER

Set Variable SRCSHARE to SOURCE

Set Variable SRCEXE to VISUALNOTEPAD.EXE -M

REM  Set up environmental variables required for SU.

Set Variable SETCMD to SET
SU_COMMANDLINE=\\%SRCSERVER%\%SRCSHARE%\%SRCEXE%

Set Variable SETDOM to SET SU_DOMAIN=GARYMIL_PC

Set Variable SETPASS to SET SU_PASSWORD=password

Set Variable SETUSER to SET SU_USERNAME=SUACCT

REM  Place the command line parameters into variables; this
REM  makes them easier to modify.


Set Variable ARGS to
"%SETUSER%&&%SETPASS%&&%SETDOM%&&%SETCMD%&&START /B

     "Installing Application" %TEMP%\SU.EXE -cb -l -e"
```

This code is spaced so that it is easier to read. Lines are broken for layout only: entries should be on a single line. If you want to skip this section, go to page 413.

```
REM  Finally, execute the SU command.

Execute CMD.EXE /C %ARGS% (Wait)

End Block

REM  If the command line is a -M then just update the
REM  machine portions.

If CMDLINE Contains "-M" then

    If System Doesn't Have NT Administrator Rights Abort Installation

    Check free disk space

    Include Script: %_SMSINSTL_%\INCLUDE\uninstal.ipf

    Install File C:\Program Files\Visual Notepad\Visual Notepad
Notes.vnp to %MAINDIR%\Program Files\Visual Notepad

    Install File C:\Program Files\Visual Notepad\Visual Notepad.exe
to %MAINDIR%\Program Files\Visual Notepad\Visual Notepad

    If System Has Windows 95 Shell Interface Start Block
```

This code is spaced so that it is easier to read. Lines are broken for layout only: entries should be on a single line. If you want to skip this section, go to page 413.

SMS Installer Script   *(continued)*

```
      Get Registry Key
Software\Microsoft\Windows\CurrentVersion\Explorer\Shell Folders
place in Variable STARDIR

      Get Registry Key
Software\Microsoft\Windows\CurrentVersion\Explorer\Shell Folders
place in Variable DESKTOP

      Get Registry Key
Software\Microsoft\Windows\CurrentVersion\Explorer\Shell Folders
place in Variable STARTUPDIR

      Get Registry Key
Software\Microsoft\Windows\CurrentVersion\Explorer\Shell Folders
place in Variable GROUPDIR

      Get Registry Key
Software\Microsoft\Windows\CurrentVersion\Explorer\Shell Folders
place in Variable CSTARTDIR

      Get Registry Key
Software\Microsoft\Windows\CurrentVersion\Explorer\Shell Folders
place in Variable CDESKTOP

      Get Registry Key
Software\Microsoft\Windows\CurrentVersion\Explorer\Shell Folders
place in Variable CSTARTUPDIR

      Get Registry Key
Software\Microsoft\Windows\CurrentVersion\Explorer\Shell Folders
place in Variable CGROUPDIR

      Set Variable CGROUP_SAVE to %GROUP%
```

> This code is spaced so that it is easier to read. Lines are broken for layout only: entries should be on a single line. If you want to skip this section, go to page 413.

```
    Set Variable GROUP to %GROUPDIR%\%GROUP%

    Create Shortcut from %MAINDIR%\Program Files\Visual
Notepad\Visual Notepad.exe to %CGROUPDIR%\Visual Notepad

  Else

      Add Icon "Shortcut to Visual Notepad" to Program Manager Group
"%GROUP%"

      Command: "%MAINDIR%\Program Files\Visual Notepad\Visual
Notepad.exe" c:\program files\visual notepad\visual notepad
notes.vnp  Dir: %MAINDIR%\Program Files\Visual Notepad

  End Block

 Edit 3 registry keys

 Edit 16 registry keys

 Edit 3 registry keys

REM  These three are manually added to the package when it is
REM  created; you can query these keys to determine the
REM  installation status of a given piece of software. This is
REM  what we are doing in the PACKAGE.SCR script.

  Self-Register OCXs/DLLs

 End Block

Include Script: %_SMSINSTL_%\INCLUDE\rollback.ipf
```

This code is spaced so that it is easier to read. Lines are broken for layout only: entries should be on a single line. If you want to skip this section, go to page 413.

C H A P T E R   8

Configuring Secure-Channel Windows NT Client Authentication at Awesome Computers

By Alan von Weltin, MCS— Greater Philadelphia

Windows NT user authentication on a wide area network (WAN) can occur on either the local or the remote network. When IT groups configure remote sites, they sometimes assume (mistakenly) that the most efficient way to handle remote-user authentication is to have it take place on backup domain controllers (BDCs) at the remote site. But this can sometimes cause problems—slow user logons, disrupted logon scripts, and overused WAN links—in which case it may be better to authenticate over a secure channel to a local domain controller at, for instance, a headquarters office. This chapter describes how, explains the role of Windows Internet Naming Service (WINS) in the authentication process, and provides recommendations and tools for managing secure channels on remote networks.

In Focus

Enterprise
Awesome Computers is a large hardware sales corporation with locations throughout the United States, Europe, and Asia.

Network
10 major sales locations connected by a WAN serve as regional offices; supporting 175 branch offices; one headquarters site in Puyallup, WA.

Challenge
Users complained that the logon process took too long and that they could not get a logon script when they booted up.

Solution
Awesome Computers used the DOMMON and NETDOM utilities to configure secure channels for authentication. They used the SETPREFDC utility to initiate efficient secure channel acquisition.

What You'll Find In This Chapter

- How the authentication process is effected within large, dispersed organizations.

- Methods and recommendations for establishing secure channels so that they are used for authentication.

- What to look for when assessing existing secure channels, and how to establish new ones.

The Windows NT Client Authentication Process

Simply putting a BDC for the master account domain at a remote site does not ensure that local user authentication is handled there. This is because of how the authentication process works. This section explains the process, starting with *discovery*, during which the Windows NT workstation establishes and validates connections with a domain controller (DC). When you understand the process, you will see how it can happen that even though a secure connection already exists for authentication, it is not used.

The discussion is based on Windows NT Workstation machine accounts located in resource domains and workstations configured as h-node clients (the default for workstations configured as WINS clients). See the *Microsoft Windows NT Server 4.0 Resource Kit* for a full description of Windows Internet Naming Service (WINS) and of NetBIOS node types.

Sending Logon Requests to Domain Server

Before a client can log onto the network, it must validate its machine account by creating a secure channel with a resource domain DC (see Figure 8.1).

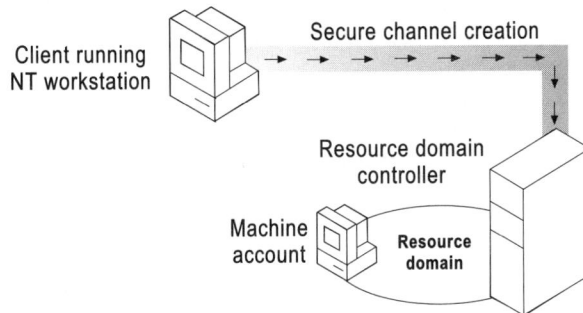

Figure 8.1 Client sends broadcasts to resource domain controller.

On request, WINS sends the client a list of *resource domain <1C>* entries, ordering them from the most recently refreshed entries down to entries that have been replicated into the WINS database. The client sends local broadcasts to these entries, continuing down until an attempt succeeds.

The first step in assessing your authentication process, then, is to review your WINS architecture and make sure clients are directed to the proper WINS server.

Establishing a Secure Channel between Trusting Domains

Next, a secure channel must be established between the resource domain DC and the master account domain DC (see Figure 8.2).

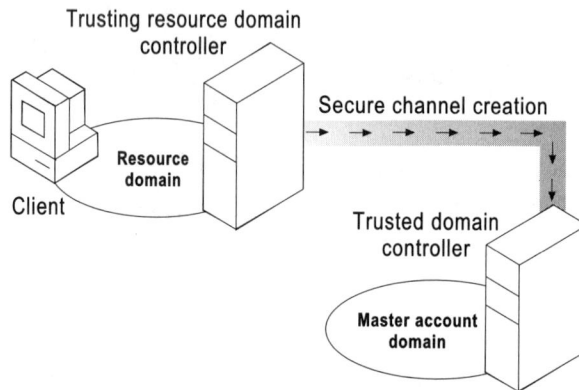

Figure 8.2 Domain server discovery process.

In a process similar to the client discovery process, resource servers query the WINS for *account domain <1C>* entries (rather than *resource* entries) and send out local broadcasts to establish a secure channel between the client and a trusting resource domain DC. When this succeeds, a logon screen is displayed. Step by the step, the process is:

1. H-node clients (default for WINS users) query WINS for *resource domain <1C>* entries to obtain a list of domain controllers. M-node clients use a broadcast query to obtain the list.

2. The client sends a local NetLogon broadcast to the first *resource domain <1C>* entry, and works its way down the list until a resource domain DC responds to the logon request by validating the client account.

3. At the client's request, the resource domain DC displays a list of trusted domains in the user's logon dialog box.

4. To log on, the user enters the USERID, selects an account domain name, then enters the password.

Validating Logon

The resource domain DC relays the user's logon request to the master account domain DC and passes back the validation information (the name of the server that validated the account) to the user over the pre-established trusted connection path to the account DC. For the purposes of understanding this process so that you can change it for WAN environments, this is a critical step because it defines *where user account authentication requests are sent*. It is explained further in the next section.

The client uses the supplied name of the account domain DC and is logged onto the master account domain. If a logon script has been defined, it is now executed.

Resource Domain to Account Domain Trust Communications

On boot up, a resource domain DC discovers and establishes a secure channel to a master account domain DC for trust communications and to route user requests for account authentication. To do this, it uses its defined name-resolution node type (m, h, etc.) to obtain the list of master account domain DCs. It then sends a local NetLogon broadcast to the first *account domain DC <1C>* name, continuing through the list until a master account domain controller validates the NetLogon request. It uses this trusted connection to route user logon requests.

This process is repeated each time a domain controller is restarted, the secure channel connection is lost and must be re-established, or the NetLogon service stops and is restarted.

Server Acquisition Order

Windows NT Workstations and resource domain DCs work through the server list supplied by WINS from most recently refreshed entry to least recently refreshed and then to entries obtained from replication with other WINS servers. The first entry is always the primary domain controller (PDC).

This order provides the key for configuring authentication to occur over secure channel connections, because it indicates where you have to place entries for secure channels so that they are chosen over other entries.

Monitoring and Managing Secure Channel Connections

Because remote site users encountered problems associated with inefficiently configured authentication, Awesome Computers ran a quick check of secure channel status using the Windows NT Server Resource Kit DOMMON utility. This graphical domain-monitoring tool displays the secure channels between clients and domains, and between DCs and other domains. Here is how they used the NETDOM and NLTEST utilities to reset the improperly connected channels they found with DOMMON.

To Check/Reset Secure Channel Status

To check and reset the secure channel, they used NETDOM—a command line utility used to reset a BDC secure channel—to issue these commands from the resource domain:

```
NETDOM MASTER MASTERDOMAIN /QUERY
```

```
NETDOM MASTER MASTERDOMAIN /RESET
```

NLTEST is a command-line utility used to test trust relationships and the state of DC replication in a Windows NT domain. Awesome Computers used it to find out if a secure channel was already established and, if so, which master account controller it used:

```
NLTEST /SC_QUERY:MASTERDOMAIN
```

For more information on how to use NETDOM and NLTEST, see their help files and these Knowledge Base articles:

- Q175025, Title: How to Build and Reset A Trust Relationship from a Command Line
- Q156684, Title: How to Use NLTEST to Force a New Secure Channel
- Q158148, Title: Domain Secure Channel Utility—Nltest.exe
- Q181171, Title: Secure Channel Manipulation with TCP/IP

To Configure Secure Channels

Once Awesome Computers saw the difference that secure-channel authentication made, they reconfigured so that user authentication occurs over secure channels on regional BDCs, rather than on each remote site BDC. To monitor and change secure-channel connections, they:

- Got a copy of the SETPREFDC utility from Microsoft Technical Support (MTS—http://support.microsoft.com/support/) and installed it on all resource domain DCs.

> **Note** Microsoft Technical Support considers SETPRFDC and NLTEST to be "Informational Resources," not tools, and does not support them. Only experienced administrators should use them.

- Created a list of preferred master account DCs for each resource domain DC.
- Created an AT command for each resource domain DC that issues a call to SETPREFDC using the names of the preferred partners. For example:

```
Setprefdc.exe MasterDomainName MasterDomainController1
MasterDomainController2 MasterDomainController3)
```

- Configured the AT command to run at an interval based on their network replication schedule.

SETPREFDC checks for the current secure-channel partner against its list of preferred partners. If the partner is not in the list, SETPREFDC prompts the resource domain DC to query the master domain again for a list of DCs, then checks entries until it finds a match. If it finds no match, it chooses the DC from the master domain that responded first.

SETPREFDC should be installed and run on every resource domain DC. The server must have at least SP2 installed—SP3 is recommended.

More Information

For more information on this subject refer to these articles:

- "Systems Engineering—Under the Hood of Client Logon (Windows 95 and Windows NT 3.51 and 4.0)" on TechNet
- Q165202, Title: WinNT Client Logon in Resource and Master Domain Environment

CHAPTER 9

Deploying Microsoft Cluster Server at Five Lakes Printing

By The Enterprise Services Assets Team

To keep the network running, systems administrators conduct regular backups, monitor for potential service or server outages, and quickly resolve issues that affect system availability. Another method for ensuring the manageability, scalability, and availability of enterprise systems is clustering—connecting a group of independent systems, so they can work together as a single entity. This chapter explains what Five Lakes Printing found when they considered using Microsoft Cluster Server (MSCS) to provide server failover and increased system availability.

In Focus

Enterprise

Five Lakes Printing is a large contract printer based in Michigan.

Network

Two Windows NT servers, Windows NT 2500 clients, 300 print queues.

Challenge

Network print servers experienced overloads and often went out of service.

Solution

Network administrators decided to cluster the print servers using Microsoft Windows NT Server 4.0 Enterprise Edition with Microsoft Cluster Server, configured in passive/active mode: the active server provides the printing services, the passive server is available as a backup.

What You'll Find In This Chapter

- An explanation of clustering and how various cluster configurations work.

- Strategies for designing a cluster environment.

- Procedures for testing failover scenarios.

Achieving Failover with Cluster Server

Microsoft Cluster Server (MSCS) connects two servers so that their data can be accessed and managed as a single system. The resulting *cluster* consists of a network link between two servers (nodes), and each node's link with a shared small computer system interface (SCSI) hard drive, where the shared cluster data is stored.

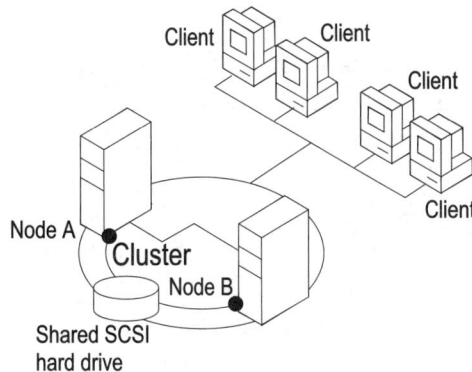

Figure 9.1 An MSCS configuration.

To perform failover, MSCS:

- Automatically detects a node failure and transfers its data onto the other node. Users experience only a momentary pause in service.

- Allows resources, including network applications and services, to remain available even when a server is taken offline for maintenance or other reasons.

- Enables cluster-aware applications to load-balance and scale across multiple servers within a cluster. To be cluster-aware, an application must use cluster application programming interface (API) calls and resource dynamic-link library (DLL) functions to access cluster features.

Cluster resources can use three failover techniques: **mirrored disk**, **shared device**, and **shared nothing**. **Mirrored-disk** failover allows each server to maintain its own disks and run software that copies the data from one server onto another. **Shared device** failover permits nodes to access data on any device. Because access must be synchronized, this method requires specialized software called Distributed Lock Manager (DLM), which tracks references to cluster hardware resources. **Shared nothing** failover requires that each server own its own disk resources; it uses DLM to transfer ownership of a disk from one server to another.

MSCS supports the shared nothing model; it supports the shared device model as long as applications supply DLM. The latter arrangement can affect performance because DLM generates some additional traffic between nodes and serializes access to hardware resources.

A fault-tolerant system (of which MSCS is a component) can be described as one with less than 30 seconds of downtime in a year. Fault tolerance requires a range of technologies:

- Uninterruptible power supply (UPS)
- Redundant power supply
- Error correction code (ECC) memory
- Redundant array of inexpensive disks (RAID) storage
- Fault-tolerant network interface cards (NICs)
- Redundant network fabric
- High-availability software (in this case, MSCS)

This table highlights the failover scenarios in which you can use MSCS:

Points of failure and how to work around them.

Point of failure	Microsoft Cluster Server solution	Other possible solutions
Network component, such as a hub, router, etc.	None	Spare components, redundant routes, etc.
Power supply	None	UPS
Server hardware, such as CPU, memory, network card, etc.	Failover	None
Non-shared disk	Failover	None
Shared disk	None	RAID
Server connection	Failover	None
Server software, such as the operating system, a service, or an application	Failover	None

Planning Failover with MSCS at Five Lakes Printing

Here are the steps that Five Lakes Printing used to evaluate MSCS and plan for their own implementation.

Select Applications to Cluster

The first step involves selecting the types of system applications and services that need to be highly available, such as mission-critical applications and file shares. One way to determine the level of criticality for each service is to rank them according to their value to end users and how much they cost your business when they are down.

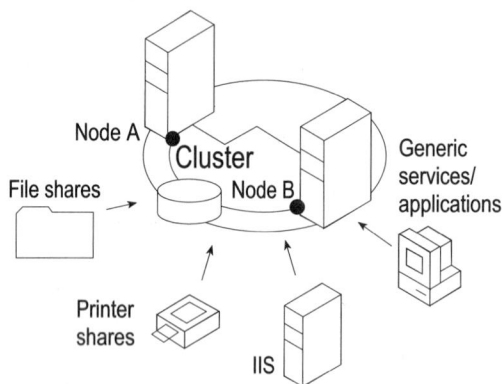

Figure 9.2 Examples of server applications for clustering.

Three types of server applications benefit from MSCS:

- **Core Windows NT Server, Enterprise Edition services.** File shares, print queues, Internet/intranet sites managed by Microsoft Internet Information Server (IIS), Microsoft Message Queue Server services, and Microsoft Transaction Server services.

- **Generic applications and services.** Resources that you want to cluster for basic error detection, automatic recovery, and management.

- **Cluster-aware applications.** Applications that use clustering APIs to access cluster features.

Choose a Cluster Model for Failover

How your system handles failover is determined by the function and performance requirements of the applications and services you select for clustering. This section explains the five cluster models (A through E, below) you can choose from when implementing MSCS.

Model A: High-Availability Solution with Static Load Balancing

This model achieves failover by having each node maintain its own resources *and* the resources of another node. Use this model for resources that require high availability, such as file and print shares. Network performance depends on the types of resources you choose and the capacity of the nodes.

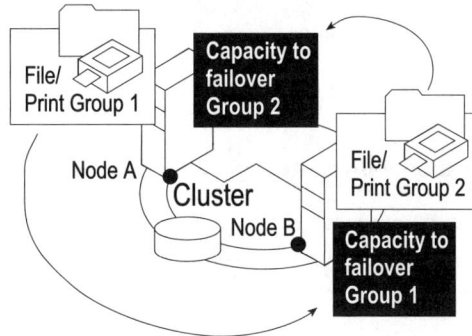

Figure 9.3 Cluster model for high availability and static load balancing.

If a node fails, its file and print groups are transferred to the other node to maintain. When the failed node returns on-line, the groups fail back to the original node and performance returns to normal.

Model B: Hot Spare Solution with Maximum Availability

This model achieves failover by having one cluster node provide all the resources, keeping another node (a hot spare) available in case the main node fails. Because this requires a second server you have to weigh its cost against the need for continuous high availability of critical resources.

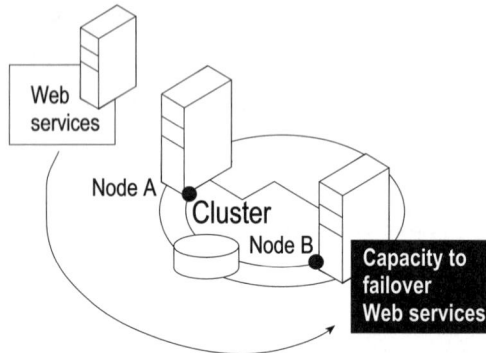

Figure 9.4 Cluster model using hot spare for maximum availability.

Use this model if you have resources for which high availability is critical (such as Web servers that customers use to place orders) and your business cannot tolerate degraded performance during failover.

Model C: Partial Cluster Server Solution

This model also achieves failover by using a hot spare for high availability resources but uses the designated primary server to run non-cluster-aware applications. This means you don't have to purchase a server to run only non-cluster-aware applications, but it also means that if the primary fails the non-clustered resources will unavailable until it is brought back online.

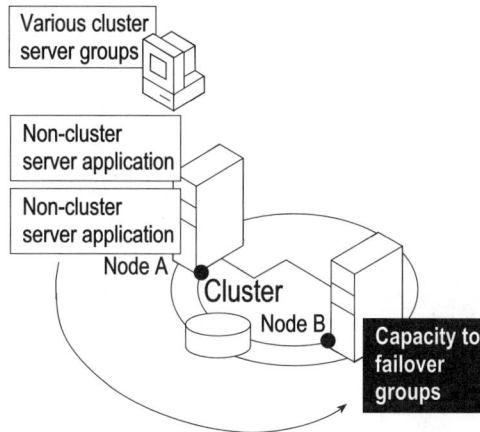

Figure 9.5 Partial cluster model.

This model is useful if you have non-cluster-aware applications you can afford to lose temporarily if the primary fails.

Model D: Virtual-Server-Only Solution (No Failover)

This model does not provide failover (because it uses only one server) but it increases the performance of specific resources and allows you to manage them with MSCS clustering strategy. Five Lakes Printing used this model to group file and print shares resources (virtual servers) so that users could access them more easily. The section "Define Resource Groups" (page 436) explains how to build groups.

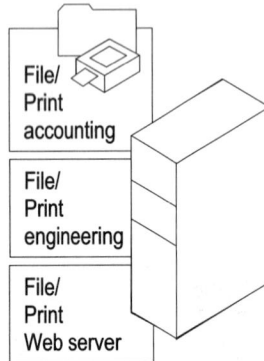

Figure 9.6 Cluster model using only a virtual server (no failover).

One advantage to using this model is that if you do add another server to your system, groups are already created—the only thing you have to configure are the failover policies.

Model E: Hybrid Solution

This model incorporates the advantages of the other four by combining multiple failover scenarios into a single cluster. Use it if you have a variety of resources that require maximum failover and you have the hardware required to support it. While it is effective from the failover point of view, putting both shares on a single node can reduce performance.

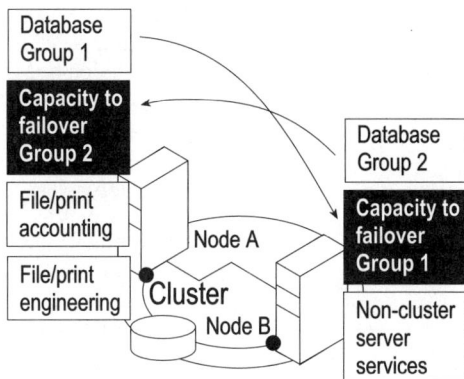

Figure 9.7 Hybrid cluster model.

This model provides static load balancing for two database shares by logically grouping file and print share resources to create two virtual servers for user and administrative convenience on Node A, and a non-cluster-aware application group with no failover protection on Node B.

Identify Which Resources to Cluster

The next step is to decide which file shares, printers, and applications to cluster. Do this by evaluating their availability requirements—their importance to end users and your company's operation. For a resource to be failed over by MSCS it must use Transmission Control Protocol/Internet Protocol (TCP/IP) for network communication and be configured to store data on a shared SCSI drive.

Types of resources that can be clustered.

Resource type	Description
Distributed Transaction Coordinator	Clustered installation of Microsoft Distributed Transaction Coordinator (DTC)
File share	File shares accessible by a network path, such as *servername**sharename*
Generic application	Network or desktop applications, such as a database program
Generic service	Windows NT services, such as a logon-authentication service
IIS virtual root	Microsoft IIS 3.0 (or later) virtual roots for World Wide Web (WWW), File Transfer Protocol (FTP), and Gopher
IP address	Internet Protocol (IP) network address
Microsoft Message Queuing Server	Clustered installation of Microsoft Message Queuing Server
Network name	The virtual-server computer name for a network device or service
Physical disk	Disk resources on the shared SCSI bus for shared folders or storage
Print spooler	Printer queues for network-attached printers
Time service	Special resource that maintains time consistency between cluster nodes

For these resources to be defined within a cluster and have basic failover functionality, MSCS includes generic resource DLLs. You can also write your own resource DLLs for non-cluster-aware applications or services to take better advantage of MSCS features.

List all server-based applications and sort them according to cluster share groups, virtual servers, or non-cluster applications. Your network capacity is the total of these three resource types.

Build Dependency Trees for Resources to Define Resource Dependencies

Dependency trees show the relationships of the resources that reside in the same group on a node. You can refer to them to make sure you do not create share clusters that have dependencies between critical resources, such as file and print shares.

Refer to these rules as you build dependency trees:

- Do not include the cluster name and cluster IP address in the dependency tree or group—they are created automatically during installation.
- A resource can depend on any number of other resources. Use lines to link a resource to all of its dependencies.
- Resources in the same dependency tree must all be online on the same node of a cluster. Make sure to include all resource dependencies.
- A resource can be active or online on only one node in the cluster at a time.
- Resources of a dependency tree can be contained in only one cluster group.
- You can bring a resource online only after all of the resources that it depends on are online. The hierarchy in the tree should display dependent resources *above* the resources on which they depend.

- You must take a resource offline before taking off any resources on which it depends. Place resources that have other resources dependent on them at the bottom of the tree.

- Do not link critical resources with high availability needs to other resources in the group. You cannot put multiple resources of these types within a single cluster: Microsoft Distributed Transaction Coordinator (MSDTC), Microsoft Message Queuing Server (MSMQ), and the Time Service resource.

Figure 9.8 shows the dependency scheme for all resource types. Dashed lines show "typical" but not required links:

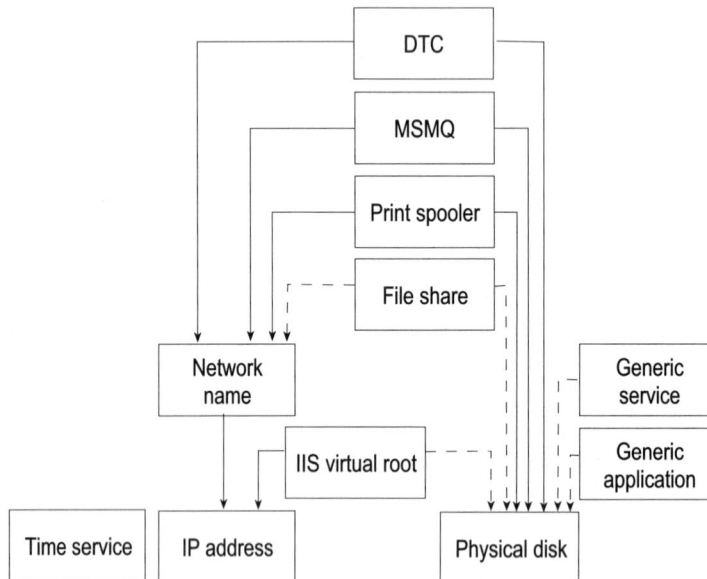

Figure 9.8 Dependency scheme for all resource types.

Sample Dependency Trees

Figures 9.9 and 9.10 display the relationship between two file shares and an IIS virtual root. Tree A in Figure 9.9 represents a single dependency tree. Because the resources all belong to one group, dependencies cannot be divided across cluster nodes.

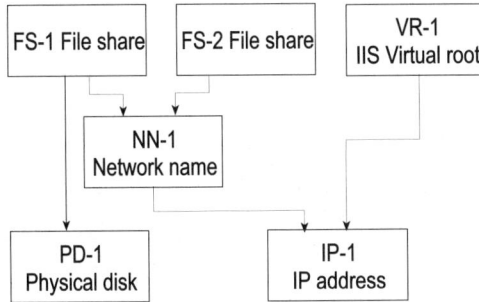

Figure 9.9 Sample dependency Tree A.

With minor modifications to Tree A, you can build dependencies across the nodes to create static load balancing (see Figure 9.10). Defining a second IP address resource (IP-2) creates two independent dependency trees that can be defined in separate groups, allowing the file shares to be active on one node while the virtual root is active on another.

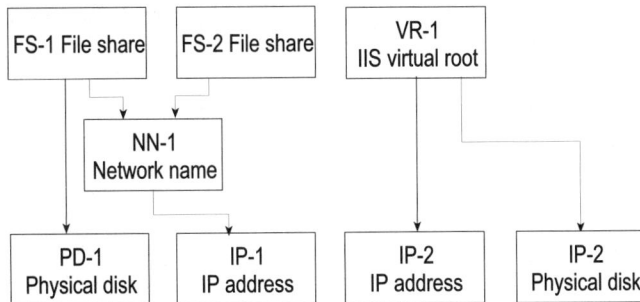

Figure 9.10 Sample dependency Tree B.

Defining Resource Properties

Once you have mapped your resources using dependency trees, you should define general, advanced, and resource-specific properties. These properties are set when you implement MSCS on your system. For a detailed description of these properties see "Setting Properties" in Chapter 4 of the *Microsoft Cluster Server Administrator's Guide*.

Define Resource Groups

A group links the dependencies for a collection of dependent or related resources to be managed as a single unit—typically all the resources needed to run a specific application or service. Grouping is the primary means of achieving static load balancing. Careful lab testing and resource monitoring can help you determine a an optimal-performance grouping system for your system.

Resource group definition rules:

- A group can be active on only one cluster node at a time.
- Resources within the same group can be owned by only one node in the cluster.
- A resource cannot span groups.
- A dependency tree cannot span groups.

Define Group Properties

You must define group properties (general, failover, and failback) before you can set them during the implementation stage. Do this in conjunction with establishing a failover policy (described in the next section). For a detailed description of these properties see the MSCS on-line help or the *Microsoft Cluster Server Administrator's Guide*.

Establish Failover Policies

Failover policies determine how groups behave during failover. The online and offline transitions occur in a predefined order: a resource is brought online after all resources it depends on are brought online, and a resource is taken offline before any resource it depends on is taken offline. Failback is when a group returns to the node it was active on prior to a failover.

The cluster service automatically initiates failover when it detects a failure on one of the cluster nodes. Because each cluster node monitors its own processes and the other node processes, the need for failover is detected with minimal delay. In most cases, MSCS can detect a node has failed and begin failover in less than 10 seconds.

A failover policy is defined as the maximum number of times (the *threshold*) that a group is allowed to failover in a specified number of hours (the *period*) before it is taken offline. When a group exceeds the failover policy MSCS leaves it offline. Assign an appropriate failover policy to each resource group in MSCS.

Implementing Failover Using MSCS

With the information you have gathered in the planning stage, you can configure MSCS according to your failover design. Implementing failover involves configuring servers, software, and clusters on MSCS.

Configuring Hardware

You have to make configuration changes to your system hardware to ensure proper failover.

Standard Server Hardware

Although you can configure MSCS using the minimum requirements (two nodes configured similarly, one SCSI disk on a shared bus, and one network interface card for each node), you can achieve more effective high availability by analyzing your system and eliminating all single points of failure. This table summarizes single points of failure and possible options for addressing them.

Protecting against single points of failure.

Point of failure	Typical solution	Preferable solution	Optimal solution
Cluster power source	Use an uninterruptible power supply (UPS) with power conditioning capabilities to protect the entire cluster from AC power problems (brownouts, surges, power loss).	Use a UPS for each node of the cluster and any external drive cabinets so that there are backup UPS units in case of failure.	Use UPS systems with redundant power paths: AC power to the UPS systems from different circuits or power grids; generator backups for the AC power source.
Cabinet power supply	Use multiple power cords connected to independent power sources for each cabinet in the cluster.	Use multiple internal power supplies and multiple power cords connected to independent power sources, for each cabinet in the cluster.	Use multiple, hot-pluggable, internal power supplies and multiple power cords connected to independent power sources, for each cabinet in the cluster.
Cluster inter-connect	Use a single network interface card (NIC) per cluster node. This interface is configured as both the public network for client-to-cluster connectivity and as the private network for node-to-node communications. **See Note on the next page.**	Use dual NICs per cluster node, with one NIC dedicated to the private network and the other to the public network. 32-bit (or faster) PCI network cards are recommended to minimize failures due to adapter congestion.	Use at least two NICs per cluster node—one dedicated to the private network and the other to the public network configured as a backup route in the event that the private network fails. 32-bit (or faster) PCI network cards are recommended to minimize failures due to adapter congestion.

Protecting against single points of failure.   *(continued)*

Point of failure	Typical solution	Preferable solution	Optimal solution
Cluster inter-connect *(continued)*	**Note:** This configuration is not recommended because congestion on the public network could result in the delay or loss of cluster heartbeat messages, in turn causing unexpected resource failover conditions. 32-bit (or faster) PCI network cards are recommended to minimize failures due to adapter congestion.		
Client-to-cluster connectivity	Use a routed TCP/IP network with redundant routers on the cluster's public network subnet. Multiple gateways ensure connectivity in the event of a router failure.	Use a routed TCP/IP network with multiple gateways on every server and client subnet.	Use physically multi-homed clients and servers with fully redundant network paths.
Server memory	Use 8-bit, no parity.	Use 9-bit, with 1-bit parity to allow detection of single-bit memory errors.	Use Error Correction Code (ECC) memory. ECC detects double-bit errors and corrects single-bit errors.

Protecting against single points of failure.   *(continued)*

Point of failure	Typical solution	Preferable solution	Optimal solution
Private disk storage	Use one or more high-performance, physical disks for each server's local storage. (SCSI disks are recommended for best performance but are not required.) Configure the disks to the operating system as either independent volumes or a non-fault-tolerant Redundant array of Inexpensive disks (RAID 0). Each physical disk represents a single point of failure.	Use multiple, high-performance, physical disks for each server's local storage—use the Windows NT fault-tolerant disk driver to configure the disks as RAID 1 or RAID 5 volumes. A single disk failure does not cause a node failure; however, the node needs to be brought down in order to replace a failed drive.	Use multiple, high-performance, physical disks for each server's local storage—use hardware RAID support to combine the disks into fault-tolerant volumes (for example, RAID 1 or 5). Hot-swap capability allows failed disks to be replaced without taking down the node.
Shared disk storage	On the shared bus, use one or more physical disks configured as either independent volumes or non-fault-tolerant RAID (RAID 0). Note that shared disks must be addressable through a SCSI interface. **See Note on the next page.**	Use hardware RAID to create a fault-tolerant disk volume. This volume acts as the quorum device and hosts application data for a single resource group. Note that using the Windows NT fault-tolerant disk driver to create a volume is not supported on the shared bus.	Use hardware RAID to create multiple, fault-tolerant disk volumes. The availability of multiple volumes allows the cluster to be arranged in an active-active configuration.

Protecting against single points of failure.   *(continued)*

Point of failure	Typical solution	Preferable solution	Optimal solution
Shared disk storage *(continued)*	**Note:** This configuration is not recommended because failure of a disk or volume results in a loss of service for all resources hosted on it; they are not restartable on another node of the cluster and data loss is likely. You should make the shared disk hosting the quorum resource fault-tolerant, because the quorum contains the cluster configuration data and loss of this device results in the loss of the entire cluster.		
SCSI Connectivity	Each server connected to the local shared bus must contain a high-performance, single-ended SCSI controller card. Use multiple controller cards or a card that supports multiple SCSI buses if local disk storage is SCSI —local storage cannot be located on the shared bus.	Each server contains one or more high-performance, differential SCSI controller cards. Each of these cards may be used to support multiple SCSI buses.	Use fiber channel technology to create a shared bus.

Many configuration options meet the minimum requirements of MSCS but Microsoft provides technical support only for configurations that have passed cluster validation testing (use the Hardware Compatibility List (HCL) at http://www.microsoft.com/ntserver/info/hwcompatibility.htm as a reference for assembling valid clusters).

To be valid, configurations must use the same hardware for both nodes of the cluster, a hardware RAID controller, and a PCI network interface card on the cluster interconnect. The HCL also lists various system components such as SCSI adapters, fiber channel adapters, and RAID devices that have passed Cluster Component Candidate testing.

Peripherals

You should connect peripherals (printers, fax devices, modems, tape drives) directly to the network (if applicable) or to another, non-clustered server—that is, treat peripherals as "local" resources rather than cluster resources. There is no facility to failover peripherals if a node fails, and adding a local resource to a cluster can severely restrict some administrative operations. For instance, if you add a fax server to one of the cluster nodes you can no longer perform scheduled maintenance on the fax server during the day because taking down its node results in a loss of service.

RAID Array Configuration and Partitioning

Configure disks on the shared bus as fault-tolerant volumes so that when you create additional shared volumes the cluster can use an active-active configuration. (See the table above.)

Recommendations:

- Format each volume for NTFS only.
- Use a single partition on each disk (logical partitions cannot be failed over independently).
- Permanently assign the same drive letter to a given shared disk on each node.

SCSI Conventions

Your system must have at least one shared SCSI bus formed by a PCI-based SCSI controller. To form a shared bus:

- Change the value of one of the SCSI IDs. The IDs must be different before the controllers can be connected to the same bus; the default is 7.
- Disable each controller's boot-time for the SCSI bus reset operation (use the manufacturer's configuration utilities).

Capacity Requirements

Cluster configuration involves balancing each node's capacity so that resources perform optimally and either node can temporarily run the resources of the other during failover. The capacity requirements for cluster nodes are:

- **Hard-disk-storage.** Each node in a cluster must have enough hard-disk capacity to store permanent copies of all applications and other resources required to run all groups. Plan disk space allowances so that either node can efficiently run all resources during failover.

- **CPU.** Failover can strain the CPU processing capacity of an MSCS server when the server takes control of the resources from a failed node. If you don't plan properly, the CPU of a surviving node can be pushed beyond its practical capacity during failover, slowing response time. Plan your CPU capacity on each node so that it can accommodate new resources without greatly affecting responsiveness.

- **RAM.** Each node in your cluster should have enough RAM to handle all applications that run on either node. Also, make sure to set the Windows NT paging files appropriately for each node's physical memory.

IP Addresses

MSCS does not support DHCP-assigned IP addresses for the cluster administration address (associated with the cluster name), or for any IP address resources. To configure Windows NT on each node, use either static IP addresses (which ensures the highest degree of availability) or DHCP permanently-leased IP addresses (with a slight chance of failure).

Private Network Addressing

If you configure a cluster with a private interconnect it is good practice to assign addresses from one of the private networks defined by the Internet Assigned Numbers Authority (IANA). Refer to RFC 1597 "Address Allocation for Private Internets" and RFC 1631 "The IP Network Address Translator (NAT)" located at http://safety.net/rfc.html. RFC 1597 defines three network classes for private networks as listed below.

- 10.0.0.0 – 10.255.255.255 (Class A), Subnet Mask: 255.0.0.0
- 172.16.0.0 – 172.31.255.255 (Class B), Subnet Mask: 255.255.0.0
- 192.168.0.0 – 192.168.255.255 (Class C), Subnet Mask 255.255.255.0

Do not assign default gateways or WINS servers to the adapters on the private interconnect: it causes the server name to be registered as a multi-homed value and registers the public and private addresses in WINS. Clients select addresses randomly and will not be able to connect with the server if they select a private address.

Using a Public Network (Subnet)

To move from a private to the public network see RFC 1631, "The IP Network Address Translator (NAT)" (http://safety.net/rfc1631.txt). You should reserve IP addresses from the public network subnet for the cluster: one for each physical node, one for the cluster, and one for each resource group that includes an IP address resource.

Naming Conventions

For proper failover, clients must connect using the virtual server names instead of connecting directly to the cluster nodes. You should establish strict naming conventions for each server type as a means of differentiating them, because no automated method exists for hiding the physical server names from the browse list.

Configuring Software

Windows NT Server Configuration

Before installing MSCS, you must install Microsoft Windows NT Server, Enterprise Edition on the non-shared disk(s) of each node, and you must apply Service Pack 4. Make sure that no paging files or system files reside on the shared disk(s). For more detailed information on configuring servers, see your *Microsoft Server Administrator's Guide*.

Non-Clustered Applications

If you have resources that you do not want to run in the context of a resource group, install them on a local, non-shared disk.

Configuring Clusters

Use the information you gathered during the planning stage to implement resources, dependencies, and groups.

Determining Resource Parameters

To optimize performance on your system, you need to observe a fully configured cluster running on hardware from the Hardware Compatibility List. To optimize, try changing the defaults for polling intervals, and for the pending timeout, RestartThreshold, and RestartPeriod parameters.

You can tune the values of the LooksAlive or IsAlive polling intervals to determine how quickly a cluster service becomes aware of a resource failure. For more information on setting polling intervals using Cluster Administrator, see Chapter 4 of the *Microsoft Cluster Server Administrator's Guide* or the Cluster Administrator Help.

Tune the Pending Timeout parameter for each resource using the worst case restart time. You should consider that restart times vary with the size of a resource's transaction logs (for example, Microsoft SQL Server and Microsoft Exchange). Calculate the timeout for the node under maximum load to avoid setting the parameter too low, which can cause the cluster service to put a resource in a failed or offline state even if a failure has not occurred.

The RestartThreshold and RestartPeriod parameters are calculated in combination (and in conjunction with the Pending Timeout value) to define how many attempts are made to restart a resource before the group is moved to another node. (Note: >= indicataes *greater than or equal to*.)

RestartPeriod >= RestartThreshold x Pending Timeout

For example, a resource has a 10-second restart time and a worst case restart time of 30 seconds. If three restart attempts are allowed, you should set the RestartPeriod to no less than 90 seconds:

RestartPeriod >= 3 x 30 seconds

Setting RestartPeriod too low can create problems. Consider what happens if you set it to 45 seconds for the case above. A nominal restart time (10 seconds) needs about 30 seconds to make three restart attempts, after which the threshold is reached and the resource group is failed over. If the server is heavily loaded, however, three restarts can never complete in 45 seconds, so the process will never meet the RestartThreshold and the process will keep trying restarts on the same node indefinitely.

Implementing Dependencies

As you implement the resource dependencies you established during the planning stage, keep in mind that the relationships are transitive. For instance, if the print spooler resource is dependent on a network name that is in turn dependent on an IP address resource, you don't have to define a dependency relationship between the print spooler and the IP address. See "Setting Properties," in Chapter 4 of your the *Cluster Server Administrator's Guide*.

Implementing Groups

You have to determine the FailoverThreshold and FailoverPeriod parameters for groups the same way you determined them for individual resources. Use the worst case failover time for the entire resource group.

FailoverPeriod >= FailoverThreshold x (worst-case Group Failover Time)

For example, don't set the FailoverPeriod lower than 180 seconds for a group with a worst case failover time of 45 seconds and a threshold of four restart attempts:

FailoverPeriod >= 4 x 45 seconds

See "Setting Properties," in Chapter 4 in the *Cluster Server Administrator's Guide*.

Establishing Administrative Procedures

Here are some recommended administrative procedures for MSCS.

Proper Startup/Shutdown Procedures

MSCS startup and shutdown procedures mostly depend on the hardware platform you are using. Because cluster nodes access information on SCSI disks, in most cases you should power up shared SCSI drives *before* the cluster nodes and wait about a minute to give the nodes adequate time to properly spin-up and become fully operational. You should shut down cluster nodes completely before you power off the shared SCSI drives.

In addition, before you perform system maintenance on a node you should transfer all failover groups to the other node. Transfer them back to the original node when the maintenance is complete.

Maintaining Shared Applications

The proper maintenance procedures for applications installed on the cluster's shared SCSI drives depend largely on the application. If registry changes are required and the application resource is configured to replicate registry entries, installation on the active node may be all that is required. Cluster-aware applications are better equipped to support this type of installation method. If the application is not cluster-aware, you may have to install the software on both nodes.

Backup Procedures

For MSCS: back up the operating system for each cluster node, the data on the SCSI bus drive, and the data on each node's local drive.

Operating System

Windows NT 4.0, Enterprise Edition includes a separate utility, Cluster Configuration Backup (ClusConB) for backing up your cluster configuration. For more information, see the MSCS Release notes (\MSCS\Readme.doc) in CD 2. Use the same process to back up and restore cluster nodes that you use for other Windows NT Server installations: use Windows NT Backup for the registry and boot and system drives. You can also use RDISK.EXE to keep a current emergency repair disk (ERD) for *both* nodes.

Because the hardware settings and the disk signatures for the shared SCSI bus are stored in the registry, you cannot restore the Windows NT backup onto another computer. For instance, if a cluster node fails and you replace it with a new node, you must reinstall Windows NT Server, Enterprise Edition on the new node computer. If the other cluster node is still functional you can run Cluster Administrator on it, and evict the replaced node, install MSCS on the new node, join the existing cluster, and restore applications and data.

Knowledge Base articles on restoring Windows NT after replacing hardware.

Article ID	Title
Q112019	Changing Primary Disk System After Installation
Q130928	Restoring a Backup of Windows NT to Another Computer
Q139822	How to Restore a Backup to Computer with Different Hardware
Q139820	Moving or Removing Disks & Fault Tolerant Drive Configurations
Q113976	Using Emergency Repair Disk With Fault Tolerant Partitions

Shared SCSI Bus Drive

You can back up data on the shared SCSI bus drives from the node that owns the disk resource you want to back up and you can back up data from a remote computer to a hidden administrative share using a network connection. For instance, you can use the New Resource wizard to create FBackup$, GBackup$, and HBackup$ file shares for the root of drives F, G, and H. The shares are not displayed in the Windows NT browse list and can be configured so that only members of the Backup Operators group can access them.

For more information, see Chapter 6, "Backing Up and Restoring Network Files," in *Windows NT Server Version 4.0 Concepts and Planning,* and Chapter 5, "Preparing for and Performing Recovery" in the *Windows NT Server Resource Guide.*

Local Drives

It is also critical to back up data on the shared local drive. It is acceptable, but not the best approach, to install backup hardware and software on each node and let each node back up its data. A better solution is identify a non-clustered Windows NT Server and schedule it to copy data regularly from the shared drive to a backup server, from which you can back up a copy.

Using Cluster Administrator

Cluster Administrator performs most of the MSCS administrative functions. It is installed by default on both cluster nodes when you install MSCS. You can also install it on any Windows NT 4.0 Workstation or Server computer on the network. There are a few things to watch out for when using the Cluster Administrator.

Verify Resource Settings

Make sure you accurately enter directory and file names for resources you create. If you make a mistake while entering a file share or generic application name, Cluster Administrator does not verify them.

Increase Size of Quorum Log File

When a node is unavailable, MSCS writes all configuration changes and management data to a file called the quorum log. If both nodes are offline, the first node back online checks this log for any configuration changes before it brings the cluster online.

Entries are removed from the log once all nodes have processed any changes. But if a node is down for a long time or there are a large number of resources in the cluster (such as a cluster print server with numerous printers) the log file can fill and data can be lost. You can increase the log file size (default 64 KB) to prevent this.

Additional clustering tasks can be performed by the Cluster Administrator executable program located in the %systemroot%\system32 folder. For more information see the *MSCS Administrator's Guide*.

Disaster Recovery Procedures

MSCS is only one part of a fault-tolerant system. You should follow traditional disaster recovery guidelines when using it, such as:

- Perform regular system backups (including registries) and store copies of backup tapes offsite.

- Purchase and configure a spare cluster configuration to protect against failure of original equipment.

- Implement cluster shared disks as hardware RAID devices (the first release of MSCS does not support software-based RAID). This is especially important for the quorum log because without this redundancy SCSI disks represent a single point of failure for the cluster.

- Create a distributed system with components in different data centers. This is not possible with a traditional SCSI-based cluster because of the extremely restricted distance limitations imposed by the SCSI bus.

Fiber channel solutions are currently being developed to deploy MSCS as fault resistant in building-wide (or larger) disaster scenarios, but current fiber channel implementations often depend on a fiber channel hub, which can represent a new single point of failure. This issue should be addressed in future releases.

Maintenance Procedures

When maintenance is scheduled on one of the cluster nodes, transfer all resources and applications to the other node. When maintenance is complete, transfer them back to the original node and begin maintenance procedures on the second node. When you are done, load-balance resources manually or let them failback to their preferred node. You must synchronize firmware and software upgrades on both nodes of a cluster.

MSCS Mode Requirements

MSCS supports two modes of operation: active/active (both nodes provide services to users) and active/passive (one node does the work and the other is on standby). For capacity planning, use Performance Monitor to ensure that each node can accommodate the applications and services running on the other node. On a Windows NT 4.0 system you should at a minimum monitor these counters:

Memory

- **Pages/sec.** Number of requested pages accessed from disk because RAM was not immediately available (acceptable range is 0 - 20).

- **Available Bytes.** Amount of available physical memory (acceptable value is 4 MB or higher).

- **Committed Bytes.** Amount of virtual memory that is committed to physical RAM or to pagefile space (should be less than the amount of physical RAM).

- **Pool Non-paged Bytes.** Amount of RAM in the non-paged pool system memory area; space acquired by operating system components as they accomplish their tasks (value should not increase).

Processor

- **% Processor Time.** Amount of time the processor is busy (should not exceed 75%).

- **% Privileged Time.** Amount of time the processor spends performing operating system services (should not exceed 75%).

- **% User Time.** Amount of time the processor spends on user services, such as running a word processor (should not exceed 75%).

- **Interrupts/sec.** Number of interrupts the processor is servicing from applications or hardware devices (depends on the processor, but should be fairly low).

- **System:Processor Queue Length.** Number of requests the processor has in its queue (should not exceed two).

Disk

- **% Disk Time.** Amount of time the disk drive is busy servicing read and write requests (acceptable value is less than 50%).

- **Disk Queue Length.** Number of pending disk I/O requests for the disk drive (acceptable range is 0-2).

- **Avg. Disk Bytes/Transfer.** Average number of bytes transferred to or from the disk during read/write operations (depends on the disk subsystem, but value should be high).

- **Disk Bytes/sec.** Rate at which bytes are transferred to or from disks during read/write operations (depends on the disk subsystem, but value should be high).

These counters provide a good measuring stick for system performance, but you may want to monitor other counters depending on the applications and services that are clustered. Collect erformance data at peak and off-peak periods for a specified timeline to see how the system is faring. For more information on performance tuning see the *Windows NT Server Resource Kit*.

Printing

If you use MSCS as a print server be aware of these limitations:

- You must stop and restart the print spooler to add printer ports remotely for both Windows NT Server 4.0 or Windows NT 4.0, Enterprise Edition. If you have multiple remote locations and cannot interrupt user printing during peak business hours, you'll have to add ports during non-business hours.

- You should place all printer ports and drivers on both cluster nodes so that they are available during system maintenance or failures.

Testing MSCS on Your System

As soon as a cluster is implemented, you should perform several tests.

Validating Installation and Configuration

Most support problems are related to initial installation and hardware configuration. To identify and eliminate these problems as early as possible, implement a basic acceptance test immediately after installing the cluster.

Testing Failover Scenarios

You also need to test for potential failover scenarios. For instance, you should verify that the disk and cluster resources are available on the correct node after a system failure. Test this before you install applications or configure other resources. The table below shows you how to use Cluster Administrator on a remote computer to test for failover.

Validating failover scenarios.

| | *******************************Failover scenario******************************* | | | |
Test categories	Node A owns all resources. Fail to Node B.	Node A owns all resources. Node B fails.	Node B owns all resources. Fail to Node A.	Node B owns all resources. Node A fails.
Group move (administrative)	X		X	
Resource failure (administrative)	X		X	
Node failure—system restart	X	X	X	X
Node failure—Windows NT trap	X	X	X	X
Node failure—system reset	X	X	X	X
Node failure—power down	X	X	X	X

Note The default configuration for resource failure is to restart upon failure. Unless you modify these parameters, the disk resources must be failed four times in succession for a failover to occur (using the Initiate Failure command).

Designate a node as the failing node, then perform an orderly operating system shutdown on it to test the system restart. To initiate a Windows NT blue screen trap test, use the "KILL" utility in the Windows NT Resource Kit to terminate the WINLOGON process.

Most server hardware includes a system-reset switch for rebooting without completely shutting off the power. The system reset and power down tests help determine if a complete loss of power to one node affects the SCSI bus termination.

This level of validation testing can effectively eliminate hardware configuration or software installation as problem sources.

Testing Units

You should perform unit tests on each virtual server you created in the planning stage *before* you fully implement MSCS on your system. It is the best source of information for determining static load balancing. Use these guidelines (tests vary depending on resource type):

- **Resource parameters.** Verify that restarts function correctly and that failover occurs according to the period and threshold settings for each resource. Carefully validate the Pending Timeout setting for startup *and* shutdown of each resource—when resources exceed this parameter they are placed in a failed state and loss of service results. You should also account for the loss of other non-critical network services, such as name servers, that may coincide with a failover.

- **Resource dependencies.** Ensure that all dependencies between resources are configured and functioning properly. Take each resource in the dependency tree offline and bring it back online to verify that it behaves appropriately during startup and shutdown.

- **Resource failures.** Wherever possible, induce resource failures without using Cluster Administrator. For example, you can fail network name and IP address resources by introducing duplicates on the network. These are generally more meaningful test cases than artificially initiated failures.

- **Group parameters.** Ensure that all group parameters are functioning as specified. Test to see that failback to a preferred node works even in abnormal startup conditions. For instance, check the low virtual-memory state during the saving of a system dump file that follows a blue-screen trap.

- **Failover scenarios.** Repeat all of the failure scenarios described in the section on validating failover scenarios table above.

- **Checkpoint restart.** Test the worst case restart times for applications (such as Microsoft SQL Server or Exchange) that perform checkpoints and use a transaction log.

- **Scalability boundary cases.** Design scalability tests to account for worst-case growth predictions to take into account the fact that some virtual servers are designed to support a variable number of associated resources. For instance, a virtual server that hosts home directory shares uses one disk resource, one network name resource, one IP address resource, and a variable number of shares. On the other hand, a virtual server for print services uses fixed MSCS resources but the number of printers defined on the spooler varies greatly.

- **Client load.** Some resources may perform differently when placed under a heavy client load. In most cases it is impractical to set up a lab with the hundreds (or thousands) of clients necessary to duplicate a worst-case load scenario. If available, you can use benchmarking or load simulation tools to simulate the impact of a large number of clients, which requires fewer machines. Another (less reliable) approach is to track carefully the load signature with varying numbers of smaller client loads and extrapolate the worst-case conditions.

- **Client response.** For testing, use the client software that you used to connect to the cluster during production. Although you may not be able to change client behavior in response to a restart or failover, it is very important to understand and document it. For instance, at the first threshold, a loss of service may not be visible to the client. At a second threshold, a dialog box may appear giving the client the opportunity to retry an operation. But by the third threshold, retries may no longer be successful and the client may be required to restart. You can use this type of information to implement a failover scenario that minimizes impact to users.

- **Rolling upgrade.** Before implementing MSCS, you should include a process for upgrading or applying patches to the hardware or applications without a loss of service—a rolling upgrade. Test this process as much as is practicable.

- **Symmetry.** Because most cluster configuration is not node-specific (with the exception of preferred owners) you don't have to repeat unit testing scenarios with resources that are active on the alternate node.

If, while you are executing your test plan, you think of other tests you would like to run, document them and perform them during integration testing.

Testing for Proper Integration

Usually, traditional test plans use integration testing to exercise and verify the functionality of modules after you have combined them in the unit tests. In a cluster environment, the situation is somewhat different because combining virtual servers on a cluster should not result in any functional changes from the client's perspective.

So integration testing in a cluster is designed to ensure that each virtual server functions the same while coexisting with other virtual servers as it did during unit testing. Some performance impact is to be expected, but there should be no functional changes as a result of grouping virtual servers.

To conduct an integration test, configure all virtual servers to a single node and re-verify the unit test cases in the worst-case scenario. To produce a system-wide, worst-case load signature, make sure that you execute scalability and client load scenarios in parallel.

P A R T   3

Deploying Windows NT— Automated Installation

Here's a scenario that offers maximum job security: you are systems administrator for a huge enterprise, you don't have enough help, you have to install new software on a half a million desktops. Remember the good old days, the ones where you went around to each machine on each desk and cranked through installation scripts screen after screen? They weren't that good after all, were they? Or at least they wouldn't be so good now, when the proliferation of PCs, software, service packs, updates, and add-ons would make software distribution resemble the job of painting a huge bridge—you labor and sweat for years, and long before you are done it is already time to start again.

Of course no one thinks in terms of individual setups anymore. There are automated methods. This section goes into great detail as it explains two of the best ones for Windows NT. Chapter 10 walks you through the Microsoft Automated Installation Framework (MSIF). Microsoft Consulting Services combined its vast experience in the field with the standard practices outlined in the deployment guide to create this collection of components that make PC installation and configuration automatic and dynamic. Chapter 11 provides a template for an unattended modular build of Windows NT, service packs, and application software. Each of these chapters provides enough details, tips, and code samples to make mastering these tools easy. Say, maybe *these* are the good old days.

C H A P T E R   1 0

Windows NT 4.0 Automated Installation Framework

By Matthew D. Storer, MCS— Great Lakes

There are a number of tools and methods for building an automated Microsoft Windows NT 4.0 installation and most of them are clearly documented in the *Automating Microsoft Windows NT Setup Deployment Guide*, which can be downloaded from http://www.microsoft.com/ntworkstation/info/Deployment-guide.htm. The guide requires a deep knowledge Windows NT 4.0 setup files, which can sometimes intimidate technical managers and engineers. Microsoft Consulting Services (MCS) has developed a framework called the Windows NT 4.0 Automated Installation Framework (MSIF)—a collection of components that make PC installation and configuration automatic and dynamic—to provide a quick sample implementation based on standard practices outlined in the deployment guide *and* MCS deployment experience.

The *Customizing the Windows NT 4.0 Upgrade Process* framework (also available at http://www.microsoft.com/ntserver) focuses on building and managing complex automated upgrades.

What You'll Find In This Chapter

- **A quick discussion of the need for automated installation.**

- **A description of Microsoft Consulting Services' Windows NT 4.0 Automated Installation Framework (MSIF), concentrating on its component-based design and how it operates.**

- **Instructions on how to install, use, and extend MSIF.**

- **Code samples, settings, and explanations.**

Warning This chapter makes recommendations for tuning the Windows NT registry using the Registry Editor. Using the Registry Editor incorrectly can cause serious, system-wide problems that require you to reinstall Windows NT. Microsoft cannot guarantee that any problems resulting from the use of Registry Editor can be solved. Use this tool at your own risk.

Hands-On Installation

Today, large deployment-project rollout schedules often require many Windows NT installations and upgrades to be completed per day, so many that the hands-on approach, which takes hours of dedicated technician time and introduces more chances for mistakes, is neither feasible nor economical.

Hands-on installation traditionally has involved copying an image from hard disk to hard disk or over the network. As operating systems have become more sophisticated, utilities have been created to take an image from one hard drive to another by copying sectors. A hard drive duplication installation of Windows NT presents two issues: the impact of the hardware it is installed on, and the need for a unique Security ID (SID) in each instance of the operating system so that all Windows NT operating systems can communicate. The second condition requires each computer to have a unique Windows NT installation for proper support and operation. In sum, you need an easier and more efficient method.

Windows NT 4.0 Automated Installation Framework (MSIF)

The Microsoft Windows NT 4.0 Automated Installation Framework (MSIF) is a collection of components that work together to install and configure computers automatically. The components are installed independent of each other, which gives you flexibility at each stage of the process: installing the operating system, configuring, and installing applications. This design also reduces overall implementation costs by reusing previously developed installation components.

Although simple, MSIF objectives require enterprise participation to be successful: you have to plan and develop your solution using the MSIF specifications. MSIF is a *framework*; it requires standard installation practices, and installation and configuration documentation, but it offers fast installation and configuration.

The process is sequential and simple. Create a share point on an image server, copy a Windows NT 4.0 Workstation or Server image to the share point, install the sample MSIF components to the share point, modify the components, and independently automate each application installation. Then all you have to do is insert the modified boot disk and start the installation.

You can find a copy of the MSIF boot disk files on the companion CD in the directory \MSIF.

A framework installation involves five stages (explained more fully below):

- Boot disk and configure hard drive
- Windows NT operating system installation
- Windows NT configuration and application installation
- Technician configuration
- Quality assurance

Boot Disk and Configure Hard Drive

The boot disk addresses the installation's first action item—"reformatting" the hard drive and loading the appropriate network drivers. After the network drivers are loaded, the boot disk connects to the MSIF share point and downloads a set of MSIF script files created for the system (the computer hardware/software combination) being installed.

Windows NT Operating System Installation

The boot disk then starts the Windows NT operating system installation using standard unattended command line parameters. Near the end of Windows NT setup, an MSIF script file is executed that forces Windows NT to automatically log on after reboot, bypass Windows NT Tip of the Day, and begin running each application installation sequentially.

Windows NT Configuration and Application Installation

After Windows NT setup completes and reboots, MSIF runs the application installation in two phases separated by an operating system reboot. This makes it possible to install applications that require a reboot before they can be configured. The last step of the MSIF framework removes all of the MSIF automated programming changes.

Technician Configuration

Although the system has been automatically installed and configured, you still may have to perform several steps by hand. Technicians may be needed to create an Emergency Repair disk, or perform other tasks that cannot be automated.

Quality Assurance

Now that the machine has been completely set up, you need to test it to ensure that all of the bits have been copied and installed correctly. All or part of this testing can be automated, but if it is done by a technician, try to draw QA testers from groups other than the configuration team, whose members are too involved with the implementation to test it objectively.

Setup and Configuration

The first step to setting up the MSIF framework is to select an image server and create a network share from which the entire installation is performed. Next, copy the Windows NT 4.0 operating system (Workstation or Server) to the share. Then install the MSIF framework. Finally, update the MSIF boot disk with the appropriate network driver and the MSIF template scripts customized. These steps are explained in greater detail below.

Required Materials

You need a server with ample disk space and network connectivity, any licensed copy of Windows NT 4.0, the MSIF boot disk, and an image of each application that needs to be installed.

Step 1: Create Image Server Share Point

The image server is a critical MSIF framework component.

Optimization Suggestions

Here are some suggestions to optimize the mass installation process:

1. To minimize connectivity problems, the server should be a Windows NT Server 3.51 or higher.

2. To maximize throughput, use high-speed network adapters and hubs/switches.

3. To utilize available physical network bandwidth, install the server on an isolated network segment or at least on a dedicated routed network segment.

4. To get the best Windows NT performance, select **System Properties** from Control Panel and configure the server for **Average Boost**. Then from Control Panel, select **Network** then **Services**, and configure the server for **File and Print**.

5. To reduce access to the server during production loads, use the image server only for production loads—not for testing, general file sharing, or even as an application server.

6. To reduce the number of files copied during Windows NT setup, you can remove some directories. For example, once you have identified which network interface cards (NICs) you need to load, you can delete all of the NICs that you do not need. They are listed under the I386\DRVLIB.NIC.

Required Steps

1. From the Windows NT Explorer, create a directory called MSIF.

2. Share the directory as MSIF.

3. Set appropriate permissions on directory and share.

Step 2: Copy Windows NT Image to Share Point

After you have created the share point, copy a subset of the Windows NT operating system source files into it. In addition to the standard Windows NT installation files, this directory will also host various unattended files such as CMDLINES.TXT and other third party OEM video and network drivers as described in *Microsoft Windows NT Workstation: Deployment Guide*. The example framework provided also includes a "co-installation" of a Windows NT service pack. When copying files, make sure that you are actually copying *all* files (some Windows Explorer views "hide" DLL and SYS files.)

Required Steps

1. From the root of the share point, create a directory called NT4WKS for Windows NT 4.0 Workstation or NT4SRV for Windows NT 4.0 Server.

2. From the Windows NT 4.0 source, copy the entire I386 directory to either NT4WKS (workstation) or NT4SRV (server).

3. From the root of the share point, create a directory called NT4SP3 (or the latest Windows NT service pack version) for Windows NT 4.0 Service Pack 3.

4. From the Windows NT 4.0 Service Pack 3 source, copy the entire set of files to the NT4SP3 directory.

Step 3: Install MSIF Framework

After you have copied the Windows NT source files to the image server, run SETUP.BAT from the SETUP directory on the MSIF boot disk. This file creates the OEM directory in the NT4WKS\I386 and NT4SRV\I386 directories, copies the standard MSIF CMDLINES.TXT into the OEM and $$ directories, moves the Windows NT service pack (if one is found) to the $$ directory, creates the TEMPLATES directory in the root of the share point, and copies MSIF sample scripts into the TEMPLATES directory.

Required Step

1. From the MSIF boot disk SETUP directory, run SETUP.BAT [*drive:*], where [*drive:*] is the drive letter mapped to the share point. At a minimum, SETUP.BAT requires that NT4WKS or NT4SRV exist under the root of the MSIF share and that you have placed the Windows NT service pack in NT4SPx (where x is the version number of the service pack).

Step 4: Customize MSIF Framework

When you have installed the MSIF framework and copied the Windows NT operating system files to the share point, you need to customize the MSIF boot disk and sample scripts. This generally requires three customizations: rebuild the disk partition, customize the template, and add support for network drivers.

Required Steps: Rebuild Disk Partition

Most hard drives require modification to support a network-based unattended installation of Windows NT 4.0. The disk partition can be configured in a variety of ways and the number of steps and tools used to accomplish this vary from deployment to deployment. The three most common reasons a hard drive requires repartitioning:

- It has Windows 95 FAT32 file system installed, which cannot be accessed by Windows NT 4.0.

- Its partitioning scheme is not desirable. For example, a standard configuration may require a 1-GB logical C drive.

- It does not have any partition information, so the primary partition needs to be created from scratch.

Because you will most likely have to modify the sample boot disk provided, here are several methods to automate the creation of new partitions and logical disk drives.

DEBUG.EXE with Input Test File

You can use this command to turn a hard drive into a totally raw disk. It should work on any machine with any types or numbers of partitions. The DEBUG script was taken from the Microsoft Developer Network. (For more information on it, search on *debug partition table* in the MSDN Knowledge Base.) The sample framework uses this command in conjunction with FDISK.EXE 1 /PRI:500 /Q. The contents of DELPART.TXT are shown on page 507.

Command Line:

DEBUG.EXE < DELPART.TXT

FDISK.EXE with Unsupported Command Line Parameters

You can use this command to create a new primary partition of a specific size. The switches listed below can simplify the unattended load process, but Microsoft does directly not support them. The sample framework uses this command in conjunction with DEBUG.EXE < A:\DELPART.TXT. The FDISK command is detailed under AUTOEXEC.BAT in the "Boot Disk/Hard Drive MSIF Files" section, page 495.

Command Line:

FDISK 1 /PRI:<size in MB> /Q (to create a primary partition)

FDISK 1 /EXT:<size in MB> /Q (to create an extended partition)

FDISK 1 /LOG:<size in MB> /Q (to create a logical drive)

FDISK.EXE with Input Text File

You can create one or more input answer files to delete existing partition information and create new ones. When you create new partitions, remember to set the primary partition as active.

Command Line:

FDISK.EXE < FDISK.TXT

Required Steps: Add Custom Template

Templates determine which set of MSIF installation scripts to run. For more information on templates refer to page 479; for information on the MSIF boot disk refer to page 476.

1. To prepare a new template, create a new directory under TEMPLATE on the image server share point. Give it a name that uniquely identifies it and is no longer than eight characters. This is the name used as the TEMPLATE value in the MSIF boot disk process.

2. Copy the template scripts from the TEMPLATES\SAMPLE directory to the new directory. Customize a copy of them so that you can keep an original version.

3. Open AUTOEXEC.BAT located in the root of the MSIF boot disk and locate the "ECHO MSIF Configuration Template Menu:" line. Using the example provided and the name of the new template directory, update the sample or add your choice. Then add or update the "if "%OPTION%" == "1" SET TEMPLATE=CPQ5200A" statement substituting the correct OPTION number and template name.

Add your own
template here.

```
REM 1. Prompt for Information.
ECHO.
ECHO MSIF Configuration Template Menu:
ECHO.
ECHO 1) Compaq LTE 5200 (CPQ5200A)
ECHO 2) Dell OptiPlex GXa (DELLA)
ECHO 3) Boot to DOS
ECHO.
ENQUIRE "Enter choice (1, 2, or 3) = ", OPTION
if "%OPTION%" == "1" SET TEMPLATE=CPQ5200A
if "%OPTION%" == "2" SET TEMPLATE=DELLA
if "%OPTION%" == "3" GOTO END
```

Change to
TEMPLATE=*new template*.

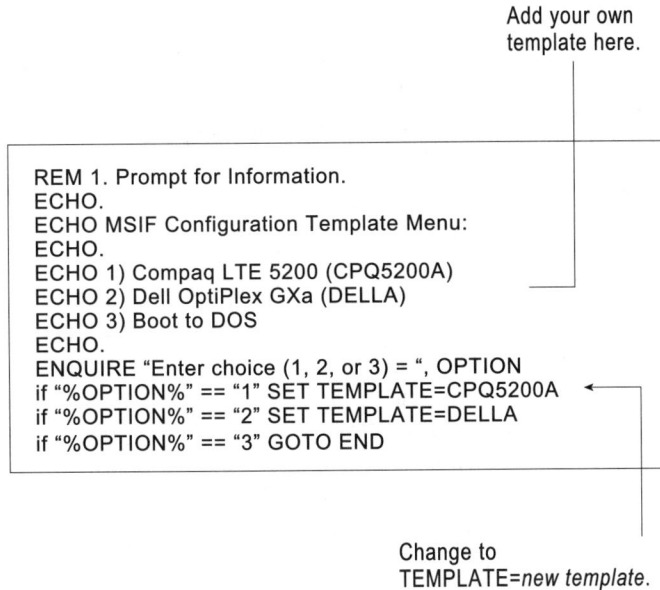

Figure 10.1 Example MSIF boot disk AUTOEXEC.BAT file: where to place custom template.

Required Steps: Add Network Adapter Card Driver

The boot disk stores all of the necessary files for MS-DOS networking under A:\NET. It uses NetBEUI as the network protocol and stores each NIC driver, PROTOCOL.INI, and SYSTEM.INI, in a unique subdirectory of A:\NET identified by the name of the MSIF template. The sample boot disk provided uses an NE2000-compatible MS-DOS network driver.

To add a new NIC to the boot disk is simple.

To use the NE2000 with NetBEUI:

1. Locate the root of A:\NET directory.
2. Change the name of the sample CPQ5200A to the name of your template.

To use a different NIC with NetBEUI:

1. Locate the root of A:\NET directory.
2. Change the name of the sample CPQ5200A (or create a new directory) to the name of your template, which is the name you assigned during the "Add Custom Template" step above.
3. Copy the MS-DOS NIC driver, SYSTEM.INI, and PROTOCOL.INI to the new template directory. If you do not have a SYSTEM.INI or PROTOCOL.INI, use the sample ones and edit the driver name.

To use a different NIC and protocol such as Transmission Control Protocol/Internet Protocol (TCP/IP):

1. Create a new network boot disk from scratch using the NCADMIN.EXE tool that ships with Windows NT Server 4.0.
2. Copy all of the files in the root of the MSIF sample disk to the root of the new boot disk. **DO NOT COPY** A:\NET subdirectory.
3. On the new boot disk, locate the root of A:\NET directory.
4. Create a new subdirectory using the new template name (the name you assigned during the "Add Custom Template" step above).

5. Move the MS-DOS NIC driver, SYSTEM.INI, and PROTOCOL.INI from the root of the A:\NET directory to the new template directory.

6. Edit the relocated SYSTEM.INI. Delete the values to the right of these entries:

   computername=

   username=

   workgroup=

   logondomain=

Component Architecture

The flowchart in Figure 10.2 graphically represents the MSIF process. The rest of this section describes each of the steps, or components, in detail.

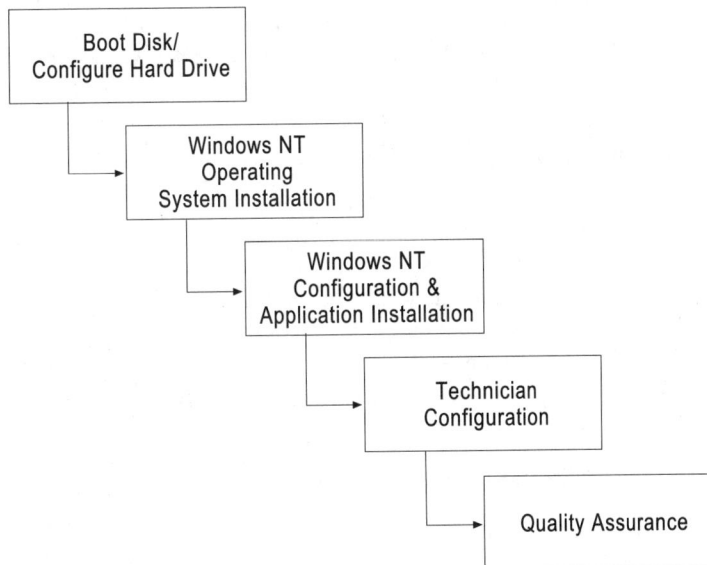

```
┌──────────────────────┐
│     Boot Disk/        │
│ Configure Hard Drive  │
└──────────┬───────────┘
           │    ┌──────────────────────┐
           └──▶ │    Windows NT         │
                │    Operating          │
                │ System Installation   │
                └──────────┬───────────┘
                           │    ┌──────────────────────┐
                           └──▶ │   Windows NT          │
                                │ Configuration &       │
                                │ Application Installation│
                                └──────────┬───────────┘
                                           │    ┌──────────────────────┐
                                           └──▶ │    Technician         │
                                                │   Configuration       │
                                                └──────────┬───────────┘
                                                           │    ┌──────────────────────┐
                                                           └──▶ │   Quality Assurance   │
                                                                └──────────────────────┘
```

Figure 10.2 The MSIF process.

Boot Disk/Configure Hard Disk

The MSIF boot disk is used to boot up MS-DOS 6.22 operating on the target computer, create new disk partition, format the new partition, load network drivers and connect to the MSIF share point, and finally, start the installation of Windows NT. If you don't have to reconfigure the partition schema on your computer you can skip steps 1 and 2 below.

Process

The sample MSIF boot disk functions as if the Windows NT operating system will be installed in drive C, which needs to be recreated (re-partitioned). The boot disk goes through the following process:

1. MS-DOS Boot

The boot disk loads MS-DOS 6.22 operating system, HIMEM.SYS, EMM386.EXE, and IFSHLP.SYS (see page 495 for a sample file). The batch file AUTOEXEC.BAT is executed from the boot disk.

2. Determine Boot Status

This section tracks the installation progress so that the system can be rebooted at desired intervals. It stores the state of the STATUS environment variable in A:\STATUS.BAT as one of three values: STEP1, STEP2, or BYPASS. A GOTO statement is used to run the corresponding step established by the STATUS variable. Below is a sample of the commands used. The first line defaults STATUS to equal STEP1 in the case that the STATUS.BAT has been deleted. (These STEPS are part of the framework; you can modify them to suit your needs.)

```
SET STATUS=STEP1

IF EXIST A:\STATUS.BAT CALL A:\STATUS.BAT

CLS

@ECHO.
```

```
@ECHO Window NT 4.0 Automated Installation Framework

@ECHO Boot Disk - %STATUS%, Revision 4.0

@ECHO ------------------------------------------------------------

@ECHO.

IF %STATUS%==STEP2 GOTO STEP2

IF %STATUS%==BYPASS GOTO BYPASS

GOTO STEP1
```

3. STEP1—Prompt for Information

This section prompts you to select an MSIF Template. This menu allows you to run more than one system configuration from the same boot disk and network share point. If you want, you can comment out the menu and set the template to a default. The command line tool *ENQUIRE.COM* is free utility used to prompt for user input and set value to an environment variable, such as OPTION. The OPTION variable uses a series of "if" statements to determine which MSIF template to invoke.

After the variant information has been collected, the environment variables are saved to a file named VARS.BAT to be used during STEP2. For this boot disk these environment variables are set:

- TEMPLATE = The MSIF unique name assigned to a particular computer configuration
- COMPUTERNAME = The computer name used by the boot disk when starting the network services and the computer name assigned to the Windows NT computer

```
REM 1. Prompt for Information.

ECHO.

ECHO MSIF Configuration Template Menu:

ECHO.

ECHO 1) Compaq LTE 5200 (CPQ5200A)

ECHO 2) Dell OptiPlex GXa (DELLA)

ECHO 3) Boot to DOS

ECHO.

ENQUIRE "Enter choice (1, 2, or 3) = ", OPTION

if "%OPTION%" == "1" SET TEMPLATE=CPQ5200A

if "%OPTION%" == "2" SET TEMPLATE=DELLA

if "%OPTION%" == "3" GOTO END

ECHO.

ENQUIRE "Enter name of computer = ", COMPUTERNAME

ECHO.

ECHO SET TEMPLATE=%TEMPLATE%> A:\VARS.BAT

ECHO SET COMPUTERNAME=%COMPUTERNAME%>> A:\VARS.BAT

ECHO SET LOGIN=install>> A:\VARS.BAT

ECHO SET PASSWORD=install>> A:\VARS.BAT

ECHO SET WORKGROUP=usa-detroit>> A:\VARS.BAT

ECHO SET DOMAIN=loadsite>> A:\VARS.BAT

ECHO SET NETDRIVE=x:>> A:\VARS.BAT

ECHO SET NETSERVER=MSTORER_TRP>> A:\VARS.BAT

ECHO SET NETSHARE=MSIF>> A:\VARS.BAT
```

4. STEP1—Rebuild Disk Partition

This section runs DEBUG.EXE to delete the pre-existing MS-DOS or non-MS-DOS partitions and it creates a new small FAT16 MS-DOS partition using the undocumented FDISK 1 /PRI:500 command. The small partition size speeds up the initial format. Windows NT extends the partition size to its fullest potential during its load. If you want the size of drive C to remain fixed, remove the entry "ExtendOEMPartition" from UNATTEND.TXT located under the TEMPLATE directories.

- DEBUG.EXE, uses an MSDN documented input text file to "wipe" the disk
- FDISK.EXE, creates new primary MS-DOS partition (500 MB)

For more information, see the "Required Steps: Rebuild Disk Partition" section, page 470.

```
REM 2. Rebuild Disk Partition.

ECHO SET STATUS=STEP2 > A:\STATUS.BAT

a:\debug.exe < a:\delpart.txt

a:\fdisk.exe 1 /PRI:500 /Q

a:\reboot.com
```

4. STEP2—Format Disk

Begin step 2 by formatting the hard disk using the standard command line switches available and an input text file that simply contains the character *y*. This is used to respond to the question, "Do you want to continue?". /U indicates *unconditional* format and /V sets the *volume name*. FORMAT.TXT contains the string *Y*. Below is a sample of the command used:

- ECHO 1. Formating Hard Drive...
- a:\format C: /U /V:CORP < a:\format.txt

5. STEP2—Set Status Bypass Flag

The STATUS flag is set to BYPASS in the event that a technician needs to cancel the installation at this point. If STATUS=BYPASS on boot, AUTOEXEC.BAT bypasses disk partitioning and formatting. This is also handy for testing and troubleshooting.

```
ECHO 2. Setting BYPASS Flag...

ECHO SET STATUS=BYPASS > A:\STATUS.BAT

:BYPASS
```

6. STEP2—Load SmartDrive

SmartDrive optimizes memory allocation.

```
ECHO 3. Loading SmartDrive...

a:\net\smartdrv.exe /x 2048 > nul
```

7. STEP2—Set Environment Variables Stored in VARS.BAT

Using the values written to VARS.BAT earlier, the boot disk executes VARS.BAT to "set" the environment variables. This allows variables to be collected initially and used later.

```
ECHO 4. Setting Environment Variables Stored in VARS.BAT...

CALL A:\VARS.BAT
```

8. STEP2—Load Network Based on Selected Template

This copies the network adapter associated with the selected MSIF template to the A:\NET directory and updates the "clean" version of the network-adapter-specific SYSTEM.INI file with the environment variables. Note that this process looks for *computername*, *logondomain*, *username*, and *workgroup* to modify them. CHANGE.EXE is used to update the computer name in the boot disk SYSTEM.INI and in the UNATTEND.TXT file.

```
ECHO 5. Loading %TEMPLATE%...

copy a:\net\%TEMPLATE%\*.* a:\net

change a:\net\system.ini computername= computername=%COMPUTERNAME% > nul

change a:\net\system.ini logondomain= logondomain=%DOMAIN% > nul

change a:\net\system.ini username= username=%LOGIN% > nul

change a:\net\system.ini workgroup= workgroup=%workgroup% > nul

path=a:\;a:\net
```

9. STEP2—Start Network

This starts the network by logging on and then connecting to the MSIF network share.

```
ECHO 6. Starting Network...

a:\net\net logon %LOGIN% %PASSWORD% /YES /SAVEPW:NO

a:\net\net use %NETDRIVE% \\%NETSERVER%\%NETSHARE%
```

10. STEP2—Copying MSIF Template Files and Edit UNATTEND.TXT

From the connected MSIF network share, this copies down MSIF template files such as UNATTEND.TXT, INSTALL.BAT, RUNONCE.INF, etc., and updates the local copy of the UNATTEND.TXT with the new COMPUTERNAME entered earlier.

```
ECHO 7. Downloading MSIF Template Files...

C:

cd \

md msif

copy %NETDRIVE%\TEMPLATE\%TEMPLATE%\*.* c:\msif

change c:\msif\unattend.txt ComputerName= ComputerName=%COMPUTERNAME% >
nul
```

11. STEP2—Reset Status Flag

This resets the MSIF boot disk by setting the STATUS flag file equal to STEP1. Before Windows NT installation starts, the STATUS variable is set to STEP1, which in effect "resets" the boot disk to be reused on another machine. If the boot disk gets "out-of-step," then delete A:\STATUS.BAT. This resets the boot disk manually.

```
ECHO 8. Resetting MSIF Boot Disk......

ECHO SET STATUS=STEP1 > A:\STATUS.BAT
```

12. STEP2—Start Windows NT Installation

This starts installing Windows NT by copying the INSTALL.BAT down from the image server. It contains the unattended call to start the installation of the specified operating system. More information on INSTALL.BAT is on page 484.

```
ECHO 9. Starting Operating System Installation...

c:\msif\install
```

Windows NT Operating System Installation

This phase of the installation (based mostly on the *Automating Microsoft Windows NT Setup Deployment Guide*) begins when the MSIF boot disk calls the C:\MSIF\INSTALL.BAT that was copied from the MSIF image server during the initial boot process. From this point, the standard unattended installation of Windows NT occurs, taking full advantage of the OEM\CMDLINES.TXT and RUNONCE.INF concepts. Most likely, you will not need to modify the script files used in this phase. System changes and application installation changes are covered in the next section—"Windows NT Configuration and Application Installation."

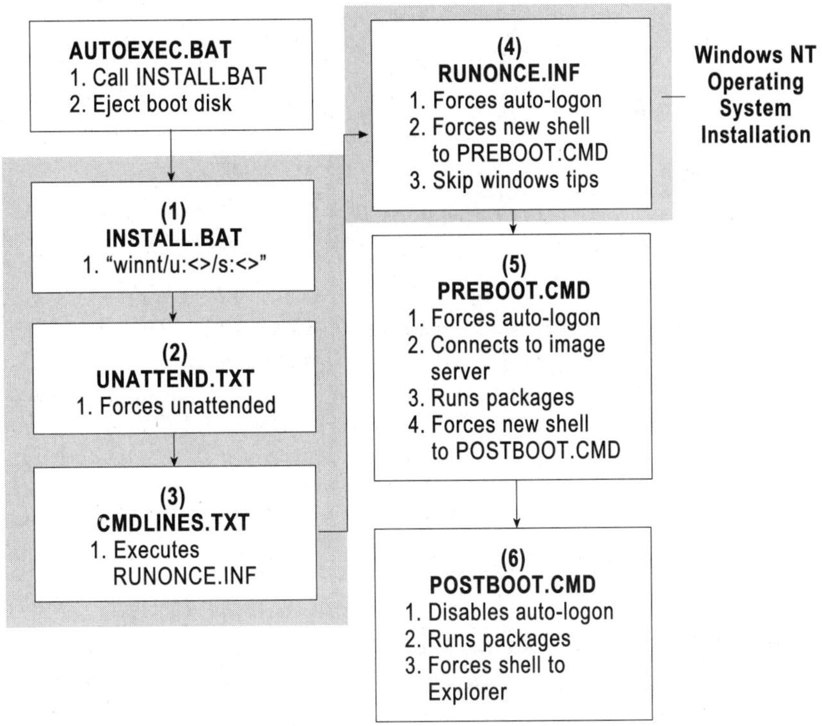

Figure 10.3 Process of Windows NT System Installation.

Process

The MSIF boot disk calls the C:\MSIF\INSTALL.BAT, which starts the Windows NT setup using unattended-mode parameters to drive the installation. When the standard Windows NT installation is finished, the boot disk process checks for the existence of CMDLINES.TXT located in i386\OEM.

If it is found, Windows NT setup executes the commands listed in it. This framework uses CMDLINES.TXT to execute an .INF file called C:\MSIF\RUNONCE.INF, which forces auto-logon, changes the default Windows NT shell, and bypasses the Windows Tips.

1. INSTALL.BAT

INSTALL.BAT runs the Windows NT operating system installation in unattended mode. Specifically, C:\MSIF\INSTALL.BAT calls WINNT.EXE, the Windows NT setup executable. The standard Windows NT setup runs in "unattended" mode, reading all of its settings from the MSIF template file C:\MSIF\UNATTEND.TXT. Specifically, the "/u:C:\MSIF\Unattend.txt" component instructs Windows NT setup to run in unattended mode and to retrieve its settings from C:\MSIF\UNATTEND.TXT. The last component, "/s:X:\Nt4Wks\i386", simply complements the unattended mode by providing the source location of the Windows NT core operating system files (/s is required for a completely unattended mode).

```
X:\Nt4Wks\i386\WinNT /u:C:\MSIF\Unattend.txt /s:X:\Nt4Wks\i386
```

2. UNATTEND.TXT

The sample framework uses a generic UNATTEND.TXT file that includes most of the standard automated entries. For more information on how to customize this file, refer the *Guide to Automating Windows NT Setup*. UNATTEND.TXT is detailed in the "Windows NT Operating System Installation Files" section, page 508.

3. CMDLINES.TXT

Next, the content of CMDLINES.TXT is executed at the end of the standard Windows NT setup. This file is located in the i386\OEM directory. The OEM and CMDLINES.TXT are not installed automatically; MSIF installs them for you if you follow the steps in the "Setup and Configuration" section below. Windows NT runs CMDLINES.TXT before it reboots the last time. For purposes of this framework, CMDLINES.TXT was modified to call C:\MSIF\RUNONCE.INF and install the latest Windows NT service pack in silent mode.

```
[Commands]

"rundll32 setupapi,InstallHinfSection DefaultInstall 128
C:\MSIF\RunOnce.inf"

"C:\WINNT\NT4SP3\Update.exe -u -n -z"
```

4. RUNONCE.INF

Apply RUNONCE.INF to prepare Windows NT for continued configuration and application installation. RUNONCE.INF forces Windows NT to use both EXPLORER.EXE and PREBOOT.CMD as its shell, forces the system to auto-logon as Administrator with no password, and removes the default Windows NT Tips.

```
[AddReg]

; 1. Forces Windows NT shell from Explorer to be PREBOOT.CMD.
HKLM, "SOFTWARE\Microsoft\Windows NT\CurrentVersion\Winlogon", ->
"Shell", 0, "Explorer.exe C:\MSIF\PreBoot.cmd"


; 2. Forces default user/password and enables autologon.
HKLM, "SOFTWARE\Microsoft\Windows NT\CurrentVersion\Winlogon", ->

"DefaultUserName", 0, "Administrator"
HKLM, "SOFTWARE\Microsoft\Windows NT\CurrentVersion\Winlogon", ->
"DefaultPassword", 0, ""
HKLM, "SOFTWARE\Microsoft\Windows NT\CurrentVersion\Winlogon", ->
"AutoAdminLogon", , "1"


; 3. Disables default Windows NT Tips.
HKCU, "SOFTWARE\Microsoft\Windows\CurrentVersion\Explorer\Tips", ->
"DisplayInitialTipWindows", 65537, 0
HKCU, "SOFTWARE\Microsoft\Windows\CurrentVersion\Explorer\Tips", ->
"Show", 1, 0, 0, 0, 0
HKCU, "SOFTWARE\Microsoft\Windows\CurrentVersion\Explorer\Tips", ->
"Next", 1, 3, 0
```

Windows NT Configuration and Application Installation

This phase of the framework configures Windows NT 4.0 operating system and application installation. It is divided into two generic phases that replace the standard Windows NT Explorer shell—PreBoot and PostBoot. Figure 10.3 demonstrates the process flow.

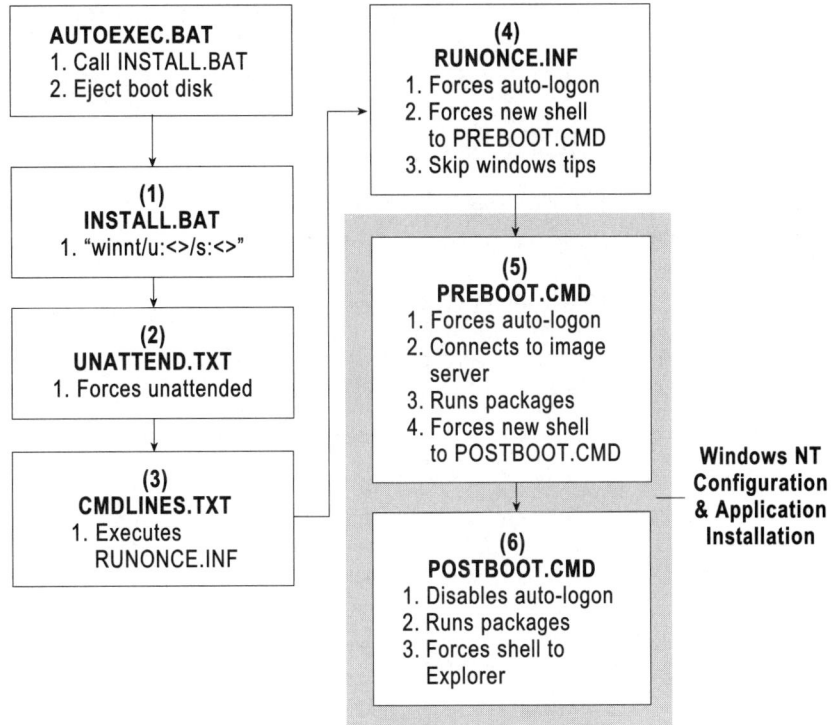

Figure 10.4 Process for Windows NT configuration and application installation.

Process

The Windows NT Explorer shell is replaced with PREBOOT.CMD by
RUNONCE.INF (RUNONCE.INF is covered in the previous section.)
PREBOOT.CMD connects to the MSIF share, downloads necessary utilities,
launches scripted application installations, and re-sets Windows NT shell to
POSTBOOT.CMD. The POSTBOOT.CMD connects to the MSIF share, launches
scripted application installations, removes the MSIF connection, re-sets the
Windows NT shell back to Windows NT Explorer, removes the autologon
settings, and reboots.

PREBOOT.CMD

1. Set Environment Variables

The Pre-Reboot phase begins by setting environment variables that are used by
this batch file and available to other installation scripts. As a part of this phase,
C:\MSIF is added to the session path.

```
echo 1. Setting environment variables...

     SET MSIF_SHARE=\\MSTORER_TRP\MSIF

     SET MSIF_DRIVE=X:

     SET MSIF_SCRIPTS=C:\MSIF

     SET MSIF_LOGIN=install

     SET MSIF_PASSWORD=install

     SET MSIF_FULLNAME=Sample Installation

     SET MSIF_ORGNAME=Microsoft Consulting Services

     SET PATH=%PATH%;C:\MSIF
```

2. Connect to MSIF Share

After the variables are set, it connects to the MSIF share point. The error checking helps with troubleshooting slow connect times.

```
echo 2. Connecting to MSIF share point...

    :NETCONN

    NET USE %MSIF_DRIVE% %MSIF_SHARE% /USER:%MSIF_LOGIN%
%MSIF_PASSWORD%

    IF ERRORLEVEL 1 Goto NetUseError

    Goto SkipNetUseError

    :NetUseError

    Echo Error connecting to image server! You may want to contact
    deployment support.

    Echo.

    Echo To retry connection, press ENTER.

    Echo To exit load, press CTRL+C.

    Pause

    GoTO NETCONN

    :SkipNetUseError
```

3. Download Utilities

Now that a network connection exists, MSIF downloads utilities located in the UTILITIES directory off of the root of the MSIF share, and copies them into C:\MSIF.

```
echo 3. Copying MSIF and other handy utilities to C:\MSIF...

    %MSIF_DRIVE%

    COPY \UTILITIES\*.* C:\MSIF
```

4. Set Windows NT Shell to Explorer

Next, PREBOOT.CMD sets the Windows NT shell back to Windows NT
Explorer to reduce the possibility of getting errors during application installation.

```
echo 4. Setting Windows NT shell to Explorer...

    rundll32 setupapi,InstallHinfSection DefaultInstall 128 ->

    %MSIF_SCRIPTS%\Explorer.INF
```

5. Package Installations and Configurations

This is where you add your own scripted application installations. The example
below uses the Microsoft Office 97 installation script as an example. The goal
here is to abstract the framework from the detail programming of the actual
installation script. So a batch file called OFF97ADM.BAT (meaning Office 97
Administrative installation) is used to "call" the Office 97 installation script
located in OFF97ADM directory off of the root MSIF share. The SLEEP 5 allows
each application script 5 seconds before starting the next one—this "slows down"
the process and keeps the installation linear.

```
echo 5. Running Pre-Reboot package installations and configurations...


    echo Office 97 Professional Edition

        %MSIF_DRIVE%

        CD \OFF97ADM

        CALL OFF97ADM.BAT

        SLEEP 5
```

6. Prepare System for Post-Reboot Phase

This step applies PREBOOT.INF changes, removes the network connection, and reboots the computer.

```
echo 6. Preparing system for Post-Reboot phase...

        rundll32 setupapi,InstallHinfSection DefaultInstall 128 ->

        %MSIF_SCRIPTS%\PreBoot.INF

        C:

        NET USE %MSIF_DRIVE% /D

        START SHUTDOWN.EXE /L /R /T:5 /Y
```

PREBOOT.INF changes the Windows NT shell to POSTBOOT.CMD, sets default logon user to Administrator, sets the default logon password to blank, and enables the AutoAdminLogon flag.

```
[AddReg]

; 1. Change Windows NT shell from PREBOOT.CMD to POSTBOOT.CMD

HKLM,"SOFTWARE\Microsoft\Windows NT\CurrentVersion\Winlogon", ->

"Shell",0,"Explorer.exe C:\MSIF\PostBoot.cmd"


; 2. Forces default user / password and enables autologon

HKLM,"SOFTWARE\Microsoft\Windows NT\CurrentVersion\Winlogon", ->

"DefaultUserName",0,"Administrator"

HKLM,"SOFTWARE\Microsoft\Windows NT\CurrentVersion\Winlogon", ->

"DefaultPassword",0,""

HKLM,"SOFTWARE\Microsoft\Windows NT\CurrentVersion\Winlogon", ->

"AutoAdminLogon", ,"1"
```

POSTBOOT.CMD

This is phase 2 of the application installation and configuration section. Post-Reboot performs essentially the same processes as does Pre-Reboot, but it sets the Windows NT shell back to Windows NT Explorer and removes the autologon registry settings. This phase allows configuration of applications that require a reboot.

1. Set Environment Variables

The Post-Reboot phase begins by setting environment variables that are used by this batch file and are available to other installation scripts. As a part of this phase, C:\MSIF is added to the session path.

```
echo 1. Setting environment variables...

    SET MSIF_SHARE=\\[SERVER_NAME]\MSIF

    SET MSIF_DRIVE=X:

    SET MSIF_SCRIPTS=C:\MSIF

    SET MSIF_LOGIN=install

    SET MSIF_PASSWORD=install

    SET MSIF_FULLNAME=Sample Installation

    SET MSIF_ORGNAME=Microsoft Consulting Services

    SET PATH=%PATH%;C:\MSIF
```

2. Connect to MSIF Share

After the variables are set, MSIF connects to the MSIF share point. The error checking helps with troubleshooting slow connect times.

```
echo 2. Connecting to MSIF share point...

    :NETCONN

    NET USE %MSIF_DRIVE% %MSIF_SHARE% /USER:%MSIF_LOGIN%
    %MSIF_PASSWORD%

    IF ERRORLEVEL 1 Goto NetUseError

    Goto SkipNetUseError

    :NetUseError

    Echo Error connecting to image server! You may want to
    contact deployment support.

    Echo.

    Echo To retry connection, press ENTER.

    Echo To exit load, press CTRL+C.

    Pause

    GoTO NETCONN

    :SkipNetUseError
```

3. Set Windows NT Shell to Explorer

Next, POSTBOOT.CMD sets the Windows NT shell back to Windows NT Explorer to reduce the possibility of getting errors during application installation.

```
echo 4. Setting Windows NT shell to Explorer...

    rundll32 setupapi,InstallHinfSection DefaultInstall 128 ->

    %MSIF_SCRIPTS%\Explorer.INF
```

4. Package Installations & Configurations

This is where you add your own scripted application installations. Refer to the "POSTBOOT" section above for an example.

5. Prepare System for Final Reboot

This step applies POSTBOOT.INF changes, removes the network connection, and reboots the computer.

```
echo 5. Preparing system for Final Reboot...

    rundll32 setupapi,InstallHinfSection DefaultInstall 128 ->

    %MSIF_SCRIPTS%\PostBoot.INF

    C:

    NET USE %MSIF_DRIVE% /D

    C:\MSIF\SHUTDOWN.EXE /L /R /T:10 /Y

    POSTBOOT.INF removes the default logon password and disables the
AutoAdminLogon flag.
```

```
[AddReg]

; 1. Removes default AutoLogon on settings from WinLogon.

HKLM,"SOFTWARE\Microsoft\Windows NT\CurrentVersion\Winlogon","DefaultPas
sword",0,""

HKLM,"SOFTWARE\Microsoft\Windows NT\CurrentVersion\Winlogon","AutoAdminL
ogon",,"0"
```

File Samples

Boot Disk/Hard Drive MSIF Files

CONFIG.SYS

```
FILES=30

DEVICE=A:\DOS\HIMEM.SYS /TESTMEM:OFF

DEVICE=A:\DOS\EMM386.EXE NOEMS

DOS=HIGH,UMB

DEVICEHIGH=A:\NET\IFSHLP.SYS

LASTDRIVE=Z
```

AUTOEXEC.BAT

```
@ECHO OFF

REM

========================================================================

REM     Author: Microsoft Consulting Services
```

> This code is spaced so that it is easier to read. Lines are broken for layout only: entries should be on a single line. If you want to skip this section, go to page 506.

AUTOEXEC.BAT   *(continued)*

```
REM    Date:          May 1, 1998

REM    Description:   AUTOEXEC.BAT recreates disk partition, formats

                      disk, loads network drivers, connects to image

                      server, copies installation instructions to

                      hard drive, and starts Windows NT installation.

REM
```

```
REM
```

```
REM  Determine Boot Status.

REM

REM  This section is used to keep track of the progress of the

REM  installation for the purpose of forcing the system to reboot

REM  at desired intervals. It uses the STATUS environment

REM  variable to do this.

REM
```

This code is spaced so that it is easier to read. Lines are broken for layout only: entries should be on a single line. If you want to skip this section, go to page 506.

AUTOEXEC.BAT   *(continued)*

```
REM  The state of this variable is stored in A:\STATUS.BAT and

REM  will be one of three values: STEP1, STEP2 or BYPASS.  If

REM  the boot disk becomes confused as to which step it is trying

REM  to execute, simply delete the STATUS.BAT file and the boot

REM  disk will begin at STEP1.


REM

REM

==================================================================

SET STATUS=STEP1

IF EXIST A:\STATUS.BAT CALL A:\STATUS.BAT

CLS

@ECHO.

@ECHO Windows NT 4.0 Automated Installation Framework

@ECHO Boot Disk - %STATUS%, Revision 4.0

@ECHO -------------------------------------------------------------

@ECHO.

IF %STATUS%==STEP2 GOTO STEP2

IF %STATUS%==BYPASS GOTO BYPASS

GOTO STEP1
```

This code is spaced so that it is easier to read. Lines are broken for layout only: entries should be on a single line. If you want to skip this section, go to page 506.

AUTOEXEC.BAT   *(continued)*

```
:STEP1

REM

==================================================================

REM

REM  Prompt for Information and Rebuild Disk Partition.

REM

REM 1. Prompt for Information. System uses a freeware utility called

REM    ENQUIRE.COM to prompt for input and set environment variables

REM    based on the input. For purposes of this boot disk the following

REM    environment variables are set:

REM

REM    - TEMPLATE, used to load the correct MSIF template and MS-DOS

REM      network interface card.

REM    - COMPUTERNAME, this is used in SYSTEM.INI and UNATTEND.TXT

REM

REM    After variant information has been collected, the boot disk saves
```

This code is spaced so that it is easier to read. Lines are broken for layout only: entries should be on a single line. If you want to skip this section, go to page 506.

AUTOEXEC.BAT   *(continued)*

```
REM    the environment variables to a VARS.BAT file to be used during

REM    STEP2.

REM

REM 2. Rebuild Disk Partition. This section runs DEBUG.EXE to delete the

REM    pre-existing MS-DOS or non-DOS partitions and it creates a new

REM    small FAT16 MS-DOS partition using the undocumented

REM    FDISK 1 /PRI:500 command. The small partition size speeds up the

REM    initial formatting. Windows NT extends the partition size to its

REM    fullest potential during the load.

REM

REM    - DEBUG.EXE, uses an MSDN documented input text file to

REM      "wipe" the disk

REM    - FDISK.EXE, creates new primary MS-DOS partition (500 MB).

REM

REM
```

This code is spaced so that it is easier to read. Lines are broken for layout only: entries should be on a single line. If you want to skip this section, go to page 506.

```
REM 1. Prompt for Information.

ECHO.

ECHO MSIF Configuration Template Menu:

ECHO.

ECHO 1) Compaq LTE 5200 (CPQ5200A)

ECHO 2) Dell OptiPlex GXa (DELLA)

ECHO 3) Boot to DOS

ECHO.

ENQUIRE "Enter choice (1, 2, or 3) = ", OPTION

if "%OPTION%" == "1" SET TEMPLATE=CPQ5200A

if "%OPTION%" == "2" SET TEMPLATE=DELLA

if "%OPTION%" == "3" GOTO END

ECHO.

ENQUIRE "Enter name of computer = ", COMPUTERNAME

ECHO.

ECHO SET TEMPLATE=%TEMPLATE%> A:\VARS.BAT

ECHO SET COMPUTERNAME=%COMPUTERNAME%>> A:\VARS.BAT

ECHO SET LOGIN=install>> A:\VARS.BAT

ECHO SET PASSWORD=install>> A:\VARS.BAT

ECHO SET WORKGROUP=usa-detroit>> A:\VARS.BAT
```

This code is spaced so that it is easier to read. Lines are broken for layout only: entries should be on a single line. If you want to skip this section, go to page 506.

AUTOEXEC.BAT   *(continued)*

```
ECHO SET DOMAIN=loadsite>> A:\VARS.BAT

ECHO SET NETDRIVE=x:>> A:\VARS.BAT

ECHO SET NETSERVER=[SERVER_NAME]>> A:\VARS.BAT

ECHO SET NETSHARE=MSIF>> A:\VARS.BAT


REM 2. Rebuild Disk Partition.

ECHO SET STATUS=STEP2 > A:\STATUS.BAT

a:\debug.exe < a:\delpart.txt

a:\fdisk.exe 1 /PRI:500 /Q

a:\reboot.com




:STEP2

REM
============================================================================

REM

REM Format Disk, Load Network, and Run Operating System Installation

REM

REM 1. Formats disk using the standard command-line switches available
```

This code is spaced so that it is easier to read. Lines are broken for layout only: entries should be on a single line. If you want to skip this section, go to page 506.

AUTOEXEC.BAT   *(continued)*

```
REM    and an input text file that simply contains the character "y".

REM    This is used to respond to the question, "Do you want to

REM    continue?"

REM

REM 2. BYPASS: can be used to "bypass" disk partitioning and formatting

REM    during testing and troubleshooting.

REM

REM 3. SmartDrive is loaded to optimize the memory allocation.

REM

REM 4. Set environment variables stored in VARS.BAT.

REM

REM 5. Loads the network adapter associated with the selected MSIF

REM    template, then updates the "clean" version of the network-

REM    adapter-specific SYSTEM.INI file with the environment variables.

REM

REM 6. Starts the network by logging on and then connecting to the MSIF

REM    network share.

REM
```

This code is spaced so that it is easier to read. Lines are broken for layout only: entries should be on a single line. If you want to skip this section, go to page 506.

```
REM 7. Copies down MSIF template files to C:\MSIF and edits the "clean"

REM    copy of the UNATTEND.TXT with new computername.

REM

REM 8. Resets the MSIF boot disk by setting the STATUS flag file equal

REM    to STEP1.

REM

REM 9. Start Windows NT load.

REM

REM
```

==

```
ECHO Preparing Computer's Hard Drive and Network...



ECHO 1. Formating Hard Drive...

a:\format C: /U /V:CORP < a:\format.txt



ECHO 2. Setting BYPASS Flag...
```

This code is spaced so that it is easier to read. Lines are broken for layout only: entries should be on a single line. If you want to skip this section, go to page 506.

AUTOEXEC.BAT *(continued)*

```
ECHO SET STATUS=BYPASS > A:\STATUS.BAT

:BYPASS


ECHO 3. Loading SmartDrive...

a:\net\smartdrv.exe /x 2048 > nul


ECHO 4. Setting Environment Variables Stored in VARS.BAT...

CALL A:\VARS.BAT


ECHO 5. Loading %TEMPLATE%...

copy a:\net\%TEMPLATE%\*.* a:\net

change a:\net\system.ini computername= computername=%COMPUTERNAME% > nul

change a:\net\system.ini logondomain= logondomain=%DOMAIN% > nul

change a:\net\system.ini username= username=%LOGIN% > nul

change a:\net\system.ini workgroup= workgroup=%workgroup% > nul

path=a:\;a:\net

CLS
```

This code is spaced so that it is easier to read. Lines are broken for layout only: entries should be on a single line. If you want to skip this section, go to page 506.

AUTOEXEC.BAT   *(continued)*

```
ECHO ----------------------------------------------------------------

ECHO.

ECHO                                 WARNING!

ECHO.

ECHO    Please remove diskette from the A: drive once the NT
        installation starts.

ECHO.

ECHO ----------------------------------------------------------------

ECHO.


ECHO 6. Starting Network...

a:\net\net logon %LOGIN% %PASSWORD% /YES /SAVEPW:NO

a:\net\net use %NETDRIVE% \\%NETSERVER%\%NETSHARE%


ECHO 7. Downloading MSIF Template Files...

C:

cd \

md msif
```

This code is spaced so that it is easier to read. Lines are broken for layout only: entries should be on a single line. If you want to skip this section, go to page 506.

AUTOEXEC.BAT   *(continued)*

```
copy %NETDRIVE%\TEMPLATE\%TEMPLATE%\*.* c:\msif

change c:\msif\unattend.txt ComputerName= ComputerName=%COMPUTERNAME% >
nul


ECHO 8. Resetting MSIF Boot Disk......

ECHO SET STATUS=STEP1 > A:\STATUS.BAT


ECHO 9. Starting Operating System Installation...

c:\msif\install


:END
```

STATUS.BAT

Default setting on initial boot:

```
SET STATUS=STEP1
```

DELPART.TXT

```
a 100

int 13


rax

0301

rbx

0200

f 200 1 200 0

rcx

0001

rdx

0080

p

q
```

Windows NT Operating System Installation

INSTALL.BAT

```
X:\Nt4Wks\i386\WinNT /u:C:\MSIF\Unattend.txt /s:X:\Nt4Wks\i386
```

UNATTEND.TXT

```
[Unattended]

OemPreinstall = yes

NoWaitAfterTextMode = 1

NoWaitAfterGUIMode = 1

OEMSkipEula = yes

FileSystem = ConvertNTFS

ExtendOEMPartition = 0

ConfirmHardware = no

NtUpgrade = no

Win31Upgrade = no

TargetPath = WINNT

OverwriteOemFilesOnUpgrade = no


[OEM_Ads]

Banner = "Windows NT 4.0 *Automated Installation Framework"


[UserData]

FullName = "Build 1.0, rev 1"

OrgName = "Microsoft Corporation"
```

```
ComputerName = MCSTEST

ProductId = "222-222222"


[GuiUnattended]

OemSkipWelcome = 1

OEMBlankAdminPassword = 1

TimeZone = "(GMT-05:00) Eastern Time (US & Canada)"


[Display]

ConfigureAtLogon = 0

BitsPerPel = 10

XResolution = 800

YResolution = 600

VRefresh = 60

AutoConfirm = 1


[Network]

DetectAdapters = ""

InstallProtocols = ProtocolsSection

InstallServices = ServicesSection
```

```
JoinWorkgroup = "USA-DETROIT"


[ProtocolsSection]

NBF = NBFParamSection


[NBFParamSection]


[ServicesSection]
```

CMDLINES.TXT

```
[Commands]

"rundll32 setupapi,InstallHinfSection DefaultInstall 128
C:\MSIF\RunOnce.inf"

"C:\WINNT\NT4SP3\Update.exe -u -n -z"
```

RUNONCE.INF

```
; Windows NT 4.0 Automated Installation Framework

; RunOnce

;

; 1. Forces Windows NT shell from Explorer to be PREBOOT.CMD

; 2. Forces default user / password and enables autologon

;     - Sets Default User to Administrator
```

```
;      - Sets Default Password to blank

;      - Enables AutoLogon

; 3. Disables default Windows NT Tips

; ----------------------------------------------------------


[Version]

Signature = "$Windows NT$"


[DefaultInstall]

AddReg = AddReg

DelReg = DelReg

UpdateInis = UpdateInis


[AddReg]

; 1. Forces Windows NT shell from Explorer to be PREBOOT.CMD

HKLM, "SOFTWARE\Microsoft\Windows NT\CurrentVersion\Winlogon", "Shell",
0, "Explorer.exe C:\MSIF\PreBoot.cmd"


; 2. Forces default user / password and enables autologon
```

```
HKLM, "SOFTWARE\Microsoft\Windows NT\CurrentVersion\Winlogon",
"DefaultUserName", 0, "Administrator"

HKLM, "SOFTWARE\Microsoft\Windows NT\CurrentVersion\Winlogon",
"DefaultPassword", 0, ""

HKLM, "SOFTWARE\Microsoft\Windows NT\CurrentVersion\Winlogon",
"AutoAdminLogon", , "1"


; 3. Disables default Windows NT Tips

HKCU, "SOFTWARE\Microsoft\Windows\CurrentVersion\Explorer\Tips",
"DisplayInitialTipWindows", 65537, 0

HKCU, "SOFTWARE\Microsoft\Windows\CurrentVersion\Explorer\Tips", "Show",
1, 0, 0, 0, 0

HKCU, "SOFTWARE\Microsoft\Windows\CurrentVersion\Explorer\Tips", "Next",
1, 3, 0


[DelReg]


[UpdateInis]
```

PREBOOT.CMD

```
@echo OFF

REM =================================================================

REM

REM      File:   PREBOOT.CMD

REM      Date:   May 1, 1998

REM      Author: Microsoft Consulting Services

REM

REM      Desc:   This file begins Pre-Reboot phase of the unattended load

REM              of applications and system configuration. It is the

REM              first of two Windows NT shells. RunOnce.Inf executed at

REM              the end of the standard Windows NT load (executed via

REM              cmdlines.txt) sets PREBOOT.CMD as the new

REM              Windows NT shell.

REM

REM              PreReboot (PREBOOT.CMD) performs the following steps:

REM

REM              1. Sets standard MSIF environment variables.

REM              2. Connects to MSIF share point.  This share has the
```

This code is spaced so that it is easier to read. Lines are broken for layout only: entries should be on a single line. If you want to skip this section, go to page 518.

PREBOOT.CMD *(continued)*

```
REM            operating system, applications, and any

REM            specific system configuration information.

REM         3. All standard utility files such as SHUTDOWN and

REM            DELTREE are copied down from \UTILITIES to C:\MSIF.

REM         4. Resets Windows NT shell back to Explorer while

REM            executing PREBOOT.CMD. This eliminates the possibility

REM            of applications being installed "restarting" the

REM            Windows NT shell during their installation process.

REM         5. Installs all of the Pre-Reboot packages destined to

REM            run before reboot.

REM         6. Sets Windows NT shell to POSTBOOT.CMD for Post-Reboot

REM            and restarts the computer.

REM

REM ================================================================
```

This code is spaced so that it is easier to read. Lines are broken for layout only: entries should be on a single line. If you want to skip this section, go to page 518.

PREBOOT.CMD   *(continued)*

```
cls

echo.

echo Windows NT 4.0 Automated Installation Framework

echo PreBoot Phase

echo ---------------------------------------------------------------------



echo 1. Setting environment variables...

    SET MSIF_SHARE=\\[SERVER_NAME]\MSIF

    SET MSIF_DRIVE=X:

    SET MSIF_SCRIPTS=C:\MSIF

    SET MSIF_LOGIN=install

    SET MSIF_PASSWORD=install

    SET MSIF_FULLNAME=Sample Installation

    SET MSIF_ORGNAME=Microsoft Consulting Services

    SET PATH=%PATH%;C:\MSIF
```

This code is spaced so that it is easier to read. Lines are broken for layout only: entries should be on a single line. If you want to skip this section, go to page 518.

```
echo 2. Connecting to MSIF share point...

    :NETCONN

    NET USE %MSIF_DRIVE% %MSIF_SHARE% /USER:%MSIF_LOGIN%
%MSIF_PASSWORD%

    IF ERRORLEVEL 1 Goto NetUseError

    Goto SkipNetUseError

    :NetUseError

    Echo Error connecting to image server! You may want to contact
deployment support.

    Echo.

    Echo To retry connection, press ENTER.

    Echo To exit load, press CTRL+C.

    Pause

    GoTO NETCONN

    :SkipNetUseError




echo 3. Copying MSIF and other handy utilities to C:\MSIF...

    %MSIF_DRIVE%

    COPY \UTILITIES\*.* C:\MSIF
```

> This code is spaced so that it is easier to read. Lines are broken for layout only: entries should be on a single line. If you want to skip this section, go to page 518.

```
echo 4. Setting Windows NT shell to Explorer...

    rundll32 setupapi,InstallHinfSection DefaultInstall 128
%MSIF_SCRIPTS%\Explorer.INF




echo 5. Running Pre-Reboot package installations and configurations...


    echo Office 97 Professional Edition

        %MSIF_DRIVE%

        CD \OFF97ADM

        CALL OFF97ADM.BAT

        SLEEP 5




echo 6. Preparing system for Post-Reboot phase...

    rundll32 setupapi,InstallHinfSection DefaultInstall 128 ↵

    %MSIF_SCRIPTS%\PreBoot.INF

    C:

    NET USE %MSIF_DRIVE% /D
```

This code is spaced so that it is easier to read. Lines are broken for layout only: entries should be on a single line. If you want to skip this section, go to page 518.

PREBOOT.INF

```
; Windows NT 4.0 Automated Installation Framework.

; Pre-Reboot Phase.

;

; 1. Forces Windows NT shell to be POSTBOOT.CMD.

; 2. Forces default user/password and enables autologon.

;      - Sets Default User to Administrator

;      - Sets Default Password to blank

;      - Enables AutoLogon

; -----------------------------------------------------------------------


[Version]

Signature = "$Windows NT$"


[DefaultInstall]

AddReg = AddReg

DelReg = DelReg

UpdateInis = UpdateInis


[AddReg]
```

```
; 1. Change Windows NT shell from PREBOOT.CMD to POSTBOOT.CMD

HKLM,"SOFTWARE\Microsoft\Windows NT\CurrentVersion\Winlogon", ↵
"Shell",0,"Explorer.exe C:\MSIF\PostBoot.cmd"


; 2. Forces default user / password and enables autologon

HKLM,"SOFTWARE\Microsoft\Windows NT\CurrentVersion\Winlogon", ↵
"DefaultUserName",0,"Administrator"

HKLM,"SOFTWARE\Microsoft\Windows NT\CurrentVersion\Winlogon", ↵
"DefaultPassword",0,""

HKLM,"SOFTWARE\Microsoft\Windows NT\CurrentVersion\Winlogon", ↵
"AutoAdminLogon", ,"1"


[DelReg]

[UpdateInis]
```

POSTBOOT.CMD

```
@echo OFF

REM

▪▪▪▪▪▪▪▪▪▪▪▪▪▪▪▪▪▪▪▪▪▪▪▪▪▪▪▪▪▪▪▪▪▪▪▪▪▪▪▪▪▪▪▪▪▪▪▪▪▪▪▪▪▪▪▪▪▪▪▪▪▪▪▪▪▪▪▪▪▪▪▪▪▪▪▪▪

REM     File:   POSTBOOT.CMD

REM     Date:   May 1, 1998
```

> This code is spaced so that it is easier to read. Lines are broken for layout only: entries should be on a single line. If you want to skip this section, go to page 524.

POSTBOOT.CMD   *(continued)*

```
REM  Author: Microsoft Consulting Services

REM

REM  Desc: This file begins the Post-Reboot phase of the unattended

REM  load of applications and system configuration.  POSTBOOT is the

REM  second of 2 Windows NT shells run.

REM

REM  Post-Reboot (POSTBOOT.CMD) performs the following steps:

REM

REM  1. Sets standard MSIF environment variables.

REM  2. Resets Windows NT shell back to Explorer while executing

REM     POSTBOOT.CMD.  This eliminates the possibility of

REM     applications being installed "restarting" the Windows NT

REM     shell during their installation process.

REM  3. Connects to MSIF share point.  This share has the

REM     operating system, applications, and any
```

This code is spaced so that it is easier to read. Lines are broken for layout only: entries should be on a single line. If you want to skip this section, go to page 524.

POSTBOOT.CMD   *(continued)*

```
REM     specific system configuration information.

REM  4. Installs all of the Post-Reboot packages destined for

REM     after reboot.

REM  5. Disables auto-logon, disconnects MSIF network

REM     drive and restarts the computer.

REM

REM
```

```
cls

echo.

echo Windows NT 4.0 Automated Installation Framework

echo Post-Reboot

echo -----------------------------------------------------------------



echo 1. Setting environment variables...

    SET MSIF_SHARE=\\[SERVER_NAME]\MSIF

    SET MSIF_DRIVE=X:
```

This code is spaced so that it is easier to read. Lines are broken for layout only: entries should be on a single line. If you want to skip this section, go to page 524.

POSTBOOT.CMD   *(continued)*

```
    SET MSIF_SCRIPTS=C:\MSIF

    SET MSIF_LOGIN=install

    SET MSIF_PASSWORD=install

    SET MSIF_FULLNAME=Sample Installation

    SET MSIF_ORGNAME=Microsoft Consulting Services

    SET PATH=%PATH%;C:\MSIF



echo 2. Connecting to MSIF share point...

    :NETCONN

    NET USE %MSIF_DRIVE% %MSIF_SHARE% /USER:%MSIF_LOGIN%
%MSIF_PASSWORD%

    IF ERRORLEVEL 1 Goto NetUseError

    Goto SkipNetUseError

    :NetUseError

    Echo Error connecting to image server! You may want to contact
deployment support.

    Echo.

    Echo To retry connection, press ENTER.

    Echo To exit load, press CTRL+C.
```

This code is spaced so that it is easier to read. Lines are broken for layout only: entries should be on a single line. If you want to skip this section, go to page 524.

POSTBOOT.CMD   *(continued)*

```
Pause

GOTO NETCONN

:SkipNetUseError



echo 3. Setting Windows NT shell to Explorer...

    rundll32 setupapi,InstallHinfSection DefaultInstall 128 ↵
%MSIF_SCRIPTS%\Explorer.INF



echo 4. Running Post-Reboot package installations and configurations...


REM     echo IntelliMouse Driver

REM     %MSIF_DRIVE%

REM     CD \IMOUSE21

REM     CALL IMouse21.BAT

REM     SLEEP 5



echo 5. Preparing system for Final Reboot...
```

This code is spaced so that it is easier to read. Lines are broken for layout only: entries should be on a single line. If you want to skip this section, go to page 524.

POSTBOOT.CMD   *(continued)*

```
        rundll32 setupapi,InstallHinfSection DefaultInstall 128 ↵
%MSIF_SCRIPTS%\PostBoot.INF

        C:

        NET USE %MSIF_DRIVE% /D

        C:\MSIF\SHUTDOWN.EXE /L /R /T:10 /Y
```

POSTBOOT.INF

```
; Windows NT 4.0 Automated Installation Framework

; Post-Reboot Phase

;

; 1. Removes default AutoLogon on settings from WinLogon

;      - Removes Default Password

;      - Disables AutoLogon

; --------------------------------------------------------------------


[Version]

Signature = "$Windows NT$"


[DefaultInstall]

AddReg = AddReg
```

```
DelReg = DelReg


[AddReg]

; 1. Removes default AutoLogon on settings from WinLogon

HKLM,"SOFTWARE\Microsoft\Windows NT\CurrentVersion\Winlogon", ↵

"DefaultPassword",0, ""

HKLM,"SOFTWARE\Microsoft\Windows NT\CurrentVersion\Winlogon", ↵

"AutoAdminLogon",, "0"


[DelReg]
```

EXPLORER.INF

```
; Microsoft Windows NT Installation Framework

; Microsoft Consulting Services

; Revision 4.0

; Explorer.Inf - Configure Windows NT Shell to Explorer

;

; 1. Sets Windows NT shell to Explorer while load is in operation

; ----------------------------------------------------------------


[Version]
```

```
Signature = "$Window NT$"


[DefaultInstall]

AddReg = AddReg

DelReg = DelReg


[AddReg]

; 1. Sets Windows NT shell to Explorer while load is in operation

HKLM, "SOFTWARE\Microsoft\Windows NT\CurrentVersion\Winlogon", ↵

"Shell",0, "Explorer.exe"


[DelReg]
```

UNATTEND.TXT Parameters (TechNet)

Windows NT Command Line

Windows NT 4.0 uses an unattended method of setup with the /U switch. The syntax is:

```
winnt /u:<answer file> /s:<location of source files>
```

-or-

```
Winnt32 /u:<answer file> /s:<location of source files>
```

The *<answer file>* is a text file that contains all the answers a user normally would be required to enter during Windows NT setup. You can create this file with a text editor or with Setup manager (SETUPMGR.EXE, in the resource kit). Listed below are all valid answer file parameters along with their possible values. For a further explanation of these values, go to http://www.microsoft.com and download the self-extracting file DEPLOY.EXE.

Sample UNATTEND.TXT File

```
;[Unattended]

;Method = Express|Custom

;NtUpgrade = Yes|No

;Win31Upgade = Yes|No

;TargetPath = *|<Path Name>|Manual

;OverwriteOemFilesOnUpgrade = Yes|No

;ConfirmHardware = Yes|No

;OEMPreinstall = Yes|No

;NoWaitAfterTextMode =  (0 = stop, 1 = Reboot)

;NoWaitAfterGuiMode = (0 = stop, 1 = Reboot)

;FileSystem = ConvertNTFS|LeaveAlone

;ExtendOemPartition = (0 = no, 1 = Yes)


;
```

This code is spaced so that it is easier to read. Lines are broken for layout only: entries should be on a single line. If you want to skip this section, go to page 547.

```
*\PARTNER

*\;

*\; OemSkipEula is undocumented at this time and is

*\; supported only for Premier accounts.

*\;

*\;OemSkipEula = Yes|No

*\

;

; Descriptions are from the COMPUTER Section of TXTSETUP.SIF

; =========================================================

; ComputerType = "AST Manhattan SMP","RETAIL"

; ComputerType = "Compaq SystemPro Multiprocessor or 100%
Compatible","RETAIL"

; ComputerType = "Corollary C-bus Architecture","RETAIL"

; ComputerType = "Corollary C-bus Micro Channel Architecture","RETAIL"

; ComputerType = "IBM PS/2 or other Micro Channel-based PC","RETAIL"

; ComputerType = "MPS Uniprocessor PC","RETAIL"

; ComputerType = "MPS Multiprocessor PC","RETAIL"

; ComputerType = "MPS Multiprocessor Micro Channel PC","RETAIL"

; ComputerType = "NCR System 3000 Model 3360/3450/3550","RETAIL"
```

> This code is spaced so that it is easier to read. Lines are broken for layout only: entries should be on a single line. If you want to skip this section, go to page 547.

UNATTEND.TXT   *(continued)*

```
; ComputerType = "Olivetti LSX5030/40","RETAIL"

; ComputerType = "Standard PC","RETAIL"

; ComputerType = "Standard PC with C-Step i486","RETAIL"

; ComputerType = "Wyse Series 7000i Model 740MP/760MP","RETAIL"


;KeyBoardLayout = <Layout description>

; Example;

;   KeyBoardLayout = "US-International"


;[GuiUnattended]=========================================


;[GuiUnattended]

;OemSkipWelcome = (0 = no, 1 = Yes)

;OemBlankadminPassword = (0 = no, 1 = Yes)

;TimeZone = <Time Zone>

; The following are strings for AdvServerType

; AdvServerType = LANMANNT

; AdvServerType = LANSECNT

; AdvServerType = SERVERNT
```

This code is spaced so that it is easier to read. Lines are broken for layout only: entries should be on a single line. If you want to skip this section, go to page 547.

UNATTEND.TXT   *(continued)*

```
; Definition of Server Type

; LANMANNT=PDC

; LANSECNT=BDC

; SERVERNT=Standalone




;[UserData]================================================


;[UserData]
;FullName = <user name>

;OrgName = <company name>

;ComputerName = <computer name>

;ProductID = <product ID> (CD-key)

;

; Note if PID is for an OEM version of WINDOWS NT the algorithm

; for the PID is: xxxyy-OEM-0000016-zzzzz

;

; x = Julian calendar date for the day

; y = The current year (last two digits)

; z = Any numeric combination you want
```

This code is spaced so that it is easier to read. Lines are broken for layout only: entries should be on a single line. If you want to skip this section, go to page 547.

UNATTEND.TXT   *(continued)*

```
;

;

;[LicenseFilePrintData]══════════════════════════════

;[LicenseFilePrintData]

; AutoMode ═ PerServer or PerSeat

; AutoUser ═ xxxx or PerServer


;[NetWork]═══════════════════════════════════════════

;[NetWork]

;Attend ═ Yes|No

; This value should not be specified for a complete unattended install.

;

;JoinWorkGroup ═ <workgroup name>

;JoinDomain ═ <Domain name>

;CreateComputerAccount ═ <user_name, password>

;InstallDC ═ <domain name>

;InstallAdapters ═ <Install adapters section>
```

> This code is spaced so that it is easier to read. Lines are broken for layout only: entries should be on a single line. If you want to skip this section, go to page 547.

```
;

; If not AUTODETECTED do not use

; this option

;

;DetectAdapters = <detect adapters section>|""

;

;InstallProtocols = <Protocol(s) list section>

;InstallServices = <Sevices list section>

;InstallInternetServer <internet information server parameters>

;DoNotInstallInternetServer = Yes|No

;[detect adapters section]

;

; Used only if the adapter AUTODETECTED by setup.

;

;DetectCount = <Number of detection attempts>

;LimitTo = <netcard inf option>

;Example;

; LimitTo = DECETHERWORKSTURBO
```

This code is spaced so that it is easier to read. Lines are broken for layout only: entries should be on a single line. If you want to skip this section, go to page 547.

UNATTEND.TXT   *(continued)*

```
;[Install adapters section]

; Examples;

;   DECETHERWORKSTURBO = DECETHERWORKSTURBOParams

;   EE16 = EE16Params


;[DECETHERWORKSTURBOParams]

;InterruptNumber = 5

;IOBaseAddress = 768                      ;Note!! all numbers in these sections

;MemoryMappedBaseAddress = 851968   ;are converted from hex to decimal

;!AutoNetInterfaceType = 1              ;(768 = 300h). You can get these

;!AutoNetBusNumber = 0                  ;values from the registry of a

;                                                  ;computer with the adapter installed.


;[EE16Params]

;!AutoNetInterfaceType = 1

;Transceiver = 3

;!AutoNetBusNumber = 0
```

This code is spaced so that it is easier to read. Lines are broken for layout only: entries should be on a single line. If you want to skip this section, go to page 547.

```
;IoChannelReady = 2

;IoBaseAddress = 784

;InterruptNumber = 10



;[Protocol(s) list section]

; OEM File listing for protocols

;

; TCPIP - OEMNXPTC.INF

; NETBEUI - OEMNXPNB.INF

; IPX - OEMNSVNW.INF

; DLC - OEMNXPDL.INF

; Point to Point Protocol - OEMNXPPP.INF

; STREAMS - OEMNXPST.INF

; Apple Talk - OEMNXPSM.INF

;



; TC = TCPIPParams

; NBF = NetBeuiParams

; NWLNKIPX = NWLINKIPXParams
```

This code is spaced so that it is easier to read. Lines are broken for layout only: entries should be on a single line. If you want to skip this section, go to page 547.

```
; DLC = DLCParams

; RASPPTP = RASPPTPParams

; STREAMS = STREAMSParams

; ATALK = ATALKParams


;[TCPIPParams]

; DHCP = yes|no

; IPAddress = www.xxx.yyy.zzz

; Subnet = www.xxx.yyy.zzz

; Gateway = www.xxx.yyy.zzz

; DNSServer = www.xxx.yyy.zzz www.xxx.yyy.zzz www.xxx.yyy.zzz

; WINSPrimary = www.xxx.yyy.zzz

; WINSSecondary = www.xxx.yyy.zzz

; DNSName = <DNS name server>

; ScopeID = This_is_the_scope_id


;[NetBeuiParams]

; No parameters needed


;[NWLINKIPXParams]
```

This code is spaced so that it is easier to read. Lines are broken for layout only: entries should be on a single line. If you want to skip this section, go to page 547.

```
; No parameters needed


;[DLCParams]

; No parameters needed


;[RASPPTPParams]

; No parameters needed


;[STREAMSParams]

; No parameters needed


;[ATALKParams]

; You need to figure out how to set the default zone and adapter. This

; is needed for printing. Many high-end publishing companies use Apple

; printers on their networks and need this protocol to print. See the

; Windows NT Setup Guide for details on settings such as these.


;[Sevices list section]

; NWWKSTA = InstallCSNW

; SNMP = InstallSNMP
```

This code is spaced so that it is easier to read. Lines are broken for layout only: entries should be on a single line. If you want to skip this section, go to page 547.

UNATTEND.TXT   *(continued)*

```
; RAS = InstallRemoteAccess

; NETMON = InstallNetMon

; STCPIP = InstallSimpleTCP

; TCPPRINT = InstallTCPPrint

; INETSTP = InstallInternetServer

; SAP = InstallSAP


;[InstallCSNW]

; DefaultLocation = <server location (usually preferred server)>

; DefaultScriptOption = 0|1|3

;   0 = No scripts will be run

;   1 = Netware 3.X level scripts

;   3 = Either Netware 3.X or 4.X level scripts can be run


;[InstallSNMP]

; Accept_CommunityName = Name1, Name2, Name3 (Max is 3)

; Send_Authentication = yes | no

; AnyHost = yes | no

; Limit_Host = host1, host2, host3 (Max is 3)

; Community_name = <Community name>
```

This code is spaced so that it is easier to read. Lines are broken for layout only: entries should be on a single line. If you want to skip this section, go to page 547.

```
; Traps = IPaddress | IPXaddress (max of 3 IP or IPX addresses)

; Contact_Name = <user name>

; Location = <computer location>

; Service = Physical, Applications, Datalink, Internet, EndToEnd


;[Modem]================================================

;[Modem]

;InstallModem = <Modem parameter section>

; Example;

;    InstallModem = MyModem

;

;[ModemParameterSection]

;<Com Port Number> = <Modem description>

; Example;

;    Com2 = "Hayes V-Series Ultra Smartmodem 9600"

;

;

;[InstallRemoteAccess]

;
```

This code is spaced so that it is easier to read. Lines are broken for layout only: entries should be on a single line. If you want to skip this section, go to page 547.

UNATTEND.TXT   *(continued)*

```
; PortSections = <port section name>

; DialoutProtocols = TCPIP|IPX|NetBEUI|All

; DialInProtocols = TCPIP|IPX|NetBEUI|All

; NetBEUIClientAccess = Network|ThisComputer


; TCPIPClientAccess = Network|ThisComputer

; IPXClientAccess = Network|ThisComputer

; UseDHCP = Yes|No

; StaticAddressBegin = <IP address>  (used only if UseDHCP = No)

; StaticAddressEnd = <IP address>   (used only if UseDHCP = No)

; ExcludeAddress = <IP address1 - IP address2>

;  The above is used to exclude a range of addresses when a range

;  has been assigned manually. Requires that StaticAddressBegin and

;  StaticAddressEnd are specified already.

;

; ClientCanRequestIPAddress = Yes|No

; AutomaticNetworkNumbers = Yes|No

; NetworkNumberFrom <IPX Net Number>

; AssignSameNetworkNumber = Yes|No
```

This code is spaced so that it is easier to read. Lines are broken for layout only: entries should be on a single line. If you want to skip this section, go to page 547.

UNATTEND.TXT   *(continued)*

```
; ClientsCanRequestIpxNodeNumber = Yes|No


; [port section name]

; PortName = COM1|COM2|COM3-COM25

; DeviceType = modem  (presently only value available)

; DeviceName = "Hayes V-Series Ultra Smartmodem 9600"

; PortUsage = DialOut|DialIn|DialInOut


;[InstallNetMon]


;[InstallSimpleTCP]


;[InstallTCPPrint]


;[<internet information server parameters>]

;

; (0 = do not install, 1 = install)

; InstallINETSTP = 0|1

; InstallFTP = 0|1

; InstallWWW = 0|1
```

This code is spaced so that it is easier to read. Lines are broken for layout only: entries should be on a single line. If you want to skip this section, go to page 547.

```
; InstallGopher = 0|1

; InstallADMIN = 0|1

; InstallMosaic = 0|1

; InstallGateway = 0|1

; InstallDNS = 0|1

; InstallHELP = 0|1

; InstallSMALLPROX = 0|1

; InstallCLIENTADMIN = 0|1

; WWWRoot = <www root directory i.e.  C:\INETSRV\WWW>

; FTPRoot = <FTP root directory i.e.  C:\ftp>

; GopherRoot = <gopher root directory i.e  C:\INETSRV\GOPHER>

; InstallDir = <Internet services install directory>

; EmailName = <E-mail Name i.e. john@org.com>

; UseGateway = 1

; GatewayList = \\gateway1 \\gateway2 \\gateway3

; DisableSvcLoc = 1

; GuestAccountName <name>

; GuestAccountPassword <password string>


;[InstallSAP]
```

This code is spaced so that it is easier to read. Lines are broken for layout only: entries should be on a single line. If you want to skip this section, go to page 547.

```
;[DisplayDrivers]==========================================


; [DisplayDrivers]

; <Display driver description> = Retail|Oem


;[Display]============================================


;[Display]

;

; For this to fully automate, the ConfigureAtLogon cannot be used.

;

; ConfigureAtLogon = (0 = during setup, 1 = at first logon)

;

;BitsPerPel = <Valid bits per pixel>

;XResolution = <Valid X resolution>

;YResolution = <Valid Y resolution>

;VRefresh = <Valid refresh rate>

;Flags = <Valid flags>
```

This code is spaced so that it is easier to read. Lines are broken for layout only: entries should be on a single line. If you want to skip this section, go to page 547.

UNATTEND.TXT   *(continued)*

```
;AutoConfirm = (0 = do not use specified settings,

;                  1 = use pre-defined settings)

;InstallDriver (0 = No, 1 = Yes)

;InfFile = <inf file name 1>,<inf file name 2>,.......

;InfOption = <inf option 1>,<inf option 2>,.........

; Example:

;   InstallDriver = 1

;   InfFile = S3.inf, Matrox.inf

;   InfOption = s3 765, Millenium 3D


;[KeyBoardDrivers]========================================


;[KeyBoardDrivers]

;"XT, AT, or Enhanced Keyboard (83-104 keys)" = "RETAIL"


; Descriptions are from the KEYBOARD Section of TXTSETUP.SIF

; ========================================================

; "XT, AT, or Enhanced Keyboard (83-104 keys)" = "RETAIL"
```

This code is spaced so that it is easier to read. Lines are broken for layout only: entries should be on a single line. If you want to skip this section, go to page 547.

UNATTEND.TXT   *(continued)*

```
;[PointingDeviceDrivers]===================================


;[PointingDeviceDrivers]


; Descriptions are from the MOUSE Section of TXTSETUP.SIF

;     =====================================================

; "Microsoft Mouse Port Mouse (includes BallPoint)" = "RETAIL"

; "Logitech Mouse Port Mouse" = "RETAIL"

; "Microsoft InPort Bus Mouse" = "RETAIL"

; "Microsoft Serial Mouse" = "RETAIL"

; "Microsoft BallPoint Serial Mouse" = "RETAIL"

; "Logitech Serial Mouse" = "RETAIL"

; "Microsoft (Green Buttons) or Logitech Bus Mouse" = "RETAIL"

; "No Mouse or Other Pointing Device" = "RETAIL"

; "Microsoft Mouse Port Mouse (includes BallPoint)" = "RETAIL"


;[MassStorageDrivers]===================================


;[MassStorageDrivers]
```

This code is spaced so that it is easier to read. Lines are broken for layout only: entries should be on a single line. If you want to skip this section, go to page 547.

UNATTEND.TXT   *(continued)*

```
; Descriptions are from the SCSI Section of TXTSETUP.SIF

; ==========================================================

; "Adaptec AHA-151X/AHA-152X or AIC-6260/AIC-6360 SCSI Host

;  Adapter" = "RETAIL"

; "Adaptec AHA-154X/AHA-164X SCSI Host Adapter" = "RETAIL"

; "Adaptec AHA-174X EISA SCSI Host Adapter" = "RETAIL"

; "Adaptec AHA-274X/AHA-284X/AIC-777X SCSI Host Adapter" = "RETAIL"

; "Adaptec AHA-294X/AHA-394X or AIC-78XX PCI SCSI Controller" = "RETAIL"

; "Adaptec AHA-2920 or Future Domain 16XX/PCI/SCSI2Go SCSI Host

;  Adapter" = "RETAIL"

; "AMD PCI SCSI Controller/Ethernet Adapter" = "RETAIL"

; "AMIscsi SCSI Host Adapter" = "RETAIL"

; "BusLogic SCSI Host Adapter" = "RETAIL"

; "BusLogic FlashPoint" = "RETAIL"

; "Compaq 32-Bit Fast-Wide SCSI-2/E" = "RETAIL"

; "Compaq Drive Array" = "RETAIL"

; "Dell Drive Array" = "RETAIL"

; "DPT SCSI Host Adapter" = "RETAIL"

; "Future Domain TMC-7000EX EISA SCSI Host Adapter" = "RETAIL"

; "Future Domain 8XX SCSI Host Adapter" = "RETAIL"
```

This code is spaced so that it is easier to read. Lines are broken for layout only: entries should be on a single line. If you want to skip this section, go to page 547.

```
; "IBM MCA SCSI Host Adapter" = "RETAIL"

; "IDE CD-ROM (ATAPI 1.2)/Dual-channel PCI IDE Controller" = "RETAIL"

; "Mitsumi CD-ROM Controller" = "RETAIL"

; "Mylex DAC960/Digital SWXCR-Ex Raid Controller" = "RETAIL"

; "NCR 53C9X SCSI Host Adapter" = "RETAIL"

; "NCR C700 SCSI Host Adapter" = "RETAIL"

; "NCR 53C710 SCSI Host Adapter" = "RETAIL"

; "Symbios Logic C810 PCI SCSI Host Adapter" = "RETAIL"

; "Olivetti ESC-1/ESC-2 SCSI Host Adapter" = "RETAIL"

; "QLogic PCI SCSI Host Adapter" = "RETAIL"

; "MKEPanasonic CD-ROM Controller" = "RETAIL"

; "Sony Proprietary CD-ROM Controller" = "RETAIL"

; "UltraStor 14F/14FB/34F/34FA/34FB SCSI Host Adapter" = "RETAIL"

; "UltraStor 24F/24FA SCSI Host Adapter" = "RETAIL"




;[DetectedMassStorage]=====================================



;[DetectedMassStorage]
```

This code is spaced so that it is easier to read. Lines are broken for layout only: entries should be on a single line. If you want to skip this section, go to page 547.

```
;[OEMAds]=====================================================


;[OEMAds]

;Banner = <text string> (must be enclosed in quotes and have

;                              the string 'Windows NT')

; Example;

;   Banner = "My own Windows NT setup"

;Logo = <file name>

;Background = <file name>
```

Handy Miscellaneous Registry Settings

Controlling Which Accessories are Installed

For your reference, here is Knowledge Base article Q156813.

Title: Controlling which Accessories are Installed During Setup.

The information in this article applies to:

- Microsoft Windows NT Workstation versions 4.0
- Microsoft Windows NT Server versions 4.0

Summary

By default unattended setup does not provide a way to control what accessory applications are installed on the Start Menu\Programs\Accessories menu.

More Information

> **Warning** Modifying .INF files incorrectly can cause serious, system-wide problems that may require you to reinstall Windows NT to correct them. Microsoft cannot guarantee that any problems resulting from .INF file modifications can be solved. Use this method at your own risk.

Each application or group of applications on the Accessories menu has an associated Information File (.INF). Each .INF uses the variable InstallType to determine if the application is to be installed.

There are three values that InstallType can equal:

- 0 = Manual only
- 10 = Typical or Custom
- 14 = Typical, Custom, or Portable

The following INF files use the InstallType variable. The list of INF files can be found under the [BaseWinOptionsInfs]in the SYSSETUP.INF.

- accessor.inf
- communic.inf
- games.inf
- imagevue.inf
- mmopt.inf
- multimed.inf
- optional.inf
- pinball.inf
- wordpad.inf

The following example is the section for Free Cell from the GAMES.INF for
Windows NT 4.0 Server. By default games are not installed on server. Since
Unattended Setup uses *Typical* for installation purposes a value of 10 can be used
for InstallType. By default InstallType for Free Cell is 0.

```
[Freecell]

OptionDesc          = %Freecell_DESC%

Tip                 = %Freecell_TIP%

IconIndex           = 62 ;Windows mini-icon for dialogs

Parent              = Games

;

; This is the value that is changed.

; To install Free Cell change InstallType from 0 to 10

;

InstallType         = 0 ;Manual only

CopyFiles           = FreecellCopyFilesSys, FreecellCopyFilesHelp

AddReg              = FreecellAddReg

UpdateInis          = FreecellInis

Uninstall           = FreecellUninstall

Upgrade             = FreecellUpgrade

Detect              = %11%\freecell.exe
```

Additional Information

To take advantage of the InstallType variable for manual or unattended installations of Windows NT a certain amount of preparation is needed.

1. The contents of the i386 directory from the Windows NT 4.0 CD needs to be copied to a distribution share.

2. For each .INF file that needs to be modified the file first needs to be expanded and the original file renamed.

   EXPAND GAMES.IN_ GAMES.INF

   RENAME GAMES.IN_ GAMES.SAV

Note The Windows NT version of EXPAND.EXE needs to be used.

---

3. Edit the INF file and change the InstallType value.

   0 = Manual only

   10 = Typical or Custom

   14 = Typical, Custom, or Portable

KBCategory: **kbsetup**

KBSubcategory: **ntsetup ntdriver ntreskit**

Additional reference words: **prodnt 4.00**

Registry Punch—Windows NT Source Path

```
; Windows NT 4.0 Automated Installation Framework

; File Format: INF

;

; 1. Forces Windows NT source path to \\[SERVER_NAME]\MSIF\NT4Wks\i386

; -------------------------------------------------------------------


[Version]

Signature = "$Windows NT$"


[DefaultInstall]

AddReg = AddReg

DelReg = DelReg

UpdateInis = UpdateInis


[AddReg]

; 1. Forces Windows NT source path to be S:\NT4Wks\i386

HKLM,"Software\Microsoft\Windows\CurrentVersion\Setup","SourcePath",0, ↵

"\\[SERVER_NAME]\MSIF\NT4Wks\i386"

HKLM,"Software\Microsoft\Windows NT\CurrentVersion","SourcePath",0, ↵
```

```
"\\[SERVER_NAME]\MSIF\NT4Wks\i386"


[DelReg]


[UpdateInis]
```

Registry Punch—Default Screen Saver
REGEDIT4

```
; Windows NT 4.0 Automated Installation Framework

; File Format: REG

;

; 1. Sets the default Screen Saver information to be copied to each

;    user account when logging in for the first time at a machine.

; 2. Sets the default Screen Saver information for the Local

;    Administrator account by saving settings to current user when

;    logged on as Administrator during initial installation.

; ----------------------------------------------------------------



; 1. Sets the default Screen Saver information to be copied to each
```

```
;      user account when logging in for the first time at a machine.

[HKEY_USERS\Default User\Control Panel\Desktop]

"ScreenSaveTimeOut"="300"

"ScreenSaveActive"="1"

"ScreenSaverIsSecure"="1"

"SCRNSAVE.EXE"="C:\\WINNT\\System32\\logon.scr"


; 2. Sets the default Screen Saver information for the Local

;      Administrator account by saving settings to current user when

;      logged on as Administrator during initial installation.

[HKEY_CURRENT_USER\Control Panel\Desktop]

"ScreenSaveTimeOut"="600"

"ScreenSaveActive"="1"

"ScreenSaverIsSecure"="1"

"SCRNSAVE.EXE"="C:\\WINNT\\System32\\logon.scr"
```

Registry Punch—Disable Browse Master/LMAnnouce
REGEDIT4

```
; Windows NT 4.0 Automated Installation Framework

; File Format: REG

;

; 1. Disables MaintainServerList and IsDomainMaster

; 2. Disables LMAnnounce

; ------------------------------------------------------------------


; 1. Disables MaintainServerList and IsDomainMaster

[HKEY_LOCAL_MACHINE\SYSTEM\CurrentControlSet\Services\Browser\
Parameters]

"MaintainServerList"="OFF"

"IsDomainMaster"="FALSE"


; 2. Disables LMAnnounce

[HKEY_LOCAL_MACHINE\SYSTEM\CurrentControlSet\Services\LanmanServer\
Parameters]

"Lmannounce"=dword:00000000
```

Registry Punch—Disable Pop-Up Print Notification

REGEDIT4

```
; Windows NT 4.0 Automated Installation Framework

; File Format: REG

;

; 1. Sets Pop-Up Print Notification off.

; ----------------------------------------------------------------

[HKEY_LOCAL_MACHINE\SYSTEM\CurrentControlSet\Control\Print\Providers]

"NetPopup"=dword:00000000
```

Quick Reference for Unattended Installation

Here is a summary of tools and methods created by MCS. It is not comprehensive, but it lists some things you can use to get started.

Summary of tools and methods created by MCS.

Steps	Method	Notes
Basic installation	WINNT /U:UNATTENDED.TXT	Allows unattended installation of basic environment (in other words, SCSI, keyboard, display drivers; creation or joining domains or standalone; installation of services such as, DHCP, WINS, SNMP, DNS)
		All unattended Windows NT installation starts from here.
		See *Windows NT Deployment Guide*, Automating Windows NT Setup.
Personalizing after basic installation	Use \I386\OEM\CMDLINES.TXT to set RunOnce registry key to run a personalized batch file, For example: *RUNONCE.CMD*	Create a batch file called whatever you want (for example, RUNONCE.CMD) having the calls to utility and commands you need to personalize your setup (for example, DHCP configuration of range and scope, adding users, creating shares and printers, and so on).

Summary of tools and methods created by MCS. *(continued)*

Steps	Method	Notes
Personalizing after basic installation *(continued)*		The key in registry is: HKEY_LOCAL_MACHINE\Software\Microsoft\CurrentVersion\Windows\RunOnce. To allow the batch to run, you also need to set: HKEY_LOCAL_MACHINE\Software\Microsoft\CurrentVersion\Winlogon\AutoAdminLogon=1 and to set a valid DefaultUsername, DefaultPassword and DefaultDomain. Keep in mind that for this to work correctly work you must have DontDisplayLastUsername=0. Without it you'll get a "wrong password" message.
Personalizing: disk label	Command LABEL in batch file	For example: *LABEL E: USER*

Summary of tools and methods created by MCS. *(continued)*

Steps	Method	Notes
Personalizing: BOOT.INI timeout	Use Rundll32 Setupapi	The second way to apply it is in CMDLINES.TXT when you do an OEM preinstall. You could use the same .INF file, but you would have to copy ATTRIB.EXE to the OEM directory, and put the following in CMDLINES.TXT: *.\attrib.exe c:\boot.ini -s -h –r* *rundll32 setupapi,InstallHinfSection DefaultInstall 128 .\bootini.inf* *.\attrib.exe c:\boot.ini +s +h +r* You could also execute the attrib and rundll32 commands in a batch file done with a runonce after setup, or via an SMS job.

Summary of tools and methods created by MCS.   *(continued)*

Steps	Method	Notes
Personalizing: Renaming accounts or changing password	Use CUSRMGR.EXE by G. Zanzen	For example: *CUSRMGR -u Administrator -r BNAdmin* *CUSRMGR -u BNAdmin -P BNAdmin*
Personalizing: Managing users and groups	ADDUSERS (NTRK) USRTOGRP (NTRK) NET USER NET GROUP NET LOCALGROUP	See references in the *Windows NT Resource Kit* For example, Disabling Guest account: *net user GUEST /ACTIVE:NO*
Personalizing: Creating shares	NET SHARE RMTSHARE (NTRK)	See references in the *Windows NT Resource Kit*

Summary of tools and methods created by MCS.   *(continued)*

Steps	Method	Notes
Personalizing: Installing printers	DRVMAN.EXE to install driver ADDPRINT.EXE to set up print share	For example: *c:\batch\DRVMAN install "HP LaserJet 4" d:\i386* For example: *c:\batch\ADDPRINT "HP LaserJet 4" "STAMPANTE-RADAR" "HP LaserJet 4" LPT1: winprint raw*
Personalizing: Account policies	NET ACCOUNT PASSPROP (NTRK)	For example: *C:\winnt\system32\net accounts /MAXPWAGE:90 /MINPWLEN:8 /UNIQUEPW:3 /DOMAIN* For example: *PASSPROP /COMPLEX*
Personalizing: Setting trust relationships	NETDOM (NTRK)	See Knowledge Base article Q175025, Title: How to Build and Reset a Trust Relationship from a Command Line
Personalizing: Adding rights to users	Use NTRIGHTS.EXE by G. Zanzen	For example: *NTRights +r SeServiceLogonRight -u BNAdmin* *NTRights +r SeServiceLogonRight -u Supervisor* *NTRights +r SeServiceLogonRight -u TESEO_DOM_CENTR\BNAdmin*

Summary of tools and methods created by MCS.   *(continued)*

Steps	Method	Notes
Personalizing: Removing OS/2 subsystem	DEL ..\System32\OS2ss.EXE	For example: *del c:\winnt\system32\os2ss.exe*
Personalizing: Removing POSIX subsystem	DEL ..\System32\PSXss.EXE	For example: *del c:\winnt\system32\psxss.exe*

C H A P T E R   1 1

Windows NT Workstation Unattended Modular Build

By David Skinner, MCS— UK

This chapter provides a template for an unattended modular build of Windows NT, service packs, and application software. The procedural information is broken out into four sections:

- The need for automation
- Overview of standard unattended Windows NT installation
- Design qualities of a modular build
- Walkthroughs and examples of a modular build

Other sections following these provide tips (there are also tips in the procedures), a complete listing and explanation of answer file settings, information on MS-DOS utilities, and a discussion of the ScriptIT utility. The discussion assumes that you are familiar with the manual installation and configuration of Windows NT.

What You'll Find In This Chapter

- An automated solution for "hands-free" installation and configuration of Windows NT Workstation, service packs, and application software.

- Illustration of the standard Windows NT 4.0 (Server and Workstation) functionality for unattended operating system installation and configuration using an answer file and special OEM directory structure.

- Tips on common procedures for Windows NT (and application) configuration.

Warning This chapter makes recommendations for tuning the Windows NT registry using the Registry Editor. Using the Registry Editor incorrectly can cause serious, system-wide problems that require you to reinstall Windows NT. Microsoft cannot guarantee that any problems resulting from the use of Registry Editor can be solved. Use this tool at your own risk.

The Need for Automation

As the PC has become "ubiquitous" it has also evolved into a system several orders of magnitude more powerful than its pioneering predecessor. Operating systems such as Microsoft Windows NT Workstation provide a multi-tasking environment with seamless connectivity to external network systems. Applications such as Microsoft Office leverage this power to provide users with state-of-the-art productivity tools. In addition to boosted productivity, this progress has introduced a problem: rather than plugging in and setting up a few terminals, IT groups now have to install great numbers of increasingly complicated machines.

Deployment Challenges

The increasing internal complexity of operating systems and application software, combined with evolving hardware standards, makes it difficult for companies to adopt and adhere to a consistent PC deployment method.

Typically, companies deploying large numbers of Windows NT Workstations face these challenges:

- Varying PC hardware configuration: CPU, video, hard disk size, hard disk controller, network interface, mouse (PS/2, serial, etc.).
- Different software and configuration requirements from department to department.
- Installation and configuration of application software that does not support automated installation.

Providing an Automated Solution

This chapter describes a process that builds on the Windows NT setup program's unattended installation facility to create a modular unattended deployment process for *hands-free* installation and configuration of Windows NT Workstation, service packs, and application software.

Developing an automated build has some costs, but it offers:

- **Standardization.** Even when hardware differs, you can configure both the operating system and applications to company standards, providing a mechanism for centralized version and quality control.

- **Reduced Configuration Errors.** Automating configuration reduces the risk of error.

- **Faster Deployment.** Eliminating human input during the build reduces the need for someone to wait, and allows concurrent deployment scheduling.

- **Increased Supportability.** If there are future support problems, you have a known reference for system configuration.

- **Recovery.** If there are future hardware failures, you can quickly re-deploy the operating system and applications.

- **Cost Effective.** Fewer people are required to manage and deliver the rollout, making outsourcing an option. For example, you can provide the hardware supplier with the automated build mechanism, so that new hardware arrives already configured.

Windows NT Unattended Installation

This section illustrates the standard Windows NT 4.0 (Server and Workstation) functionality for unattended operating system installation and configuration through the use of an answer file and special OEM directory structure.

Answer File

An answer file is a text file that can be used to provide some or all of the configuration information required to automate the Windows NT operating system installation and configuration.

Although the syntax of this file is relatively simple, its hundreds of configuration options (listed later in the "Answer File Information" section) can make it lengthy and cryptic. A GUI-mode tool (Setup Manager) provided on the Windows NT CD (in \SUPPORT\DEPTOOLS\i386) presents configuration options as a series of dialogs or checkboxes and automatically generates an answer file.

Here is a simple (commented) answer file for an example:

```
[Unattended]

OemPreinstall = yes               ;Enables use of $OEM$

NoWaitAfterTextMode = 1           ;Automatic reboot after text mode

NoWaitAfterGUIMode = 1            ;Automatic reboot after GUI mode

FileSystem = ConvertNTFS          ;Convert FAT to NTFS

ExtendOEMPartition = 0            ;Do not extend partition

ConfirmHardware = no              ;Do not ask user to confirm

NtUpgrade = no                    ;Do not allow upgrade of NT

Win31Upgrade = no                 ;Do not upgrade from Win3.x

TargetPath = winntw               ;Installation directory

OverwriteOemFilesOnUpgrade = no
```

```
[GuiUnattended]

OemSkipWelcome = 1              ;Do not display welcome page

OEMBlankAdminPassword = 1       ;Do not specify Admin password

TimeZone = "(GMT) Greenwich Mean Time; Dublin, Edinburgh, London"


[Display]

ConfigureAtLogon = 0

BitsPerPel = 8

XResolution = 800

YResolution = 600

VRefresh = 60

AutoConfirm = 1                 ;Do not ask user to confirm video


[Network]

DetectAdapters = ""             ;Auto-detect NIC from drvlib

InstallProtocols = ProtocolsSection


[ProtocolsSection]

TC = TCParamSection
```

```
[TCParamSection]

DHCP = no

IPAddress = 123.456.789.1

Subnet = 987.654.321.0

Gateway = 123.456.789.5

DNSServer = 123.456.788.750, 123.456.788.751

WINSPrimary = 123.456.788.700

WINSSecondary = 123.456.788.701
```

Once a valid answer file has been generated, you can use it to automate the installation by passing it as a command-line parameter to the standard Windows NT setup routine. For example:

```
WINNT /B /U:A:\UNATTEND.TXT /S:D:\I386
```

OEM Directory Structure

Another powerful feature of the unattended setup routine is the OEM directory structure. OEM enables additional files that are required for the build but not provided on the original Windows NT distribution medium, to be seamlessly copied to the destination hard disk using a series of predefined directory names.

Figure 11.1 illustrates a sample OEM structure. The table below explains the directory names. To utilize this structure, OEM must reside *directly* beneath the Windows NT distribution files (in this case, i386), and the OEMPreInstall parameter in the answer file must be set to *Yes*. (You must manually create the OEM structure.)

```
\Nt4
    \1386
        \$OEM$
            \$$

            \C
```

Figure 11.1 Sample OEM structure.

OEM directory definitions.

Directory name	Description
OEM	Root of OEM deployment directory structure. All directories and files are automatically distributed to locations (defined below) on local hard disk.
$$	Equates to the directory where Windows NT will be installed. Any files or directories residing beneath "$$" are copied into %systemroot%.
<letter>	Directories with a name of a single alphabetic character (A...Z) translate to the root directory on the local hard disk of the same name. This provides a simple mechanism to copy complete disk structures.
TextMode	Directory containing drivers for OEM hardware abstraction layers (HALs), mass storage, and pointing devices installed during text mode setup.
Display	Directory containing drivers for OEM video adapters.
Net	Directories containing additional network drivers that were not supplied on the retail CD.

In addition to the reserved directory names, OEM provides increased functionality through the use of two reserved file names:

OEM—CMDLINES.TXT

This text file, located in the root of the OEM structure, enables a series of commands to be executed immediately after the automated installation of Windows NT has completed. This is used to initialize phase 3 of the modular build process.

In the example below, the CMDLINES.TXT file is configured to silently install Service Pack3. It assumes that the Service Pack 3 directory has been copied into OEM\nt4sp3.

```
[Commands]

".\nt4sp3\update.exe -u -f -n"
```

OEM—$$RENAME.TXT

This text file enables automatic translation of MS-DOS style 8.3 filename formats into Windows NT long format, so that you can deploy long filenames from file systems that do not inherently provide support for them. The example below shows that this file is in section/value format, where *section* represents directory and *value* represents filename translation.

```
[GSCRIPTS]

SCRIPT~1="Example Long Script Name"



[GSCRIPTS\TEMP]

SCRIPT~2="Another long example"
```

Design Qualities

The primary goal of the modular unattended build is to provide a single, cohesive mechanism for automating the delivery of Windows NT with application software, and customizing it on a departmental or group basis.

To achieve this goal without additional infrastructure management tools such as Systems Management Server, the deployment mechanism needs these modular qualities:

- Design of the deployment directory structure must enable functional grouping of operating system, application, and configuration files. This simplifies management, and enables operating system and application installation files to reside on separate physical resources.

  For example, all Windows NT installation files could be supplied on a bootable CD. Once installed, Windows NT could connect to a network-based deployment server to install the application software.

  Figure 11.2 illustrates a simple (single CD) modular directory structure that includes application and operating system files. CoreApps represents the root of the application structure, beneath which applications are stored in individual directories. Installation scripts for each application are stored in cmdFiles. The Windows NT files (including OEM) are stored beneath *Nt4*.

```
\BuildNT (G)
\CoreApps
    \cmdFiles
    \Ie30
    \vb5
    \Vc5
\Nt4
    \I386
        \$0em$
        \Drvlib.nic
        \Inetsrv
        \System32
```

Figure 11.2 Single-CD modular directory structure.

- All scripts used to control the installation process are Windows NT command files, which are simple and "open," reducing the need for development specialists. Resource kit utilities provide any additional functionality beyond the scope of command files (registry modification, for example).

- Instead of being hard-coded to retrieve files from specific hard disk locations, scripts retrieve this information from a configuration file generated at the beginning of the modular installation process. This enables you to deploy the build from different servers or distribution media (such as CD) without modifying script logic.

- Modular functionality ensures that a configuration script introduces only a single change to the build. As you can see (Figure 11.3) this is achieved by creating a parent/child relationship between the control logic that defines how the build is configured and the configuration script that performs the individual change. This allows you to reuse configuration scripts in multiple parts of the build.

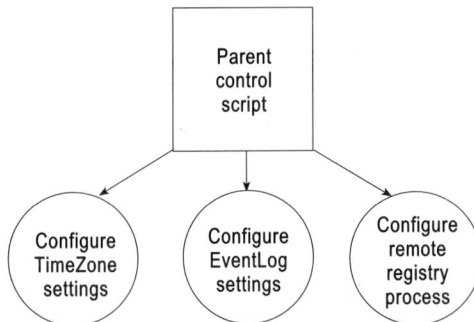

Figure 11.3 Modular configuration script functionality.

- Whenever possible, use the vendor-supplied installation routines to install and configure all applications. If the setup routine does not provide direct support for unattended installations (sometimes referred to as *silent* installations) the process can be automated through the use of an additional tool—ScriptIT.

This design avoids snapshot installation/deployment tools because they limit integration options. They record the state of the computer before and after manual installation of an application package, then write the differences (files, registry) between these recordings to an installation file. This assumes that the contents of the install-file represent the same set of system changes that would result from execution of the traditional setup routine, so if the package is applied to a new computer it will "install" the application without user intervention.

Unfortunately, this is true only if the package is installed into identical environments with identical configuration requirements. This approach eliminates the "intelligence" of the application's own setup routine, which may configure the application differently if it detects the presence of additional software it can inter-operate with.

Modular Framework—Overview

To develop a modular build it is necessary to combine the above ideals with existing Windows NT installation mechanics in a framework that models the natural (physical) stages of a manual deployment.

Figure 11.4 illustrates a five-phase model that represents the life cycle of a Windows NT installation/configuration, from PC preparation to complete installation. Phases are explained below:

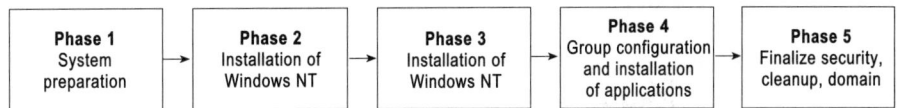

Figure 11.4 Five-phase model.

Phase 1

Phase 1 sets up and prepares the PC to receive Windows NT: an MS-DOS boot disk partitions and formats the destination hard disk for use with the FAT file system, a logical drive connection is established to the deployment device, basic configuration information is requested from the installation engineer (computer name, configuration group, IP address, etc.), and configuration information is written to appropriate files on the local hard disk. This information is used throughout the remainder of the build process, eliminating the need for further human interaction. You can pre-encode the information onto the boot disk, eliminating all human interaction, but this requires creating a uniquely prepared disk for *each* workstation

Phase 2

Phase 2 executes the traditional unattended Windows NT installation routine, using a combination of floppy-less and unattended installation mechanics to provide a completely hands-free OS installation.

Phase 3

Phase 3 enables you to implement company-wide granular configuration changes to Windows NT. For example, if your company has many departments, each with differing configuration requirements, the configuration in this phase must be common across all departments. Typical examples include browser participation, event log settings, etc.

Phase 4

Phase 4 enables group-specific configuration of Windows NT, and installation of application software through the use of package scripts. This makes it possible to use a single deployment server to provide multiple Windows NT configurations, based on group information supplied in phase 1.

Phase 5

Phase 5 configures security and domain membership properties of the workstation.

You could perform these functions as part of phase 3, but you would have to build the workstation within the domain it is joining. Separating this process allows the workstation to be built outside the domain (by an outsource partner, for example) and to join the domain upon connection to the corporate network.

Creating a Modular Unattended Build

The next sections discuss each phase in turn and provide tricks, tips, and scripts you can use in many other scenarios.

The examples that follow are based on the assumption that you want to roll out Windows NT workstation with the following applications (chosen to illustrate different installation techniques): Office97, Outlook98, Visio, and WinZIP. Windows NT is to be configured as follows:

- Support for 3Com 3c90x and 3c509 network adapters
- Event Log maximum size set to 1 MB
- Windows NT configured for UK locale
- BOOT.INI timer delay reduced to 5 seconds
- Membership in the TSTDOM domain

Getting Started

First you have to construct a skeleton deployment directory structure. It should be appropriately modularized so that operating system, application, and command-script files can reside (as far as practically possible) in separate directories. Figure 11.5 shows the directory structure used during this example.

```
\Buildsvr on `Zippy' (H:)
    \Answer
    \Apps
        \cmdFiles
        \Office97
        \ol98
        \visio5
        \WinZip
    \Nt4
        \1386
            \$0em$
            \$$
                \System32
            \C
                \Build
                    \Drivers
                        \Audio
                    \Groups
                        \Example1
                    \Gscripts
            \Net
            \NT4sp3
        \Drvlib.ric
        \Inetsrv
        \System32
```

Figure 11.5 Directory structure used in the example.

The examples and discussion in the rest of this section refer to the Figure 11.5 directory structure residing on a file server. In practice it can reside on any storage device that accessible to Windows NT and MS-DOS by a logical drive letter.

Notes on Figure 11.5, working down from the top:

- **Answer.** The directory containing the skeleton answer files for use in phase 1.
- **cmdfiles.** Scripts to control the installation of application software.
- **Office97/ol98/visio5/WinZip.** Application directories.
- **Drivers.** Subdirectories for drivers that cannot be installed by the answer file.
- **Example1.** Configuration group directories containing department-specific scripts.
- **Gscripts.** Location of control script for phase 3.
- **Net.** Directory containing the OEM network drivers (not supplied with Windows NT) used by the answer file in phase 2.
- **Drvlib.nic.** Standard directory from the distribution CD, but trimmed to include only required drivers.

Preparing Windows NT Installation Files

Copy the contents of the i386 (and subdirectories) from the original Windows NT distribution CD into the corresponding i386 directory on the distribution server.

TIP: Replacement Driver required for NTFS conversion—SETUPDD.SYS

There is a known problem with automatic conversion and extension of FAT to NTFS in Windows NT prior to Service Pack 3. To avoid this issue, copy the SETUPDD.SYS file from Service Pack 3 into the Windows NT distribution directory. For more information, see Knowledge Base article Q143473, Title: Unattended Setup Stops and Says Press Any Key to Shut Down.

TIP: Reducing files copied during setup

During the text mode portion of unattended setup, Windows NT copies all files from the DRVLIB.NIC distribution directory onto the local hard disk. This directory contains all network drivers supplied with Windows NT and is approximately 20 MB. You can optimize network download times and storage overhead by removing non-required drivers from this directory.

If you don't need Internet services you can delete the contents of INETSRV but leave the directory name: this prevents a "file not found" error during Windows NT installation. If you remove the name, you can avoid the error message by removing (or commenting out) the INETSRV entry in DOSNET.INF.

Preparing Application Directories

Create a directory structure to enable modular storage of application software. Copy the applications into unique (obvious) directories within the application structure, and to put the installation scripts in cmdFiles.

Create the OEM structure

Create the OEM structure beneath i386, ensuring the syntax and relative position of directories is correct.

TIP: Enabling processing of OEM structure during setup

To enable processing of the OEM structure, make sure the OemPreInstall=YES value is specified in the answer file.

TIP: OEM NIC drivers

Ensure that all OEM NICs are placed in unique sub-directories beneath NET.

Unattended Answer Files

Use Setup Manager to create an unattended answer file for each PC with a different hardware configuration. Store these files in the *Answer* directory on the deployment server.

TIP: Removing EndUser License Dialog

Even though you are configuring Windows NT for unattended installation, by default it displays the End User License Agreement dialog and waits for a response. You can avoid this by adding the "OEMSkipEULA = yes" value to the [Unattended] section of the answer file. If Setup Manager later modifies the answer file, it deletes this line and you will have to put it back in.

TIP: How to determine NIC parameters

When you are specifying the configuration parameters for OEM network cards, you may have trouble finding the appropriate values. You can find them by manually installing the NIC drivers and examining the registry key: HKEY_LOCAL_MACHINE\System\CurrentControlSet\<service name>\ Parameters, where *<service name>* is the name of the network driver.

Boot disk

Create an MS-DOS boot disk with device drivers to enable logical drive connection to the distribution device. Include hard disk preparation utilities in addition to the START.BAT file (and utilities) required in phase 1.

Phase 1—System Preparation Walkthrough

Phase 1 begins with an MS-DOS boot disk that is configured with the appropriate device drivers to provide connectivity to the distribution device. In the example case, the deployment server is Windows NT, so the disk is configured with Microsoft Networking for MS-DOS, and contains the necessary files for hard disk preparation (FDISK and Format). It also stores START.BAT—the batch file (command script) that controls phase 1.

START.BAT depends on three MS-DOS utilities stored on the boot disk: GetLine, Set_Ini!, and ShowMenu. These are highlighted in this section and detailed in "MS-DOS Utilities" section beginning on page 673. Figure 11.6 outlines boot disk functionality.

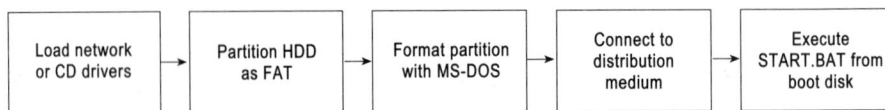

```
┌──────────────┐   ┌──────────────┐   ┌──────────────┐   ┌──────────────┐   ┌──────────────┐
│ Load network │──▶│ Partition HDD│──▶│Format partition│─▶│  Connect to  │──▶│   Execute    │
│or CD drivers │   │   as FAT     │   │ with MS-DOS  │   │ distribution │   │START.BAT from│
│              │   │              │   │              │   │   medium     │   │  boot disk   │
└──────────────┘   └──────────────┘   └──────────────┘   └──────────────┘   └──────────────┘
```

Figure 11.6 Boot disk functionality.

Here is a typical AUTOEXEC.BAT file from a network boot disk:

```
@ECHO OFF

ECHO Network Install - BOOT DISK

SMARTDRV C+                          ;See [1] below


NET START

NET USE K: \\FILESERV\NTBUILD

A:\START.BAT                         ;See [2] below
```

Notes on sample AUTOEXEC.BAT file:

[1]—Smartdrv with write-behind caching to improve file-copy speed during initial MS-DOS-based phase.

[2]—This is the Windows NT pre-configuration script. It generates answer files and initiates phase 2.

Partitioning the Hard Disk

To receive Windows NT for the first time, the PC must have an MS-DOS formatted FAT partition large enough to contain Windows NT and the associated OEM directory structure and temporary files. During phase 2, if you set *FileSystem = ConvertNTFS* in the answer file, Windows NT automatically converts FAT to NTFS.

TIP: How to install Windows NT on disks <2 GB

On hard drives larger than 2 GB, MS-DOS cannot access data beyond the 2-GB boundary (beyond 1-GB on some systems). During FAT to NTFS conversion, Windows NT provides a feature to extend the installation partition to the maximum size of the disk. This feature is enabled by the *OemExtendPartition = 1, nowait* parameter in conjunction with *FileSystem = ConvertNTFS*. Both parameters are in the [Unattended] section of the answer file. On hard disks larger than 4 GB, SP4 is required in conjunction with this feature.

TIP: Decreasing disk preparation time

If you use the feature outlined above you can reduce the time it takes to prepare and format the initial FAT partition by defining a partition large enough to support the installation of phase 2, and allowing Windows NT to extend the partition before applications are installed.

START.BAT—Generating Configuration Information

START.BAT, located on the boot disk, generates all configuration information required for subsequent phases. The information is stored in two files placed on the root of the newly prepared hard disk:

- **C:\UNATTEND.TXT**—A Windows NT answer file with configuration information unique to the current PC, generated by copying a skeleton answer file from the *Answer* directory on the distribution server onto the local hard disk and merging machine- and user-specific information. To modify section/value format text files within batch files, use the MS-DOS utility SET_INI!.

- **C:\NETWORK.BAT** or **C:\CDROM.BAT**—An MS-DOS batch file with environment variables used to determine drive paths (for the distribution server), computer name, domain name, and configuration group (enables support for multi-department/user configurations discussed in phase 4). The file name indicates the type of distribution device used for deployment.

You can configure START.BAT to provide *all* configuration information automatically, but to do it you need to create a unique boot disk for each workstation/user. Figure 11.7 illustrates START.BAT logic.

```
              ┌─────────────┐
              │   Define    │
              │configuration│
              │  files and  │
              │display menu │
              └─────────────┘
                     │
          ┌──────────◇──────────┐
   CDROM──│     Decision        │──NETWORK
          └──────────◇──────────┘
       │                        │
┌─────────────┐          ┌─────────────┐
│  Generate   │          │  Generate   │
│ CDROM.BAT   │──────────│ NETWORK.BAT │
│from user    │          │from user    │
│   input     │          │   input     │
└─────────────┘          └─────────────┘
                │
         ┌─────────────┐
         │ Display NIC │
         │ choice menu │
         └─────────────┘
                │
      ┌─────────◇─────────┐
3Com──│    Decision       │──Generic NIC
9c90x └─────────◇─────────┘
    │                     │
┌─────────────┐    ┌─────────────┐
│  Copy 3com  │    │ Copy generic│
│skeleton file│────│NIC skeleton │
│ and merge   │    │  file and   │
│ user data   │    │   merge     │
└─────────────┘    │  userdata   │
                   └─────────────┘
         ┌─────────────┐
         │Start phase2 │
         │by calling   │
         │ WINNT.EXE   │
         └─────────────┘
```

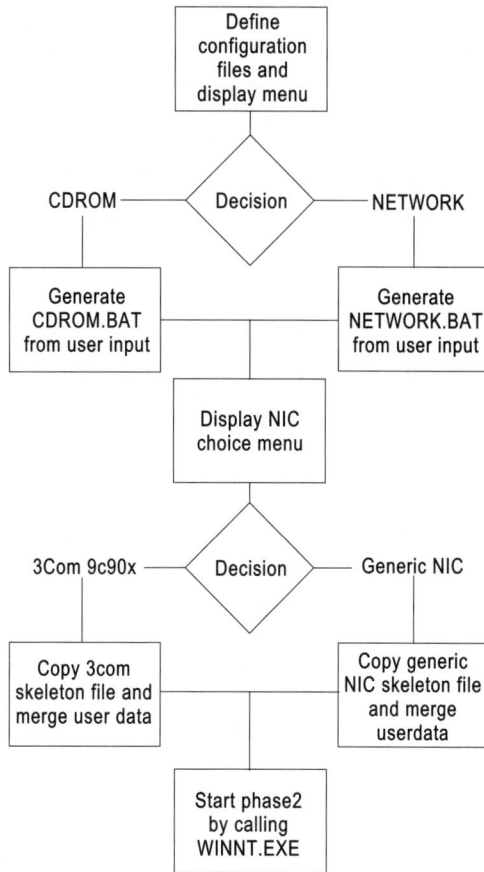

Figure 11.7 START.BAT logic.

START.BAT—Listing

In this example, START.BAT is configured to request a minimal set of configuration data from an installation engineer and write it to the files described above.

```
@echo off

SET netfile=C:\NETWORK.BAT                    ;See [1] below

SET cdfile=C:\CDROM.BAT

SET ansfile=C:\UNATTEND.TXT

@ERASE %NETFILE%

@ERASE %CDFILE%

@ERASE %ANSFILE%

CLS


:main

ECHO.

ECHO Example Main Menu

ECHO.

ECHO [A] Network Installation

ECHO [B] CDROM Installation

ECHO.

ECHO Use cursor keys to select, or ESC to cancel:


SHOWMENU A B /E=choice                        ;See [2] below

IF ERRORLEVEL 27 GOTO exit
```

This code is spaced so that it is easier to read. Lines are broken for layout only: entries should be on a single line. If you want to skip this section, go to page 591.

START.BAT   *(continued)*

```
IF %choice% == A GOTO getNetInfo

IF %choice% == B GOTO getCDROMInfo


:getNetInfo

GETLINE Domain Name:  /L=15 /E=DOMAIN

IF ERRORLEVEL 27 GOTO exit


GETLINE Configuration Group: /L=10 /E=GROUP  ;See [3] below

IF ERRORLEVEL 27 GOTO exit


GETLINE Source UNC Path: /L=30 /E=SRCUNC

IF ERRORLEVEL 27 GOTO exit


GETLINE Logical Drive: /L=2 /E=SRCDRV        ;See [4] below

IF ERRORLEVEL 27 GOTO exit


ECHO SET GROUP=%GROUP%>%NETFILE%

ECHO SET SRCUNC=%SRCUNC%>>%NETFILE%          ;See [5] below

ECHO SET SRCDRV=%SRCDRV%>>%NETFILE%
```

This code is spaced so that it is easier to read. Lines are broken for layout only: entries should be on a single line. If you want to skip this section, go to page 591.

START.BAT   *(continued)*

```
ECHO SET DOMAIN=%DOMAIN%>>%NETFILE%

GOTO adapters


:getCDROMInfo

GETLINE Domain Name:  /L=15 /E=DOMAIN

IF ERRORLEVEL 27 GOTO exit


GETLINE Configuration Group: /L=10 /E=GROUP   ;See [3] below

IF ERRORLEVEL 27 GOTO exit


GETLINE CDROM Drive Letter: /L=2 /E=SRCDRV

IF ERRORLEVEL 27 GOTO exit


ECHO SET GROUP=%GROUP%>%CDFILE%

ECHO SET SRCDRV=%SRCDRV%>>%CDFILE%

ECHO SET DOMAIN=%DOMAIN%>>%CDFILE%

GOTO adapters


:adapters

CLS
```

This code is spaced so that it is easier to read. Lines are broken for layout only: entries should be on a single line. If you want to skip this section, go to page 591.

START.BAT   *(continued)*

```
ECHO.

ECHO Main Build Menu

ECHO.

ECHO [A] Example Machine with 3c90x Network Card

ECHO [B] Example Machine with autodetected network card

ECHO.


SHOWMENU A B /E=choice

IF ERRORLEVEL 27 GOTO exit


GETLINE Computer Name:  /L=15 /E=CNAME

IF ERRORLEVEL 27 GOTO exit


IF %choice% == A GOTO 3com

IF %choice% == B GOTO autoDetect


:3com

ECHO Mode: 3c90x

COPY %SRCDRV%\ANSWER\3C90X.TXT %ANSFILE%

GOTO modifyComputerName
```

This code is spaced so that it is easier to read. Lines are broken for layout only: entries should be on a single line. If you want to skip this section, go to page 591.

START.BAT   *(continued)*

```
:autoDetect

ECHO Mode: Auto

COPY %SRCDRV%\ANSWER\GENERIC.TXT %ANSFILE%

GOTO modifyComputerName


:modifyComputerName

SET_INI! %ANSFILE% [UserData] "ComputerName = %CNAME%"   ;See [6] below


:runNTInstall

:.\NT4\I386\WINNT /B /S:.\NT4\I386 /U:%ANSFILE%          ;See [7] below


:exit
```

Notes on START.BAT—Listing:

[1]—Paths of all files generated by this script are stored in environment variables for easy maintenance. Any legacy configuration files are erased from the destination hard disk to ensure consistency.

[2]—The SHOWMENU utility provides menu handling facilities within the batch file. It stores the user input in an environment variable called *choice*, which can be queried by traditional IF statements. The use of ERRORLEVEL enables phase 1 to be aborted with the ESCAPE key.

[3]—*Group* refers to the *groups* directory structure beneath OEM. This environment variable is used by phase 3 to detect the appropriate configuration group for phase 4.

[4]—GetLine is a command-line utility that enables the retrieval of keyboard input during a batch file. It stores the input in an environment variable defined by **/E** switch.

[5]—Environment variables are written to the NETWORK.BAT file.

[6]—The answer file is personalized with ComputerName information. This technique can be extended to include any data that must be unique. For example: Internet Protocol (IP) address.

[7]—Phase 2 is initialized.

NETWORK.BAT—Listing

```
SET GROUP=example1

SET SRCUNC=\\ZIPPY\BUILDSRV

SET SRCDRV=T:

SET DOMAIN=TSTDOM
```

UNATTEND.TXT—Listing

```
[Unattended]

OemSkipEula = yes

OemPreinstall = yes

NoWaitAfterTextMode = 1

NoWaitAfterGUIMode = 1

FileSystem = ConvertNTFS

ExtendOEMPartition = 1, nowait

ConfirmHardware = no

NtUpgrade = no
```

```
Win31Upgrade = no

TargetPath = \winnt

OverwriteOemFilesOnUpgrade = no

KeyboardLayout = "United Kingdom"


[OEM_Ads]

Banner = "Windows NT Workstation * Example Build"

Background = buildbmp.bmp


[UserData]

FullName = "Example UserName"

OrgName = "Example OrgName"

ComputerName = EXCOMP1


[GuiUnattended]

OemSkipWelcome = 1

OEMBlankAdminPassword = 1

TimeZone = "(GMT) Greenwich Mean Time"


[Display]
```

```
ConfigureAtLogon = 0

BitsPerPel = 4

XResolution = 640

YResolution = 480

VRefresh = 60

AutoConfirm = 1


[Network]

InstallAdapters = SelectedAdaptersSection

InstallProtocols = ProtocolsSection

InstallServices = ServicesSection

JoinWorkgroup = TSTWRK


[SelectedAdaptersSection]

3C905 = OEMAdapterParamSection, \$OEM$\NET\3c90x\


[OEMAdapterParamSection]


[ProtocolsSection]

TC = TCParamSection


[TCParamSection]

DHCP = YES


[ServicesSection]
```

Starting Phase 2

Once the answer and configuration files have been generated, START.BAT invokes the Windows NT setup routine and specifies the answer file as a command-line parameter. For example:

```
%SRCDRV%\NT4\I386\WINNT /B /S:%SRCDRV%\NT4\I386 /U:%ANSFILE%
```

Phase 2—Installation of Windows NT Walkthrough

Based on a traditional unattended Windows NT setup, Phase 2 is a combination of floppy-less and unattended installation mechanics. Before the unattended installation starts, the setup routine copies all files from the distribution server (including those ordinarily located on the retail Windows NT boot disks), and creates directories on the local hard disk.

Directories created by setup.

Filename	Description
\LDR	A copy of SETUPLDR.BIN.
\TXTSETUP.SIF	Windows NT Setup Information File.
\WIN_NT.~LS	Temporary directory into which distribution i386 contents are decompressed.
\WIN_NT.~BT	Temporary directory into which files normally located on NT boot floppies are copied.
\$	Temporary directory into which all files and subdirectories of OEM are copied.
\WIN_NT.~BT\WINNT.SIF	Generated by WINNT; a combination of basic setup data and the newly generated UNATTEND.TXT.
\WIN_NT.~BT\BOOTSECT.DAT	DOS boot sector, saved as file. Loads and executes \LDR, beginning text mode portion of setup.
\WIN_NT.~LS\system32	Contents of second NT boot disk.
BOOT.INI	Modified to reference BOOTSECT.DAT.

After files have been copied, the boot sector and BOOT.INI files are modified; the system is rebooted and the initial text mode portion of Windows NT setup begins. The load process proceeds as follows:

1. NT executive/kernel—Loads NTKRNLMP.EXE.
2. Hardware abstraction layer—HAL486C.DLL, HALAPIC.DLL, HALMCA.DLL, HALMPS.DLL, HALMPSM.DLL, HALNCR.DLL – depending on hardware detected.
3. SETUPREG.HIV—A small registry containing a minimal *currentcontrolset* with i8042, PCMCIA and setupDD configuration.
4. Locale specific data—Loads locale-specific codepage data.
5. Setup font—Loads VGAOEM.FON for use during GUI-mode setup.
6. Windows NT kernel mode setup—Loads SETUPDD.SYS, a kernel mode driver that performs operating system installation.
7. Video driver—Loads VGA.SYS and VIDEOPRT.SYS
8. Keyboard driver—Loads i8042prt.sys, KBDCLASS.SYS and KBDxx where *xx* represents country.
9. FAT driver—Loads FASTFAT.SYS.
10. SCSI port driver—AIC78XX.SYS, AMI0NT.SYS, etc.—depending on hardware detected.
11. IDE/ESDI HDD controllers—Loads ATDISK.SYS.
12. MCA HDD controllers—Loads ABIODISK.SYS.
13. ATAPI CDROM—Loads ATAPI.SYS.
14. NTFS driver—Loads NTFS.SYS.

After the low-level hardware drivers are installed (HAL, disk controllers, bus, keyboard, etc.) the hard disk is checked for errors, and the files needed to boot Windows NT into GUI are copied (from the temporary) into the destination directory specified by the answer file. Then the remaining contents of the temporary directory \$ are distributed to their appropriate locations and the computer is rebooted.

On reboot, Windows NT enters GUI mode setup. The video, network, computer-name, and locale details are automatically configured using the answer file. The remaining Windows NT programs and accessories are copied from temporary into the destination directory. Finally, the contents of the CMDLINES.TXT file are processed. This applies the Windows NT Service Pack and makes registry changes to initialize phase 3. When this is complete, temporary directories are deleted and the operating system is rebooted.

On reboot, Windows NT automatically initializes phase 3.

OEM Directory Structure

The unattended installation makes extensive use of the OEM directory structure. All files required for the installation or subsequent configuration of Windows NT are located within OEM. This ensures that they are copied to the local hard drive as an integral part of the installation. The following sub-sections detail the additional files and modifications required for the example installation.

OEM Contents

- **CMDLINES.TXT**—A text file containing commands that are executed upon completion of GUI mode setup. As shown below, this file makes two registry changes using REGEDIT and begins a silent installation of Service Pack 3.

```
[Commands]
".\regedit /s .\run.reg"
".\regedit /s .\autolog.reg"
".\nt4sp3\update.exe -u -f -n"
```

- **REGEDIT.EXE.** The Windows NT registry editor, copied into the root of OEM for convenient use within CMDLINES.TXT.

- **RUN.REG.** A text file that is processed by RegEdit, and modifies the registry to automatically execute the phase 3 command script at next logon.

```
REGEDIT4
[HKey_Local_Machine\SOFTWARE\Microsoft\Windows\CurrentVersion\Run]
"NTConfiguration"="C:\\BUILD\\GSCRIPTS\\PHASE3.CMD"
```

TIP: Run and RunOnce Registry Keys

You can use an alternative registry key (RunOnce) for this purpose. The advantage is that once the auto-executed application has been executed, its registry presence is automatically removed. The disadvantage of this key is that it executes application *before* the desktop is completely initialized, and, more importantly, its contents can be executed prematurely as discussed in Knowledge Base article Q173039, Title: RUNONCE Key Is Processed Immediately When RUNDLL32 Is Called.

- **AUTOLOG.REG.** A text file that is processed by RegEdit; it modifies the registry to allow Windows NT to logon automatically as administrator at next reboot.

```
REGEDIT4

[HKey_Local_Machine\SOFTWARE\Microsoft\Windows NT\CurrentVersion\Winl
ogon]

"DefaultUserName"="administrator"

"DefaultPassword"=""

"AutoAdminLogon"="1"
```

- **NT4SP3 (directory).** A directory containing all files from Service Pack 3.

TIP: Reducing file transfers during SP3 installation

Inclusion of Service Pack 3 directly beneath the OEM structure (as opposed to OEM\C) reduces number of file transfers during phase 2. This is because the service pack is applied directly from \$\NT4SP3, as opposed to being moved to a permanent directory first.

- **NET (directory)**—A directory containing a series of subdirectories (with drivers) for each network card not supported by the retail NIC drivers. This directory is referenced in the unattended answer files.

OEM\$$\System32 Contents

The files and directories within this portion of the OEM structure are automatically copied into the System32 path of Windows NT installation directory. They provide core services to the configuration scripts of future phases.

- **NETDOM.** A command-line utility from the NT Resource Kit (supplement 2) that enables Windows NT to join a domain within a command-script.

- **REG.** A command-line utility from the NT Resource Kit that enables registry modification from within a command script.

- **SLEEP.** A command-line utility from the NT Resource Kit that can be used within command-scripts to cause periods of delay. This is used during application installation phase to reduce the amount of CPU activity in script loops.

- **NTRIGHTS.** A command-line utility from the NT Resource Kit that enables the granting and revoking of user rights from a command script.

- **SHUTDOWN.** A command-line utility that enables the shutdown and reboot of Windows NT from a command-script.

- **ScriptIT.** A utility that enables the automation of dialogs from the script file. This utility is used to configure aspects of Windows NT that cannot generally be automated, and to install applications that are not supplied with unattended installation routines.

OEM\C\BUILD—Contents

OEM is used to deliver a build structure to the local 'C' drive. This structure contains the configuration scripts for phase 3 onwards, and drivers that will be installed onto Windows NT after phase 2.

```
\$oem$
    \$$
    \Apps
        \System32
    \C
        \Build
            \Drivers
                \Audio
            \Groups
                \Example1
            \Gscripts
    \Net
    \NT4sp3
```

Figure 11.8 Directory names in build structure.

Notes on Figure 11.8:

- **Audio.** Contains drivers that were not supplied on the retail CD and cannot be installed in phase 2.

- **Groups.** Root directory for all department-specific parent scripts. Each subdirectory contains a PHASE4.CMD file and generally multiple package files.

- **Gscripts.** Directory containing phase 3 (cross department) configuration scripts and all configuration scripts.

Logic Overview

Figure 11.9 is an overview of stages in phase 2, which uses the traditional Windows NT unattended installation routine. Phase 3 is initialized by setting the HKEY_LOCAL_MACHINE\SOFTWARE\Microsoft\Windows\CurrentVersion\Run registry key to C:\\BUILD\\GSCRIPTS\\PHASE3.CMD, configuring auto-admin logon and rebooting the workstation.

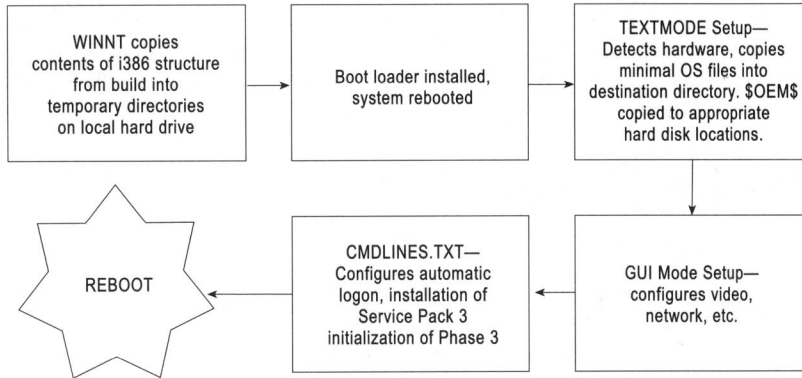

Figure 11.9 Phase 2 overview.

Phase 3—Global Windows NT Configuration Walkthrough

Phase 3 allows you to apply company-wide Windows NT configuration parameters and install drivers—tasks not supported by the unattended answer file. *Do not use this phase to install application software.*

Phase3.CMD, the parent control routine responsible for managing phase 3, is located in the C:\BUILD\GSCRIPTS directory. It establishes connection with the deployment device based on presence and the contents of the NETWORK.BAT or CDROM.BAT file generated in phase 1.

Once connection is established, Phase3.CMD calls a sequence of child (configuration) scripts that perform the configuration. In this example the configuration scripts modify the boot-loader timeout to 5 seconds, configure Windows NT locale information for UK, and limit the size of Event Log files.

When these scripts have been executed, phase 3 removes itself from the "Run" registry key and copies the appropriate phase 4 control script into the Windows NT common "Startup" group before rebooting the workstation.

Each configuration group (department) has its own phase 4 control file, located in a separate subdirectory beneath the "groups" directory. Phase3.CMD uses the %GROUP% environment variable obtained during phase 1 (and stored in CDROM.BAT or NETWORK.BAT) to determine which phase 4 control file to copy.

PHASE3.CMD—File Listing

```
@ECHO OFF

SET netFILE=C:\NETWORK.BAT

SET cdFILE=C:\CDROM.BAT                    ;See [1] below

SET oemBuildPath=C:\BUILD


IF EXIST %cdFILE% GOTO runCDFILE

IF EXIST %netFILE% GOTO runNETFILE         ;See [2] below

GOTO noConfigFile
```

PHASE3.CMD   (continued)

```
:runCDFILE

CALL %cdFILE%                                 ;See [3] below

GOTO okCONTINUE


:runNETFILE

CALL %netFILE%

SLEEP 30

NET USE /persistent:no

NET USE %SRCDRV% %SRCUNC%                      ;See [4] below

IF NOT EXIST %SRCDRV%\*.* GOTO noNetworkPath

GOTO okCONTINUE


:okCONTINUE

CALL %oemBuildPath%\gscripts\bootldr.cmd  ;See [5] below

CALL %oemBuildPath%\gscripts\locale.cmd

CALL %oemBuildPath%\gscripts\eventlog.cmd


ECHO Y|REG DELETE "HKLM\SOFTWARE

\Microsoft\Windows\CurrentVersion\Run\NTConfiguration"
```

This code is spaced so that it is easier to read. Lines are broken for layout only: entries should be on a single line. If you want to skip this section, go to page 607.

```
REM ** PREPARE FOR PHASE4 **

REGEDIT /S C:\BUILD\gScripts\AUTOLOG.REG

COPY %oemBuildPath%\GROUPS\%GROUP%\PHASE4.CMD "%WINDIR%

\PROFILES\ALL USERS\START MENU\PROGRAMS\STARTUP"

IF ERRORLEVEL=1 GOTO noPhase4


SHUTDOWN /L /R /T:0 /Y

GOTO end


:noConfigFile

CLS

COLOR C

ECHO ******************** ERROR ******************************

ECHO Cannot Find C:\CDROM.BAT OR C:\NETWORK.BAT

ECHO Ensure BOOTDISK has created files...

ECHO *********************************************************

PAUSE

COLOR

GOTO END
```

This code is spaced so that it is easier to read. Lines are broken for layout only: entries should be on a single line. If you want to skip this section, go to page 607.

PHASE3.CMD   (continued)

```
:noPhase4

CLS

COLOR C

ECHO ******************** ERROR *****************************

ECHO Cannot find script to initialise phase4

ECHO %oemBuildPath%\GROUPS\%GROUP%\PHASE4.CMD is missing!

ECHO ***********************************************************

PAUSE

COLOR

GOTO END

:noNetworkPath

CLS

COLOR C

ECHO ************************** ERROR **************************

ECHO Cannot establish connection to network server resource:

ECHO %SRCDRV% %SRCUNC%

ECHO ***********************************************************

PAUSE

COLOR

GOTO END

:END
```

This code is spaced so that it is easier to read. Lines are broken for layout only: entries should be on a single line. If you want to skip this section, go to page 607.

Notes on PHASE3CMD.CMD—File Listing:

[1]—All file paths are represented by environment variables.

[2]—Checks for presence of configuration files generated in phase 1. If neither is found, an error is reported. This could be extended to cover the eventuality of both files being present.

[3]—File is executed, instantiating the variables it contains.

[4]—Test valid network connection.

[5]—Child configuration scripts are executed.

The configuration scripts executed as part of the phase 3 parent routine are explained in the following sections.

BOOTLDR.CMD—File Listing

This uses RunDLL32 (the Windows NT utility for executing exported functions in DLLs) to configure the Windows NT setup engine for processing BOOT.INF (shown below), which contains changes relevant to BOOT.INI.

```
@echo off

echo Modifying BOOT.INI to 5 Seconds

START /WAIT ATTRIB -R -S -H C:\BOOT.INI

START /WAIT rundll32 setupapi,InstallHinfSection DefaultInstall 128
C:\BUILD\GSCRIPTS\boot.inf

START /WAIT ATTRIB +R +S +H C:\BOOT.INI
```

BOOT.INF—File Listing

```
; Example INF file to modify boot loader for

; 5 second delay

[Version]

Signature = "$Windows NT$"


[DefaultInstall]

AddReg = AddReg

DelReg = DelReg

UpdateInis = UpdateInis


[AddReg]

[DelReg]

[UpdateInis]

"C:\boot.ini","boot loader",,"timeout=5"
```

EVENTLOG.CMD—File Listing

The following script configures each workstation's Event Log so that the Application, System, and Security logs won't exceed 1 MB each:

REM Event Log Settings

REG UPDATE "HKLM\SYSTEM\CURRENTCONTROLSET\
SERVICES\EVENTLOG\APPLICATION\MAXSIZE=1048576"

REG UPDATE "HKLM\SYSTEM\CURRENTCONTROLSET\
SERVICES\EVENTLOG\APPLICATION\RETENTION=0"

REG UPDATE "HKLM\SYSTEM\CURRENTCONTROLSET\
SERVICES\EVENTLOG\SECURITY\MAXSIZE=1048576"

REG UPDATE "HKLM\SYSTEM\CURRENTCONTROLSET\
SERVICES\EVENTLOG\SECURITY\RETENTION=0"

REG UPDATE "HKLM\SYSTEM\CURRENTCONTROLSET\
SERVICES\EVENTLOG\SYSTEM\MAXSIZE=1048576"

REG UPDATE "HKLM\SYSTEM\CURRENTCONTROLSET\
SERVICES\EVENTLOG\SYSTEM\RETENTION=0"

LOCALE.CMD—File Listing

This script configures the default-user and administrator locales for use in the UK.
(This example shows a UK set up.)

: Define locale changes from US to UK

REM= Update Local Admin

REG UPDATE "HKCU\Control Panel\International\iCountry=44"

REG UPDATE "HKCU\Control Panel\International\iDate=1"

REG UPDATE "HKCU\Control Panel\International\iMeasure=0"

REG UPDATE "HKCU\Control Panel\International\iNegCurr=1"

REG UPDATE "HKCU\Control Panel\International\iTime=1"

REG UPDATE "HKCU\Control Panel\International\iTLZero=1"

REG UPDATE "HKCU\Control Panel\International\Locale=00000809"

REG UPDATE "HKCU\Control Panel\International\s1159=AM"

REG UPDATE "HKCU\Control Panel\International\s2359=PM"

REG UPDATE "HKCU\Control Panel\International\sCountry=United Kingdom"

REG UPDATE "HKCU\Control Panel\International\sCurrency=£"

REG UPDATE "HKCU\Control Panel\International\sLanguage=ENG"

REG UPDATE "HKCU\Control Panel\International\
sLongDate=dd MMMM yyyy"

REG UPDATE "HKCU\Control Panel\International\sShortDate=0"

REM= Update Default

REG UPDATE "HKU\Default\Control Panel\International\iCountry=44"

REG UPDATE "HKU\Default\Control Panel\International\iDate=1"

REG UPDATE "HKU\Default\Control Panel\International\iMeasure=0"

REG UPDATE "HKU\Default\Control Panel\International\iNegCurr=1"

REG UPDATE "HKU\Default\Control Panel\International\iTime=1"

REG UPDATE "HKU\Default\Control Panel\International\iTLZero=1"

REG UPDATE "HKU\Default\Control Panel\International\Locale=00000809"

REG UPDATE "HKU\Default\Control Panel\International\s1159=AM"

REG UPDATE "HKU\Default\Control Panel\International\s2359=PM"

REG UPDATE "HKU\Default\Control Panel\International\
sCountry=United Kingdom"

REG UPDATE "HKU\Default\Control Panel\International\sCurrency=£"

REG UPDATE "HKU\Default\Control Panel\International\sLanguage=ENG"

REG UPDATE "HKU\Default\Control Panel\International\
sLongDate=dd MMMM yyyy"

REG UPDATE "HKU\Default\Control Panel\International\sShortDate=0"

Phase 4—Application Installation Walkthrough

Phase 4 automates Windows NT configuration and the installation of application software for specific department (group) requirements. It allows you to use a single build mechanism to deploy different configurations (operating system and applications) simply by specifying a configuration "group" on the boot disk.

The individualized sets of command scripts for each group are located in a group-name directory beneath "Groups" on the build tree. The example in Figure 11.10 shows that one group directory (*Example1*) has been created. This approach keeps the control-logic for different customizations separate, reducing the likelihood of cross-group errors resulting from manual script modifications.

```
\$oem$
    \$$
        \System32
    \C
        \Build
            \Drivers
                \Audio
            \Groups
                \Example1
            \Gscripts
```

Figure 11.10 Command script directory structure.

Three-Tier Command-Scripts

In addition to the group directory structure, a three-tier command-script architecture is implemented, which introduces the concept of a "package."

A package is a logical grouping of configuration changes—software installation or Windows NT configuration modifications—that are either strongly related or must be performed before a reboot. Figure 11.11 shows that a package has a parent/child relationship with multiple configuration scripts that perform the actual configuration change.

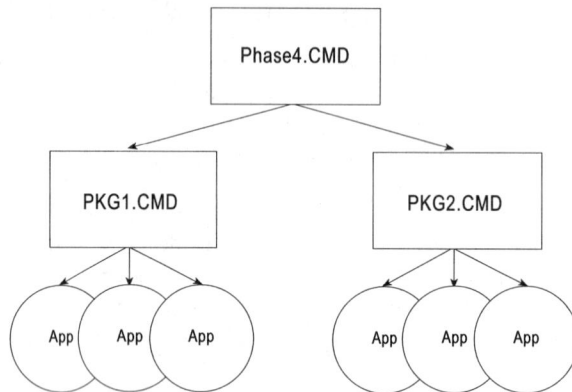

Figure 11.11 Parent/child package relationship.

Aside from the advantages of modularity, packages enable phase 4 to persist over the multiple reboots that may result from the installation of application software. One of the most important features of a package is that it can be executed only once; subsequent execution attempts are ignored. This reduces complexity of the phase 4 parent control routine.

Phase 4—Parent Control

Phase4.CMD, the parent control script for phase 4, reads the NETWORK.BAT (or CDROM.BAT) configuration file and establishes logical drive connectivity with the distribution device. Then it changes the working directory to the local configuration group (*Example1*) as defined by the %GROUP% variable, and sequentially executes each package file within the group.

Phase 4 is initialized using the startup group, as opposed to the "Run" or "RunOnce" registry keys. This has a couple advantages:

- All packages are executed after the desktop environment is fully initialized, significantly reducing the likelihood of failure if the setup routine requires desktop interaction.
- Some software applications have a two-part installation process that modifies the Run/RunOnce key and causes a reboot. Upon logon, the software application finalizes its configuration. If phase 4 used these keys, the two-part installer (from the previous reboot) and a new package file might execute concurrently, creating an inconsistent configuration. Use of the startup feature prevents this problem.

Once all child scripts have been executed, phase 4 passes execution control to PHASE5.CMD.

Package Script—File Listing (PKG1)

In addition to calling child configuration routines, a package has other configurable properties.

Configurable package properties.

Parameter/value	Definition
REBOOT=YES	Package reboots workstation, without returning control to parent.
REBOOT=WAIT	Package waits for application installation routine to reboot workstation. Control does not return to parent.
REBOOT=NO	Package terminates, returning control to parent.
AUTOLOGON=YES	Configure registry for auto-admin logon.
AUTOLOGON=NO	Do not configure registry for auto-admin logon.

The PKG1.CMD file from Example1 group, is listed and annotated below. The other package files (PKG2.CMD, for example) have this format and different header and child-script calls.

```
@ECHO OFF


SET reboot=WAIT                          ;See [1] below

SET autoLogon=YES

SET oemBuildPath=C:\BUILD
```

```
IF NOT DEFINED oemBuildPath GOTO definedError   ;See [2] below

IF NOT DEFINED reboot GOTO definedError

IF NOT DEFINED autoLogon GOTO definedError


IF NOT EXIST %oemBuildPath% GOTO pathError

IF EXIST %oemBuildPath%\%0 GOTO exit             ;See [3] below


ECHO Installing Package %0

REM ** CALL CHILD CONFIGURATION SCRIPTS HERE **


CALL %SRCDRV%\CMDFILES\OFF97.CMD                 ;See [4] below

CALL %SRCDRV%\CMDFILES\OL98.CMD


:updateStatus

ECHO Package Install Complete>%oemBuildPath%\%0 ;See [5] below


:autoLogonCheck

IF %autoLogon%==NO goto rebootCheck

REG UPDATE "HKLM\SOFTWARE\Microsoft\Windows NT\CurrentVersion

\Winlogon\DefaultUserName=administrator"
```

```
REG UPDATE "HKLM\SOFTWARE\Microsoft\WindowsNT\CurrentVersion
\Winlogon\DefaultPassword="
REG UPDATE "HKLM\SOFTWARE\Microsoft\Windows NT\CurrentVersion
\Winlogon\AutoAdminLogon=1


:rebootCheck
IF %reboot%==NO GOTO exit
IF %reboot%==WAIT GOTO rebootWait
ECHO Forcing System Shutdown ...                    ;See [6] below
START /WAIT SHUTDOWN /L /R /T:5 /Y
GOTO exit


:rebootWait
SLEEP 5                                             ;See [7] below
ECHO Waiting for reboot...
GOTO rebootWait


:definedError
COLOR 4F
```

```
ECHO *************************** ERROR ************************

ECHO Environment Variable Not Defined In Package: %0

ECHO Package Installation Failed!

ECHO ************************************************************

PAUSE

GOTO exit


:pathError

COLOR 4F

ECHO ************************** ERROR ****************************

ECHO Directory %oemBuildPath% not found!

ECHO Package Installation Failed!

ECHO ************************************************************

PAUSE

GOTO exit


:exit
```

Notes on Package Script—File Listing (PKG1):

[1]—Environment variables as defined in the table above this sample. Reboot is configured to WAIT because Outlook 98 (deployed in this package) forces a system reboot.

[2]—Error checking.

[3]—Test to determine if package has been executed before.

[4]—Installation of application software.

[5]—Write completion data to prevent subsequent execution.

[6]—Reboot workstation.

[7]—Loop until application causes reboot.

Example Phase 4 Control File

The phase 4 control file establishes logical drive connection to the deployment server, reads the configuration batch file from hard disk, then executes package files in sequence. Here is an example file:

```
@ECHO OFF

SET netFILE=C:\NETWORK.BAT

SET cdFILE=C:\CDROM.BAT                          ;See [1] below

SET oemDrive=C:

SET buildPath=BUILD
```

PHASE 4 SCRIPT   (continued)

```
SET oemBuildPath=%oemDrive%\%buildPath%

IF EXIST %cdFILE% GOTO runCDFILE

IF EXIST %netFILE% GOTO runNETFILE              ;See [2] below

GOTO noConfigFile


:runCDFILE

CALL %cdFILE%

GOTO okCONTINUE


:runNETFILE

CALL %netFILE%

SLEEP 30                                        ;See [3] below

NET USE /persistent:no

NET USE %SRCDRV% %SRCUNC%

IF NOT EXIST %SRCDRV%\*.* GOTO noNetworkPath

GOTO okCONTINUE


:okCONTINUE

%oemDrive%                                      ;See [4] below
```

This code is spaced so that it is easier to read. Lines are broken for layout only: entries should be on a single line. If you want to skip this section, go to page 623.

PHASE 4 SCRIPT   (continued)

```
CD %oemBuildPath%\Groups\%group%

IF %ERRORLEVEL% GEQ 1 GOTO groupError


CALL pkg1.cmd                                          ;See [5] below

CALL pkg2.cmd




CD %oemBuildPath%\gscripts

PHASE5.CMD


GOTO end


:noConfigFile

CLS

COLOR C

ECHO ************************ ERROR ***************************

ECHO Cannot Find C:\CDROM.BAT OR C:\NETWORK.BAT

ECHO Ensure BOOTDISK has created files...

ECHO **********************************************************

PAUSE
```

> This code is spaced so that it is easier to read. Lines are broken for layout only: entries should be on a single line. If you want to skip this section, go to page 623.

PHASE 4 SCRIPT   (continued)

```
COLOR

GOTO END


:noPhase4

CLS

COLOR C

ECHO *********************** ERROR *************************

ECHO Cannot find script to initialise phase4

ECHO %oemBuildPath%\GROUPS\%GROUP%\PHASE4.CMD is missing!

ECHO ********************************************************

PAUSE

COLOR

GOTO END


:noNetworkPath

CLS

COLOR C
```

This code is spaced so that it is easier to read. Lines are broken for layout only: entries should be on a single line. If you want to skip this section, go to page 623.

PHASE 4 SCRIPT   (continued)

```
ECHO *************************** ERROR ****************************

ECHO Cannot establish connection to network server resource:

ECHO %SRCDRV% %SRCUNC%

ECHO ****************************************************************

PAUSE

COLOR

GOTO END


:groupError

CLS

COLOR C

ECHO ********************** ERROR *******************************

ECHO Cannot Change to Group Directory

ECHO %oemBuildPath%\Groups\%group%

ECHO ****************************************************************

PAUSE

COLOR

GOTO END


:END
```

This code is spaced so that it is easier to read. Lines are broken for layout only: entries should be on a single line. If you want to skip this section, go to page 623.

Notes on Example Phase 4 Control File:

[1]—All file paths are represented by environment variables.

[2]—Checks for presence of configuration files generated in phase 1. If neither is found, an error is reported. This can be extended to cover the eventuality of both files being present.

[3]—Test valid network connection.

[4]—Change working directory to appropriate configuration group as defined by *%group%*.

[5]—Execute packages then pass control to phase 5.

Installing Third-Party Applications

To keep the build as flexible and extensible as possible, vendor-supplied installation routines are used for all application software. No snapshot technology is used. Given the complexity of modern applications, and their potential interoperability with other software, this approach ensures that applications configure themselves appropriately with respect to other software on the workstation.

Most installation routines supplied with software support unattended setup (sometimes referred to as batch-mode, silent, or quiet setup), but if you have to install one that doesn't you can automate the process with ScriptIT (see page 676).

Even when applications support unattended installation, their preparation and deployment mechanics can vary. Here is a general guideline for integrating applications into the build:

1. Copy the contents of the original distribution into a unique directory on the deployment server.

2. Generate an unattended configuration file (sometimes called a *response file*) for the application. You may need additional tools to do this. Wherever possible, ensure that the application does not automatically reboot Windows NT; if you can't avoid this, make the application the last entry in the package file and set the package header to WAIT.

3. Create a configuration script that executes the installation routine (using a response file) and store the script in the application scripts folder on the deployment server (*cmdFiles*, in the example).

If the installation routine does not support unattended setup, step 2 is replaced by the manual generation of a ScriptIT script that contains automated responses to the setup dialogs. This file is stored in the same location as (3).

The next sections illustrate this process by showing the installation of four commercial applications with different installation routines.

Installing Microsoft Office 97 with Service Release 1

Microsoft Office is supplied with an installation routine that supports unattended setup when used in conjunction with the Network Installation Wizard. This is an Office Resource Kit tool (available from http://www.microsoft.com/office/ork) that modifies the administrative installation table file (.STF) for the Office setup program, enabling automated configuration of information that ordinarily requires interaction.

Here are the steps needed to integrate Office 97 into the modular build:

1. Create a unique directory beneath **Apps** called *Office97*, and copy the entire contents of the Office97 CD into it.

2. Create a unique directory beneath **Office97** called *SR1*, and copy the contents of Service Release 1 into it.

3. Use the Network Installation Wizard to pre-configure all necessary options for Office97. Be sure to save the modified configuration files to the Office97 directory on the deployment server.

4. Create a configuration script to install Office97 and Service Release 1, and store it in the application scripts directory. An example script is shown below:

```
@echo off

echo Installing Office97 /w Service Pack1

start /wait %SRCDRV%\apps\OFFICE97\SETUP /B2 /Q1N


rem Install Service Release

start /wait %SRCDRV%\apps\OFFICE97\SR1\SR1 /q
```

Installing Visio5

Visio5 uses InstallShield technology to perform its setup and configuration. InstallShield has built-in support for unattended installations using response files, and requires no additional tools for configuration.

Here are the steps needed to integrate Visio5 (or any InstallShield application that supports unattended installation) into the modular build:

1. Create a unique directory beneath **Apps**, called *Visio5* and copy the entire contents of the Visio5 distribution into it.

2. Using a pre-built workstation that does not currently have Visio installed, connect to the distribution directory and execute the Visio setup routine, specifying the **-r** switch to enable automatic generation of a response file.

3. Complete the attended Visio installation. Your responses to configuration questions are recorded to the response file SETUP.ISS that has been placed in the %SYSTEMROOT% directory.

4. When you have configured Visio, copy the response file from %SYSTEMROOT% into the Visio5 directory on the distribution server that contains the SETUP executable.

5. Create a command script to install Visio5, and store it in the application scripts directory. Here is an example script:

```
@echo off
echo Installing Visio5
START /WAIT %SRCDRV%\apps\VISIO5\SETUP -S
:loopBack
sleep 30
IF EXIST "%TEMP%\_ISTMP0.DIR" GOTO loopBack
:end
```

TIP: Preventing premature script continuation

Using the START /WAIT parameter in the installation script causes Windows NT to stop processing further command-script lines until SETUP is terminated. During installation of an InstallShield-driven application, the SETUP executable may initialize another process to perform the actual installation, terminating the original process. If SETUP.EXE terminates before the application is installed, Windows NT resumes (premature) execution of phase 4 command scripts.

To prevent this, the script checks for the presence of a temporary directory (_ISTMP0.DIR) created by InstallShield in the %temp% directory. InstallShield automatically removes this directory when the installation is complete, so its is used to determine script termination.

TIP: Using *sleep* to reduce CPU utilization

The *sleep* command is used to reduce the high CPU utilization that would result from a loop structure in a command-script.

Installing Outlook 98

Due to the complexity and potential configuration variance possible in Outlook 98, you should use the Outlook Deployment Kit to manage the installation. It enables the pre-configuration of both Outlook 98 and Internet Explorer 4.01 by generating the executables, configuration data, and setup routine for automated deployment.

Here are the steps needed to integrate Outlook 98 into the modular build:

1. Create a unique directory beneath **Apps** called *OL98* but do not copy any files into it.

2. Install the Outlook Deployment Kit on a workstation that has network connectivity to the build server.

3. Execute the ODK on the local workstation and specify all the configuration parameters (including *silent installation* option) for Outlook 98. During this process, you will be prompted for a directory to store the packaged Outlook 98 product. Specify the directory created in step 1. When you have specified all the configuration information, the ODK will populate the directory with all files required for the deployment.

4. Create a command script to install Outlook 98, and store it in the application scripts directory. Here is an example script:

```
@echo off

echo Installing Outlook98

start /wait %SRCDRV%\apps\OL98\CD\EN\PACKAGES\SETUP
```

TIP: Outlook reboot cannot be suppressed via ODK

You can specify a command-line parameter that suppresses an automatic reboot of the operating system, but it has no effect in an ODK environment. To keep this from derailing the build, make sure Outlook 98 is the last application in a package, and reset the *Reboot* package header to WAIT.

Installing WinZIP

WinZIP is an example of an application that does not have an unattended installation routine, but you can still automate installation by creating a ScriptIT script.

Here are the steps needed to integrate WinZIP into the modular build:

1. Create a unique directory beneath **Apps**, called *WinZIP* and copy the entire contents of the WinZIP distribution into it.

2. Manually install WinZIP using the keyboard to interact with the dialogs. Record the window titles and keystrokes required, then use this information to create a script file and store it in the *cmdFiles* directory. Here is an example script file:

```
[SCRIPT]

RUN=%SRCDRV%\apps\WinZIP\SETUP.EXE

WinZip Setup+Setup will={ENTER}

WinZip Setup+Thank you=!N

License Agreement and Warranty Disclaimer=!Y

WinZip Setup+Select=!C!N

WinZip Setup+Click=!E!N

WinZip Setup+Installation={ENTER}
```

3. Create a command script to begin the WinZIP installation, and store it in the application scripts directory. Here is an example script:

```
@echo off

echo Installing WinZIP

START /WAIT SCRIPTIT %SRCDRV%\apps\cmdFiles\WinZIP.TXT
```

Phase 5—Finalize/Domain Membership Walkthrough

This is the final stage of the modular build process. It joins the workstation to an existing domain, sets the local administrator password to the word SECRET, enables a legal warning message, and removes the BUILD structure on the local hard disk.

Joining the Domain

In a traditional unattended Windows NT setup, automated membership of a domain is achieved through the Windows NT answer file. Unfortunately, this requires that the workstation must be able to communicate with the domain controller for the remainder of the build process, imposing domain-dependence.

Often, this is not practical. For example, if you want to replace 2000 legacy PCs with new equipment, you can supply the hardware vendor with the unattended build, and ask that the hardware be pre-loaded before delivery. But to use the traditional mechanism (with domain dependency), the vendor must also be supplied with a valid backup domain controller (BDC).

To eliminate this problem, the modular build process does not use the Windows NT answer file to perform domain membership. Instead it uses a Resource Kit (Supplement 2) utility called NETDOM, which permits computer-account creation and domain membership from within a command-script.

Computer Account

For a workstation to join a domain, a computer account must already exist on the domain controller. There are two ways to create this account:

1. The NETDOM utility can automatically create the account prior to joining the domain, although to do this you have to encode an administrative user ID and password into the build scripts, presenting a possible security issue.

2. Before the workstation joins the domain, the administrator can manually create the accounts. This removes any security issues, and ensures that only valid computers join the domain.

Administrative Password

Prior to PC deployment, it is advisable to set a password for the local administrator account using the NET USER command. In the simple example shown in the "CHGPASS—Listing" section (page 636) the password is changed to the word SECRET.

TIP: Automated secure passwords

If a more secure (unique) password is required for each workstation, it would be easy to author a password generation program that creates a unique password based on computer name. These passwords could be cryptic and unique, and the administrator could obtain them by entering the computer name into the password generator.

Phase 5 CMD—Listing

Below is a simple phase 5 parent script. Like the previous scripts, it employs a parent/child relationship to effect the various configuration changes.

TIP: Existing network connections causes *join* failure

Notice that this phase establishes no logical drive network connections. A workstation cannot join a domain until all existing network connections are terminated. If you don't establish any, you won't have to terminate any.

```
@ECHO OFF

SET netFILE=C:\NETWORK.BAT

SET cdFILE=C:\CDROM.BAT

SET oemBuildPath=C:\BUILD


IF EXIST %cdFILE% GOTO runCDFILE

IF EXIST %netFILE% GOTO runNETFILE

GOTO noConfigFile


:runCDFILE

CALL %cdFILE%

GOTO okCONTINUE


:runNETFILE

CALL %netFILE%

GOTO okCONTINUE
```

This code is spaced so that it is easier to read. Lines are broken for layout only: entries should be on a single line. If you want to skip this section, go to page 636.

PHASE 5 SCRIPT   (continued)

```
:okCONTINUE


ERASE /Q "%WINDIR%
        \PROFILES\ALL USERS\START MENU\PROGRAMS\STARTUP\PHASE4.CMD"


CALL %oemBuildPath%\GSCRIPTS\JOINDOM

IF %ERRORLEVEL% EQU 2453 GOTO joinFAILED

IF %ERRORLEVEL% EQU 5 GOTO noCompACCT

IF %ERRORLEVEL% NEQ 0 GOTO genericERROR

REG UPDATE "HKLM\SOFTWARE\Microsoft\Windows NT

\CurrentVersion\Winlogon\DefaultDomainName=%DOMAIN%"



CALL %oemBuildPath%\GSCRIPTS\CHGPASS

CALL %oemBuildPath%\GSCRIPTS\LEGAL



RD /S /Q %oemBuildPath%

SHUTDOWN /L /R /T:0 /Y

GOTO end



:noConfigFile
```

> This code is spaced so that it is easier to read. Lines are broken for layout only: entries should be on a single line. If you want to skip this section, go to page 636.

```
CLS

COLOR C

ECHO **************** ERROR *****************************

ECHO Cannot Find C:\CDROM.BAT OR C:\NETWORK.BAT

ECHO Ensure BOOTDISK has created files...

ECHO *******************************************************

PAUSE

COLOR

GOTO END


:joinFAILED

CLS

COLOR C

ECHO****************** ERROR *****************************

ECHO Cannot Find Domain %DOMAIN%

ECHO*******************************************************

PAUSE

COLOR

GOTO END
```

This code is spaced so that it is easier to read. Lines are broken for layout only: entries should be on a single line. If you want to skip this section, go to page 636.

PHASE 5 SCRIPT   (continued)

```
:noCompACCT

CLS

COLOR C

ECHO**************** ERROR *****************************

ECHO Cannot join domain - NO COMPUTER ACCOUNT

ECHO*******************************************************

PAUSE

COLOR

GOTO END


:genericERROR

CLS

COLOR C

ECHO**************** ERROR *****************************

ECHO Cannot join domain - Generic Error.  Consult NETDOM tool.

ECHO*******************************************************

PAUSE

COLOR

GOTO END

:END
```

This code is spaced so that it is easier to read. Lines are broken for layout only: entries should be on a single line. If you want to skip this section, go to page 636.

JOINDOM—Listing

Here is a child script that executes the NETDOM utility with appropriate parameters, and uses the DOMAIN environment variable defined during phase 1 to specify the domain name.

```
@ECHO OFF

NETDOM /DOMAIN:%DOMAIN% MEMBER /JOINDOMAIN
```

CHGPASS—Listing

Here is a child script that changes the password of the local administrator to SECRET using the built-in NET USER command.

```
@ECHO OFF

NET USER ADMINISTRATOR SECRET
```

LEGAL—Listing

This script adds a legal warning message to the Windows NT logon process.

```
@ECHO OFF

REG UPDATE
"HKLM\SOFTWARE\Microsoft\Windows NT\CurrentVersion\Winlogon\LegalNoticeC
aption=Example Legal Notice"

REG UPDATE
"HKLM\SOFTWARE\Microsoft\Windows NT\CurrentVersion\Winlogon\LegalNoticeT
ext=Example Legal Notice Text"
```

Tips on Common Procedures

How to Determine Which Registry Keys an Application Uses

To develop an in-depth understanding of Windows NT (and application) configuration, you have to understand the significance and use of individual registry keys. Many software products do not provide detailed registry information, so you sometimes have to use tools to get this information.

Warning Incorrect modification of the registry can lead to system instability and/or loss of application functionality. Before implementing registry changes, make sure the software vendors support the modifications you make.

During the normal execution of an application, both Windows NT and the application will make regular reference to the registry. There are two easy ways to discover which registry keys are being accessed:

Real Time Monitoring. REGMON is a real-time registry monitor available from the System Internals Web site (http:\\www.sysinternals.com). It displays all activity in an easy to read format, showing the process that accessed the registry, data that was read/written, and whether the access was successful. You can store captured data in text files for later analysis.

Snapshot Analysis. Windows NT has a snapshot/deployment tool called SYSDIFF (in support\deptools\i386 directory on the distribution CD), which you can use to record the various registry (and file) changes made during manual configuration of Windows NT or applications.

638 Managing a Microsoft Windows NT Network

For example, suppose a Windows NT workstation is configured to operate at a video resolution of 640x480, and you want to determine which registry modifications are required to automate the configuration to 800x600. You can do this by using SYSDIFF this way:

1. SYSDIFF /SNAP BASE.IMG

   Causes SYSDIFF to record the state of all files and registry settings to the BASE.IMG file.

2. Change video resolution using the control panel in the usual manner.

3. C. SYSDIFF /DIFF BASE.IMG NEW.IMG

   Causes SYSDIFF to read the current state of all files and registry, compare them to the contents of BASE.IMG, and write the differences to NEW.IMG.

4. SYSDIFF /INF NEW.IMG C:\

   Causes SYSDIFF to generate a OEM directory on C:\. Within this structure, the file NEW.INF contains all the registry changes made during stage 2. You can manually transpose these into the configuration script format used throughout the modular build process.

Note It is possible that additional (non-related) registry activity will occur before the difference snapshot is taken, resulting in an .INF file that contains data that does not directly relate to the original configuration change. Prior to including all information in a configuration file, it is important to analyze and understand the impact of the registry changes you intend to make.

How to Automate SHARE Creation

You can use the NET SHARE command to create network shares within configuration scripts. The example below creates a share called EXAMPLE, which points to directory C:\EX.

```
NET SHARE EXAMPLE=C:\EX
```

How to Automate User Account Creation

You can use the NET USER command to create local user accounts within configuration scripts. The example below creates a user called *tester*, with comment, password expiration, home directory, and profile path configured:

```
NET USER tester /add /comment:"Example Account for User"

/expires:never

/homedir:\\zippy\%username%$

/profilepath:\\zippy\profile
```

How to Remove the Recycle Bin from the Desktop

You can do this by creating a configuration script that deletes the following registry key:

```
HKEY_LOCAL_MACHINE\SOFTWARE\Microsoft\Windows\CurrentVersion

\Explorer\Desktop\NameSpace

\{645FF040-5081-101B-9F08-00AA002F954E}"
```

How to Prevent Windows NT Workstation from Providing Browser Services

Use this configuration script prevents Windows NT from providing browser services to the other computers on the network:

```
REG UPDATE "HKEY_LOCAL_MACHINE\System\CurrentControlSet\Services

\Browser\Start=4"

REG UPDATE "HKEY_LOCAL_MACHINE\System\CurrentControlSet\Services

\Browser\Parameters\MaintainServerList=No"
```

How to Assign System Rights to Users During Setup

You can use the NTRIGHTS utility (in the resource kit) to assign system rights to users. The example below assigns user TESTUSER the right to shut down the system:

```
Ntrights -u testuser +r SeShutDownPrivilege
```

How to Automate Printer Creation

You can use the ZAK utility CON2PRT to create printers within a configuration script. Here is an example:

```
CON2PRT /CD \\PRNTSVR\HP550C
```

How to Prevent a Computer from Appearing on a Browse List

Use the NET CONFIG command to prevent workstations or servers appearing in browse lists. Here is an example:

```
NET CONFIG SERVER /HIDDEN:YES
```

How to Install AGP Graphics Drivers

Video adapters that use the new AGP standard require the added functionality of the hardware abstraction layers (HALs) supplied in Windows NT SP3 or later. Since SP3 is applied after the answer file has been processed, AGP video cards cannot simply be added into the answer file. There are two ways to solve this problem:

- Copy the HAL(s) from SP3 into the distribution directory, and create an answer file with the appropriate configuration data for the video card. Here is a list of HALS:

486c_up	= hal486c.dll
astmf_mp	= halast.dll
cbus2_mp	= halcbus.dll
cbusmc_mp	= halcbusm.dll
e_isa_up	= hal.dll
mca_up	= halmca.dll
mps_up	= halapic.dll
mps_mp	= halmps.dll
mps_mca_mp	= halmpsm.dll
ncr3x_mp	= halncr.dll
oli5030_mp	= haloli.dll
syspro_mp	= halsp.dll
wyse7000_mp	= halwyse7.dll

Since most new video cards are supplied with an interactive installation routine, use ScriptIT to install the drivers after SP3 has been applied. A discussion of ScriptIT begins on page 676.

How to Install Sound Cards

The answer file does not support sound card installation, but you can easily automate the process with ScriptIT. Here is a script that installs the wave drivers for the Sound Blaster AWE card.

```
[SCRIPT]

RUN=CONTROL.EXE

Control Panel=##MU{enter}

Multimedia Properties={RIGHT 4}!A

Add={ENTER}C:\Build\Drivers\Audio\Creative\NT40\{ENTER}

Add Unlisted or Updated Driver=#{DOWN} {ENTER}

Sound Blaster Base I/O Address={ENTER}

Sound Blaster 16 Configuration={ENTER}

System Setting Change=!D

Multimedia Properties=!+{F4}

Control Panel=!+{F4}


[ADLIB]

Driver Exists=!N

File Installation Error={ENTER}
```

How to Set DNS Search Order

The Windows NT answer file does not provide a mechanism to specify the search order of Domain Name System (DNS) suffix. You can automate this using a configuration script as follows:

```
REG UPDATE "HKLM\SYSTEM\CurrentControlSet\Services\TCPIP

\Parameters\SearchList=EXAMPLE1.COM EXAMPLE2.COM"
```

How to Activate a Control Panel Applet

Use the RunDLL32 command from a configuration script. This is a utility that enables the execution of exported functions in a dynamic link library. The *shell32* library is used to load various control panel applets defined in the table beginning on the next page.

Note Some applets have multiple panels, and are accessed by specifying an index value.

Control panel applets.

Panel	Filename	Index
Mouse properties	MAIN.CPL	@0
Keyboard properties	MAIN.CPL	@1
Printers	MAIN.CPL	@2
Fonts	MAIN.CPL	@3
Power supply (UPS)	UPS.CPL	@0
Time/date	TIMEDATE.CPL	@0
Telephony	TELEPHON.CPL	@0
System panel	SYSDM.CPL	@0
Server manager	SRVMGR.CPL	@0
Services panel	SRVMGR.CPL	@1
Devices panel	SRVMGR.CPL	@2
Ports	PORTS.CPL	@0
Network panel	NCPA.CPL	@0
Modem	MODEM.CPL	@0
Multimedia properties	MMSYS.CPL	@0
Sound properties	MMSYS.CPL	@1
Regional settings	INTL.CPL	@0

Control panel applets.   *(continued)*

Panel	Filename	Index
PCMCIA devices	DEVAPPS.CPL	@0
SCSI adapters	DEVAPPS.CPL	@1
Tape devices	DEVAPPS.CPL	@2
Display properties	DESK.CPL	@0
Console properties	CONSOLE.CPL	@0
Add/remove programs	APPWIZ.CPL	@0

The following example activates the multimedia control panel and displays multimedia properties:

```
rundll32.exe shell32.dll,Control_RunDLL mmsys.cpl @0
```

How to Configure Crash Recovery

The system control panel provides various options to define what Windows NT will do in the event of a crash. The example below configures Windows NT to write the crash details to the event log and automatically reboot:

```
REG UPDATE "HKLM\SYSTEM\CURRENTCONTROLSET\CONTROL\CRASHCONTROL\
LOGEVENT=1"

REG UPDATE "HKLM\SYSTEM\CURRENTCONTROLSET\CONTROL\CRASHCONTROL\
AUTOREBOOT=1"
```

How to Remove Briefcase from the Installation

By default, the briefcase application (SYNCAPP.EXE) is installed onto each user's desktop. You can disable this by editing the TXTSETUP.SIF and LAYOUT.INF files on the distribution server, and inserting a semicolon before each line that begins with SYNCAPP.EXE.

Answer File Information

An answer file consists of section headers, parameters, and values for those parameters. Most of the section headers are predefined (although users can define some of them). You don't have to specify parameters and keys in the UNATTEND.TXT file if your installation does not require them. The file format is based on the sectioned, parameter/value schema as used in Windows .INI files.

[Unattended]

This header identifies whether an unattended installation is being performed. If it does not exist, the UNATTEND.TXT file is ignored. Parameters that can exist in this section are discussed below.

OemPreinstall

Value: Yes | No

Determines whether an OEM pre-installation is being performed. When the value is *Yes*, any existing subdirectories are copied. *No* means a regular unattended Setup is being performed and only the Inetsrv, System32 and Drvlib.nic subdirectories are copied.

NoWaitAfterTextMode

Value: 0 | 1

Determines whether the text mode portion of Setup should automatically boot into GUI mode. It is valid only when OemPreinstall = *Yes*. The default behavior is to halt after text mode during a pre-installation. *0* indicates that Setup should halt after text mode and *1* indicates that Setup should automatically reboot into GUI mode after text mode is complete.

`NoWaitAfterGuiMode`

`Value: 0 | 1`

Determines whether the GUI mode portion of Setup should automatically reboot to the logon screen. It is valid only when OemPreinstall = Yes. The default behavior is to halt at the end of GUI mode Setup. *0* indicates that Setup should halt after GUI mode and *1* indicates that Setup should automatically reboot after GUI mode is complete.

`FileSystem`

`Value: ConvertNTFS | LeaveAlone`

Specifies whether the primary partition should be converted to NTFS or left alone. In general, partitions greater than 512 MB should be converted to NTFS. If this value is set to "ConvertNTFS" it is done after the first reboot of an unattended setup.

`ExtendOemPartition`

`Value: 0 | 1`

Enables installation of Windows NT on a hard disk larger than 2 GB. This key causes text mode Setup to extend the partition containing the temporary Windows NT sources into any available unpartitioned space that physically follows it on the disk. The temporary install source must be a primary partition limited to 1024 cylinders. Writing beyond the 1024th cylinder causes the installation to fail. *0* implies that the partition will not be extended, and 1 indicates that it should be extended. When the value is *1*, the FileSystem key must be set to ConvertNTFS. When the value is set to *1*, OemPreinstall must be equal to *yes*.

ConfirmHardware

Value: Yes | No

Determines whether a user should manually confirm hardware and mass storage devices detected by the Setup program. *Yes* indicates that a user must manually confirm the hardware detected and *No* implies that Setup should install the detected devices. For a complete unattended installation, this key should be set to *No*.

NtUpgrade

Values: Yes | No | Manual | Single

Determines whether a previous version of Windows NT Workstation or Server should be upgraded. It should be set in order to perform an upgrade. *Yes* indicates that the detected Windows NT installation should be upgraded. If multiple installations are detected, the first installation found is upgraded. *No* implies that the upgrade should be aborted if a Windows NT installation is found—this is the appropriate value when OemPreinstall = *Yes*. *Manual* implies that the user must specify which previous installation should be upgraded. *Single* indicates that the upgrade should continue only if a single Windows NT installation is found. If multiple installations are found, the user must manually select which installation to upgrade.

Win31Upgrade

Values: Yes | No

This key determines whether previous installations of 16-bit should be upgraded to Windows NT. *Yes* indicates that the Windows installation should be upgraded, and *No* means do not upgrade the installation if found.

```
OverwriteOemFilesOnUpgrade
```

```
Values: Yes | No
```

Determines whether OEM-supplied files that have the same name as Windows NT system files should be overwritten during an unattended upgrade or not. *Yes* means overwrite the files and *No* means do not. The default behavior is to overwrite OEM-supplied files.

```
TargetPath
```

```
Values: * | <path name> | Manual
```

Determines which directory Windows NT should be installed into and implies that Setup should generate a unique directory name for the installation. This is usually WINNT.x where x is *0*, *1*, and so on. *<path name>* is user-defined installation directory. *Manual* indicates that Setup should prompt the user to enter the installation path. *Do not use drive letters in this value.*

```
ComputerType
```

```
Values: <hal description> [, Retail | OEM]
```

Indicates the type of hardware abstraction layer (HAL) to be loaded by the Setup Loader, and installed by text-mode Setup. If this key is not present, Setup attempts to detect the type of computer and install the appropriate retail HAL. Only valid when OemPreinstall = *Yes*. The *<hal description>* string identifies the HAL to be installed. It must match one of the strings in the [Computer] section of the TXTSETUP.SIF file (for a retail HAL), or the TXTSETUP.OEM file (for an OEM HAL). *Retail* informs Setup that the HAL to be installed is part of the Windows NT product. *OEM* indicates that the HAL to be loaded is OEM-supplied. If the HAL is OEM-supplied, the driver name must also be listed in the [OemBootFiles] section of the UNATTEND.TXT file.

```
KeyboardLayout
```

```
Value: <layout description>
```

Indicates the type of keyboard layout to be installed. If this key does not exist, Setup will detect and install a keyboard layout. *<layout description>* must match one of the right hand strings (in "") in the ["Keyboard Layout"] section of the TXTSETUP.SIF file.

[MassStorageDrivers]

This section contains a list of SCSI drivers to be loaded by the Setup Loader, and installed during text mode Setup. If this section is missing or empty, Setup attempts to detect the SCSI devices on the computer, and install the corresponding retail drivers.

```
<mass storage driver description>
```

```
Value: RETAIL | OEM
```

This string identifies the driver to be installed. It must match one of the strings defined in the right-hand side of the [SCSI] section of the TXTSETUP.SIF file (for a retail driver), or the TXTSETUP.OEM file (for an OEM driver). You can specify multiple <mass storage driver description>s. *RETAIL* indicates that the driver is part of the retail Windows NT product. *OEM* indicates that the driver is OEM-supplied. If the value is *OEM*, the driver must also be listed in the [OemBootFiles] section of the UNATTEND.TXT file.

[DisplayDrivers]

This section contains a list of display drivers to be loaded by the Setup Loader, and installed during text mode Setup. It is valid only when OemPreinstall = *Yes*. If this section is missing or empty, Setup attempts to detect the display devices on the computer, and installs the corresponding retail drivers. You can get the same functionality by using the settings in the [Display] section described on page 656.

```
<display driver description>
```

```
Value: RETAIL | OEM
```

This string identifies the driver to be installed. It must match one of the strings defined in the right-hand side of the [Display] section of the TXTSETUP.SIF file (for a retail driver), or the TXTSETUP.OEM file (for an OEM driver). You can specify multiple *<display driver description>*s. *RETAIL* indicates that the driver is part of the retail Windows NT product. *OEM* indicates that the driver is OEM-supplied.

[KeyboardDrivers]

This section contains a list of Keyboard drivers to be loaded by the Setup Loader, and installed during text mode Setup. It is valid only when OemPreinstall = *Yes*. If this section is missing or empty, Setup attempts to detect the keyboard devices on the computer and installs the corresponding retail drivers.

```
<keyboard driver description>
```

```
Value: RETAIL | OEM
```

This string identifies the driver to be installed. It must match one of the strings defined in the right-hand side of the [Keyboard] section in TXTSETUP.SIF file (for a retail driver) or the TXTSETUP.OEM file (for an OEM driver). You can specify multiple *<keyboard driver description>*s. *RETAIL* indicates that the driver is part of the retail Windows NT product. *OEM* indicates that the driver is OEM-supplied.

[PointingDeviceDrivers]

This section contains a list of pointing device drivers to be loaded by the Setup Loader, and installed during text-mode Setup. It is valid only when OemPreinstall = *Yes*. If this section is missing or empty, Setup attempts to detect the pointing devices on the computer, and installs the corresponding retail drivers.

```
<pointing device driver description>
```

Value: RETAIL | OEM

This string identifies the driver to be installed. It must match one of the strings defined in the right-hand side of the [Mouse] section of the TXTSETUP.SIF file (for a retail driver), or the TXTSETUP.OEM file (for an OEM driver). You can specify multiple *<pointing device driver description>*s. *RETAIL* indicates that the driver is part of the retail Windows NT product. *OEM* indicates that the driver is OEM-supplied.

[OEMBootFiles]

This section is used to specify OEM-supplied boot files. It is valid only if OemPreinstall = *Yes* and the files listed here have been placed in the OEM\Textmode directory of the OEM's distribution share point.

```
Txtsetup.oem
```

This file contains descriptions of all the OEM-supplied drivers listed in this section and instructions on how to install them. It must exist if this section is listed.

```
<hal file name>
```

This maps to a HAL description that has been defined by the ComputerType key in the [Unattended] section of the UNATTEND.TXT file.

```
<scsi driver file name>
```

This maps to a mass storage driver description defined in the [MassStorageDriver] section of the UNATTEND.TXT file. There can be multiple *<scsi driver file name>*s listed in the [OemBootFiles] section.

[OEM_Ads]

This section instructs Setup that the default end-user interface will be modified by the keys below.

Banner

Values: <text string>

Specifies a text string to be displayed in the upper left corner of the computer screen. The text must contain the *Windows NT* sub-string or it will be ignored. To specify more than one line, you can separate the lines using asterisks (*).

Logo

Values: <file name> [,<resource id>]

Specifies a bitmap to be displayed in the upper right corner of the screen. If this line has only one field, it is assumed to be a .BMP file located in the OEM directory of the distribution share point. However, if two fields are specified, the first field is the name of a DLL and the second is a base-10 number that represents the resource ID of the bitmap in the DLL. The DLL specified should be located in the OEM directory.

Background

Values: <file name> [,<resource id>]

Specifies a background bitmap to be displayed. If this line has only one field, it is assumed to be a .BMP file located in the OEM directory of the distribution share point. However, if two fields are specified, the first field is the name of a DLL and the second is a base-10 number that represents the resource ID of the bitmap in the DLL. The DLL specified should be located in the OEM directory.

[GuiUnattended]

OemSkipWelcome

Value: 0 | 1

Used to specify whether the introductory *Welcome to Windows NT Setup* page is skipped. Default behavior is to show the page.

OEMBlankAdminPassword

Value: 0 | 1

Specifies whether the user should be shown the Administrator Password Wizard page. Default behavior is to show the page. In Windows NT 4.0 you cannot automate the setup of the administrator password unless you specify it to be blank (OEMBlankAdminPassword = 1). The only way to set this is to let Windows NT prompt for it either during GUI mode or after the install is complete.

TimeZone

Value: <text string>

Determines the time zone of the computer. If the key is empty, the user is prompted to indicate a time zone.

DetachedProgram

Value: <detached program string>

Used to indicate the path of the custom program that should run concurrently with the Setup program. If the program requires any arguments, the *Arguments* key must be specified.

[UserData]

FullName

Value: <string>

This is used to specify the user's full name. If the key is empty or missing, the user is prompted to enter a name. This should contain the name of the person or company to which the software is registered, *not* the name of the user who will be using the machine or the user account.

OrgName

Value: <string>

Specifies an organization name. If this is empty, the user is prompted to enter one.

ComputerName

Value: <string>

Specifies the computer name. If this is empty or missing, the user is prompted to enter one.

ProductID

Value: <string>

Specifies the Microsoft product identification (productID) number. It is on the CD jewel case.

[Display]

This section is used to specify display settings for the particular graphics devices being installed. In order for this to work properly, the user must know what settings are valid for the graphics. If the pre-specified settings are not valid, the user is prompted to select them.

`ConfigureAtLogon`

`Value: 0 | 1`

Specifies when the graphics devices are configured: *0* indicates configure during Setup and *1* indicates configure during the first logon by the user. For a fully automated installation this key should not be used.

`BitsPerPel`

`Value: <valid bits per pixel>`

Specifies the <valid bits per pixel> for the graphics device being installed.

`Xresolution`

`Value: <valid x resolution>`

Specifies a <valid x resolution> for the graphics device being installed.

`Yresolution`

`Value: <valid y resolution>`

Specifies a <valid y resolution> for the graphics device being installed.

```
Vrefresh
```

```
Value: <valid refresh rate>
```

Specifies a <valid refresh rate> for the graphics device being installed.

```
AutoConfirm
```

```
Value: 0 | 1
```

Indicates whether the graphics device should be configured using pre-specified display settings. *0* implies do not use the pre-specified settings and *1* means use them. AutoConfirm = *1* requires that all the necessary parameters have already been specified in the UNATTEND.TXT file.

```
[Display]

    BitsPerPel = 8

    XResolution = 1024

    YResolution = 768

    VRefresh = 70

    Flags = 0

    AutoConfirm = 1
```

[Modem]

This section header is used to identify whether a modem should be installed. It is used by Remote Access Service (RAS) to install a modem if DeviceType = *Modem* in the list of RAS parameters. This section cannot be empty if you want to install modems using RAS in unattended mode.

```
InstallModem
```

```
Value: <modem parameter section>
```

Defines a section where modem installation parameters are defined. The key must exist in order to install any modems.

```
[<modem parameter section>]
```

This lists the keys and values required to install a modem on a particular COM port. If this section is blank, RAS performs modem detection on its pre-configured ports and installs any modems it finds.

```
<COM port number>
```

```
Values: <Modem description> [, <Manufacturer>, <Provider>]
```

The <COM port number> key specifies the COM ports on which modems are installed. The COM port numbers must match ports configured or to be configured by the RAS installation. *<Modem description>* must match a modem description in a MDMXXXXX.INF file that corresponds to the modem to be installed. This string must be enclosed in quotation marks. The *<Manufacturer>* and *<Provider>* fields are optional; they identify the manufacturer and provider of a particular modem in cases where the *<modem description>* string is not unique to a particular manufacturer.

[Network]

This section informs Setup that networking should be installed. If empty, the user is presented with various error messages. If this section header is missing, network installation is skipped.

```
Attended
```

```
Value: Yes | No
```

Specify this key if you want the user to install networking manually during an unattended installation.

`JoinWorkgroup`

`Value: <workgroup name>`

Used to define the workgroup in which the computer will participate.

`JoinDomain`

`Value: <domain name>`

Use this to define the domain in which the computer will participate.

`CreateComputerAccount`

`Values: <username>, <password>`

Allows the machine account to be created during setup. The *username* and *password* are for a domain account that has the right to "Add Workstations To Domain." Note that for this value to work, the network card must be able to contact the domain controller. This is crucial for computers that are using only Transmission Control Protocol/Internet Protocol (TCP/IP) and when the domain controller is on a different segment. There must be a way to resolve the IP address. If the account does not have the right to add workstations to the domain or cannot contact the domain controller, setup informs you that it failed to create the account and returns to the **Join Domain** dialog.

`DetectAdapters`

`Value: <detect adapters section> | ""`

Used to detect network adapter cards installed on a computer. Either this key or the InstallAdapters key must exist in order to install network cards. If the value is "" the first card detected will be installed.

```
InstallAdapters
```

```
Value: <install adapters section>
```

Defines a section in which the network adapters to be installed are listed. Adapters are not detected, but if this key is present the adapters listed in the section are installed by default.

```
InstallProtocols
```

```
Value: <protocols section>
```

Defines a section in which the network protocols to be installed are listed.

```
InstallServices
```

```
Value: <services section>
```

Defines a section listing the network services to be installed. These services can be installed during unattended setup:

- NWWKSTA = Client service for NetWare
- SNMP = SNMP service
- RAS = Remote Access Service
- NETMON = Network monitor
- STCPIP = Simple TCPIP
- TCPPRINT = TCPIP Printing service
- INETSTP = Install Internet server
- SAP = SAP service

[<Detect Adapters Section>]

This section is pointed to by the DetectAdapters key described earlier.

```
DetectCount
```

```
Value: <number of detection attempts>
```

Indicates the number of detection attempts Setup should make.

```
LimitTo
```

```
Value: <netcard inf option>
```

This specifies a list of netcard information options to which the detection should be limited. To find the options for particular cards look in the [Options] section of the corresponding OEMNADXX.INF file.

[<Install Adapters Section>]

```
<Netcard Inf option>
```

```
Value: <netcard parameter section>
```

This points Setup to the section that contains descriptions for a particular network adapter card. To find the options for particular cards look in the [Options] section of the corresponding OEMNADXX.INF files.

```
<oem path>
```

This points to the location of the OEM-supplied files. If the path starts with a drive letter, then the literal path is used to find the OEM driver; if it starts with a back slash (\), then the path given is appended to the path to the installation source.

[<netcard Parameters Section>]

This section contains the parameters for a network adapter card for which the *<netcard inf option>* has been specified in the [*<Detect Adapters Section>*] or the [*<Install Adapters Section>*] of the UNATTEND.TXT file. You can find these values by parsing the appropriate OEMNADXX.INF or OEMSETUP.INF file for the network card. Or you can look in the registry of a Windows NT machine with the adapter already installed and functioning properly. Use REGEDT32.EXE and look in:

```
HKEY_LOCAL_MACHINE\system\currentcontrolset\services\
<%netcardkeyname%>X
```

where X = *1* or ordinal of adapter installed. In this key, look at the parameter's key and note the values. Note: All values in the registry appear as hexadecimal but they are converted to decimal in your UNATTEND.TXT file. For instance, the value of IOBaseAddress =0x300 in the registry must be set to IOBaseAddress = 768 in the answer file. Example:

[EE16Params]

!AutoNetInterfaceType = 1

Transceiver = 3

!AutoNetBusNumber = 0

IoChannelReady = 2

IoBaseAddress = 768

InterruptNumber = 10

[<Protocols Section>]

This section contains a list of .INF file options for network protocols and the corresponding UNATTEND.TXT file section in which the parameters for the particular protocol are listed.

NBF

Value: <Netbeui Parameters>

Indicates that NetBEUI should be installed in unattended mode. The corresponding parameter section must exist or Setup fails.

NWLNKIPX

Value: <IPX Parameters>

Indicates that IPX should be installed in unattended mode. The corresponding parameter section must exist or Setup fails.

TC

Value: <Tcpip Parameters>

This key indicates that TCP/IP should be installed in unattended mode. The corresponding parameter section must exist or Setup fails.

DLC

Value: <DLC Parameters>

This key indicates that DLC should be installed in unattended mode. The corresponding parameter section must exist or Setup fails.

```
RASPPTP   (Point to Point Protocol)
```

```
Value: <Ras PTPP Parameters
```

Indicates that RAS Point-to-Point Protocol should be installed in unattended mode. The corresponding parameter section must exist or Setup fails.

```
STREAMS
```

```
Value: <Streams parameters>
```

Indicates that STREAMS should be installed in unattended mode. The corresponding parameter section must exist or Setup fails.

```
ATALK   (Apple talk protocol)
```

```
Value: <ATALK parameters>
```

Indicates that Apple-Talk Protocol should be installed in unattended mode. The corresponding parameter section must exist or Setup fails.

[<NetBEUI Parameters>]

This parameter is left empty because NetBEUI does not require any extra parameters to be installed.

[<IPX Parameters>]

This parameter is left empty because IPX does not require any extra parameters to be installed.

[<TCPIP Parameters>]

DHCP

Value: Yes | No

Specifies whether Dynamic Host Configuration Protocol (DHCP) should be used.

ScopeID

Value: <scope ID>

Specifies the computer's scope identifier if required on a network that uses NetBIOS over TCP/IP. If DHCP = *No*, the following keys must be specified:

IPAddress

Value: <IP address>

Used to specify the IP address for the computer.

Subnet

Value: <subnet address>

Specifies the subnet mask address.

Gateway

Value: <gateway address>

Identifies the default gateway address for the computer.

DNSServer

Value: <IP Addresses>

Used to specify up to 3 DNS servers.

```
WINSPrimary
```

```
Value: <IP Address>
```

Used to specify the IP address of the primary WINS server.

```
WINSSecondary
```

```
Value: <IP address>
```

Used to specify the IP address of the secondary WINS server.

```
DNSName
```

```
Value: <DNS domain name>
```

This key is used to specify the DNS domain name.

[<Services Section>]

```
NETMON
```

```
Value: <Netmon Parameters section>
```

Points to <Netmon Parameters>.

```
STCPIP
```

```
Value: <Simple TCPIP Parameters section>
```

Points to <Simple TCPIP Parameters>.

```
TCPPRINT
```

```
Value: <TCPIP Printing Parameters section>
```

Points to <TCPIP Printing Parameters>.

```
INETSTP
```

```
Value: <Internet server parameters section>
```

Points to <Internet server parameters>.

```
SAP

Value: <SAP Parameters section>
```

Points to <SAP Parameters>.

```
SNMP

Value: <Snmp Parameters>
```

Points to <Snmp Parameters>.

```
RAS

Value: <Ras Parameters>
```

Points to <Ras Parameters>.

```
NWWKSTA

Value: <NetWare Client Parameters>
```

Points to <NetWare Client Parameters>.

[Netmon Parameters Section]

No values are needed here but the section header must exist for the service to install.

[Simple TCPIP Parameters Section]

No values are needed here but the section header must exist for the service to install.

[TCPIP Printing Parameters Section]

No values are needed here but the section header must exist for the service to install.

[SAP Parameters Section]

No values are needed here but the section header must exist for the service to install.

[<NetWare Client Parameters>]

```
!DefaultLocation
```

```
Value: <server_location>
```

This identifies the default logon server for the NetWare client. For NDS logins use this syntax: !DefaultLocation = "*ABC\MARKETING.US."

```
!DefaultScriptOptions
```

```
Values: 0 | 1 | 3
```

Defines the default action to perform with scripts. *0* implies that no scripts will be run, *1* indicates that only NetWare 3.x-level scripts will be run, and *3* implies that either NetWare 3.x or NetWare 4.x-level scripts can be run.

```
[<Snmp Parameters>]
```

```
Accept_CommunityName
```

```
Value: <community names>
```

Specifies a maximum of three community names from which the computer on which the Simple Network Management Protocol (SNMP) service is running accepts traps. Separate the *<community names>* with commas.

Send_Authentication

Value: Yes | No

This indicates whether an authentication trap should be sent when an unauthorized community or host requests information.

Any_Host

Value: Yes | No

This specifies whether the computer on which the SNMP service is being installed should accept SNMP packets from any host.

Limit_Host

Values: <host names>

You can specify up to three *<host names>*, separated by commas. This key is valid when Any_Host = *No*.

Community_Name

Value: <community name>

Indicates the *<community name>* for the computer.

Traps

Values: <IP addresses> | <IPX addresses>

Use this to specify up to three IP or IPX addresses to which traps should be sent.

Contact_Name

Value: <name>

Use this to specify the computer user's name.

```
Location
```

```
Value: <computer location>
```

Use this to specify the physical location of the computer.

```
Service
```

```
Values: Physical, Applications, Datalink, Internet, End-to-End.
```

Any combination of the five SNMP services listed here can be specified as values. They must be separated by commas.

[<RasParameters>]

```
PortSections
```

```
Values: <port section name>
```

Use this to define a port section name. You can specify multiple port section names but they must be separated by commas. See *[<port section names>]* definition below.

```
DialoutProtocols
```

```
Value: TCP/IP | IPX | NETBEUI | ALL
```

ALL implies all installed protocols.

```
DialinProtocols
```

```
Value: TCP/IP | IPX | NETBEUI | ALL
```

ALL implies all installed protocols.

NetBEUIClientAccess

Value: Network | ThisComputer

The default is *Network*.

TcpIpClientAccess

Value: Network | ThisComputer

The default is *Network*.

UseDHCP

Value: YES | NO

The default is *Yes*.

StaticAddressBegin

Value: <IP_address>

This key is required if UseDHCP = *NO*.

StaticAddressEnd

Value: <IP_address>

This key is required if UseDHCP = *NO*.

ExcludeAddress

Value: <IP_address1 - IP_address2>

Use this to exclude a range of IP addresses when you are assigning a range of IP addresses manually. It requires that StaticAddressBegin and StaticAddressEnd be specified already.

```
ClientCanRequestIPAddress
```

Value: YES | NO

The default is *No*.

```
IpxClientAccess
```

Value: Network | ThisComputer

The default is *Network*.

```
AutomaticNetworkNumbers
```

Value: YES | NO

The default is *YES*.

```
NetworkNumberFrom
```

Value: <IPX_net_number>

Valid numbers range from 1 to 0xFFFFFFFE. This key is required if
AutomaticNetworkNumbers = *NO*.

```
AssignSameNetworkNumber
```

Value: YES | NO

The default is *YES*.

```
ClientsCanRequestIpxNodeNumber
```

Value: YES | NO

The default is *NO*.

[<port section name>]

PortName

Value: COM1 | COM2 | COM3-COM25

Indicates the names of the ports to be configured in a particular port section.

DeviceType

Value: Modem

This key indicates the type of device RAS should install. Currently, the only available device type is a modem.

PortUsage

Value: DialOut | DialIn | DialInOut

This defines the dialing properties for the ports being configured.

MS-DOS Utilities

SHOWMENU

This makes it easy to create interactive menus within a batch file environment. Menu items are passed to SHOWMENU as parameters and the user selects the appropriate item using the cursor. The items can be stored in an environment variable, aiding clarity of script.

```
Syntax:
```

```
SHOWMENU Choice1 [Choice2] [Choice3] .. [/E=VarName]
```

If **/E** switch is not specified, MS-DOS ErrorLEVEL is set to the choice sequence number. ErrorLEVEL is set to *0* if the menu terminated with escape.

If the **/E** is specified, an environment variable [VarName] is created and contains value of user-selected item. ErrorLEVEL is set to *27* if the menu terminated with escape. Here is an example:

```
SHOWMENU A B /E=choice
```

```
IF ERRORLEVEL 27 GOTO exit
```

```
IF %choice% == A GOTO getNetInfo
```

```
IF %choice% == B GOTO getCDROMInfo
```

GETLINE

This enables easy retrieval of keyboard input within a batch file environment. User response is stored in an environment variable, aiding clarity of script.

```
Syntax:
```

```
GetLine
[Prompt][/L=n][/D=String][/I=String][/X=string][/U][/P][/E=VarName]
```

```
[Prompt] = Optional input prompt, displayed prior to accepting input.
```

[/L] = Defines maximum length of input string.

[/D] = Provides a default response.

[/X] = Defines prohibited ASCII characters.

[/I] = Defines allowed ASCII characters.

[/P] = Private input (no echo).

If the **/E** switch is specified, an environment variable [VarName] is created that contains the value of user input. If Escape is pressed, the environment variable is not changed. An MS-DOS ErrorLevel of *0* on exit signifies the environment has been changed.

If the **/E** switch is not specified, the MS-DOS ErrorLEVEL is set to the first letter of the response, or *0* if Escape was pressed. Here is an example:

```
GETLINE Computer Name:   /L=10 /E=CNAME
```

SET_INI!

SET_INI! enables modification of text files stored in .INI format from within a batch file.

Syntax:

```
Set_ini! IniFileSpec [Section] "Parameter=Value"
```

```
IniFileSpec - Complete DOS path to the '.INI' file which will be
modified.
```

[Section] - Represents the section within the '.INI' file which will be modified.

"Parameter=Value" - Section parameter which will be modified.

NOTES:

- If no parameter value is specified (for example: *Parameter=*) the line is removed from file.
- [Section] is optional, enabling the utility to be used with non .INI files.
- New sections are added at the end of the .INI file.
- New parameters are added at the beginning of the section.

Here is an example:

```
SET_INI! %ANSFILE% [UserData] "ComputerName = %CNAME%"
```

SCRIPTIT

ScriptIT is a command-line utility for automating interactive software installations and system configuration tasks. It automates any traditional window or dialog interaction by sending keystrokes from a specially defined script file to the window or dialog that requires automation.

ScriptIT uses a script file to determine the sequence of keyboard events it will generate and the windows into which it will insert keystrokes. The example below illustrates a simple ScriptIT script that opens Notepad, types *Hello* and saves the file as C:\TEST.TXT:

```
[SCRIPT]

run=NOTEPAD.EXE

Untitled - Notepad=Hello

Untitled - Notepad=!FA

Save As=C:\TEST.TXT+{ENTER}
```

ScriptIT scripts are simple text files that must begin with a section labeled [SCRIPT]. A list of values/parameters that (with the exception of *run*) relate to window name/keyboard action begins on page 678.

In the above example, ScriptIT runs the notepad executable, and waits for the presence of a window called "Untitled – Notepad". When this is found, ScriptIT sends five keystrokes (which represent the word hello) to that window. It repeats this process on the next line, sending the key sequence <ALT>FA (activating the *File->Save AS* keyboard shortcut), then ENTER.

Once a script file has been generated, ScriptIT can process it simply by specifying it as a command-line parameter. For example: SCRIPTIT EXAMPLE.TXT.

As the example script shows, ScriptIT can simulate the use of all keys on the PC keyboard, including the non-printable characters. The tables below list various key-to-value translations.

Control and shift keys.

Key	Precede with
Alt key	!
Control key	^
Shift key	+

Key-to-value translations.

Key	SendKey equivalent	Description
~	{~}	Sends a tilde (~)
!	{!}	Sends an exclamation point (!)
^	{^}	Sends a caret (^)
+	{+}	Sends a plus sign (+)
{	{ { }	Sends a left brace ({)
}	{ } }	Sends a right brace (})
Alt	{ALT}	Sends an alt keystroke
Backspace	{BACKSPACE} or {BS}	Sends a backspace keystroke
Clear	{CLEAR}	Clears the field
Delete	{DELETE} or {DEL}	Sends a delete keystroke
Down arrow	{DOWN}	Sends a down arrow keystroke

Key-to-value translations.   *(continued)*

Key	SendKey equivalent	Description
End	{END}	Sends an end keystroke
Enter	{ENTER} or ~	Sends an enter keystroke
Escape	{ESCAPE} or {ESC}	Sends an esc keystroke
F1 through F16	{F1} through {F16}	Sends the appropriate function keystroke
Help	{HELP}	Sends a help (F1) keystroke
Home	{HOME}	Sends a home keystroke.
Insert	{INSERT} or {INS}	Sends an insert keystroke
Left arrow	{LEFT}	Sends a left arrow keystroke
Page down	{PGDN}	Sends a page down keystroke
Page up	{PGUP}	Sends a page up keystroke
Right arrow	{RIGHT}	Sends a right arrow keystroke
Space	{SPACE} or {SP}	Sends a spacebar keystroke
Tab	{TAB}	Sends a tab keystroke
Up arrow	{UP}	Sends an up arrow keystroke

Sending Window Commands

In addition to sending keystrokes, ScriptIT has several commands that enable it to determine or change the state of a given window. For example, the following script runs Notepad, then hides the window:

```
[SCRIPT]

run=NOTEPAD.EXE

Untitled - Notepad=~WINHIDE
```

Additional ScriptIT window-based commands.

Tilde command	Description
~exit	Exits the script immediately. For example: `Untitled - Notepad=~exit` Tells your script to exit when it sees the **Untitled—Notepad** window.
~wait	Causes a five-second delay in the execution of the script.
~winwaitactive	By default, if a window exists (hidden or visible) ScriptIT attempts to send keystrokes to it, even if it isn't ready to accept input. This command causes ScriptIT to pause execution until the specified window receives the focus. For example: `Untitled - Notepad=~winwaitactive#Hello` Causes ScriptIT to wait until the Untitled—Notepad window gets the focus. Once that happens, the script continues by sending the string "Hello" to the Notepad window. This feature is useful when a window exists but it is not ready to receive keystrokes because the setup program is busy doing something else, such as copying files.

Additional ScriptITwindow-based commands.   *(continued)*

Tilde command	Description
~winwaitclose	Causes the script to pause until the window is closed. For example: `Setup=~winwaitclose` Causes the script to pause until the **Setup** window closes. This is very useful when setup programs have multiple windows open. ScriptIT tries to continue when it sees a window title that it needs to send keystrokes to; however, a previous step may not have finished. Using `~winwaitclose` allows you to pause the script until the previous step completes.
~winclose	Causes ScriptIT to close the window and terminate the executable that created it. For example: `Untitled—Notepad=~winclose` Causes ScriptIT to shut down the Notepad instance that created that window.
~winhide	Causes ScriptIT to make the specified window invisible. For example: `Untitled - Notepad=~winhide` Causes ScriptIT to hide the window titled **Untitled—Notepad**. The window is still there, but the user cannot see it.

Additional ScriptITwindow-based commands.   *(continued)*

Tilde command	Description
~winshow	Causes ScriptIT to show the specified window if it is currently hidden. For example: `Untitled - Notepad=~winshow` Causes ScriptIT to make the hidden **Untitled—Notepad** window visible again.
~winmin	Causes ScriptIT to display the specified window as an icon. For example: `Untitled - Notepad=~winmin` Causes ScriptIT to minimize the specified **Notepad** window.
~winmax	Causes ScriptIT to display the specified window as a full-screen window. For example: `Untitled - Notepad=~winmax` Causes ScriptIT to maximize the specified **Notepad** window.

You can find more detailed information on ScriptIT and a copy of the software at http://www.microsoft.com/ntserver.

Just a Little More Before You Head out the Door

Yes, you have been a diligent reader, and no doubt a faithful systems administrator. Long gone are the days when you were a Senior Systems Analyst and you could spill your soft drink on your keyboard and not a soul would know. Maybe right now you're refining your skills, sitting back at your desk tapping your monitor's screen with your big toe as you read this book. But no matter where you are in the IT food chain, there are always problems to solve. Maybe your support staff is frustrated with too many users who need immediate help but can't seem to provide *any* information useful in troubleshooting their problem. Maybe an integration project is about to be dropped in your lap: incorporate the network of your company's latest acquisition into the enterprise network. They use *what*? What happened to those good old days? Long gone.

The first section of this book delved into setting up a management infrastructure using SMS. This last section goes a little deeper, providing detail on how to use SMS more effectively. Chapter 12 describes two simple issues and provides tools for configuring remote control settings and getting the right information to help desk staff. Chapter 13 looks at the workaround procedure for configuring a Novell 4.1*x* server to function as an SMS logon and distribution server.

C H A P T E R   1 2

Simple Management Tools at Magnificent Bank

*By Rick Varvel,
MCS—Portland*

Chapter 1 looked at setting up operational procedures in your organization, outlining best practices in running an efficient network. Chapter 2 stepped back and looked at a Microsoft Systems Management Server (SMS) deployment, using site hierarchy to inventory hardware and software and distribute packages while minimizing bandwidth utilization. But what happens on the day-to-day level as you *tune* your management infrastructure? This chapter describes two simple issues and the tools to troubleshoot them: getting unique SMS computer (machine) IDs and adjusting client remote control settings. Microsoft Consulting Services (MCS) developed both the GetSMSID and RCPATCH tools while working with Magnificent Bank to streamline network management.

In Focus

Enterprise
Magnificent Bank, based in Tombstone, Arizona, has over 150 branch offices throughout the Southwest and Mexico.

Network
Branch offices connect over a wide area network (WAN), with 3200 users sharing 1500 computers.

Challenge
Effectively managing the network remotely while minimizing support needed to configure SMS clients, and the potential errors introduced by end user modifications.

Solution
Magnificent Bank used the GetSMSID and RCPATCH tools created by MCS.

What You'll Find In This Chapter

- **Description and steps for using GetSMSID—a tool that end users can use to get SMS-related information.**

- **Description and steps for using RCPATCH—a tool for changing the remote control settings.**

Warning This chapter makes recommendations for tuning the Windows NT registry using the Registry Editor. Using the Registry Editor incorrectly can cause serious, system-wide problems that require you to reinstall Windows NT. Microsoft cannot guarantee that any problems resulting from the use of Registry Editor can be solved. Use this tool at your own risk.

Determining SMS Unique IDs Using GetSMSID

SMS administrators and helpdesk staff need to know each computer's SMS unique ID (SMSID) in order to inventory hardware and software, distribute packages, troubleshoot, and so forth. If you distribute GetSMSID to each desktop, end users can determine at a glance their computer's SMS unique ID, the SMS domain, and other SMS-related information to assist helpdesk staff in troubleshooting the SMS client's installation.

SMS 1.2 identifies each computer in the SMS database using a unique number, which is stored in C:\SMS.INI under the [SMS] section:

```
[SMS]

BuildNo=786

SPNumber=0

INIFileVersion=66302

CopyListVersion=835643765

SiteCode=SKZ

SMS Unique ID=SKZ01234

SMSPath=C:\MS\SMS
```

SMS uses the SMSID to target computers for software distribution, among other things. In most cases a computer has only one user, so it is possible to send software to either a group of SMSIDs or a group of users based on an SMS machine group or query. However, if a computer has multiple users, SMS lists *only the last user to logon,* making it impossible to distribute software reliably by user name.

This can be an issue for companies (such as utility companies, hospitals, and banks) that have hundreds of computers that are shared by multiple users operating on different shifts. By running GetSMSID on each of these computers, you can target computers for software distribution regardless of who has or is logged on.

Another common daily management scenario is troubleshooting remote control problems (see also the "Adjusting SMS Remote Control Settings Using RCPATCH" section on page 691), which often are related to Internet protocol (IP) addressing issues. GetSMSID can determine the computer's current IP address, which you can then compare with the SMS inventory database, confirming consistency. The Help Desk could ask end users to use the PING utility from a command prompt to get the address, but users often consider this an "advanced" technique beyond the scope of their *perceived* abilities.

In addition, GetSMSID also reports (see the interface in Figure 12.1):

- SMS domain name
- SMS service pack installed on the client
- SMS client setup phase
- Current SMS logon server
- Amount of free disk space
- Computer name
- Domain Name System (DNS) host name and domain names

The SMS domain name is unrelated to the DNS domain name.

Figure 12.1 GetSMSID client configuration.

Requirements for GetSMSID

GetSMSID is a 32-bit Windows application written with Microsoft Visual Basic 5.0, and does not run on Windows 3.1or Windows for Workgroups because they are 16-bit environments. It has been successfully tested on Windows 98 and Windows 2000 Beta2 but not deployed on either platform. (You can find a copy of GetSMSID on the companion CD, under the \SMSTools\GetSMSID directory.) To produce accurate results, you must have:

- SMS.INI installed on your C drive.
- An active network connection.
- IP loaded.
- Visual Basic 5.0 runtime file (MSVBVM50.DLL) in Path or in the same directory as GetSMSID or GetSMSIDnoip (see the next section: "If Obtaining IP Addresses Causes Problems").

Note In order to obtain the service pack number, setup phase condition, or current logon server information, you must have SMS build 786 because previous versions of SMS did not record this information in SMS.INI.

In addition to Magnificent Bank, the tool is currently being used by several large enterprises and has been tested on the Windows 95 and Windows NT 4.0 platforms. It has been distributed successfully in the following ways:

- Pushed out to the client via SMS or a logon script
- Distributed as an e-mail attachment or link
- Run from a server

The last option works well for situations in which the client does not have MSVBVM50.DLL installed locally. To use the "Run from server" option, simply copy MSVBVM50.DLL and GetSMSID (or GetSMSIDnoip—see below for details) files into a shared directory on a file server and then inform users how to connect to the share and run either GetSMSID or GetSMSIDnoip depending on their hardware platform.

If Obtaining IP Address Causes Problems

The IP address is obtained using the VB 5 Winsock control. If for some reason the IP address information does not appear or is inaccurate, you can use a second version of the program, GetSMSIDnoip.EXE (also found on the companion CD, under the \SMSTools\GetSMSID directory).

Adjusting SMS Remote Control Settings Using RCPATCH

SMS remote control settings provide the ability for you to troubleshoot and assist users *remotely,* but they need to be configured properly. Changing the default remote control settings in an SMS client requires end users to use the Help Desk application that ships with SMS because there is no automated method of modifying the settings. Unfortunately, end users can make these changes incorrectly, requiring valuable support time and resources to fix them.

RCPATCH allows you to avoid this by creating an SMS package and job to automate the process of changing remote control settings. The benefits include:

- Reducing the time required to alter default remote control settings
- Helping to create and maintain consistent remote control settings for a large group of computers
- Modifying features not supported by default

Caution This section provides procedures, files, and information on modifying SMS remote control settings as a technical example—*only knowledgeable personnel should follow the steps outlined.* It is recommended that you thoroughly test the automated remote control changes prior to production use.

Using RCPATCH

RCPATCH is a 32-bit application that can be used to modify the settings in the SMS.INI [Sight] section in both Windows 95 and Windows NT workstations. If your organization uses Windows NT Workstation 4.0 and also limits user access to the file system, you must install SMS Service Pack 2 or later on the server and *create two blank files* on each workstation to run SMS on these computers. Name these **SMS.INI** and **SMS.NEW** and set them with read/write access. RCPATCH and SMS use these two files as though they resided on an Windows NT 4.0 workstation that does not have the root of drive C: set to read-only access.

SMS remote control settings are determined by the values stored in the [Sight] section of the SMS.INI file. RCPATCH makes a line-by-line comparison of the settings in the [Sight] section of SMS.INI and the settings in the [Sight] section of RCPATCH.TXT. If they are the same, the original line is written; otherwise the line in RCPATCH.TXT is written, resulting in an SMS.INI file that contains a [Sight] section matching the RCPATCH.TXT contents.

To implement RCPATCH:

1. Use NOTEPAD or another text editor to modify the RCPATCH.TXT file to reflect the settings you want.
2. Create a directory and copy RCPATCH.EXE, RCPATCH.TXT, and RCPATCH.BAT to that directory.
3. Create an SMS package pointing to RCPATCH.BAT.
4. Create an SMS job to distribute the package created in Step 3.

Note RCPATCH.TXT must be placed in the same directory as Windows. Type **rcpatch /?** (from a command prompt) for instructions.

Using the Sample Installation Files

You can find the sample files on the companion CD under the \SMSTools\RCPatch directory. RCPATCH.TXT and RCPATCH.BAT are included for reference. In some cases you can use them as is, but in most cases you will need to modify them.

- RCPATCH.EXE
- RCPATCH.TXT (change settings in this file to reflect your required remote control settings)
- RCPATCH.BAT (sample .BAT file that can be used to create an SMS package)

If you use a .BAT file to call RCPATCH.EXE and it does not display anything on the screen, you can use Package Command Manager (running as a service on Windows NT workstations) to push RCPATCH out as a background task. The sample RCPATCH.BAT file included on the companion CD has been tested in such an environment.

More Information

Information Related to GetSMSID

- See Dan Appleman's *Programmer's Guide to the Win32* API, especially Chapter 4: VB5INI Application Example. Although not expressly geared to VBA developers, this book (published by Ziff-Davis Press) is a solid resource for any application developer who wants to call functions in the Windows API from any dialect of BASIC.

See these items on TechNet:

- Q160215, Title: HOWTO: Obtain the Host IP address Using Windows Sockets.
- Q145679, Title: HOWTO: Use the Registry API to Save and Retrieve Settings.
- Q178755, Title: HOWTO: Enumerate the Values of a Registry Key.

Information Related to RCPATCH

See these items on TechNet:

- "Windows NT 4.0 Remote Troubleshooting and Diagnostics."
- "Automated Client Upgrade Process For Windows 95 and Windows NT Workstation 4.0 Through Systems Management Server."
- *Microsoft Systems Management Server 1.2 Reviewer's Guide*.
- *Microsoft Systems Management Server 1.2 Resource Guide*, "Troubleshooting Remote Control."
- *Microsoft Systems Management Server 1.2 Resource Guide*, Chapter 11, "Working with Remote Control."
- Q191441, Title: Systems Management Server 1.2 Service Pack 4 Fixlist.
- Q153825, Title: List of Fixed Bugs in Systems Management Server Version 1.2.
- Q161216, Title: SMS: Client Setup Fails to Update Sms.ini on Windows NT System.
- Q123317, Title: SMS: Enabling Help Desk Options from Logon Servers Unsupported.
- *Systems Management Server Tools and Utilities* "Updated Tracer Utility— SMSTRACE.EXE."
- Q170440, Title: SMS: Remote Controlling a Multihomed Windows NT Client Computer.

C H A P T E R   1 3

Managing and Integrating a Legacy Novell NetWare 4.1*x* Environment with SMS at All-Terrain Trucking

By Rick Varvel, MCS—Portland

This chapter looks at how All-Terrain Trucking integrated Microsoft Systems Management Server (SMS) into their Novell NDS environment to help with hardware and software inventory collection, software distribution, and remote control. Although SMS 1.2 supports Novell 3.*x* servers as both SMS logon and distribution servers, this capability does not extend to Novell 4.1*x* servers, and All-Terrain Trucking had versions of both. This chapter provides techniques developed by MCS for configuring 4.1*x* server so that it appears as a 3.*x* server to SMS.

In Focus

Enterprise
All-Terrain Trucking, based in Tallahassee, Florida, supports operations in 24 branch offices throughout the eastern seaboard and mid-Atlantic states.

Network
A mix of 5000 desktop computers and 65 servers spread across a central location and 24 branch offices. Hub-and-spoke network connected over frame relay.

Challenge
Maintaining software and hardware inventory, performing remote troubleshooting and distributing software packages to Microsoft Windows 9*x* and Windows NT 4.0 clients over an integrated network containing Microsoft and Novell NetWare 4.1*x* servers without replacing the branch office Novell servers.

Solution
Configure Novell 4.1*x* servers to function as SMS logon and distribution servers.

What You'll Find In This Chapter

- **Steps for configuring a Novell 4.1x server as an SMS logon server.**

- **Steps for configuring the Windows NT environment.**

- **Best practices for configuring SMS 1.2.**

- **Configuration troubleshooting tips.**

Preliminary Notes

Caution To configure a Novell 4.1*x* server to support Systems Management Server, you must carefully plan and implement modifications to the Novell logon scripts and other system-related files.

Even when a Novell 4.1*x* server is successfully configured as an SMS logon server, these issues remain:

- Windows NT workstations running the Novell client and processing Novell logon scripts cannot run the SMS portion of the logon script (SMSLS.SCR), which means they cannot be inventoried in this way.

  To correct this, you can run RUNSMS.BAT manually from a Novell 4.1*x* or a Windows NT Server, or you can configure workstations to logon to a Windows NT Server and process the SMS portion of a Windows NT logon script (SMSLS.BAT).

- If you set up Windows NT workstation clients to run RUNSMS.BAT from a Novell server, you must also change site properties.

- Program Group Control does not work from a Novell *4.1x* server.

- Microsoft Technical Support does not officially support the configuration outlined in this article.

Profile of All-Terrain Trucking

All-Terrain Trucking wanted to set up SMS 1.2 in its Novell 4.1*x* NDS environment to collect inventory from 5,000 desktops. The network consists of two primary locations separated by T3 links, and 24 remote offices connected by frame relay running at approximately 768 Kbps each. One Novell server in each location (26 in all) is designated as an SMS logon server, *but only two* of the 26 (PDX01 and PDX02, in the primary sites—see Figure 13.1) are configured to be SMS distribution servers. A third distribution server resides on SMS01.

All Novell SMS logon servers run version 4.11, but the techniques outlined in this chapter apply to any Novell 4.1*x* server. The basic steps are covered in the "Configuring the Novell 4.1*x* NDS Environment," "Configuring the Windows NT Environment," and "Configuring SMS 1.2 sections."

Except for 150 PCs in the information technology (IT) department, all computers run Windows 95 with the Novell Client32 configured as *the primary* networking client, and the Client for Microsoft Networks as the secondary. The IT department computers run Windows NT 4.0, using the Microsoft Novell Client as the primary networking client and the Client for Microsoft Networks as the secondary.

PCs running Windows NT workstation process the Novell logon script but are redirected to a Windows NT server (the SMS central site) to execute the SMS inventory process.

All Windows NT users are located in a single master account domain and SMS is configured in a separate resource domain. Since Exchange is used for e-mail, all users have both a Novell and a Windows NT account. All inventory information is stored on a single SMS central site server. (Server configuration details are detailed in the remainder of this chapter.)

Windows NT 4.0 workstations use SMS01 as a distribution server; Windows 95 computers use either PDX01 or PDX02, depending on their location. All-Terrain Trucking has some Windows for Workgroup computers, but network administrators did not add them to the inventory because they are phasing out these older clients.

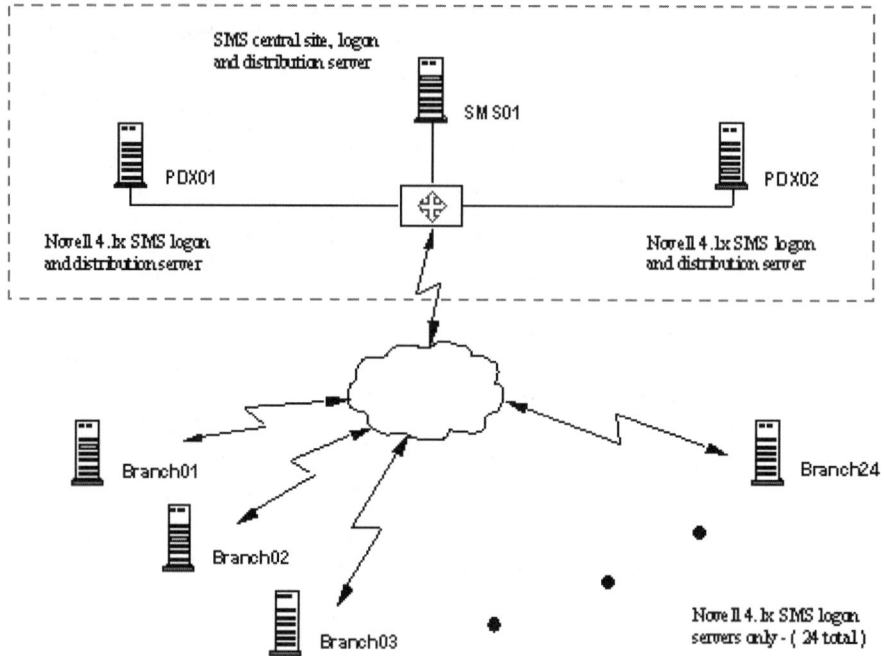

Figure 13.1 All-Terrain Trucking SMS configuration.

Configuring the Novell 4.1*x* NDS Environment

Because SMS 1.2 supports Novell 3.*x* servers as both logon and distribution servers, but does not support Novell 4.1*x* servers, you have to configure the Novell 4.1*x* server to operate in "bindery mode" so that it *appears as a* 3.*x* server to SMS. This section covers the configuration steps to do this. If you have multiple Novell 4.1*x* servers, you need to perform all steps on each of them *except* for modifying SMSLS.SCR. Changes to SMSLS.SCR are made on the SMS site server and replicated to each Novell SMS logon server during the SMS site maintenance cycle. If you want a Novell 4.1*x* server to function as a distribution server as well, use the logon server configuration steps, then send out an SMS job to place a package on it as you would for a Windows NT distribution server.

Configuring a Novell *4.1x* server as an SMS logon server is probably the most difficult of the three sections because it contains numerous small details, any of which can cause the process to fail if performed incorrectly or out of sequence.

Designating Novell Servers as SMS Logon Servers

This step is subject to basic SMS architecture design principles. Keep in mind that SMS logon servers require maintenance overhead, so it is a good idea to have as few as possible. For example, if 26 remote logon servers are connected to the primary site server on 56-Kbps lines, the primary site server takes more than an hour to cycle through all logon servers to verify that all SMS support files are intact. The more time spent on this frequent process, the less is available for other things such as package creation, job distribution, and reporting. Minimize SMS logon servers unless you have numerous remote offices, each with numerous users: in this case placing an SMS logon server at each remote location will improve performance.

Under normal operation, each client downloads about 2 MB of inventory information each time it connects to an SMS logon server, which can take 5 to 10 minutes over a 56-Kbps link. Utilities such as SKIPINV.EXE, from the *Microsoft BackOffice Resource Kit, Second Edition,* can reduce this time to seconds by detecting whether it is an inventory day and foregoing the download if is not. Changing the inventory-scanning interval from weekly to monthly also helps.

Establishing a *3.x* Bindery Context

Novell NDS users log on to a hierarchical organizational database rather than to an individual server database (as they did with Novell 3.*x*). A user's location in the tree is called a **context** (the full path to the container in which an object is valid). For instance, in Figure 13.2 the user account ALEX is valid in the context of .SALES.MYCO. The table below defines common NDS bindery terms.

Common NDS terminology.

Leaf object	An object such as a server, user, printer, etc. Leaf objects cannot contain other leaf objects or other containers.
Container	A unit holding different types of objects such as organizational units (OUs) and leaf objects.
Organization container (O)	The top level container. There is usually only one organization container per NDS tree.
Organizational unit container (OU)	There can be multiple OUs per organization and they can be nested. OUs can contain leaf objects but not O containers.
Context	The full path to the container in which an object is valid. For example, in Figure 13.2, SALES.MYCO is considered the context in which the user account ALEX is valid.
Partition	A logical representation of a portion of the NDS database.
Replica	A physical representation of one or more partitions residing on a Novell 4.1*x* server.

Novell 3.*x* databases are called **binderies**. For applications such as SMS that are designed to communicate with them, Novell NDS supports a **bindery context**, which presents the Novell 4.1*x* server to SMS as if it were a Novell 3.*x* server. The bindery context is usually entered in the form **.GroupOU.DepartmentOU.Organization**, but it can also be set higher or lower in the tree. For instance, in Figure 13.2, .DEV.IS.MYCO, PDX.DEV.IS.MYCO and IS.MYCO are all potentially valid bindery contexts.

In order to set a bindery context on a Novell 4.1*x* server, the server must contain a replica of one or more partitions, each of which represents the portion of the NDS hierarchy you want to associate a bindery context with.

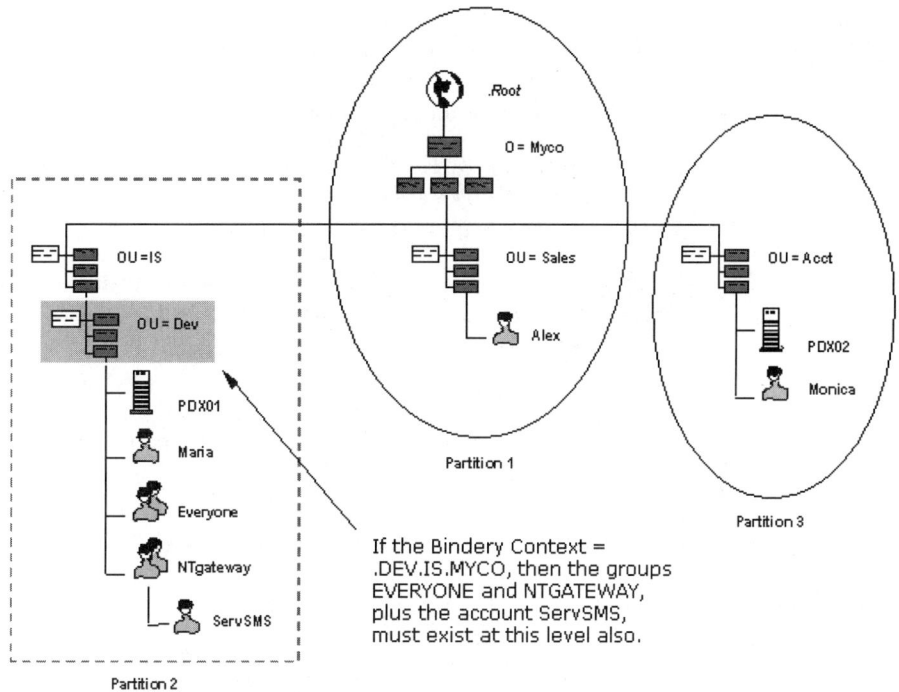

Figure 13.2 Bindery context example.

In this example, if server PDX01 contains a replica of Partition 1 and 2, and server PDX02 has a replica only of Partition 3, the valid bindery contexts are:

For PDX01

- .DEV.IS.MYCO
- .IS.MYCO
- .MYCO
- .SALES.MYCO

For PDX02

- .ACCT.MYCO

A Novell 4.1*x* server configured as an SMS logon server must have a replica of the partition that contains the NDS context you are trying to set a bindery context for. Each bindery context points to a specific context within the NDS hierarchy.

In Figure 13.2, PDX01 is the Novell 4.1*x* server, and .DEV.IS.MYCO is the context where the user (Maria) to be inventoried exists. The various SMS/GSNW user and support groups are also created in .DEV.IS.MYCO.

A bindery context is not inclusive (it does not flow down the tree); it is effective only for the context in which you set it. For instance, it you set the bindery context in Figure 13.2 to .IS.MYCO instead of .DEV.IS.MYCO, Maria would not be able to participate in the SMS inventory process because SMS would connect to the Novell 4.1*x* server in the context of .IS.MYCO, and Maria is a member of .DEV.IS.MYCO, and bindery context is not inherited.

Although bindery contexts are not inclusive, you can combine the ones you set on a server into a single bindery by entering them on the same line and separating them with a semicolon.

For example, to have both Alex and Maria (Figure 13.2) participate in an SMS inventory the following conditions must be true:

- Server PDX01 has a replica of both Partition 1 and Partition 2.

- The command SET BINDERY CONTEXT = .MYCO;.DEV.IS.MYCO;.SALES.MYCO is run on server PDX01.

- The appropriate SMS service account and support groups are configured in the bindery context (this topic is discussed in detail in following sections).

To decide where to set the bindery context, determine the NDS context(s) for all user leaf objects that will participate in SMS inventory. For example, on the Novell 4.1*x* SMS logon server:

- SET BINDERY CONTEXT = .MYCO prevents Maria and Alex from participating in the SMS inventory because they are in the DEV and SALES containers respectively, and therefore not visible to SMS.

- SET BINDERY CONTEXT = .MYCO;.DEV.IS.MYCO allows only Maria to participate in the SMS inventory.

- SET BINDERY CONTEXT = .MYCO;.DEV.IS.MYCO;.SALES.MYCO allows both Maria and Alex to participate in the SMS inventory.

Creating a Bindery Context

This requires administrative privileges on each server targeted to be a Novell SMS logon server. It is easier to use an organizational administrative account to configure the server, but if this is prevented by political or security issues, then administrative access is sufficient.

Complete these steps on each server:

1. Log on to a workstation with an Admin-level account and connect to a Novell server. Open RCONSOLE and establish a connection to the Novell server on which you want to create a bindery context.
2. Enter **SET BINDERY CONTEXT=.GROUP.DEPT.ORG** and press ENTER. **GROUP** is the Novell OU that contains the users who process the SMS portion of the Novell logon script. Example: **.DEV.IS.MYCO**.

   If multiple OUs are participating in processing the script, separate them with semicolons. Example:

   ```
   SET BINDERY CONTEXT=.GROUP1.DEPT.ORG;.GROUP2.DEPT.ORG.
   ```

3. Map a drive to the SYS volume of the server you want to set the bindery context on. Edit the file AUTOEXEC.NCF and enter the line necessary to create a bindery context (the same command you entered in Step 2). Be sure to save your changes.

Note You can establish a bindery context from the command line but it is valid only for the current session—when a server reboots the bindery context is deleted. To make sure SMS remains stable, you have to modify the AUTOEXEC.NCF file and enter the necessary instructions for establishing the bindery context.

Creating a Novell Service Account

Before installing an SMS central or primary site server you need to create a service account so that SMS can access system resources. To configure a Novell server to function as an SMS logon server you need to create an identical service account (in both name and password) in the bindery context.

The account **ServSMS** is used in the bindery context example. Accounts begin with the letters **serv** so that all service accounts created on Windows NT (for example, ServSQL, ServEXCH, etc.) sort alphabetically when viewed with User Manager for Domains. You can use your existing service account as long as Windows NT and Novell have the same names and passwords.

The Novell service account must be created in the bindery context of the Novell SMS logon server; it must have a *Supervisor* equivalency and all permissions for all volumes on the server.

When you create the SMS service account on the Novell SMS logon server, *do not* enable the connection limit feature. SMS initiates and uses multiple Novell logons during the normal course of operations.

To create the SMS service account, use the NWADMIN or NETADMIN. You must use the SYSCON utility to grant Supervisor equivalency because the Supervisor object exists only in the bindery context (not in NDS). On Novell 4.1*x* servers you can't use Syscon. Instead, locate SYSCON.EXE (along with the supporting files SYS$MSG.DAT and IBM$RUN.OVL) on a Novell 3.*x* server and copy the files to the Novell SMS logon server's SYS:\Public directory.

Creating SMS Related Groups in NDS

SMS 1.2 has no concept of a Novell 4.1*x* directory database. It views each Novell SMS logon server as a separate 3.*x*-style server with its own database (bindery) and expects to communicate with it using standard Novell 3.*x* procedures.

Each Novell 3.*x* server contains a group called EVERYONE and a user account called SUPERVISOR by default. Novell 4.1*x* does not include either by default, but emulates a 3.*x* server by establishing a bindery context within the Novell 4.1*x* NDS hierarchy.

Using SYSCON, you must create two groups (NTGATEWAY and EVERYONE) in the bindery context. Gateway Services for NetWare (GSNW) running on the SMS site server uses the NTGATEWAY group to communicate with the Novell 4.1*x* server during SMS logon server configuration routine site maintenance, and when pushing out software packages.

The EVERYONE group corresponds to the same group on a Novell 3.*x* server. SMS uses this group to grant permissions to the various SMS directories created on Novell SMS logon servers. *Do not add any users to the EVERYONE group.*

Once you have created the two groups, you need to add the SMS service account to the NTGATEWAY group.

Note You must create the NTGATEWAY and EVERYONE groups within the bindery context. Example: in Figure 13.2, if your bindery context is set to **.DEV.IS.MYCON**, and you create the groups in **.IS.MYCO** or **.SALES.IS.MYCO**, then SMS cannot communicate with your Novell 4.1*x* server.

Modifying the Novell Logon Script

For a Novell 4.1*x* server to function as an SMS logon server, you must modify the script or scripts that users run when they log on to Novell. Many companies have both a system logon script and departmental logon scripts. It is more efficient to modify the script at the system level than on a container by container basis at the departmental level. Whichever method you use, add code to the Novell logon script in a portion of the script that is run by everyone (for instance, near the top of the script before any group assignments are made).

Note You can also modify these scripts by clicking **Use All Detected Servers** in the **Domain Properties** dialog box during SMS site setup but this *is not recommended* because it gives you no control over which Novell 4.1*x* servers become SMS logon servers—SMS makes every Novell server it finds an SMS logon server.

Code to Modify the Novell Server Logon Script

Use this code sample to modify the logon script for the Novell server you have designated as the SMS logon server. A detailed breakdown of each section of code (including whether the section is required or optional) is given in the sections that follow.

```
IF MEMBER OF "GP_SKIP_SMS" THEN
IF "%OS" = "WINNT" THEN
#NET USE T: \\YourNTSMSLogonServer\SMS_SHR
#T:\RUNSMS.BAT
#NET USE /D T:
ELSE
```

```
MAP ROOT T:=\\YourNovellSMSLogonServer\SYS\PUBLIC
#T:\SMSSAFE.BAT
MAP DEL T:

DOS SET SMSDRIVE="T:"
MAP %<SMSDRIVE>=YourNovellSMSLogonServer/YourNovellSMSVolume:
SET SMS_LOGON="%<SMSDRIVE>\SMS\LOGON.SRV"
INCLUDE %<SMS_LOGON>\SMSLS.SCR
DOS SET SMS_LOGON=
MAP DEL %<SMSDRIVE>
DOS SET SMSDRIVE=
END
END
```

Note Except for server-specific strings, you should enter the code exactly as it is displayed, in upper case and not indented. If you don't, the results are unpredictable. For example, testing for group membership may fail.

Code to Skip the SMS Logon Script (Optional)

Use this to handle situations where it is undesirable to run SMS inventory. Example: roaming technicians and computers that fail on inventory because of unresolved hardware conflicts.

```
IF MEMBER OF "GP_SKIP_SMS" THEN
```

Code to Collect Inventory From Windows NT Workstations (Optional)

Use this portion of code to support Windows NT workstations that log on to a Novell SMS logon server, because Windows NT workstations are not inventoried from a Novell logon script by default. You can inventory the workstations by mapping them to a Windows NT server from within a Novell logon script. Drive **T** is an example: you can use any drive letter that is valid in your environment.

```
IF "%OS" = "WINNT" THEN
#NET USE T: \\YourNTSMSLogonServer\SMS_SHR
#T:\RUNSMS.BAT
#NET USE /D T:
```

Code to Avoid Hardware Lockups (Optional)

Use this code segment to run SMSSAFE.BAT, which disables certain hardware inventory checks that are known to cause problems. If you have no known hardware conflicts this code segment is not necessary. For more information refer to section "Avoiding Lockups during Hardware Inventories" on page 712. Drive **T** is an example: you can use any drive letter that is valid in your environment.

```
MAP ROOT T:=\\YourNovellSMSLogonServer\SYS\PUBLIC
#T:\SMSSAFE.BAT
MAP DEL T:
```

Default SMS logon script (Required)

This is the default SMS logon script. It is the minimum code required to add a client to the SMS inventory database. Before you can use the logon script, you must replace each logon script variable with the value that pertains to your Novell 4.1x SMS logon server in the Domain Properties dialog box. For instance, in Figure 13.3 below the Novell SMS logon server is PDX01 and the \SMS directory structure is located on VOL1.

```
DOS SET SMSDRIVE="T:"

MAP %<SMSDRIVE>=YourNovellSMSLogonServer/YourNovellSMSVolume:

SET SMS_LOGON="%<SMSDRIVE>\SMS\LOGON.SRV"

INCLUDE %<SMS_LOGON>\SMSLS.SCR

DOS SET SMS_LOGON=

MAP DEL %<SMSDRIVE>

DOS SET SMSDRIVE=

END
```

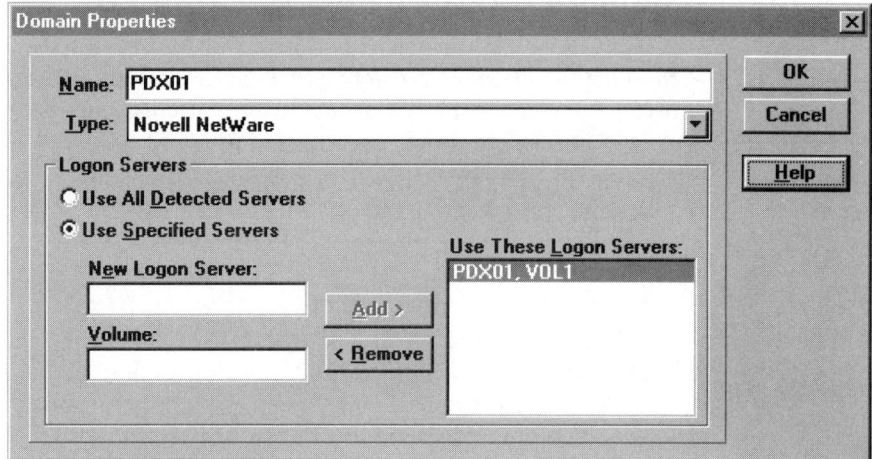

Figure 13.3 Modifying domain properties.

Examples of logon script variables.

Logon script variable	Replace with:
YourNTSMSLogonServer	The name of the SMS logon server you want Windows NT workstation users to connect to. Example: *#NET USE T: \\SMS01\SMS_SHR*
YourNovellSMSLogonServer	The name of the Novell 4.1x server you want to configure as an SMS logon server (that is: the name of the Novell 4.1x server you specify in the **Domain Properties** dialog box when configuring the SMS site to support Novell logon servers). Example: *MAP ROOT T:=\\PDX01\SYS\PUBLIC*
YourNovellSMSVolume	The name of the volume that contains the \SMS directory structure (that is: the name of the Novell 4.1x volume you specified in the **Domain Properties** dialog when configuring the SMS site to support Novell logon servers). Example: *MAP %<SMSDRIVE>=PDX01/VOL1:*

Avoiding Lockups during Hardware Inventories

A hardware inventory scan is performed when users run the SMSLS.SCR file from the Novell logon script (every 7 days by default). During this process SMS may encounter situations it cannot resolve, such as interrupt conflicts.

Note If you do not experience lockups when you collect a hardware inventory, skip to the "Modifying SMSLS.SCR" section on page 717.

If SMS cannot access specific hardware, it writes an entry into a file called SMSSAFE.TMP in C:\MS\SMS\DATA. It uses this entry to keep track of where hardware detection failed so that it can skip this hardware during subsequent logons. This process usually works properly, but in cases when it does not, users' computers lock up each time hardware inventory is taken.

Note Once setup successfully completes, the contents of SMSSAFE.TMP are written to SMS.INI in the workstation's Status section, for example:

```
[Workstation Status]
GamePorts=CRASHED
PrinterPorts=CRASHED
```

To avoid these lockups, you can create your own SMSSAFE.TMP file and send it to clients before performing the initial hardware scan (see the three files displayed below). The Novell logon script calls the SMSSAFE.BAT file to create the necessary SMS directory structure on drive C, then pushes out MSSAFE.TMP and SMSSAFE.TXT. Each time the computer's hardware is inventoried, the logon script calls SMSSAFE.BAT and, if it finds SMSSAFE.TXT, it exits, otherwise the remainder of SMSSAFE.BAT is processed.

Note Any hardware component that is skipped using SMSSAFE.TMP does not appear in an SMS inventory, so you may want to target only the computers with known hardware conflicts rather than every computer in the organization.

SMSSAFE.BAT

```
@ECHO OFF

IF EXIST "C:\MS\SMS\DATA\SMSSAFE.TXT" GOTO END

MD C:\MS

MD C:\MS\SMS

MD C:\MS\SMS\DATA

COPY O:\SMSSAFE.TXT C:\MS\SMS\DATA >NUL

COPY O:\SMSSAFE.TMP C:\MS\SMS\DATA >NUL

:END

CLS
```

SMSSAFE.TMP

```
GamePorts=CRASHED

PrinterPorts=CRASHED
```

SMSSAFE.TXT

The existence of this file indicates that the SMS Game Port and Printer Port tests have been bypassed.

To push the SMSSAFE.TMP file to SMS client computers that are hanging during hardware inventory collection, perform these steps on each Novell 4.1*x* SMS logon server:

1. Edit SMSSAFE.TMP to skip the hardware test that is causing the SMS hardware inventory to hang (usually GamePorts or PrinterPorts).

2. Copy SMSSAFE.BAT, SMSSAFE.TMP and SMSSAFE.TXT to \\YourNovellSMSLogonServer\SYS\PUBLIC.

3. Modify the logon script to call SMSSAFE.BAT (this can be part of the SMS portion of the logon script or placed before it in the Novell logon script).

To determine where SMS hardware inventory is hanging

1. Open a command window.

2. Type the command **INVDOS /f /v /e > c:\inv.txt** (or **INVWIN32 /f /i /v /e > c:\inv.txt** on Windows NT computers) and press ENTER. Insert a space between command line variables or they will not be recognized.

   This forces a hardware inventory, run in verbose mode, and redirects the output to a text file called INV.TXT located in the root of drive C.

3. Review the c:\inv.txt file and locate the line where inventory failed.

For reference, the output of **INVDOS /f /i /v > inv.txt** is displayed below.

INV.TXT
Hardware inventory phase

```
<< SCANNING WORKSTATION HARDWARE >>

ComputerName

ComputerConfig

CPU Speed Test

CPU = PENTIUM  75MHz

BiosInfo

Keyboard

Dma

Disks

DriveA

DriveB

DriveC

Volume COMPRESSED

DriveH

Volume

ConventionalMemory

CMOSMemory
```

```
ExtendedMemory

XMSMemory

DPMIMemory

EMMMemory

MouseInfo

Video

CommPorts

PrinterPorts

GamePorts

DeviceInfo

TSRInfo

IRQInfo
```

Note Any of the inventory items can conflict. The last item listed in INV.TXT usually refers to the item causing the conflict. For example, if a Game Port and an NIC card share the same interrupt, the last entry in INV.TXT would be GamePorts because SMS would hang when testing the interrupt and not write any more entries.

Modifying SMSLS.SCR

On a Windows NT SMS logon server, clients run SMSLS.BAT or SMSLS.CMD from a Windows NT logon script. On a Novell SMS logon server, clients run the Novell equivalent of SMSLS.BAT called SMSLS.SCR, which is copied to the Novell SMS logon server by default. It will not function correctly with the Novell Client32 or Novell IntraNetware client until you modify it by adding .COM and .EXE extensions to all occurrences of dosver, netspeed, NLSMSG16, CLI_DOS, INVDOS, and clrlevel. If you don't, users will experience lockups during logon as soon as the SMS portion of the Novell logon script runs.

The best way to avoid this is to create a Novell group, add a few users, and use it to work out kinks in logon-script processing before you add the rest of the users.

Changes to the SMSLS.SCR are displayed in italics:

```
REM   Copyright (C) 1994-1995 Microsoft Corporation

REM

REM   This file is the Systems Management Server (SMS) logon script

REM   include file for NetWare workstations.

REM   It installs the SMS client components and collects hardware

REM   and software inventory data.
```

```
write ""

write "Microsoft Systems Management Server (SMS)"

write ""


REM  This file contains the SMS login script for NetWare,

REM  and will be included from the system login script.


if <SMSLS> == "" goto START

set SMS_VERBOSE="/v"

write "Executing SMS logon script for netware."

goto START



START:


REM  If operating system is Windows NT then exit.

if <OS> = "Windows_NT"  GOTO NT
```

```
REM  Determine the DOS version and exit if Chicago.

#%<SMS_LOGON>\dosver.com

set SMS_ERR=ERROR_LEVEL


REM  Check for a slow network connection to the server and

REM  possibly exit. If not, spawn the executable files for CLI_DOS

REM and INVDOS located on this server.


#%<SMS_LOGON>\netspeed.com

set SMS_ERR=ERROR_LEVEL


if <sms_err> < "1" then GOTO NET_DOS


if <sms_err> = "2" then begin

    #%<SMS_LOGON>\x86.bin\NLSMSG16.EXE 6 /C YN /T Y,30 /M "Slow network
detected. Continue"

    set SMS_ERR=ERROR_LEVEL

    if <sms_err> < "2" then GOTO NET_DOS

end
```

```
            goto END


        NET_DOS:

        #%<SMS_LOGON>\x86.bin\CLI_DOS.EXE /p:%<SMS_LOGON>\    %<SMS_VERBOSE>

        #%<SMS_LOGON>\x86.bin\INVDOS.EXE /i /l:%<SMS_LOGON>\ %<SMS_VERBOSE>

        GOTO END


        NT:

        #%<SMS_LOGON>\x86.bin\NLSMSG16.EXE 11 /M "This version of SMS does not
        support Windows NT workstations"

        #%<SMS_LOGON>\x86.bin\NLSMSG16.EXE 12 /M "that are clients to a Novell
        NetWare server."

        GOTO END


        END:

        #%<SMS_LOGON>\clrlevel.com

        set SMS_ERR=

        set SMS_VERBOSE=
```

The master copy of SMSLS.SCR is stored on the SMS site server in \SMS\SITE.SRV\MAINCFG.BOX\CLIENT.SRC. Edit this copy, *not* the copy stored in \SMS\LOGON.SRV on each Novell SMS logon server.

Changes made to the master copy of SMSLS.SCR are replicated to all the Novell SMS logon servers in your site during the next site maintenance cycle. To force replication, initiate a watchdog cycle with this command:

```
sendcode sms_site_config_manager 192
```

SENDCODE.EXE is located on the SMS installation CD under \SUPPORT\DEBUG\X86 and is not installed by default. You must copy it from the SMS CD and place it in the \SMS\SITE.SRV\X86.BIN directory on the SMS site server.

Note   If you apply a service pack to SMS, it overwrites the master copy of SMSLS.SCR (which in turn overwrites all copies of the file within the SMS hierarchy) with an SMSLS.SCR that does not contain any of the .COM or .EXE extensions required (as shown above). This causes user computers to lock up on the next logon.

To avoid user computer lockups in this situation:

1. Save a copy of \SMS\SITE.SRV\MAINCFG.BOX\CLIENT.SRC \SMSLS.SCR as \SMS\SITE.SRV\MAINCFG.BOX\CLIENT.SRC \SMSLS.SAV

2. Apply the SMS service pack.

3. Immediately delete the new master copy of \SMS\SITE.SRV\MAINCFG.BOX\CLIENT.SRC \SMSLS.SCR supplied by the service pack.

4. Copy \SMS\SITE.SRV\MAINCFG.BOX\CLIENT.SRC \SMSLS.SAV to \SMS\SITE.SRV\MAINCFG.BOX\CLIENT.SRC \SMSLS.SCR

5. Force a watchdog cycle using sendcode sms_site_config_manager 192 to push the file out to all the Novell SMS logon servers.

Because you need to allow enough time for changes to reach each Novell SMS logon server, it is a good idea to apply service packs at night or on weekends. You also need to allow time for the saved copy of the SMSLS.SCR file to overlay the service pack copy. If you are in a time crunch, you can copy the file manually to the \SMS\LOGON.SRV directory on each Novell SMS logon server.

Creating INVDOS.PIF to Close a DOS Command Window

When the SMS portion of the Novell logon script executes, the SMSLS.SCR file calls a number of other files that collectively manage the computer. One of these (INVDOS.EXE—hardware inventory) is called last and when it is called from a Novell SMS logon server it leaves an MS-DOS command window open on the screen for Novell Client32 networking clients (not for Microsoft Client for Novell Networks). The window doesn't stop the logon process but it does annoy users and there is a procedure below for closing it automatically.

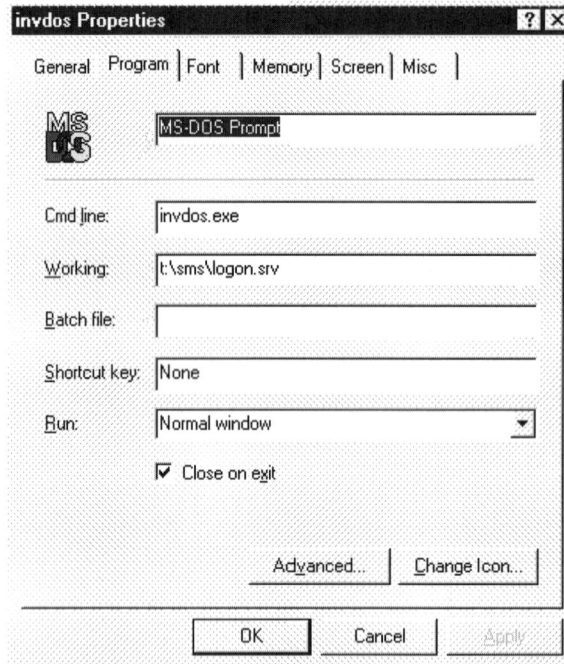

Figure 13.4 Configuring invdos Properties.

Here is how to force INVDOS.EXE to close the command window when it exits. Drive **T** is an example: you can use any drive letter that is valid in your environment as long as the drive letter specified in INVDOS.PIF (for example: Working: T:\SMS\LOGON.SRV) matches the drive letter used in the SMS portion of the Novell logon script (for example: DOS SET SMSDRIVE=T:).

1. Log on to a Windows 95 computer.
2. Copy C:\WINDOWS\DOSPROMPT.PIF to C:\WINDOWS\INVDOS.PIF.
3. Right click INVDOS.PIF and select **Properties**.
4. Click the **Program** tab.
5. Change the command line to *INVDOS.EXE*.
6. Change working to *x:\SMS\LOGON.SRV* where *x* is the drive letter you assigned in the SMS portion of your Novell logon script (for example, **DOS SET SMSDRIVE="T:"**). See the "Modifying the Novell Logon Script" section (on page 707) for more detailed instructions.
7. Click the **Close on Exit** box
8. Click **OK** to save changes.
9. Edit SMSLS.SCR and modify the line that calls INVDOS.EXE to call INVDOS.PIF (for example: #%<SMS_LOGON>\x86.bin**INVDOS.PIF** /i /l:%<SMS_LOGON>\ %<SMS_VERBOSE>). See the "Modifying SMSLS.SCR" section on page 717 for details.
10. Copy INVDOS.PIF in C:\WINDOWS to the SMS site server, placing it in \SMS\SITE.SRV\MAINCFG.BOX\CLIENT.SRC\X86.BIN.

    The file is replicated to the other Novell SMS logon servers during the next site maintenance cycle.

This causes the logon script to call SMSLS.SCR, which calls INVDOS.PIF, which calls INVDOS.EXE, which closes all active windows. Refer to Figure 13.4 on page 722 for details on how to configure INVDOS.PIF.

Modifying Rights on SMS Logon Server Support Directories

When a Novell 4.1*x* server is configured as an SMS logon server, SMS support directories and files are copied from the SMS site server to the Novell volume specified in the domain properties window of the SMS administrator. The EVERYONE group created in the bindery context of the Novell SMS logon server has rights to the \SMS directory structure by default. After you have used the SMS Administrator program to configure the Novell 4.1*x* server to be an SMS logon server, and the \SMS logon server directory structure has propagated out to it, you need to give access rights to users who process the SMS portion of the Novell logon script.

In the example below, the Novell NDS organization was given the appropriate rights to each of the \SMS directory structures. You can use this method, or, if you want to be more granular, you can assign rights at the OU level, but this requires more maintenance and is more work to set up initially.

Listed below are the rights necessary to use SMS for any person that will be processing the SMS portion of the logon script. Be sure to replace **YourOrgNameHere** with the name of your Novell NDS organization.

SMSRIGHT.BAT

```
REM SMSRIGHT.BAT

@ECHO OFF


RIGHTS %1\SMS RF /NAME=.YourOrgNameHere

RIGHTS %1\SMS\LOGON.SRV RF /NAME=.YourOrgNameHere

RIGHTS %1\SMS\LOGON.SRV\APPCTL.BOX RF /NAME=.YourOrgNameHere

RIGHTS %1\SMS\LOGON.SRV\CCR.BOX RWCEMF /NAME=.YourOrgNameHere

RIGHTS %1\SMS\LOGON.SRV\DESPOOLR.BOX RWCEMF /NAME=.YourOrgNameHere

RIGHTS %1\SMS\LOGON.SRV\INVENCFG.BOX RF /NAME=.YourOrgNameHere

RIGHTS %1\SMS\LOGON.SRV\INVENTRY.BOX RWCEMF /NAME=.YourOrgNameHere

RIGHTS %1\SMS\LOGON.SRV\ISVMIF.BOX RWCEMF /NAME=.YourOrgNameHere

RIGHTS %1\SMS\LOGON.SRV\MSTEST RF /NAME=.YourOrgNameHere

RIGHTS %1\SMS\LOGON.SRV\PCMINS.BOX RF /NAME=.YourOrgNameHere

RIGHTS %1\SMS\LOGON.SRV\PCMPKG.SRC RWCEMF /NAME=.YourOrgNameHere

RIGHTS %1\SMS\LOGON.SRV\SMSID RWCEMF /NAME=.YourOrgNameHere

RIGHTS %1\SMS\LOGON.SRV\APPCTL.BOX\DATABASE RF /NAME=.YourOrgNameHere

RIGHTS %1\SMS\LOGON.SRV\APPCTL.BOX\INIFILES RF /NAME=.YourOrgNameHere

RIGHTS %1\SMS\LOGON.SRV\APPCTL.BOX\SCRIPTS RF /NAME=.YourOrgNameHere
```

To assign appropriate rights to the SMS directories on a Novell SMS logon server:

1. Run *SMSRIGHT.BAT \\servername\volume* > *c:\temp\volumename.txt* on the Novell SMS logon server. The servername and volume you pass in to SMSRIGHT.BAT must contain the \SMS\ LOGON.SRV directory structure.

2. Review c:\temp\volumename.txt for any errors assigning rights.

Configuring the Windows NT Environment

This section uses All-Terrain Trucking (5,000 clients) to show how to configure the Windows NT environment. For administrative purposes, the company decided to handle all package creation, job distribution, and inventory collection from a single SMS site server.

The server was configured as follows:

Hardware

- Dual-processor Pentium Pro (200 MHz)
- 1 GB RAM (error correcting)
- Array A = Raid 1 (9 GB)
- Array B = Raid 1 (9 GB)
- Array C = Raid 5 (18 GB)
- (All arrays configured in hardware.)
- Single Ethernet NIC (100BaseT) with IP and IPX protocols. IPX configured to use 802.3 instead of Auto for frame type detection.

Software

- NT 4.0 with SP3
- SQL 6.5 with SP4
- SMS 1.2 with SP3
- Gateway Services for NetWare
- SNMP = Public and host SYSMGR.ALLTERRAIN.ORG
- Using SQL Administrator, change the amount of memory available to SQL from 8,192 (2-K pages) to 292,968 (2-K pages) which equals 599 MB
- Bumped open SQL objects to 7,000

These specifications are for an SMS site with 8,000 workstations. Although All-Terrain has only 5,000 users, the server was sized for 8,000 to allow room for growth and a possible merger with another SMS site. Use the tables below to determine the correct settings for your environment.

Physical memory requirements.

SQL overhead	17 MB
SQL use	599 MB
Primary SMS site	18 MB
SMS administrator	16 MB
Windows NT operating system	16 MB
Additional services	16 MB
Total physical memory	**682 MB**

Physical disk space requirements.

SMS data device	8,000 workstations in inventory x 60 K = 480,000 K = 480 MB (rounded up to 500 MB)
SMS log device	20% of SMS data device = 20% of 500 MB = 100 MB
tempdb data device	20% of SMS data device = 20% of 500 MB = 100 MB
tempdb log device	20% of tempdb data device = 20% of 100 MB = 20 MB
SMS root directory	130 MB
History files	8,000 x 100k = 800,000 K = 800 MB
Windows NT operating system physical disk requirements	124 MB
Package requirements	3.0 GB
Total physical disk requirements	**4.75 GB**

Configuration.

Drives	Drive letter	Size	Contents
	N/A	~36 MB	Hardware manufacturer system files.
Array A (0 & 1) mirrored	C: (partition 1)	2 GB	Operating system and swap file.
Array A (0 & 1) mirrored	D: (partition 2)	7 GB	\SMSAPPS directory. This is used to store all packages created with SMS. (The name \SMSAPPS is optional.
Array B (2 & 3) mirrored	E:	9 GB	SQL server and all SQL log files (SMS.LOG, TEMPDB.LOG, etc.)
5 internal in RAID 5	F:	18 GB	SMS and all SQL database files (SMS.DAT, TEMPDB.DAT, etc.)

Configuring SMS 1.2

To configure an SMS site server to support Novell 4.1*x* servers as SMS logon servers, you need to:

- Install Gateway Services for NetWare (GSNW) on the SMS site server: in Control Panel, click **Network-Services**, **Add**. Then select **Gateway Services for Netware** and click **OK**

- Create individual Novell SMS domains for each logon server. Open SMS administrator and go to the **Site Properties-Domain Properties** dialog box.

- Specify the appropriate Novell server name and volume for each logon server. Open SMS administrator and go to the **Site Properties-Domain Properties** dialog box.

Troubleshooting

Configuring SMS to support Novell 4.1*x* involves several detailed steps, any one of which can derail the process if performed incorrectly or out of sequence. Troubleshooting procedures are not well documented. The most informative tools are the event log on the SMS site server, the GSNW **New Share** dialog, and SMSTRACE. This section briefly discusses how to track down and solve the most common problems with connectivity, rights, and simple mistakes.

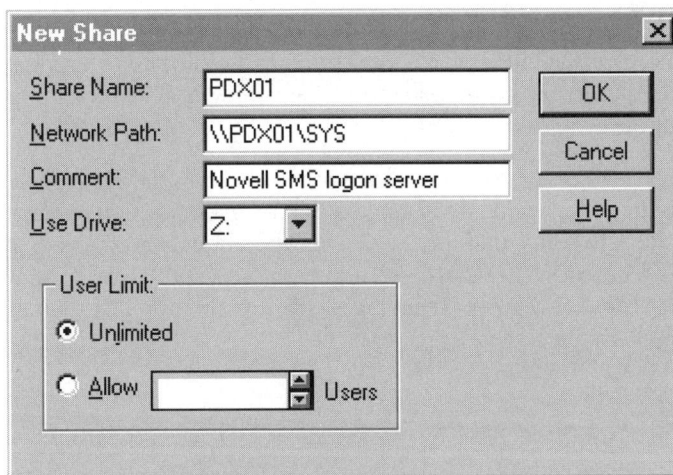

Figure 13.5 New Share dialog box.

Testing Connectivity

When GSNW is enabled, SMS communicates with Novell 4.1*x* using a bindery context. A simple way to test this connection is to check the configuration properties in the **Configure Gateway** dialog box in Control Panel, GSNW. If the bindery context is set up correctly you should be able to map a drive by clicking **Add** and typing the appropriate information.

You may be unable to establish a share with a Novell SMS logon server if:

- The bindery context is not established at the correct level.
- An EVERYONE group has not been added in the bindery context.
- An NTGATEWAY group has not been added in the bindery context.
- The Novell SMS service account has not been added to the NTGATEWAY group.

Another source of connection problems is Novell's use of Ethernet frames—Novell 3.*x* servers use 802.3 by default, and 4.1*x* servers use 802.2. Windows NT defaults to auto detect for the frame type when installing support for IPX, and in some cases auto detect does not work. To eliminate frame type detection as a possible cause, you can modify the IPX frame so that it uses the same type of frame as the Novell SMS logon server.

Checking Rights

Problems are rare once connectivity is established and rights are set in the SMS logon server directory structure. They are possible though, and here is an example of one.

Users logged into Novell SMS logon server \\PDX01 for over a month with no issues, then suddenly began experiencing connection problems. A quick visual check revealed that the server was operational and that a drive could be mapped to it. The \SMS\ LOGON.SRV directory structure also appeared to be intact. HMAN.LOG showed that the SMS site server could communicate with the Novell SMS logon server.

Upon closer inspection it was determined that the rights to the \SMS\
LOGON.SRV directory structure contained only the EVERYONE group (the
orgname was missing as a trustee). This happened because the server was running
out of space and a Novell administrator moved the entire \SMS directory to
another drive. When SMS performed its scheduled site maintenance, it noticed the
\SMS directory structure was missing and rebuilt it. By default it supplied rights
only to the EVERYONE group. Running SMSRIGHT.BAT fixed the problem.

Looking for Simple Mistakes

Problems caused by simple mistakes are usually accidental and they may not
appear right away. A common cause is poor communication between remote
Novell administrators (in branch offices) and the SMS administrator.

Communication and documentation can fix these sorts of problems. For instance,
when you edit AUTOEXEC.NCF and put in the bindery context, be sure to put in
a comment stating its purpose and a contact name. Do this for the Novell logon
script too.

If inventory collection suddenly stops for no apparent reason, check to see that the
SMS client computer is still communicating with the Novell SMS logon server.
Look at the SMS log files first, on the client and the server. Use Notepad to check
the client's \MS\SMS\LOGS\CLI_MON.LOG; use SMSTRACE to view
HMAN.LOG on the server. Also check for any communication problems with the
Novell SMS logon server.

SMSTRACE.EXE allows real-time monitoring of SMS logs. It is on the SMS
installation CD under \SUPPORT\DEBUG\X86, but it is not installed by
default—you have to copy it. Put it in the \SMS\SITE.SRV\X86.BIN directory on
the SMS site server. If you put it in another directory you must also copy over
BASE.DLL and MFC.DLL.

If one or more Novell SMS logon servers mysteriously stop functioning, possible causes are:

- The \SMS\LOGON.SRV directory was deleted or rights to the directory structure were modified.
- The SMS portion of the Novell logon script was commented out or removed.
- The bindery context was deleted.
- The Novell server was upgraded and \SMS\LOGON.SRV was not transferred to the new server.
- The Novell server was renamed.

More Information

Refer to these Microsoft Knowledge Base articles for more information:

- Q152469, Title: Hardware Inventory Hangs at 30% When Detecting the Game Port.
- Q157838, Title: SMS: NetWare Client32 for Windows 95 Stops Responding on Logon.
- Q156402, Title: SMS: PCM Looks in Wrong Path for Default Distribution Server.
- Q154411, Title: SMS Err Msg: Unable to Initialize IPX Protocol.
- Q159539, Title: SMS: File Transfer Fails with Client Running NetWare Client32.
- Q159540, Title: SMS: HelpDesk Cannot Reconnect to Windows 95 with Client32.
- Q182593, Title: SMS Err: "Unable to Initialize NetBIOS Protocol" on Win95 Client.

Appendixes

A P P E N D I X   A

References and Resources

This list contains references to Microsoft support offerings and other sources of information on Microsoft Windows NT Server and Microsoft Systems Management Server found through Microsoft Press, on the Microsoft Web site, or on TechNet.

Support and technical resources	Where found
Microsoft Support: Pointer to Support Online and support options	http://www.microsoft.com/support/
Microsoft Support Online: Access to Microsoft Technical Support's entire collection of problem-solving tools and technical information, including the Knowledge Base, troubleshooting wizards, service packs, and other downloads	http://support.microsoft.com/support/
Premier Technical Account Management	http://www.microsoft.com/Enterprise /support/TAM.htm
Basic and Enhanced Supportability Review	Consult your Microsoft Consulting Services liaison or Technical Account Manager for additional information

(continued)

Support and technical resources	Where found
Microsoft Enterprise Services: Worldwide services and support for large organizations	http://www.microsoft.com/Enterprise /support.htm
Premier Technical Support	http://www.microsoft.com/Enterprise /support/techsupport.htm
Premier Technical Account Management	http://www.microsoft.com/Enterprise /support/TAM.htm
Basic and Enhanced Supportability Review	Consult your Microsoft Consulting Services liaison or Technical Account Manager for additional information
Microsoft Certified Solution Providers	http://www.microsoft.com/mcsp/
Microsoft Certified Professional (MCP) training	http://www.microsoft.com/mcp/
Microsoft Training and Certification	http://www.microsoft.com/train_cert/

(continued)

Support and technical resources	Where found
Microsoft Certified Technical Education Centers (CTECs)	http://www.microsoft.com/train_cert /train/ctec.htm

Microsoft Press:
  Look for the following titles:
 	
  Networking Essentials, Second Edition
 	
  Microsoft Windows NT Network Administration Training
 	
  Microsoft TCP/IP Training
 	
  Microsoft Windows NT Server   4.0 Enterprise Technologies Training
 	
  BackOffice Resource Guide, Second Edition
 	
  Microsoft Windows NT Server 4.0 Resource Kit
 	
  Microsoft Windows NT Server Resource Kit Version 4.0, Supplement One
 	
  Microsoft Windows NT Server Resource Kit Version 4.0, Supplement Two
 	
  Microsoft Windows NT Workstation 4.0 Resource Kit
 	
  ALS Microsoft Windows NT Technical Support
	1-800-MSPRESS (677-7377)
	
	http://mspress.microsoft.com/
	
	For a complete listing of available titles on Windows NT, go to:
	http://mspress.microsoft.com/ findabook/list/subject_5T.htm

(continued)

Support and technical resources	Where found
Microsoft Windows NT Technical Support Training	
Microsoft Systems Management Server Training	
Microsoft Press ResourceLink: Provides direct access to complete resource kits, training kits, and other titles, as well as the latest technical updates and tools	http://mspress.microsoft.com/reslink/
Microsoft BackOffice Web site	http://www.backoffice.microsoft.com
Microsoft Windows NT Web site	http://www.microsoft.com/ntserver/
Microsoft Systems Management Server Web site	http://www.microsoft.com/smsmgmt/
Microsoft Security Advisor Web site	http://www.microsoft.com/security
Microsoft TechNet: The central information and community resource designed for IT professionals	http://www.microsoft.com/technet/
Microsoft Developer Network (MSDN)	http://msdn.microsoft.com/developer/
Microsoft Year 2000 Readiness Disclosure and Resource Center	http://www.microsoft.com/technet/topics/ year2k/default.htm

General information	Where found
Microsoft Solutions Framework: *To help you plan an enterprise architecture that adapts to (or drives) industry change, consistently build business-driven applications, and manage your computing environment*	http://www.microsoft.com/msf/ You can also find an overview article on TechNet.
"Managing Infrastructure Deployment Projects"	Search TechNet
Internet Connection Services for Microsoft RAS, Standard Edition	Search TechNet, under Windows NT Server Manuals
Microsoft Cluster Server Administrator's Guide	Search TechNet, under Windows NT Server Manuals
"Automating Microsoft Windows NT Setup Deployment Guide"	http://www.microsoft.com/ntworkstation /info/Deployment-guide.htm
"Customizing the Windows NT 4.0 Upgrade Process"	http://www.microsoft.com/ntserver You can also search on TechNet
Overview of Windows NT registry and Registry Editor	See "Appendix A – Windows NT Registry" in Windows NT Server Concepts and Planning Manual (also on TechNet)

Windows NT Server-related tools (noted in this volume)	Where found
Network Monitor	See "Chapter 10 - Monitoring Your Network" in Windows NT Server *Concepts and Planning Manual* (also on TechNet)
	Microsoft Windows NT Server 4.0 Resource Kit Supplement 1, "Chapter 7: Monitoring Bandwidth and Network Capacity"
C2CONFIG.EXE	Found in the *Microsoft Windows NT 4.0 Resource Kit, Supplement Three*
NLTEST.EXE	Query TechNet using the "Q" number
Refer to Q158148, Title: Domain Secure Channel Utility – NLTEST.EXE	*For the most up-to-date collection of Knowledge Base articles, search Microsoft Technical Support online: http://support.microsoft.com/support /a.asp?M=F*
KIX32.EXE	Found in the *Microsoft Windows NT 4.0 Resource Kit, Supplement Three*
NETDOM.EXE	Found in the *Microsoft Windows NT 4.0 Resource Kit, Supplement Three*
REGBACK.EXE	Found in the *Microsoft Windows NT 4.0 Resource Kit, Supplement Three*
REGMON	http://www.sysinternals.com
ROBOCOPY.EXE	Found in the *Microsoft Windows NT 4.0 Resource Kit, Supplement Three*

Windows NT Server-related tools (noted in this volume)	Where found
SCRIPTIT.EXE	http://www.microsoft.com/ntserver
See also:	Query TechNet using the "Q" number
Q191605, Title: Incorporating ScriptIt with Unattended Installation	*For the most up-to-date collection of Knowledge Base articles, search Microsoft Technical Support online:*
Q191667, Title: How to Use ScriptIt to Install FPNW via Unattended Installation	*http://support.microsoft.com/support /a.asp?M=F*
SU.EXE (Switch User utility) and SUSS.EXE (SU Service)	*Microsoft Windows NT Server 4.0 Resource Kit—Supplement Two*
WINDIFF.EXE	Found in the *Microsoft Windows NT 4.0 Resource Kit, Supplement Three*

General Windows NT networking information	Where found
Microsoft Windows NT Server: Communication services technical details	http://www.microsoft.com/ntserver /commserv/techdetails/default.asp
Look for these whitepapers:	
"Virtual Private Networking Overview"	You can also search TechNet.
"Internet Connection Service"	
"Routing and Remote Access"	
"Understanding Point-To-Point Tunneling Protocol (PPTP)"	
"Using Point-to-Point Tunneling Protocol"	
"Unicast Routing Principles"	
"TCP/IP Implementation Details"	

(continued)

General Windows NT networking information	Where found
"Guide To Microsoft Windows NT 4.0 Profiles and Policies"	http://microsoft.com/ntserver/ management/deployment/planguide/ prof_policies.asp
"Windows NT 4.0 Remote Troubleshooting and Diagnostics"	Search on TechNet
Windows NT Server: *Security services technical details*	http://microsoft.com/ntserver/security/ default.asp
Windows NT Server downloads Web page	http://microsoft.com/NTServer/all/downloads.a sp
Microsoft Windows Hardware Compatibility List (HCL)	http://www.microsoft.com/hwtest/hcl/
"Active Directory Service Interfaces— The Easy Way to Access and Manage LDAP-Based Directories (Windows NT 4.0)"	Search TechNet.
"Planning for Windows NT Server 5.0"(Windows 2000)	http://microsoft.com/ntserver/ management/deployment/planguide/ PlanForNT5.asp
Also listed as:	
"Planning Windows NT Server 4.0 Deployment with Windows NT Server 5.0 in Mind"	Search TechNet.

(continued)

General Windows NT networking information	Where found
"Configuring DHCP"	*Microsoft Windows NT Sever 4.0 Resource Kit: Networking Guide*
"Browsing and Windows 95 Networking"	http://www.microsoft.com/win32dev/netwrk/browse1.htm http://www.microsoft.com/win32dev/netwrk/browse2.htm
"Performance Analysis and Optimization of MS Windows NT Server, Part 1"	Search on TechNet.
"Appendix A - RAS Registry Values"	
NetLogon: Q163204, Title: Increase Domain Logon Timeout over Network Q151259, Title: New Netlogon Registry Entry for Dialup Routers *Pulse:* Q150350, Title: NetLogon Maximum Value of Pulse Should Exceed 3600 Q102717, Title: Windows NT UAS Replication (Windows NT and LAN Manager) Q135360, Title: Periodic Re-Transmit Times for Packets	Query TechNet using the "Q" number, or search on the registry subkey. *For the most up-to-date collection of Knowledge Base articles, search Microsoft Technical Support online: http://support.microsoft.com/support /a.asp?M=F*

(continued)

General Windows NT networking information	**Where found**

DisablePasswordChange:

Q154501, Title: How to Disable Automatic Machine Account Password Changes

Q175468, Title: Effects of Machine Account Replication on a Domain

ExpectedDialupDelay:

Q152719, Title: WAN and Trust: Traffic on the Wire

Q154355, Title: How to Tune Trusts for Dialup Routers in a WAN

Q163204, Title: Increase Domain Logon Timeout over Network

DisableServerThread:

Q131902, Title: Printer Browse Thread May Cause Extensive Network Traffic

BcastQueryTimeout & BcastNameQueryCount:

"Windows NT 3.5, 3.51, 4.0 - TCP/IP Implementation Details"

"Windows NT Server 4.0 - WINS Architecture and Capacity Planning"

Q120642, Title: TCP/IP & NBT Configuration Parameters for Windows NT

(continued)

General Windows NT networking information	Where found

AutoDisconnect:

Q97559, Title: How Remote Access Service Processes Datagram Traffic

Q97599, Title: Windows NT RAS Registry Parameters

Q181407, Title: Troubleshooting Proxy RAS Autodial and Autodisconnect

Q134346, Title: Remoteboot Workstation Cannot Reconnect After Net 808 Errors

Q103003, Title: REG: Network Services Entries, Part 7

Q117304, Title: RAS Event ID (Error Code) Information

Q138365, Title: How the Autodisconnect Works in Windows NT

Q105134, Title: AutoDisconnect Default Incorrect in Online Help

EnableRaw:

Q127023, Title: Raw SMB Requests Across Router Results in Session Termination

(continued)

General Windows NT networking information	Where found

SizReqBuf:

Q177266, Title: Remote Directory Lists Are Slower Than Local Directory Listings

RPC_Binding_Order:

Q174701, Title: XCLN: Troubleshooting RPC Problems for Exchange Clients

NetServerEnum:

Q131902, Title: Printer Browse Thread May Cause Extensive Network Traffic

Q136712, Title: Common Questions About Browsing with Windows NT

"Appendix F: Browser Traffic"

MaintainServerList:

Q136712, Title: Common Questions About Browsing with Windows NT

MasterAnnounce:

Q191611, Title: Symptoms of Multihomed Browsers

ReplicationGovernor:

Q140422, Title: Domain Synchronization Over a Slow WAN Link

(continued)

General Windows NT networking information	Where found

TCPWindowSize, TCPRecvSegmentSize, & TCPSendSegmentSize:

Q102973, Title: REG: TCP/IP Transport Entries, Part 1

Q140552, Title: How to Optimize Windows NT to Run Over Slow WAN Links w/TCP/IP

Q120642, Title: TCP/IP & NBT Configuration Parameters for Windows NT

WAN planning and design	Where found
Q120151, Title: Browsing a Wide Area Network with WINS	Query TechNet using the "Q" number.
Q154355, Title: How to Tune Trusts for Dialup Routers in a WAN	*For the most up-to-date collection of Knowledge Base articles, search Microsoft Technical Support online:*
Q152719, Title: WAN and Trust: Traffic on the Wire	*http://support.microsoft.com/support /a.asp?M=F*
Q134985, Title: Browsing & Other Traffic Incur High Costs over ISDN Routers	
Q140552, Title: How to Optimize Windows NT to Run Over Slow WAN Links w/TCP/IP	
Q159168, Title: Multiple Default Gateways Can Cause Connectivity Problems	

Tuning Windows NT Server for dial-on-demand & slow links	Where found
Enterprise Networking, by Daniel Minoli.	ISBN 0-89006-621-3
The Simple Book, by Marshall T. Rose.	ISBN 0-13-451659-1
DNS and Bind, by Paul Albitz and Cricket Liu.	ISBN 1-56592-236-0
How to Manage Your Network Using SNMP, by Marshall T. Rose and Keith McCloghrie.	
The Basics Book of Frame Relay, by Motorola Press University.	ISBN 0-201-56377-0
The Open Book, by Marshall T. Rose.	ISBN 0-13-643016-3
TCP/IP Explained, by Phillip Miller.	ISBN 1-55558-166-8
RFC 1001 and RFC 1002: Protocol Standard for a NetBIOS Service on a TCP/UDP Transport.	
RFC 1541: Dynamic Host Configuration Protocol.	

(continued)

Tuning Windows NT Server for dial-on-demand & slow links	Where found
Q164308, Title: Windows NT 4.0 Clients May Refresh WINS Entries Frequently	Query TechNet using the "Q" number.
Q139270, Title: How to Change Name Resolution Order on Windows 95 and Windows NT	*For the most up-to-date collection of Knowledge Base articles, search Microsoft Technical Support online: http://support.microsoft.com/support /a.asp?M=F*
Q120642, Title: TCP/IP & NBT Configuration Parameters for Windows NT	
Q102878, Title: Information on Browser Operation	
Q134985, Title: Browsing & Other Traffic Incur High Costs over ISDN Routers	
Q102981, Title: REG: Workstation Service Entries	
Q131902, Title: Printer Browse Thread May Cause Extensive Network Traffic	
Q124184, Title: Service Running as System Account Fails Accessing Network	
Q154501, Title: How to Disable Automatic Machine Account Password Changes	

Directory replication & synchronization	Where found
"Synchronization over WAN and Remote Area Service"	"Chapter 2 – Network Security and Domain Planning" in *Microsoft Windows NT Server 4.0 Resource Kit, Networking Guide*
"Implementing Directory Services Using MS Windows NT Server - Part 2"	Search on TechNet.
Q140422, Title: Domain Synchronization Over a Slow WAN Link	Query TechNet using the "Q" number *For the most up-to-date collection of Knowledge Base articles, search Microsoft Technical Support online: http://support.microsoft.com/support /a.asp?M=F*

Systems Management Server—network traffic related information	Where found
"Deploying Applications and Content Using Systems Management Server 1.2"	Search TechNet
"Distributing Software over Slow Links"	http://www.microsoft.com/smsmgmt /support/out_of_band.asp?A=5&B=3
Q191317, Title: SMS: "Not Mandatory Over Slow Link" Check Box Has Been Removed Q185805, Title: SMS: Disabling the Mandatory Countdown Timer in PCM Q185346, Title: SMS: Logon Script Takes a Long Time over RAS or Slow Connection	Query TechNet using the "Q" number. *For the most up-to-date collection of Knowledge Base articles, search Microsoft Technical Support online: http://support.microsoft.com/support /a.asp?M=F*
"Remote Control Troubleshooting"	http://www.microsoft.com/smsmgmt /support/remotecontrol.asp?A=5&B=3

General Systems Management Server information	Where found
SMS Installer Download	http://backoffice.microsoft.com/downtrial /moreinfo/smsinst.asp
Q191441, Title: Systems Management Server 1.2 Service Pack 4 Fixlist	Query TechNet using the "Q" number. *For the most up-to-date collection of Knowledge Base articles, search Microsoft Technical Support online: http://support.microsoft.com/support /a.asp?M=F*
"Chapter 3—Understanding Sites" in the *Microsoft Systems Management Server Planning Guide*	Search on TechNet
"Chapter 3—Installing and Upgrading Sites, Servers, and Clients" in the *Microsoft Systems Management Server 1.2 Resource Guide* (of the *BackOffice Resource Kit, Second Edition*)	Search on TechNet
Q125487, Title: SMS Administrator Unable To Retrieve Machine List Q110352, Title: Optimizing Microsoft SQL Server Performance Q138347, Title: SMS: Procedure for Backing up and Restoring a Secondary site	Query TechNet using the "Q" number. *For the most up-to-date collection of Knowledge Base articles, search Microsoft Technical Support online: http://support.microsoft.com/support /a.asp?M=F*

(continued)

General Systems Management Server information	Where found
"Automated Client Upgrade Process For Windows 95 and Windows NT Workstation 4.0 Through Systems Management Server"	Search on TechNet
"Remote Control Troubleshooting"	http://www.microsoft.com/smsmgmt /support/remotecontrol.asp?A=5&B=3
"Package Definition Files"	http://www.microsoft.com/smsmgmt /support/PDFs.asp?A=5&B=5
"Troubleshooting Remote Control" in the *Microsoft Systems Management Server 1.2 Resource Guide*	Search on TechNet
"Working with Remote Control" in the *Microsoft Systems Management Server 1.2 Resource Guide*	Search on TechNet
"Updated Tracer Utility - SMSTRACE.EXE"	Search on TechNet
Q161216, Title: SMS: Client Setup Fails to Update Sms.ini on Windows NT System. Q123317, Title: SMS: Enabling Help Desk Options from Logon Servers Unsupported. Q170440, Title: SMS: Remote Controlling a Multihomed Windows NT Client Computer	Query TechNet using the "Q" number. *For the most up-to-date collection of Knowledge Base articles, search Microsoft Technical Support online: http://support.microsoft.com/support /a.asp?M=F*

(continued)

General Systems Management Server information	Where found
SMS and Novell NetWare and NDS related information	Where found
SKIPINV.EXE	*Microsoft BackOffice Resource Guide, Second Edition* (Utilities)
Configuring Systems Management Server and Novell's NDS	http://www.microsoft.com/smsmgmt /support/ndswp.asp?A=5&B=3
Q152469, Title: Hardware Inventory Hangs at 30% When Detecting the Game Port	Query TechNet using the "Q" number.
Q157838, Title: SMS: NetWare Client32 for Windows 95 Stops Responding on Logon	*For the most up-to-date collection of Knowledge Base articles, search Microsoft Technical Support online:*
Q156402, Title: SMS: PCM Looks in Wrong Path for Default Distribution Server	*http://support.microsoft.com/support /a.asp?M=F*
Q140802, Title: Package Command Manager (PCM) is Limited to 10 Servers	
Q154411, Title: SMS Err Msg: Unable to Initialize IPX Protocol	
Q159539, Title: SMS: File Transfer Fails with Client Running NetWare Client32	
Q159540, Title: SMS: HelpDesk Cannot Reconnect to Windows 95 with Client32	
Q182593, Title: SMS Err: "Unable to Initialize NetBIOS Protocol" on Win95 Client	

Windows NT security	Where found
"Microsoft Report on C2 Evaluation of Windows NT"	http://www.microsoft.com/security
C2CONFIG.EXE	Found in the *Microsoft Windows NT 4.0 Resource Kit, Supplement Three*
"Guide To Windows NT 4.0 Profiles and Policies"	http://www.microsoft.com/ntserver /management Search also on TechNet
Appendix D, "Security In a Software Development Environment," in the *Microsoft Windows NT Resource Kit Version 3.5 Update*	Search on TechNet
Internet Explorer Administration Kit Web site	http://ieak.microsoft.com
Q161990, Title: How to Enable Strong Password Functionality in Windows NT Q189746, Title: How to Use Proxy Server with Content Replication System. Q143475, Title: Windows NT System Key Permits Strong Encryption of the SAM. Q189595, Title: PPTP Performance & Security Upgrade for WinNT 4.0 Release Notes Q167029, Title: Resource and Master Domain DCs Do Not Load-Balance Validation Q188855, Title: Security Privilege Must Be Enabled to View Security Event Log	Query TechNet using the "Q" number. *For the most up-to-date collection of Knowledge Base articles, search Microsoft Technical Support online: http://support.microsoft.com/support /a.asp?M=F*

(continued)

Windows NT security	Where found
Chapter 11, "Registry Editor and Registry Administration," in the *Microsoft Windows NT Version 3.5 Resource Guide*	Search on TechNet
"Creating Certificate Hierarchies with MS Certificate Server Version 1.0"	Search on TechNet
Chapter 6, "Backing Up and Restoring Network Files" in *Microsoft Windows NT Server Concepts and Planning* manual	Search on TechNet

Secure client logon	Where found
Q175025, Title: How to Build and Reset A Trust Relationship from a Command Line	Query TechNet using the "Q" number.
Q156684, Title: How to Use NLTEST to Force a New Secure Channel	*For the most up-to-date collection of Knowledge Base articles, search Microsoft Technical Support online:*
Q158148, Title: Domain Secure Channel Utility—NLTEST.EXE	*http://support.microsoft.com/support /a.asp?M=F*
Q181171, Title: Secure Channel Manipulation with TCP/IP	
Q165202, Title: WinNT Client Logon in Resource and Master Domain Environment	
"Systems Engineering—Under the Hood of Client Logon (Windows 95 and Windows NT 3.51 and 4.0)"	Search on TechNet

Microsoft Cluster Server-related information	Where found
"Setting Properties" in Chapter 4 of the *Microsoft Cluster Server Administrator's Guide*	Search on TechNet
Hardware Compatibility List (HCL)	http://www.microsoft.com/ntserver/info/hwcompatibility.htm
Chapter 6, "Backing Up and Restoring Network Files," in *Microsoft Windows NT Server Version 4.0 Concepts and Planning*	Search on TechNet
Chapter 5, "Preparing for and Performing Recovery" in the *Microsoft Windows NT Server Resource Kit Resource Guide*	Search on TechNet
Q112019, Title: Changing Primary Disk System After Installation	Query TechNet using the "Q" number
Q130928, Title: Restoring a Backup of Windows NT to Another Computer	*For the most up-to-date collection of Knowledge Base articles, search Microsoft Technical Support online:*
Q139822, Title: How to Restore a Backup to Computer with Different Hardware	*http://support.microsoft.com/support/a.asp?M=F*
Q139820, Title: Moving or Removing Disks & Fault Tolerant Drive Configurations	
Q113976, Title: Using Emergency Repair Disk With Fault Tolerant Partitions	
Internet Assigned Numbers Authority (IANA): RFC 1597 and RFC 1631.	http://www.safety.net/rfc.htm

Windows NT Server 4.0 Service Pack 4	Where found
"List of Bugs Fixed in Windows NT 4.0 Service Packs (Part 1)" also Microsoft Knowledge Base (KB) article Q150734	http://support.microsoft.com/support /kb/articles/q150/7/
	You can also search TechNet for this article and the following using the Qxxxxxx number.
	For the most up-to-date collection of Knowledge Base articles, search Microsoft Technical Support online: http://support.microsoft.com/support/
"List of Bugs Fixed in Windows NT 4.0 Service Packs (Part 2)" also KB article Q194834	http://support.microsoft.com/support /kb/articles/Q194/8/
"Windows NT 4.0 Service Pack 4 README.TXT File (40-bit)"	http://support.microsoft.com/support /ntserver/content/servicepacks /readme
"How do I install Service Pack 4?"	http://support.microsoft.com/support /ntserver/content/servicepacks /instalsp
"Before Installing a Windows NT Service Pack" also KB article Q165418	http://support.microsoft.com/support /kb/Articles/Q165/4/18

(continued)

Windows NT Server 4.0 Service Pack 4	Where found
"Eight Steps to Take Before Installing Windows NT 4.0 Service Pack 4"	Search on TechNet.
"Year 2000 Information for Windows NT 4.0 Service Pack 4 Installation"	Search on TechNet.
"Common Service Pack Questions and Answers"	Search on TechNet.
Full download page for Windows NT Service Pack 4 (starts with license agreement)	http://support.microsoft.com/support/ ntserver/content/servicepacks/ sp4start.asp?PR=NTS&T1=7d&FR=0& A=T&T=B&S=F&
"Repairing Windows NT After the Application of Service Pack 3" also KB article	Search on TechNet
"Tips for Deploying MS Windows NT Server 4.0 Service Pack 3"	Search on TechNet.
"How to Search Windows NT Articles by Topic"	http://support.microsoft.com/support/ kb/articles/q102/6/52.asp?FR=0

List of Knowledge Base article fixes in Service Pack 4	Where found
The titles below are separated by keyword topic.	http://support.microsoft.com/support /kb/articles/q150/7/34.asp
	You can also search TechNet for this article and the following using the Qxxxxxx number.
	For the most up-to-date collection of Knowledge Base articles, search Microsoft Technical Support online: http://support.microsoft.com/support /a.asp?M=F

16-Bit Windows Version 3.x-Based Applications

Q142026, Title: Err: "Hidden Console of WOW VDM" Running 16-bit or MS-DOS App

Q154791, Title: MS-DOS-based Applications May Not Find All Files

Q167969, Title: Under Windows NT, Win16 Applications Opening MS-DOS Devices Fail

Q169020, Title: 32-bit Help Fails to Start When 16-bit Help Is Running

Q170753, Title: Window Focus Set to Invoke Wrong 16-bit Application Through DDE

Q174233, Title: KeInitSystem Function Returns Uninitialized Stack on Alpha

Q174234, Title: Computer Hangs with Intensive 16-bit Code Running in a VDM

Q174266, Title: "Print Screen" from MS-DOS Application May Print Twice

List of Knowledge Base article fixes in Service Pack 4   *(continued)*

Q176211, Title: Console-mode Apps May Run Slowly on Multiprocessor Computers

Q177631, Title: Comdlg32 Fails to Display Drives Mapped by SUBST Command

32-Bit Windows-Based Applications

Q146965, Title: GetAdmin Utility Grants Users Administrative Rights

Q167871, Title: Error When Connecting to a Share on WinNT 4.0 NTFS Partition

Q170057, Title: Dr. Watson Dialog Box Stops Responding

Q170509, Title: Memory Leak in SERVICES.EXE Causes Performance Degradation

Q170510, Title: Double-Clicking the Mouse Button Acts as a Single Click

Q171996, Title: Winsock Function Calls Generate Non-Paged Pool Memory Leak

Q173993, Title: Dialog Message Not Sent Correctly from 32-bit to 16-bit App

Q173994, Title: GetTextExtentPoint32W May Fail with Unicode Characters > 0x

Q174531, Title: DirectDraw Fails Surface Creation with Large Dimensions

Q176319, Title: Docfile Standard Marshalling Returns 0x800706f4

Q177684, Title: Application Using SetOwner May Hang Windows NT User Interface

Backup Issues (NTBACKUP.EXE)

Q170566, Title: Ntbackup.exe Log Has Additional Space at Beginning of Each Line

Q170568, Title: Seagate Tape Drive Light Stays Lit After Exiting NTBACKUP

Boot Process and Startup

Q157913, Title: Services Set to Interact With Desktop May Fail to Start

Q163855, Title: STOP 0x0000001e May Occur in Srv.sys w/ Down Level Client

Q174932, Title: STOP 0x0000000A with Halmps.dll When Restarting

List of Knowledge Base article fixes in Service Pack 4 *(continued)*

Configuration and Tuning

Q174625, Title: Environment Variables May Prevent Logging On

Q175745, Title: Memory Leak When Using Win32 GetClipboardFormat API

Domain Administration

Q166822, Title: Remote Password Change Works Incorrectly to Down-Level Server

Q171308, Title: Explorer File Properties Dialog Version Tab Missing

Q172003, Title: Macintosh Change Password Fails on Down Trusted Domain PDC

Q173385, Title: System Policy Editor Will Not Allow More Than 255 Characters

Q174058, Title: Delayed Worker Threads Causes a STOP 7A

Q174076, Title: Invalid Password Message When Strong Passwords Are Required

Q174205, Title: LSASS May Use a Large Amount of Memory on a Domain Controller

Q174840, Title: Disabling Buttons in the Windows NT Security Dialog Box

Q175468, Title: Effects of Machine Account Replication on a Domain

Q175641, Title: LMCompatibilityLevel and Its Effects

Q178109, Title: Roving Profiles for Windows 95 Clients Stop Working

Q190928, Title: Poledit Spin Boxes Limit Max Value to 9999

MS-DOS-Based Applications

Q171940, Title: MS-DOS Application I/O Operations Cause Floppy Drive Access

Device Drivers

Q138791, Title: SCSI Printing Devices Requiring Wide SCSI May Fail

Q154094, Title: Using Iomega ATAPI Zip Drives with Windows NT

List of Knowledge Base article fixes in Service Pack 4   *(continued)*

Q157032, Title: Services for Macintosh May Cause STOP 0x0A During High Load

Q167703, Title: Canon Bubble Jet BJC-4300 Does Not Support Ledger Paper

Q170572, Title: Unable to Format a 1.44-MB Disk on an LS-120 After SP3

Q174187, Title: WinNT Does Not Display IBM PS/2 TrackPoint as the Mouse Driver

Q174764, Title: Memory Leak in Ntfs.sys

Q175321, Title: SNA Client Sessions Hang Until SNA Server Is Restarted

Q177257, Title: STOP 0x0000000A or Difficulty Recognizing IDE CD-ROM Drives

File Systems

Q165387, Title: Sharing Violation When Deleting a Folder

Q169404, Title: NTFS Directory Corruption with Frequent File Creation

Q169608, Title: Occasional File Corruption When Using Unbuffered I/O

Q171213, Title: Copy to Removable Drive in Explorer May Fail After Media Swap

Q172930, Title: Removing Bypass Traverse Checking Causes Copy to Drop Streams

Q173322, Title: How to Disable Autochk During a Windows NT Reboot

Q174502, Title: Fault Tolerant Recovery Does Not Reoccur After Shut Down

Q171458, Title: Windows NT May Fail On Request to Open Large Files

Q172705, Title: Explorer Access Violates When Viewing a File's Properties

Q177591, Title: Service Pack Version Truncated in About Box

Q185727, Title: BUG: closesocket() Fails with 10038 After _open_osfhandle()

Interoperability

Q146095, Title: STOP: 0x0000000A or STOP: 0x0000001E in Tcpip.sys

Q147222, Title: Group of Hotfixes for Exchange 5.5 and IIS 4.0

List of Knowledge Base article fixes in Service Pack 4   *(continued)*

Q150953, Title: Nwuser.exe Send Function Truncates Messages to 38 Characters

Q165404, Title: NTVDM AV on Servers with Exchange cc:Mail Connector

Q173526, Title: "Serious Disk Error" When Saving Word 6.0 Document on Windows NT

Q173533, Title: WinNT Radius Client Sends Incomplete Accounting Information

Q173998, Title: Middle East/Thai Windows NT May Print Incorrect Characters

Q174478, Title: Minimizing or Maximizing Does Not Redraw Window Properly

Q174541, Title: Publisher 3.0/4.0 Does Not Print Brick or Vertical Line Patterns

Q175877, Title: CSNW Connection Leak When Running 16-bit Applications

Q178202, Title: Fix for Loss of Data Records or Partial Records Written to Disk

Q180356, Title: NWConv Fails to Apply Correct Group Permissions

Macintosh Connectivity

Q171989, Title: Windows NT Services for Macintosh May Not Start in Desired Zone

Q177644, Title: Commenting Macintosh File Changes Date and Time Stamp

Q177660, Title: Access Violation Occurs in Sfmprint.exe on Busy Print Server

Q178364, Title: Macintosh Clients See Files on WinNT Server Constantly Moving

Q180716, Title: SFM Fails to Accept Associations with Two-Character Extensions

Q180717, Title: SFM: File Date and Time Stamp Change with Get Info

Q180718, Title: SFM: Disconnect Macintosh Clients before Dismounting Volume

Q185722, Title: SFM Rebuilds Indexes upon Restarting of Windows NT

Q188315, Title: Stop Error Message in Sfmsrv.sys

Network Issues (Services and Protocols)

Q109993, Title: Winsock Application Causes 0x0000000A Blue Screen STOP Message

List of Knowledge Base article fixes in Service Pack 4   *(continued)*

Q125020, Title: NetBIOS SEND WAIT Call Returns Before RECEIVE is Sent

Q141496, Title: DHCP Client Comment Disappears When Obtaining IP Address

Q154990, Title: SETPASS May Change Password of Wrong User

Q155701, Title: Invalid UDP Frames May Cause WINS to Terminate

Q156655, Title: Memory Leak and STOP Screens Using Intermediate NDIS Drivers

Q157911, Title: Deadlock in Service Control Manager During System Shut Down

Q161968, Title: NetBT Tears Down TCP Session with Many Concurrent File Transfers

Q167110, Title: WinNT Err. Msg: Stop 0x1E in FPNWSRV.SYS

Q167395, Title: RIP Routes May Expire Early When Running Windows NT 4.0 RIP

Q168662, Title: DLC May Fail When Connecting Through an IBM 2210 Router

Q169847, Title: SNMP SysUpTime Counter Resets After 49.7 Days

Q171997, Title: WINS Replication Does Not Start As Scheduled

Q172030, Title: WinNT Err Msg: Stop 0xA in TCPIP.SYS

Q172290, Title: Routing and Remote Access "Out of Buffers" Event Logs

Q172512, Title: Routing and Remote Access Event ID 20100

Q172613, Title: Errors Connecting Through RAS When Password Expires

Q173525, Title: WINS Client May Switch Primary and Secondary WINS Servers

Q173676, Title: Client Cannot Resolve MX Record via Microsoft DNS Server

Q173753, Title: Duplicate IP Addresses After Upgrading DHCP Clients to SP2

Q173941, Title: Windows NT DNR Does Not Cache Short Names

Q174676, Title: NetWare Authentication Failure When Logging On to NetWare Server

Q174869, Title: WINS Client Sends Refresh Requests to Secondary WINS Server

List of Knowledge Base article fixes in Service Pack 4   *(continued)*

Q175035, Title: Diskless Workstations Cannot Find BOOTP Server with DHCP

Q176082, Title: RRAS Server Updates Link State Database but Not Route Table

Q176209, Title: RAS or RRAS Server Fails to Answer Incoming Calls

Q176502, Title: RAS Authentication Rechallenge Resets Compression Flag

Q177125, Title: User Cannot Log On to LAN Because of RAS Logon Failures

Q177654, Title: Slow Network Performance Using NetBEUI Across Bridges

Q181120, Title: Manual Dial Dialog Fails to Appear when Logging On

Q184026, Title: NetDDE Causes Dr. Watson When Closing Incomplete Connections

Q151677, Title: NWLink SPX Ignores Allocation Number Sent By Peer

Q152079, Title: SNMP Traps Contain Invalid Agent ID Field

Q157123, Title: Communicating with SNA Hosts May Cause STOP 0x0A in DLC.SYS

Q163662, Title: Running Multiple Instances of an Application Causes STOP x50

Q166846, Title: Cannot Reconnect to TN3270 Server with Close Listen Sockets

Q170534, Title: Microsoft FTP Client Echoes Gateway Password on the Screen

Q174465, Title: Bad SAP Packet Causes 0x0000000A In Afd.sys

Q177113, Title: Incomplete Print Jobs Using JetDirect over SPX

Q177245, Title: Multiprocessor Computer May Hang Because of Tcpip.sys

Q177653, Title: CRT Conflict with Getservbyname

Q177680, Title: With GSNW, WinNT Client Cannot See All Files on NetWare Server

Q178381, Title: SNMP Leaks Memory If the OID Cannot Be Decoded

Q179092, Title: NWLNKIPX Sends Broadcast RIPX Packets Over the Network

Q181799, Title: RPC/TCP Connection Attempt Made Only to First Address

Q178110, Title: FPNW Does Not Allow OS/2 Clients to Open Files

List of Knowledge Base article fixes in Service Pack 4   *(continued)*

Printing

Q141708, Title: Printing to LPD Printer Is Slow or Fails with Windows NT

Q143160, Title: Enterprise Server Stops During Print Spooling

Q149658, Title: TCP/IP Printing Causes File Cache to Grow

Q151778, Title: Huge Downlevel Print Job Causes File Cache to Grow

Q152764, Title: Garbled Characters Appear in Windows NT Print Queue

Q152993, Title: Raster Fonts Print Different on Windows NT 4.0 Than on 3.51

Q154475, Title: Add Printer Wizard Printer Browse List Not in Alphabetical Order

Q161969, Title: LPR Printing Device Reports an Error If Printer Not Available

Q164438, Title: FPNW Print Jobs Do Not Print or Errors Occur in FPNW Interface

Q169131, Title: Print Setup Dialog Box May Take a Long Time to Display

Q172147, Title: Add Printer Wizard Hangs When Searching for Remote Printers

Q174333, Title: Installing Win95 Print Drivers on WinNT 4.0 Asks for Wrong Disk

Q174510, Title: Print Job Corruption Printing on Fast Hardware Across Slow Link

Q174540, Title: Extra Page Printed on Epson Stylus Color Printers

Q174871, Title: Printer Shares Lost after Changing Server Name

Q175637, Title: Poor Print Quality with Epson Stylus Pro XL ESC/P 2

Q175643, Title: CR Interpreted As CR/LF When Text Job Is Converted to PCL or PS

Q176087, Title: LPRMON Status Strings Are No Longer Localized on German Version

Q177445, Title: Use LoadLibraryEx When Loading Printer Drivers

Q177471, Title: EBCDIC Characters not Properly Converted to ANSI Characters

List of Knowledge Base article fixes in Service Pack 4   *(continued)*

Q179156, Title: Updated TCP/IP Printing Options for Windows NT 4.0 SP3 and Later

Q181022, Title: Err: Cannot Write to LPTx Printing to Parallel Port

Q183292, Title: Print Preview Frequently Causes Access Violation in Spooler

Remote Access Service

Q112547, Title: Dial-Up Networking Hangs After Failed Multilink Attempt

Q123597, Title: WinNT Err Msg: Error 614 Out of Buffers When Using RAS Script

Q160517, Title: RRAS May Decrement Local Static Route Metric

Q169822, Title: DSMN RAS Dial-in Properties Deletes NetWare Compatibility

Q177670, Title: RRAS Does Not Enforce Strong Encryption for DUN Clients

Q178205, Title: Connecting to a Server is Slow over RAS Using LMHOSTS File

Q186904, Title: MPROUTER Access Violation on Invalid Radius Response

Q186905, Title: Radius Client Uses 100 Percent CPU on Invalid Response

Q187940, Title: Input Filters over IPX WAN Routing May Fail to Filter Packets

Security

Q175020, Title: BUG: Remote COM Server Shuts Down After 6 Minutes

Q129457, Title: Anonymous Connections May Be Able to Obtain the Password Policy

Q147706, Title: How to Disable LM Authentication on Windows NT

Q154087, Title: Access Violation in LSASS.EXE Due to Incorrect Buffer Size

Q154174, Title: Invalid ICMP Datagram Fragments Hang Windows NT, Windows 95

Q154694, Title: New Policy Available to Hide Go To on Tools Menu

Q173817, Title: Savedump.exe Now Provides More Security to Memory.dmp

List of Knowledge Base article fixes in Service Pack 4   *(continued)*

Q175048, Title: CACLS Quits on Access Denied Errors with /c

Q182918, Title: Account Lockout Event also Stored in Security Event Log on DC

Q183054, Title: Taking Ownership Remotely May Set Owner Incorrectly

Q184017, Title: Administrators Can Display Contents of Service Account Passwords

Setup

Q158548, Title: Sysdiff Changes Dates on Files It Applies to Windows NT

Q159839, Title: Sysdiff Does Not Add Empty Directories

Q174927, Title: Error Message During Setup of Noncritical Changes

Q175266, Title: Creating Many Partitions Causes Double Drive Letters

Server-Related Issues

Q154162, Title: Memory Leak in Perfmon.exe Occurs Monitoring WINS Counters

Q154398, Title: BDC Secure Channel May Fail if More Than 250 Computer Accounts

Q154984, Title: DNS Server May Not Recursively Resolve Some Names

Q154985, Title: DNS Registry Key Not Updated When Changing Zone Type

Q157182, Title: FPNW Causes STOP 0x50 When Connection Is Closed Twice

Q158706, Title: Netmon Performance Counters Support a Maximum of Eight Adapters

Q159599, Title: WINS Consistency Checking May Not Start at Scheduled Time

Q163055, Title: DHCP Client May Fail with WinNT 4.0 SP2 Multinetted DHCP Server

Q167038, Title: RAS Clients Run Winsock and RPC Applications Slowly

Q167629, Title: Predictable Query IDs Pose Security Risks for DNS Servers

Q167708, Title: BootP Client Names Disappear in DHCP Manager

List of Knowledge Base article fixes in Service Pack 4   *(continued)*

Q168076, Title: WINS Fails to Converge

Q169274, Title: TCP/IP Causes Time Wait States to Exceed Four Minutes

Q169461, Title: Access Violation in DNS.EXE Caused by Malicious Telnet Attack

Q170518, Title: DNS Admin Fails When Managing Large Number of Zones

Q170965, Title: SFM Time and Date Stamp Change Copying Between Volumes Locally

Q171180, Title: Non-Paged Pool Memory Leak in IRP Pool Tag

Q174509, Title: Stop 0x0000000A in Ndiswan.sys with Digiboard ISDN Board

Q176973, Title: Stop 0x0000000A in Netbt.sys on BDC When WINS Server Shuts Down

Q178393, Title: SQL Server Hangs When Sending a Message Using SQLMail

Q178546, Title: CSNW Does Not Display Directory Name with Extended Characters

Q179995, Title: Memory Leak in FPNW Causes Windows NT Server to Hang

Q180532, Title: Xircom PC Card Fails to Function

Q180963, Title: Denial of Service Attack Causes Windows NT Systems to Restart

Q181311, Title: Data Corruption Occurs with Record Locking on FPNW Server

Q181928, Title: Using POLEDIT to Save Policy Files on NetWare Servers May Fail

Q182205, Title: Clients Cannot Send Mail Attachments Through Modem Sharing

Q182227, Title: DNS Server Does Not Check for Delegations Before Forwarding

Q182441, Title: Full Synchronization from WinNT PDC to LanMan Server May Fail

Q182816, Title: WINS PriorityClassHigh Parameter Does Not Work After Restarting

Q183677, Title: Client Authentication with Personal Certificates Fail

Q183718, Title: CACLS Not Resolving Principle Names Correctly

List of Knowledge Base article fixes in Service Pack 4   *(continued)*

Q183832, Title: GetHostName() Must Support Alternate Computer Names

Q184219, Title: Access Violation in Microsoft TAPI Browser 2.0

Q184228, Title: Dr. Watson in Nwssvc.exe Deleting Queue and Printer from FPNW

Q184229, Title: Copying Files to a Macintosh Volume Changes Date and Time Stamp

Q184344, Title: Reconcile on DHCP Scope Does Not Work Correctly for BOOTP Client

Q184353, Title: DHCP ALT+H Shortcut Key for HELP Is Not Available

Q184414, Title: Access Violation When Printing PostScript to SFM Print Server

Q184744, Title: DHCP Server Leaks Registry Quota on Alpha Version of Windows NT

Q184754, Title: Several Threads Created in LRPC Running Stress Test in IIS

Q184832, Title: Intermittent Name Conflicts with WINS Server

Q185051, Title: Restarting Cluster Service Causes Services.exe to Crash

Server and Workstation-Related Issues

Q129047, Title: Synchronizing DNS Information in Registry with Boot Files

Q137565, Title: System Error 53 When Connecting to a FQDN

Q143478, Title: Stop 0A in Tcpip.sys When Receiving Out Of Band (OOB) Data

Q151860, Title: STOP 0x0A While Writing to the Middle of a Cached File

Q153161, Title: WinNT Systems Running RAS May Exhaust Available DHCP Leases

Q153296, Title: Write Cache on IDE/ATAPI Disks Is Not Flushed on Shut Down

Q154387, Title: TAPISRV.EXE Thread Uses Excessive CPU Time

Q154460, Title: Denial of Service Attack Against WinNT Simple TCP/IP Services

Q154552, Title: NETSTAT Causes Memory Leak

List of Knowledge Base article fixes in Service Pack 4   *(continued)*

Q155495, Title: Reference Counter Overflow in Security Descriptor Causes STOP

Q158396, Title: Explorer Hangs When Creating a New Folder On a MAC Volume

Q158516, Title: Access Violation in RPCRT4.DLL When Pickling Buffered RPC Data

Q158581, Title: Icon Position Not Stored When Using Roaming Profiles

Q158682, Title: Shortcuts Created Under Windows NT 4.0 Resolve to UNC Paths

Q159595, Title: Missing Uppercase "A" Character in the 1257 Font

Q159909, Title: STOP 0x0000000A May Occur on Multiprocessor Systems

Q163251, Title: STOP 0xA Due to Buffer Overflow in NDISWAN.SYS

Q163852, Title: Invalid Operand with Locked CMPXCHG8B Instruction

Q164023, Title: Fix for Gethostbyname() IP Address Order on Local Multihomed Mac

Q164253, Title: WinNT Err. Msg: Event ID 2018 When Srv.sys Is out of Memory

Q164314, Title: WinNT Err Msg: STOP 0x0000001E in Win32k.sys When Moving Mouse

Q165005, Title: Windows NT Slows Down Because of Land Attack

Q165181, Title: EISA Configuration Boot Code Is Replaced on Mirror Drives

Q165439, Title: Parsing LMHOSTS with Invalid Entries Can Cause Stop 0x1E

Q165664, Title: RPC Encoding API "MesInqProcEncodingId" May Not Work

Q165989, Title: GetPeerName() Returns WSAENOTCONN After Select() Returns Success

Q166571, Title: Creating an SFM Volume on Large Partition Causes a Stop 0x24

Q169888, Title: User-Define Path Dropped When User and System Paths Too Large

Q170626, Title: DDEML: Memory Leak in Global Shared Memory

Q170817, Title: Windows NT Causes APC Smart UPS Battery to Discharge

List of Knowledge Base article fixes in Service Pack 4   *(continued)*

Q170880, Title: Diskdump.sys Common Buffer Size Is Changed

Q171181, Title: Deadlock in TCP/IP on Multiprocessor Computers

Q171295, Title: Fault Tolerant Systems May Encounter Problems with WinNT SP3

Q171307, Title: How to Disable SAP Broadcast for RPC Service

Q171386, Title: Connectivity Delay with Multiple Redirectors Installed

Q171564, Title: TCP/IP Dead Gateway Detection Algorithm Updated for Windows NT

Q171790, Title: Time Incorrect After Restarting Multiprocessor System

Q172122, Title: Toshiba I586 Pro 230 MHz System and the National 307 Chip

Q172511, Title: Stop 0x0000000A w/ Services for Macintosh & McAfee Anti-Virus

Q172885, Title: NetWare Print Server Names With Periods Truncated in Explorer

Q172982, Title: 16-bit ShellExecute Fails if Application Exists in Long Path

Q173277, Title: No Memory.dmp File Created with RAM Above 1.7 GB

Q173881, Title: STOP 0x0000000A in Netbt.sys on a Multiprocessor Computer

Q173997, Title: Drive Letter Not Displayed in Error Message Box

Q174020, Title: STOP 0x0000001E During Forced Shutdown and Program Exit

Q174534, Title: BitBlt May Not Work When Raster Operation Mode Is NOTSRCCOPY

Q174535, Title: Access Violation When TCMAPP Exceeds 16 Users

Q174543, Title: Enabling the Shift Lock Feature on Windows NT 4.0

Q174830, Title: NMI Error Message on Blue Screen May Be Garbled

Q174844, Title: Spooler Service Causing Access Violation

Q174929, Title: No Response to ARP Causes Duplicate IP Addresses on Network

List of Knowledge Base article fixes in Service Pack 4   *(continued)*

Q175225, Title: Disabling Context Menus Does Not Disable Key Combinations

Q175667, Title: Error Message: Copy Profile Error

Q175687, Title: Win32k.sys Causes STOP 0x0000001e and 0x0000000a On SMP

Q175738, Title: Collate Feature May Not Work with PostScript Printing

Q176081, Title: Access Violation in Explorer.exe Removing a Share

Q176322, Title: The Far East GetTextExtent API Fails with Null LPNFit

Q176976, Title: Wrong Return Value from MkParseDisplayName

Q176977, Title: STOP 0x00000023 FAT_FILE_SYSTEM with Corrupted Floppy Disk

Q177647, Title: Nonpaged Pool Size Incorrectly Displayed in Performance Monitor

Q177650, Title: Remote Shutdown Fails If User Is Logged On Without Rights

Q177651, Title: AT Command Handles Quotation Marks Differently

Q177655, Title: Negative Values in Performance Monitor Data

Q177668, Title: Calibration Does Not Change When You Calibrate Foot Pedals

Q177676, Title: Stop 0x00000024 May Occur When Bypass Traverse Checking Disabled

Q177757, Title: Dr. Watson Does Not Report Service Pack Number

Q177868, Title: SnmpMgrTrapListen API Returns ERROR_SERVICE_NOT_ACTIVE Error

Q178113, Title: Specifying a Group Name in LMHOSTS File May Cause STOP 0xA

Q178208, Title: CrashOnAuditFail with Logon/Logoff Auditing Causes Blue Screen

Q178413, Title: Windows NT System May Hang When Running a Filter Driver

Q178414, Title: Archive Bit Is Not Reset When a File Is Renamed

Q178550, Title: IP Address Conflict with Address 0.0.0.0

List of Knowledge Base article fixes in Service Pack 4   *(continued)*

Q178557, Title: Dr. Watson May Display Message Box Even When Disabled

Q178636, Title: Directory Listing Not Correct When Using Russian Characters

Q178723, Title: Problems with "Run Only Allowed Windows Application"

Q178741, Title: Event Log Opening Problem Causes Services.exe Failure

Q179107, Title: STOP 0x0000000A in Raspptpe.sys on a Windows NT PPTP Server

Q179129, Title: STOP 0x0000000A or 0x00000019 Due to Modified Teardrop Attack

Q179147, Title: Access Denied Starting Program

Q179187, Title: Problems Using TAPI 2.1

Q179190, Title: NWRDR May Send Excessive GetNearestServer Requests

Q179433, Title: Cache Manager May Cause Data Corruption on SMB Servers on FAT

Q179553, Title: Access Violation in PolEdit When Defining Allowed Windows Apps

Q179741, Title: STOP 0x0A Due to Duplicate Free in Afd.sys

Q179827, Title: Registry Handle Leak Causes Random Blue Screens

Q179873, Title: Files Open with UNC Path May Be Closed Prematurely

Q179983, Title: RDR Sessions on UNC Name Images May Log Off Prematurely

Q180622, Title: STOP:0x0000001E with STATUS_INSUFFICIENT_RESOURCES in Sfmsrv.sys

Q180648, Title: Windows NT 4.0 Traps with a Stop 0x24 or Stop 0xA

Q180854, Title: Access Violation in Winlogon with Third-Party Gina.dll

Q180875, Title: Russian Clients May Have File I/O Problems on an FPNW Server

Q181859, Title: Stop 0x0000000A When Using UltraBac to Back Up a SQL Server

List of Knowledge Base article fixes in Service Pack 4   *(continued)*

Q182005, Title: Euro Currency Not Available in Windows NT Character Sets

Q182047, Title: DHCP Server Performance Degraded by Large Number of Scopes

Q182288, Title: RPC May Cause System to Stop Responding during Shutdown

Q182322, Title: SNMP Appends Garbage to Data in Response to SNMP Get

Q182333, Title: Excessive Processor Usage on Print Servers

Q182444, Title: NBF MaxFrameSize Calculated Incorrectly on Token Ring

Q182781, Title: Client Connections to Multihomed Server Not Load Balanced

Q182817, Title: CSNW: Unable to Rename File on NetWare Server

Q182825, Title: NET USE Returns Error 53 When Host Has 3 or more NICs

Q183069, Title: Ensoniq PCI Sound Card Experiences Static When Disk Is Accessed

Q183335, Title: Calling Card and Area Code Not Dialed Using Both TAPI Options

Q183419, Title: Memory Leak in Spoolss.exe Causes Performance Degradation

Q183581, Title: Out of Virtual Memory Messages During Windows NT Installation

Q183651, Title: Default Memory Settings for Lexmark Optra S 1250 Incorrect

Q183652, Title: Access Violation When More Than 200 Adapters Are Installed

Q183653, Title: Client Authentication Fails Connecting to Netscape Server

Q183654, Title: IBM DTTA-351010 10.1 GB Drive Capacity Is Inaccurate

Q183656, Title: XCOPY Returns "Invalid Parameter" When Using Date Switch

Q183657, Title: Unable to Insert OLE Objects into Application Documents

Q183664, Title: NDS Logon Scripts Do Not Execute Correctly

Q183699, Title: Winsdmp.exe Inefficiently Dumps WINS Databases with Large ID

Q183704, Title: Hide Drives Policy in Common.adm Has No VALUEOFF Statement

Q183705, Title: RPC Mishandles Changes in the Number of IP Addresses

List of Knowledge Base article fixes in Service Pack 4   *(continued)*

Q183709, Title: Printing from Xerox 3006 May Cause Paper Jams

Q183812, Title: Problems When a Connection over an ISDN Bridge Is Not Closed

Q183819, Title: DCOM over HTTP Method Calls May Hang for up to 15 Minutes

Q183840, Title: Stop 0xC000021A When Starting Task Manager with CTRL+ALT+DEL

Q183859, Title: Integrity Checking on Secure Channels with Domain Controllers

Q183930, Title: FIX: IP Is Mangled When Using UDP on Multihomed Computers

Q184072, Title: HasOverlappedIoCompleted, GetOverlappedResult Give Wrong Value

Q184101, Title: Small Single and Double-Precision Values Are Rounded to Zero

Q184132, Title: Err Msg: Value Entered Does Not Match with the Specified Type

Q184139, Title: Stopping RPC Locator Service Causes Error 2186

Q184213, Title: SystemFileCacheInformation Can Be Changed Without Privilege

Q184232, Title: DCOMCNFG Saves Incorrect Display Name in Services

Q184278, Title: Server in One Domain May Disconnect Client in Another Domain

Q184350, Title: WordPerfect Suite 6.0 Setup Fails with Multiple CD-ROMs

Q184537, Title: Very Large Files Cause Performance Problems

Q184538, Title: Error Message: A Controller for This Domain Could Not Be Found

Q184752, Title: Xerox PCL Does Not Print Landscape

Q184758, Title: STOP 0x78 When NonPagedPoolSize > 7/8 of Physical Memory

Q184794, Title: STOP 0x50 May Be Caused by PPTP Registry Entries

Q184954, Title: Computer Hangs While Booting with HP 6L Printer out of Paper

Q185203, Title: SPOOLSS Hangs When Printing a File With a Corrupted EMF Record

List of Knowledge Base article fixes in Service Pack 4   *(continued)*

Q185668, Title: IntelliMouse TrackBall Wheel Does Not Work with Service Pack 3

Q187392, Title: PATCH: Stop 0x0000000A in Wind32k.sys xxxDDETrackWindowDying

Q192127, Title: BUG: RpcTestCancel() Always Returns Error Code 5

Stop Messages/Blue Screen

Q172762, Title: Continuous Bhnt.sys Load and Unload Causes STOP 0xA and 0x7F

Q174555, Title: STOP 0x0000001E When IIS Service Is Stopped

Q185300, Title: STOP 0x24 in Ntfs.sys Function NTFSMoveFile()

Q185624, Title: Calls to NtQueryVolumeInformationFile May Cause Stop 0x0000001E

Q193532, Title: Stop 0x0000000A When Running Executable from Floppy Disk

Q193548, Title: Stop 0x0000002E Using Qlogic Driver Version 2.29

TCP/IP

Q162230, Title: Fragmentation and Performance Issues with PPTP Connections

Workstation-Related Issue

Q183676, Title: Window Position of Windisk.exe Causes Access Violation

Internet Information Server 3.0 Related Issues

Q143484, Title: IIS Services Stop with Large Client Requests

Q185870, Title: IIS: SQL Server Insert Error Regarding Column Name Mismatch

Q189462, Title: Only Partial Pages Displayed or Error "The Connection Was Reset"

Internet Information Server 4.0 Related Issues

Q183283, Title: IE Through Proxy Server to IIS May Stop on Page with Scripts

Q184288, Title: GP Fault May Occur with IIS on Multi-processor System

List of Knowledge Base article fixes in Service Pack 4   *(continued)*

Q184891, Title: Server.HTMLEncode Garbles Extended Characters

Q185219, Title: IIS 4.0 with Multiple Certificates May Return Error

Q185349, Title: Problems Remotely Accessing W3 or FTP Perfmon Counters

Q186929, Title: LowercaseFiles Registry Key Has Added Functionality

Q188806, Title: "::$DATA" Data Stream Name of a File May Return Source

Q189262, Title: FTP Passive Mode May Terminate Session

Q190009, Title: Client Cert. Mapping Only Works w/First Page on Proxy Connection

Q190010, Title: Logging Performs Unwanted Flushes of Log Data Buffer

Q190015, Title: Setting LogonMethod to Batch Causes "Parameter is Incorrect"

Q193525, Title: Access Violation Occurs When Viewing Web Sharing Tab

Q193526, Title: W3SVC Counters Fail after a Successful Install

Q193528, Title: Internet Service Manager Does Not Allow Wildcard Redirections

Q193613, Title: ADSI Paths Greater than 80 Characters Causes Access Violation

Q193614, Title: Viewing Computer from MMC Causes Access Violation to Occur

Q193688, Title: HTMLA: Object Already Exists When Creating New Web Sites

Q193689, Title: IIS Security: Mapping IDC Reveals Paths for Web Directories

Q193793, Title: ":$DATA" Data Stream Name Returns Source of a Remote File

Q193812, Title: Extended Characters in URL Translated into UTF-8 Characters

Q194393, Title: New Window From Here Option in MMC May Cause Fatal Error

Q194787, Title: XFOR: IIS 4.0 SMTP Does Not Retry Delivery on HELO/EHLO Failures

List of Knowledge Base article fixes in Service Pack 4   *(continued)*

Microsoft Commercial Internet Server Issues

Q190785, Title: IMS Not Trying Next MX Record If Session to Port 25 Established

Q193686, Title: SMTP Services Do Not Start Automatically After One Is Stopped

Q193687, Title: Invalid Handle Exception Error During SMTP Server Maintenance

Q194785, Title: XFOR: Windows NT Option Pack Certificate Causes MCIS SSL to Fail

Q194786, Title: XFOR: MCIS SMTP Service Strands Messages

Proxy Server Issues

Q176922, Title: Multiple IP Addresses Cause Dynamic Packet Filter to Fail

Q189276, Title: ODBC Causes Access Violation in 16-Bit Winsock

Site Server 3.0 issue

Q187999, Title: "Access Denied" w/ Personalization & Membership Authentication

General Service Pack 4 Fix

Q192292, Title: Unpredictable TCP Sequence Numbers in SP4

Q142047, Title: Bad Network Packet May Cause Access Violation (AV) on DNS Server

Q142615, Title: Event Log Service Fails to Check Access to Security Log File

Q142635, Title: Cannot Change the Drive Letter of Removable Drives

Q159310, Title: Updated Version of Dns.exe Fixes Several Problems

Q167040, Title: PPTP Performance Update for Windows NT 4.0 Release Notes

Q168748, Title: Java Applets Cause IE 3.02 to Stop Responding w/ SP3

Q169291, Title: Using Scopes with Different Subnet Masks in a Superscope

Q169839, Title: XFOR: Cannot Enable (Appletalk) MTA Service NT SP3

List of Knowledge Base article fixes in Service Pack 4   *(continued)*

Q170517, Title: Cannot Log on Using IPX After Installing SP3 on Windows NT 4.0

Q173059, Title: Security Events Are Not Logged During Audit

Q173523, Title: IIS 3.0 Can Fail in Low Memory Conditions

Q174748, Title: XADM: ESEUTIL /g Returns Error -1022

Q175093, Title: User Manager Does Not Recognize February 2000 As a Leap Year

Q177154, Title: Access Control Causes Reverse Proxy to Fail

Q177677, Title: TSR Applications Hang While Login.exe Is Running

Q177906, Title: Caching Does Not Work Under Reverse Proxying

Q177983, Title: Stop 0xA in Netbt.sys with Greater Than 64 Adapters

Q178302, Title: XADM: Upgrade to Exchange 5.5 Fails If Virus Software Is Enabled

Q178471, Title: STOP 0XA Caused by Race Condition in VDM and Process Delete

Q179157, Title: Stop 0xA in Tcpip.sys When Source Routing Data Exceeds 18 Bytes

Q180122, Title: After Changing the Time, Windows NT May Skip a Day

Q180168, Title: Novell Client 32 for Win95 Displays Duplicate Files on FPNW

Q182540, Title: WinNT x86 MPS HAL Can Fail To Map System Relative IRQs

Q182644, Title: DNR Sorts IP Address for Multihomed Hosts Before Returning List

Q183123, Title: Find Files Displays Garbled Date if Year is 2000 or Greater

Q183125, Title: Shell Doc Property Dialog Custom Date Incorrect after Year 2000

Q183749, Title: Access Violation in INETINFO:TerminateExtension

Q183755, Title: More Than One Internal IP with Socks Enabled Causes Dr. Watson

Q183875, Title: DHCP Server Leases Excluded Addresses if the Scope Is Expanded

List of Knowledge Base article fixes in Service Pack 4   *(continued)*

Q183886, Title: Access Violation in LSASS When Logging on System

Q184835, Title: Explorer on Windows 95 DFS Client May Hang

Q184836, Title: Application Access Violates When Session Is Terminated

Q184875, Title: API Function BroadcastSystemMessage() Always Returns 1 (Success)

Q184879, Title: Windows NT Logon Dialog May Disappear

Q184881, Title: Reverse Lookups with BIND Earlier Than 4.8.3 Fail

Q184937, Title: Session Between Multihomed Computers May End Unexpectedly

Q184996, Title: Incomplete List of NetWare Server Volumes with CSNW/GSNW

Q184998, Title: RDR May Read or Write from Wrong File If File Is Memory Mapped

Q185081, Title: No Domain Controllers Found When Logging on Using RAS

Q185137, Title: Log Logical Record Request May Be Sent to Wrong Server

Q185142, Title: NetWare API Log Logical Record May Incorrectly Succeed

Q185212, Title: Cluster Server Does Not Support More than 900 Shares

Q185260, Title: User Accounts May Get Locked out After Entering Wrong Password

Q185323, Title: Pool NonPaged Bytes Not Accurately Calculated for User Mode

Q185355, Title: Printers Folder Displays Printer Error When Printer Is Busy

Q185559, Title: Negative Value in NtGdiFastPolyPolyline Causes Blue Screen

Q185568, Title: WlxCloseUserDesktop Function Unavailable for GINA Writers

Q185571, Title: Printing from Lotus Freelance 97 Produces Thin Horizontal Line

Q185605, Title: Stop Error Caused by Invalid Use of Private Video Driver Handle

Q185625, Title: Windows NT Client Logon Fails with EnableSecuritySignature Set

List of Knowledge Base article fixes in Service Pack 4   *(continued)*

Q185682, Title: Bugcheck When IPX Is Bound to Only Ndiswan Adapter

Q185723, Title: Explorer File Copy from Windows 95 Share Fails

Q185729, Title: Computer Becomes Unresponsive During CGI Stress Test

Q185734, Title: DNS Server Access Violation in Dns!sendNbstatResponse Routine

Q185735, Title: Explorer Crashes When Dragging Lotus Notes Files over Toolbar

Q185736, Title: Applications May Appear Hung or Unresponsive on Windows NT 4.0

Q185765, Title: HP LaserJet 4Si Driver Unprintable Region is Incorrect

Q185773, Title: NTFS Corruption on Drives > 4 GB Using ExtendOEMPartition

Q185787, Title: STOP 0x0000002E on Alpha with ISA Sound Card

Q185788, Title: Windows NT Hangs on Boot on DEC Alpha Clustered Servers

Q185791, Title: STOP on DEC Miata and Rawhide Platforms Using Graphics Tablet

Q185867, Title: STOP 0x0000000A in Win32k.sys After Installing Korean Office 97

Q185892, Title: Unwanted Popup Message While Printing to an LPR Printer

Q185944, Title: Stop 0x7B After Installing Windows NT on an ALR Evolution-V ST

Q185945, Title: Access violation in win32k!HMMarkObjectDestroy in JPN and KOR NT

Q186051, Title: Archive Bit Is Not Set with File or Directory Rename

Q186078, Title: Name Resolution May Fail If NetBios Name Has ASCII Character

Q186081, Title: STOP 0x0000000A When Restoring Tape

Q186101, Title: FTP Client Does Not Show the Correct Transfer Size for Files

Q186150, Title: NetBEUI May Hang When Using Arcnet Under Heavy Network Traffic

Q186158, Title: Blue Screen When Shutting Down with RAS Connection Established

List of Knowledge Base article fixes in Service Pack 4   *(continued)*

Q186217, Title: 3C509 Is Not Autodetected During Setup on ThinkPad 760EL & XL

Q186241, Title: Dr. Watson May Cause CPU Usage to Spike

Q186247, Title: Users Are Unable to Print to Server

Q186339, Title: Adobe ATM 4.1 OpenType Fonts Not Showing up in Font Menu

Q186357, Title: RPC UseWinsockForIP is Only Applicable to UDP and IPX

Q186416, Title: System Hang Results from Large Number of Notify Syncs

Q186434, Title: Slow Network Default Profile Operation

Q186439, Title: Removing Server Service Results in Memory Leak

Q186455, Title: Mgmtapi.dll Opens Trap Socket in Exclusive Mode

Q186463, Title: Windows NT Replies to Address Mask Requests

Q186473, Title: You Can Delete All Records on a WINS Server Using SNMP

Q186494, Title: Event ID 517 Not Created When Security Log Is Cleared

Q186495, Title: WOW Leak Launching Many Instances of a 16-Bit Application

Q186669, Title: FPNW Logout.exe Incorrectly Reports Year After Jan. 1, 2000

Q186743, Title: International Characters Print Incorrectly in Schedule Plus

Q186746, Title: International Calling Codes Updated in Service Pack 4

Q186770, Title: Windows NT Hangs Trying to Access SuperDisk SLS-120 Disk Drive

Q186805, Title: Intermittent Stop 0xA in Srv.sys on Shutdown

Q186820, Title: DNS Server Returns Wrong Response When WINS Lookup Is Enabled

Q186860, Title: Update Memory Settings and Add Exec Paper Size to Sharp Models

Q186873, Title: Netbios Delays Sending/Receiving Packets When Session Is Lost

List of Knowledge Base article fixes in Service Pack 4   *(continued)*

Q186963, Title: Incorrect Dimensions in Executive Form with Mannesmann Driver

Q187277, Title: The FTP PORT Command Fails in IIS 3.0

Q187302, Title: Stop 0x00000040 in NetBT Protocol

Q187493, Title: Some Netscape Client Certificates Rejected by IIS

Q187508, Title: FTP Server Fails to Respond If First Binding Does Not Work

Q187518, Title: Apps Using Beep API on Multiprocessor Systems May Crash

Q187519, Title: NTBackup Will Not Run from Command Line with Blank Space

Q187520, Title: Tandberg SL5 Tape Device Not Auto-Detected in Window NT 4.0

Q187555, Title: WINS Incorrect Version ID Assigned During Scavenging

Q187576, Title: Stop 0x0000000A May Occur in TCP/IP

Q187577, Title: STOP 0xA Because of Spin Lock in Sfmatalk.sys on DEC Alpha

Q187615, Title: Setup Hangs When System Includes More Than Two RAW Drives

Q187669, Title: Unable to Use NetBIOS Resources over SLIP

Q187672, Title: Access Violation in RAS Using Multilink

Q187686, Title: LookupAccountSid Causes Access Violation on Multihomed System

Q187696, Title: Changes to Calculator in Service Pack 4

Q187705, Title: Application Error in CorelWEB.GALLERY

Q187708, Title: Cannot Connect to SQL Virtual Server via Sockets in Cluster

Q187709, Title: Domain Name Resolver Caches Responses

Q187769, Title: Application Error in NTVDM Running cc:Mail Utilities

Q187802, Title: DHCP Assigns "Bad_Address" to "Host Unreachable"

List of Knowledge Base article fixes in Service Pack 4   *(continued)*

Q187830, Title: Performance Decrease Transmitting Data over the Network

Q187856, Title: IIS: Limit SSL Message Size to 16 KB for Netscape

Q187884, Title: CoCreateInstance on Multiple Threads Causes Hangs or Failures

Q187936, Title: Application May Hang Calling LogonUser() API

Q187939, Title: IPX May Not Work When Packet Size Is Larger Than Receive Buffer

Q187941, Title: An Explanation of the New CHKDSK /C and /I Switches

Q187947, Title: 100 Percent CPU System Handle Problem

Q187964, Title: MGI PhotoSuite May Paste Screenshots as Garbage or an AV Occurs

Q188000, Title: Cannot Enter Stand-Alone Dieresis Character on Swiss Keyboards

Q188027, Title: Performance, Audit Logging, and Fixes to the DHCP Service

Q188303, Title: Random Stop 0x50 Errors on Cirrus Video Adapters

Q188312, Title: Lexmark Optra E+ Unprintable Region Is Incorrect

Q188414, Title: Random Stop 0x0000000A When Running IPX over Token Ring

Q188424, Title: Multilayered Display Driver Produces Black Line in Word

Q188571, Title: STOP 0x0000000A in Netbt.sys Caused by Invalid DNS Record

Q188652, Title: Error Replicating Registry Keys

Q188700, Title: Screensaver Password Works Even if Account Is Locked Out

Q188838, Title: Task Manager CPU Usage Only Displays Eight Processors

Q188879, Title: RPC Endpoint Mapper Will Not Register All Interfaces

Q188896, Title: Access Violation in Explorer.exe Changing Share Permissions

Q189010, Title: SBS: RAS Leases Six Addresses from DHCP

List of Knowledge Base article fixes in Service Pack 4   *(continued)*

Q189011, Title: Using Performance Monitor Remotely Causes Access Violation

Q189012, Title: Clicking Default Scope Does Not Open Active Lease Window

Q189013, Title: Atapi.sys Does Not Support Multiple Logical Devices

Q189032, Title: Floating Point Arguments Won't Pass Between NT RPC and IBM RPC

Q189061, Title: Repeated Regsavekey/Regrestorekey Actions Corrupt Registry Hive

Q189080, Title: TCP Connection May Drop When Transferring Large Amounts of Data

Q189114, Title: NetDDE Refuses Incoming WM_DDE_INITIATEs from Windows 95

Q189119, Title: UserEnv Returns Corrupted Profile for All Failures

Q189171, Title: WinSock Applications May Fail or Stop Responding

Q189225, Title: LMMIB2 Unable to "Walk" from .1.3.6.1.4.1.77.1.4.4

Q189245, Title: Lmmib2.dll Does Not Support All Objects

Q189283, Title: No More Than About 570 Reservations Visible in a DHCP Scope

Q189290, Title: Loss of Desktop After Logon When Using a Filter Gina.dll

Q189291, Title: Hang in Winlogon on Workstation Locked Dialog Box

Q189395, Title: Support for Canadian ACNOR Keyboard

Q189471, Title: WpuOpenCurrentThread Does Not Work

Q189522, Title: Network Drive Letters in PATH Statement Causes Excessive Traffic

Q189579, Title: F11 and F12 Keys Do Not Function in MS-DOS Applications

Q189606, Title: Browser Service Fails to Start or Stop Button Is Unavailable

Q189612, Title: Access Violation Occurs in Windows NT Explorer (Explorer.exe)

Q189756, Title: PerfMon Percentage of Registry Quota in Use Displayed Wrong

List of Knowledge Base article fixes in Service Pack 4   *(continued)*

Q189988, Title: CMPXCHG8B CPUs in Non-Intel/AMD x86 Compatibles Not Supported

Q190011, Title: Perl Script Mappings Converted to Uppercase During Upgrade

Q190288, Title: SecHole Lets Non-administrative Users Gain Debug Level Access

Q190354, Title: Unattended Setup of MSCS with -JOIN Parameter Requires Input

Q190449, Title: Corrupted SAM Hangs Windows NT Server

Q190506, Title: WINS Replication Problem Events 4262, 4261, and 1c Replication

Q190552, Title: WinNT 4.0 DHCP Client Modified to meet RFC 2131

Q190791, Title: STATUS_CANT_WAIT Returned from an NTCreateFile Call

Q190834, Title: SCSI Adapter Is No Longer Visible from SCSI Adapters Utility

Q190931, Title: Snmptrap.exe Ignores SNMP Trap PDU Greater Than 4,096 Bytes

Q190932, Title: SNMP Service Ignores SNMP Trap PDU Greater Than 4,096 Bytes

Q191088, Title: Printer Prompts for Paper with Dutch Workstations

Q191098, Title: Large File Copy Operation Causes Available Bytes to Drop

Q191284, Title: STOP 0x0000001E in Netbt.sys

Q191285, Title: Services for Macintosh Index Corruption on Large Volumes

Q191309, Title: ALT+Numeric Keypad Problem When CHCP Command is Used

Q191362, Title: FPNW Pass-Through Authentication from Trusted Domain May Fail

Q191387, Title: Unable to Run 16-bit Apps If FILES= Is Greater Than 255

Q191418, Title: Arcs Print Incorrectly with EMF on PCL Printers

Q191419, Title: GP Fault or Access Violation When Buffer Too Small

Q191428, Title: WINS Replication Fails If More Than 30 Partners Are Configured

List of Knowledge Base article fixes in Service Pack 4   *(continued)*

Q191614, Title: Able to Commit More Memory Than Is Available

Q191634, Title: Group Policies Cause Excessive \PIPE\samr Connections on PDC

Q191689, Title: Incorrect Font Characteristics May Be Used on Imported Graphics

Q191751, Title: Smoothing Fonts Disabled Using ETO_GLYPHINDEX

Q191756, Title: Stop 0x1E Switching Between System Menus in Application Window

Q191767, Title: LogicalDisk Partition Missing in Performance Monitor

Q191768, Title: Date of Print Job May Be Displayed Incorrectly in Print Queue

Q191775, Title: WINS Service Fails to Start With More Than 99 PNG Entries

Q191830, Title: Memory Leak Due to Repeated Logon/Logoff May Corrupt Profiles

Q191832, Title: Access Violation in Hangul Version of Lotus Organizer 97

Q191834, Title: Network Problems That Occur When Logging Off May Corrupt Profile

Q191850, Title: Convert Reports Cannot Create Elementary File System Structures

Q191852, Title: Bhnetb.dll Leaks Memory in Winlogon.exe Process with NetMon

Q191896, Title: Printing to NT LPD Server from SUN OS 4.1.4 May Not Process C/R

Q191915, Title: Screen Saver Time-out is Limited to 60 Minutes

Q191992, Title: NdrConvert Causes Access Violation in RPC Client on WinNT 4.0

Q192051, Title: LDAP Does Not Authenticate on French WinNT Due to Encryption

Q192056, Title: Point and Print Functionality with More Than 20 Driver Files

Q192104, Title: Windows NT Does Not Start If Primary Partition Is Above 2 GB

Q192126, Title: Add Workstation Fails with RestrictAnonymous

Q192132, Title: STA Threads Lose Thread Token

List of Knowledge Base article fixes in Service Pack 4   *(continued)*

Q192229, Title: Login Script Group Membership Mapping on BDC Fail If PDC Is Down

Q192265, Title: Srvinfo.exe Does Not Close Registry Handles with SMTP Service

Q192266, Title: Sockets-based Child Processes Are Not Stopped

Q192267, Title: Various STOP Errors When Opening Files on Novell NetWare Servers

Q192293, Title: IIS Stops ODBC Logging after Failing to Communicate with SQL

Q192409, Title: Open Files Can Cause Kernel to Report INSUFFICIENT_RESOURCES

Q192453, Title: MoveFile API from Windows 95 with Invalid UNC Causes STOP 0xa

Q192457, Title: Downloaded File May Be Saved in Incorrect Folder with IE

Q192460, Title: Matrox Video Driver Causes STOP 0x00000050

Q192547, Title: WINSADMIN Writes Invalid SP Time to Registry

Q192690, Title: Search: Unable to Connect to Catalog Server via Search MMC

Q192736, Title: STOP 0x0000000A Blue Screen on Alpha AXP

Q192749, Title: Multiple SSL Connections May Cause Error Starting Security Sys

Q192773, Title: Cluster Server Memory Leak When MTS Explorer Is Running

Q192774, Title: Stop 0x0000000A in Tcpip.sys Processing an ICMP Packet

Q192786, Title: Event ID 11 Changed to an Informational Message

Q193056, Title: Problems in Date/Time after Choosing February 29 in a Leap Year

Q193064, Title: Pressing Cancel Button in Date/Time Utility Changes Date

Q193090, Title: Inetmib1.dll Causes Memory Leak in Winlogon.exe Process

Q193106, Title: Filesystem Filter Drivers may Unload Unexpectedly

Q193121, Title: Cannot Connect to DFS Leaf a Second Time if Server is NetWare

Q193157, Title: TCP/IP Does Not Allow MAC Addresses to Change Dynamically

List of Knowledge Base article fixes in Service Pack 4   *(continued)*

Q193169, Title: Script Mappings Are Not Removed from the Registry after Migration

Q193206, Title: Acquiring SNMP Info For OSPF in RRAS Hangs

Q193209, Title: Gethostbyname Not Working Correctly with Only DUN Installed

Q193233, Title: Rpcss.exe Consumes 100% CPU Due to RPC Spoofing Attack

Q193271, Title: Cannot Create Virtual Directory in Administrator Program

Q193371, Title: WINS/DHCP Admin Show Expiration Dates 2000 - 2009 with One Digit

Q193436, Title: DHCP Client Shuts Down After Two Declines

Q193499, Title: Multiple RRAS Client Disconnects Cause Increased CPU Usage

Q193529, Title: Modem Sharing Clients Cause Stop 0x000001E on SBS

Q193530, Title: Access Violation in WINSCL When Using CR or SDB Parameter

Q193596, Title: RASMAN Registry Values Cannot Be Set Higher Than 0xFF

Q193646, Title: Event ID 10005 from DCOM After Installing IIS

Q193654, Title: Services Continue to Run After Shutdown Initiated

Q193655, Title: Multiple Entries for AUTOCHK Abort in System Log

Q193779, Title: Cluster Server Drive Letters Do Not Update Using Disk Admin

Q193781, Title: Cache Manager May Cause Data Corruption

Q193806, Title: CSNW Error 85, Local Device Already in Use

Q193891, Title: HTTP Through Firewall and "Bypass Proxy for Local Intranet"

Q193899, Title: Event ID 1008, 4005 with Missing TCP/IP Performance Counters

Q193921, Title: Virtual Server Is No Longer Viewable Through MMC

Q194130, Title: SNMP Edit Box Drops a Character When Writing to the Registry

Q194133, Title: Remote Shell (RSH) Commands Hang w/ Multiple Sessions Running

List of Knowledge Base article fixes in Service Pack 4   *(continued)*

Q194168, Title: Dns.exe Dr. Watson When Changing the TTL of a Cached Record

Q194193, Title: STOP 0xA in Sfmatalk.sys When Copying Files on an SFM Volume

Q194194, Title: DNS Fails with Error 1201 If Secondary Zone File Not Specified

Q194200, Title: Cannot Change WinNT Passwords from Exchange and Outlook Clients

Q194228, Title: Rule Containing Multiple Clauses Only Functions Properly Once

Q194322, Title: T/R NIC May Fail Windows Hardware Quality Lab (WHQL) Test

Q194336, Title: ERROR: Destroyed NTFS Directory

Q194340, Title: Access Violation when Using Rcp.exe to Copy to Unix

Q194341, Title: Simple TCP/IP Services Can Be Driven to 100% CPU

Q194424, Title: DHCP Server May Fail to Record Lease

Q194429, Title: TCPIP Timewaitstate may not remain in 2*msl

Q194431, Title: Applications May be able to "Listen" on TCP or UDP Ports.

Q194465, Title: PPTP May Refuse Connections When VPNs Are Free

Q194726, Title: FPNW Client Does Not Get Correct Time or Date After Y2K

Q194850, Title: IMS: SMTPSVC May Display BCC Addresses on Outgoing Messages

Q194919, Title: Windows NT Boot Process Hangs Because of DST Manipulation

Q195083, Title: Access Violation Installing News Service on DEC Alpha Computer

Q195084, Title: Cannot Send SSL Messages after Installing New Certificate

APPENDIX B

Configuring the Server Proxy Feature for Exchange Server 4.0 - 5.5

Configuring Server Proxy

Follow these instructions *exactly* or Microsoft Exchange will not function with the Server Proxy feature.

1. Install and configure the Microsoft Proxy Server.
2. Select **Client Configuration** in the Winsock Proxy Properties dialog. Type *IP Address* in the Client Connects to Microsoft Winsock Proxy Server by... field.
3. Install the WinSock Proxy (WSP) Client on the Exchange Server computer *even if it is already installed*. To do this, connect to the MSPCLNT share on the Proxy Server and run SETUP.EXE from the root directory.
4. Change the DNS settings on the Exchange Server computer. You *must* define an Internet DNS server address on the Exchange server or it will not be able to send mail correctly. In Control Panel/Network/TCPIP click the **DNS** tab. Enter the DNS server address(es) for your Internet Service Provider.

   If your DNS server does not function properly, use the MSN DNS servers below to test name resolution:

   204.255.246.17

   204.255.246.18

5. Test the WSP client on the Exchange Server. At the MS-DOS prompt type:

   FTP FTP.MICROSOFT.COM

   If the WSP client is functioning the response should be similar to:

   Connected to ftp.microsoft.com.

   220 ftp Microsoft FTP Service (Version 3.0).

   User (ftp.microsoft.com:(none)):

6. Once the WSP client is running, you have to create *two* WSPCFG.INI files in the Proxy Server on the Exchange Server.

The first WSPCFG.INI file is for use with the Exchange SMTP service. To create it, copy and paste the four lines below to Notepad (use copy/paste—**do not type in the information**) and save the file as WSPCFG.INI in the directory where MSEXCIMC.EXE is located:

[MSEXCIMC]

ServerBindTcpPorts=25

Persistent=1

KillOldSession=1

The SMTP port (25) on the Exchange Server is now bound to Proxy Server port 25.

The second WSPCFG.INI file is for use with the Exchange store (STORE.EXE). To create it, copy and paste the four lines below to Notepad (use copy/paste—**do not type in the information**) and save the file as WSPCFG.INI in the directory where STORE.EXE is located:

[STORE]

ServerBindTcpPorts=110,119,143

Persistent=1

KillOldSession=1

Additional ports, such as ports 119 and 143 above, can be listed because STORE.EXE provides Network News Transfer Protocol (NNTP) on port 119, POP mail on port 110, etc.

7. Verify that the two WSPCFG.INI files do not have a .TXT extension, which can happen if your Explorer interface uses default settings. If the file appears as WSPCFG.INI.TXT, rename it.

8. If you are using Access Control on the Winsock Proxy service follow the steps below. If you are not using it, go to step 9.

   If Access Control is enabled on the Winsock Proxy service, you must grant the user account that starts the Exchange services access to the Proxy Server.

   This must be a *domain user account*, not a local account on the Exchange server. If it is a local account, create a new user account on the domain. In Control Panel, click **Services** then click **Startup**.

   In the Winsock Proxy **Properties** dialog click **Permissions** and assign the new account unlimited access.

9. Reboot the Exchange server.

   Once the Exchange server restarts, it should automatically listen on the external interface of the Proxy Server.

10. Test connectivity to the Exchange services from a machine that is *directly connected* to the Internet.

    On the test computer, select Run from the Start menu and enter: **TELNET.EXE**

    Form the **Connect** menu select **Remote System**. Enter these variables:

    HOST NAME: External IP address of the proxy server

    PORT: 25

    TERM TYPE: vt100

    When you are connected, a blank screen is displayed. Press the ENTER key and wait about 30 seconds. You should see a message from the Exchange SMTP service indicating a good setup. If not, re-check your settings.

    You can also try port 110 to test the POP service.

Configuring Your DNS Mail Exchange (MX) Record

1. If you are using your Internet Service Provider's DNS server, you must contact them and ask to add **MX** and **A** DNS resource records for your domain so other Internet mail servers can contact your Exchange server. These records must refer to the IP address of the Proxy Server's external network adapter *not* to the internal IP address of the Exchange Server or to SMTP server itself.

   For example, if your registered Internet domain name is *mydomain.com* and your internal Exchange server uses a DNS host name of *exchange1*, you would need to use an **MX** record (it stands for *mail ex-changer*) to provide other Internet hosts the name of your internal Exchange server. In this case, an **MX** record added in the *mydomain.com* zone could provide the information:

   mydomain.com IN MX 10 exchange1.mydomain.com

2. Next you need to create an **A** record (it stands for *address*) for *exchange1.mydomain.com* that uses the Proxy Server's external IP address. For example, if that is 127.34.56.89 you would add this **A** record to the *mydomain.com* zone:

   exchange1.mydomain.com   IN A 127.34.56.89

3. In addition, you can add or create a **PTR** record (it stands for *pointer*) to the *mydomain.com* zone to provide reverse lookup. A valid **PTR** record would be:

   89.56.34.127.in-addr.arpa   IN PTR exchange1.mydomain.com

More Information

Except for step 6, these server proxy setup instructions also apply to other, third-party SMTP mail servers, although WSPCFG.INI settings will differ. WSPCFG.INI settings for other products (including SMTP servers) see Knowledge Base article Q177153, Title: Additional Proxy Server 2.0 Configurations.

If dynamic packet filtering is enabled on the proxy server (recommended), the proxy server will dynamically open all necessary ports when they are requested. No special configuration is needed.

You do not have to configure a DNS address on other proxy clients. This is required only on the Exchange server computer.

Index

Symbols and Numbers

A

Inventory of hardware and software, supporting with SMS, 7

inventory record, sending from the secondary site to the primary, 90

inventory reporting, transferring to primary site servers, 73

inventory-scanning interval, changing from weekly to monthly, 700

IP, network layer security for, 313

IP addresses
    determining the current with GetSMID, 688
    problems obtaining with GetSMID, 690
    specifying, 665
    support by MSCS, 444–45

IPCP protocol, providing PPP configurations to remote clients, 372

IP forwarding, 371

IP GRE packets, 311

IP Network Address Translator (NAT), 445

IPSEC (Internet Protocol Security), 313, 314

IpxClientAccess parameter in the [<RasParameters>] section of the answer file, 672

IPX, installing in unattended mode, 663

[<IPX Parameters>] section of the answer file, 664

IsAlive polling interval, tuning the values of, 446

ISDN adapter pools, avoiding, 310

IsDomainMaster, disabling, 554

ISLOGON.BAT used at PGHCC, 49–50

isql script, recreating the structure of a restored SMS database, 76

ISS (Internet Security System), 226–28

_ISTMP0.DIR temporary directory, checking for the presence of, 627

IT group
    controlling access to information, 280
    roles for, 5

ITSEC Home page, 297

J

Job Automation Developer, test group roles and responsibilities, 25

Job Automation Tester/QA, 12, 25

job triggers, distributing, 15

JOINDOM, 636

JoinDomain parameter in the [Network] section of the answer file, 659

JoinWorkgroup parameter in the [Network] section of the answer file, 659

JSCRIPT, enabling to manipulate IIS admin objects, 352

K

Kane Security Analyst (KSA), 226–27

kbdclass.sys, loading, 596

kbdxx, loading, 596

Kerberos Authentication Protocol Web site, 298

keyboard, simulating the use of all keys on, 677–79

keyboard driver, loading, 596

[KeyboardDrivers] section of the answer file, 651

keyboard input, retrieving during a batch file, 587, 591

KeyboardLayout parameter in the [Unattended] section of answer file, 650

Keyboard properties panel, 644

Key Manager, 342, 367

key request process, template for documenting, 342

key-to-value translations in ScriptIT, 678–79

Key Vision, 353–54

KILL utility, terminating the WINLOGON process, 456

KIX32.EXE, 385, 740

KIX32 script, 392

KIXDOSMS.SCR used at PGHCC, 70

KIXSCRIPT.SCR used at PGHCC, 64–69

KiXTart scripting utility, 39, 49

Knowledge Base article
    Q110352, 83
    Q125487, 83
    Q138347, 87
    Q156813, 547

Knowledge Base article, fixes in Service Pack 4, 759–94

KSA (Kane Security Analyst), 226–27

L

L2TP, security features of, 314

LABEL command in a batch file, 557

Lante Corporation, 163, 215

last logged on user, blocking the display of, 196

Layer 2 VPN protocols (PPTP/L2TP), combining with IPSEC, 313

LDAP, supporting, 361

LDAP-based directory, 361–64, 366

leaf objects, 700–703

legacy configuration files, erasing from the destination hard disk, 586, 590

LegalNoticeText value, 340

Legal Notice (Windows NT security setting), 247

LEGAL script, 636

<letter> directories, 570

Lightweight Directory Access Protocol (LDAP). See LDAP

Limit_Host parameter in the [<NetWare Client Parameters>] section of the answer file, 669

Limit the Duration of Passwords Granted to Third Parties or Consultants with an Expiration Flag (Windows NT security setting), 260

LimitTo parameter of the [<Detect Adapters Section>] of the answer file, 661

live monitoring after software release, 15

LMAnnounce, disabling, 554

Load and Unload Device Drivers (Windows NT security setting), 256

Microsoft Press offers *comprehensive* learning solutions to help new users, power users, and professionals get the most from *Microsoft technology.*

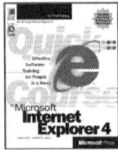

Quick Course® Series
Fast, to-the-point instruction for new users

Starts Here® Series
Interactive instruction on CD-ROM that helps students learn by doing

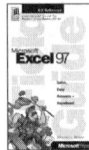

Field Guide Series
Concise, A–Z references for quick, easy answers—anywhere

Web Titles
Timely books on a wide variety of Internet topics

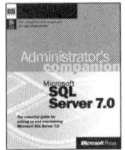

Administrator's Companion
Details every significant aspect of the product deployment cycle

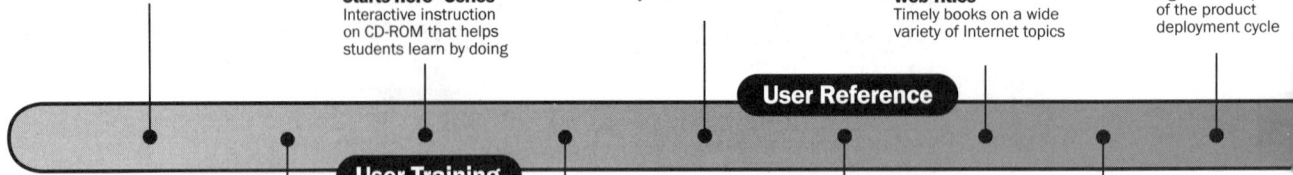

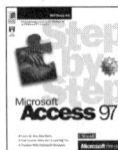

User Reference

User Training

Step by Step Series
Self-paced tutorials for classroom instruction or individualized study

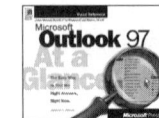

At a Glance Series
Quick visual guides for task-oriented instruction

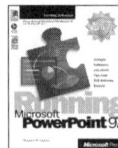

Running Series
A comprehensive curriculum alternative to standard documentation books

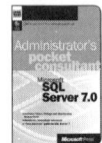

Administrator's Pocket Consultant
Quick answers for everyday network management issues

With **over 200** *print,*
multimedia, and online resources—
whatever your training or
reference need or learning style,
we've got a solution to help
you *start faster and go farther.*

Notes from the Field
Microsoft Consulting Services'
best practices for supporting
enterprise technology

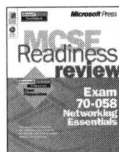

Readiness Reviews
Microsoft Certified
Professional exam
practice on CD-ROM

Resource Kits
Comprehensive technical
information and tools to
plan, deploy, and manage
Microsoft technology

**Microsoft®
Professional Editions**
Technical information
straight from the source

Professional

Developers

**Technical
References**
Highly focused
IT reference
and solutions

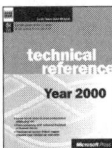

**Strategic
Technology Series**
Easy-to-read overviews
for decision makers

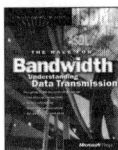

**Microsoft Certified
Professional Training Kits**
The Microsoft Official
Curriculum for certification
exams

Developer Learning Tools
Learning packages designed to
build mastery of programming
fundamentals

**Microsoft
Programming Series**
The foundations of
software development

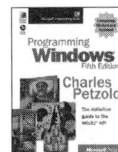

*Look for them at your bookstore
or computer store today!*

Microsoft Press

mspress.microsoft.com

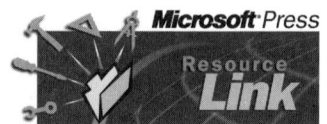

MICROSOFT LICENSE AGREEMENT
Book Companion CD

IMPORTANT—READ CAREFULLY: This Microsoft End-User License Agreement ("EULA") is a legal agreement between you (either an individual or an entity) and Microsoft Corporation for the Microsoft product identified above, which includes computer software and may include associated media, printed materials, and "online" or electronic documentation ("SOFTWARE PRODUCT"). Any component included within the SOFTWARE PRODUCT that is accompanied by a separate End-User License Agreement shall be governed by such agreement and not the terms set forth below. By installing, copying, or otherwise using the SOFTWARE PRODUCT, you agree to be bound by the terms of this EULA. If you do not agree to the terms of this EULA, you are not authorized to install, copy, or otherwise use the SOFTWARE PRODUCT; you may, however, return the SOFTWARE PRODUCT, along with all printed materials and other items that form a part of the Microsoft product that includes the SOFTWARE PRODUCT, to the place you obtained them for a full refund.

SOFTWARE PRODUCT LICENSE

The SOFTWARE PRODUCT is protected by United States copyright laws and international copyright treaties, as well as other intellectual property laws and treaties. The SOFTWARE PRODUCT is licensed, not sold.

1. **GRANT OF LICENSE.** This EULA grants you the following rights:

   a. **Software Product.** You may install and use one copy of the SOFTWARE PRODUCT on a single computer. The primary user of the computer on which the SOFTWARE PRODUCT is installed may make a second copy for his or her exclusive use on a portable computer.

   b. **Storage/Network Use.** You may also store or install a copy of the SOFTWARE PRODUCT on a storage device, such as a network server, used only to install or run the SOFTWARE PRODUCT on your other computers over an internal network; however, you must acquire and dedicate a license for each separate computer on which the SOFTWARE PRODUCT is installed or run from the storage device. A license for the SOFTWARE PRODUCT may not be shared or used concurrently on different computers.

   c. **License Pak.** If you have acquired this EULA in a Microsoft License Pak, you may make the number of additional copies of the computer software portion of the SOFTWARE PRODUCT authorized on the printed copy of this EULA, and you may use each copy in the manner specified above. You are also entitled to make a corresponding number of secondary copies for portable computer use as specified above.

   d. **Sample Code.** Solely with respect to portions, if any, of the SOFTWARE PRODUCT that are identified within the SOFTWARE PRODUCT as sample code (the "SAMPLE CODE"):

   i. **Use and Modification.** Microsoft grants you the right to use and modify the source code version of the SAMPLE CODE, *provided* you comply with subsection (d)(iii) below. You may not distribute the SAMPLE CODE, or any modified version of the SAMPLE CODE, in source code form.

   ii. **Redistributable Files.** Provided you comply with subsection (d)(iii) below, Microsoft grants you a nonexclusive, royalty-free right to reproduce and distribute the object code version of the SAMPLE CODE and of any modified SAMPLE CODE, other than SAMPLE CODE, or any modified version thereof, designated as not redistributable in the Readme file that forms a part of the SOFTWARE PRODUCT (the "Non-Redistributable Sample Code"). All SAMPLE CODE other than the Non-Redistributable Sample Code is collectively referred to as the "REDISTRIBUTABLES."

   iii. **Redistribution Requirements.** If you redistribute the REDISTRIBUTABLES, you agree to: (i) distribute the REDISTRIBUTABLES in object code form only in conjunction with and as a part of your software application product; (ii) not use Microsoft's name, logo, or trademarks to market your software application product; (iii) include a valid copyright notice on your software application product; (iv) indemnify, hold harmless, and defend Microsoft from and against any claims or lawsuits, including attorney's fees, that arise or result from the use or distribution of your software application product; and (v) not permit further distribution of the REDISTRIBUTABLES by your end user. Contact Microsoft for the applicable royalties due and other licensing terms for all other uses and/or distribution of the REDISTRIBUTABLES.

2. **DESCRIPTION OF OTHER RIGHTS AND LIMITATIONS.**

   - **Limitations on Reverse Engineering, Decompilation, and Disassembly.** You may not reverse engineer, decompile, or disassemble the SOFTWARE PRODUCT, except and only to the extent that such activity is expressly permitted by applicable law notwithstanding this limitation.

   - **Separation of Components.** The SOFTWARE PRODUCT is licensed as a single product. Its component parts may not be separated for use on more than one computer.

   - **Rental.** You may not rent, lease, or lend the SOFTWARE PRODUCT.

- **Support Services.** Microsoft may, but is not obligated to, provide you with support services related to the SOFTWARE PRODUCT ("Support Services"). Use of Support Services is governed by the Microsoft policies and programs described in the user manual, in "online" documentation, and/or other Microsoft-provided materials. Any supplemental software code provided to you as part of the Support Services shall be considered part of the SOFTWARE PRODUCT and subject to the terms and conditions of this EULA. With respect to technical information you provide to Microsoft as part of the Support Services, Microsoft may use such information for its business purposes, including for product support and development. Microsoft will not utilize such technical information in a form that personally identifies you.

- **Software Transfer.** You may permanently transfer all of your rights under this EULA, provided you retain no copies, you transfer all of the SOFTWARE PRODUCT (including all component parts, the media and printed materials, any upgrades, this EULA, and, if applicable, the Certificate of Authenticity), **and** the recipient agrees to the terms of this EULA.

- **Termination.** Without prejudice to any other rights, Microsoft may terminate this EULA if you fail to comply with the terms and conditions of this EULA. In such event, you must destroy all copies of the SOFTWARE PRODUCT and all of its component parts.

3. **COPYRIGHT.** All title and copyrights in and to the SOFTWARE PRODUCT (including but not limited to any images, photographs, animations, video, audio, music, text, SAMPLE CODE, REDISTRIBUTABLES, and "applets" incorporated into the SOFTWARE PRODUCT) and any copies of the SOFTWARE PRODUCT are owned by Microsoft or its suppliers. The SOFTWARE PRODUCT is protected by copyright laws and international treaty provisions. Therefore, you must treat the SOFTWARE PRODUCT like any other copyrighted material **except** that you may install the SOFTWARE PRODUCT on a single computer provided you keep the original solely for backup or archival purposes. You may not copy the printed materials accompanying the SOFTWARE PRODUCT.

4. **U.S. GOVERNMENT RESTRICTED RIGHTS.** The SOFTWARE PRODUCT and documentation are provided with RESTRICTED RIGHTS. Use, duplication, or disclosure by the Government is subject to restrictions as set forth in subparagraph (c)(1)(ii) of the Rights in Technical Data and Computer Software clause at DFARS 252.227-7013 or subparagraphs (c)(1) and (2) of the Commercial Computer Software—Restricted Rights at 48 CFR 52.227-19, as applicable. Manufacturer is Microsoft Corporation/One Microsoft Way/Redmond, WA 98052-6399.

5. **EXPORT RESTRICTIONS.** You agree that you will not export or re-export the SOFTWARE PRODUCT, any part thereof, or any process or service that is the direct product of the SOFTWARE PRODUCT (the foregoing collectively referred to as the "Restricted Components"), to any country, person, entity, or end user subject to U.S. export restrictions. You specifically agree not to export or re-export any of the Restricted Components (i) to any country to which the U.S. has embargoed or restricted the export of goods or services, which currently include, but are not necessarily limited to Cuba, Iran, Iraq, Libya, North Korea, Sudan, and Syria, or to any national of any such country, wherever located, who intends to transmit or transport the Restricted Components back to such country; (ii) to any end-user who you know or have reason to know will utilize the Restricted Components in the design, development, or production of nuclear, chemical, or biological weapons; or (iii) to any end-user who has been prohibited from participating in U.S. export transactions by any federal agency of the U.S. government. You warrant and represent that neither the BXA nor any other U.S. federal agency has suspended, revoked, or denied your export privileges.

DISCLAIMER OF WARRANTY

NO WARRANTIES OR CONDITIONS. MICROSOFT EXPRESSLY DISCLAIMS ANY WARRANTY OR CONDITION FOR THE SOFTWARE PRODUCT. THE SOFTWARE PRODUCT AND ANY RELATED DOCUMENTATION IS PROVIDED "AS IS" WITHOUT WARRANTY OR CONDITION OF ANY KIND, EITHER EXPRESS OR IMPLIED, INCLUDING, WITHOUT LIMITATION, THE IMPLIED WARRANTIES OF MERCHANTABILITY, FITNESS FOR A PARTICULAR PURPOSE, OR NONINFRINGEMENT. THE ENTIRE RISK ARISING OUT OF USE OR PERFORMANCE OF THE SOFTWARE PRODUCT REMAINS WITH YOU.

LIMITATION OF LIABILITY. TO THE MAXIMUM EXTENT PERMITTED BY APPLICABLE LAW, IN NO EVENT SHALL MICROSOFT OR ITS SUPPLIERS BE LIABLE FOR ANY SPECIAL, INCIDENTAL, INDIRECT, OR CONSEQUENTIAL DAMAGES WHATSOEVER (INCLUDING, WITHOUT LIMITATION, DAMAGES FOR LOSS OF BUSINESS PROFITS, BUSINESS INTERRUPTION, LOSS OF BUSINESS INFORMATION, OR ANY OTHER PECUNIARY LOSS) ARISING OUT OF THE USE OF OR INABILITY TO USE THE SOFTWARE PRODUCT OR THE PROVISION OF OR FAILURE TO PROVIDE SUPPORT SERVICES, EVEN IF MICROSOFT HAS BEEN ADVISED OF THE POSSIBILITY OF SUCH DAMAGES. IN ANY CASE, MICROSOFT'S ENTIRE LIABILITY UNDER ANY PROVISION OF THIS EULA SHALL BE LIMITED TO THE GREATER OF THE AMOUNT ACTUALLY PAID BY YOU FOR THE SOFTWARE PRODUCT OR US$5.00; PROVIDED HOWEVER, IF YOU HAVE ENTERED INTO A MICROSOFT SUPPORT SERVICES AGREEMENT, MICROSOFT'S ENTIRE LIABILITY REGARDING SUPPORT SERVICES SHALL BE GOVERNED BY THE TERMS OF THAT AGREEMENT. BECAUSE SOME STATES AND JURISDICTIONS DO NOT ALLOW THE EXCLUSION OR LIMITATION OF LIABILITY, THE ABOVE LIMITATION MAY NOT APPLY TO YOU.

MISCELLANEOUS

This EULA is governed by the laws of the State of Washington USA, except and only to the extent that applicable law mandates governing law of a different jurisdiction.

Should you have any questions concerning this EULA, or if you desire to contact Microsoft for any reason, please contact the Microsoft subsidiary serving your country, or write: Microsoft Sales Information Center/One Microsoft Way/Redmond, WA 98052-6399.

start faster

go

farther

Register Today!

Return this
Managing a Microsoft® Windows NT® Network
registration card today

Microsoft® Press

mspress.microsoft.com

0-7356-0647-1

Managing a Microsoft® Windows NT® Network

FIRST NAME | MIDDLE INITIAL | LAST NAME

INSTITUTION OR COMPANY NAME

ADDRESS

CITY | STATE | ZIP

E-MAIL ADDRESS | ( ) PHONE NUMBER

U.S. and Canada addresses only. Fill in information above and mail postage-free.
Please mail only the bottom half of this page.

**start faster
go
farther**

For information about Microsoft Press® products, visit our Web site at

mspress.microsoft.com

Microsoft·Press

BUSINESS REPLY MAIL

FIRST-CLASS MAIL   PERMIT NO. 108   REDMOND WA

POSTAGE WILL BE PAID BY ADDRESSEE

NO POSTAGE
NECESSARY
IF MAILED
IN THE
UNITED STATES

MICROSOFT PRESS
PO BOX 97017
REDMOND, WA 98073-9830